UNDERSTANDING

ARGUMENT

A Text with Readings

UNDERSTANDING

ARGUMENT

A Text with Readings

Dorothy U. Seyler

*Northern Virginia
Community College*

McGraw-Hill, Inc.
New York   St. Louis   San Francisco   Auckland   Bogotá
Caracas   Lisbon   London   Madrid   Mexico City   Milan   Montreal
New Delhi   San Juan   Singapore   Sydney   Tokyo   Toronto

This book was developed by STEVEN PENSINGER, Inc.

UNDERSTANDING ARGUMENT: A TEXT WITH READINGS

Permissions Acknowledgments appear on pages 505–508, and on this page by reference.

This book is printed on acid-free paper.

1 2 3 4 5 6 7 8 9 0 DOC DOC 9 0 9 8 7 6 5 4 3

ISBN 0-07-056438-8

This book was set in Sabon by The Clarinda Company.
The editors were Steve Pensinger and Tom Holton;
the designer was Robin Hoffmann;
the production supervisor was Leroy A. Young.
R. R. Donnelley & Sons Company was printer and binder.

Library of Congress Cataloging-in-Publication Data

Seyler, Dorothy U.
    Understanding argument: a text with readings / Dorothy U. Seyler.
        p.   cm.
    Includes index.
    ISBN 0-07-056438-8
        1. English language—Rhetoric.   2. Persuasion (Rhetoric).
    3. College readers.   I. Title.
    PE1431.S37   1994
    808'.0427—dc20
                                                            93-10907

About the Author

Dorothy U. Seyler is Professor of English at Northern Virginia Community College. A Phi Beta Kappa graduate of the College of William and Mary, Dr. Seyler holds advanced degrees from Columbia University and the State University of New York at Albany. She taught at Ohio State University, the University of Kentucky, and Nassau Community College before moving with her family to Northern Virginia.

She has coauthored *Introduction to Literature* and *Language Power*, both now in second editions, and is the author of *Read, Reason, Write*, in its third edition, *The Writer's Stance, Patterns of Reflection,* and *Doing Research*. In addition, Professor Seyler has published articles in professional journals and popular magazines. She enjoys tennis and traveling, and writing about both.

Contents

Declene of ~~...~~

Preface

Writing effective arguments is a challenge. We need to appreciate this challenge of supporting intelligent positions on issues, and then find the strategies for rising to the challenge. Perhaps the most important first step to meeting the challenge lies in accepting that arguing well is not easy. Asserting a position may be easy, but supporting it convincingly is another matter. We all need to accept the complexity of most issues, find the gray areas rather than thinking in absolutes, respect the opposition, and determine the kind of evidence that is needed to support a given assertion. No small assignment, but help is here, help in *Understanding Argument*.

A text that will help students understand argument needs to provide a clear explanation of the nature of argument, guidelines for constructing good arguments, models of argument to read and study, and information and ideas about some timely—and timeless—issues. *Understanding Argument* provides these elements in a text of ten chapters divided into two parts.

Part I, composed of three chapters, contains the textual guide to argument. Chapter 1's explanation of the nature of argument blends both classical and Toulmin patterns without placing a heavy emphasis on terminology. Rather, the concern is to demonstrate the basic shape of arguments, to emphasize the need to pinpoint the assumptions underlying any argument, and to recognize the most frequent patterns of argument. Chapter 1 also reviews the most common logical fallacies and includes a section on how to evaluate the uses of authority and statistics.

Armed with an understanding of the nature of argument, students can proceed to the second chapter, which guides them in the process of reading and analyzing the arguments of others. This chapter teaches students to read actively, to summarize accurately, and to recognize the elements of style that shape, tone, and convey a writer's attitude. Both Chapters 1 and 2 contain exercises throughout to provide opportunities to learn through practice.

The final chapter in Part I is the "nuts and bolts" guide to writing effective arguments. After reminding students of the important ways that audience influences the shape of an argument, the chapter provides specific guidelines for composing arguments based on the writer's argumentative purpose. The chapter includes two annotated student arguments, guidelines for handling sources, and a guide to the process of revising. *Understanding Argument* does not include fourteen pages on how to write a research essay, fourteen (or twelve or twenty) virtually useless pages. Students using this text in a course that requires a documented argument can, for one combined price, obtain this text and the full-fledged research handbook *Doing Research*.

Chapters 4 through 10, comprising Part II of *Understanding Argument,* organize fifty-seven articles around seven issues, issues that have a cross-disciplinary flavor and that are examined from several perspectives. Some argument texts pair two articles on a topic, implying that taking a stand on an issue is a simple matter of being for or against something. In *Understanding Argument,* the articles in each chapter reveal several "sides" as well as several approaches to key issues and illustrate that many current debates reflect classic philosophical differences or turn on different definitions of key terms. The articles gathered here also reveal how interconnected many current issues are, that conflicts over First Amendment rights, for example, invade education as college administrators seek ways to make today's multicultural campuses into a community. Although most essays are current, several now classic works are also included so that students can develop a historical context for current debates. The essays vary in length and difficulty, so that readers can develop skills over the period of the semester. To aid both students and instructors working with this text, each article is preceded by a headnote to provide context and is followed by questions for analysis and discussion. Each chapter in Part II concludes with suggestions for writing.

No book of value is written alone. I am pleased to acknowledge the contributions of others in shaping this text. My thanks are due once again to the library staff at the Annandale Campus of Northern Virginia Community College, especially Marian Delmore, Ruth Stanton, and Janice Jeffries, who cheerfully helped me locate needed information. As always my editor Steve Pensinger deserves a special thank you for helping develop the idea of the book into this text, and Tom Holton should be recognized for supervising the preparation of the book, the second book of mine that he has handled so skillfully at McGraw-Hill. My daughter Ruth also made an important contribution by reading many proposed articles and listening to my discussions of their various merits. My friend Sue Walker, who contributed good ideas to the design of *Doing Research,* gave us the idea for the cover of *Understanding Argument,* a cover that would both compliment that of *Doing Research* and be appropriate for this text. I also appreciate the many fine suggestions of the following reviewers: Robert Esch, University of Texas at El Paso; C. Jeriel Howard, Northeastern Illinois University; James Howland, California Polytechnic Institute; Stanley J. Kozikowski, Bryant College; Barry M. Maid, University of Arkansas at Little Rock; and Deanne Milan, San Francisco City College.

Finally, I want to thank all my students, who have taught me much about argument, but especially Patti Bailey and Paul Duke, whose essays appear in the text.

Dorothy U. Seyler

PART I

ELEMENTS OF ARGUMENT

CHAPTER 1

EXPLORING THE
NATURE OF
ARGUMENT

 ost of us, at some time, have felt that we were foolishly uninformed, incapable of defending our views, or lacking the ammunition to counter someone else's foolishness. We leave the theater with friends and discover that we are alone in not liking the film, but when asked to explain why, we can only respond, lamely, "I just didn't like it." Over pizza later, we sit silently, because we don't know about the consequences of the national debt or we don't know how to defend our views on congressional term limits. Fortunately there is a way out of these uncomfortable situations. We become well informed by reading analytically and by listening with a critical ear to debates of current issues. We develop the confidence to present our views and challenge others' ideas when we understand how to construct effective arguments and counterarguments.

Good evidence and good sense are powerful tools against the emotional appeals of advertising and political demagoguery. They are essential tools of the enlightened citizenry a democracy demands. The ability to shape an intelligent argument will command the respect of those knowledgeable, thoughtful people whose opinions of us matter. Mature people do not need to agree on all issues to respect one another's good sense, but they do have little patience with uninformed and illogical statements masquerading as argument. There are good reasons for understanding argument.

THE SHAPE OF ARGUMENT

Although arguments come in various patterns to accomplish various purposes, their basic structure remains the same. *An argument consists of evidence presented in support of an assertion or claim that is either stated or implied.* For example:

1. Conclusion: We should not go skiing today
   Evidence: because it is too cold.

2. Evidence: Because some laws are unjust,
   Conclusion: civil disobedience is sometimes justified.

3. Evidence: All human life is sacred.
   Implied Conclusion: Therefore abortion is wrong.

Actually, the shape of argument is a bit more complex than these examples suggest. Each argument has a third element that is not stated in the above examples. This third part is the "glue" that connects the support—the evidence or reasons—to the argument's assertion and thus fulfills the logic of the argument. This glue, what British philosopher Stephen Toulmin calls the argument's *warrant,* is the belief, principle, or assumption that allows us to assert that our evidence or reasons do indeed support our conclusion. See Figure 1.1 for a model of Toulmin's argument structure.

Look again at each of the sample arguments to see what principles or assumptions must be accepted to make each argument work:

1. Conclusion: We should not go skiing today.
   Evidence: It is too cold.
   Underlying assumption (warrant): When it is too cold, skiing is not fun; the activity is not sufficient to keep one from becoming uncomfortable.

2. Conclusion: Civil disobedience is sometimes justified.
   Evidence: Some laws are unjust.

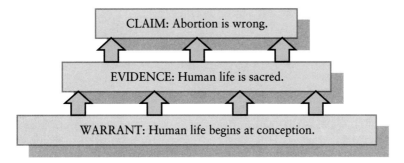

Figure 1.1 The Toulmin Structure of Argument

Underlying assumption (warrant):	To get unjust laws changed, people need to be made aware of the injustice. Acts of civil disobedience will get people's attention and make them aware that the laws need changing.
3. Conclusion:	Abortion is wrong.
Evidence:	Human life is sacred.
Underlying assumption:	Human life begins at conception.

Assumptions play an important role in shaping an argument, so you need to be sure to clarify those assumptions upon which an argument rests. Note, for instance, another assumption operating in the first argument, namely, that the temperature considered "uncomfortable" for the speaker will also be uncomfortable for her companions, an uncertain assumption. In the second example, the assumption is less debatable, for acts of civil disobedience usually get media coverage and serve to dramatize the participants' views. (Not everyone may agree that the laws are unjust, but that is another argument.) The underlying assumption in the third example underscores the importance of becoming aware of each argument's glue, for often the warrants themselves need to be defended or supported in some way. The debate over when human life begins is at the center of the debate over abortion rights.

EXERCISE: CREATING ARGUMENTS

For each of the following claims, give one statement that can serve as evidence for the claim and then state the underlying assumption, or warrant, that completes the argument.

1. Professor White is not a good teacher.
2. Colleges should admit students only on the basis of academic merit.
3. The Washington Redskins are a great football team.
4. Americans need to reduce the fat in their diets.

Exploring further the shape of argument, we need to consider the kinds of statements that can function as reasons and conclusions. An argument's conclusion must be an assertion that can be debated, a statement to which we can respond "I agree" or "I disagree." Arguments are not about questions (Are you going to the dorm?), personal preferences (My favorite dessert is pecan pie), or facts (There are twenty-six chairs in Room 110). These are not arguable assertions; they do not need support from reasons and evidence. The statement "I liked President Reagan" states a personal preference, but the statement "President Reagan was a great president" is open to debate and thus could be the conclusion to, or claim of, an argument.

Sometimes we present arguable assertions in statements that are qualified to sound like personal preferences. If you were to write, "I believe that high school students should be required to do more homework," you would have made an assertion that can—and should—be supported with reasons. Placing such qualifiers as "I believe," "I think," or "I feel" in an assertion does not free you from the need to support assertions. The statement "I believe that President Reagan was a great president" calls for a defense with evidence and reasons.

Conclusions to arguments must, then, be either inferences or judgments, for these are debatable assertions. And the support provided for conclusions will be composed of facts, opinions based on facts (inferences), or opinions based on values, beliefs, or ideas (judgments)—or some combination of the three. Let's consider what kinds of statements each of these terms describes.

Facts

Facts are statements that are readily verifiable. Factual statements refer to what can be counted or measured or confirmed by reasonable observers or trusted experts.

There are twenty-six desks in Room 110.
In the U.S. about 400,000 people die each year as a result of smoking.

These are factual statements. We can verify the first by observation, by counting. The second fact comes from medical records; we rely on trusted record-keeping sources and medical experts for verification. By definition, we do not argue about the facts. In a dispute over "facts," one person has the facts and the other does not. Usually. Sometimes "facts" change, as we learn more about the universe we live in. For example, only in the last thirty years has convincing evidence been gathered to demonstrate the relationship between smoking and various illnesses of the heart and lungs. Further, except for the trivia buff, facts are useful only when we understand what they mean. How many desks there are in Room 110 really does not matter unless more students arrive for class than there are desks for them to use.

Inferences

Inferences are opinions based on facts. They are the conclusions we draw from an analysis of facts.

> There will not be enough desks in Room 110 for upcoming fall-semester classes.
> Smoking is a serious health hazard.

Predictions of an increase in student enrollment for the coming fall semester lead to the inference that most English classes scheduled in Room 110 will run with several more students per class than last year. The dean should order new desks. Similarly, we infer from the numbers of deaths that smoking is a health problem, for more people are dying from tobacco than from AIDS, or murder, or car accidents, causes of death that get media coverage but do not produce nearly as many deaths.

　　Inferences vary in their closeness to the facts supporting them. That the sun will "rise" tomorrow is an inference, but we count on its happening, acting as if it is a fact. However, the first inference stated above is based not just on the fact of twenty-six desks but on another inference, a projected increase in student enrollment, and two assumptions. The argument looks like this:

Fact:	There are twenty-six desks in Room 110.
Inference:	There will be more first-year students next year.
Assumptions:	1. English will remain a required course.
	2. No additional classrooms are available for English classes.
Conclusion:	There will not be enough desks in Room 110 for upcoming fall-semester classes.

This inference could be challenged by a different analysis of the facts supporting enrollment projections. Or, if additional rooms can be found, the dean will not need to order new desks. Inferences can be part of the support of an argument, or they can be the conclusion of an argument.

Judgments

Judgments are opinions based on values, beliefs, or philosophical concepts. (Judgments also include opinions based on personal preferences, but we have already excluded these from argument.) Judgments concern right and wrong, good and bad, better or worse, should and should not. When support other than purely personal preferences can be presented, judgments are arguable:

> English classes in Room 110 should not exceed an enrollment of twenty-six students.
>
> Cigarette advertising should be eliminated, and the federal government should develop an antismoking campaign.

To support the first judgment, we need to explain what constitutes overcrowding, or what constitutes the best class size for effective teaching. If we can support our views on effective teaching, we may be able to convince the college president that ordering more chairs for Room 110 is not the best solution to an increasing enrollment in English classes. The second judgment also offers a solution to a problem, in this case a national health problem. To reduce the number of deaths, we need to reduce the number of smokers, either by encouraging smokers to quit or not to start. The underlying assumption: Advertising does affect behavior.

EXERCISE: FACTS, INFERENCES, AND JUDGMENTS

Compile a list of three statements of fact, three inferences, and three judgments. Try to organize them into three related sets, as illustrated here:

- Smoking is prohibited on flights within the United States.
- Secondhand smoke is a health hazard.
- Smoking should be prohibited on all flights, national and international.

We can classify judgments to see better what kind of assertion we are making and, therefore, what kind of support we need to argue effectively.

FUNCTIONAL JUDGMENTS (guidelines for judging how something or someone works or could work):

> Jack Nicklaus is the best golfer to play the game.
> Antismoking advertising will reduce the number of smokers.

AESTHETIC JUDGMENTS (guidelines for judging art, literature, music, or natural scenes):

> The sunrise was beautiful.
> *The Great Gatsby*'s structure, characters, and symbols are perfectly wedded to create the novel's vision of the American dream.

ETHICAL JUDGMENTS (guidelines for group or social behavior):

> Lawyers should not advertise.
> It is discourteous to talk during a film or lecture.

MORAL JUDGMENTS (guidelines of right and wrong for judging individuals and for establishing legal principles):

> Taking another person's life is wrong.
> Equal rights under the law should not be denied on the basis of race or sex.

Functional and aesthetic judgments generally require defining key terms and establishing criteria for the judging or ranking made by the assertion. How, for example, do we compare golfers? On the amount of money won? The number of tournaments won? Or the consistency of winning throughout one's career? What about the golfer's quality and range of shots? Ethical and moral judgments may be more difficult to support because they depend not just on how terms are defined and criteria established but on values and beliefs as well. Why shouldn't lawyers advertise? How will society be hurt by this action? If taking another person's life is wrong, why isn't it wrong in war? Or is it? These are all difficult questions that require thoughtful responses.

EXERCISES: LABELING JUDGMENTS AND UNCOVERING ASSUMPTIONS

1. Categorize the judgments you wrote for the previous exercise (p. 8) as either aesthetic, moral, ethical, or functional; or compile a list of three judgments that you then categorize.
2. For each judgment listed for exercise 1, generate one statement of support, either a fact or inference or another judgment. Then state the warrant (underlying assumption) required to complete each argument.

TYPES OF ARGUMENT

We can understand more about the nature of argument by examining traditional forms of argument—induction, deduction, analogy, and causal arguments—observing, in addition, how each contains the basic shape of argument explained above.

Induction

Induction is the process by which we reach inferences—opinions based on facts, or on a combination of facts and less debatable inferences. The inductive process moves from particular to general, from support to assertion. We infer something to be so based on the facts we have gathered and studied. In general, the more evidence, the more convincing the argument. No one wants to debate tomorrow's sunrise; the evidence for counting on it is too convincing. Most inferences, though, are drawn from less evidence, so we need to examine inductive arguments closely to judge their reasonableness.

The pattern of induction looks like this:

Facts:	There is the dead body of Smith.
	Smith was shot in his bedroom between the hours of 11:00 p.m. and 2:00 a.m., according to the coroner.
	Smith was shot by a .32 caliber pistol.
	The pistol left in the bedroom contains Jones's fingerprints.
	Jones was seen, by a neighbor, entering the Smith home at around 11:00 p.m. the night of Smith's death.
	A coworker heard Smith and Jones arguing in Smith's office the morning of the day Smith died.
Conclusion:	Jones killed Smith.

The facts are presented. The jury infers that Jones is a murderer. Unless there is a confession or a trustworthy eyewitness, the conclusion is an inference, not a fact. This is the most logical explanation; that is, the conclusion meets the standards of simplicity and frequency while accounting for all of the known evidence.

The following paragraph illustrates the process of induction, in this case of generalizing from facts about a social condition:

American society has become increasingly violent in the last twenty-five years, in that people of many ages and backgrounds seem more ready to use violence to solve problems. According to figures quoted in a 1986 article by Adam Smith, each year in America now about 10,000 people die from gun deaths, in contrast to 3 in Great Britain and 17 in West Germany. An increasing number of victims are children and teenagers who are settling quarrels over drug territories or girlfriends by shooting. Sometimes the victims are parents, the murderers their children who are ending arguments over money or the use of the car. And sometimes the victims are children. In the first three months of 1989 in Washington, DC, over 100 people were murdered, many teenagers, many deaths drug-related. A youngster in a Maryland community shot both parents in a quarrel over money. A Virginia teenager shot his stepmother and left her body in a truck by the roadside. The trial of a Manhattan man who beat his adopted daughter to death is only one recent celebrated case of child beating. Further, in 1989 CBS reported that suicides have increased since 1986. Added to that are the Los Angeles area freeway shootings by frustrated drivers. The causes for this increase in violence are certainly numerous and complex, but the conclusion that "average" citizens, not crooks, are increasingly resorting to violence seems inescapable.

Observe that the writer organizes evidence by type of violence. Notice also that all facts relate to the issue of increasing violence among ordinary people. The writer does not get sidetracked into statistics for armed robberies or gang killings. A good inductive argument is based on a sufficient volume of *relevant* evidence. The basic shape of this inductive argument is illustrated in Figure 1.2.

Deduction

Although induction can be described as an argument that moves from particular to general, from facts to inference, deduction cannot accurately be described as the reverse. Deductive arguments are more complex than suggested by such a description. *Deduction is the reasoning process that*

Figure 1.2 The Shape of an Inductive Argument

Conclusion:	American society has become increasingly violent.
Support:	The facts presented in the paragraph.
Assumption:	The facts are representative, not isolated incidents, and thus reveal a trend, justifying the conclusion drawn.

draws a conclusion from the logical relationship of two assertions, usually one broad judgment or definition and one more specific assertion, often an inference. Suppose on the way out of American history class, you say "Abraham Lincoln certainly was a great leader." Someone responds with the expected question: "Why do you think so?" You explain: "He was great because he performed with courage and a clear purpose in a time of crisis." Your explanation contains a conclusion and an assertion about Lincoln (an inference) in support. But behind your explanation rests an idea about leadership, in the terms of deduction, a *premise.* The argument's basic shape is illustrated in Figure 1.3.

What we see above is another example of the basic shape of argument, but the deductive argument is traditionally arranged somewhat differently. The two reasons are called *premises;* the broader one, called the *major premise,* is written first and the more specific one, the *minor premise,* comes next. The premises and conclusion are expressed to make clear that assertions are being made about categories or classes. To illustrate:

Major premise:	All people who perform with courage and a clear purpose in a crisis are great leaders.
Minor premise:	Lincoln was a person who performed with courage and a clear purpose in a crisis.
Conclusion:	Lincoln was a great leader.

If these two premises are correctly, that is, logically, constructed, then the conclusion follows logically, and the deductive argument is *valid.* This does not mean that the conclusion is necessarily *true.* It does mean that if you accept the truth of the premises, then you must accept the truth of the conclusion, because in a valid argument the conclusion follows logically, necessarily. How do we know that the conclusion must follow if the argu-

Figure 1.3 The Shape of a Deductive Argument

<u>Conclusion:</u>	Lincoln was a great leader.
<u>Reasons:</u>	1. People who perform with courage and clear purpose in a crisis are great leaders. 2. Lincoln was a person who performed with courage and a clear purpose in a crisis.
<u>Assumption:</u>	The relationship of the two reasons leads, logically, to the conclusion.

ment is logically constructed? Let's think about what each premise is saying and then diagram each premise to represent each assertion visually.
The first premise says that all people who act a particular way are people
who fit into the category called "great leaders":

The second premise says that Lincoln, a category of one, belongs in the
category of people who act in the same particular way that the first
premise describes:

If we put the two diagrams together, we have the following set of circles,
demonstrating that what the conclusion asserts follows from the premises:

Some deductive arguments merely look right, but the two premises do not lead logically to the conclusion that is asserted, so we must read each argument carefully or diagram each one to make certain that the conclusion follows from the premises. Consider the following argument: Unions must be communistic because they want to control wages. The sentence contains a conclusion and one reason, or premise. From these two parts of a deductive argument we can also determine the unstated premise, just as we could with the Lincoln argument: Communists want to control wages. If we use circles to represent the three categories of people in the argument and diagram the argument, we see a different result from the Lincoln argument:

Diagramming the argument reveals that it is invalid; that is, it is not logically constructed because the statements do not require that the union circle be placed inside the communist circle. We cannot draw the conclusion we want from just any two premises, only from those that provide a logical basis from which a conclusion can be reached.

We must first make certain that deductive arguments are properly constructed or valid. But suppose the logic works and yet you do not agree with the conclusion? Your complaint, then, must be with one of the premises, a judgment or inference that you do not accept as true. Consider, as an example, the following argument:

Major premise:	(All) dogs make good pets.
Minor premise:	Fido is a dog.
Conclusion:	Fido will make a good pet.

This argument is valid. (Diagram it; your circles will fit into one another just as with the Lincoln argument.) However, you are not prepared to agree, necessarily, that Fido will make a good pet. The problem is with the major premise. For the argument to work, the assertion must be about *all* dogs, but we know that not all dogs will be good pets.

When composing a deductive argument, your task will be to defend the truth of your premises. Then, if your argument is valid (logically constructed), readers will have no alternative but to agree with your conclusion. If you disagree with someone else's logically constructed argument, then you must show why one of the premises is not true. Your counterargument will seek to discredit one (or both) of the premises. The Fido argument can be discredited by your producing examples of dogs that have not made good pets.

A deductive argument can serve as the core of an entire essay, an essay that supports the argument's conclusion by developing support for each of the premises. Since the major premise is either a broad judgment or a definition, it will need to be defended on the basis of an appeal to values or beliefs that the writer expects the reader to share. The minor premise, usually an inference about a particular situation (or person), would be supported by relevant evidence, as with any inductive argument. You can see this process at work in the Declaration of Independence. Questions follow the Declaration to guide your analysis of this famous example of the deductive process.

❖

The Declaration of Independence

In Congress, July 4, 1776
The unanimous declaration of the thirteen
United States of America

When in the course of human events, it becomes necessary for one people to dissolve the political bands which have connected them with another, and to assume among the powers of the earth, the separate and equal station to which the Laws of Nature and of Nature's God entitle them, a decent respect to the opinions of mankind requires that they should declare the causes which impel them to the separation.

We hold these truths to be self-evident, that all men are created equal, that they are endowed by their Creator with certain unalienable rights, that among these are life, liberty and the pursuit of happiness. That to secure these rights, governments are instituted among men, deriving their just powers from the consent of the governed. That whenever any form of government becomes destructive of these ends, it is the right of the people to alter or to abolish it, and to institute new government, laying its foundation on such principles and organizing its powers in such form, as to them shall seem most likely to effect their safety and happiness. Prudence, indeed, will dictate that governments long established should not be changed for light and transient causes; and accordingly all experience hath shown, that mankind are more disposed to suffer, while evils are sufferable, than to right themselves by abolishing the forms to which they are accustomed. But when a long train of abuses and usurpations, pursuing invariably the same object evinces a design to reduce them under absolute despotism, it is their right, it is their duty, to throw off such government, and to provide new guards for their future security. Such has been the patient sufferance of these Colonies; and such is now the necessity which constrains them to alter their former systems of government. The history of the present King of Great Britain is a history of repeated injuries and usurpations, all having in direct object the establishment of an absolute tyranny over these States. To prove this, let facts be submitted to a candid world.

3   He has refused his assent to laws, the most wholesome and necessary for the public good.

4   He has forbidden his Governors to pass laws of immediate and pressing importance, unless suspended in their operation till his assent should be obtained; and when so suspended, he has utterly neglected to attend to them.

5   He has refused to pass other laws for the accommodation of large districts of people, unless those people would relinquish the right of representation in the Legislature, a right inestimable to them and formidable to tyrants only.

6   He has called together legislative bodies at places unusual, uncomfortable, and distant from the depository of their public records, for the sole purpose of fatiguing them into compliance with his measures.

7   He has dissolved representative houses repeatedly, for opposing with manly firmness his invasions on the rights of the people.

8   He has refused for a long time, after such dissolutions, to cause others to be elected; whereby the legislative powers, incapable of annihilation, have returned to the people at large for their exercise; the State remaining in the meantime exposed to all the dangers of invasion from without and convulsions within.

9   He has endeavoured to prevent the population of these States; for that purpose obstructing the laws of naturalization of foreigners; refusing to pass others to encourage their migration hither, and raising the conditions of new appropriations of lands.

10   He has obstructed the administration of justice, by refusing his assent to laws for establishing judiciary powers.

11   He has made judges dependent on his will alone, for the tenure of their offices, and the amount and payment of their salaries.

12   He has erected a multitude of new offices, and sent hither swarms of officers to harass our people, and eat out their substance.

13   He has kept among us, in times of peace, standing armies without the consent of our legislatures.

He has affected to render the military independent of and superior to   14
the civil power.

He has combined with others to subject us to a jurisdiction foreign to   15
our constitution, and unacknowledged by our laws; giving his assent to
their acts of pretended legislation:

For quartering large bodies of armed troops among us: 16

For protecting them, by a mock trial, from punishment for any mur-   17
ders which they should commit on the inhabitants of these States:

For cutting off our trade with all parts of the world: 18

For imposing taxes on us without our consent: 19

For depriving us, in many cases, of the benefits of trial by jury: 20

For transporting us beyond seas to be tried for pretended offences: 21

For abolishing the free system of English laws in a neighbouring   22
Province, establishing therein an arbitrary government, and enlarging its
boundaries so as to render it at once an example and fit instrument for introducing the same absolute rule into these Colonies:

For taking away our Charters, abolishing our most valuable laws,   23
and altering fundamentally the forms of our governments:

For suspending our own Legislatures, and declaring themselves in-   24
vested with power to legislate for us in all cases whatsoever.

He has abdicated government here, by declaring us out of his protec-   25
tion and waging war against us.

He has plundered our seas, ravaged our coasts, burnt our towns, and   26
destroyed the lives of our people.

He is at this time transporting large armies of foreign mercenaries to   27
complete the works of death, desolation and tyranny, already begun with
circumstances of cruelty and perfidy scarcely paralleled in the most bar-
barous ages, and totally unworthy the head of a civilized nation.

He has constrained our fellow citizens taken captive on the high seas   28
to bear arms against their country, to become the executioners of their
friends and brethren, or to fall themselves by their hands.

He has excited domestic insurrections amongst us, and has endeav-   29
oured to bring on the inhabitants of our frontiers, the merciless Indian savages, whose known rule of warfare, is an undistinguished destruction of all
ages, sexes, and conditions.

In every stage of these oppressions we have petitioned for redress in   30
the most humble terms: our repeated petitions have been answered only by
repeated injury. A prince whose character is thus marked by every act
which may define a tyrant is unfit to be the ruler of a free people.

Nor have we been wanting in attention to our British brethren. We   31
have warned them from time to time of attempts by their legislature to extend an unwarrantable jurisdiction over us. We have reminded them of the
circumstances of our emigration and settlement here. We have appealed to
their native justice and magnanimity, and we have conjured them by the

ties of our common kindred to disavow these usurpations, which would inevitably interrupt our connections and correspondence. They too have been deaf to the voice of justice and of consanguinity. We must, therefore, acquiesce in the necessity, which denounces our separation, and hold them, as we hold the rest of mankind, enemies in war, in peace friends.

32   We, therefore, the Representatives of the United States of America, in General Congress assembled, appealing to the Supreme Judge of the world for the rectitude of our intentions, do, in the name, and by the authority of the good people of these Colonies, solemnly publish and declare, That these United Colonies are, and of right ought to be Free and Independent States; that they are absolved from all allegiance to the British Crown, and that all political connection between them and the State of Great Britain, is and ought to be totally dissolved; and that as Free and Independent States, they have full power to levy war, conclude peace, contract alliances, establish commerce, and to do all other acts and things which Independent States may of right do. And for the support of this declaration, with a firm reliance on the protection of Divine Providence, we mutually pledge to each other our lives, our fortunes, and our sacred honor.

Questions

1. What is the Declaration's central deductive argument? State the argument in the shape illustrated above: major premise, minor premise, conclusion. Construct a valid argument. (If necessary, draw circles representing each of the three terms in the argument to check your version for validity.)

   (*Hint:* Start with the conclusion: George III's government should be overthrown.)
2. Which paragraphs are devoted to supporting the major premise? What kind of support has been given?
3. Which paragraphs are devoted to supporting the minor premise? What kind of support has been given?
4. Why has more support been given for one premise than the other?

EXERCISES: COMPLETING AND EVALUATING DEDUCTIVE ARGUMENTS

Turn each of the following statements into valid deductive arguments. (You have the conclusion and one premise, so you will have to determine what missing premise would complete the argument. Draw circles if necessary to test for validity.) Then decide which arguments have premises that could be supported by noting the kind of support that might be provided. Explain why you think some arguments have insupportable premises. Here is an example:

Premise:	All Jesuits are priests.
Premise:	No women are priests.
Conclusion:	No women are Jesuits.

Since the circle for women must be placed outside the circle for priests, it must also be outside the circle for Jesuits. Hence the argument is valid. The first premise is true by definition; the term *Jesuit* refers to an order of Roman Catholic priests. The second premise is true for the Roman Catholic Church, so if the term *priest* is used only to refer to people with a religious vocation in the Roman Catholic Church, then the second premise is also true by definition.

1. Mrs. Ferguson is a good teacher because she can explain the subject matter clearly.
2. Segregated schools are unconstitutional because they are unequal.
3. Michael must be a good driver because he drives fast.
4. The media clearly have a liberal bias because they make fun of Dan Quayle.

Analogy

The argument from analogy is an argument based on comparison. Analogies assert that since A and B are alike in several ways, they must be alike in another way as well. The argument from analogy concludes with an inference, an assertion of a significant similarity in the two items being compared. The other similarities asserted in the argument serve as evidence in support of the inference. The shape of an argument by analogy is illustrated in Figure 1.4.

Figure 1.4 The Shape of an Argument by Analogy

Evidence:	A has characteristics 1, 2, 3, and 4. B has characteristics 1, 2, and 3.
Conclusion:	B has characteristic 4 (as well).
Assumption:	If B has three characteristics in common with A, it must have the key fourth characteristic as well.

Although analogy is sometimes an effective approach to an issue because clever, imaginative comparisons are often moving, analogy is not as rigorously logical as either induction or deduction. Frequently an analogy is based on only two or three points of comparison, whereas a sound inductive argument presents many examples to support its conclusion. Further, to be convincing, the points of comparison must be fundamental to the two items being compared. An argument for a county cat leash law developed by analogy with dogs may cite the following similarities:

- Cats are pets, just like dogs.
- Cats live in residential communities, just like dogs.
- Cats can mess up other people's yards, just like dogs.
- Cats, if allowed to run free, can disturb the peace (fighting, howling at night), just like dogs.

Does it follow that cats should be required to walk on a leash, just like dogs? If such a county ordinance were passed, would it be enforceable? Have you ever tried to walk a cat on a leash? In spite of legitimate similarities brought out by the analogy, the conclusion does not logically follow because the arguer is overlooking a fundamental difference in each animal's personality. Dogs can be trained to a leash; most cats (Siamese are one exception) cannot be so trained. Such thinking will produce sulking cats and scratched owners. But the analogy, delivered passionately to the right audience, could lead community activists to lobby for a new law.

Observe that the problem with the cat-leash-law analogy is not in the similarities asserted about the items being compared but rather in the underlying assumption that the similarities logically support the argument's conclusion. A good analogy asserts many points of comparison and finds likenesses that are essential parts of the nature or purpose of the two items being compared. The best way to challenge another's analogy is to point out a fundamental difference in the nature or purpose of the compared items. For all of their similarities, when it comes to walking on a leash, cats are *not* like dogs.

EXERCISE: ANALYZING AN ARGUMENT BY ANALOGY

Study the process of analogy in the following brief argument and then answer the questions that follow.

College newspapers should not be under the supervision or control of a faculty sponsor. After all, no governmental sponsor controls the *New York Times,* fortunately, or we would no longer have a free press in this country. We need a free college press, too, one that can attack college policies when they are wrong.

Questions

1. What are the two items being compared? List them as reasons to show the shape of the argument.
2. What is the claim of the analogy? State it as a conclusion to complete the shape of the argument.
3. Is the analogy a sound argument? If so, explain why. If not, explain what is wrong with the comparison.
4. What audience might be moved by this analogy?

Arguments about Cause

Because we want to know *why* things happen, arguments about cause abound. We want to understand past events (Why was Kennedy assassinated?), to explain current situations (Why have SAT scores dropped?), and to predict the future (Will the economy improve if there is a tax cut?). All three questions ask for a causal explanation, including the last one. To answer the last question with a yes (or no) is to assert that a tax cut is (or is not) a cause of economic improvement.

Causal arguments are similar in their purpose rather than in their structure. Causal arguments explain either why a particular situation or phenomenon occurred (or will occur) or what produced (or will produce) a general state of affairs. Napoleon's loss at Waterloo is a particular situation, although it certainly developed from more than one cause. Dropping SAT scores is a general educational problem; good sense tells us that there is more than one cause for this problem, too. One consideration in any causal argument you may undertake is how broad a generalization you can support. For example, although low SAT's is a national problem, a school administrator in Texas may feel that from her research she can explain the causes only in her community, not in the entire nation.

When looking for the cause of A, we are looking for an *agent:* a person, a situation, another event that brought A into existence. To discover that a lit cigarette dropped in a bed caused a particular house fire is, presumably, to have found the fire's cause. But if we continue to probe the situation, we uncover a more complicated sequence of causes. Why did the person in bed drop the cigarette? Because he fell asleep, we learn. Why did he fall asleep, unaware of his cigarette? Because, old and ill, he had taken a sleeping pill to help induce sleep. Did the sleeping pill cause the fire? Did his illness or age cause the fire? Where do we stop in the chain of causes?

The answer to the last question is that it depends, finally, on the purpose of the argument. Further, distinguishing among types of causes, or complex causal relationships, reveals that events do not occur in a vacuum. There are *conditions* surrounding an event, making the assigning of one cause difficult at best. In the example above, the man's age and illness are existing conditions that contributed to, although they did not directly cause, the fire. We also speak of *influences* when discussing cause. The sleeping pill certainly influenced the man's behavior that led to the fire. To change the example, you might say that a particular teacher influenced your decision to attend the college you chose. The teacher is not the cause of your attending the college but rather an influence on your decision. Some conditions and influences may qualify as *remote causes. Proximate causes* are more immediate, usually closer in time to the event or situation. The man's dozing off with a lighted cigarette is a proximate cause of the fire. Moving to the final step in the process, we come to the *precipitating cause,* the triggering event—in this example, the cigarette's igniting the combustible mattress fabric. Isolating a precipitating cause is usually necessary to prevent events from recurring, but often we need to go further back to determine remoter causes or conditions, especially if we are interested in assigning responsibility for what has occurred.

Consider Craig's situation. Last week he had a rear-end collision with the car in front of him. The precipitating cause was his car's closeness to the car in front, too close to make stopping without a collision possible. If Craig wants to avoid another accident of this kind, he should not get too close to the car ahead of him. However, the car is not responsible for the accident because it was too close; Craig must accept responsibility for putting his car in a situation conducive to rear-end collisions. Craig may prefer to believe that his car developed a will of its own or was suddenly possessed by the devil, but neither the state trooper nor Craig's insurance company will accept that explanation of cause.

In summary, a good causal argument is based, first, on the recognition of the complexity of causation, a recognition that keeps us from rushing in to assert only one cause for most events or situations. Second, a good causal argument distinguishes carefully among types of causes. Word choice is crucial to presenting a clear and convincing argument. Do you want to argue that A, and A alone, caused B, that A was one of several contributing causes, or that A was an influence? Finally, a good causal argument demonstrates more than just a *time relationship* or *correlation* between A and B. It proves *agency.* March precedes April, but March does not cause April to arrive. Further, good SAT scores do not cause good college grades. There is a correlation between good scores and good grades, but that is not the same thing as cause. (It is wise to infer, though, that whatever knowledge or skills produce good scores also produce, or at least contribute to, good grades.)

Keep in mind, as well, that the most convincing causal arguments are about believable causal agents, agents that are consistent with our knowledge of human behavior and scientific laws. Most people do not believe that personalities are shaped by astrological signs, or that scientific laws, as we understand them at present, are suspended in the Bermuda Triangle, allowing planes and ships to vanish or enter a fourth dimension.

John Stuart Mill, a nineteenth-century British philosopher, explained in detail various ways of investigating and demonstrating causal relationships. One way to isolate cause is to demonstrate that one agent is *common* to similar outcomes. For instance, twenty-five employees attend a company luncheon. Later in the day ten report to area hospitals, and another four complain the next day of having experienced vomiting the night before. Public health officials will soon want to know what these people ate for lunch. Different people during the same twelve-hour period had similar physical symptoms of food poisoning. The common factor may well have been the tuna salad that they ate for lunch.

Another way to isolate cause is to recognize one key *difference*. If two situations are alike in every way but one, and the situations result in different outcomes, then the one way they differ must have caused the different outcome. Studies in the social sciences are often based on the single-difference method. To test for the best teaching methods for math, an educator could set up an experiment with two classrooms similar in every way except that one class devotes fifteen minutes three days a week to instruction by drill. If the class receiving the drill scores much higher on a standard test given to both groups of students, the educator could argue that math drills make a measurable difference in learning math. But the educator should be prepared for skeptics to challenge the assertion of only one difference between the two classes. Could the teacher's attitude toward the drills make a difference in student learning? If the differences in student scores are significant, the educator probably has a good argument, even though a teacher's attitude cannot be controlled in the experiment.

Finally, one can develop a causal argument around a technique we all use for problem solving: *the process of elimination*. When something happens, we examine all possible causes and eliminate them, one by one, until we are satisfied that we have isolated the actual cause (or causes). When the FAA has to investigate a plane crash, it uses this process, exploring possible causes such as mechanical failure, weather, human error, or terrorism. Sometimes the process isolates more than one cause, or points to a likely cause without providing unequivocal proof.

In the following article, Lester Thurow uses the process-of-elimination method to isolate what he argues is the major cause for existing differences in men's and women's earnings. Use the questions that follow the article to guide your analysis of his argument.

Why Women Are Paid Less Than Men

Lester C. Thurow

A professor at the MIT Sloan School of Management and consultant to governments and private corporations, Lester C. Thurow (b. 1938) has written extensively on economic and public-policy issues. "Why Women Are Paid Less Than Men" was published in the New York Times *on March 8, 1981.*

1   In the 40 years from 1939 to 1979 white women who work full time have with monotonous regularity made slightly less than 60 percent as much as white men. Why?

2   Over the same time period, minorities have made substantial progress in catching up with whites, with minority women making even more progress than minority men.

3   Black men now earn 72 percent as much as white men (up 16 percentage points since the mid-1950s) but black women earn 92 percent as much as white women. Hispanic men make 71 percent of what their white counterparts do, but Hispanic women make 82 percent as much as white women. As a result of their faster progress, fully employed black women make 75 percent as much as fully employed black men while Hispanic women earn 68 percent as much as Hispanic men.

4   This faster progress may, however, end when minority women finally catch up with white women. In the bible of the New Right, George Gilder's *Wealth and Poverty*, the 60 percent is just one of Mother Nature's constants like the speed of light or the force of gravity.

5   Men are programmed to provide for their families economically while women are programmed to take care of their families emotionally and physically. As a result men put more effort into their jobs than women. The net result is a difference in work intensity that leads to that 40 percent gap in earnings. But there is no discrimination against women—only the biological facts of life.

6   The problem with this assertion is just that. It is an assertion with no evidence for it other than the fact that white women have made 60 percent as much as men for a long period of time.

7   "Discrimination against women" is an easy answer but it also has its problems as an adequate explanation. Why is discrimination against women not declining under the same social forces that are leading to a lessening of discrimination against minorities? In recent years women have

made more use of the enforcement provisions of the Equal Employment Opportunities Commission and the courts than minorities. Why do the laws that prohibit discrimination against women and minorities work for minorities but not for women?

When men discriminate against women, they run into a problem. To   8 discriminate against women is to discriminate against your own wife and to lower your own family income. To prevent women from working is to force men to work more.

When whites discriminate against blacks, they can at least think that   9 they are raising their own incomes. When men discriminate against women they have to know that they are lowering their own family income and increasing their own work effort.

While discrimination undoubtedly explains part of the male-female   10 earnings differential, one has to believe that men are monumentally stupid or irrational to explain all of the earnings gap in terms of discrimination. There must be something else going on.

Back in 1939 it was possible to attribute the earnings gap to large   11 differences in educational attainments. But the educational gap between men and women has been eliminated since World War II. It is no longer possible to use education as an explanation for the lower earnings of women.

Some observers have argued that women earn less money since they   12 are less reliable workers who are more apt to leave the labor force. But it is difficult to maintain this position since women are less apt to quit one job to take another and as a result they tend to work as long, or longer, for any one employer. From any employer's perspective they are more reliable, not less reliable, than men.

Part of the answer is visible if you look at the lifetime earnings profile   13 of men. Suppose that you were asked to predict which men in a group of 25-year-olds would become economically successful. At age 25 it is difficult to tell who will be economically successful and your predictions are apt to be highly inaccurate.

But suppose that you were asked to predict which men in a group of   14 35-year-olds would become economically successful. If you are successful at age 35, you are very likely to remain successful for the rest of your life. If you have not become economically successful by age 35, you are very unlikely to do so later.

The decade between 25 and 35 is when men either succeed or fail. It   15 is the decade when lawyers become partners in the good firms, when business managers make it onto the "fast track," when academics get tenure at good universities, and when blue collar workers find the job opportunities that will lead to training opportunities and the skills that will generate high earnings.

If there is any one decade when it pays to work hard and to be consis-   16 tently in the labor force, it is the decade between 25 and 35. For those who succeed, earnings will rise rapidly. For those who fail, earnings will remain flat for the rest of their lives.

17   But the decade between 25 and 35 is precisely the decade when women are most apt to leave the labor force or become part-time workers to have children. When they do, the current system of promotion and skill acquisition will extract an enormous lifetime price.

18   This leaves essentially two avenues for equalizing male and female earnings.

19   Families where women who wish to have successful careers, compete with men, and achieve the same earnings should alter their family plans and have their children either before 25 or after 35. Or society can attempt to alter the existing promotion and skill acquisition system so that there is a longer time period in which both men and women can attempt to successfully enter the labor force.

20   Without some combination of these two factors, a substantial fraction of the male-female earnings differentials are apt to persist for the next 40 years, even if discrimination against women is eliminated.

Questions

1. What is Thurow's explanation for the discrepancy between the earnings of white women and white men, for the apparent single difference that accounts for the lower earnings?

2. Thurow's conclusion about women's lower earnings can be expressed as two-thirds of a deductive argument: Women fail to achieve big earnings because they are not working and advancing between the ages of twenty-five and thirty-five. What, then, is the major premise? How does Thurow support the minor premise?

3. Thurow's support for the major premise is a series of assertions in paragraph 15. Are these facts or assumptions? Is it true that most people who are going to be successful are so by age thirty-five?

4. *Consider:* What are other facts about jobs that men and women hold that may account for some of the discrepancy in pay?

THE LANGUAGE OF ARGUMENT

Our discussion of argument has rested on the definition of argument as rational discourse; that is, a claim or assertion is put forward and then defended with reasons, with logic and evidence. When we talk about the red-hot argument in yesterday's government class, though, we are not referring to the "bare-bones" shapes examined in this chapter. Sometimes the term *persuasion* is used to distinguish the heated debate from the carefully reasoned argument. But the arguer wants to be persuasive, too, to win over listeners or readers. Thus the term *argument* is usually considered to be the broader term, incorporating the persuasive goal.

Acknowledging that the arguer wants to be convincing does not mean that "anything goes." Abusive language, vicious or condescending attacks on all who disagree with your views are unacceptable strategies in good argument. Purposely ignoring relevant evidence or distorting the facts through the manner of presentation are also unacceptable, because such strategies are unethical. The ability to recognize the manipulative techniques of con artists is one of the rewards of understanding argument. To employ such strategies in your arguments is to lose the attention and respect of others who understand argument, who expect a reasoned presentation of ideas and evidence. Remember that even your best efforts at convincing argument will not persuade everyone. If you present your views in a clear and honest manner, you will at least win the respect of those readers who cannot, finally, accept your position. If, however, you are crude, mean-spirited, or manipulative, you will win few to your side and lose the respect of most. The good writer will of course seek to organize and develop an argument in a skillful, persuasive way, but there is a big difference between effectively presenting one's reasons and resorting to emotional appeals or illogic to try to win the debate.

You will find that many good writers of argument go out of their way to establish common ground with readers who may disagree with them or who otherwise may feel threatened and become defensive. Recognizing that readers who feel the need to defend their position will not be open to new information or different ideas, good writers often seek a conciliatory tone and approach. In his book *On Becoming a Person,* psychologist Carl R. Rogers recommends developing conciliatory arguments, arguments that are presented in nonthreatening language, that fairly express opposing views, and that stress the common ground that opposing sides may share.

Consider, for example, the openings of two articles on city life. First, Henry Fairlie begins his article, "The Idiocy of Urban Life," this way:

> Between about 3 a.m. and 6 a.m. the life of the city is civil. Occasionally the lone footsteps of someone walking to or from work echo along the sidewalk. All work that has to be done at those hours is useful—in bakeries, for example. Even the newspaper presses stop turning forests into lies. Now and then a car comes out of the silence and cruises easily through the blinking traffic lights. The natural inhabitants of the city come out from damp basements and cellars. With their pink ears and paws, sleek, well-groomed, their whiskers combed, rats are true city dwellers. Urban life, during the hours when they reign, is urbane.

Fairlie concludes his negative view by describing life in the city as an "existence of unreality, pretense, and idiocy."

C. R. Creekmore, on the other hand, opens his article, "Cities Won't Drive You Crazy," by writing:

> Trapped in one of those Olympian traffic jams on the Garden State Parkway in New Jersey, I waited to pay my toll for the Newark exit. Horns, insults, and exhaust fumes had settled in a noisy, dark-tempered cloud. As I finally reached the end of the exact-change line, I faced a sudden dilemma. There was the automatic toll collector, side-by-side with a human toll taker standing in his little booth. I stared into the impersonal mouth of the collection machine, then at the person, and chose him. The man looked shocked. He regarded the quarter I thrust at him as if it were a bug. "Grow up!" he screamed at me with a sense of indignation that I assumed was generated by a life dedicated to the parkway system. "Grow up and use the machine!"
>
> To me, the incident has always summed up the essence of what cities are: hotbeds of small embarrassments, dehumanizing confrontations, monetary setbacks, angry people and festering acts of God.
>
> Many Americans agree with this stereotype and believe firmly that the dirty, crowded, dangerous city must gradually destroy an urbanite's psyche. . . . A large body of research, conducted in the past 15 years by a diverse group of social scientists, challenges these heartfelt prejudices.

Fairlie's images of the city and those foolish enough to live there may amuse those who already share his views, but they are not likely to please—and thus persuade—those who enjoy urban living. Few city dwellers will appreciate the idea that they are less social or urbane than rats. By contrast, Creekmore begins by relating a personal experience that can explain the negative view many hold of cities, a view that he describes as "heartfelt," if misguided. His opening says to readers: "I understand how you feel about cities, but let's look at some facts that may lead to a different view." Purposely employing the conciliatory approach may save you from producing arguments that do not work.

ARGUMENTS THAT DO NOT WORK: LOGICAL FALLACIES

A thorough study of the shape of argument needs to include a study of logical fallacies because so many "arguments" fail to meet standards of sound logic and good sense. Before examining specific types of arguments that do not work, let's consider briefly why people offer arguments that aren't sensible.

Causes of Illogic

One frequent cause for illogical debate is simply a lack of knowledge of the subject. Some people have more information than others, either from formal study or wide-ranging experiences. The younger you are, the less you can be expected to know about or understand complex issues. On the other hand, if you want to debate a complex or technical issue, then you cannot use ignorance as an excuse for producing a weak argument. To illustrate: Following the 1992 riots in Los Angeles, then press secretary Marlin Fitzwater asserted that welfare programs of the 1960s and 1970s caused the riots. When reporters asked which programs, Fitzwater responded that he did not have a list with him! Instead of ducking the need for evidence, you want to read as much as you can, listen carefully to discussions, ask questions, and, when called on to write, select topics about which you have knowledge or which you are willing to study before writing.

Ego problems are another cause of weak arguments. Those with poor self-esteem often have difficulty in debates because they attach themselves to their ideas and then feel personally attacked when someone disagrees with them. Usually the next step is a defense of their views with even greater emotion and irrationality, even though self-esteem is enhanced when others applaud our knowledge and thoughtfulness, not emotion and irrationality.

A third cause of irrationality is the collection of prejudices and biases that we carry around, having absorbed them "ages ago" from family and community. Prejudices range from the worst ethnic, religious, or sexist stereotypes to political views we have adopted uncritically (Democrats are all bleeding hearts; Republicans are all rich snobs), to perhaps less serious but equally insupportable notions (if it's in print, it must be right; if it's not meat and potatoes, it is not really dinner). People who see the world through distorted lenses cannot possibly acquire and assess facts and reason logically from them.

Finally, many bad arguments stem from a human need for answers—any answers—to the questions that deeply concern us. We want to control our world because that makes us feel secure, and having answers makes us feel in control. This need can lead to illogic from oversimplifying problems, from refusing to settle for qualified answers to questions.

The causes of illogic, not surprisingly, lead us to a twofold classification of bad arguments: logical fallacies that result from (1) oversimplifying the issue or from (2) ignoring the issue by substituting emotion for reason.

Fallacies Resulting from Oversimplifying

ERRORS IN GENERALIZING Errors in generalizing include overstatement and hasty or faulty generalization. All have in common an error in the inductive pattern of argument. In each fallacy, the inference drawn from the evidence is unwarranted, either because too broad a generalization is made or because the generalization is drawn from incomplete or incorrect evidence. *Overstatement* occurs when the argument's assertion is an unqualified generalization—that is, it refers to all members of a category or class, although the evidence justifies an assertion about only some in the class. Overstatements are frequently signaled by words such as *all, every, always, never,* or *none.* But remember that assertions such as "children love clowns" are understood to refer to "all children," even though the word *all* does not appear in the sentence. It is the writer's task to qualify statements appropriately, using words such as *some, many,* or *frequently,* as appropriate. Overstatements are discredited by finding only one exception to disprove the assertion. One frightened child who starts to cry when the clown approaches will destroy the argument. For example:

- Lawyers are only interested in making money.
  (What about Ralph Nader who works to protect consumers, or public defenders who take cases of those unable to pay for a lawyer?)

Hasty or *faulty generalizations* may be qualified assertions, but they still oversimplify by arguing from insufficient evidence or from ignoring some relevant evidence. For example:

- Political life must lead many to excessive drinking. In the last six months the paper has written about five members of Congress who have either confessed to alcoholism or have been arrested on DWI charges.
  (Five is not a large enough sample from which to generalize about *many* politicians. Also, the five in the newspaper are not a representative sample; they have made the news because of their drinking.)

FORCED HYPOTHESIS The *forced hypothesis* is also an error in inductive reasoning. The explanation (hypothesis) offered to account for a particular situation is "forced," or illogical, because either (1) sufficient evidence does not exist to draw any conclusion or (2) the evidence can be explained more simply or more sensibly by a different hypothesis. This logical fallacy often results from failure to consider other possible explanations; we can discredit a forced hypothesis by providing alternative conclusions that are more sensible or just as sensible as the one offered. Consider the following example:

- Professor Redding's students received either A's or B's last semester. He must be an excellent teacher.
  (The grades alone cannot support the conclusion.
  Professor Redding could be an excellent teacher; he could have started with excellent students; he could be an easy grader.)

NON SEQUITUR The term *non sequitur,* meaning literally "it does not follow," could apply to all arguments that do not work, but the term is usually reserved for those arguments in which the conclusions are not logically connected to the reasons, those arguments with the "glue" missing. In a hasty generalization, for example, there is a connection between support (five politicians in the news) and conclusion (many politicians with drinking problems), just not a convincing connection. With the *non sequitur* there is no recognizable connection, either because (1) whatever connection the arguer sees is not made clear to others or (2) because the evidence or reasons offered are irrelevant to the conclusion. For example:

- Donna will surely get a good grade in physics; she loved her biology class.
  (Loving one course, even one science course, does not support the conclusion that the student will get a good grade in another course. If Donna is not good at math, she definitely will not "love" physics.)

SLIPPERY SLOPE The *slippery slope* argument asserts that we should not proceed with or permit A because, if we do, the terrible consequences X, Y, and Z will occur. This type of argument oversimplifies by assuming, without evidence and usually by ignoring historical examples, existing laws, or any reasonableness in people, that X, Y, and Z will follow inevitably from A. This kind of argument rests on the belief that most people will not want the final, awful Z to occur. The belief, however accurate, does not provide a sufficiently good reason for avoiding A. One of the best-known examples of slippery slope reasoning can be found in the gun-control debate:

- If we allow the government to register handguns, next it will register hunting rifles; then it will prohibit all citizen ownership of guns, thereby creating a police state or a world in which only outlaws have guns.
  (Surely no one wants the final dire consequences predicted in this argument. However, handgun registration does not mean that the consequences will follow. The United States has never been a police state, and its system of free elections guards against such a future. Also, citizens have registered cars, boats, and planes for years without any threat of these belongings being confiscated.)

FALSE DILEMMA The *false dilemma* oversimplifies an issue by asserting only two alternatives when there are more than two. The either/or thinking of this kind of argument can be an effective tactic if undetected. If the arguer gives us only two choices and one of those is clearly unacceptable, then the arguer can push us toward the preferred choice. For example:

- The Federal Reserve System must lower interest rates, or we will never pull out of the recession.

  (Clearly, staying in a recession is not much of a choice, but the alternative may not be the only or the best course of action to achieve a healthy economy. If interest rates go too low, inflation can be triggered. Other options include the government's creating new jobs or patiently letting market forces play themselves out.)

FALSE ANALOGY When examining the shape of analogy, we also considered the problems with this type of argument. (See p. 20.) Remember that you challenge a false analogy by noting many differences in the two items being compared or by noting a significant difference that is being ignored.

POST HOC FALLACY The term *post hoc,* from the Latin *post hoc, ergo propter hoc* (literally, "after this, therefore because of it") refers to a common error in arguments about cause. One oversimplifies causation by confusing a time relationship with cause. Reveal the illogic of *post hoc* arguments by pointing to other possible causes:

- We should throw out the entire city council. Since the members were elected, the city has gone into deficit spending.

  (Assuming that deficit spending in this situation is bad, was it caused by the current city council? Or did the current council inherit debts? Or is the entire region suffering from a recession?)

Fallacies Resulting from Ignoring the Issue

There are many arguments that divert attention from the issue under debate. Of the seven discussed here, the first three try to divert attention by introducing a separate issue or "sliding by" the actual issue; the following four seek diversion by appealing to the audience's emotions or prejudices. In the first three the arguer tries to give the impression of presenting an argument; in the last four the arguer charges forward on emotional manipulation alone.

BEGGING THE QUESTION To assume that part of your argument is true without supporting it is to *beg the question.* Arguments seeking to pass off as proof statements that must themselves be supported are often introduced with such phrases as "the fact is" (to introduce opinion), "obviously," and "as we can see." For example:

- Clearly, lowering grading standards would be bad for students, so a pass-fail system should not be adopted.

  (Does a pass-fail system lower standards? No evidence has been given. If so, is that necessarily bad for students?)

RED HERRING The *red herring* is a foul-smelling argument indeed. The debater introduces a side issue, some point that is not relevant to the debate:

- The senator is an honest woman; she loves her children and gives to charities.

  (The children and charities are side issues; they do not demonstrate honesty.)

STRAW MAN The *straw man* argument attributes to opponents erroneous and usually ridiculous views that they do not hold so that their position can be easily attacked. We can challenge this illogic by demonstrating that the arguer's opponents do not hold those views or by demanding that the arguer provide some evidence that they do:

- Those who favor gun control just want to take all guns away from responsible citizens and put them in the hands of criminals.

  (The position attributed to proponents of gun control is not only inaccurate but actually the opposite of what is sought by gun-control proponents.)

AD HOMINEM One of the most frequent of all appeals to emotion masquerading as argument is the *ad hominem* argument (literally, argument "to the man"). Sometimes the debate turns to an attack of a supporter of an issue; other times, the illogic is found in name calling. When someone says that "those crazy liberals at the ACLU just want all criminals to go free," or a pro-choice demonstrator screams at those "self-righteous fascists" on the other side, the best retort may be silence, or the calm assertion that such statements do not contribute to meaningful debate.

COMMON PRACTICE OR BANDWAGON To argue that an action should be taken or a position accepted because "everyone is doing it" is illogical. The majority is not always right. Frequently when someone is defending an action as ethical on the ground that everyone does it, the action isn't ethical and the defender knows it isn't. The bandwagon argument is a desperate one:

- There's nothing wrong with fudging a bit on your income taxes. After all, the superrich don't pay any taxes, and the government expects everyone to cheat a little.

  (First, not everyone cheats on taxes; many pay to have their taxes done correctly. And if it is wrong, it is wrong regardless of the number who do it.)

AD POPULUM Another technique for arousing an audience's emotions and ignoring the issue is to appeal "to the people," to the audience's presumed shared values and beliefs. Every Fourth of July, politicians employ this tactic, appealing to God, mother, apple pie, and "traditional family values." As with all emotional gimmicks, we need to reject the argument as illogical.

- Good, law-abiding Americans must be sick of the violent crimes occurring in our once godly society. But we won't tolerate it anymore; put the criminals in jail and throw away the key.

  (This does not contribute to a thoughtful debate on criminal justice issues.)

EVALUATING THE USE OF AUTHORITY AND STATISTICS

Because many arguments provide statistical information and the inferences of authorities as support, a study of argument is incomplete without a discussion of how we evaluate such evidence. We do know that movie stars and sports figures are not authorities on cereals and soft drinks. But what about *real* authorities? When we present the opinions or research findings of authorities as support for an assertion, we are saying to readers that the authority is trustworthy and the opinions sound. But what we are saying is actually an assumption, part of the glue joining support to claim, and as such it can be challenged. If the source of evidence can be shown to lack authority, then the logic of the argument is invalid. Thus, we need to make careful judgments about the authority of evidence in any argument, including our own.

There are key questions we need to ask to evaluate evidence or opinions "on authority." First, is the study current? That is, is the evidence still valid? If the authority presents a case study or gives examples, is the evidence representative? Can the inferences presented by the authority be drawn, logically, from the examples? Second, is the writer actually viewed as an authority? Does he or she have legitimate credentials: degrees, publications in respected journals, a good reputation with peers? And finally, on the topic under debate, do authorities agree? If there is considerable disagreement over an issue, then the quoting of one authority doesn't prove much. Remember that disagreements abound in the social sciences; the experts just do not agree on what the evidence means. *Writers of argument must be able to justify their authorities.* Challengers know to take a close look at the uses of authority in any argument.

We should also know that—to use the cliché—although statistics don't lie, people lie with statistics. Numbers—statistical information and the results of polls—are facts, but when they are presented in an argument, they are being used by a person interested in supporting a position. Without fudging the numbers, writers, highly motivated to prove their point, can manipulate statistical information.

Be alert to three techniques for distorting numerical evidence. First, writers can select only the numbers that serve their purpose, that support their position. For example, in a review of Charles Murray's study of social welfare programs, *Losing Ground,* MIT economist Lester Thurow argues that Murray presents a "selective collection of 'evidence'" to give support to the Reagan political agenda. Thurow then offers the following analysis of Murray's misrepresentation of evidence:

> For example, the book contains only three words concerning the elderly: "I shall be discussing the working-age poor and discriminated against, not the elderly." Thus he does not tell us that poverty among the elderly has declined from 25.3% (twice the national average) in 1969 to 14.1% (less than the national average) in 1983. Nor does he tell us that although the elderly used to have median per capita incomes well below those of the nonelderly, their median per capita incomes are now equal to—and perhaps even slightly superior to—those of the nonelderly. In other words, the biggest social welfare success story isn't in the analysis.

Writers can also alter the reader's sense of how big or how small the numbers are by the form of presentation. Numbers can be presented as fractions, whole numbers, or percentages. If you want to emphasize budget increases, present whole numbers, billions of dollars. If you want to deemphasize budget increases, use percentages. Finally, writers can affect our response to statistics by their word choice. One can write of "a *mere* 3 percent increase," while another stresses "the *enormous* $5 billion increase."

These examples suggest the kinds of questions to ask about statistical presentations. What relevant information has not been provided? When you read "two out of three chose the Merit combination of low tar and good taste," you must ask "Two-thirds of how many altogether?" When you read that the number of women earning more than $25,000 a year has doubled in the last ten years, instead of thinking that women are finally catching up, ask "how many women actually earn more than $25,000?" And what percentage of the total workers with that salary or more do they represent? Also consider when the information was obtained, if the sample was randomly selected, if the sample was large enough to be significant, and if like items are being compared. These are the questions you need to ask when you read the arguments of others and when you look for evidence to support your own arguments.

EXERCISE: EVALUATING THE LOGIC
OF ARGUMENTS

Read and evaluate the following article (from the *New York Times,* December 12, 1984) by Stanley S. Scott, vice-president and director of corporate affairs for Philip Morris Company. Determine the claim of his argument and then consider the logic of his reasons and the significance of his evidence.

1   The civil rights act, the voting rights act and a host of antidiscrimination laws notwithstanding, millions of Americans are still forced to sit in the back of planes, trains and buses. Many more are subject to segregation in public places. Some are even denied housing and employment: victims of an alarming—yet socially acceptable—public hostility.

2   This new form of discrimination is based on smoking behavior.

3   If you happen to enjoy a cigarette, you are the potential target of violent antismokers and overzealous public enforcers determined to force their beliefs on the rest of society.

4   Ever since people began smoking, smokers and nonsmokers have been able to live with one another using common courtesy and common sense. Not anymore. Today, smokers must put up with virtually unenforceable laws regulating when and where they can smoke—laws intended as much to discourage smoking itself as to protect the rights of nonsmokers. Much worse, supposedly responsible organizations devoted to the "public interest" are encouraging the harassment of those who smoke.

5   This year, for example, the American Cancer Society is promoting programs that encourage people to attack smokers with canisters of gas, to blast them with horns, to squirt them with oversized water guns and burn them in effigy.

6   Harmless fun? Not quite. Consider the incidents that are appearing on police blotters across America:

> In a New York restaurant, a young man celebrating with friends was zapped in the face by a man with an aerosol spray

can. His offense: lighting a cigarette. The aggressor was the head of a militant antismoker organization whose goal is to mobilize an army of two million zealots to spray smokers in the face.

In a suburban Seattle drug store, a man puffing on a cigarette while he waited for a prescription to be filled was ordered to stop by an elderly customer who pulled a gun on him.

A 23-year-old lit up a cigarette on a Los Angeles bus. A passenger objected. When the smoker objected to the objection, he was fatally stabbed.

A transit policeman, using his reserve gun, shot and fatally wounded a man on a subway train in the Bronx in a shootout over smoking a cigarette.

The basic freedoms of more than 50 million American smokers are at   7
risk today. Tomorrow, who knows what personal behavior will become socially unacceptable, subject to restrictive laws and public ridicule? Could travel by private car make the social engineers' hit list because it is less safe than public transit? Could ice cream, cake and cookies become socially unacceptable because their consumption causes obesity? What about sky diving, mountain climbing, skiing and contact sports? How far will we allow this to spread?

The question all Americans must ask themselves is: can a nation that   8
has struggled so valiantly to eliminate bias based on race, religion and sex afford to allow a fresh set of categories to encourage new forms of hostility between large groups of citizens?

After all, discrimination is discrimination, no matter what it is   9
based on.

CHAPTER 2

READING AND
RESPONDING TO
ARGUMENTS

Because they understand how written works are put together, good writers usually make good readers. The reverse is also true: Reading well can lead to writing well. The close connection between reading and writing skills results in writing assignments in reading courses and reading assignments in writing courses. Whether your primary purpose is the study of argument or the study of writing, you will be assigned readings for several reasons.

First, readings are assigned to illustrate various forms of writing. They serve students as models of the kinds of writing they will be asked to create. The various pieces interspersed throughout Chapter 1, for example, illustrate types of argument. In addition to studying the whole essay, models should be examined for the ways they organize and present evidence and for their uses of language. We also read for information, for facts and ideas, for new ways of analyzing issues. There is much to be learned about history, about philosophy and politics, and about your contemporary society in the collection of arguments in this text.

Finally, we read in order to write, to find topics to write about, information to incorporate in our writing, and ideas to respond to. Reading spurs writing. Journalists prepare stories about the homeless. One reader responds with a letter to the editor in which he compares the homeless to the squirrels on Capitol Hill. A student, to complete an argument assignment, writes a refutation of the letter, an essay that is then reproduced in this text (see pp. 87–91), providing reading for other students. You will be called upon to respond to your reading or incorporate sources into your writing in various ways. This chapter examines some of the specific ways that you may be asked to respond, but first let's consider the reading process itself.

ACTIVE READING

Responses to written works vary depending in part on your purposes in reading. Most readers skim more of the daily paper than they read. When first examining texts or library materials, you are wise to use a "flip-and-skim" approach to see what the work contains and how it may be useful to you. But once you become engaged in a particular work that you must know well, then accuracy, not speed, should be the goal. You can improve your reading skills by adhering to the following steps to accurate, engaged reading:

1. *Become a part of the writer's audience.* We need to understand and accept that writers do not have all of us in mind when they write. Specialists writing to other experts assume knowledge that some readers may not have. Writers from earlier times assume readers who share a culture that we today may not understand very well. You prepare yourself to join a writer's audience by learning as much as you can about the writer, about the time the piece was written, and about the anticipated audience. For writings in this text, you will be aided by introductory notes; be sure to study them.
2. *Read with an open mind.* Good readers seek new knowledge and ideas; they do not "rewrite" a work to suit themselves. Remember that not all who write will share your views or express themselves as you do. Your task as an engaged reader is to read what is on the page, giving the writer a fair chance to develop ideas, giving yourself the thoughtful reflection needed to comprehend those ideas.

3. *Consider the title.* Titles are the first words writers give us about their work. Take time to look for clues in the title that may reveal both the work's subject and perhaps the writer's approach or attitude as well.

4. *Read slowly.* The initial goal of reading is understanding the writer's message, not completing an assignment as quickly as possible. Only when you slow down will you be able to observe the key words that connect a writer's ideas, establish the relationships among the parts of a written work, and create the work's tone.

5. *Use a dictionary and other appropriate reference works.* Reading a work containing words that you do not know is like trying to play tennis with some of the strings missing from your racket. When reading Gans's essay in Chapter 3, you may need to look up the word *pejorative.* You should also obtain information about any particular examples writers use, about the people, places, events, or concepts they refer to but do not explain. If you miss the point of an illustration, you may miss the point of the entire work.

6. *Be alert to the use of figurative language and other writing strategies.* Remember that recognizing a work's tone is important to understanding a writer's position and that figurative language helps shape tone. Watch for such elements as metaphors, irony, and understatement. (See pp. 55–58.)

7. *Make notes.* Use more than just your eyes when you read. The more senses you engage, the more active your involvement in the reading process. As you read, underline key sentences such as each paragraph's topic sentence and the writer's thesis, if stated. When you look up a word's definition, write the definition in the margin so that you can reread that section with understanding. Make whatever other notes that will help you become more fully engaged in the reading process. Don't just underline a writer's main idea; note in the margin that it *is* the main idea. When you recognize that a writer is providing a series of examples or a list of reasons, label them as "examples" or "reasons" and then number each one in the margin. Draw pictures to illustrate concepts; draw arrows to connect examples to ideas.

8. *Keep a reading journal.* In addition to taking notes in the margin of your text, you may want to develop the useful habit of writing regularly in a journal. A reading journal records your responses to reading assignments but is more informal and personal than class notes. Keeping a journal gives you the opportunity to record impressions and feelings, initial reactions to assignments, perhaps ideas that will eventually shape your next essay. Purchase a sectional notebook for class and devote one section to class notes, another to entries on your reading. Write on one side of the page only, leaving the blank side

for additions, perhaps after the reading has been discussed in class or you have read it a second time. If you develop the habit of writing regularly, chances are that both your reading and writing skills will improve.

RESPONDING TO READING

To say that you will be assigned readings for models, to gain new knowledge about issues, and to generate writing is to suggest that not all responses to reading are appropriate for academic writing. You may read romance novels or science fiction for fun; you may read *People* magazine so that you can join in casual conversations about the lives of movie or sports celebrities. These are legitimate activities of self-expression, but in the classroom self-expression may not be the primary goal. You are most likely to be asked *what* a work says or *how* it contrasts with another work, or *if* the argument is sound, not whether you liked the essay. The following pages explain and illustrate various responses to reading typical of academic work. First, though, read Michael Korda's essay and answer the questions that follow.

❖

How to Be a Leader

Michael Korda

Editor-in-chief of the publishing firm Simon and Schuster, Michael Korda (b. 1933) is author of Power *(1975) and the novels* Worldly Goods *(1982),* Queenie *(1985), and* The Fortune *(1989). This essay appeared in* Newsweek *on January 5, 1981.*

At a moment when we are waiting to see whether we have elected a President or a leader, it is worth examining the differences between the two. For not every President is a leader, but every time we elect a President we hope for one, especially in times of doubt and crisis. In easy times we are ambivalent—the leader, after all, makes demands, challenges the status quo, shakes things up.

Leadership is as much a question of timing as anything else. The leader must appear on the scene at a moment when people are looking for leadership, as Churchill did in 1940, as Roosevelt did in 1933, as Lenin did in 1917. And when he comes, he must offer a simple, eloquent message.

1

2

3   Great leaders are almost always great simplifiers, who cut through argument, debate and doubt to offer a solution everybody can understand and remember. Churchill warned the British to expect "blood, toil, tears and sweat"; FDR told Americans that "the only thing we have to fear is fear itself"; Lenin promised the war-weary Russians peace, land and bread. Straightforward but potent messages.

4   We have an image of what a leader ought to be. We even recognize the physical signs: leaders may not necessarily be tall, but they must have bigger-than-life, commanding features—LBJ's nose and ear lobes, Ike's broad grin. A trademark also comes in handy: Lincoln's stovepipe hat, JFK's rocker. We expect our leaders to stand out a little, not to be like ordinary men. Half of President Ford's trouble lay in the fact that, if you closed your eyes for a moment, you couldn't remember his face, figure or clothes. A leader should have an unforgettable identity, instantly and permanently fixed in people's minds.

5   It also helps for a leader to be able to do something most of us can't: FDR overcame polio; Mao swam the Yangtze River at the age of 72. We don't want our leaders to be "just like us." We want them to be like us but better, special, more so. Yet if they are *too* different, we reject them. Adlai Stevenson was too cerebral. Nelson Rockefeller, too rich.

6   Even television, which comes in for a lot of knocks as an image-builder that magnifies form over substance, doesn't altogether obscure the qualities of leadership we recognize, or their absence. Television exposed Nixon's insecurity, Humphrey's fatal infatuation with his own voice.

7   A leader must know how to use power (that's what leadership is about), but he also has to have a way of showing that he does. He has to be able to project firmness—no physical clumsiness (like Ford), no rapid eye movements (like Carter).

8   A Chinese philosopher once remarked that a leader must have the grace of a good dancer, and there is a great deal of wisdom to this. A leader should know how to appear relaxed and confident. His walk should be firm and purposeful. He should be able, like Lincoln, FDR, Truman, Ike and JFK, to give a good, hearty, belly laugh, instead of the sickly grin that passes for good humor in Nixon or Carter. Ronald Reagan's training as an actor showed to good effect in the debate with Carter, when by his easy manner and apparent affability, he managed to convey the impression that in fact he was the President and Carter the challenger.

9   If we know what we're looking for, why is it so difficult to find? The answer lies in a very simple truth about leadership. People can only be led where they want to go. The leader follows, though a step ahead. Americans *wanted* to climb out of the Depression and needed someone to tell them they could do it, and FDR did. The British believed that they could still win the war after the defeats of 1940, and Churchill told them they were right.

A leader rides the waves, moves with the tides, understands the deepest yearnings of his people. He cannot make a nation that wants peace at any price go to war, or stop a nation determined to fight from doing so. His purpose must match the national mood. His task is to focus the people's energies and desires, to define them in simple terms, to inspire, to make what people already want seem attainable, important, within their grasp.

Above all, he must dignify our desires, convince us that we are taking part in the making of great history, give us a sense of glory about ourselves. Winston Churchill managed, by sheer rhetoric, to turn the British defeat and the evacuation of Dunkirk in 1940 into a major victory. FDR's words turned the sinking of the American fleet at Pearl Harbor into a national rallying cry instead of a humiliating national scandal. A leader must stir our blood, not appeal to our reason.

For this reason, businessmen generally make poor leaders. They tend to be pragmatists who think that once you've explained why something makes sense, people will do it. But history shows the fallacy of this belief. When times get tough, people don't want to be told what went wrong, or lectured, or given a lot of complicated statistics and plans (like Carter's energy policy) they don't understand. They want to be moved, excited, inspired, consoled, uplifted—in short, led!

A great leader must have a certain irrational quality, a stubborn refusal to face facts, infectious optimism, the ability to convince us that all is not lost even when we're afraid it is. Confucius suggested that, while the advisers of a great leader should be as cold as ice, the leader himself should have fire, a spark of divine madness.

He won't come until we're ready for him, for the leader is like a mirror, reflecting back to us our own sense of purpose, putting into words our own dreams and hopes, transforming our needs and fears into coherent policies and programs.

Our strength makes him strong; our determination makes him determined; our courage makes him a hero; he is, in the final analysis, the symbol of the best in us, shaped by our own spirit and will. And when these qualities are lacking in us, we can't produce him; and even with all our skill at image building, we can't fake him. He is, after all, merely the sum of us.

Questions

1. Which newly elected president does Korda refer to in sentence 1? How do you know?
2. What is Korda's subject? What is his main idea or point, his thesis? (Be sure to state the thesis as a complete sentence.)

3. What, according to Korda, are the chief characteristics of a leader? List both the traits needed by a leader and the traits that keep one from being a good leader.
4. What is Korda's primary method of developing and supporting his thesis?
5. What is the relationship between leaders and their followers? What do followers want from a leader? What does a leader need from potential followers to be successful?

Reinforcing the Reading Process

After reading complex material, even when following guidelines for active reading, you may still feel uncertain about the thoroughness of your understanding. Understanding a writer's subject and purpose can be aided by a preliminary analysis of the work's thesis, evidence, and organization.

WHAT IS THE THESIS? Often the first question an instructor asks to initiate class discussion of an assigned essay is: "What is the thesis?" The *thesis* is the main idea or chief point a writer wants to establish. In argument, the thesis is the writer's primary assertion or claim. A thesis is not the same as the writer's subject; rather, it is what the writer wants to assert about the subject. Korda's subject is leadership; what he asserts about the nature of leadership is his thesis. If you answer the instructor's question by saying that Korda is examining leadership or leadership traits, you are off to a good start in determining the thesis, but you need to ask, and then answer, the question: "What does Korda assert about the traits required for leadership?"

As you read, try to locate a sentence or two that seem to establish the writer's position on his or her subject, but keep in mind that a thesis does not have to be stated specifically in an article. Sometimes an author's thesis is implied, so you will have to formulate a thesis statement after you finish reading. Make sure always to state a work's thesis as a complete sentence. Doing so will help you get beyond a statement of subject to an assertion. The difference between Korda's subject and his thesis illustrates the distinction:

Subject: The Nature of Leadership

Thesis: Great leaders need to come at the right time and have several key traits that include special talents, firmness, and the ability to simplify, to use power, and to inspire others.

HOW IS THE THESIS DEVELOPED? After finding a writer's thesis or writing a sentence that expresses the work's main idea, you can usefully examine the kinds of evidence provided to develop and support the writer's claim. If you have trouble deciding on the thesis, you may benefit by starting with an analysis of how the essay is developed and then work toward an appropriate generalization. Does the writer provide a series of examples? If so, what do they demonstrate? Is the article developed by one lengthy illustration? Does the author present a sequence of connected ideas, or reasons? Korda presents several ideas about leadership and timing and illustrates his ideas with specific examples of presidents and prime ministers. If you are the type of reader who remembers specific details but has trouble seeing what the particulars add up to, make a list of the work's facts and examples and then reflect on what assertion the details would support.

WHAT IS THE WORK'S SHAPE OR ORGANIZATION? An analysis of a work's structure can also help you to understand what you have read. Becoming aware of shape will enable you to distinguish between main ideas and evidence, to follow the steps in an argument, to recognize the writer's purpose. The more precisely you understand what an author is doing and how she or he is accomplishing that task, the better you will grasp the author's message. Some patterns used repeatedly include:

1. *Chronology.* Arguments can employ time sequence by following, for example, the process of a particular case through the legal system or by reviewing the historical development of a particular debate. In "How to Get the Poor Off Our Conscience," John Kenneth Galbraith organizes his discussion of solutions to the problem of poverty by beginning with the Bible and then proceeding through the centuries to conclude with several contemporary positions, including his own.

2. *General to particular.* A frequent structure in essay writing is to begin with a generalization, one's thesis, and then to present evidence—particulars—in support of the position. If several distinct reasons are given to support a claim, they may be introduced one at a time, with support given for each reason before the writer moves on to the next point. In their critique of euthanasia (see pp. 291–97), Drs. Singer and Siegler first refute each of the two reasons usually given in support of euthanasia and then proceed to explain and support each of their several reasons for opposing euthanasia.

3. *Particular to general.* Reversing the pattern to begin with evidence and then conclude with the claim is also a common pattern, especially when the issue is controversial. The advantage of this approach lies in enticing readers by presenting facts first and stating controversial opinions last.

4. *Question-answer; problem-solution.* Arguments frequently follow the pattern of beginning with a question to be answered or reminding readers of a current problem, and then offering an answer to the question or a solution to the problem. The question-answer structure is used by researchers reporting the results of experiments in the sci-

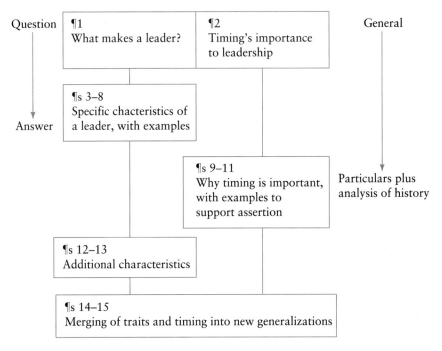

Figure 2.1 Diagram of "How to Be a Leader"

ences and social sciences and by writers debating the meaning of terms or concepts. Korda is essentially answering the question, "What are the characteristics of a leader?" When Charles Krautham-mer argues that we must make illegal drugs seem less glamorous (see pp. 228–30), he is offering a solution to the problem of the crime and violence generated by illegal drugs.

Keep these patterns in mind as you read and develop the habit of ex-amining a work's structure to aid reading comprehension. You can make marginal notes that emphasize organization, or even diagram the work's organization to observe its parts and their relationships, as illustrated in Figure 2.1.

WRITING SUMMARIES AND PARAPHRASES

Reading actively and then reinforcing the reading process should give you the understanding needed to write a summary of the work. The ability to write clear and accurate summaries is an important skill; most students will have occasion to write summaries in at least one of these four situations:

1. To have a record of what you have read to prepare for class discussion or for future study or research
2. To respond to a test question calling for information from assigned reading
3. To demonstrate that assigned material has been read and understood ("Prepare a 100-word summary of each article on the reading list.")
4. To reproduce the main ideas of a work that you will also examine in some other way, perhaps in a comparative analysis of two arguments or a refutation of an argument

For each of these purposes, you need a *summary,* a brief statement that accurately reproduces, in your own words, the main points of the work, a statement that does not misrepresent or distort the writer's ideas in any way. If you are summarizing a writer's ideas in an argument, before proceeding to challenge them, fairness requires that you first represent the writer's position accurately. If an instructor assigns a summary of course readings, then be sure to write a nonevaluative restatement of each writer's ideas. To prepare good summaries, follow these guidelines for writing:

Guidelines for Writing a Summary

1. Maintain a direct, objective style without resorting to overly simplistic sentences.
2. Begin with the writer's thesis and then present additional key points following the order of the original article.
3. Exclude specific examples, illustrations, or background sections.
4. Combine main ideas into fewer sentences than were used in the original.
5. Select precise, accurate verbs to show the relationship of ideas (Korda *asserts,* or Korda *argues*) rather than vague verbs that provide only a list of ideas (Korda *talks* about or Korda *says* that).

With these writing guidelines in mind, read the following summary of Michael Korda's "How to Be a Leader" (pp. 41–43) and consider why it needs revision.

Summary 1

In Michael Korda's "How to Be a Leader" (*Newsweek,* 1981), Korda talks about leadership. He says that we don't know yet if the new president will be a leader. Leadership has to do with timing. He says that leaders are simplifiers, out of the ordinary,

special, know how to use power, not clumsy, easygoing. He
goes on to say that leaders should move us and not be pragmatic like businessmen. Korda concludes that leaders are "merely
the sum of us."

We can agree that the writer of this summary has read and basically understood Korda's essay. However, the summary lacks focus and can even
be said to be misleading. The summary can be greatly improved by eliminating the unimportant second sentence and combining the first and third
sentences into a more precise, forceful thesis statement. Next, the sentences
stating key qualities of a leader can be better organized into those qualities
leading to admiration and those enabling the leader to motivate others.
The quality of "easygoing" needs refinement, for to have the "divine madness" of a leader is certainly not to be easygoing. Finally, the concluding
sentence needs a major overhaul so as not to misleadingly suggest that, in
spite of the qualities listed, a leader is not really special. Here is a much-
improved version:

Summary 2

In Michael Korda's "How to Be a Leader" (*Newsweek*, 1981),
Korda asserts that leadership does not exist in a political position but in both particular leadership qualities and in timing.
He explains that leaders must have a clear identity and be able
to inspire others but that leaders must also come at a time
when people want to be led. Korda argues that great leaders
need traits that make them stand out: special talents, grace,
firmness; they also need to be able to inspire others by simplify-
ing issues, using power effectively, stirring their followers, and
convincing them that problems can be solved. Korda concludes
by returning to the issue of timing and stressing the need for
followers to show some of the courage and strength they want
in a leader so that both can move forward.

Occasionally a summary of a page or more, rather than a paragraph,
may be required. In a longer summary, key terms and phrases may be presented in direct quotation, and the author's methods of development and
kinds of evidence may be described. To expand on the paragraph summary
of Korda's essay, one could explain that Korda uses famous leaders to illustrate the traits needed for leadership and contrasts positive traits found
in great presidents and prime ministers with negative traits found in those
presidents who were not great leaders.

Although the terms *summary* and *paraphrase* are often used interchangeably, they are not exact synonyms. A *paraphrase*, like a summary, is

a nonevaluative restatement of someone's writing, usually a complex passage, a brief essay, or a poem. The goal of a paraphrase is to represent accurately, but in simpler words and sentences, the work in question. Paraphrase differs from summary in that it frequently contains more words than the original passage.

To illustrate, we will examine the following paragraph from Jean-Jacques Rousseau's *The Social Contract*. In this paragraph Rousseau raises the question of the right, if any, that the strong man has to require obedience and offers the argument that might does not justify obedience:

> Let us assume for a moment that some such Right does really exist. The only deduction from this premise is inexplicable gibberish. For to admit that Might makes Right is to reverse the process of effect and cause. The mighty man who defeats his rival becomes heir to his Right. So soon as we can disobey with impunity, disobedience becomes legitimate. And, since the Mightiest is always right, it merely remains for us to become possessed of Might. But what validity can there be in a Right which ceases to exist when Might changes hands? If a man be constrained by Might to obey, what need has he to obey by Duty? And if he is not constrained to obey, there is no further obligation on him to do so. It follows, therefore, that the word Right adds nothing to the idea of Might. It becomes, in this connection, completely meaningless.

To paraphrase this paragraph we can write:

> Rousseau says that it is illogical to assert that the mighty ruler has any right to require obedience, that only "gibberish" follows such an assumption because to say that "Might makes Right" is to say that might can cause right whereas the reverse is actually true. That is, being in the right should give power, but strength or power does not give right. If might makes right, then any mighty man can, by defeating a rival, take his right away. But such a position encourages the mighty to disobey those with a right to obedience and makes disobedience legitimate. Besides, how can there be any "rightness" in obeying someone if that rightness ends as soon as a stronger person takes it away? If we obey only because the strong make us obey them, then there is no duty to obey, only pressure from the mighty's strength. When might changes hands, then, we are no longer obligated to obey the one who has might and thinks he also has right. To have might, therefore, is to have power but not to have right; it is meaningless to talk of right as necessarily a part of might.

The paraphrase is longer than Rousseau's original, for the goal is to clarify complex political philosophy, not to highlight main ideas, as in a summary. When engaged in active reading, let the kind of marking you do of the text guide your decision to write a summary or a paraphrase. If you easily find a work's thesis and can indicate the main points in support of it, then you have the elements of a summary. But if you find yourself making long notes in the margin, then you probably need to paraphrase those passages to be certain that you understand what you are reading. Also, when an instructor asks you to restate a writer's ideas, think about whether you need a summary or a paraphrase. If you are asked to restate a writer's argument, the instructor wants a summary; if an instructor asks you to explain, in your own words, the reasoning of a complex argument, the instructor wants a paraphrase.

EXERCISE: SUMMARY AND PARAPHRASE

1. The following editorial, "Hate Crimes and Free Speech," appeared in the *Washington Post* on June 23, 1992, immediately after the Supreme Court's ruling on a case involving "hate crime." Summarize the editorial in one paragraph—no more than five or six sentences. Be sure to begin your summary with the thesis.

1   Robert Viktora ought to be prosecuted. He and several other teenagers were arrested two years ago and charged with burning a makeshift cross in the yard of a black family in their St. Paul, Minn., neighborhood. He might have been charged with making terroristic threats, arson or criminal damage to property, all punishable by imprisonment and fines. But instead he was charged with racially motivated assault—a count he has not yet challenged—and hate crime. The latter makes it a misdemeanor to place "on public or private property a symbol, object, characterization or graffiti, including, but not limited to, a burning cross or Nazi swastika, which one knows or has reasonable grounds to know arouses anger, alarm or resentment in others on the basis of race, color, creed, religion or gender." Yesterday a unanimous U.S. Supreme Court ruled that ordinance unconstitutional on First Amendment grounds.

2   The ruling is sweeping and reassuring, since the most recent controversial Supreme Court opinions upholding unpopular symbolic speech were the flag-burning cases, decided on a 5-4 vote. But the justices were not unanimous in their reasoning. Four would have held that the St. Paul prohibition is not aimed at "fighting words," utterances that are intended and likely to incite immediate violent response, for which there is no constitutional protection. Five joined an opinion written by Justice Scalia, who

reasons that even if the prohibited conduct is the equivalent of fighting words, the ordinance is unconstitutional because it prohibits symbolic speech on the grounds of content. Thus, for example, while a city can regulate all noisy sound trucks it cannot make a distinction based on content and regulate only noisy sound trucks blaring messages against the incumbent government. Similarly, while fighting words in general can be regulated, a community cannot frame an ordinance in terms of the content of the speech itself. St. Paul cannot then penalize fighting words because they might provoke violence on the basis of race, religion or ethnic background and leave undisturbed similar speech expressing hostility on the basis of political affiliation, union membership or homosexuality.

This ruling will force reconsideration of hundreds of laws and speech   3
codes in public universities. All regulations that impose content-based restrictions on speech are in jeopardy. They should be. Criminal conduct such as the arson, trespass and threats involved in the Minnesota cross burning must be prosecuted. But the placing of a swastika in one's window, the drawing of a caricature that exaggerates ethnic or racial appearance and the carrying of a sign that says: "Girls are smarter than boys"—all of which would have been criminal under the contested ordinance—constitute protected speech. The preservation of a forum in which even insulting, hurtful and outrageous ideas can be expressed is an essential price of our system; without it free speech would be fatally undermined.

2. The following passage is from the essay "A Free Man's Worship" by the British philosopher Bertrand Russell. Paraphrase the paragraph, choosing your words carefully and increasing the number of sentences to make Russell's ideas clear.

   Brief and powerless is Man's life; on him and all his race the slow, sure doom falls pitiless and dark. Blind to good and evil, reckless of destruction, omnipotent matter rolls on its relentless way; for Man, condemned to-day to lose his dearest, to-morrow himself to pass through the gate of darkness, it remains only to cherish, ere yet the blow falls, the lofty thoughts that ennoble his little day; disdaining the coward terrors of the slave of Fate, to worship at the shrine that his own hands have built; undismayed by the empire of chance, to preserve a mind free from the wanton tyranny that rules his outward life; proudly defiant of the irresistible forces that tolerate, for a moment, his knowledge and his condemnation, to sustain alone, a weary but unyielding Atlas,* the world that his own ideals have fashioned despite the trampling march of unconscious power.

* Brother of Prometheus, condemned to support the sky on his shoulders; thus anyone bearing a heavy load.—Ed.

ANALYZING A WRITER'S STYLE

Understanding style, that is, how a piece has been written, can further strengthen a reader's understanding of content by making clear the writer's attitude toward his or her subject. Analyzing techniques of style also helps us understand why some arguments are so persuasive, even those with which we disagree. Remember that writers who do not resort to name calling and other logical fallacies designed to manipulate will still compose their arguments with care, using appropriate rhetorical strategies to move readers to embrace their views. This applies even to the research team reporting and drawing conclusions from its experimentation, for the unemotional scientific report is designed to establish credibility through objectivity. All writers, in short, select a style; readers need to recognize each writer's strategies for creating tone and affecting their readers.

Word Choice

The first element of style to examine closely is word choice. Consider the following sentences on the subject of scofflaws by Frank Trippett:

> [I]t is painfully apparent that millions of Americans who would never think of themselves as lawbreakers, let alone criminals, are taking increasing liberties with the legal codes that are designed to protect and nourish their society. Indeed, there are moments today—amid outlaw litter, tax cheating, illicit noise and motorized anarchy—when it seems as though the scofflaw represents the wave of the future.

Does Trippett approve of scofflaws? Is he a sociologist reporting on changes in American society? Trippett's word choice tells us that the answer to both questions is no; Trippett disapproves strongly of Americans ignoring the laws. How do we know? His word choice. The laws exist to "protect" and "nourish" us, but we are "lawbreakers," even "criminals." We are outlaws and cheaters who engage in "illicit" behavior and "anarchy." The words selected to describe laws are positive; those that describe scofflaws are negative.

Two terms that are helpful in analyzing word choice are *denotation* and *connotation*. Words with similar meanings have similar denotations, but not all words with similar denotations have the same connotation. A word's connotation is what the word suggests, what we associate the word with, that goes beyond its formal definitions. The words *house* and *home,* for example, both refer to a building or structure in which people live. But the word *home* also suggests concepts and feelings of family and security. Thus the word *home* has a strong positive connotation, whereas *house* has little if any connotative significance. *House* brings to mind a picture of a physical structure but little else because the word doesn't carry the emotional baggage that words with connotations carry. Consider Trippett's use of both *lawbreakers* and *criminals*. Although these words are synonyms, for most people *criminals* has a strong negative connotation, but *lawbreakers* is a more neutral, technical label. For Trippett, Americans who cheat on taxes and run red lights are not merely lawbreakers but criminals; the difference is connotation.

In addition to responding to a writer's choice of connotative language, we need to observe the *level of diction* used. Are the writer's words primarily typical of conversational language (that is, colloquial) or of a more formal style? Does the writer use slang words or technical words? Is the word choice concrete and vivid or abstract and intellectual? These differences help to shape a work's tone and affect our response to what we read. For example, Michael Korda's colloquial style is created in large part by his word choice. Korda says that a leader "must know how to use power." He could have said, if he wanted to sound more formal, that a leader "must have the ability to exercise power." The second option isn't technical or scholarly, but it definitely is more formal than what Korda chose to write. Consider for contrast Lincoln's word choice in "The Gettysburg Address": "on this continent" rather than "in this land," "we take increased devotion" rather than "we become more committed." Lincoln is consistently formal and abstract in his address.

One way to produce an informal style is to choose simple words: *use* instead of *exercise*. To create greater informality (a colloquial style), a writer can use contractions: *can't* for *cannot, we're* for *we are*. Korda uses fourteen contractions in his short essay on leadership, but there are no contractions in "The Gettysburg Address." Contractions are one of the chief marks of colloquial style; you may be wise to keep them to a minimum in your academic writing.

Sentence Structure

Choosing the words to convey attitude and shape a desired style is only part of the writing task; writers also think carefully about the arrangement of words into sentence structures. Examining a writer's choice of structures will reveal how sentence patterns affect style and tone. Are the writer's sentences generally long, short, or varied in length? Are the structures primarily:

- *Simple* (one independent clause)
  Leadership is as much a question of timing as anything else.

- *Compound* (two or more independent clauses)
  The Industrial Revolution was under way, and the British could see the changes in their lives.
- *Complex* (at least one independent and one dependent clause)
  When times get tough, people don't want to be told what went wrong.

The longer the sentence and more complex the structure, the more formal the style. Long compound sentences joined by *and* do not increase formality much because these sentences are really two or more short, simple sentences hooked together. But simple sentences, those with one independent clause, that have been expanded by many modifiers will create a formal style. The following simple sentence from Korda's "How to Be a Leader," for example, is more complicated than the sample compound sentence above:

- *Expanded simple sentence*

  [A] leader is like a mirror, reflecting back to us our own sense of purpose, putting into words our own dreams and hopes, transforming our needs and fears into coherent policies and programs.

In "The Gettysburg Address" three sentences range from 10 to 16 words, six from 21 to 29 words, and the final sentence is an incredible 82 words. All but two of Lincoln's sentences are either complex or compound-complex sentences. Korda's typical sentence lengths and structures contrast with Lincoln's and reflect the important role sentences play in creating style. Korda has some sentences of over 20 words, but most range between 10 and 16 words, and some are as brief as 4 words.

Other elements of sentence structure shape a writer's style. Although many English teachers work hard to rid student writing of *sentence fragments* (incomplete sentences), professional writers know that the occasional fragment can be used effectively for emphasis. Korda writes:

Adlai Stevenson was too cerebral. Nelson Rockefeller, too rich.

The second sentence is, technically, a fragment, but because its structure is so much like the previous sentence, we tend to add the missing verb *was* ourselves. The brevity, repetition of structure, and involvement of the reader all contribute to an emphatic conclusion to Korda's fifth paragraph.

An overly simplistic sentence structure, just like an overly simplistic vocabulary, can be used to show that the writer thinks the subject is silly or childish or insulting. In one essay, syndicated columnist Ellen Goodman objects to society's oversimplifying of addictions and need to believe in quick and lasting cures. To emphasize her point, she presents several well-known examples, but notice her style:

> Hi, my name is Jane and I was once a bulimic but now I am an exercise guru. . . . Hi, my name is Oprah and I was a food addict but now I am a size 10.

Metaphors

When Korda writes that a leader is like a mirror, he is using a metaphor, or more specifically a simile. Similes and metaphors are more alike than different. Both draw a comparison between two things that are not really alike but seem, in the writer's mind, to be alike in some significant way. The difference between metaphors and similes is only one of expression. Metaphors state directly, or imply, the comparison; similes express the comparison by using a connector such as *like* or *as*. We can see the difference between metaphors and similes by using Korda's idea:

Simile: A leader is like a mirror.

Metaphor: A leader mirrors the desires of his or her followers.

When we analyze style, observing how often a writer uses metaphors (or similes) is important, but more important is the impact of the chosen metaphors. The comparisons that writers make reveal much about their perceptions of and attitudes toward their subjects. Korda's simile of a leader as a mirror captures perfectly his perception that a leader is but a good reflection of the desires of his or her followers.

Metaphors, like connotative words, are so powerful, so emotionally compelling, that we respond to them even if we are not conscious of their use. But to be fully aware of a writer's attitude, we need, first, to recognize that words or phrases are metaphorical and, next, to take time to "open up" the metaphor: to state the two items being compared, to understand the point of the comparison, and to consider the emotional effect of the comparison. During World War II, E. B. White, the essayist and author of children's books, defined democracy in one of his *New Yorker* columns. His definition contains a series of metaphors, including the statement that democracy "is the hole in the stuffed shirt through which the sawdust slowly trickles." This clever and complex metaphor, when examined, makes a important statement about democracy. We can "open up" (a metaphor, too) or explain the metaphor thus:

Just as one can punch a hole in a scarecrow's shirt and discover that there is only sawdust inside, nothing to be frightened of, so the idea of equality in a democracy "punches" a hole in the notion of an aristocratic ruling class and reveals that aristocrats, underneath, are ordinary people, just like the rest of us.

Note that one source of power in a metaphor lies in its compression.

EXERCISE: ANALYZING METAPHORS

Here are two more of White's metaphors on democracy. Open up each one by explaining the line in a few sentences.

Democracy is "the dent in the high hat."
Democracy is "the score at the beginning of the ninth."

Organization and Examples

While looking closely at a writer's word choice and sentence structure, do not neglect the work's organization and the choice of examples, for both reveal attitude and shape the reader's response. When analyzing organization, consider both volume and placement. Is the writer expansive, using many words to develop a point? Or is the style economical—brief, concise? Are some points developed at length while others are passed over quickly? The amount of development can tell us something about a writer's attitude. When a writer briefly presents some evidence, he may be signaling that he considers the facts to be well known or the reasons to be self-evident. On the other hand, he may be assuming agreement where none exists or have inadequate evidence to develop the point. If we conclude that either one of these latter explanations is appropriate, then we have found a flaw in the argument. Blocking the work's structure, as illustrated earlier in this chapter, can help us see what sections are getting the greatest development, hence the greatest emphasis, in an argument.

The examples chosen to illustrate points also merit our attention. Can we agree that the examples are representative, and thus fair, or is the writer distorting the realities of the issue to support her point? For example, a writer arguing in favor of the death penalty may refer to murderers such as Charles Manson to persuade readers that such people deserve the ultimate punishment. By contrast, a writer arguing against the death penalty may choose to discuss the 1992 execution of Roger Coleman in Virginia, a case involving a poor person with a court-appointed lawyer and some discrepancies in the details of the case. Readers uncertain of their position on capital punishment may well be swayed by each writer's choice of example.

Repetition

Some repetition of key words and phrases will occur in well-written and unified essays. Some writers, though, go beyond this technique of effective writing and use repetition to produce an effective cadence, like a drum beating in the background, keeping time with the speaker's fist pounding the lectern for emphasis. In his repetition of the now-famous phrase, "I have a dream," Martin Luther King, Jr., gave stirring expression to his vision of an ideal America. In the following paragraph a student tried her hand at repetition to give emphasis to her definition of liberty:

> Liberty is having the right to vote and not having other laws restrict that right; it is having the right to apply to the university of your choice without being rejected because of race. Liberty exists when a gay person has the right to a teaching position. Liberty exists when a woman who has been offered a job does not have to decline for lack of access to day care, or when a sixteen-year-old boy from a ghetto can continue his education rather than being compelled to go to work to help support his family.

These examples suggest that repetition generally gives weight and seriousness to a work and thus is appropriate when serious issues are being debated in a forceful manner.

Hyperbole, Understatement, and Irony

Three other techniques for shaping tone and expressing attitude include hyperbole (overstatement), understatement, and verbal irony. The three are similar in that all function by creating a discrepancy between what the writer says and what the writer actually means for the reader to understand. *Hyperbole* is the easiest of the three to recognize, for the writer so overstates the case that we recognize the satiric intent. Although hyperbole can be used to satirize, usually the tone is light because of the humorous quality in overstatement. Complaining about today's "food chic," Russell Baker writes:

In the past 20 years the compendium of fatal foods has, at one time or another, included everything consumed by the human race. The only way to live forever, it seemed, was never to eat again.

Understatement and irony can also be used with a light hand but often create a more serious or biting tone. To play down what is important is to give emphasis to the issue's seriousness. Recall Ellen Goodman's sentences from her argument on addiction (see p. 55). They can also be used as examples of understatement, for the word choice and sentence structure, by playing down the complex causes for addiction and the difficulties of becoming—and staying—cured, aid her argument for giving serious attention to the physical and psychological problems of addiction.

Hyperbole expresses more than is meant, and understatement expresses less; *verbal irony* can be defined as expressing the opposite of what is meant. Recognizing verbal irony in writing takes skilled reading and some practice. When the exasperated parent says to the scruffy-jeans-and-sweatshirt-dressed teenager, "Dressed for dinner, I see," the teenager can tell from the tone of voice and body language, as well as the social context, that the parent really wants the outfit changed before the family goes to dinner. In writing, the body language is missing and the tone somewhat harder to "hear," so we have to rely on the context of the passage, and indeed the subject and purpose of the entire piece, to determine if irony is present. Consider as an example the title Grace Lichtenstein chose for an essay on college sports: "Playing for Money." In one sense the statement is without irony, for the athletes do play a game. In another sense, though, the title is ironic, for Lichtenstein makes clear in her argument that college sports are not "play," but serious business for the athletes, the coaches, and the colleges. The bringing together of presumably disparate items, "play" and "money," ironically underscores a major problem Lichtenstein finds in college athletics. Recognizing irony in argument is an important reading skill to develop, for to miss the irony is to misunderstand the writer's position.

Quotation, Italicization

Finally, writers can use several visual techniques that signal readers to give special attention to certain words. A writer can place a word or phrase in quotation marks and thus question its validity or its meaning in that context. Herbert Gans, for example, writes in his essay on the underclass (see Chapter 3) that:

America has a long history of insults for the "undeserving" poor.

By using quotation marks around the word "undeserving," Gans establishes that he questions the distinction some make between the deserving and undeserving poor. The expression *so-called* has the same effect.

Italicizing (or underscoring when typing) a key word or phrase gives it added emphasis. Korda uses italics twice in his essay:

Yet if they [leaders] are *too* different, we reject them.

Americans *wanted* to climb out of the Depression. . . .

These visual techniques have a place in writing, but writers need to be careful not to rely too heavily on such devices. Strategies that are overworked lose their power.

EXERCISE: RECOGNIZING ELEMENTS OF STYLE

Name the technique or techniques used in each of the following passages, and briefly explain the idea of the passage.

1. Censorship is a contagious disease.
2. The bias and therefore the business of television is to *move* information, not collect it.
3. If guns are outlawed, only the government will have guns. Only the police, the secret police, the military. The hired servants of our rulers. Only the government—and a few outlaws.
4. Having read all the advice on how to live 900 years, what I think is that eating a tasty meal once again will surely doom me long before I reach 900 while not eating that same meal could very well kill me. It's enough to make you reach for a cigarette!
5. If you are desperate for a quick fix, either legalize drugs or repress the user. If you want a civilized approach, mount a propaganda campaign against drugs.

COMPARATIVE ANALYSIS

Sometimes instructors assign summaries to confirm students' accurate reading. Other times, instructors want students to do more with required reading, so they assign an analysis of style, or a combination of summary and style analysis. (To be prepared for class discussion, you will want to be able to discuss both what a work says and how it is developed.) A third response to reading is the comparative analysis, a study of two (or more) works on the same topic. Comparative analyses can take two approaches to the readings. One type of analysis is a comparison or, more typically, a contrast of styles. Your task is to explain how the two works differ in the presentation of their arguments, not in the writers' attitudes toward the topic. To develop a contrast-of-styles analysis, select three or four elements of style that are significant in the works and organize your analysis around those elements so that your organization reinforces your purpose in writing. If you write about first one work and then the other, chances are good that you will summarize each work rather than explain differences in style. The following pattern illustrates an effective organization for a comparative analysis:

Introduction:	Statement of purpose: To show differences in style of writer A and writer B
A1 and B1	Sentence structures of writer A and writer B
A2 and B2:	Word choice of writer A and writer B
A3 and B3:	Metaphors used by writer A and by writer B
Conclusion:	Explanation of the effect of differences in the two styles

The second type of comparative analysis examines similarities or differences in content rather than in style, or differences in both content and presentation. Preparing this type of analysis is much the same as that illustrated above. First you need to read each source carefully and be certain that you can state each thesis and analyze each work's development. Then you need to organize your analysis so that key points of similarity or difference are apparent, as the outline above illustrates. If you are going to focus on differences primarily, then begin by noting, briefly, the similarities. Devote most of your analysis to the major points of difference. Perhaps each work is similar in structure: A thesis is developed by the author presenting and providing evidence to support three reasons. However, the authors have different positions on the issue, offer different reasons, and in one case draw different conclusions from the same evidence. Your analysis might follow this pattern:

Introduction:	Statement of your subject and purpose and brief explanation of the two sources' similarities in structure
A1 and B1:	Explanation of different claims of writer A and writer B
A2 and B2:	Explanation of different reasons presented by writer A and writer B
A3 and B3:	Analysis of different conclusions from similar evidence given by writer A and writer B

Conclusion: Discussion of how such differences may be accounted
                     for; that is, how do two people manage to see an issue
                     so differently

EVALUATION

Writing summaries and analyses of others' arguments provides good training in accurate reading and in understanding how argumentative essays
can be put together. To prepare good summaries and analyses, you need to
read sympathetically, to identify with the views and styles of other writers,
a discipline that may help you become more open to other points of view
and will certainly help you become a better judge of argument. For to evaluate another's argument is much more complicated than simply to decide
that you "like" or "dislike" the argument, that you agree or disagree with
the writer's position. A good evaluation must be grounded in accurate
reading and sound analysis because evaluators must be able to defend their
judgments.

An evaluation may answer one or more of the following questions: Is
the argument logical? Is it developed and supported sufficiently to be convincing? Does it achieve its purpose? The columnist who challenges a previously published editorial has analyzed the editorial and found it deficient
in some way. The columnist may fault the editor's logic and show how the
editorial develops a weak argument. The columnist may object to the editor's lack of adequate or relevant support for the editorial's claim. The
columnist may demonstrate that the editor gets sidetracked, that the editorial does not develop the issue that it presumably sets out to develop. In
each case the columnist makes a negative judgment about the editorial, but
that judgment is an informed one based on the columnist's knowledge of
language, of the principles of good argument, and of the concepts of unity
and direction in writing.

Evaluating an argument can take several forms. Sound arguments
may become sources for papers we write. The challenge of another's logic
or evidence leads to a refutation. Arguments that we have fundamental objections to spur us to write our own arguments supporting a different
claim. Chapter 3 provides guidelines for preparing these various kinds of
argumentative essays. But before turning to Chapter 3, read and respond
to the following article, using the accompanying questions and exercises as
guides.

Politicians of Silence

A. M. Rosenthal

*A Canadian educated at City College in New York City, A. M.
Rosenthal (b. 1922) is a columnist for the New York Times. Much of
his career in journalism was spent as a foreign correspondent, for which
reporting he won a Pulitzer Prize in 1960. The following column
appeared in the Times on March 13, 1992.*

1   I hope it will not annoy the Presidential candidates and other seekers
of political office if I bring up a subject that they hardly mention as they
dash around campaigning.

2   Drugs. You remember—drugs, as in drug addiction, drug crime, drug
disease, drug homeless, drug madness, drug guns, drug blood and drug babies. And as in The War Against Drugs, declared by Washington, way
back, about three years ago.

3   Maybe it is not worth talking about anymore. Maybe the Bush Administration was right: declare victory, put it on the back burner and put
out the pilot light. Then announce a new war, against a different national
killer, like the capital gains tax or something.

4   And maybe all those state legislatures and governors were right to
answer recession pressure by whacking away at treatment of drug addicts.

5   After all, it is a proven fact that drug addicts are too zonked out to
vote. And it is another proven fact that middle- and upper-class Americans
do not worry about drugs unless they hit their own families or neighborhoods.

6   So politicians assume, doubtless correctly, that Americans are too
stupid to understand that one day some addict from a mean street somewhere might wander into their neighborhood and teach them a civics lesson by sticking a knife in their ribs.

7   Not everybody has forgotten. In New York City, about 750 people
got together Wednesday at a benefit dinner organized by Tina Brown, editor
of *Vanity Fair*, and by the Morgans Hotel Group. The purposes were to
help the work against drugs with time and money, and honor Dr. Mitchell
S. Rosenthal. In the past 25 years, he has not forgotten for an hour.

8   Dr. Rosenthal is head of Phoenix House, largest of the 250 American
therapeutic communities. They are based on a no-magic treatment for addiction.

9   The prescription is for about one year of hard work—all day, every
day in a disciplined environment—that has two objectives. The first is to
equip addicts mentally, physically and spiritually to keep off drugs, forever.

The second is to give them the education, work habits and self-respect needed to earn a living in the world outside. 10

No magic, no guarantee. But 70 percent of the addicts who stick it out for a year stay clean and useful to themselves and society. Each addict costs about $45 a day in philanthropic or tax money. Pennies, compared with the tens of billions spent building prisons and stocking them with addicts on a perpetual round trip between street and cell. 11

Education against drugs, by schools and volunteer groups like the Partnership for a Drug-Free America, is making drugs less chic in schools. 12

But about 6.5 million drug users so abuse themselves that they cannot function in or for the American community. They fill jails, clog hospitals with needle-AIDS and TB, crowd shelters and provide morgues with a steady, dependable supply of the corpses of their victims. 13

Therapeutic communities will not end the drug problem, but they will help, a lot. Dr. Rosenthal says about 100,000 beds are needed. About a tenth that number exist now, more than half in New York and California. 14

And meanwhile the housing, land and shops for vocational training are available in closed military bases. The therapeutic communities plead helplessly for this wasted resource. 15

Since so many politicians are reluctant to bring up drugs now, how about legalizing the whole thing so we can stop bothering our heads? Dr. Rosenthal, like most drug experts, says it would be suicide for America. But then, nothing is perfect. 16

Oh, certainly, there would be more drug use and abuse. But to keep drugs out of sight of most Americans, electrified walls could be built around the poor white or black and Hispanic neighborhoods infected by drug addicts. 17

Then armed guards could be posted at gates. Addicts could be shot if they tried to get out. Other residents would have to show passes from the special legalization police. 18

Behind the walls, addicts could kill each other off; burying them would be cheaper than treatment. Maybe bounties could be paid for death certificates of crack babies. They would just drag through life anyway. 19

Yes, come to think of it now, it could work. Trees could even be planted near the walls. 20

Reading and Analyzing

1. What is Rosenthal's subject? What is his thesis? Does Rosenthal state his thesis in the essay, or did you have to write a thesis statement for the essay?

2. Explain the details of the program for drug addicts at Phoenix House. How successful has the project been?

3. What does Rosenthal accomplish by paragraph 3? The paragraph consists of three sentences; describe the sentence structures used. What kind of expression is "The War Against Drugs"? What does the author gain by using capitalization?

4. How would you describe the tone of the opening five paragraphs? What techniques does the author use to create tone and convey attitude?

5. What kind of evidence does Rosenthal provide to develop his claim?

6. Paragraph 3 contains a sentence or two that might, initially, be viewed as Rosenthal's thesis. Is his thesis stated in this paragraph? If not, how did you decide that the author does not express his views here?

7. Paragraph 16 also states a position that might be taken as the author's thesis. Is his thesis stated here? If not, what led you to conclude that Rosenthal does not hold the view expressed in this paragraph? What techniques does the author use in paragraphs 16 through 20?

Responding to the Writer's Ideas

1. Given the success rate at Phoenix House, do you think the project should be expanded? Why or why not?

2. Should closed military bases be used for therapeutic communities? Does this seem like a good idea for using those facilities? Why or why not?

Writing Suggestions

1. Write a one-paragraph (six to seven sentences) summary of Rosenthal's column. Include in your summary a brief comment on the strategies he used to develop his argument.

2. Block the structure of the essay and then diagram the structure, indicating the paragraphs that are devoted to each part of the piece. (See p. 46 for a sample diagram.)

3. In an essay, analyze Rosenthal's style. Select three to four techniques that you consider central to his style and explain how they work in the column. Be sure to illustrate each stylistic technique with examples from the column.

4. Evaluate Rosenthal's argument. How effective is his approach in achieving his purpose? Be sure to consider his audience and purpose carefully, including the length and nature of his column.

CHAPTER 3

PREPARING GOOD
ARGUMENTS

The basics of good writing remain much the same even in works as seemingly different as the personal essay, the argumentative essay, and the research paper. Good writing is focused, organized, and concrete. Essays are focused and unified when all material included effectively develops and supports a clear main idea, the claim of your argument. A clear organization that is appropriate for the work's subject and purpose provides unity; specifics both develop the work's main idea and engage the reader. Sound principles, that are well-known to you. But how, exactly, are they achieved in the argumentative essay? That is the key question this chapter will address by establishing specific guidelines for writing the most typical kinds of arguments. Whatever your particular

subject and purpose in writing—and whether your topic is assigned or selected by you—you are not ready to plan your essay until you have reflected on your audience.

CONSIDERING AUDIENCE

Argument presupposes an audience, and thus the likelihood of counterarguments. We do not argue with ourselves; we explain our positions on tax
increases or protecting endangered species to convince others to share our
positions. (You may want to have a "debate" with yourself to clarify your
thinking on an issue, but the place for self-examination is in your journal,
or in class discussion. When you are ready to compose an essay, then you
are writing for others.)

Imagine Your Readers

Too often students plunge into writing without thinking much about their
audience, for, after all, their "audience" is only the instructor who has
given the assignment, just as their purpose in writing is to complete the assignment and get a grade. These views of audience and purpose can result
in some weak argumentative essays for several reasons. First, if you are not
envisioning readers who may disagree with your views, you may not work
to develop the best defense and to consider how you can eliminate potential counterarguments. Second, you may ignore your essay's needed introductory material on the assumption that the instructor, knowing the assignment, has a context for understanding your writing. Remember,
though, that instructors expect complete essays that can be read with understanding by anyone, not just someone who knows the assignment. Instructors want students to practice writing good opening paragraphs that
introduce the topic and make the essay's purpose clear. Finally, if you are
thinking only of completing an assignment, not of expressing your views
convincingly, your argument is not likely to be the forceful piece that will
demonstrate quality writing. Once engaged in a writing task, try to forget
that you are a student and think of yourself as a writer keen on composing
the best possible argument on your topic.

Now that you have taken off your student's hat and put on your
writer's hat, try to imagine your classmates as part of the audience so that
you are writing to many readers with varied beliefs and values. Imagine
readers who are intelligent, thoughtful, prepared to listen and learn, but in
need of sound reasoning and convincing evidence before embracing your
position. It is best to imagine readers holding a range of views: Some will
probably never agree with you regardless of how persuasively you argue,

many are skeptical and need convincing, and only a few already share your views but are nonetheless looking for good arguments that they can use to support their thinking. If most of your readers already agree with you, there really is little point in writing; you would be "preaching to the choir," as the saying goes. Those who are strongly opposed to your position won't be moved by your writing, but you still want to win their respect with a good defense of your claim. Those in the middle, the fence-sitters, represent the most important audience; they are the ones you can influence if you argue effectively.

Select an Appropriate Persona

The elements of style—word choice, sentence structure, examples, and so on—examined in Chapter 2, together with the logic and structure of your argument, establish the tone of your essay, the "voice" that readers will hear. You want to think carefully about that voice, the person they will imagine as they read your argument. The term for this "person" is *persona*. Sometimes writers create a persona quite different from themselves as part of their persuasive strategy. Jonathan Swift, for instance, does not "speak" as a minister or a man active in politics in his essay "A Modest Proposal" (see pp. 372–79); instead, he manufactures a very different person to carry his satire. You may want to try this strategy in a paper; it is a writing challenge but also fun. Most of the time, however, your persona will be someone more closely resembling yourself. Still, you have different roles in your life, and you use different voices as appropriate in those roles. You speak (presumably) with courtesy and intelligence to teachers and employers, but you may use slang with friends, or speak condescendingly (surely not often!) to a younger brother or sister. What persona is appropriate for the argumentative essay?

Unless you plan to create an unusual persona to achieve a special effect, you probably want to use the serious voice you normally use for serious discussions with other adults; this is the persona that will help establish your credibility. Still, there are degrees of formality and several different tones from which to choose. Let's consider three variations of this voice for three different college audiences.

First, a researched argument—one that draws heavily on sources and contains formal documentation—usually employs the most formal style and objective tone. Remember that the research essay is offered to the entire scholarly community, or to one subject specialty within that community. Writers are careful to use specialized terms correctly, to follow the conventions of documentation, to avoid a chatty style by not using contractions *(can't, won't)* or leaning too heavily on the personal pronoun *(I),* and to eliminate humor or sarcasm or preachiness. Still, the clearest writing is simple and direct, so do not try to sound scholarly if this results in an artificial, "puffed-up" voice.

The argumentative essay—without formal documentation, possibly drawing on personal experience for support, and directed to a general audience that includes your instructor and classmates—can be written in a more informal style and can range in tone from dispassionate to righteously indignant. Nonetheless, respect for your audience and your topic requires that you avoid nastiness or silliness. Use *I* when appropriate: when drawing on your experience or separating your views from others. Avoid overuse of *I,* however; do not keep attaching *I think* or *I feel* to statements. (It is your essay; readers know that you are expressing your thoughts and feelings.) Use specialized terms when appropriate, but consider the need to define such terms for a general audience.

Finally, consider how you might prepare an argument on a campus issue for your college newspaper. In this writing situation, you want to be especially careful about style and tone. Many campus issues are just as serious as those debated in society as a whole, issues such as who should speak at commencement or if hate speech should result in suspension. Such topics require the same seriousness, thoughtfulness, and control of emotion that one expects in debates of capital punishment and euthanasia. Other topics, though, may allow for a more playful approach. A negative attitude toward what you consider a silly new parking regulation can be expressed, for example, in a scornful or mocking tone through such strategies as negative connotation, irony, and understatement. Just be careful that you do not end up sounding as silly as the regulation by first doing your homework on the issue to learn the reasons for the new regulation.

Recognize the Role of Counterarguments

What can you expect your diverse readers to know about your topic? Whether you are writing on a current problem or a centuries-old philosophical debate, you must expect most readers to have some knowledge of the issues. Their knowledge does not free you from the responsibility of developing your argument fully, however. In fact, their knowledge imposes additional demands on you. What your readers know may be little more than an overview of the issue from television coverage or the emotional outbursts of a family member whose views are quite different from yours. Sometimes what people "know" are bits and pieces of misinformation and prejudice, but they hold on to their views strongly nonetheless. For example, one would have to be from Mars not to be aware of the arguments on both sides of the abortion-rights issue. Outside abortion clinics and legislatures, supporters of both positions shout at one another about the rights of the fetus and the rights of women to control their bodies. To address this topic without challenging the arguments of the opposition would do little to convince skeptical readers.

Similarly, one can no longer debate the issues of gun control without referring to the Constitution's Second Amendment or to this country's death rate from handguns. In a plea to ban handguns, Republican Senator John Chafee wrote the following:

> There will be those who will argue that there exists a fundamental constitutional right to bear arms. But if there is one argument that is utter nonsense, this is it. Not only have its proponents not read their Constitution lately, but they haven't followed more than 50 years of remarkably unanimous court holdings against that erroneous supposition.
>
> As for those who will argue that handguns in the home are needed for protection, they haven't reviewed the horrific statistics detailing that handguns are far, far more likely to kill a loved one than an intruder.

Senator Chafee understands that he must address the two arguments most frequently put forward by opponents of handgun control. An awareness of audience tells us that to prepare a good argument, we must include a challenge to the reasons offered by opposing viewpoints.

UNDERSTANDING YOUR WRITING PURPOSE

To establish specific guidelines for writing argument, we need to distinguish among several types of argumentative purposes and then to consider what each type requires to accomplish its purpose. To make these distinctions, let's review some of the arguments presented in Chapter 1. The claim that violence in our society is increasing, an inductive argument, calls for gathering and analyzing relevant facts. The Declaration of Independence, an expanded deductive argument, needs to combine reasons with facts to support a claim based on values. The purpose of the first type of argument is to report on what is or is not, what has happened or will happen. It is the argument we find in history texts and in the reports of investigations in the sciences and social sciences. The purpose of the second type of argument is to establish a principle, defend a position. A variation of the position paper is the argument whose purpose is to establish a new or, in the writer's view, more appropriate definition of a key term. Defining one's terms in any debate is vitally important, but sometimes the argument itself is over how a term should be used. The demands of writing a definition paper are sufficiently different from the position paper to warrant separate discussion in this chapter.

Two other kinds of arguments bear separate consideration as well. Sometimes our purpose is not to support, in general, a position we hold but to challenge a specific argument someone else has written, to refute that person's logic or use of evidence. We observed in Chapter 2 that reading spurs writing; the refutation essay is one important response to reading. Finally, many arguments are about what should or should not be done in public life or by governmental bodies. They are not about "right" positions but rather about how to solve problems. To support public-policy claims effectively, writers must do more than reason about what is right or good; they must also consider feasibility: What will it cost? Can the solution be implemented? Let's consider, in turn, how each of these argumentative purposes can best be developed into effective essays.

The Investigative Argument

The first step to preparing an inductive argument—an investigation of facts from which an inference is drawn—is to evaluate the soundness of your conclusion or claim in relation to the evidence you have obtained or expect to obtain. Have you appropriately qualified your claim to avoid overstatement or a forced hypothesis? The numbers may not support the claim that (all) Americans are worse off financially in the 1990s than they were in the 1980s, but they may support the more limited claim that *some* Americans, or specific segments of the population, are worse off.

Your next task is to see what evidence you have and what more you will need to support your claim. You should make two lists: (1) a list of the evidence you already have, facts drawn from previous knowledge and from preliminary reading or investigation; and (2) a list of the *kinds* of evidence you still need to produce a good argument. The second list is the more difficult because you must ask yourself tough questions about how much evidence is necessary, what kinds of specifics are needed, and how they should be gathered. Suppose you are working with the issue of financial well-being in the 1990s, and you have some statistics from your reading which have led to the topic selection. What more do you need, and where will you find the information? You may want to compare median incomes of families for several years in the 1980s and 1990s. You could also compare the percentage of Americans in various income brackets for the representative years; that is, has the percentage of American families with an income of less than $10,000 increased in the 1990s? These figures are available in such reference sources as the *Statistical Abstract of the United States* (published annually). Figures are also available by race and by sections of the country. You may also want to look at unemployment

rates, at the numbers of jobs lost as a result of the recession, even at inflation rates, for all of these have an impact on the financial potential of
Americans at a given time. It is always best to get your statistics from publications of the Census Bureau or from the *Statistical Abstract* rather than
in bits and pieces from different books and articles. Remember that figures
you use from someone's argument must be studied carefully and evaluated
by you for reliability. And if you are doing an investigation of attitudes on
your campus and gathering your own figures through questionnaires
and/or interviews, you will need to devise objective procedures so as not to
bias your results.

Once you have completed your investigation, you will need to think
carefully about how to present evidence to readers. Few readers are content to read a list of disorganized details from which they are supposed to
draw the same conclusion as the writer. Here are some guidelines for writing your paper.

Guidelines for Preparing an Investigative Paper

1. *Begin with an opening paragraph that introduces your topic in an interesting way.* Possibilities include beginning with a startling statistic
   or explaining how the essay's facts will impact on readers.
2. *Devote space early in your paper to explaining your methods or
   procedures,* if you have conducted your own investigation to generate facts. For example, if you have obtained information through
   questionnaires or interviews, recount the process: the questions, the
   number of people involved, the basis for selecting those people, and
   so on.
3. *Classify the evidence that you present.* Devising a meaningful organization is part of the originality of your study and will make your argument more forceful. It is the way you see the issue and want readers to see it. If you are contrasting incomes, for example, organize by
   points of contrast. To present all the statistics from the 1980s first
   and then the 1990s dilutes the purpose of contrast and challenges
   readers to remember which numbers from the first part of the paper
   are to be compared to those in the second half.
4. *Consider presenting evidence in several ways, including charts and
   tables as well as within paragraphs.* Readers are used to visuals, especially in technical reports and works containing a fair amount of
   numbers.
5. *Analyze evidence.* Do not ask your reader to do the thinking that is
   your job initially. Explain how your evidence *is* evidence by discussing the connection between facts and the inference they are supporting. In a study of selling techniques used in computer ads in business magazines, a student finds four major selling techniques, one of

which he classifies as "corporate emphasis." Alan begins his paragraph on corporate emphasis thus:

In the technique of corporate emphasis, the advertiser discusses the whole range of products and services that the corporation offers, instead of specific elements. This method relies on the public's positive perception of the company, the company's accomplishments, and its reputation.

Alan then provides several examples of ads in this category, including an IBM ad:

In one of its eight advertisements in the study, IBM points to the scientists on its staff who have recently won the Nobel Prize in physics.

But Alan does not stop there. He explains the point of this ad, connecting the ad to the assertion that this technique emphasizes the company's accomplishments:

The inference we are to draw is that IBM scientists are hard at work right now in their laboratories developing tomorrow's technology to make the world a better place in which to live.

The Position Paper

The position paper is more philosophical, more abstract, than the investigative paper. It asserts what is right or wrong, good or bad, for us as individuals or as a society. The position paper asserts a claim on such varied issues as capital punishment, euthanasia, pornography, and endangered species. A claim of principle is supported in large part by a logical sequencing of reasons. However, arguments in support of a principle also rely on relevant facts; remember that most of the Declaration of Independence is a list of specific abuses experienced by the colonists. The position paper may be the most difficult of argument assignments because it may be perceived to be the easiest. To argue effectively for a principle requires more than a forceful statement of one's personal values and beliefs.

Your first step in preparing a position paper should be to explore the reasons for your position. You may want to list the reasons and evidence you would consider using to defend your claim. Then make a list of the reasons most frequently used by the opposition. The second list will eventually help you prepare counterarguments, but first it will help test your commitment to your position. If you find the opposition's arguments persuasive, ones that you do not see how to challenge, you may need to re-think your position. Ideally, your two lists will confirm your views but also increase your respect for opposing views and guide you to some compromises, or at least to a conciliatory tone when you begin to write.

Armed with a reconfirmed position and a list of reasons for your claim, you can now plan your paper. You need to decide which reasons you will include and how you will develop each one. You also need to plan how you will challenge the opposition's arguments and then how you will weave all of this into a unified essay. Studying the guidelines and the sample student essay that follow should help you with the task.

Guidelines for Preparing a Position Paper

1. *Begin with an opening paragraph or two that introduce your topic in an interesting way.* Possibilities include a statement of the issue's seriousness or reasons why the issue is currently being debated. Sometimes we are spurred to write by a recent event that receives media coverage because it dramatizes the issue; recounting such an event provides an effective opening. In her essay on gun control, Patti questions the costs—in human suffering—generated by the freedom to own guns and then recounts a recent incident to illustrate her concern.

2. *Decide where to place your thesis statement, your position on the issue.* Your best choices are either early in your essay (paragraph 1 or 2) or at the end of your essay, after you have made your case. The second approach can be an effective alternative to the more common pattern of stating one's thesis early in an essay.

3. *Organize your reasons in a meaningful way.* One good plan is to move from the least important to the most important reason, followed by challenges to potential counterarguments. Another structure is to organize by the arguments of the opposition, explaining why each of their reasons fails to hold up. Ernest van den Haag uses this second pattern in "The Ultimate Punishment: A Defense"; see pp. 252–58.

4. *Provide a logical defense of or specifics in support of each reason.* You have not finished your task by simply asserting three or four or five reasons for your claim. You must also offer facts or examples or a logical explanation of each reason. For example, you have not defended your views on capital punishment by asserting that it is right or just to take the life of a murderer. Why is it right or just? Executing the murderer will not bring the victim back to life. Do two wrongs make a right, or a further wrong? These are some of the thoughts your skeptical reader will have, and continue to hold, unless you explain why these thoughts are inappropriate. Similarly, you

cannot convincingly assert that the death penalty acts as a deterrent to subsequent murders unless you have evidence that it does act as a deterrent. If you want to use this reason, you must do some research on the issue of deterrence. And remember that quoting another writer's opinion on your topic does not provide proof for one of your reasons. Even though the writer quoted may be well-known and respected, presenting the writer's views in your argument merely demonstrates that someone else agrees with your position. It does not provide evidence that your shared views should be accepted.

5. *Maintain the appropriate level of seriousness for an argument of principle.* Of course word choice must be appropriate for a serious discussion, but in addition be sure to present reasons that are also appropriately serious. If, for example, you are defending the claim that songs should not be subject to labeling about their content because the result is a kind of censorship that is inconsistent with First Amendment rights, do not trivialize your argument by including the point that young people are tired of parents' and other adults' controlling their lives. It may be true that teenagers are tired of parental control, but that is another issue for another paper; it is inappropriate in a paper debating First Amendment issues. Similarly, it would be demeaning to argue for death sentencing on the grounds of the cost of life imprisonment; to put a price tag on a human life is offensive to most readers.

6. *Examine your reasons and support carefully to avoid logical fallacies.* Qualify your statements and control your language. In the heat of debate over cherished values and beliefs, we are prone to sweeping generalizations and verbal attacks on opponents, but these strategies rarely win converts. For example, you cannot effectively argue against limits on the speech of college students by asserting that the First Amendment guarantees free speech and that we are either free or not free. A moment's reflection reminds us that many laws do restrict free speech and that there is no absolute freedom for individuals within a group because the group's needs impose restrictions on individuals. There are laws against libel, against the advertising of certain products on television, against yelling fire in a crowded theater—when there is no fire.

STUDENT ESSAY

Gun Control: One Side of a Loaded Issue

Patti Bailey

As Americans, we enjoy many constitutional rights. The freedom of gun ownership is one such right, but is the choice many Americans make today to arm themselves truly worth the costs?

Subject is introduced by questioning the problems of gun ownership.

Evidence of innocent lives lost in shooting incidents strongly suggests it is not. A report aired by the television show <u>60 Minutes</u> on February 10, 1992, cited the following statistic: "One child is killed every day in an accident involving a handgun." The death toll in Washington, DC, has now risen well above the 300 mark, many of these deaths brought on by the availability of handguns. One violent incident earlier this year [1992] involved a couple in suburban Maryland who were viciously attacked in their own home in a quiet neighborhood. The husband was shot by an unknown as-

The problems are illustrated with recent incidents.

sailant upon opening the door; his wife, running out of the house to get help, was chased
down by the gunman and shot to death on the
front porch of their neighbor's house. These
are just a few examples of violence in our society involving handguns. Surely they must give
pause to those who insist on their "right" to
own guns.

Opponents of any gun-control legislation

Student ex-
amines the
Second
Amendment
as support
for gun
ownership.

cite the Second Amendment to the Constitution
of the United States: "A well-regulated militia, being necessary to the security of a free
state, the right of the people to keep and bear
arms, shall not be infringed." Depending upon
the side you are on, this statement is interpreted in different ways. The National Rifle Association and its supporters place great emphasis on the words "the right of the people to
keep and bear arms," while those in favor of
gun control view these rights as being related
to the state and the military. Who is right? Is
the Second Amendment, as it is written, still

applicable in this day of violence and blood-
shed? How should it be interpreted to best
serve public safety? What measures should be
taken to ensure public safety while protecting
the rights of those who wish to arm themselves?

Here are some reasonable proposals that
balance rights with the realities of our time,
of a time far different than that of the early
years of the Republic. First, longer waiting
periods to allow time for more thorough background checks must be instituted. The longer it
takes to obtain a gun, the less likely it is to
be used in passion. Even if this saves but a
few lives, it will be worth it. Those who truly
desire to own a gun for legitimate purposes--
self—protection, antique collections, or compe-
tition--should be willing to sacrifice time in
the interest of public safety. Second, following registration, some form of participation in
a gun-safety program should be mandatory, particularly for first-time purchasers. Because of
the rapid rise in accidental deaths of children

Proposals for controlling gun ownership in light of the needs of our time.

Proposals include registration, education, and prohibition of semiautomatic assault rifles.

from handguns, these education programs should be extended to school-aged children as well. We educate our children in the dangers of drugs, alcohol, and tobacco; we now need to add an education in firearms as well. I am not saying that we should teach them how to use a gun correctly; that instruction is up to the parents who choose to have guns in the house. Recent evidence suggests that because of television, children's perceptions of guns lie more in fantasy than ever before. What I am suggesting is some kind of instruction in the difference between play guns and real guns, what to do if they find a gun, and how to avoid getting into situations that could be fatal. Finally, a law outlawing the use of semiautomatic assault rifles must be passed. There is no justification for the average American citizen to own such a weapon.

Opponents of gun control argue that if you take away guns, you must also take away knives and other objects that could be used as weapons.

This is a silly distraction from an already complex issue. In the heat of the moment, you may
have a second chance against someone attacking
with a knife. With a gun there are few second
chances, as the potential for death is vastly
increased. Opponents also liken gun control to
censorship. If I couldn't speak, perhaps my
quality of living would be reduced, but I would
still be breathing. Without some form of gun
control, I might not be so lucky.

Student concludes by countering opponents of any restrictions on gun ownership.

The Definition Essay

"Define your terms" is not idle advice for good writing. People disagree more than we sometimes think over the meanings of terms such as *leader* or *patriot* or *good* teacher. The deductive argument about Lincoln's leadership, illustrated in Chapter 1 (see pp. 12–13), turns on a definition of leadership. To support that argument successfully, you need to explain and defend a definition of leadership as well as demonstrate Lincoln's leadership traits.

For another example of the importance of definition, think again about Lester Thurow's unfavorable review of Charles Murray's *Losing Ground* discussed in Chapter 1 (see p. 35). Thurow objects to Murray's excluding of the elderly from his analysis of social welfare programs. It may be that Murray is fudging numbers to support his thesis that welfare programs have failed, but it may also be that Murray does not believe that programs such as social security fit the definition of a welfare program, even though it is one of the government's most costly social programs. Thurow's response to Murray might be that any government program supported by taxpayers that then benefits a particular group (the elderly, the poor, homeowners, students) is by definition a social welfare program. To defend himself against some of Thurow's objections, Murray should have explained why he was going to exclude certain programs from the "social welfare" category. He needed, in short, to give his definition of social welfare.

Even if Murray had defined his terms, he and Thurow would probably have been at odds. Sometimes the real debate is the definition itself, not what does or does not fit the definition. Although Michael Korda in "How to Be a Leader" (pp. 41–43) gives many examples of well-known leaders, he is more interested in defining the term *leader* than in arguing that his examples belong in the category. His purpose is to establish criteria for judging all potential leaders, past, present, and future, in order to present the general traits of the class. The argument that depends on defining terms has become the definition argument.

In the following article, Herbert Gans defines the term *underclass* and explains what its current usage tells us about American society. Study his definition argument carefully, using the questions that follow to help your study, for we will draw guidelines for writing a definition argument from his and Korda's examples.

❖

So Much for the "Underclass"?

Herbert J. Gans

Born in Germany in 1927, Herbert J. Gans became a U.S. citizen in 1945. After obtaining his Ph.D., Gans worked in city and regional planning and urban studies before joining the sociology department at Columbia University in 1971. He has continued to work in urban studies as a consultant and a research fellow at the Center for Policy Research. Gans has written many articles and books including The Urban Villagers *(1962; revised edition 1982) and* Deciding What's News *(1979). The following article appeared in the* Washington Post *on September 10, 1990.*

Sticks and stones may break my bones, but names can never hurt me goes the old proverb. But like many old proverbs, this one is patent nonsense, as anyone knows who has ever been hurt by ethnic, racist or sexist insults and stereotypes.

The most frequent victims of insults and stereotypes have been the poor, especially those thought to be undeserving of help because someone decided—justifiably or not—that they had not acted properly. America has a long history of insults for the "undeserving" poor. In the past they were bums, hoboes, vagrants and paupers; more recently they have been culturally deprived and the hard-core poor. Now they are "the underclass."

Underclass was originally a 19th-century Swedish term for the poor. In the early 1960s, the Swedish economist Gunnar Myrdal revived it to describe the unemployed and unemployables being created by the modern economy, people who, he predicted, would soon be driven out of that economy unless it was reformed. Twenty years later, in Ronald Reagan's America, the word sprang to life again, this time not only to describe but also to condemn. Those normally consigned to the underclass include: women who start their families before marriage and before the end of adolescence, youngsters who fail to finish high school or find work, and welfare "dependents"—whether or not the behavior of any of these people is their own fault. The term is also applied to low-income delinquents and criminals—but not to affluent ones.

"Underclass" has become popular because it seems to grab people's attention. What grabs is the image of a growing horde of beggars, muggers, robbers and lazy people who do not carry their part of the economic load, all of them threatening nonpoor Americans and the stability of American society. The image may be inaccurate, but then insults and pejoratives don't have to be accurate. Moreover, underclass sounds technical, academic, and not overtly pejorative, so it can be used without anyone's biases showing. Since it is now increasingly applied to blacks and Hispanics, it is also a respectable substitute word with which to condemn them.

5   There are other things wrong with the word underclass. For one, it lumps together in a single term very diverse poor people with diverse problems. Imagine all children's illnesses being described with the same word, and the difficulties doctors would have in curing them.

6   For example, a welfare recipient often requires little more than a decent paying job—and a male breadwinner who also has such a job—to make a normal go of it, while a high school dropout usually needs both a better-equipped school, better teachers and fellow students—and a rationale for going to school when he or she has no assurance that a decent job will follow upon graduation. Neither the welfare recipient nor the high school dropout deserves to be grouped with, or described by, the same word as muggers or drug dealers.

7   Labeling poor people as underclass is to blame them for their poverty, which enables the blamers to blow off the steam of self-righteousness. That steam does not, however, reduce their poverty. Unfortunately, underclass, like other buzzwords for calling the poor undeserving, is being used to avoid starting up needed antipoverty programs and other economic reforms.

8   Still, the greatest danger of all lies not in the label itself but in the possibility that the underclass is a symptom of a possible, and dark, American future: that we are moving toward a "post-post-industrial" economy in which there may not be enough decent jobs for all. Either too many more jobs will move to Third World countries where wages are far lower or they will be performed by ever more efficient computers and other machines.

9   If this happens, the underclass label may turn out to be a signal that the American economy, and our language, are preparing to get ready for a future in which some people are going to be more or less permanently jobless—and will be blamed for their joblessness to boot.

10   Needless to say, an American economy with a permanently jobless population would be socially dangerous, for all of the country's current social problems, from crime and addiction to mental illness would be sure to increase considerably. America would then also become politically more dangerous, for various kinds of new protests have to be expected, not to mention the rise of quasi-fascist movements. Such movements can already be found in France and other European countries.

11   Presumably, Americans—the citizenry and elected officials both—will not let any of this happen here and will find new sources of decent jobs, as they have done in past generations, even if today this requires a new kind

of New Deal. Perhaps there will be another instance of what always saved America in the past: new sources of economic growth that cannot even be imagined now.

The only problem is that in the past, America ruled the world eco- 12 nomically, and now it does not—and it shows in our lack of economic growth. Consequently, the term underclass could become a permanent entry in the dictionary of American pejoratives.

Questions

1. What does Gans accomplish in his opening paragraph?
2. Where does he introduce his specific topic?
3. Gans never announces his purpose or states a one-sentence thesis; how do you know what his purpose and his claim are? What clues are provided in the first two paragraphs to make his views clear?
4. What kind of information does Gans give readers in paragraph 3? What do we learn about the term in his paragraph?
5. What are the term's characteristics that make it appealing to users? What characteristics make its use, in Gans's view, wrong?
6. What does the word's use tell us about America's possible economic future? What should the term tell us that we need to do?

Gans's definition essay gives us, along with Korda's, good ideas for developing this type of argument. Whether you are defining a technical or a widely used abstract term, you must know how the term is commonly used and what additional meanings it may have or may have had in the past. You also need to be clear about your purpose in writing. Do you wish to challenge the current use of the term, or add your perspective to readers' understanding of a complex, frequently debated concept such as *justice?* Is your focus going to be on the word's denotative meanings or the connotations the word carries? One of Gans's concerns with the use of *underclass,* for example, is the term's negative connotation. Here are some suggestions for developing a definition argument.

Guidelines for Preparing a Definition Argument

1. *Begin with an opening paragraph or two that introduce your subject in an interesting way.* Possibilities include the occasion—an event in the news or something you read, for example—that has led to your writing; or a misunderstanding about the term's meaning that you want to correct.

2. *Do not begin by quoting or paraphrasing a dictionary definition of the term.* "According to Webster . . ." is an approach lacking originality and reader interest.

3. *State your thesis—your definition of the term—early in your essay, if you can do so in a sentence or two.* (You may find that there are too many parts to your definition to combine into one or two sentences.) If you do not state a brief thesis, then be certain to establish your purpose in writing early in your essay.

4. *Use several strategies for developing a definition that is concrete and specific.* Consider using a number of the following means of development:

- *Word origin or history of usage*
  The word's original meaning can be instructive. If the word has changed meanings over time, explore those changes as clues to how the word should be used, especially if you are going to object to the word's current use (as Gans does with *underclass*).

- *Descriptive details*
  Be specific. For example, list traits of a leader or patriot or courageous person; explain the behaviors that make a wise or courteous person; describe the situations that demonstrate the existence of liberty. Use negative traits as well as positive ones; that is, what is not contained in the word.

- *Comparison and contrast*
  Clarify and limit your definition by contrasting it with words of similar meaning. For example, what are the subtle but important differences between *freedom* and *liberty?* Between *courtesy* and *manners?* Between *knowledge* and *wisdom?*

- *Metaphors*
  Consider the use of figurative comparisons. Whether expressed as metaphors or similes, they are effective because they are concrete and vivid. (For example, Korda says that a leader is like a mirror.)

- *Examples*
  Illustrate your definition with actual or hypothetical examples. Korda uses actual leaders to illustrate the traits of leadership. Gans uses generic examples when he lists the types of people placed together in the category *underclass*.

- *Function or use*
  A frequent strategy for defining is explaining the item's use or function: A pencil is a writing instrument. A similar approach can give insight into general or abstract terms as well. For example, what is accomplished by courteous or patriotic behavior? Gans employs this strategy, in a sense, when he explains what the use of the term *underclass* tells us about our attitudes toward the poor and about our economic condition.

The Refutation Essay

When your primary purpose in writing is to challenge someone's argument rather than to present your own argument, you are writing a refutation. A good refutation does not merely point an accusing finger at another's argument. Rather, it demonstrates, in an orderly and logical way, the weaknesses of logic or evidence in the argument, or it both analyzes weaknesses and builds a counterargument. Refutations usually challenge a specific, written argument, but they can also challenge a prevailing attitude or belief that is, in the writer's view, contrary to the evidence. Study Paul Duke's refutation of a letter to the editor and the following guidelines to prepare a good refutation essay.

Guidelines for Preparing a Refutation Essay

1. *Read accurately.* Make certain that you have understood your opponent's argument. If you assume views not expressed by the writer and accuse the writer of holding those illogical views, you are guilty of the straw man fallacy, of attributing and then attacking a position that the person does not hold. Take time, therefore, to determine the writer's thesis, look up terms and references you do not know, and examine the logic and evidence thoroughly.
2. *Pinpoint the weaknesses in the original argument.* Analyze the argument to determine, specifically, what flaws the argument contains. If the argument contains logical fallacies, make a list of the ones you plan to discredit. Examine the evidence presented; is it insufficient, unreliable, or irrelevant? Has the writer oversimplified the issues or presented an unworkable solution? Are the assumptions joining claim and evidence faulty? Decide, before drafting your refutation, exactly what elements of the argument you intend to challenge.
3. *Write your thesis.* After analyzing the argument and deciding on the weaknesses to be challenged, write a thesis which establishes that your disagreement is with the writer's logic, assumptions, or evidence, or a combination of these.
4. *Draft your essay, using the following three-part organization.* (1) *The opponent's argument.* Usually you should not assume that your reader has read or remembered the argument you are refuting. Thus at the beginning of your essay, you need to state, accurately and fairly, the main points of the argument to be refuted. (2) *Your thesis.* Next make clear the nature of your disagreement with the argument you are refuting. Your thesis might assert, for example, that a writer has not proved his assertion because he has provided evidence that is outdated, or that the argument is not sound because it rests on an unacceptable definition, or that the argument is filled with logical fallacies that discredit the piece. (3) *Your refutation.* The specifics of

your counterargument will depend upon the nature of your disagreement. If you are challenging the writer's evidence, then you must present the more recent evidence or explain why the evidence used is unreliable or misleading. If you are challenging assumptions, then you must explain why they do not hold up. If your thesis is that the piece is filled with logical fallacies, then you must present and explain each fallacy.

STUDENT ESSAY

If You Can't Say Anything Nice,

Don't Say Anything

Paul Duke

In the January 2, 1989, issue of the <u>Wash-</u>
<u>ington Post</u>, Christian Brahmstedt wrote a let-
ter to the editor entitled "Help Those Who
Help, Not Hurt, Themselves" in which he addresses the growing problem of homelessness in
the Washington, DC, area and offers a solution
to this mounting problem. Brahmstedt's article
is riddled with fallacious and illogical arguments that rely on emotional appeals rather
than a factual and logical argument.

Brahmstedt seeks to clarify the difference between the poor and the homeless. He
states that the poor are more justly represented by new families struggling and working hard
to achieve financial independence, whereas the
homeless are people who "do not seek work or
pride. They are satisfied to beg and survive on

Introduction makes clear the specific article to be refused.

Thesis establishes that this refutation will focus on the article's illogic.

Second paragraph gives a clear summary of Brahmstedt's argument.

others' generosity." Brahmstedt then compares
the homeless to squirrels that he sees on Capitol Hill begging for food; regardless of how
much the squirrels are fed, they simply return
the next morning for more. Both the squirrels
and the homeless have learned only to beg for
sustenance rather than to fend for themselves.
Brahmstedt offers the solution that everyone
simply stop giving donations to the homeless
and thereby force them to earn a living. The
writer concludes with the suggestion that these
donations would be put to better use if they
were given to the poor families who are struggling with two jobs just to make ends meet.

The third
paragraph's
topic sen-
tence pro-
vides a tran-
sition to the
student's
refutation
of Brahm-
stedt's logic.

Aside from the numerous <u>ad hominem</u> fallacies and generally offensive tone of his letter, Brahmstedt's argument is weak and logically invalid. In his attempt at separating the
poor from the homeless, Brahmstedt has already
undermined his own argument. He asserts that we
have all been part of the poor at one time or
another but that we are proud and work hard

until we escape from that category. While I

don't doubt that many have done just that, I am

equally certain that many have not. Children of

wealthy families or students with job contacts

with large corporations certainly have an easi-

er time of it, and few people are thrown out

into the world with absolutely no financial aid

from home. It is likewise an overstatement to

say that all homeless people do not seek work

or pride, and it is a faulty generalization to

assume that homeless people are satisfied with

begging for a living. Here Brahmstedt applies a

straw man tactic to apply unfounded attributes

to the many homeless people of the Washington

area.

Student uses terms to label fallacies.

Brahmstedt continues his illogic with a

false analogy of the homeless to squirrels.

Certainly squirrels beg for food; it is far

easier than going to find it yourself, after

all. But squirrels are only simple animals that

are incapable of thinking, much less learning

the value of the independence that Brahmstedt

Student ex-plains why the author's statements are fallacies.

desires. The homeless beg for their food only because they have no other means of getting it. The homeless may have struggled harder than many of Brahmstedt's "poor," but they were the less fortunate ones. Many homeless are mentally ill and cannot work. They are a more diverse group than the squirrels on Capitol Hill. To imply that the homeless are as incapable as squirrels and are trained like dogs is an outrageous slander.

In his equally illogical solution, Brahmstedt contends that by refusing aid to the homeless, they will be forced to earn a living like respectable citizens. This non sequitur

Student concludes by challenging the logic of Brahmstedt's conclusion.

assumes that none of the homeless has tried to become independent, and it goes back to Brahmstedt's original error in assuming that all of the homeless enjoy begging and living on the streets. The final step in the writer's solution is to divert the donations from the homeless to the "poor" as Brahmstedt defines them. Here it seems that Brahmstedt has forgotten the problem

he was originally addressing, for if the donations given to the destitute homeless have
caused the homeless to become dependent on
those donations for survival, then it makes
sense that the struggling and hard-pressed poor
would simply use these diverted funds in the
same way, and soon the poor and the homeless
would simply change places.

The Problem-Solution Paper

Many of the arguments over public policy can usefully be understood as arguments over solutions to problems. For example, the claim "we need a balanced-budget amendment" offers a solution to the problem of the spiraling national debt and the high interest payments needed to sustain that debt. Most people agree—at least in theory—that the national debt is a problem, but not all would agree that an amendment is the solution. When arguing about public-policy issues, you want to think first about what situation you are addressing and why you think the situation is a problem in need of change.

Many arguments for solutions concentrate on the nature of the problem, for how we define a problem has much to do with what kinds of solutions become appropriate. For example, some people are concerned about our ability to feed a growing population, especially given weather changes and other agricultural problems. But many will argue that the problem is not an agricultural one (how much food can we grow) but a political one (to whom will the food be distributed and at what cost). If the problem is agricultural, we need to worry about available farmland, water supply, and farming technology. If the problem is political, we need to worry about price supports, distribution to poor countries, and grain embargoes used for political leverage. To support a policy claim, you may first need to define the problem.

The argument for solutions can take many forms, depending upon your primary purpose in writing. Possibly as many as six steps may be needed to support a proposed solution. When preparing such an argument, consider each of the six steps outlined in the following guidelines and decide which ones are relevant to your problem and your purpose in writing. Then organize your paper according to the steps you have selected as appropriate. Do not jump back and forth among the various steps; instead, discuss each step in turn.

Guidelines for Preparing a Problem-Solution Paper

1. *Demonstrate that a problem situation exists.* In many cases you can count on an audience who knows the world well enough to be aware of a situation that is considered a problem. Sometimes, though, people have to be warned of a problem before they are prepared to consider solutions to the problem. For example, studies reveal that many parents and students are satisfied with what the students are learning in high school in spite of comparative testing that shows American students ranking far behind their counterparts in other countries. Some people still need to be convinced that American education has some serious problems to be addressed. If you want to argue for in-

creasing requirements in math and science, you may have to begin by reminding readers that we have a problem. Most will understand that inadequate preparation in math and science is a problem but may have to be persuaded to a sense of national urgency.

2. *Explain the cause or causes of the problem.* If your proposed solution is tied to removing the cause(s) of the problem, then you need to establish cause and prove it early in your essay. Remember, though, that some problems are created from many causes over a period of time; it may now be fruitless to try to pinpoint causes. Republicans and Democrats spend considerable energy blaming one another for inflation, recession, and crime. Sometimes one suspects that their fussing is a smoke screen for their lack of solutions. If cause is important, argue for it; if it is irrelevant, move to your solution.

3. *Explain your solution.* If television violence contributes to violence in society, then your proposal is simple: Eliminate violence from television programs. Ways to implement the solution may be open to debate, but the solution is clear-cut. Solutions to the problems of drunk driving or drugs in our society are far less obvious. Problems resulting from multiple causes will produce many proposed solutions. Before you seek to defend your solution against others, consider including the next two steps in your argument.

4. *Explain the process for achieving your solution.* Sometimes we have good proposals to offer but must defer to others for ways to achieve those proposals. If you have not examined the political or legal steps necessary to implement your solution, then this step cannot be part of your purpose in writing. However, anticipating a skeptical audience that says "How are we going to do that?" you would be wise to think about precise steps for achieving your solution. When proposing to eliminate violent TV programs, you might suggest, for example, that an appropriate government agency be commissioned to establish standards or guidelines for the TV industry and create a review board to rule when controversy arises. Showing your readers that you have thought ahead to the next step in the process can be an effective method of persuasion.

5. *Support the feasibility of your solution.* Offering a method for implementing your solution is a plus for your argument; demonstrating the feasibility of your method is even more convincing. Consider Prohibition, for instance. The method for eliminating alcohol was simple: Make it illegal. But the method did not work; it wasn't feasible, in this case because it wasn't acceptable to the majority of Americans. When supporting the feasibility of your proposal, consider the cost of implementing your solution, the relative complexity of your proposal, and its acceptability to the majority of persons affected by the proposed solution.

6. *Demonstrate that your proposed solution is better than others.* Anticipate challenges to your solution by comparing it with others that have been or might be suggested and by showing how yours is better. One measure of a solution's worth is its feasibility; if it won't work, then it is a lousy idea. Another measure must be the proposal's potential effectiveness. Can you show how your solution will avoid the limited effectiveness of other solutions that have been tried? Of course another defense is that it is the right thing to do. Values also belong in public-policy debates, not just issues of cost and political acceptability.

USING SOURCES: A NOTE ON STYLE

Most arguments need supporting facts, some of which may not be commonly known. This means that writers of argument frequently must do research, checking information in various reference sources, perhaps reading relevant articles such as those in this text. When drawing on sources in your arguments, you need to consider the expectations of readers and the conventions of presenting sources. First, let's examine the general principles; then review some conventions of form.

Two principles should guide your use of sources, whether your argument is an essay or a more formal research paper. The first is *fairness. Both information—other than common knowledge—and ideas taken from sources, whether paraphrased or quoted, must be acknowledged.* In research essays the pattern of acknowledgment will be one of the accepted forms of documentation. In a less formal essay, acknowledgment is also necessary. The second principle is *context.* You never want to just "dump" source material on your reader without making clear who has gathered the facts or presented the ideas. Put yourself in your readers' place. Readers need to be guided through your argument; they need you to distinguish clearly between your ideas and the ideas of others

In both kinds of papers the best way to present material from sources is to introduce the borrowed material with the author's name, what is called an *introductory tag.* And if the borrowed material must be presented in several sentences, guide readers through that material by continuing to refer to the author so that they know exactly what has come from each source and what has come from you. To illustrate, study the excerpt that follows from another student refutation of the letter to the editor regarding the homeless. To develop her refutation, Trang Nguyen chose to obtain some facts that would challenge the letter writer's views of the homeless. Trang wrote in part:

The homeless are not a homogenous category of people but rather a group of varied types. Often the homeless are the sick, the disabled, or the vulnerable. According to W. R. Breakey, who led a study in 1989 of the homeless in the Baltimore area, 50 percent of these vagrants had a major mental illness. Another study of the homeless conducted by P. Koegel in the Los Angeles area revealed that 60 percent of the homeless had a chronic psychiatric disorder.

Trang uses the information from her reading to challenge the writer's concept of the homeless, but she makes clear who are the authors of the borrowed information. If this were part of a formal research paper, additional documentation would be needed.

Observe as well that Trang presents the borrowed information in her own words. It is safe to say that student writers use direct quotation entirely too much. Unless you can justify quoting, because there is something special about the original wording, then paraphrase the material and use an introductory tag. And *always* use an introductory tag with any direct quotations.

Sometimes you may want to introduce borrowed material with information in addition to the author's name. You can give readers additional context by providing the author's credentials (for example, geologist Dale Russell who is Curator of Fossil Vertebrates at Canada's National Museum of Natural Sciences) or the title of the source used (for example, In *A Distant Mirror* Barbara Tuchman argues that . . .). There are conventions for referring to people and to works that you need to follow in all your papers.

References to People

- In a first reference, give the person's full name: Barbara Tuchman, Dale Russell. In second and subsequent references, use only the last name (surname): Tuchman, Russell.
- Do not use *Mr., Mrs.,* or *Ms.*
- Never refer to an author by her or his first name. Write Tuchman, not Barbara; Russell, not Dale.

References to Titles of Works

Titles of works must always be written as titles. Titles are indicated by capitalization and by either quotation marks or underlining. (Underlining in handwritten or typed papers represents italic type in printed works.)

CAPITALIZING TITLES

- The first and last words are capitalized.
- The first word of a subtitle is capitalized.
- All other words in titles are capitalized except:
  Articles (*a, an, the*)
  Coordinating conjunctions (*and, or, but, nor, for, yet, so*)
  Prepositions of five or fewer letters (for example, *in, for, with;* prepositions of more than five letters are capitalized: *Between, Through, Before*)

TITLES REQUIRING QUOTATION MARKS   Titles of works published *within* other works, for example, within a book, magazine, or newspaper, are indicated by quotation marks. Thus essay, article, chapter, short story, and poem titles are placed within quotation marks.

TITLES REQUIRING UNDERLINING (ITALICS IN PRINT)   Titles of works that are separate publications and, by extension, titles of items such as artworks and films are underlined. Thus play, novel, nonfiction and textbook, magazine, and newspaper titles are underlined.

A CHECKLIST FOR REVISION

Good writers know that drafting their paper is only one step to preparing a completed project and that the revision stage may be the most important. Actually you should approach revision as three separate stages: *rewriting* (adding, deleting, or moving parts of the draft around); *editing* (a rereading to correct errors from misspellings to awkward sentences; and *proofreading* the final copy. Trying to combine the first two steps can lead to incomplete revision; ignoring the third step can result in a discouraging grade. Use the following guidelines, grouped by these three steps, to take you from a draft to a completed paper.

Rewriting

Read your draft through and make changes—adding, deleting, moving parts around—as a result of answering the following questions:

PURPOSE AND AUDIENCE

1. Is my draft long enough to fulfill the assignment requirements and my purpose in writing?

2. Are terms defined and concepts explained appropriately?
3. Have I responded to the counterarguments with which my audience will be familiar?

CONTENT

1. Do I have a clearly stated thesis?
2. Have I presented sufficient evidence to support my claim?
3. Are there any irrelevant sections that should be deleted?

STRUCTURE

1. Are paragraphs ordered to develop the topic logically?
2. Does the content of each paragraph help develop the thesis?
3. Is everything in each paragraph on the same subtopic to create paragraph unity?
4. Do body paragraphs have a balance of the general and the concrete?
5. Are there any paragraphs that should be combined? Are there any very long paragraphs that should be divided? (Length alone is not a reason to divide; check long paragraphs for unity.)

Make any large-scale changes involving length, content, organization, and paragraphing first, considering as you rewrite if you are assuming information or understanding in readers that it is your task to provide. After making changes, read the draft through again to assess your new version. Complete your revision by judging your draft according to the following questions:

COHERENCE

1. Have connecting words been used and key terms repeated to produce paragraph coherence?
2. Have transitions been used to show connections between paragraphs?

SOURCES

1. When drawing on sources, have I paraphrased instead of quoting whenever possible?
2. Have I avoided long quotations?
3. Have I used introductory tags to create a context for source material?
4. Have I referred to authors and their sources correctly?

After making the additional changes generated by the above questions, you are ready for editing.

Editing

Although you may have corrected various errors and stylistic weaknesses as you made major revisions, you are wise to examine the now-completed second draft for specific "smaller"—but still important—kinds of problems. Students often say that they would be happy to edit their papers if they only knew what to look for. Their point is well taken. What often passes for editing is an examination of content, what you have just done to revise your first draft. Here are five specific elements of writing that you should examine, one by one, to perform a thorough editing of your paper.

TONE Read your draft through to assess the paper's tone. Have you avoided humor or sarcasm, except as a part of your topic? Have you avoided condescending to readers or ridiculing the opposition? Do you maintain an appropriate level of seriousness throughout? (Do not be flip; do not complain.)

SENTENCE STYLE Examine your draft *sentence by sentence,* testing your sentences against the following questions:

1. Are the sentences grammatically complete, except for those fragments purposely used for emphasis? Look for any sentences beginning with words such as *because* and *although.* These words introduce dependent clauses that must be attached to an independent clause to make a complete sentence.
2. Are there instances of wordiness, clichés, trite expressions, or inflated phrases that can be eliminated? Examine your writing for phrases such as the following, and observe the simpler alternatives that can be substituted:

Wordy, trite, inflated	*Revision*
very unique	unique
the study tends to suggest	the study suggests
in this day and age	today, now, currently
conduct an examination of	examine
at the present time	now
fewer in number	fewer
of great importance	important
in today's modern society	today

3. Do you need to increase sentence variety? Consider varying both length and structure. Begin some sentences with clauses or phrases to avoid having most start with subject and verb.

4. Most important, do sentences present ideas clearly, and with precision? Look specifically at uses of *this* and *which*. Do not use *this* to refer vaguely to a complex idea in the preceding sentence, and avoid attaching a *which* clause, as a vague comment, onto a complex statement.

DISCRIMINATORY LANGUAGE Edit to eliminate all discriminatory language, language that stereotypes people by race, sex, nationality, religion, age, or handicap. Most people recognize ethnic or racial slurs and would not write such statements, but sometimes attitudes about young, old, or handicapped people can slip unnoticed into writing, and of course sexist writing is a particular problem because English lacks a neuter pronoun to refer to people. Remember that it is unacceptable to use *he* to refer to a noun that could be male or female. Here are a few ways around the problem:

- Use *people, humans,* or *human beings* instead of *man.*
- Use nonsexist terms for types of workers: Instead of *manpower,* use *workers, staff,* or *personnel.* Instead of *policeman,* use *police officer;* instead of *housewife,* use *homemaker* and so forth.
- Eliminate *he* and *his* to refer to a noun that could be male or female by pluralizing the noun and then using the plural pronouns *they* or *their.* Alternatively, recast the sentence to avoid the use of a pronoun. *He or she* can be used sparingly but not more than once in a sentence.

WORD CHOICE Examine your word choice, and edit as necessary according to your answers to these questions:

1. Are specialized terms used correctly?
2. Have I avoided an excessive use of specialized terms and selected instead, where possible, simpler words?
3. Have I used, as much as possible, specific, concrete words instead of general, abstract words? Look for too much reliance on such words as *thing, factor,* and *aspect.*
4. Have I used correctly those troublesome words called *homonyms: there, their, they're; you're, your; where, were; its, it's; affect, effect;* and so forth?

CONVENTIONS OF FORM Finally, review the guidelines in this chapter for referring to people and to titles of works and check your work against those guidelines.

Proofreading

When your editing is completed, prepare a final draft of your paper. Select quality paper and use a typewriter with a new ribbon or a good printer. Then proofread the final copy carefully, making necessary corrections neatly in ink. For pages with several errors, print a corrected page or re-type the page.

PART 2

ARGUMENTS
FOR
ANALYSIS

CHAPTER 4

DEBATING
EDUCATION
ISSUES: WHAT
ARE THE
PROBLEMS?
WHAT ARE THE
SOLUTIONS?

How do you improve educational opportunities for disadvantaged students, raise standards and improve the discipline of learning so that American students will be able to compete in the world marketplace, provide instruction for citizenship in a multiethnic society, and shore up the self-esteem of students—all at the same time? If you have the answer, education departments and school boards around the country are waiting to hear from you.

How to educate young people and how to manage a universal educational system have been debated in educational journals, the popular media, and PTA meetings for a long time, but the breadth and stridency of the debate have increased dramatically in recent years, particularly since the 1983 report on America's schools, *A Nation at Risk*. Since 1983, the indicators—dropping SAT scores, poor showings by American students on international tests in math and science, complaints by college professors of students' lack of preparation for college work—reflect only a worsening report card for our schools. So, what are we to do?

Numerous solutions have been put forward: spend more money on education, pay teachers better to attract better teachers, extend the school day or the school year, reverse the dumbing down of textbooks, require more homework, require exit exams for promotion and graduation, develop a national curriculum on the Japanese model, institute a voucher system for school choice, even improve nutrition in the school lunch. How do we sort through these different proposals and evaluate them against the goals of education and the many demands on our schools?

There are at least three issues to be considered in deciding on the best solutions to the problems. The first is feasibility—money and politics. We have no more money, as some would put it, to "throw at the problem" unless the nation reorders its priorities and/or finds the will to increase taxes. (To find more money for education without increasing taxes means reducing entitlement programs. This means shifting money away from the elderly; however, the elderly vote whereas young people of school age do not.) Other political issues include the vocal teachers' federations and entrenched education departments that control teacher certification and have much to say about the length of the school day or year and about teacher evaluation. Daniel Singal believes that part of the problem lies in teacher certification requirements; he acknowledges the political challenge in changing the system.

The second issue involves what to teach and how to motivate students to learn what is taught. Writers who address this issue range from calling for more academic courses—math, science, English, history, and a foreign language every year—to demanding a uniform curriculum to making students read more, and more difficult, works and write more, and more demanding, papers. These writers also make suggestions for motivating students to fulfill the more demanding requirements. Several authors in this chapter focus their attention on this issue, notably Diane Ravitch, Charles Fowler, Richard Lynn, Nathan Caplan et al., and Daniel Singal. Each of these writers makes curriculum suggestions and addresses the problem of motivation. Caplan's article, based on extensive research, is the most positive: "Indochinese Refugee Families and Academic Achievement" argues that American schools can teach when students value learning, do homework, and have involved parents. Most of the writers who address this issue are concerned with raising standards; they inevitably cite our poor performance internationally and the need to have competent workers to compete in the global village.

The third issue is how to teach, or how to focus the material to meet some of the other goals of education mentioned in paragraph 1. Many who question the wisdom of a national curriculum and achievement testing are concerned that inner-city and rural schools do not have the resources—the money for books and equipment, qualified teachers, an atmosphere for learning—needed to present a more rigorous curriculum, with the result that many students in such schools will not measure up, losing opportunities for college entrance, losing self-esteem. (A possible counter to this position is that if these, and other, students are not prepared for the skilled jobs of the twenty-first century, they will live adult lives with little to feel good about. See the discussion of future jobs in Chapter 9.) One alternative to higher academic standards is to place more emphasis on affective education, to argue for the importance of spending time on group social skills and on developing a sense of self. Many educators feel strongly that the call for a more rigorous academic curriculum will lead to drills and memorization rather than to developing the imaginative and intuitive parts of the human personality. An educational philosophy that stresses personal growth and self-knowledge will be uncomfortable with one that emphasizes gaining knowledge and intellectual skills. Finally, those educators who want students to learn about and accept the many different cultures that make up the human community may also object to a uniform, academic course of study because they want time, particularly in literature and social studies classes, to explore many cultures, and they fear that a uniform course of study will turn out to be the traditional, Western civilization course of study. The last two articles in this chapter, one by Joseph Banks, the other by Albert Shanker, debate the role of multiculturalism in our schools.

Clearly these three issues can be separated only as an organizational strategy, for they intersect at many points, making the task of developing a coherent, fair, and feasible plan for educational change seem almost insurmountable. But since the alternative, to plod along as we are now, is untenable, we must bring our collective energies to bear on finding ways to improve our schools.

❖

Back to Basics: Test Scores Don't Lie

Diane Ravitch

Educated at Wellesley and Columbia and long an adjunct professor at Columbia University's Teachers College, Diane Ravitch (b. 1938) is currently an assistant secretary in the U.S. Department of Education.
Among her many publications are The Troubled Crusade: American Education 1945–1980 *(1983) and* The Schools We Deserve: Reflections on the Educational Crisis of Our Time *(1985). In the following article, published in* The New Republic *on March 6, 1989, Ravitch argues that it is not the tests that need changing but American attitudes toward education.*

1   When I was in public high school in Texas in the 1950s, one of the last things a girl wanted was a reputation as a good student. Girls who got good grades were "brains," and brains were socially handicapped. Most girls strived to cultivate the June Allyson image: a follower, not a leader; cute and not too smart, or at least not so smart that the guys felt threatened.

2   Apparently—despite the women's movement and the presence of significant numbers of successful women as role models—it is still considered inappropriate in most schools and colleges for girls to seem "smart." As a female student at Hunter High School in New York City recently explained, "I make straight A's, but I never talk about it. . . . It's cool to do really badly. If you are interested in school and you show it, you're a nerd." In elite institutions, where students are chosen for their academic ability, girls are more willing to challenge the boys academically than they are in nonselective schools and colleges. But with the demise of most single-sex girls' schools and colleges, there are now even fewer institutions where girls can be leaders and achievers without feeling like freaks. The popular culture—through television, movies, magazines, and videos—incessantly drums in the message to young women that it is better to be popular, sexy, and "cool" than to be intelligent, accomplished, and outspoken: Madonna has replaced June Allyson.

3   In 1986 researchers Signithia Fordham and John U. Ogbu found a similar anti-academic ethos among both male and female students at an all-black high school in Washington, D.C. They noted that able students

faced strong peer pressure not to succeed in school. If they did well in their studies, they might be accused of "acting white." Fordham and Ogbu observed that "peer group pressures against academic striving take many forms, including labeling (e.g., 'brainiac' for students who receive good grades in their courses), exclusion from peer activities or ostracism, and physical assault."

These attitudes, whether expressed by boys or girls, blacks or whites, discourage academic achievement. If boys or girls who study are derided as "goobs" and "dweebs"—two of the many pejorative terms for good students catalogued in a recent *New York Times* survey of teenage slang— then most boys and girls are going to avoid studying. Permissive parents and permissive educators don't help the situation by leaving adolescents adrift in a culture shaped largely by the mass media. A national mathematics assessment released in 1988 revealed that American teenagers know the basics taught in elementary school, but their academic performance trails off as they get older and peer pressures begin to take effect. Only half of all 17-year-olds "reached a level of proficiency associated with material taught in junior high school mathematics."

Unfortunately, outside the cultural bubble inhabited by Madonnas and dweebs lies a real world, and in that world poor academic achievement is not without conseqences. Last March a comparison of students in 17 nations reported that our fifth-graders ranked eighth out of the 17; our ninth-graders ranked 16th out of 17 (beating out Hong Kong only); and our 12th-graders ranked last in biology, third from last in chemistry, and fourth from last in physics. Just a few weeks ago another international test of mathematics and science was released by the Educational Testing Service, with the same dismal results. Compared to 13-year-old students in Ireland, South Korea, Spain, the United Kingdom, and four provinces in Canada, our students scored last in mathematics and well below the mean in science.

There is a growing real world correspondence between our declining test results and our declining economic prowess. Those countries that promote hard work and self-discipline in school have surged ahead, eroding the technological edge that we once enjoyed. According to the *New York Times,* Japan's annual share of American patents grew over the past 15 years from 4 percent to 19 percent, while our own share dropped from 73 percent to 54 percent. Experts point to the lack of a well-educated labor force as one of the prime causes of our diminishing economic position. Government policy is partially responsible, as are inadequate levels of savings and investment. But we have wounded ourselves, socially and economically, by failing to nurture scientists, engineers, inventors, and, in fact, a general citizenry who can read, write, compute, and adeptly use technology. In the 17-nation science study, the bottom quarter in the ninth grade of U.S. schools is described as "scientifically illiterate."

7   So what are we doing about it? Among the nations that regularly lead the world in international competitions, like Korea and Japan, there is a strong core curriculum that begins in elementary school. U.S. educators should be demanding that all future teachers get a solid liberal education, one that includes math, science, history, literature, and foreign language; and some educators are. Educators and concerned citizens should also be insisting that all children learn science and mathematics and history and literature and a foreign language in every grade from elementary school onward; but few educators are, because they either don't believe in doing so or know there aren't enough qualified teachers to offer such a rich curriculum.

8   What we shouldn't be doing is denying that a problem exists, or jettisoning objective measures that reveal our educational shortcomings. Yet that has been one effect of the anti-testing movement, which just won a federal court order in New York banning the use of Scholastic Aptitude Tests as the sole criterion for awarding state scholarships, on the grounds that the SAT (the nation's most widely used college admission test) discriminates against girls. Judge John M. Walker, noting that boys get higher scores than girls, ruled that this use of the test to distribute scholarships violates the equal protection clause of the Constitution.

9   Down this path lies a great deal of foolishness. Racial and gender disparities crop up on most objective measures of academic performance. On the science tests that were given to students in 17 nations, boys outscored girls in every country, and the gap increased with each age level; only among the most advanced seniors in Hong Kong and Sweden—and only on the biology exam—did girls outscore boys. In the history assessment, boys usually outscored girls, and sometimes the differences were startling. For example, in a national history assessment in 1987, boys were more likely than girls to locate the Rocky Mountains on a map, to know that Columbus discovered the New World before 1750, and to know that the Great Depression occurred between 1900 and 1950. Are these gender-biased questions? It doesn't seem so.

10   Some of the differences between the genders and the races on tests of subject matter can be accounted for by different course-taking patterns. For example, white males tend to take more advanced courses in science than do females and members of minority groups. Something else is amiss, however, because even when girls and blacks and Hispanics take physics, the white males still outperform them by a considerable margin. Since I don't believe that white males have a genetic edge, I have to conclude that deeply ingrained self-deprecation and ever present peer pressures combine to depress the aspirations and achievements of girls and minority students.

11   Thus, if the SAT were abolished, there would still be gender disparities and racial disparities on other tests. But since I happen to think that the SAT has outlived its usefulness as a college admission test, I am not

going to raise a hue-and-cry about its potential demise. Far better in determining whether a student deserves admission to a selective institution would be a test that measures what he or she has actually studied—or should have studied—in science, history, literature, mathematics, and foreign language. Because the SAT is content-free (except in its mathematical questions), high schools can afford to ignore content. If the SAT were replaced by achievement tests, high schools would be likelier to teach the subjects that matter, and students would be likelier to take them. Both developments would narrow the achievement gap that places us at a disadvantage in international comparisons.

But no matter what kind of test is used, we will continue to have serious cultural problems undermining educational achievement: the negative attitudes of students who jeer at those who do well in school; the negative attitude of parents who urge their sons to strive and achieve but not their daughters; and the negative attitude of educators who accept the destructive peer culture, not acknowledging their responsibility to establish a climate in which academic achievement, hard work, and brainpower are honored.   12

We could tackle the achievement gap by following the lead of Judge Walker in New York and rejecting the validity of all tests in which white males consistently outperform females and members of minority groups. Maybe we could even stop participating in international assessments that tell us how badly we are doing compared with other countries.   13

Or we could take a hard look at the social and cultural attitudes among teenagers and adults that discourage girls, blacks, and Hispanics from seeing themselves as future engineers, doctors, and scientists; and then we could think hard about ways to change the peer pressures that put down academic achievement. We will continue to lose ground and squander our educational resources until teenagers and their parents come to recognize that academic achievement requires the same motivation and active involvement as achievement in sports or music.   14

Reading and Analyzing

1. What, exactly, is Ravitch's subject? That is, what problem in American education does she examine?
2. What has caused the problem, or what is the cause of the problem that Ravitch chooses to emphasize?
3. State the author's thesis, the claim of her argument, in a sentence or two.
4. Analyze Ravitch's opening. What does she accomplish in her first two paragraphs? How do paragraphs 3 and 4 expand her opening? What does she use to develop these two paragraphs?

5. What female image is presented by June Allyson? By Madonna?

6. What strategies does Ravitch use in presenting source material? How does she guide readers through borrowed material?

7. What are the social and economic consequences of the educational problem examined here?

8. How does Ravitch explain racial and gender disparities on standardized tests? What is *not* a cause of these disparities in her view?

9. What is the author's attitude toward the SAT test? Is the test biased? Is it useful? Should it be replaced? If so, with what?

10. What responses to the problem does Ravitch think are mistakes? Why?

11. What solutions does she offer?

Responding to the Writer's Ideas

1. Does Ravitch's analysis of attitudes toward good grades correspond to your experience in high school? If so, how did you cope with the situation?

2. Do you think that the SAT test should be replaced by achievement tests? Or, should achievement tests be required by colleges in addition to the SAT? Why or why not?

3. Ravitch blames parents as well as teenagers for the decline in academic performance. Is this an appropriate charge? If parents are not an immediate cause, in what ways can they influence what happens—or does not happen—in school?

4. The author wants to see science, math, literature, history, and a foreign language taught in every year from elementary school on. Do you agree with this suggestion? Why or why not?

5. In one study, one-fourth of ninth graders were described as "scientifically illiterate." Does this fact surprise you? Dismay you? Do you know people who fit into this category? Explain your reactions.

❖

Why Johnny Can't Read,
But Yoshio Can

Richard Lynn

Born in London and educated at King's College, Cambridge, Richard Lynn (b. 1930) lives in Northern Ireland and teaches in the psychology department at the University of Ulster. His research, which has concentrated on national differences, has led to his most recent book, Educational Achievement in Japan *(1988). The following essay, drawn from his book and published in the* National Review *on October 28, 1988, not only contrasts Japanese and American schools but argues for changes in the latter.*

There can be no doubt that American schools compare poorly with Japanese schools. In the latter, there are no serious problems with poor discipline, violence, or truancy; Japanese children take school seriously and work hard. Japanese educational standards are high, and illiteracy is virtually unknown.

The evidence of Japan's high educational standards began to appear as long ago as the 1960s. In 1967 there was published the first of a series of studies of educational standards in a dozen or so economically developed nations, based on tests of carefully drawn representative samples of children. The first study was concerned with achievement in math on the part of 13- and 18-year-olds. In both age groups the Japanese children came out well ahead of their coevals in other countries. The American 13-year-olds came out second to last for their age group; the American 18-year-olds, last. In both age groups, European children scored about halfway between the Japanese and the Americans.

Since then, further studies have appeared, covering science as well as math. The pattern of results has always been the same: the Japanese have generally scored first, the Americans last or nearly last, and the Europeans have fallen somewhere in between. In early adolescence, when the first tests are taken, Japanese children are two or three years ahead of American children; by age 18, approximately 98 percent of Japanese children surpass their American counterparts.

Meanwhile, under the Reagan Administration, the United States at least started to take notice of the problem. In 1983 the President's report, *A Nation at Risk,* described the state of American schools as a national

111

disaster. A follow-up report issued by the then-secretary of education, Mr. William Bennett, earlier this year claims that although some improvements have been made, these have been "disappointingly slow."

5   An examination of Japan's school system suggests that there are three factors responsible for its success, which might be emulated by other countries: a strong national curriculum, stipulated by the government; strong incentives for students; and the stimulating effects of competition between schools.

6   The national curriculum in Japan is drawn up by the Department of Education. It covers Japanese language and literature, math, science, social science, music, moral education, and physical education. From time to time, the Department of Education requests advice on the content of the curriculum from representatives of the teaching profession, industry, and the trade unions. Syllabi are then drawn up, setting out in detail the subject matter that has to be taught at each grade. These syllabi are issued to school principals, who are responsible for ensuring that the stipulated curriculum is taught in their schools. Inspectors periodically check that this is being done.

7   The Japanese national curriculum ensures such uniformly high standards of teaching that almost all parents are happy to send their children to the local public school. There is no flight into private schools of the kind that has been taking place in America in recent years. Private schools do exist in Japan, but they are attended by less than 1 percent of children in the age range of compulsory schooling (six to 15 years).

8   This tightly stipulated national curriculum provides a striking contrast with the decentralized curriculum of schools in America. Officially, the curriculum in America is the responsibility of school principals with guidelines from state education officials. In practice, even school principals often have little idea of what is actually being taught in the classroom.

9   America and Britain have been unusual in leaving the curriculum so largely in the hands of teachers. Some form of national curriculum is used throughout Continental Europe, although the syllabus is typically not specified in as much detail as in Japan. And now Britain is changing course: legislation currently going through Parliament will introduce a national curriculum for England and Wales, with the principal subjects being English, math, science, technology, a foreign language, history and geography, and art, music, and design. It is envisioned that the new curriculum will take up approximately 70 percent of teaching time, leaving the remainder free for optional subjects such as a second foreign language, or extra science.

10   Under the terms of the new legislation, schoolchildren are going to be given national tests at the ages of seven, 11, 14, and 16 to ensure that the curriculum has been taught and that children have learned it to a satisfactory standard. When the British national curriculum comes into effect, America will be left as the only major economically developed country without one.

To achieve high educational standards in schools it is necessary to   11
have motivated students as well as good teachers. A national curriculum
acts as a discipline on teachers, causing them to teach efficiently, but it
does nothing to provide incentives for students, an area in which American
education is particularly weak.

One of the key factors in the Japanese education system is that sec-   12
ondary schooling is split into two stages. At the age of 11 or 12, Japanese
children enter junior high school. After three years there, they take competitive entrance examinations for senior high schools. In each locality
there is a hierarchy of public esteem for these senior high schools, from the
two or three that are regarded as the best in the area, through those considered to be good or average, down to those that (at least by Japanese
standards) are considered to be poor.

The top schools enjoy national reputations, somewhat akin to the   13
famous English schools such as Eton and Harrow. But in England the
high fees exacted by these schools mean that very few parents can afford
them. Consequently there are few candidates for entry, and the entrance
examinations offer little incentive to work for the great mass of children.
By contrast, in Japan the elite senior high schools are open to everyone.
While a good number of these schools are private (approximately 30 percent nationwide, though in some major cities the figure is as high as 50
percent), even these schools are enabled, by government subsidies, to
keep their fees within the means of a large proportion of parents. The
public schools also charge fees, but these are nominal, amounting to only
a few hundred dollars a year, and loans are available to cover both fees
and living expenses.

Thus children have every expectation of being able to attend the best   14
school they can qualify for; and, hence, the hierarchical rankings of senior
high schools act as a powerful incentive for children preparing for the entrance examinations. There is no doubt that Japanese children work hard
in response to these incentives. Starting as early as age ten, approximately
half of them take extra tuition on weekends, in the evenings, and in the
school holidays at supplementary coaching establishments known as *juku*,
and even at that early age they do far more homework than American children. At about the age of 12, Japanese children enter the period of their
lives known as *examination hell*: during this time, which lasts fully two
years, it is said that those who sleep more than five hours a night have no
hope of success, either in school or in life. For, in addition to conferring
great social and intellectual status on their students, the elite senior high
schools provide a first-rate academic education, which, in turn, normally
enables the students to get into one of the elite universities and, eventually,
to move into a good job in industry or government.

Although Japanese children are permitted to leave school at the age   15
of 15, 94 percent of them proceed voluntarily to the senior high schools.

Thus virtually all Japanese are exposed in early adolescence to the powerful incentive for academic work represented by the senior-high-school entrance examinations. There is nothing in the school systems of any of the Western countries resembling this powerful incentive.

16   The prestige of the elite senior high schools is sustained by the extensive publicity they receive from the media. Each year the top hundred or so schools in Japan are ranked on the basis of the percentage of their pupils who obtain entry to the University of Tokyo, Japan's most prestigious university. These rankings are widely reported in the print media, and the positions of the top twenty schools are announced on TV news programs, rather like the scores made by leading sports teams in the United States and Europe. At a local level, more detailed media coverage is devoted to the academic achievements of all the schools in the various localities, this time analyzed in terms of their pupils' success in obtaining entry to the lesser, but still highly regarded, local universities.

17   Thus, once Japanese 15-year-olds have been admitted to their senior high schools, they are confronted with a fresh set of incentives in the form of entrance examinations to universities and colleges, which are likewise hierarchically ordered in public esteem. After the University of Tokyo, which stands at the apex of the status hierarchy, come the University of Kyoto and ten or so other highly prestigious universities, including the former Imperial Universities in the major provincial cities and the technological university of Hitosubashi, whose standing and reputation in Japan resembles that of the Massachusetts Institute of Technology in the United States.

18   Below these top dozen institutions stand some forty or so less prestigious but still well-regarded universities. And after these come numerous smaller universities and colleges of varying degrees of standing and reputation.

19   To some extent the situation in Japan has parallels in the United States and Europe, but there are two factors that make the importance of securing admission to an elite university substantially greater in Japan than in the West. In the first place, the entire Japanese system is geared toward providing lifelong employment, both in the private sector and in the civil service. It is practically unheard of for executives to switch from one corporation to another, or into public service and then back into the private sector, as in the United States and Europe. Employees are recruited directly out of college, and, needless to say, the major corporations and the civil service recruit virtually entirely from the top dozen universities. The smaller Japanese corporations operate along the same lines, although they widen their recruitment net to cover the next forty or so universities in the prestige hierarchy. Thus, obtaining entry to a prestigious university is a far more vital step for a successful career in Japan than it is in the United States or Europe.

Secondly, like the elite senior high schools, the elite universities are meritocratic. The great majority of universities are public institutions, receiving substantial government subsidies. Again, as with the senior high schools, fees are quite low, and loans are available to defray expenses. In principle and to a considerable extent in practice, any young Japanese can get into the University of Tokyo, or one of the other elite universities, provided only that he or she is talented enough and is prepared to do the work necessary to pass the entrance examinations. Knowing this, the public believes that *all* the most talented young Japanese go to one of these universities—and, conversely, that anyone who fails to get into one of these schools is necessarily less bright. Avoiding this stigma is, of course, a further incentive for the student to work hard to get in.

The third significant factor responsible for the high educational standards in Japan is competition among schools. This operates principally among the senior high schools, and what they are competing for is academic reputation. The most prestigious senior high school in Japan is Kansei in Tokyo, and being a teacher at Kansei is something like being a professor at Harvard. The teachers' self-esteem is bound up with the academic reputation of their schools—a powerful motivator for teachers to teach well.

In addition to this important factor of self-esteem, there is practical necessity. Since students are free to attend any school they can get into, if a school failed to provide good-quality teaching, it would no longer attract students. In business terms, its customers would fade away, and it would be forced to close. Thus the essential feature of the competition among the Japanese senior high schools is that it exposes the teachers to the discipline of the free-enterprise system. In the case of the public senior high schools, the system can be regarded as a form of market socialism in which the competing institutions are state-owned but nevertheless compete against each other for their customers. Here the Japanese have been successfully operating the kind of system that Mikhail Gorbachev may be feeling his way toward introducing in the Soviet Union. The Japanese private senior high schools add a further capitalist element to the system insofar as they offer their educational services more or less like firms operating in a conventional market.

The problem of how market disciplines can be brought to bear on schools has been widely discussed in America and also in Britain ever since Milton Friedman raised it a quarter of a century or so ago, but solutions such as Friedman's voucher proposal seem as distant today as they did then. Although the proposal has been looked at sympathetically by Republicans in the United States and by Conservatives in Britain, politicians in both countries have fought shy of introducing it. Probably they have concluded that the problems of getting vouchers into the hands of all parents, and dealing with losses, fraud, counterfeits, and so forth, are likely to be too great for the scheme to be feasible.

24   The Japanese have evolved a different method of exposing schools to market forces. Subsidies are paid directly to the schools on a per-capita basis in accordance with the number of students they have. If a school's rolls decline, so do its incomes, both from subsidies and from fees. This applies to both the public and private senior high schools, although the public schools obviously receive a much greater proportion of their income as subsidies and a smaller proportion from fees.

25   A similar scheme is being introduced in Britain. The Thatcher government is currently bringing in legislation that will permit public schools to opt out of local-authority control. Those that opt out will receive subsidies from the central government on the basis of the number of students they have. They will then be on their own, to sink or swim.

26   There is little doubt that this is the route that should be followed in America. The exposure of American schools to the invigorating stimulus of competition, combined with the introduction of a national curriculum and the provision of stronger incentives for students, would work wonders. Rather than complaining about Japanese aggressiveness and instituting counterproductive protectionist measures, Americans ought to be looking at the source of Japan's power.

Reading and Analyzing

1. What is Lynn's subject? Be specific, keeping in mind that this is an argument, not just an analysis of Japanese schools.
2. Who is Lynn's audience? What are his expectations regarding the readers of *U.S. News and World Report*?
3. Examine Lynn's introduction. What does he accomplish in his first four paragraphs?
4. Paragraph 5 is a sentence that sounds like a thesis. What needs to be added to it to complete the claim of Lynn's argument?
5. How is Lynn's essay organized? Analyze the structure, noting the paragraphs devoted to each subtopic.
6. What are the three characteristics of Japanese schools that make them successful? Examine each characteristic in detail, listing points of difference between Japanese and American schools.
7. Lynn also mentions European schools. Are they more like Japanese or American schools? How do European students' performance on tests compare to Americans? In what way are American schools different from both Japanese and European schools?
8. How would you describe Lynn's tone? Is he angry, serious, preachy, satiric, something else?

Responding to the Writer's Ideas

1. Lynn gives credit to the "Japanese national curriculum" for ensuring "uniformly high standards of teaching." He suggests then that the standard curriculum is the major cause for Japan's quality schools. Might there be other causes? If the United States were to adopt a standard curriculum, would that guarantee improved schools?

2. Many American educators, including Diane Ravitch, favor a national curriculum and regular testing of achievement. Others oppose such a change. What, in your view, might be the advantages of a uniform curriculum? What might be the disadvantages?

3. Of the three characteristics of Japanese schools examined by Lynn, which, in your view, seems the most compelling reason for the Japanese students' superior performance? Why?

4. Which of the characteristics would you like to see adopted in the United States? Why? Are there any you do not want? Why?

5. Although Japanese students can drop out of school at 15 and not attend high school, almost all continue. Do you think giving American students this choice is a good idea? Why or why not?

❖

Indochinese Refugee Families
and Academic Achievement

Nathan Caplan, Marcella H. Choy, and John K. Whitmore

Multiple authorship often signals an academic study in the sciences or social sciences. This case is no exception. The three authors worked together on their study of Indochinese refugee students in American schools at the University of Michigan's Institute for Social Research. Nathan Caplan is professor emeritus of psychology at the university and program director at the institute, Marcella Choy is a doctoral candidate in social psychology, and John Whitmore is a Southeast Asian specialist at Michigan. The results of their study were published in the February 1992 issue of Scientific American.

1   The scholastic success of Asian children is well recognized. Their stunning performance—particularly in the realm of science and mathematics—has prompted American educators to visit Japanese and Taiwanese schools in an effort to unearth the foundations of these achievements. Experts recommend that American schools adopt aspects of their Asian counterparts, such as a longer school year or more rigorous tasks, in order to raise the scholastic level of U.S. students.

2   Yet there is no need to go abroad to understand why these children do so well. The achievement of Asian-American students indicates that much may be learned about the origins of their triumph within the American school system itself. More specifically, during the late 1970s and early 1980s, devastating political and economic circumstances forced many Vietnamese, Lao and Chinese-Vietnamese families to seek a new life in the U.S. This resettlement of boat people from Indochina offered a rare opportunity to examine the academic achievement of their children.

3   These young refugees had lost months, even years of formal schooling while living in relocation camps. Like their parents, they suffered disruption and trauma as they escaped from Southeast Asia. Despite their hardships and with little knowledge of English, the children quickly adapted to their new schools and began to excel.

4   In researching the economic and scholastic accomplishments of 1,400 refugee households in the early 1980s, our group at the University of Michigan studied the forces that shaped the performance of these children. Some of the standard explanations for educational excellence—parental

encouragement and dedication to learning—applied to the young students, but other theories proved inadequate.

Although some of our findings are culturally specific, others point overwhelmingly to the pivotal role of the family in the children's academic success. Because this characteristic extends beyond culture, it has implications for educators, social scientists and policy-makers as well as for the refugees themselves. It is clear that the U.S. educational system can work— if the requisite familial and social supports are provided for the students outside school.

Our study encompassed many features of resettlement. We gathered survey and other data on 6,750 persons in five urban areas—Orange County, Calif., Seattle, Houston, Chicago and Boston—and obtained information about their background and home life as well as economic and demographic facts. We discovered that with regard to educational and social status, the refugees proved to be more ordinary than their predecessors who fled Vietnam in 1975 during the fall of Saigon. These newer displaced persons had had limited exposure to Western culture and knew virtually no English when they arrived. Often they came with nothing more than the clothes they wore.

From this larger group, we chose a random sample of 200 nuclear families and their 536 school-age children. Twenty-seven percent of the families had four or more children. At the time of the study, these young refugees had been in the U.S. for an average of three and a half years. We collected information on parents and their children during interviews conducted in their native tongues; we also gained access to school transcripts and other related documents.

All the children attended schools in low-income, metropolitan areas— environs not known for outstanding academic records. The refugees were fairly evenly distributed throughout the school levels: grades one through 11 each contained about 8 percent of the children in the study; kindergarten and 12th grade each contained about 5 percent. We converted the students' letter grades into a numerical grade point average (GPA): an A became a four; a D became a one. After calculations, we found that the children's mean GPA was 3.05, or a B average. Twenty-seven percent had an overall GPA in the A range, 52 percent in the B range and 17 percent in the C range. Only 4 percent had a GPA below a C grade.

Even more striking than the overall GPAs were the students' math scores. Almost half of the children earned As in math; another third earned Bs. Thus, four out of five students received either As or Bs. It is not surprising that they would do better in this subject. Their minds could most easily grasp disciplines in which English was not so crucial: math, physics, chemistry and science. As expected, their grades in the liberal arts were lower: in areas where extensive language skills were required, such as English, history or social studies, the combined GPA was 2.64.

10   To place our local findings in a national context, we turned to standardized achievement test scores, in particular, the California Achievement Test (CAT) results. In this arena as well, we found that the performance of the newly arrived students was exceptional. Their mean overall score on the CAT was in the 54th percentile; that is, they outperformed 54 percent of those taking the test—placing them just above the national average. Interestingly, their scores tended to cluster toward the middle ranges: they showed a more restricted scope of individual differences.

11   The national tests also reflected an above-average ability in math when the Indochinese children were compared with children taking the exam at equivalent levels. Half of the children studied obtained scores in the top quartile. Even more spectacularly, 27 percent of them scored in the 10th decile—better than 90 percent of the students across the country and almost three times higher than the national norm. The CAT math scores confirmed that the GPAs of these children were not products of local bias but of true mathematical competence.

12   Again, the lowest scores were found in the language and reading tests. In this case, the mean score was slightly below the national average. For reasons discussed earlier, this finding was expected. It remains remarkable, however, that the students' scores are so close to the national average in language skills.

13   The GPA and CAT scores show that the refugee children did very well, particularly in light of their background. A history marked by significant physical and emotional trauma as well as a lack of formal education would not seem to predispose them to an easy transition into U.S. schools. Yet even though they had not forgotten their difficult experiences, the children were able to focus on the present and to work toward the future. In so doing, they made striking scholastic progress. Moreover, their achievements held true for the majority, not for just a few whiz kids.

14   Clearly, these accomplishments are fueled by influences powerful enough to override the impact of a host of geographic and demographic factors. Using various statistical approaches, we sought to understand the forces responsible for this performance. In the process, a unique finding caught our attention, namely, a positive relation between the number of siblings and the children's GPA.

15   Family size has long been regarded as one of the most reliable predictors of poor achievement. Virtually all studies on the topic show an inverse relation: the greater the number of children in the family, the lower the mean GPA and other measures associated with scholastic performance. Typically, these reports document a 15 percent decline in GPA and other achievement-related scores with the addition of each child to the family. The interpretation of this finding has been subject to disagreement, but there is no conflict about its relation to achievement.

16   For the Indochinese students, this apparent disadvantage was somehow

neutralized or turned into an advantage. We took this finding to be an important clue in elucidating the role of the family in academic performance. We assumed that distinctive family characteristics would explain how these achievements took place so early in resettlement as well as how these children and their parents managed to overcome such adversities as poor English skills, poverty and the often disruptive environment of urban schools.

Because they were newcomers in a strange land, it was reasonable to expect that at least some of the reasons for the children's success rested on their cultural background. While not ignoring the structural forces present here in the U.S.—among them the opportunity for education and advancement—we believed that the values and traditions permeating the lives of these children in Southeast Asia would guide their lives in this country. 17

Knowledge of one's culture does not occur in a vacuum; it is transmitted through the family. Children often acquire a sense of their heritage as a result of deliberate and concentrated parental effort in the context of family life. This inculcation of values from one generation to another is a universal feature of the conservation of culture. 18

We sought to determine which values were important to the parents, how well those values had been transmitted to the children and what role values played in promoting their educational achievement. In our interviews we included 26 questions about values that were derived from a search of Asian literature and from social science research. Respondents were asked to rate the perceived importance of these values. 19

We found that parents and children rated the perceived values in a similar fashion, providing empirical testimony that these parents had served their stewardship well. For the most part, the perspectives and values embedded in the cultural heritage of the Indochinese had been carried with them to the U.S. We also determined that cultural values played an important role in the educational achievement of the children. Conserved values constituted a source of motivation and direction as the families dealt with contemporary problems set in a country vastly different from their homeland. The values formed a set of cultural givens with deep roots in the Confucian and Buddhist traditions of East and Southeast Asia. 20

The family is the central institution in these traditions, within which and through which achievement and knowledge are accomplished. We used factor analyses and other statistical procedures to determine value groupings and their relation to achievement. These analyses showed that parents and children honor mutual, collective obligation to one another and to their relatives. They strive to attain respect, cooperation and harmony within the family. 21

Nowhere is the family's commitment to accomplishment and education more evident than in time spent on homework. During high school, Indochinese students spend an average of three hours and 10 minutes per day; in junior high, an average of two and a half hours; and in grade 22 school, an average of two hours and five minutes. Research in the U.S. shows that American students study about one and a half hours per day at the junior and senior high school levels.

23   Among the refugee families, then, homework clearly dominates household activities during weeknights. Although the parents' lack of education and facility with English often prevents them from engaging in the content of the exercise, they set standards and goals for the evening and facilitate their children's studies by assuming responsibility for chores and other practical considerations.

24   After dinner, the table is cleared, and homework begins. The older children, both male and female, help their younger siblings. Indeed, they seem to learn as much from teaching as from being taught. It is reasonable to suppose that a great amount of learning goes on at these times—in terms of skills, habits, attitudes and expectations as well as the content of a subject. The younger children, in particular, are taught not only subject matter but how to learn. Such sibling involvement demonstrates how a large family can encourage and enhance academic success. The familial setting appears to make the children feel at home in school and, consequently, perform well there.

25   Parental engagement included reading regularly to young children—an activity routinely correlated to academic performance. Almost one half (45 percent) of the parents reported reading aloud. In those families, the children's mean GPA was 3.14 as opposed to 2.97 in households where the parents did not read aloud. (This difference, and all others to follow in which GPAs are compared, is statistically reliable.) It is important to note that the effects of being read to held up statistically whether the children were read to in English or in their native language.

26   This finding suggests that parental English literacy skills may not play a vital role in determining school performance. Rather, other aspects of the experience—emotional ties between parent and child, cultural validation and wisdom shared in stories read in the child's native language, or value placed on reading and learning—extend to schoolwork. Reading at home obscures the boundary between home and school. In this context, learning is perceived as normal, valuable and fun.

27   Egalitarianism and role sharing were also found to be associated with high academic performance. In fact, relative equality between the sexes was one of the strongest predictors of GPA. In those homes where the respondents disagreed that a "wife should always do as her husband wishes," the children earned average GPAs of 3.16. But children from homes whose parents agreed with the statement had an average GPA of 2.64. In households where the husband helped with the dishes and laundry, the mean GPA was 3.21; when husbands did not participate in the chores, the mean GPA was 2.79.

This sense of equality was not confined to the parents—it extended   28
to the children, especially in terms of sex-role expectations and school performance. GPAs were higher in households where parents expected both
boys and girls to help with chores. Families rejecting the idea that a college
education is more important for boys than for girls had children whose average GPA was 3.14; children from families exhibiting a pro-male bias had
a mean GPA of 2.83.

Beyond the support and guidance provided by the family, culturally   29
based attributions proved to be important to refugees in their view of
scholastic motivation. The "love of learning" category was rated most
often by both parents and students as the factor accounting for their academic success. There appeared to be two parts to this sentiment. First, the
children experienced intrinsic gratification when they correctly worked a
problem through to completion. The pleasure of intellectual growth, based
on new knowledge and ideas and combined with increased competence
and mastery, was considered highly satisfying. Second, refugee children felt
a sense of accomplishment on seeing their younger siblings learn from their
own efforts at teaching. Both learning and imparting knowledge were perceived as pleasurable experiences rather than as drudgery.

The gratification accompanying accomplishment was, in turn, found-   30
ed on a sense of the importance of effort as opposed to ability. The
refugees did not trust fate or luck as the determinant of educational outcome; they believed in their potential to master the factors that could influence their destiny. And their culture encompasses a practical approach to
accomplishment: setting realistic goals. Without the setting of priorities
and standards for work, goals would remain elusive. But anyone endorsing
the values of working in a disciplined manner and taking a long-term view
could establish priorities and pursue them.

Belief in one's own ability to effect change or attain goals has long   31
been held to be a critical component of achievement and motivation—and
our findings support this conclusion. Parents were asked a series of questions relating to their perceived ability to control external events influenc-
ing their lives. Those who had a clear sense of personal efficacy had children who attained higher GPAs.

We had some difficulty, however, interpreting the perception of effi-   32
cacy as an idea generated solely by the individual. Despite a vast social science literature asserting the contrary, we believe that these refugees' sense
of control over their lives could be traced to family identity. It seemed to
us that the sense of familial efficacy proved critical, as opposed to the more
Western concept of personal efficacy.

Other cultural values show us that the refugee family is firmly linked   33
not only to its past and traditions but to the realities of the present and to
future possibilities. This aptitude for integrating the past, present and fu-

ture appears to have imparted a sense of continuity and direction to the lives of these people.

34   Education was central to this integration and to reestablishment in the U.S. It was and still is the main avenue for refugees in American society to succeed and survive. In contrast, education in Indochina was a restricted privilege. The future of the refugee children, and of their families, is thus inextricably linked to schools and to their own children's performances within them. The emphasis on education as the key to social acceptance and economic success helps us understand why academic achievement is reinforced by such strong parental commitment.

35   Outside school, the same sense of drive and achievement can be seen in the parents. Having a job and being able to provide for the family is integral to family pride. Shame is felt by Asian families on welfare. Reflecting the same determination and energy that their children manifest in school, Indochinese parents have found employment and climbed out of economic dependency and poverty with dispatch.

36   Two of the 26 values included as a measure of cultural adaptation entailed integration and the acceptance of certain American ways of life: the importance of "seeking fun and excitement" and of "material possessions." These ideas are of particular concern because they address the future of refugee families and mark the potential power and consequence of American life on the refugees and subsequent generations. Not surprisingly, when our subjects were asked to indicate which values best characterized their nonrefugee neighbors, these two items were most frequently cited.

37   More interesting, however, was our finding that these same two values were correlated with a lower GPA. We found that parents who attributed greater importance to fun and excitement had children who achieved lower GPAs: 2.90 as opposed to 3.14. The results for material possessions were similar: GPAs were 2.66 versus 3.19.

38   It is not clear why these negative associations exist. Do they reflect less strict parents or families who have integrated so quickly that cultural stability has been lost? We believe it is the latter explanation. Refugees who held that "the past is as important as the future" had children whose GPAs averaged 3.14. Children of those who did not rate the preservation of the past as highly had an average GPA of 2.66. This item was one of the most powerful independent predictors of academic performance.

39   Our findings run contrary to expectations. Rather than adopting American ways and assimilating into the melting pot, the most successful Indochinese families appear to retain their own traditions and values. By this statement we are in no way devaluing the American system. The openness and opportunity it offers have enabled the Indochinese to succeed in the U.S. even while maintaining their own cultural traditions.

40   Although different in origins, both traditional Indochinese and mid-

dle-class American values emphasize education, achievement, hard work, autonomy, perseverance and pride. The difference between the two value systems is one of orientation to achievement. American mores encourage independence and individual achievement, whereas Indochinese values foster interdependence and a family-based orientation to achievement. And in view of the position of these refugees in society during the early phase of resettlement in this country, this approach appears to have worked well as the best long-term investment. It appears to be the reason why these children are highly responsive to American schools.

The lack of emphasis on fun and excitement also does not indicate misery on the part of these refugee children. Despite evidence that the suicide rate is growing among some Asian-American children, we found that those in our sample were well adjusted. Our interviews revealed no damaging manipulation of their lives by their parents; moreover, their love of learning sustained their academic pursuits.   41

The Indochinese values that encourage academic rigor and excellence are not culturally unique: earlier studies of other groups have found similar results. The children of Jewish immigrants from Eastern Europe, for example, excelled in the U.S. school system. In 1961 Judith R. Kramer of Brooklyn College and Seymour Leventman of the University of Pennsylvania reported that nearly 90 percent of the third generation attended college, despite the fact that the first generation had little or no education when they arrived in the U.S. Their emphasis on family and culture was held to be instrumental in this success.   42

In 1948 William Caudill and George DeVos of the University of California at Berkeley found that Japanese students overcame prejudice in U.S. schools immediately after World War II and thrived academically. Their success was attributed to cultural values and to parental involvement. More recently, a study by Reginald Clark of the Claremont Graduate School documented the outstanding achievement of low-income African-American students in Chicago whose parents supported the school and teachers and structured their children's learning environment at home.   43

These findings, as well as our own, have significance for the current national debate on education. It is clear that the American school system—despite widespread criticism—has retained its capacity to teach, as it has shown with these refugees. We believe that the view of our schools as failing to educate stems from the unrealistic demand that the educational system deal with urgent social service needs. Citizens and politicians expect teachers and schools to keep children off the streets and away from drugs, deal with teenage pregnancy, prevent violence in the schools, promote safe sex and perform myriad other tasks and responsibilities in addition to teaching traditional academic subjects.   44

As the social needs of our students have moved into the classroom,   45 they have consumed the scarce resources allocated to education and have compromised the schools' academic function. The primary role of teachers has become that of parent by proxy; they are expected to transform the attitude and behavior of children, many of whom come to school ill prepared to learn.

46   If we are to deal effectively with the crisis in American education, we must start with an accurate definition of the problem. We must separate teaching and its academic purpose from in-school social services. Only then can we assess the true ability of schools to accomplish these two, sometimes opposing, functions—or we can identify and delegate these nonacademic concerns to other institutions.

47   Throughout this article we have examined the role of the family in the academic performance of Indochinese refugees. We firmly believe that for American schools to succeed, parents and families must become more committed to the education of their children. They must instill a respect for education and create within the home an environment conducive to learning. They must also participate in the process so that their children feel comfortable learning and go to school willing and prepared to study.

48   Yet we cannot expect the family to provide such support alone. Schools must reach out to families and engage them meaningfully in the education of their children. This involvement must go beyond annual teacher-parent meetings and must include, among other things, the identification of cultural elements that promote achievement.

49   Similarly, we cannot adopt the complete perspective of an Indochinese or any other culture. It would be ludicrous to impose cultural beliefs and practices on American children, especially on those whose progress in this country has been fraught with blocked access.

50   We can, however, work to ensure that families believe in the value of an education and, like the refugees, have rational expectations of future rewards for their efforts. Moreover, we can integrate components of the refugees' experience regarding the family's role in education. It is possible to identify culturally compatible values, behaviors and strategies for success that might enhance scholastic achievement. It is in this regard that the example of the Indochinese refugees—as well as the Japanese and Jewish immigrants before them—can shape our priorities and our policies.

Reading and Analyzing

1. The authors open their article by placing their study in a context. What context of educational issues do they provide?
2. Explain the details of their study. What students were studied? Where did they live? How good was their English? What information was obtained and through what processes? Why is this back-

ground information essential for readers to have, and have early in
the paper?

3. What type of argument is this? How should the essay be classified
based on the analysis of argument in Chapter 1? Based on the guidelines for writing in Chapter 3?

4. What were the students' average GPAs? In what subjects did they
perform best? Why? Where did they place on the CAT? What is important about the students' CAT scores in math?

5. To what do the authors attribute the students' performance? On
what basis do they conclude that this cause must be a powerful influence for scholastic success?

6. What is the usual result of large families on scholastic performance?
How did family size become an advantage to the Indochinese in the
study? What did the children learn from their families? What is the
family role in their culture?

7. How much time did the students in the study spend on homework?
How does this compare to American students? What does each Indochinese family member contribute to the homework time? What is
learned in addition to the homework lessons? What values about
learning are acquired?

8. What was the effect of egalitarian values on students' academic performance? What were some other values expressed by the students
and their families?

9. Explain the concept of personal efficacy. What have social scientists
learned about its relationship to scholastic success? How do these
authors think the concept needs to be altered for the students they
studied?

10. What did the study reveal about the relationship between valuing
fun, or possessions, or the past, and academic performance?

11. Explain the difference between Indochinese and middle-class American values. How has the difference helped the Indochinese to excel?

12. What conclusions do the authors draw with regard to solving our
educational problems? Why are American schools in trouble? What
must be done to address the problem?

13. Analyze the core structure of the authors' argument. What is their
claim about American schools? What is their evidence? What is the
argument's warrant (assumption)?

Responding to the Writers' Ideas

1. What is the effect of the detailed explanation of the authors' investigation on you? Of their credentials as researchers? Of their credibility as reinforced by the journal that published their report? Do you

think that all of these elements will work together to produce confidence in the writers for most readers?

2. If you said yes to question 1, are you prepared then to agree with their conclusions about what needs to be done in our schools? If not, why not?

3. Compare this study with the arguments by Ravitch and Lynn. With which one do these authors most closely agree?

4. If positive attitudes toward learning and the active role of parents and other family members in each student's academic life are important for performance, how do we, as a society, bring about the needed changes? If you were the Secretary of Education, what would you do? If you were a high school teacher, what would you do? If you were a parent, what would you do? How could these different people try to implement the ideas in this article?

❖

The Other Crisis in American Education

Daniel J. Singal

A specialist in intellectual history, Daniel J. Singal (b. 1944) is a history professor at Hobart and William Smith College and the author of The War Within: From Victorian to Modernist Thought *(1982). He is currently at work on an intellectual biography of William Faulkner. "The Other Crisis in American Education," published in the November 1991 issue of* Atlantic Monthly, *deplores the education that today's good students are receiving.*

Two crises are stalking American education. Each poses a major threat to the nation's future. The two are very different in character and will require separate strategies if we wish to solve them; yet to date, almost without exception, those concerned with restoring excellence to our schools have lumped them together.

The first crisis, which centers on disadvantaged minority children attending inner-city schools, has received considerable attention, as well it should. Put simply, it involves students whose habitat makes it very difficult for them to learn. The key issues are more social than educational. These children clearly need dedicated teachers and a sound curriculum, the two staples of a quality school, but the fact remains that most of them will not make significant progress until they also have decent housing, a better diet, and a safer environment in which to live.

The second crisis, in contrast, is far more academic than social and to a surprising extent invisible. It involves approximately half the country's student population—the group that educators refer to as "college-bound." Although the overwhelming majority of these students attend suburban schools, a fair number can be found in big-city or consolidated rural districts, or in independent or parochial schools. Beginning in the mid-1970s these students have been entering college so badly prepared that they have performed far below potential, often to the point of functional disability. We tend to assume that with their high aptitude for learning, they should be able to fend for themselves. However, the experience of the past fifteen years has proved decisively that they can't.

For most people, any mention of the problems of American education almost immediately conjures up an image of the wretched conditions

129

in the stereotypical urban ghetto school. But can we really explain the sharp decline in college-entrance-exam scores by pointing to the inner cities, where only a tiny fraction of students even take the Scholastic Aptitude Test, or SAT? Do so many freshmen entering prestigious institutions like Harvard and Berkeley display a limited mastery of basic historical facts, not to mention of their own language, because they come from crime-ridden neighborhoods or school districts with no tax base?

5   If one looks at the aggregate statistics of American education from this perspective, the full dimensions of this other crisis become strikingly apparent. Consider the recent history of the Stanford Achievement Test, which has long served as one of the main instruments for measuring pupil progress in our schools. According to Herbert Rudman, a professor of educational psychology at Michigan State University and a co-author of the test for more than three decades, from the 1920s to the late 1960s American children taking the Stanford made significant gains in their test performance. They made so much progress, in fact, that as the test was revised each decade, the level of difficulty of the questions was increased substantially, reflecting the increasing level of challenge of the instructional materials being used in the schools.

6   From the late 1960s to the early 1980s, however, we managed to squander the better part of that progress, with the greatest losses coming in the high schools. During the past few years the Stanford and other test results have shown some improvement in math and science, and in language skills at the elementary school level. But there has been little or no movement in the verbal areas among junior high and high school students, and seasoned test interpreters have also seen a tendency for the gains made in the early years of school to wash out as the child becomes older. In effect, the test numbers substantiate what the National Commission on Excellence in Education concluded—quoting the education analyst Paul Copperman—in 1983 in *A Nation at Risk:* "Each generation of Americans has outstripped its parents in education, in literacy, and in economic attainment. For the first time in the history of our country, the educational skills of one generation will not surpass, will not equal, will not even approach, those of their parents."

The blame for this wholesale decline in test scores is often put on a throng of underachieving minority students thought to have been pulling down national test averages, but in fact just the opposite is true. To be sure, it is possible to attribute much of the relatively small initial drop in SAT scores, from 1963 to 1970, to the fact that blacks and other minorities began taking the test in larger numbers during those years, but since then the composition of the test population has not changed in any way that would dramatically affect test scores. Most important, blacks have made gradual but significant gains in the past two decades, as measured by school achievement tests like the Stanford and by college-entrance exams.

Although their average scores still fall substantially below those of whites, their combined (verbal and math) SAT scores rose by 49 points during the 1980s alone. "Perhaps the most untold story of American education in the past few years is the achievement of black students," Gregory R. Anrig, the president of the Educational Testing Service, declares. "The hard data are encouraging." The sad irony, of course, is that this progress came at a time when the Reagan Administration was proposing drastic cuts in the amount of federal scholarship aid available to students from low-income families, most likely leading many young blacks to believe that a college education was not within their reach.

While students in the bottom quartile have shown slow but steady improvement since the 1960s, average test scores have nonetheless gone down, primarily because of the performance of those in the top quartile. This "highest cohort of achievers," Rudman writes, has shown "the greatest declines across a variety of subjects as well as across age-level groups." Analysts have also found "a substantial drop among those children in the middle range of achievement," he continues, "but less loss and some modest gains at the lower levels." In other words, our brightest youngsters, those most likely to be headed for selective colleges, have suffered the most dramatic setbacks over the past two decades—a fact with grave implications for our ability to compete with other nations in the future. If this is true—and abundant evidence exists to suggest that it is—then we indeed have a second major crisis in our education system.

Sixty Lost Points on the SAT

Look at what has happened on the SAT, a test that retains its well-deserved status as the most important educational measuring device in America. Despite the test's many critics, the number of colleges relying on the SAT keeps increasing, because it provides such an accurate gauge of the basic skills needed for college-level work, among them reading comprehension, vocabulary, and the ability to reason with mathematical concepts. The SAT also has the virtue of having a rock-steady scoring system: it is calibrated, by the College Board, so that a score earned in 1991 will represent almost exactly the same level of performance as it did in, say, 1961. Thus, by tracking the percentage of students coming in above the benchmark of 600 on the College Board scale (which runs from 200 to 800), one can get a good sense of how the country's most capable students have fared over the years.

The news is not encouraging. In 1972, of the high school seniors taking the SAT 11.4 percent had verbal scores over 600; by 1983 the number had dropped to 6.9 percent, and, despite modest gains in the mid-1980s, it remains in that disheartening vicinity. That's a decline of nearly 40 percent. The decline since the mid-1960s has probably been closer to 50 percent, but unfortunately the College Board changed its reporting system in

1972, and earlier data isn't available. The math SAT presents a somewhat different story. Though the percentage scoring over 600 dropped from 17.9 in 1972 to 14.4 by 1981, it has climbed back up to 17.9 in 1991. However, an influx of high-scoring Asian-American students (who now make up eight percent of those taking the test, as compared with two percent in 1972) has apparently had much to do with this recent upsurge.

11   To grasp what these national figures really mean, it helps to approach them from the standpoint of the individual student. How, we should ask, would the drop in SAT scores affect a typical top-quartile senior at a well-regarded suburban high school in 1991? To my knowledge, no published studies have addressed this question, but the available information, including my own research, suggests that our hypothetical senior would come in roughly fifty to sixty points lower on the verbal section and twenty-five points lower on the math than he or she would have in 1970.

12   Consider the trend in average freshman scores at selective colleges. Indeed, perusing a twenty-year-old edition of *Barron's Profiles of American Colleges* is an experience equivalent to entering a different world, with tuitions much lower and SAT scores much higher than at most schools today. In 1970 students arriving at top-ranked institutions like Columbia College, Swarthmore College, the University of Chicago, and Pomona College posted average verbal SATs from 670 to 695; by the mid-1980s the scores ranged from 620 to 640, and they have stayed roughly in that neighborhood ever since. The same pattern appears at colleges a notch or two lower in the academic hierarchy. To take a few examples from different geographic areas, from 1970 to 1987 average verbal scores went from 644 to 570 at Hamilton College, from 607 to 563 at Washington University, from 600 to 560 at the University of Michigan at Ann Arbor, and from 560 to 499 at the University of California at Santa Barbara.

13   The point is *not* that these particular schools have slipped in their relative standings. They all currently receive ratings the same as or higher than those they received twenty years ago from *Barron's* in terms of competition for admission. One could pick almost any selective institution at random and find the same trend (an exception: the stronger schools in the South, where test scores held steady or rose in the wake of desegregation). Nor can one attribute the drop in scores to a change in the size of the test population or in the percentage of high school seniors taking the SAT (the latter figure has risen significantly only in the past few years, too recently to have affected the 1987 scores). To be sure, an increase in the number of minority students attending these institutions has been a factor, but the basic problem remains: with a 40 percent decline in the proportion of students scoring over 600, there are far fewer high-scoring students to go around.

14   But do these numbers matter? Does a loss of sixty points on the verbal SAT translate into a significant difference in a student's educational ex-

perience at college? The testimony of those who teach at the college level suggests that the answer is yes. When a national poll in 1989 asked professors whether they thought undergraduates were "seriously underprepared in basic skills," 75 percent said yes and only 15 percent said no. The same poll asked whether institutions of higher learning were spending "too much time and money teaching students what they should have learned in high school." Sixty-eight percent said yes. Professors feel like this, I should add, not because they are old scolds given to grousing about students but because their work brings them into daily contact with the manifold ways in which the American education system has failed these young people.

Those who tend to dismiss those sixty lost SAT points as insignificant haven't seen a college term paper lately. It's not that freshmen in 1991 are unable to read or write. Most of them possess what the National Assessment of Educational Progress calls "satisfactory" skills in this area. But is that enough for college? Do they have sufficient command of the English language to comprehend a college-level text, think through a complex issue, or express a reasonably sophisticated argument on paper? Those of us who were teaching in the early 1970s can attest that the overwhelming majority of freshmen at the more selective colleges arrived with such "advanced" skills. Now only a handful come so equipped.

The Context of Ignorance

Take reading, for example. "While the nation's students have the skills to derive a surface understanding of what they read," the NAEP recently reported, "they have difficulty when asked to defend or elaborate upon this surface understanding." That's what most college faculty would say. Emilia da Costa, a Latin America specialist who has taught at Yale for the past eighteen years, estimates that whereas 70 percent of her students can pick out the general theme of an essay or a book, only 25 percent come away with in-depth comprehension of what they read. David Samson, a former lecturer in history and literature at Harvard, likewise observes, "No one reads for nuance. They pay no attention to detail." My own experience confirms this. Countless times I have been amazed at how little students have managed to glean from a book I know they have read, to the point where they are often unable to recall the names of prominently mentioned figures. So much escapes them; even those of above-average ability absorb no more than a dusting of detail from a printed text. And without such detailed information it's impossible for them to gain a real understanding of what the author is saying.

Equally distressing is the rate at which today's students read. A friend of mine at the University of Michigan remembers that in the 1960s the normal assignment in his courses was one book a week. Now he allows two to three weeks for each title. He has also reluctantly had to adjust the level of difficulty of his assignments: even a journalist like Walter

15

16

17

Lippmann is too hard for most freshmen and sophomores these days, he finds. Again, this is typical. Twelve to fifteen books over a fifteen-week semester used to be the rule of thumb at selective colleges. Today it is six to eight books, and they had better be short texts, written in relatively simple English.

18   As one might expect, students who don't read at an advanced level can't write well either. Their knowledge of grammar is not bad, according to Richard Marius, the director of the expository writing program at Harvard, but "the number of words available to express their thoughts is very, very limited, and the forms by which they express themselves are also very limited." The average incoming Harvard student, he observes, has a "utilitarian command of language" resulting in sentences that follow a simple subject-predicate, subject-predicate format with little variation or richness of verbal expression. Harvard, of course, gets the cream of the crop. Those of us teaching at lesser institutions would be happy with utilitarian but serviceable prose from our freshmen. More often we get mangled sentences, essays composed without the slightest sense of paragraphing, and writing that can't sustain a thought for more than half a page.

19   Along with this impoverishment of language comes a downturn in reasoning skills. Da Costa laments that students are no longer trained in logical analysis, and consequently have difficulty using evidence to reach a conclusion. R. Jackson Wilson finds this to be the greatest change he has observed during a quarter century of teaching history at Smith College. "Students come to us having sat around for twelve years expressing attitudes toward things rather than analyzing," he says. "They are always ready to tell you how they feel about an issue, but they have never learned how to construct a rational argument to defend their opinions." Again, these complaints are amply substantiated by data from the National Assessment of Educational Progress. On one test of analytic writing measuring "the ability to provide evidence, reason logically, and make a well-developed point," only *four tenths of one percent* of eleventh graders performed at the "elaborated" (what I believe should be considered college-freshman) level.

20   Finally, no account of the present condition of college students would be complete without mention of the extraordinary dearth of factual knowledge they bring to college. Horror stories on this topic abound—and they are probably all true. I will never forget two unusually capable juniors, one of whom was a star political-science major, who came to my office a few years ago to ask what was this thing called the New Deal. I had made reference to it during a lecture on the assumption that everyone in the class would be well acquainted with Franklin Roosevelt's domestic program, but I was wrong: the two students had checked with their friends, and none of them had heard of the New Deal either. Another junior recently asked me to help him pick a twentieth-century American nov-

elist on whom to write a term paper. He had heard vaguely of F. Scott Fitzgerald and Ernest Hemingway, but did not recognize the names of Sinclair Lewis, John Dos Passos, Norman Mailer, William Styron, and Saul Bellow.

Indeed, one can't assume that college students know anything anymore. Paula Fass, a professor of history at the University of California at Berkeley, remains astonished that sophomores and juniors in her upper-level course on American social history are often unable to differentiate between the American Revolution and the Civil War, but rather see them as two big events that happened way back in the past. Alan Heimert, a veteran member of the Harvard English department, encounters the same mushy grasp of historical knowledge and blames it on the "trendy social-studies curriculum" now taught in most high schools which covers broad thematic topics rather than history. "They are aware that someone oppressed someone else," he says with only slight exaggeration, "but they aren't sure exactly what took place and they have no idea of the order in which it happened."

Though not always recognized, a direct connection exists between this deficit in factual knowledge and the decline in verbal skills. Most reading, after all, is at bottom a form of information processing in which the mind selects what it wants to know from the printed page and files it away for future use. In conducting that operation of selecting, interpreting, and storing information, the reader constantly relies on his or her previous stock of knowledge as a vital frame of reference. No matter how fascinating or valuable a new detail might be, a person finds it almost impossible to hold in memory and have available for retrieval unless it can be placed in some kind of larger context. Providing that basic intellectual scaffolding used to be a major function of a good high school education. Year-long survey courses in history and literature, covering the United States, Europe, and the world, were designed to ensure that college-bound students would have the necessary background to make sense of the new subject matter they would encounter in college. Yet few high schools today teach that kind of curriculum.

Little wonder that so many students experience great difficulty in absorbing detail; since they have no context in which to fit what they read, it quickly flows out of their minds. Unable to retain much, they find little profit in reading, which leads them to read less, which in turn makes it harder for them to improve their reading skills.

One often hears this generation accused of laziness. They don't perform well in school or college or later on the job, it is said, because they lack motivation. I don't happen to subscribe to that theory. The percentage of students who are truly lazy—that is, who simply have an aversion to work—is probably no greater today than it has been in the past. The real problem, I'm convinced, is that college-bound youngsters over the past two decades have not received the quality education they deserve. As R. Jackson Wilson observes of his students at Smith, this generation is typically "good-spirited, refreshingly uncowed by teachers' authority, and very willing to work." They enter college with high ambitions, only to find those ambitions dashed in many cases by inadequate skills and knowledge. The normal activities required to earn a bachelor's degree—reading, writing, researching, and reasoning—are so difficult for them that a large number (I would guess a majority at most schools) simply give up in frustration. Some actually leave; the rest go through the motions, learning and contributing little, until it's time to pick up their diplomas. We rightly worry about the nation's high school dropouts. Perhaps we should worry as well about these silent college "dropouts."

How Good Schools Buck the Trend

25   What has caused this great decline in our schools? The multitude of reports that now fill the library shelves tend to designate "social factors" as the prime culprit. Television usually heads the list, followed by rock music, the influence of adolescent peer groups, the increase in both single-parent families and households where both parents work, and even faulty nutrition.

26   Those who attribute the loss of academic performance to social factors don't take account of the small number of high schools around the country that have managed to escape the downturn. Some are posh private academies; a few are located in blue-collar neighborhoods. What they have in common is a pattern of stable or even rising test scores at a time when virtually all the schools around them experienced sharp declines. There is no indication that the children attending these exceptional schools watched significantly fewer hours of television, listened to less heavy-metal music, were less likely to have working mothers, or ate fewer Big Macs than other children. Rather, they appear to have had the good fortune to go to schools that were intent on steering a steady course in a time of rapid change, thus countering the potentially negative impact of various social factors.

27   It would seem obvious good sense to look closely at this select group of schools to determine what they have been doing right, but as far as I can determine this has been done in only two national studies. The better one was issued by the National Association of Secondary School Principals (NASSP) in 1978, under the somewhat pedestrian title *Guidelines for Improving SAT Scores.* Now out of print and hard to find, it contains one of the most perceptive diagnoses available of the underlying malady in our schools.

28   The report identifies one main characteristic that successful schools have shared—the belief that academics must invariably receive priority over every other activity. "The difference comes," we are told, "from a

singular commitment to academic achievement for the college-bound student." These schools did not ignore the other dimensions of student life. By and large, the NASSP found, schools that maintained excellence in academics sought to be excellent in everything else they did; they "proved to be apt jugglers, keeping all important balls in the air." But academic work came first.

Two other factors help account for the prowess of these schools in holding the line against deterioration. The first is a dogged reliance on a traditional liberal-arts curriculum. In an era of mini-courses and electives, the tiny group of high schools that kept test scores and achievement high continued to require year-long courses in literature and to encourage enrollment in rigorous math classes, including geometry and advanced algebra. Though the learning environment in those schools was often "broad and imaginative," in the words of the NASSP, fundamentals such as English grammar and vocabulary received heavy stress. The other key factor in preserving academic quality was the practice of grouping students by ability in as many subjects as possible. The contrast was stark: schools that had "severely declining test scores" had "moved determinedly toward heterogeneous grouping" (that is, mixed students of differing ability levels in the same classes), while the "schools who have maintained good SAT scores" tended "to prefer homogeneous grouping."   29

If attaining educational excellence is this simple, why have these high-quality schools become so rare? The answer lies in the cultural ferment of the 1960s.   30

The Incubus of the Sixties

In every conceivable fashion the reigning ethos of those times was hostile to excellence in education. Individual achievement fell under intense suspicion, as did attempts to maintain standards. Discriminating among students on the basis of ability or performance was branded "elitist." Educational gurus of the day called for essentially nonacademic schools, whose main purpose would be to build habits of social cooperation and equality rather than to train the mind. A good education, it was said, maximized the child's innate spontaneity, creativity, and affection for others. To the extent that logic and acquired knowledge interfered with that process, they were devalued.   31

This populist tidal wave receded by the late 1970s, but the mediocrity it left in its wake remains. The extent of the devastation has varied by subject area: math and the natural sciences, which continue to be blessed with relatively widespread agreement on what should be taught, have escaped the worst damage (though test scores in these areas still fall below average in comparisons with scores in other industrialized nations), while English and history now lie in ruins in all too many schools. The latter, of course, are the disciplines primarily responsible for inculcating verbal skills   32 and for supplying the broad framework of knowledge that students need for success in college. Yet it is precisely in these areas that the spirit of the sixties remains most evident, hovering over the high schools and junior highs like a ghost.

33   Consider the teaching of English. The Great Books, of course, are out of fashion. A few get assigned as a token gesture, but are rarely set in chronological order. The results of a questionnaire I recently distributed at Hobart and William Smith Colleges suggest that less than a quarter of the college-bound population now gets a real year-long survey of American literature, with probably no more than 15 percent taking such a course in British or European literature. Instead, students all too often are given works that, as the English department at one highly ranked independent school puts it, are "age-appropriate" and "reflect [a] concern for social pluralism." "Age-appropriate" means giving students assignments "that reflect their interests as adolescents, that they can read without constant recourse to a dictionary, and from which they can take whatever they are inspired to take."

34   Nor are they asked to read much. Most ninth- and tenth-grade English reading lists are limited to four or five titles a year. According to Arthur N. Applebee, the director of the National Research Center on Literature Teaching and Learning, the typical college-bound high school student reads only sixty-five pages a week (even with Advanced Placement courses factored in), or less than ten pages a night. A check of the typical high school curriculum would disclose that plays are favorite choices these days (they tend to be much shorter than novels and make easier reading), along with personal memoirs. The rich diet of fiction and poetry that used to be served up—Dickens, Twain, Poe, Hawthorne, Shakespeare, Chaucer, Thoreau, Dickinson, Milton, Melville, and Steinbeck—is increasingly hard to find.

35   These changes in the teaching of literature matter greatly because reading is the primary vehicle by which students absorb the rhythms and patterns of language. The more a person encounters sophisticated prose, the more he or she will pick up varied sentence structure, vocabulary in context, and even spelling, as well as advanced descriptive techniques and narrative strategies. Feed a student the literary equivalent of junk food and you will get an impoverished command of English, which is what we too often see in the current crop of college freshmen. And yet, because most new teachers these days are themselves the product of this new English curriculum, the trend continues to run the wrong way.

36   The rest of the English curriculum also reflects the impact of the sixties. If the reports I get from my students are accurate, it would appear that formal drills on grammar, vocabulary, spelling, and diction are infrequent these days. Teachers may toss an occasional drill into the schedule to keep parents satisfied, but the assumption is that students will absorb

these things automatically from their reading. Given what students currently read, however, that's a dubious assumption. As for writing, when it is assigned (there seems to be wide variation among schools on this), it tends to take the form of "personal expression"—with assignments calling for first-person narratives that describe what the student has seen, felt, or experienced. Essays in which the writer marshals evidence to support a coherent, logical argument are all too rare. Since that kind of exercise might dampen creativity, it must be minimized. The outcome is utterly predictable. "Analytic writing was difficult for students in all grades," the National Assessment of Educational Progress noted in summarizing the results of its various writing tests in 1984, while students "had less difficulty with tasks requiring short responses based on personal experience."

In sum, this is a generation whose members may be better equipped to track the progress of their souls in diaries than any group of Americans since the Puritans. But as for writing papers in college, or later producing the sorts of documents that get the world's work done, that's another story. In contrast, a survey conducted by the Educational Testing Service in the mid-1960s, just before countercultural innovations swept away the old curriculum, discovered that over twice as many high school students of that era said that they "frequently" wrote papers criticizing the literary works they were studying (a valuable pedagogic strategy because it forces the student to become a much closer reader) as said that they "frequently" wrote papers based on personal experience. 37

The Shock of College-Level Demands

The same tendency appears in other key subjects. Students headed for college used to get a solid grasp of both American and European history at the high school level. Now, as most people are aware, they pass through an array of social-studies courses designed to impress upon them the central values of the sixties, including concern for the natural environment, respect for people of different racial and ethnic groups, and women's rights. These values are important and should certainly be included in the curriculum. But teaching them in such a superficial manner, devoid of any historical context, simply doesn't work—as the alarming increase in racist and sexist incidents that has plagued college campuses in the past few years would suggest. Above all, this spotty social-studies approach deprives students of that vital base of in-depth knowledge they must have to succeed as undergraduates. 38

Accompanying this pervasive dumbing-down of the curriculum has been a wholesale change in school philosophy. In place of "stretching" students, the key objective in previous eras, the goal has become not to "stress" them. One hears again and again that kids growing up "need time to smell the roses." (That they are more likely to spend their free hours in front of a television or cruising a shopping mall seems never to be consid- 39 ered.) Placing serious academic demands on them, it is thought, might impede their natural development and perhaps even render them neurotic. But the stress they avoid in high school often comes back to haunt them in college. An extensive survey of college freshmen recently found that an increasing number say they are "overwhelmed by all I have to do." "We have very high suicide rates among college students now," the survey's director, Alexander Astin, says. This should come as no surprise: having had little previous experience with stress, students are not well equipped to face the normal and necessary pressures of either college or the "real world."

40   Perhaps most crucial, the sixties mentality, with its strong animus against what it defines as "elitism," has shifted the locus of concern in American education from high to low achievers. All over the country, educators today typically judge themselves by how well they can reach the least-able student in the system, the slowest one in the class. Programs to help the culturally disadvantaged and the learning-disabled have proliferated, while those for the gifted receive no more than token interest.

41   The prevailing ideology holds that it is much better to give up the prospect of excellence than to take the chance of injuring any student's self-esteem. Instead of trying to spur children on to set high standards for themselves, teachers invest their energies in making sure that slow learners do not come to think of themselves as failures. These attitudes have become so ingrained that in conversations with teachers and administrators one often senses a virtual prejudice against bright students. There is at times an underlying feeling, never articulated, that such children start off with too many advantages, and that it would be just as well to hold them back until their less fortunate contemporaries catch up with them. At a minimum, the assumption goes, students of above-average ability will in due course find their way to classy colleges and thus don't need any special consideration from their schools.

42   In adopting this posture, one must remember, the education profession has simply been carrying out its social mandate. In the wake of the sixties the country seemed to be telling the schools that the prime mission now was to produce equality rather than excellence—to lift up those on the bottom, whether they were there because of race, class, ethnicity, or low ability. As the test scores tell us, the education establishment took this mission to heart. Those in the bottom quartile have shown slow but steady progress, while those in the top quartile have exhibited a sharp decline. Only since the appearance of *A Nation at Risk,* in 1983, with its warning about "a rising tide of mediocrity" sweeping over the schools, have we started to realize the sizable hidden cost that this current educational strategy has exacted.

43   Here it is necessary to be precise: the problem is not the pursuit of

equality as such but the bias against excellence that has accompanied it. If anything, the effort to help children who start off life severely handicapped by their socioeconomic circumstances deserves more money and attention than it has received to date. However, that effort need not and must not obscure from view the quite separate problem of restoring academic quality to our schools. If real change is to occur in this regard, we must make clear to teachers and administrators that their mandate has been revised—that we want to move toward social equality *and* academic excellence.

Four Remedies

Most of the reform proposals currently on the table fail to speak to the other crisis in American education. The majority are designed to raise minimum standards or to cut the high school dropout rate. To the extent that higher-level academics gets mentioned, the discussion usually centers on such topics as critical-thinking and "process writing" skills and cooperative learning groups, as if a few minor adjustments in technique could make a significant difference. Almost no one addresses the fundamental, substantive issues that must be dealt with if we really want to restore excellence to our schools.

If that *is* our objective—if we are determined to recover the ground we have lost since 1970—then we should take the following concrete steps:

1) *Dramatically increase the quality and quantity of assigned reading for students at all grade levels.* By the senior year of high school, college-bound students should be reading the equivalent of at least twelve books a year *for class,* not counting textbooks, along with six to eight additional books under the rubrics of independent and summer reading. To build up to this amount, the reading load should be adjusted in each of the preceding grades so that students become gradually accustomed to reading more each year. (A good rule of thumb might be to have college-bound students read the same number of books each year as their grade number—eight books in the eighth grade, nine books in the ninth, and so on.) Since reading is a learned skill that can almost invariably be improved by practice, the sheer number of pages counts—the more the better. But there should also be an effort to make the assigned texts as complex and challenging as possible. In the end, nothing builds a true command of language faster than this kind of regimen.

I can already hear a chorus of educators declaring this proposal to be utterly unworkable. "Kids just don't read anymore," they will say. But the fact is that this sort of reading load, which was standard in the best American schools a quarter century ago, is still standard in some schools today. At McDonogh, an independent school just outside Baltimore that enrolls college-bound students from a wide range of ability levels, fifteen to twenty assigned books a year in English class is not unusual for eleventh and twelfth graders. College admissions officers I know rave about how well prepared McDonogh graduates are and how enthusiastic about learning. The secret, I'm convinced, is in the reading. I see no reason why other schools can't follow McDonogh's example.

48

2) *Bring back required survey courses as the staple of the high school humanities curriculum.* There are many different ways to do this. My preference would be to have one year of coordinated courses in history and English focused on the United States, another year focused on Europe, and a third year devoted to the non-European world. Issues of race and gender would naturally arise; it is hard, for instance, to cover American literature without including black and women writers, or to discuss our past without spending considerable time on slavery and segregation. But the main purpose of this curriculum would be to ensure that students enter college with a firm knowledge of how the world they will inherit has developed.

49

3) *Institute a flexible program of ability grouping at both the elementary and secondary school levels.* Few issues in education can raise tempers faster than ability grouping, and few are more badly misunderstood. The most common error is to confuse ability grouping with "tracking," a practice in which students are sorted out at an early age according to their scores on intelligence tests and placed in separate "tracks" for fast, medium, and slow learners, where they remain through high school. Reformers in the 1960s rightly objected to that kind of predestination, pointing out that minority and working-class children were often routinely put in the slow track and thus deprived of the chance to advance themselves through schooling. But unfortunately this assault on tracking soon broadened to include ability grouping, a somewhat murky term that I would contend should be defined as a system for dividing students up on the basis of their actual performance in individual subjects. Under ability grouping a student might start off in the fast group in math but the slow one in English, with the placements changing from year to year depending on his or her progress. The guiding principle is not to give privileged treatment to any one group but rather to provide instruction closely tailored to the learning needs of each child.

50

Does ability grouping work? The research can supply whatever verdict one favors. Until roughly the mid-1960s most of the studies tended to show that ability grouping was beneficial. Then came the cultural revolution of the late 1960s. For the next two decades researchers found that ability grouping was damaging to most students, especially those at the bottom. The pendulum now seems to be swinging back the other way, with a number of recent investigators suggesting that such grouping does not harm anyone and can be of great value to those of above-average ability, provided they get a special curriculum that is truly challenging rather than simply moving through the standard curriculum at a faster pace.

Moreover, these newer studies suggest that ability grouping may actually enhance the achievement of slower learners if they, too, are given a curriculum and teaching style specially designed for them. A unique program at South Mecklenburg High School, in Charlotte, North Carolina, has even found that ability grouping can significantly help those in the middle ability range, though once again the crucial element is instruction tailored to their needs.

Since the research is contradictory, perhaps the best way to decide the issue is to apply common sense. It is obvious that with children of different ability levels in the same classroom, everything will tend toward a level just a notch above the lowest common denominator. Instead of being challenged to develop their talents to the fullest, the most capable students will be forced to work, in effect, at half speed. The math problems set before them will require little effort on their part to solve; the English texts will not stretch them in the least. As a result, these students quickly discover that there is no reason for them ever to extend themselves, that they can coast through school with minimal effort.

Ability grouping continues to face formidable political opposition; last year, regrettably, the education task force of the National Governors' Association took its first major step by denouncing it (though its statement was so brief that one has difficulty telling whether it opposes ability grouping or tracking). Thus compromises may be in order. One possibility is the system of intensive courses adopted by the Waynflete School, in Portland, Maine. An intensive section in English entails a heavier than normal load of reading in more-advanced texts, more-sophisticated writing assignments, and faster-paced instruction. The key is that all students are free to try an intensive section; there is no teacher placement involved. Those doing so run little risk: since the curriculum includes the same core material covered in a regular section, students unable to handle the demands can drop back at any time during the school year.

This arrangement has several advantages. One is that the "regular" sections are truly regular, rather than "slow" or "remedial," so that those enrolled in them feel no stigma whatsoever. Better yet, students who voluntarily contract to be in a special section are especially motivated. Administrators at Waynflete report being pleasantly surprised at the number of kids with middle-range academic ability who perform well in intensive sections because they enjoy the challenge. And of course, this is a reform that can be implemented with relatively little disruption to other programs and at virtually no extra expense. It seems clear that more schools should be trying this system, yet to date, so far as I can tell, it remains unique to Waynflete.

4) *Attract more bright college graduates into the teaching profession.* It is astonishing, but all too true, that the average verbal SAT score of the young people drawn into teaching has hovered around 400 for more than

a decade. "Half of the newly employed mathematics, science, and English teachers are not qualified to teach these subjects," bemoaned *A Nation at Risk*. Clearly, if we want top-notch instruction for college-bound students in the years ahead, we must find a new supply of capable teachers.

55   To the familiar prescriptions of offering much higher pay and better working conditions I would add that it's time to abolish certification requirements for teachers, at least above the elementary school level. When they first came into being, those requirements served the important purpose of helping to raise standards, but today their only function is to discourage talented would-be teachers from entering the profession. Indeed, certification actually serves to *lower* standards: instead of acquiring a thoroughgoing knowledge of their subject, future teachers spend far too much of their time in college and graduate school taking Mickey Mouse courses on how to construct a lesson plan. Private schools do not require certification, yet they manage to attract a teaching corps of much higher quality—even at lower salaries than the public schools pay. "Our teachers never learned how to teach, which is why they teach so well," quips Laurance Levy, the former head of McDonogh's first-rate English department.

56   My impression is that many in the top quartile of the class at our best colleges would flood into teaching if they could do so on the basis of a liberal-arts bachelor's degree—and if they could avoid the kind of stifling bureaucratic control that is all too often a teacher's lot today. Some states, including New Jersey, have experimented with letting young teachers of this description loose in their classrooms, apparently with much success, though, alas, these new teachers are eventually required to obtain certification. And programs at various selective private colleges and universities permit would-be teachers to combine a liberal-arts degree and professional training. But for the most part the cumbersome, outdated apparatus of the teaching profession remains in place.

57   The solution? While it is probably not politically possible in most states to dismantle the existing system in the near future, why not set up a parallel system to provide an alternate career path for new teachers? Those liberal-arts college graduates choosing the new path would go straight to the classroom and be exempt from all formal professional training. They would, however, have more-experienced teachers in their schools serving as their mentors. Attracting these people into the profession would necessitate a much higher pay scale but also something more. When I recently asked a group of exceptionally capable students at my college if they would consider a teaching career along these lines, three quarters at first said yes, but soon reversed themselves. They had witnessed the demeaning conditions under which most teachers work, they explained, and wouldn't want the job even if salaries were more appealing. The only way to lure them into the classroom, it became clear, would be to give them considerable freedom to shape their own curricula, allow them to choose instruc-

tional materials, and spare them the petty annoyances like the ubiquitous loudspeaker announcements that can suddenly disrupt a class. If the governors really want to do something useful to upgrade education, establishing this alternative career path is perhaps the most valuable project they could take up.

A Moral Issue

The other crisis in American education has ominous implications for the well-being of our political system. According to a recent study by the Times Mirror Center for the People and the Press, titled "The Age of Indifference," young Americans aged eighteen to twenty-nine are remarkably uninformed. They do read, the survey found, but primarily lightweight publications like *People* rather than serious newspapers or periodicals. Most striking, a majority of these young adults report that they often first become aware of political candidates from television commercials. This response cuts across all educational levels: college graduates and high school dropouts alike displayed a troubling ignorance of political facts and a reliance on sound-bites as their basic source of political knowledge. The "limited appetites and aptitudes" of this generation, the Times Mirror Center concluded, are already adversely affecting "the practice of politics and the nature of our democracy."

58

One could advance a host of reasons—economic, social, and cultural—why this other crisis in education needs immediate attention. But in the end the most important is probably moral, having to do with the responsibility of each generation to look after the well-being of its children. Observing the performance of students who have been arriving at college campuses over the past decade, one can only conclude that the present generation of American parents has been failing in its obligation to provide its offspring with a high-quality education. It seems safe to predict that this failure will have specific consequences in a lower sense of professional fulfillment for these youngsters as they pursue their careers, and will hamper their ability to stay competitive with contemporaries in many European and Asian countries, where college-bound students typically do get the benefit of first-rate schools. Is it right or sensible to place our children at such a strong disadvantage before they even begin their adult lives?

59

As the United Negro College Fund aptly puts it, a mind is a terrible thing to waste. It's time to recognize that we have been wasting far too many good ones.

60

Reading and Analyzing

1. What two crises does Singal find in American education? Which one will he examine? Why does it need to be examined? What, then, is

one purpose of Singal's essay?

2. What is Singal's thesis, the claim of his argument?

3. Explain the test score evidence that he presents to demonstrate that the second crisis is indeed a serious problem. Is the evidence clear? Convincing?

4. What is the significance of a 60-point drop in verbal SAT scores for college students? How, specifically, are students' weaknesses revealed in their college work? List the particular characteristics that Singal notes.

5. What is the role of factual knowledge? Why is it so important to have background information to do college work?

6. What characteristic of the high school curriculum does Singal point to as a reason for college students' lack of factual knowledge? What possible explanation for poor student performance does he reject?

7. What was found to be the most important characteristic of good high schools? What two other factors also contribute to their success?

8. What is Singal's explanation for the majority of schools failing to ad-here to the characteristics of success? What values from the sixties have reshaped most schools?

9. What subject areas continue to be influenced by the changes of the sixties? How is the influence seen in reading and writing assign-ments? How is it revealed in social studies courses?

10. What seems to be the current philosophy regarding students and their needs?

11. Explain in your words each of Singal's four solutions to the problem.

12. What final reasons does the author give for accepting his recommen-dations for change?

13. Analyze the essay's structure. What does the author accomplish in his opening paragraphs? How does each subsection contribute to the de-velopment of his argument?

Responding to the Writer's Ideas

1. Describe the tone and approach of Singal's argument. Does his ap-proach work for his audience and purpose?

2. Has Singal convinced you that American schools are not educating its best students as well as they could—and should? If so, why? If not, why?

3. Recall your own high school experience. Did you take survey history and literature courses, or something else? How many books were as-signed reading? Were they major novels or "age appropriate"? How much writing were you assigned? Were you assigned analyses and ar-

guments or personal-experience essays? Do you think that you received a good high school education? On what have you based your answer to the last question?

4. One of Singal's proposals calls for decreasing the control of education departments in the certification of teachers. Is this a new idea to you? Has Singal convinced you that this is part of the problem? Why or why not?

5. Another proposal is for homogeneous grouping. Do you agree that this is important in providing the best education for every student, or do you share the views of those who consider this approach to be elitist, or not in harmony with social goals?

1) Outcome based Education

2) National Curriculum

3) Cultural effects on education
4) Family values re: education

The Case for Music Education

Charles Fowler

Charles Fowler (b. 1931) is director of National Cultural Resources, Inc., and a free-lance writer and arts consultant. Fowler has directed and advised on music programs in schools, was a consultant to Radio City Music Hall and the opening events at Epcot Center in 1982, and writes a column in Musical America. *The following article, published April 5, 1992, in the* Washington Post's *annual Education Review Section, presents an argument for music in the schools, an argument that often goes unheeded in difficult economic times.*

1   When students and parents are asked to rate subjects according to their importance, the arts are inevitably at the bottom of the list. Music is nice, people seem to say, but not essential. Too often it is viewed as mere entertainment—all right for whiling away leisure time, but certainly not an educational priority. This view is shortsighted. On the contrary, music education is enormously beneficial and essential for all students.

2   Music develops human perception and sensibility; it connects us to those who came before us and to those who live beside us. Like any of the arts, it can reveal the dimensions of human life that disturb (Jimi Hendrix's explosive version of "The Star-Spangled Banner" during the Vietnam War), or it can express the exhilaration of human triumph over adversity (Beethoven's Symphony No. 9).

3   Music tells us who we are. Because music is an expression of the beings who create it, it reflects their thinking and values, as well as the social milieu in which it originated. Rap represents a life style just as surely as does a Schubert song. The jazz influences that George Gershwin, Duke Ellington, Aaron Copland and other composers introduced into their music is distinctively American because it emanated from American musical traditions. Our musical traits express our character and values. They give us identity as a society.

4   When students study the music of other times and places, they may learn to respect and appreciate the people who created it. As students learn to be receptive to other people's music, they may learn to be empathetic and compassionate toward these other human beings.

5   Music provides a kind of perception that cannot be acquired any other way. Science can explain how the earth, turning on its axis, causes the sunrise. The arts explore the emotive meaning of the same phenome-

non. We need every possible way to reveal and respond to our world for one simple but powerful reason: No one way can capture it all.

The arts are forms of thought every bit as potent in what they convey   6
as mathematical and scientific symbols. They are ways we human beings "talk" to each other. They are the language of civilization through which we express our fears, our anxieties, our curiosities, our hungers, our discoveries, our hopes. The arts are modes of communication that give us access to the stored wisdom of the ages. Most important, they are ways we give form to our ideas and imagination so that they can be shared with others. When we deny children access to a major expressive mode such as music, we deprive them of the meanings that music embodies.

Music is a way we learn to release our positive energies toward an   7
aesthetic result. America suffers from a loss of quality in workmanship. Reliable, well-made products require that workers *care* about what they are doing. The study of music teaches that kind of caring. Through music performance, students gain a respect for how all the elements—the details—make up the expressive whole. In studying music, people can learn how to apply standards to their own work. They can learn to be self-critical and to be able to self-correct. And in the process, they learn how to handle frustration and failure in pursuit of their goals.

But music replenishes the human spirit. Our feelings and our spirit   8
are part of our cognitive process, but education seldom accords them the attention they deserve. We need to educate the emotive part of our being so that we have clearer perceptions of those fundamental human states that have so much to do with interpersonal relations—love, hate, anxiety, hope and a host of other feelings.

Science and technology do not tell us what it means to be human.   9
The arts do. Music is a fundamental way we express human suffering and endurance, consolation in death, reverence for God, celebration, the meaning and value of peace and love.

Both the sciences and the arts are necessary to a balanced view of the   10
world. The arts complement the rational, logical emphasis in the curriculum by allowing students contact with the irrational and intuitive aspects of life that science is hard-pressed to explain. The real world is not composed of perfect circles, squares and triangles—simple black and white absolutes. The arts deal with the ambiguous gray areas. They teach students that there are many ways to do one thing well. Such insights help students to break through the true-false, name-this, memorize-that confines of public education.

The arts are a major area of concentration for students in Germany,   11
Japan and other countries with whom we are competing. Consequently, their education is all-encompassing. In many American schools, by contrast, music and the arts are a sadly neglected educational resource. They are far more necessary than people seem to realize.

Reading and Analyzing

1. What is Fowler's claim? Where does he state his claim?
2. Fowler's opening paragraph establishes what purpose in writing? That is, what kind of argument is this?
3. Analyze the essay's structure. How does the author develop and support his claim?
4. List each of Fowler's reasons in support of his claim.
5. What contrasts does Fowler draw between music—or the arts generally—and science and technology?

Responding to the Writer's Ideas

1. For some of his reasons, Fowler provides specific examples; for others he develops the idea in another sentence or two. Does he provide sufficient evidence to support his claim? Are there additional facts that Fowler could provide, or is his claim one for which there are no "numbers," no convincing tabulations of SAT scores, for example?
2. Might part of the difficulty that many have defending music and art programs in the schools stem from the relative lack of "hard evidence" to support the worth of such programs? Are you more likely to be convinced by claims that are supported by statistical evidence? Are school boards? If so, how can the argument for arts education be most effectively made?
3. Fowler repeats a popular idea about the differences between science and the arts. Do you agree with the distinction? Does he state the difference fairly? Are there only "black and white" answers in the study of science? Can science also appeal to the intuitive in us? Explain.
4. Which of Fowler's reasons do you consider the most convincing? Which the least convincing? Why?
5. If you were a school board member, would you keep music education in the budget? Why or why not?

❖

Multicultural Education: For Freedom's Sake

James A. Banks

*Holding a doctorate from Michigan State University, James A. Banks
(b. 1941) is a professor of education and director of the Center for
Multicultural Education at the University of Washington. Banks has
consulted on social studies curricula and written extensively on
multiethnic education. Published in* Education Leadership *(December
1991/January 1992), "Multicultural Education: For Freedom's Sake"
makes a case for education with a multiethnic focus.*

In *The Dialectic of Freedom,* Maxine Greene (1988) asks, "What   1
does it mean to be a citizen of the free world?" It means, she concludes,
having the capacity to choose, the power to act to attain one's purposes,
and the ability to help transform a world lived in common with others. An
important factor that limits human freedom in a pluralistic society is the
cultural encapsulation into which all individuals are socialized. People
learn the values, beliefs, and stereotypes of their community cultures. Although these community cultures enable individuals to survive, they also
restrict their freedom and ability to make critical choices and to take actions to help reform society.

Education within a pluralistic society should affirm and help students   2
understand their home and community cultures. However, it should also
help free them from their cultural boundaries. To create and maintain a
civic community that works for the common good, education in a democratic society should help students acquire the knowledge, attitudes, and
skills they will need to participate in civic action to make society more equitable and just.

Multicultural education is an education for freedom (Parekh 1986)   3
that is essential in today's ethnically polarized and troubled world. It has
evoked a divisive national debate in part because of the divergent views that
citizens hold about what constitutes an American identity and about the
roots and nature of American civilization. The debate in turn has sparked a
power struggle over who should participate in formulating the canon used
to shape the curriculum in the nation's schools, colleges, and universities.

The Debate Over the Canon

A chorus of strident voices has launched an orchestrated and widely publi-   4
cized attack on the movement to infuse content about ethnic groups and

151

women into the school and university curriculum. Much of the current debate over multicultural education has taken place in mass media publications such as *Time* (Gray 1991), *The Wall Street Journal* (Sirkin 1990), and *The New Republic* (Howe 1991), rather than in scholarly journals and forums. The Western traditionalists (writers who defend the canon now within the schools and universities) and the multiculturalists rarely engage in reflective dialogue. Rather, scholars on each side of the debate marshal data to support their briefs and ignore facts, interpretations, and perspectives that are inconsistent with their positions and visions of the present and future.

5   In his recent book, *Illiberal Education,* D'Souza (1991) defends the existing curriculum and structures in higher education while presenting an alarming picture of where multiculturalism is taking the nation. When multiculturalists respond to such criticism, they often fail to describe the important ways in which the multicultural vision is consistent with the democratic ideals of the West and with the heritage of Western civilization. The multicultural literature pays too little attention to the fact that the multicultural education movement emerged out of Western democratic ideals. One of its major aims is to close the gap between the Western democratic ideals of equality and justice and societal practices that contradict those ideals, such as discrimination based on race, gender, and social class.

6   Because so much of the debate over the canon has taken place in the popular media, which encourages simplistic, sound-byte explanations, the issues related to the curriculum canon have been overdrawn and oversimplified by advocates on both sides. The result is that the debate often generates more heat than light. Various interest groups have been polarized rather than encouraged to exchange ideas that might help us find creative solutions to the problems related to race, ethnicity, gender, and schooling.

7   As the ethnic texture of the nation deepens, problems related to diversity will intensify rather than diminish. Consequently, we need leaders and educators of good will, from all political and ideological persuasions, to participate in genuine discussions, dialogue, and debates that will help us formulate visionary and workable solutions and enable us to deal creatively with the challenges posed by the increasing diversity in the United States and the world. We must learn how to transform the problems related to racial and ethnic diversity into opportunities and strengths.

Sharing Power

8   Western traditionalists and multiculturalists must realize that they are entering into debate from different power positions. Western traditionalists hold the balance of power, financial resources, and the top positions in the mass media, in schools, colleges and universities, government, and in the publishing industry. Genuine discussion between the traditionalists and the

multiculturalists can take place only when power is placed on the table, negotiated, and shared.

Despite all of the rhetoric about the extent to which Chaucer, Shakespeare, Milton, and other Western writers are threatened by the onslaught of women and writers of color into the curriculum, the reality is that the curriculum in the nation's schools and universities is largely Western in its concepts, paradigms, and content. Concepts such as the Middle Ages and the Renaissance are still used to organize most units in history, literature, and the arts. When content about African and Asian cultures is incorporated into the curriculum, it is usually viewed within the context of European concepts and paradigms. For example, Asian, African, and American histories are often studied under the topic, "The Age of Discovery," which means the time when Europeans first arrived in these continents.

Facing Realities

If they are to achieve a productive dialogue rather than a polarizing debate, both Western traditionalists and the multiculturalists must face some facts. The growing number of people of color in our society and schools constitutes a demographic imperative educators must hear and respond to. The 1990 Census indicated that one of every four Americans is a person of color. By the turn of the century, one of every three will be of color (The Commission 1988). Nearly half of the nation's students will be of color by 2020 (Pallas et al. 1989). Although the school and university curriculums remain Western-oriented, this growing number of people of color will increasingly demand to share power in curriculum decision making and in shaping a curriculum canon that reflects their experiences, histories, struggles, and victories.

People of color, women, and other marginalized groups are demanding that their voices, visions, and perspectives be included in the curriculum. They ask that the debt Western civilization owes to Africa, Asia, and indigenous America be acknowledged (Allen 1986, Bernal 1987). The advocates of the Afrocentric curriculum, in sometimes passionate language that reflects a dream long deferred, are merely asking that the cultures of Africa and African-American people be legitimized in the curriculum and that the African contributions to European civilization be acknowledged. People of color and women are also demanding that the facts about their victimization be told, for truth's sake, but also because they need to better understand their conditions so that they and others can work to reform society.

However, these groups must acknowledge that they do not want to eliminate Aristotle and Shakespeare, or Western civilization, from the school curriculum. To reject the West would be to reject important aspects of their own cultural heritages, experiences, and identities. The most important scholarly and literary works written by African-Americans, such as works by W.E.B. DuBois, Carter G. Woodson, and Zora Neale Hurston, are expressions of Western cultural experiences. African-American culture resulted from a blending of African cultural characteristics with those of African peoples in the United States.

Reinterpreting Western Civilization

13   Rather than excluding Western civilization from the curriculum, multiculturalists want a more truthful, complex, and diverse version of the West taught in the schools. They want the curriculum to describe the ways in which African, Asian, and indigenous American cultures have influenced and interacted with Western civilization. They also want schools to discuss not only the diversity and democratic ideals of Western civilization, but also its failures, tensions, dilemmas, and the struggles by various groups in Western societies to realize their dreams against great odds.

14   We need to deconstruct the myth that the West is homogeneous, that it owes few debts to other world civilizations, and that only privileged and upper-status Europeans and European-American males have been its key actors. Weatherford (1988) describes the debt the West owes to the first Americans. Bernal (1987), Drake (1987), Sertima (1984), and Clarke (1990) marshal considerable amounts of historical and cultural data that describe the ways in which African and Afroasiatic cultures influenced the development of Western civilization. Bernal, for example, presents linguistic and archaeological evidence to substantiate his claim that important parts of Greek civilization (technologies, language, deities, and architecture) originated in ancient Africa.

15   We should teach students that knowledge is a social construction, that it reflects the perspectives, experiences, and the values of the people and cultures that construct it, and that it is dynamic, changing, and debated among knowledge creators and users (Banks 1991). Rather than keep such knowledge debates as the extent to which African civilizations contributed to Western civilization out of the classroom, teachers should make them an integral part of teaching. The classroom should become a forum in which multicultural debates concerning the construction of knowledge take place. The voices of the Western traditionalists, the multiculturalists, textbook authors, and radical writers should be heard and legitimized in the classroom.

Toward the Democratic Ideal

16   The fact that multiculturalists want to reformulate and transform the Western canon, not to purge the curriculum of the West, is absent from most of the writings of the Western traditionalists. It doesn't support their argument that Shakespeare, Milton, and Aristotle are endangered. By the same token, the multiculturalists have written little about the intersections of multicultural content and a Western-centric canon, perhaps because

they have focused on ways in which the established Western canon should be reconstructed and transformed.

Multicultural education itself is a product of the West. It grew out of a struggle guided by Western ideals for human dignity, equality, and freedom (Parker 1991). Multicultural education is a child of the civil rights movement led by African Americans that was designed to eliminate discrimination in housing, public accommodation, and other areas. The leaders of the civil rights movement, such as Fannie Lou Hamer, Rosa Parks, and Daisy Bates, internalized the American democratic ideal stated in such important United States documents as the Declaration of Independence, the Constitution, and the Bill of Rights. The civil rights leaders of the 1960s and 1970s used the Western ideals of freedom and democracy to justify and legitimize their push for structural inclusion and the end of institutionalized discrimination and racism.

The civil rights movement of the 1960s echoed throughout the United States and the world. Other groups, such as Native Americans and Hispanics, women, and people with disabilities, initiated their own freedom movements. These cultural revitalization movements made demands on a number of institutions. The nation's schools and universities became primary targets for reform, in part because they were important symbols of the structural exclusion that victimized groups experienced, and in part because they were easily accessible.

It would be a serious mistake to interpret these cultural revitalization movements and the educational reforms they gave birth to as a repudiation of the West and Western civilization. The major goals of these movements are full inclusion of the victimized groups into Western institutions and a reform of these institutions so that their practices are more consistent with their democratic ideals. Multicultural education not only arose out of Western traditions and ideals, its major goal is to create a nation-state that actualizes the democratic ideals for all that the Founding Fathers intended for an elite few. Rather than being divisive as some critics contend, multicultural education is designed to reduce race, class, and gender divisions in the United States and the world.

Given the tremendous social class and racial cleavages in United States society, it is inaccurate to claim that the study of ethnic diversity will threaten national cohesion. The real threats to national unity—which in an economic, sociological, and psychological sense we have not fully attained but are working toward—are the deepening racial and social-class schisms within United States society. As Wilson (1987) points out in *The Truly Disadvantaged,* the gap between the rich and the poor has grown tremendously in recent years. The social-class schism has occurred not only across racial and ethnic groups, but within these groups. Hence, the rush to the suburbs has not just been a white flight, but has been a flight by the middle class of many hues. As a consequence, low-income African

Americans and Hispanics have been left in inner-city communities without the middle-class members of their groups to provide needed leadership and role models. They are more excluded than ever from mainstream American society.

Educating for Freedom

21   Each of us becomes culturally encapsulated during our socialization in childhood. We accept the assumptions of our own community culture, internalize its values, views of the universe, misconceptions, and stereotypes. Although this is as true for the child socialized within a mainstream culture as it is for the minority child, minority children are usually forced to examine, confront, and question their cultural assumptions when they enter school.

22   Students who are born and socialized within the mainstream culture of a society rarely have an opportunity to identify, question, and challenge their cultural assumptions, beliefs, values, and perspectives because the school culture usually reinforces those that they learn at home and in their communities. Consequently, mainstream Americans have few opportunities to become free of cultural assumptions and perspectives that are monocultural, that devalue African and Asian cultures, and that stereotype people of color and people who are poor, or who are victimized in other ways. These mainstream Americans often have an inability to function effectively within other American cultures, and lack the ability and motivation to experience and benefit from cross-cultural participation and relationships.

23   To fully participate in our democratic society, these students and all students need the skills a multicultural education can give them to understand others and to thrive in a rapidly changing, diverse world. Thus, the debate between the Western traditionalists and the multiculturalists fits well within the tradition of a pluralistic democratic society. Its final result will most likely be not exactly what either side wants, but a synthesized and compromised perspective that will provide a new vision for the nation as we enter the 21st century.

References

Allen, P. G. (1986). *The Sacred Hoop: Recovering the Feminine in American Indian Traditions.* Beacon Press.

Banks, J. A. (1991). *Teaching Strategies for Ethnic Studies,* 5th ed. Boston: Allyn and Bacon.

Bernal, M. (1987). *The Afroasiatic Roots of Classical Civilization,* Vol. 1: *The Fabrication of Ancient Greece 1785–1985.* London: Free Association Books.

Clarke, J. H. (1990). "African People on My Mind." In *Infusion of African and African American Content in the School Curriculum: Proceedings of the First National Conference,* edited by A. G. Hilliard III, L. Payton-Stewart, and L. O. Williams. Morristown, N.J.: Aaron Press.

The Commission on Minority Participation in Education and American Life. (May 1988). *One-Third of a Nation*. Washington, D.C.: The American Council on Education.

D'Souza, D. (1991). *Illiberal Education: The Politics of Race and Sex on Campus*. New York: The Free Press.

Drake, St. C. (1987). *Black Folk Here and There*. Vol. 1. Los Angeles: Center for Afro-American Studies, University of California.

Gray, P. (July 8, 1991). "Whose America?" *Time* 138: 13–17.

Greene, M. (1988). *The Dialectic of Freedom*. New York: Teachers College Press.

Howe, I. (February 18, 1991). "The Value of the Canon." *The New Republic:* 40–44.

Pallas, A. M., G. Natriello, E. L. McDill. (June–July 1989). "The Changing Nature of the Disadvantaged Population: Current Dimensions and Future Trends." *Educational Researcher* 18, 2: 2.

Parekh, B. (1986). "The Concept of Multi-Cultural Education." *In Multicultural Education: The Interminable Debate*, edited by S. Modgil, G. K. Verma, K. Mallick, and C. Modgil. Philadelphia: The Falmer Press, pp. 19–31.

Parker, W. P. (1991). "Multicultural Education in Democratic Societies." Paper presented at the annual meeting of the American Educational Research Association, Chicago.

Sirkin, G. (January 18, 1990). "The Multiculturalists Strike Again." *The Wall Street Journal,* p. A14.

Sertima, I. V., ed. (1984). (Ed). *Black Women in Antiquity*. New Brunswick, N.J.: Transaction Books.

Weatherford, J. (1988). *Indian Givers: How the Indians of the Americas Transformed the World*. New York: Fawcett Columbine.

Wilson, W. J. (1987). *The Truly Disadvantaged: The Inner City, the Underclass, and Public Policy*. Chicago: The University of Chicago Press.

Reading and Analyzing

1. What is Banks's thesis? Where does he state his thesis?

2. What does Banks accomplish in paragraph 1? What is added in paragraph 2? How does paragraph 3 connect to the first two paragraphs and complete Banks's introduction?

3. Into what category of writing should this article be placed? At what point in your reading is the article's type revealed? What documentation pattern does the author use?

4. What is Banks's analysis of the debate over the canon? Where has most of the debate taken place? Why, in Banks's view, is that a problem?

5. What is a major aim of multiculturalism?

6. Banks asserts that Western traditionalists predominate in positions of power. What is his evidence for this assertion?

7. What demographic numbers does Banks cite? How are they significant to his argument?

8. How does Banks want Western civilization to be presented in the classroom? Explain the idea that "knowledge is a social construction" (paragraph 5).
9. What are the historical forces that led to the multicultural revolution? What elements in American society run counter to the fulfilling of democratic ideals? How will multicultural education help fulfill those ideals?

Responding to the Writer's Ideas

1. Banks makes an assertion about the purpose of education that is an important part of his argument. Do you agree that education should free students from cultural boundaries and enable them "to make society more equitable and just"? Why or why not?
2. Banks argues that the debate is about power and that multiculturalists need to do a better job of explaining that they want to debate and expand the traditional canon, not dump it. First, is there evidence that the debate is about power? Or is that a convenient charge of any group that wants control? Is it not possible that the debate is primarily about what should be taught—and the role of education itself? Second, should Banks explain the argument of the traditionalists? Is it fair to the opposition to suggest that their position is defended only to maintain power and is based on ignorance of the views of multiculturalists? Explain your reactions to these issues.
3. Has Banks convinced you that multiculturalism is the best approach to deciding how literature and history are taught in schools and colleges? Why or why not? What can be gained by a multicultural approach? What can be gained by a "traditional canon" approach? Can the two approaches be blended into one?

❖

The Pitfalls of Multicultural Education

Albert Shanker

A former teacher, Albert Shanker (b. 1928) has been president of the American Federation of Teachers since 1974. A strong advocate for his teachers' union, Shanker has published many articles on the controversial issues of education. The following article, a condensed version of a previously published article, appeared in the December 1991 issue of Education Digest. *Here Shanker questions the presumed advantages of an education that is consciously multicultural.*

It is easy to be in favor of multicultural and global education, in principle. The trouble comes when you try to say exactly what you mean by the term so you can put it into action. 1

If you want to feel convinced about the value of multicultural and global education, all you have to do is to look at the strife bred by ethnic, racial, and religious differences. Look at Eastern Europe, at India, at some of our own cities. If only we understood where other people were coming from—if only we had more sensitivity to their cultures—we might not be so wedded to our own points of view. And we might have a better chance of avoiding the conflicts that come from ethnocentrism. 2

However, when we come to apply this principle, there are some serious problems. The New York State Regents' goal for global education, which has also been taken up by multiculturalists, makes some of these problems very clear. According to the goal, "Each student will develop the ability to understand, respect, and accept people of different races; sex; cultural heritage; national origin; religion; and political, economic, and social background, and their values, beliefs, and attitudes." 3

This goal, expressed in a lot of positive words, sounds very broad-minded, very reasonable. And up to a point, it expresses what we'd hope for from a multicultural and global education. An educated person is not narrow-minded or provincial. So, of course we don't want students to be prejudiced—to prejudge the correctness or desirability of some idea or action before they know anything about it. We want them to be open to new ideas and ways of doing things. 4

But do we really want them to "respect and accept" the "values, beliefs, and attitudes" of other people, no matter what they are? 5

Do we want them to respect and accept the beliefs that led Chinese leaders to massacre dissenting students in Tiananmen Square? And what 6 about the values and beliefs that allowed the Ayatollah Khomeini to pronounce a death sentence on Salman Rushdie and the current leaders in Iran to confirm this sentence? Is it okay to condemn an author to death because he wrote something that offends your religious beliefs?

7   Is exposing unwanted children to the elements and certain death, a custom still widely practiced in some countries in Asia and Africa, to be respected and accepted because it is part of somebody else's culture? Is female circumcision? Must we respect the custom of forcing young children in the Philippines or Thailand to work in conditions of virtual slavery? And must we look respectfully on Hitler's beliefs and actions?

8   Should we teach students to accept the sexism of the Japanese or their racist attitudes toward immigrants just because they're part of the Japanese culture? And should we encourage students, in the name of open-mindedness and cultural sensitivity, to accept Afrikaner values and the racist beliefs that undergird apartheid? (If the United States and other nations had been so "open-minded" over the years, would these values and beliefs now be changing in South Africa?)

9   People who support this kind of approach to multicultural and global education may think they are being objective—even scientific. They may think they're freeing themselves from the limitations of their own culture and its values. But by not taking a position, they are taking one. They are saying that apartheid is okay; that there is nothing wrong with murdering someone who has committed blasphemy.

10   They're also teaching their students not to make moral judgments. If any custom or law of people in any culture is as defensible as any other, what kind of judgment is possible? So, without intending to, they encourage students in prejudice of a different sort: Instead of mindlessly assuming that others' ways of doing things have to be wrong, students will mindlessly assume these ways of doing things have to be right—or at least as good as anyone else's. And by approving practices that would not be tolerated here or in any other democracy, they are saying that some people should be held to lower standards than others—a kind of moral superiority hardly consistent with multicultural and global education.

11   It's important that we teach our children about each other's and other people's customs and values. We are unlikely to survive if we don't. But this does not mean teaching students that they need not hold other people's practices—and our own—up to moral scrutiny. If we do this, we confuse objectivity with neutrality.

Reading and Analyzing

1. Shanker's opening paragraph of two sentences not only announces his subject but also establishes his attitude toward that subject. How do you know the author's position from paragraph 1?

2. What does Shanker seek to accomplish by paragraphs 2 and 4? What argument strategy is he using here?

3. Examine Shanker's choice of examples in paragraphs 6, 7, and 8. How do they help to develop his attitude toward multicultural education?

4. What, in Shanker's view, happens when you become objective about all cultures and their values? Explain his argument against multicultural education in your own words.

5. What does Shanker think we must teach students?

Responding to the Writer's Ideas

1. How effective is Shanker's conciliatory approach? Has he made his position clear?

2. Has Shanker made a convincing argument against moral neutrality? Why or why not? Has he usefully contributed to the dialogue that Banks calls for in his defense of multicultural education? What would be Banks's response to Shanker's argument?

3. Is it possible to take a multicultural approach to education without embracing an objectivity that leads to moral neutrality? If not, why not? If so, how? What guidelines would you give to teachers that might satisfy both Banks and Shanker? Or, would you argue that a reconciliation of the two views is impossible to obtain? Support your position.

WRITING SUGGESTIONS

1. Using a simple structure of listing reasons, Charles Fowler (see pp. 148–49) defends music education in the schools. Using his essay as a model, make an argument for keeping some course or program in either elementary or high school. You can argue for art education, drama productions, sports programs, band, or field trips. Try to have several reasons why you favor the program and draw on personal experience for specific details to develop and support your reasons.

2. Develop an argument that opposes "frills" in education. That is, make a case for deleting field trips or costumed "reenactments" of Thanksgiving and so on in elementary schools or for music, art, band, sports, or clubs in high school. You can work with the arts or sports or clubs in general, or for a more specific program, such as interscholastic football. Try to have several reasons why the program should be eliminated and draw on personal experience for specific details to develop and support your reasons.

3. Examine the issue of attitudes toward studying and doing well in school that Diane Ravitch (see pp. 106–09) and Caplan, Choy, and Whitmore (see pp. 118–26) raise. Limit your argument either to students or to parents. Either develop the argument that (1) students (or parents) put down learning or do not expect or desire hard work and discipline in school or (2) that Ravitch is incorrect, that students (or parents) do care about academic achievement and support the hard work needed to achieve excellence. You may choose to further limit your argument to one group of students (women, blacks, Hispanics, and so on). If you are going to disagree with Ravitch, organize your essay as a refutation of her article. Write thoughtfully, not defensively, and use your experiences as sources of evidence.

4. If you agree that attitudes toward study and academic achievement are part of the problem in schools today, then what are the solutions to this problem? Develop a problem-solution argument in which you offer suggestions for producing more positive attitudes toward academic excellence.

5. Many of the authors in this chapter refer to SAT scores and international tests in math and science as key indicators of problems in American schools. Some educators and social commentators have argued, though, that the SAT and other machine-scored tests do not adequately measure student achievement. Take a side on this issue. If you argue that these tests are not good measures, then you must explain what measurements should be used instead.

6. Some analysts of our schools' problems have urged a uniform national curriculum as a solution. Do you agree or disagree with this proposed solution borrowed from Europe and Asia? If you agree with

this proposal, then defend the idea in an essay; if you disagree, explain why the proposal is not a good solution. In the latter case, you may offer a different solution that you think is better, but you can also devote your essay entirely to explaining why the idea is not a good one for our schools.

7. One of the proposed solutions offered by Daniel Singal is for homogeneous grouping in classrooms. Is this a good proposal? Take a position for or against this idea. Be certain, whichever side you take, to distinguish homogeneous grouping from the procedure called "tracking." Since they are not the same, it is unfair argument to assert that educators in favor of the one really mean the other. (An extension of the concept of grouping is the magnet school, an entire school in one district devoted either to the very best students in the district or, sometimes, to those especially talented in math and the sciences. You may want to consider this strategy as a part of your debate.)

8. Another proposal, one that has received attention by political leaders, is the idea of a voucher system, that is, the opportunity for parents to select the school for their children, including, in some plans, the opportunity to select a private school rather than one of the area's public schools. (The voucher, then, means that the government would pay the tuition of the private school, or some portion of the school's tuition.) Are you in favor of vouchers or opposed to them? Or, do you favor the idea within the public school system but would exclude private schools from the program? Consider the reasons for your position carefully, for this is a proposal that sounds simple but could be difficult to implement. If you argue in favor of the idea, you may want to address the issue of feasibility since the lack of feasibility is one counterargument your opponents will certainly use.

CHAPTER 5

EXAMINING THE
ARGUMENTS
FOR—AND
AGAINST—
CENSORSHIP

❖

"Congress shall make no law . . . abridging the freedom of speech or of the press," stirring words from the First Amendment to the Constitution of the United States, part of the Bill of Rights demanded by the more "radical" of the revolutionary colonists who did not want to substitute one autocratic government for another. We have to wonder if those first Americans had any idea how much debate, how many court cases, these words would stir up from their time to ours.

One of the writers in this chapter, Barbara Dority ("Feminist Moralism, 'Pornography,' and Censorship"), quotes the First Amendment to emphasize that *no laws* should be passed restricting pornographic works, but

164

a moment's reflection reminds us that these words are not absolute, that laws have been passed which restrict freedom of speech and of the press. Not surprisingly, Patty McEntee, in her defense of regulating pornography ("Is Pornography a Matter of Free Expression?"), makes this very point. For example, an individual's freedom of expression is restricted by laws against inciting a riot, slander, indecency, and perjury; newspapers are not free to publish libel. Still, the protections provided under the Bill of Rights have been highly prized, so valued that many individuals and organizations fight in court to define and limit those restrictions. What, then, are the protections of free speech and the press? And what are the restrictions necessary to promote the general welfare of a civil society? The many current issues examined in this chapter must be understood within the context of the words of, and the court rulings generated by, the First Amendment.

We cannot begin the debate more traditionally or more importantly than with an excerpt from one of the most famous discussions of individual freedom, the essay *On Liberty* by John Stuart Mill. Mill's complex philosophical study establishes one side of the debate when he asserts that a society should not regulate an individual's behavior just because it believes it is in that individual's best interest. Irving Kristol ("Pornography, Obscenity, and the Case for Censorship") disagrees, calling for a liberal censorship on the argument that if we can be influenced for good by good books, we can also be influenced for ill by bad books.

Kristol introduces the word *censorship,* a troublesome word that has become an issue in itself. Kristol calls it that "dreadful word" with good reason, for many react with automatic anger and revulsion as soon as the word is used. Understanding the word's negative connotations, Patty McEntee tries to convince readers that restriction on pornography does not constitute censorship. She argues that censorship must be defined as prior restraint by government of either speech or the press. In other words, the government's control of reporters covering the Persian Gulf War is censorship, but laws regulating pornography are not. These are essentially word games, however; most people use the term *censorship* to refer to any restrictions on freedom of expression, and the term has historical connections to legislating morality. The censors of the early Roman republic took the census *and* regulated manners and morals.

Two other words also need examination; *pornography* and *obscenity* are often used interchangeably even though their definitions differ. Obscenity is indecent behavior, and that means it is illegal. Pornography is literature, art, or film that some people consider erotic and others consider obscene. Two standards for judging pornography are (1) whether the work has any artistic value and (2) whether it is consistent with community standards. Both criteria for judgment are easy to state but difficult to employ on a work-by-work basis. Hence the ongoing debates over restricting such works as the lyrics of the 2 Live Crew or the photographs or Robert Mapplethorpe. Father Conley of Fordham University seeks to address the issue of community standards in his article "The Public and Its Art."

What are the standards acceptable to a community is the issue not just with art but with language and behavior within the college community. In an attempt to create civil behavior in today's college communities, many schools have established codes of behavior with punishment, including expulsion, for nonconformity. A recent Supreme Court decision (see pp. 50–51) seems to make such codes illegal, but surely additional test cases will come along before restrictions are lifted at many schools. Two college presidents, James Laney of Emory University and Robert O'Neil formerly of the University of Virginia, debate the appropriateness of restrictions on speech or behavior that demean or ridicule students of various ethnic groups or sexual orientation.

The First Amendment speaks not only to the rights of free expression for individuals but also to a free press. A free press has been viewed as essential to a democracy, as a check on a government's control of its citizens by keeping information from them. But are citizens entitled to know *everything*—everything about the activities of the Central Intelligence Agency, everything about strategies for a war, everything about the private lives of public figures? We know that government can and will classify some information in the interest of national security; we also know that at times classified information has protected officials engaged in illegal activity. Officials protecting themselves from public scrutiny (for example, Watergate) have led to the current "industry" of investigative reporting. Unfortunately, a spinoff has been ever-greater scrutiny of the private lives of the rich and powerful. Nat Hentoff, a strong proponent of First Amendment rights, ironically reflects the complexities of First Amendment conflicts when he asserts, in "Stories the Public Has No Right to Know," that reporters ought not to tell everything they learn about public figures. Hentoff's atypical position on this issue may serve to remind us that our society is very different from the world known to—or perhaps even imagined by—the writers of the Bill of Rights.

❖

On Liberty

John Stuart Mill

*John Stuart Mill (1806–1873) rose to be an important official in the
East India Company and sought to influence social changes in his
nineteenth-century England. He has also made a permanent name for
himself as one of our most influential philosophers. Famous for a
rigorous early education conducted by his father and recounted in his*
Autobiography, *Mill reveals his breadth of knowledge and interests in
the titles of some of his published works:* A System of Logic *(1843)*,
Principles of Political Economy *(1848)*, Consideration on
Representative Government *(1861)*, The Subjection of Women *(1869)*,
and On Liberty *(1859), from which the following passages have been
excerpted. In his essay* On Liberty, *an instant success and still one of
the most important essays on personal liberty, Mill examines the issue
of what, if any, constraints should be placed on individual freedom.
Mill, a believer in utilitarian philosophy, explores the issue in the
context of individual freedom versus the social good, or the greatest
good for the greatest number.*

Introductory

The subject of this Essay is . . . Civil, or Social Liberty: the nature
and limits of the power which can be legitimately exercised by society over
the individual. A question seldom stated, and hardly ever discussed, in general terms, but which profoundly influences the practical controversies of
the age by its latent presence, and is likely soon to make itself recognized
as the vital question of the future. It is so far from being new, that, in a
certain sense, it has divided mankind, almost from the remotest ages, but
in the stage of progress into which the more civilized portions of the
species have now entered, it presents itself under new conditions, and requires a different and more fundamental treatment. . . .

In political and philosophical theories, as well as in persons, success
discloses faults and infirmities which failure might have concealed from
observation. The notion, that the people have no need to limit their power
over themselves, might seem axiomatic, when popular government was a
thing only dreamed about, or read of as having existed at some distant period of the past. Neither was that notion necessarily disturbed by such
temporary aberrations as those of the French Revolution, the worst of

which were the work of an usurping few, and which, in any case, belonged, not to the permanent working of popular institutions, but to a sudden and convulsive outbreak against monarchical and aristocratic despotism. In time, however, a democratic republic came to occupy a large portion of the earth's surface, and made itself felt as one of the most powerful members of the community of nations; and elective and responsible government became subject to the observations and criticisms which wait upon a great existing fact. It was now perceived that such phrases as "self-government," and "the power of the people over themselves," do not express the true state of the case. The "people" who exercise the power, are not always the same people with those over whom it is exercised, and the "self-government" spoken of, is not the government of each by himself, but of each by all the rest. The will of the people, moreover, practically means, the will of the most numerous or the most active *part* of the people; the majority, or those who succeed in making themselves accepted as the majority: the people, consequently, *may* desire to oppress a part of their number; and precautions are as much needed against this, as against any other abuse of power. The limitation, therefore, of the power of government over individuals, loses none of its importance when the holders of power are regularly accountable to the community, that is, to the strongest party therein. This view of things, recommending itself equally to the intelligence of thinkers and to the inclination of those important classes in European society to whose real or supposed interests democracy is adverse, has had no difficulty in establishing itself; and in political speculations "the tyranny of the majority" is now generally included among the evils against which society requires to be on its guard.

3   Like other tyrannies, the tyranny of the majority was at first, and is still vulgarly, held in dread, chiefly as operating through the acts of the public authorities. But reflecting persons perceived that when society is itself the tyrant—society collectively, over the separate individuals who compose it—its means of tyrannizing are not restricted to the acts which it may do by the hands of its political functionaries. Society can and does execute its own mandates: and if it issues wrong mandates instead of right, or any mandates at all in things with which it ought not to meddle, it practises a social tyranny more formidable than many kinds of political oppression, since, though not usually upheld by such extreme penalties, it leaves fewer means of escape, penetrating much more deeply into the details of life, and enslaving the soul itself. Protection, therefore, against the tyranny of the magistrate is not enough; there needs protection also against the tyranny of the prevailing opinion and feeling; against the tendency of society to impose, by other means than civil penalties, its own ideas and practices as rules of conduct on those who dissent from them; to fetter the development, and, if possible, prevent the formation, of any individuality not in harmony with its ways, and compel all characters to fashion themselves

upon the model of its own. There is a limit to the legitimate interference of collective opinion with individual independence; and to find that limit, and maintain it against encroachment, is as indispensable to a good condition of human affairs, as protection against political despotism.

But though this proposition is not likely to be contested in general terms, the practical question, where to place the limit—how to make the fitting adjustment between individual independence and social control—is a subject on which nearly everything remains to be done. All that makes existence valuable to any one, depends on the enforcement of restraints upon the actions of other people. Some rules of conduct, therefore, must be imposed, by law in the first place, and by opinion on many things which are not fit subjects for the operation of law. What these rules should be, is the principal question in human affairs; but if we except a few of the most obvious cases, it is one of those which least progress has been made in resolving. No two ages, and scarcely any two countries, have decided it alike; and the decision of one age or country is a wonder to another. Yet the people of any given age and country no more suspect any difficulty in it, than if it were a subject on which mankind had always been agreed. The rules which obtain among themselves appear to them self-evident and self-justifying. This all but universal illusion is one of the examples of the magical influence of custom, which is not only, as the proverb says, a second nature, but is continually mistaken for the first. The effect of custom, in preventing any misgiving respecting the rules of conduct which mankind impose on one another, is all the more complete because the subject is one on which it is not generally considered necessary that reasons should be given, either by one person to others, or by each to himself. People are accustomed to believe and have been encouraged in the belief by some who aspire to the character of philosophers, that their feelings, on subjects of this nature, are better than reasons, and render reasons unnecessary. The practical principle which guides them to their opinions on the regulation of human conduct, is the feeling in each person's mind that everybody should be required to act as he, and those with whom he sympathizes, would like them to act. No one, indeed, acknowledges to himself that his standard of judgment is his own liking; but an opinion on a point of conduct, not supported by reasons, can only count as one person's preference; and if the reasons, when given, are a mere appeal to a similar preference felt by other people, it is still only many people's liking instead of one. To an ordinary man, however, his own preference, thus supported, is not only a perfectly satisfactory reason, but the only one he generally has for any of his notions of morality, taste, or propriety, which are not expressly written in his religious creed; and his chief guide in the interpretation even of that. Men's opinions, accordingly, on what is laudable or blamable, are affected by all the multifarious causes which influence their wishes in regard to the conduct of others, and which are as numerous as those which determine their wishes on any other subject. Sometimes their reason—at other times their prejudices or superstitions: often their social affections, not seldom their anti-social ones, their envy or jealousy, their arrogance or contemptuousness: but most commonly, their desires or fears for themselves—their legitimate or illegitimate self-interest. Wherever there is an ascendant class, a large portion of the morality of the country emanates from its class interests, and its feelings of class superiority. The morality between Spartans and Helots, between planters and negroes, between princes and subjects, between nobles and roturiers, between men and women, has been for the most part the creation of these class interests and feelings: and the sentiments thus generated, react in turn upon the moral feelings of the members of the ascendant class, in their relations among themselves. Where, on the other hand, a class, formerly ascendant, has lost its ascendency, or where its ascendency is unpopular, the prevailing moral sentiments frequently bear the impress of an impatient dislike of superiority. Another grand determining principle of the rules of conduct, both in act and forbearance which have been enforced by law or opinion, has been the servility of mankind towards the supposed preferences or aversions of their temporal masters, or of their gods. This servility though essentially selfish, is not hypocrisy; it gives rise to perfectly genuine sentiments of abhorrence; it made men burn magicians and heretics. Among so many baser influences, the general and obvious interests of society have of course had a share, and a large one, in the direction of the moral sentiments: less, however, as a matter of reason, and on their own account, than as a consequence of the sympathies and antipathies which grew out of them: and sympathies and antipathies which had little or nothing to do with the interests of society, have made themselves felt in the establishment of moralities with quite as great force. . . .

5   The object of this Essay is to assert one very simple principle, as entitled to govern absolutely the dealings of society with the individual in the way of compulsion and control, whether the means used be physical force in the form of legal penalties, or the moral coercion of public opinion. That principle is, that the sole end for which mankind are warranted, individually or collectively in interfering with the liberty of action of any of their number, is self-protection. That the only purpose for which power can be rightfully exercised over any member of a civilized community, against his will, is to prevent harm to others. His own good, either physical or moral, is not a sufficient warrant. He cannot rightfully be compelled to do or forbear because it will be better for him to do so, because it will make him happier, because, in the opinions of others, to do so would be wise, or even right. These are good reasons for remonstrating with him, or reasoning with him, or persuading him, or entreating him, but not for compelling him, or visiting him with any evil, in case he do otherwise. To justify that, the conduct from which it is desired to deter him must be cal-

culated to produce evil to some one else. The only part of the conduct of any one, for which he is amenable to society, is that which concerns others. In the part which merely concerns himself, his independence is, of right, absolute. Over himself, over his own body and mind, the individual is sovereign.

It is, perhaps, hardly necessary to say that this doctrine is meant to apply only to human beings in the maturity of their faculties. We are not speaking of children, or of young persons below the age which the law may fix as that of manhood or womanhood. Those who are still in a state to require being taken care of by others, must be protected against their own actions as well as against external injury. . . .

It is proper to state that I forego any advantage which could be derived to my argument from the idea of abstract right as a thing independent of utility. I regard utility as the ultimate appeal on all ethical questions; but it must be utility in the largest sense, grounded on the permanent interests of man as a progressive being. Those interests, I contend, authorize the subjection of individual spontaneity to external control, only in respect to those actions of each, which concern the interest of other people. If any one does an act hurtful to others, there is a *primâ facie* case for punishing him, by law, or, where legal penalties are not safely applicable, by general disapprobation. There are also many positive acts for the benefit of others, which he may rightfully be compelled to perform; such as, to give evidence in a court of justice; to bear his fair share in the common defence, or in any other joint work necessary to the interest of the society of which he enjoys the protection; and to perform certain acts of individual beneficence, such as saving a fellow-creature's life, or interposing to protect the defenceless against ill-usage, things which whenever it is obviously a man's duty to do, he may rightfully be made responsible to society for not doing. A person may cause evil to others not only by his actions but by his inaction, and in neither case he is justly accountable to them for the injury. The latter case, it is true, requires a much more cautious exercise of compulsion than the former. To make any one answerable for doing evil to others, is the rule; to make him answerable for not preventing evil, is, comparatively speaking, the exception. Yet there are many cases clear enough and grave enough to justify that exception. In all things which regard the external relations of the individual, he is *de jure* amenable to those whose interests are concerned, and if need be, to society as their protector. There are often good reasons for not holding him to the responsibility; but these reasons must arise from the special expediencies of the case: either because it is a kind of case in which he is on the whole likely to act better, when left to his own discretion, than when controlled in any way in which society have it in their power to control him. . . .

There is a sphere of action in which society, as distinguished from the individual, has, if any, only an indirect interest; comprehending all that portion of a person's life and conduct which affects only himself, or, if it also affects others, only with their free, voluntary, and undeceived consent and participation. When I say only himself, I mean directly, and in the first instance: for whatever affects himself, may affect others *through* himself; and the objection which may be grounded on this contingency, will receive consideration in the sequel. This, then, is the appropriate region of human liberty. It comprises, first, the inward domain of consciousness; demanding liberty of conscience, in the most comprehensive sense; liberty of thought and feeling; absolute freedom of opinion and sentiment on all subjects, practical or speculative, scientific, moral, or theological. The liberty of expressing and publishing opinions may seem to fall under a different principle, since it belongs to that part of the conduct of an individual which concerns other people; but, being almost of as much importance as the liberty of thought itself, and resting in great part on the same reasons, is practically inseparable from it. Secondly, the principle requires liberty of tastes and pursuits; of framing the plan of our life to suit our own character; of doing as we like, subject to such consequences as may follow; without impediment from our fellow-creatures, so long as what we do does not harm them even though they should think our conduct foolish, perverse, or wrong. Thirdly, from this liberty of each individual, follows the liberty, within the same limits, of combination among individuals; freedom to unite, for any purpose not involving harm to others: the persons combining being supposed to be of full age, and not forced or deceived.

9   No society in which these liberties are not, on the whole, respected, is free, whatever may be its form of government; and none is completely free in which they do not exist absolute and unqualified. The only freedom which deserves the name, is that of pursuing our own good in our own way, so long as we do not attempt to deprive others of theirs, or impede their efforts to obtain it. Each is the proper guardian of his own health, whether bodily, or mental or spiritual. Mankind are greater gainers by suffering each other to live as seems good to themselves, than by compelling each to live as seems good to the rest. . . .

Of the Liberty of Thought and Discussion

10   The time, it is to be hoped, is gone by when any defense would be necessary of the "liberty of the press" as one of the securities against corrupt or tyrannical government. No argument, we may suppose, can now be needed against permitting a legislature or an executive, not identified in interest with the people, to prescribe opinions to them and determine what doctrines or what arguments they shall be allowed to hear. This aspect of the question, besides, has been so often and so triumphantly enforced by preceding writers that it need not be specially insisted on in this place. Though the law of England, on the subject of the press, is as servile to this day as it was in the time of the Tudors, there is little danger of its being ac-

tually put in force against political discussion except during some temporary panic when fear of insurrection drives ministers and judges from their
propriety; and, speaking generally, it is not, in constitutional countries, to
be apprehended that the government, whether completely responsible to
the people or not, will often attempt to control the expression of opinion,
except when in doing so it makes itself the organ of the general intolerance
of the public. Let us suppose, therefore, that the government is entirely at
one with the people, and never thinks of exerting any power of coercion
unless in agreement with what it conceives to be their voice. But I deny the
right of the people to exercise such coercion, either by themselves or by
their government. The power itself is illegitimate. The best government has
no more title to it than the worst. It is as noxious, or more noxious, when
exerted in accordance with public opinion than when in opposition to it. If
all mankind minus one were of one opinion, mankind would be no more
justified in silencing that one person than he, if he had the power, would
be justified in silencing mankind. Were an opinion a personal possession of
no value except to the owner, if to be obstructed in the enjoyment of it
were simply a private injury, it would make some difference whether the
injury was inflicted only on a few persons or on many. But the peculiar evil
of silencing the expression of an opinion is that it is robbing the human
race, posterity as well as the existing generation—those who dissent from
the opinion, still more than those who hold it. If the opinion is right, they
are deprived of the opportunity of exchanging error for truth; if wrong,
they lose, what is almost as great a benefit, the clearer perception and live-
lier impression of truth produced by its collision with error. . . .

We have now recognized the necessity to the mental well-being of 11
mankind (on which all their other well-being depends) of freedom of opinion, and freedom of the expression of opinion, on four distinct grounds,
which we will now briefly recapitulate:

First, if any opinion is compelled to silence, that opinion may, for 12
aught we can certainly know, be true. To deny this is to assume our own
infallibility.

Secondly, though the silenced opinion be an error, it may, and very 13
commonly does, contain a portion of truth; and since the general or prevailing opinion on any subject is rarely or never the whole truth, it is only
by the collision of adverse opinions that the remainder of the truth has any
chance of being supplied.

Thirdly, even if the received opinion be not only true, but the whole 14
truth: unless it is suffered to be, and actually is, vigorously and earnestly
contested, it will, by most of those who receive it, be held in the manner of
a prejudice, with little comprehension or feeling of its rational grounds.
And not only this, but, fourthly, the meaning of the doctrine itself will be
in danger of being lost or enfeebled, and deprived of its vital effect on the
character and conduct: the dogma becoming a mere formal profession, in-

efficacious for good, but cumbering the ground and preventing the growth of any real and heartfelt conviction from reason or personal experience.

Reading and Analyzing

1. What, stated in your own words, is Mill's subject?
2. Explain the concept of "the tyranny of the majority." Under what kind of government is this potentially an issue?
3. In what two ways can the tyranny of the majority operate in society? Which may be the more formidable? Why?
4. In paragraph 3 Mill writes that "there is a limit to the legitimate interference of collective opinion with individual independence; and to find that limit . . . is as indispensable . . . as protection against political despotism." This statement establishes not one but two principles; what are they? What is asserted and what is implied in this statement?
5. Why, in Mill's view, are limits on individual behavior necessary in a society?
6. In what two ways does a society impose "rules of conduct" on citizens? How difficult is it to determine what these rules should be? How difficult do most people think it is? How do most people arrive at their views on these rules?
7. What is the one principle that should be the basis for deciding what constraints on individuals are appropriate? What is not a sufficient reason to restrict an individual?
8. What group is excluded from this principle? Why?
9. What does Mill include in the "region of human liberty"? What should individuals be at liberty to do? Are freedom of thought and freedom of expression to be treated the same?
10. State the claim of Mill's argument.
11. What does freedom of the press provide a society?
12. Why should neither the government nor individuals repress opinion? Summarize Mill's four reasons for protecting freedom of expression of opinion.

Responding to the Writer's Ideas

1. Mill's examination of the bounds of individual liberty is necessarily abstract, since his goal is to establish a universal principle. Has he written effectively, that is, clearly and persuasively, given his purpose?

2. Mill says that "a person may cause evil to others not only by his actions but by his inaction" and should be held accountable for both kinds of injuries. Apply this concept to a specific case: Should we have a "good-Samaritan" law that would require motorists to stop to aid a motorist in trouble? (Germany has such a law.) What would Mill say? Do you agree or disagree with Mill? Why?

3. Can you think of other situations of inaction that might warrant a law under Mill's principle?

4. Cigarette advertising is currently banned from television. Should all cigarette advertising be banned? What would Mill say? What do you say? Why?

5. What part of his argument would Mill use to justify prohibiting child pornography? Do you agree with him?

6. Two authors in this chapter, Patti McEntee and Barbara Dority, debate restrictions on adult pornography. Can one—or both—of these authors draw on Mill for support? In other words, is Mill specific enough to provide guidelines on this issue?

7. Do you agree with Mill's claim? Should individuals be free to behave in ways that are "harmful" (in someone else's view) to themselves, so long as they are not harmful to others? Or, should a society seek to legislate on issues of personal morality (for example, prohibit certain sexual acts between consenting adults) or personal health (for example, severely restrict the use of tobacco)? Defend your position.

8. Which one of Mill's reasons for not repressing freedom of expression is, in your view, the most persuasive? Why?

❖

Pornography, Obscenity, and the Case for Censorship

Irving Kristol

A graduate of New York's City College, Irving Kristol (b. 1920) is founder and coeditor of Public Interest *magazine and a senior fellow at the American Enterprise Institute. Kristol is the author of many articles and several books, including* On the Democratic Idea in America *(1972) and* Two Cheers for Capitalism *(1978). His argument for some censorship, first published in 1971, is reprinted in his collection of essays* Reflections of a Neoconservative, *published in 1983.*

Being frustrated is disagreeable, but the real disasters in life begin when you get what you want. For almost a century now, a great many intelligent, well-meaning, and articulate people—of a kind generally called liberal or intellectual, or both—have argued eloquently against any kind of censorship of art and/or entertainment. And within the past ten years, the courts and the legislatures of most Western nations have found these arguments persuasive—so persuasive that hardly a man is now alive who clearly remembers what the answers to these arguments were. Today, in the United States and other democracies, censorship has to all intents and purposes ceased to exist.

Is there a sense of triumphant exhilaration in the land? Hardly. There is, on the contrary, a rapidly growing unease and disquiet. Somehow, things have not worked out as they were supposed to, and many notable civil libertarians have gone on record as saying this was not what they meant at all. They wanted a world in which *Desire under the Elms*[1] could be produced, or *Ulysses*[2] published, without interference by philistine busybodies holding public office. They have got that, of course; but they have also got a world in which homosexual rape takes place on the stage, in which the public flocks during lunch hours to witness varieties of professional fornication, in which Times Square has become little more than a hideous market for the sale and distribution of printed filth that panders to all known (and some fanciful) sexual perversions.

[1] Play by American dramatist Eugene O'Neill.—Ed.

[2] Novel by Irish author James Joyce.—Ed.

But disagreeable as this may be, does it really matter? Might not our 3
unease and disquiet be merely a cultural hangover—a "hang-up," as they
say? What reason is there to think that anyone was ever corrupted by a
book?

This last question, oddly enough, is asked by the very same people 4
who seem convinced that advertisements in magazines or displays of violence on television do indeed have the power to corrupt. It is also asked,
incredibly enough and in all sincerity, by people—for example, university
professors and schoolteachers—whose very lives provide all the answers
one could want. After all, if you believe that no one was ever corrupted by
a book, you have also to believe that no one was ever improved by a book
(or a play or a movie). You have to believe, in other words, that all art is
morally trivial and that, consequently, all education is morally irrelevant.
No one, not even a university professor, really believes that.

To be sure, it is extremely difficult, as social scientists tell us, to trace 5
the effects of any single book (or play or movie) on an individual reader or
any class of readers. But we all know, and social scientists know it too,
that the ways in which we use our minds and imaginations do shape our
characters and help define us as persons. That those who certainly know
this are nevertheless moved to deny it merely indicates how a dogmatic resistance to the idea of censorship can—like most dogmatism—result in a
mindless insistence on the absurd.

I have used these harsh terms—"dogmatism" and "mindless"—ad- 6
visedly. I might also have added "hypocritical." For the plain fact is that
none of us is a complete civil libertarian. We all believe that there is some
point at which the public authorities ought to step in to limit the "self-expression" of an individual or a group, even where this might be seriously
intended as a form of artistic expression, and even where the artistic transaction is between consenting adults. A playwright or theatrical director
might, in this crazy world of ours, find someone willing to commit suicide
on the stage, as called for by the script. We would not allow that—any
more than we would permit scenes of real physical torture on the stage,
even if the victim were a willing masochist. And I know of no one, no matter how free in spirit, who argues that we ought to permit gladiatorial con-
tests in Yankee Stadium, similar to those once performed in the Colosseum
at Rome—even if only consenting adults were involved.

The basic point that emerges is one that Walter Berns has powerfully 7
argued: No society can be utterly indifferent to the ways its citizens publicly entertain themselves.* Bearbaiting and cockfighting are prohibited

---

*This is as good a place as any to express my profound indebtedness to Walter's
Berns's superb essay "Pornography vs. Democracy," in the Winter 1971 issue of
The Public Interest.

only in part out of compassion for the suffering animals; the main reason they were abolished was because it was felt that they debased and brutalized the citizenry who flocked to witness such spectacles. And the question we face with regard to pornography and obscenity is whether, now that they have such strong legal protection from the Supreme Court, they can or will brutalize and debase our citizenry. We are, after all, not dealing with one passing incident—one book, or one play, or one movie. We are dealing with a general tendency that is suffusing our entire culture.

8   I say pornography *and* obscenity because, though they have different dictionary definitions and are frequently distinguishable as "artistic" genres, they are nevertheless in the end identical in effect. Pornography is not objectionable simply because it arouses sexual desire or lust or prurience in the mind of the reader or spectator; this is a silly Victorian notion. A great many nonpornographic works—including some parts of the Bible—excite sexual desire very successfully. What is distinctive about pornography is that, in the words of D. H. Lawrence, it attempts "to do dirt on [sex] . . . [It is an] insult to a vital human relationship."

9   In other words, pornography differs from erotic art in that its whole purpose is to treat human beings obscenely, to deprive human beings of their specifically human dimension. That is what obscenity is all about. It is light years removed from any kind of carefree sensuality—there is no continuum between Fielding's *Tom Jones*[3] and the Marquis de Sade's *Justine*.[4] These works have quite opposite intentions. To quote Susan Sontag[5]: "What pornographic literature does is precisely to drive a wedge between one's existence as a full human being and one's existence as a sexual being—while in ordinary life a healthy person is one who prevents such a gap from opening up." This definition occurs in an essay *defending* pornography—Miss Sontag is a candid as well as gifted critic—so the definition, which I accept, is neither tendentious nor censorious.

10   Along these same lines, one can point out—as C. S. Lewis[6] pointed out some years back—that it is no accident that in the history of all literatures obscene words, the so-called four-letter words, have always been the vocabulary of farce or vituperation. The reason is clear; they reduce men and women to some of their mere bodily functions—they reduce man to his animal component, and such a reduction is an essential purpose of farce or vituperation.

---

[3] Eighteenth-century novel containing a number of sexual adventures by its main character.—Ed.

[4] Novel by the eighteenth-century French writer known for perverted sexual activities. The term *sadism* comes from de Sade's name.—Ed.

[5] Short story writer, essayist, and critic.—Ed.

[6] English novelist and essayist on moral and religious issues.—Ed.

Similarly, Lewis also suggested that it is not an accident that we have no offhand, colloquial, neutral terms—not in any Western European language at any rate—for our most private parts. The words we do use are either (1) nursery terms, (2) archaisms, (3) scientific terms, or (4) a term from the gutter (i.e., a demeaning term). Here I think the genius of language is telling us something important about man. It is telling us that man is an animal with a difference: He has a unique sense of privacy, and a unique capacity for shame when this privacy is violated. Our "private parts" are indeed private, and not merely because convention prescribes it. This particular convention is indigenous to the human race. In practically all primitive tribes, men and women cover their private parts; and in practically all primitive tribes, men and women do not copulate in public.

It may well be that Western society, in the latter half of the twentieth century, is experiencing a drastic change in sexual mores and sexual relationships. We have had many such "sexual revolutions" in the past—the bourgeois family and bourgeois ideas of sexual propriety were themselves established in the course of a revolution against eighteenth-century "licentiousness"—and we shall doubtless have others in the future. It is, however, highly improbable (to put it mildly) that what we are witnessing is the Final Revolution which will make sexual relations utterly unproblematic, permit us to dispense with any kind of ordered relationships between the sexes, and allow us freely to redefine the human condition. And so long as humanity has not reached that utopia, obscenity will remain a problem.

One of the reasons it will remain a problem is that obscenity is not merely about sex, any more than science fiction is about science. Science fiction, as every student of the genre knows, is a peculiar vision of power: What it is really about is politics. And obscenity is a peculiar vision of humanity: What it is really about is ethics and metaphysics.

Imagine a man—a well-known man, much in the public eye—in a hospital ward, dying an agonizing death. He is not in control of his bodily functions, so that his bladder and his bowels empty themselves of their own accord. His consciousness is overwhelmed and extinguished by pain, so that he cannot communicate with us, nor we with him. Now, it would be, technically, the easiest thing in the world to put a television camera in his hospital room and let the whole world witness this spectacle. We do not do it—at least we do not do it as yet—because we regard this as an *obscene* invasion of privacy. And what would make the spectacle obscene is that we would be witnessing the extinguishing of humanity in a human animal.

Incidentally, in the past our humanitarian crusaders against capital punishment understood this point very well. The abolitionist literature goes into great physical detail about what happens to a man when he is hanged or electrocuted or gassed. And their argument was—and is—that what happens is shockingly obscene, and that no civilized society should be responsible for perpetrating such obscenities, particularly since in the nature of the case there must be spectators to ascertain that this horror was indeed being perpetrated in fulfillment of the law.

16   Sex—like death—is an activity that is both animal and human. There are human sentiments and human ideals involved in this animal activity. But when sex is public, the viewer does not see—cannot see—the sentiments and the ideals. He can only see the animal coupling. And that is why, when men and women make love, as we say, they prefer to be alone—because it is only when you are alone that you can make love, as distinct from merely copulating in an animal and casual way. And that, too, is why those who are voyeurs, if they are not irredeemably sick, also feel ashamed at what they are witnessing. When sex is a public spectacle, a human relationship has been debased into a mere animal connection.

17   It is also worth noting that this making of sex into an obscenity is not a mutual and equal transaction but rather an act of exploitation by one of the partners—the male partner. I do not wish to get into the complicated question as to what, if any, are the essential differences—as distinct from conventional and cultural differences—between male and female. I do not claim to know the answer to that. But I do know—and I take it as a sign that has meaning—that pornography is, and always has been, a man's work; that women rarely write pornography; and that women tend to be indifferent consumers of pornography.* My own guess, by way of explanation, is that a woman's sexual experience is ordinarily more suffused with human emotion than is man's, that men are more easily satisfied with autoerotic activities, and that men can therefore more easily take a more "technocratic" view of sex and its pleasures. Perhaps this is not correct. But whatever the explanation, there can be no question that pornography is a form of "sexism," as the women's liberation movement calls it, and that the instinct of women's liberation has been unerring in perceiving that when pornography is perpetrated, it is perpetrated against them, as part of a conspiracy to deprive them of their full humanity.

18   But even if all this is granted, it might be said—and doubtless will be said—that I really ought not to be unduly concerned. Free competition in the cultural marketplace—it is argued by people who have never otherwise had a kind word to say for laissez-faire—will automatically dispose of the problem. The present fad for pornography and obscenity, it will be asserted, is just that, a fad. It will spend itself in the course of time; people will get bored with it, will be able to take it or leave it alone in a casual way, in a "mature way," and, in sum, I am being unnecessarily distressed about

---

* There are, of course, a few exceptions. *L'Histoire d'O*, for instance, was written by a woman. It is unquestionably the most *melancholy* work of pornography ever written. And its theme is precisely the dehumanization accomplished by obscenity.

the whole business. The *New York Times,* in an editorial, concludes hopefully in this vein.

> In the end . . . the insensate pursuit of the urge to shock, carried from one excess to a more abysmal one, is bound to achieve its own antidote in total boredom. When there is no lower depth to descend to, ennui will erase the problem.

I would like to be able to go along with this line of reasoning, but I cannot. I think it is false, and for two reasons, the first psychological, the second political.

The basic psychological fact about pornography and obscenity is that it appeals to and provokes a kind of sexual regression. The sexual pleasure one gets from pornography and obscenity is autoerotic and infantile; put bluntly, it is a masturbatory exercise of the imagination, when it is not masturbation pure and simple. Now, people who masturbate do not get bored with masturbation, just as sadists do not get bored with sadism, and voyeurs do not get bored with voyeurism.

In other words, infantile sexuality is not only a permanent temptation for the adolescent or even the adult—it can quite easily become a permanent, self-reinforcing neurosis. It is because of an awareness of this possibility of regression toward the infantile condition, a regression which is always open to us, that all the codes of sexual conduct ever devised by the human race take such a dim view of autoerotic activities and try to discourage autoerotic fantasies. Masturbation is indeed a perfectly natural autoerotic activity, as so many sexologists blandly assure us today. And it is precisely because it is so perfectly natural that it can be so dangerous to the mature or maturing person, if it is not controlled or sublimated in some way. That is the true meaning of Portnoy's[7] complaint. Portnoy, you will recall, grows up to be a man who is incapable of having an adult sexual relationship with a woman; his sexuality remains fixed in an infantile mode, the prisoner of his autoerotic fantasies. Inevitably, Portnoy comes to think, in a perfectly *infantile* way, that it was all his mother's fault.

It is true that, in our time, some quite brilliant minds have come to the conclusion that a reversion to infantile sexuality is the ultimate mission and secret destiny of the human race. I am thinking in particular of Norman O. Brown,[8] for whose writings I have the deepest respect. One of the reasons I respect them so deeply is that Mr. Brown is a serious thinker who is unafraid to face up to the radical consequences of his radical theo-

19

20

21

22

---

[7] Main character in the novel *Portnoy's Complaint* by Philip Roth.—Ed.

[8] Writer who, opposing the repression of traditional patterns and values, appealed to students in the 1960s.—Ed.

ries. Thus, Mr. Brown knows and says that for his kind of salvation to be achieved, humanity must annul the civilization it has created—not merely the civilization we have today, but all civilization—so as to be able to make the long descent backward into animal innocence.

23   And that is the point. What is at stake is civilization and humanity, nothing less. The idea that "everything is permitted," as Nietzsche[9] put it, rests on the premise of nihilism and has nihilistic implications. I will not pretend that the case against nihilism and for civilization is an easy one to make. We are here confronting the most fundamental of philosophical questions, on the deepest levels. In short, the matter of pornography and obscenity is not a trivial one, and only superficial minds can take a bland and untroubled view of it.

24   In this connection, I must also point out, those who are primarily against censorship on liberal grounds tell us not to take pornography or obscenity seriously, while those who are for pornography and obscenity on radical grounds take it very seriously indeed. I believe the radicals—writers like Susan Sontag, Herbert Marcuse,[10] Norman O. Brown, and even Jerry Rubin[11]—are right, and the liberals are wrong. I also believe that those young radicals at Berkeley, some seven years ago, who provoked a major confrontation over the public use of obscene words, showed a brilliant political instinct. And once Mark Rudd[12] could publicly ascribe to the president of Columbia a notoriously obscene relationship to his mother, without provoking any kind of reaction, the SDS [Students for a Democratic Society] had already won the day. The occupation of Columbia's buildings merely ratified their victory. Men who show themselves unwilling to defend civilization against nihilism are not going to be either resolute or effective in defending the university against anything.

25   I am already touching upon a political aspect of pornography when I suggest that it is inherently and purposefully subversive of civilization and its institutions. But there is another and more specifically political aspect, which has to do with the relationship of pornography and/or obscenity to democracy, and especially to the quality of public life on which democratic government ultimately rests.

26   Though the phrase "the quality of life" trips easily from so many lips these days, it tends to be one of those clichés with many trivial meanings and no large, serious one. Sometimes it merely refers to such exter-

[9] Nineteenth-century German philosopher who stressed the will to power as the force pushing both individuals and society.—Ed.

[10] Philosopher, educator, and writer who was embraced by the New Left of the 1960s.—Ed.

[11] Student activist in the 1960s.—Ed.

[12] Student activist in the 1960s.—Ed.

nals as the enjoyment of cleaner air, cleaner water, cleaner streets. At other times it refers to the merely private enjoyment of music, painting, or literature. Rarely does it have anything to do with the way the citizen in a democracy views himself—his obligations, his intentions, his ultimate self-definition.

Instead, what I would call the "managerial" conception of democracy is the predominant opinion among political scientists, sociologists, and economists, and has, through the untiring efforts of these scholars, become the conventional journalistic opinion as well. The root idea behind this managerial conception is that democracy is a "political system" (as they say) which can be adequately defined in terms of—can be fully reduced to—its mechanical arrangements. Democracy is then seen as a set of rules and procedures, and *nothing but* a set of rules and procedures, whereby majority rule and minority rights are reconciled into a state of equilibrium. If everyone follows these rules and procedures, then a democracy is in working order. I think this is a fair description of the democratic idea that currently prevails in academia. One can also fairly say that it is now the liberal idea of democracy par excellence.

I cannot help but feel that there is something ridiculous about being this kind of a democrat, and I must further confess to having a sneaking sympathy for those of our young radicals who also find it ridiculous. The absurdity is the absurdity of idolatry—of taking the symbolic for the real, the means for the end. The purpose of democracy cannot possibly be the endless functioning of its own political machinery. The purpose of any political regime is to achieve some version of the good life and the good society. It is not at all difficult to imagine a perfectly functioning democracy which answers all questions except one—namely, why should anyone of intelligence and spirit care a fig for it?

There is, however, an older idea of democracy—one which was fairly common until about the beginning of this century—for which the conception of the quality of public life is absolutely crucial. This idea starts from the proposition that democracy is a form of self-government, and that if you want it to be a meritorious polity, you have to care about what kind of people govern it. Indeed, it puts the matter more strongly and declares that if you want self-government, you are only entitled to it if that "self" is worthy of governing. There is no inherent right to self-government if it means that such government is vicious, mean, squalid, and debased. Only a dogmatist and a fanatic, an idolater of democratic machinery, could approve of self-government under such conditions.

And because the desirability of self-government depends on the character of the people who govern, the older idea of democracy was very solicitous of the condition of this character. It was solicitous of the individual self, and felt an obligation to educate it into what used to be called "republican virtue." And it was solicitous of that collective self which we

27

28

29

30

call public opinion and which, in a democracy, governs us collectively. Perhaps in some respects it was nervously oversolicitous—that would not be surprising. But the main thing is that it cared, cared not merely about the machinery of democracy but about the quality of life that this machinery might generate.

31   And because it cared, this older idea of democracy had no problem in principle with pornography and/or obscenity. It censored them—and it did so with a perfect clarity of mind and a perfectly clear conscience. It was not about to permit people capriciously to corrupt themselves. Or, to put it more precisely: In this version of democracy, the people took some care not to let themselves be governed by the more infantile and irrational parts of themselves.

32   I have, it may be noticed, uttered that dreadful word censorship. And I am not about to back away from it. If you think pornography and/or obscenity is a serious problem, you have to be for censorship. I will go even further and say that if you want to prevent pornography and/or obscenity from becoming a problem, you have to be for censorship. And lest there be any misunderstanding as to what I am saying, I will put it as bluntly as possible: If you care for the quality of life in our American democracy, then you have to be for censorship.

33   But can a liberal be for censorship? Unless one assumes that being a liberal *must* mean being indifferent to the quality of American life, then the answer has to be yes, a liberal can be for censorship—but he ought to favor a liberal form of censorship.

34   Is that a contradiction in terms? I do not think so. We have no problem in contrasting *repressive* laws governing alcohol and drugs and tobacco with laws *regulating* (i.e., discouraging the sale of) alcohol and drugs and tobacco. Laws encouraging temperance are not the same thing as laws that have as their goal prohibition or abolition. We have not made the smoking of cigarettes a criminal offense. We have, however, and with good liberal conscience, prohibited cigarette advertising on television, and may yet, again with good liberal conscience, prohibit it in newspapers and magazines. The idea of restricting individual freedom, in a liberal way, is not at all unfamiliar to us.

35   I therefore see no reason why we should not be able to distinguish repressive censorship from liberal censorship of the written and spoken word. In Britain, until a few years ago, you could perform almost any play you wished, but certain plays, judged to be obscene, had to be performed in private theatrical clubs, which were deemed to have a "serious" interest in theater. In the United States, all of us who grew up using public libraries are familiar with the circumstances under which certain books could be circulated only to adults, while still other books had to be read in the library reading room, under the librarian's skeptical eye. In both cases, a small minority that was willing to make a serious effort to

see an obscene play or read an obscene book could do so. But the impact of obscenity was circumscribed and the quality of public life was only marginally affected.*

I am not saying it is easy in practice to sustain a distinction between liberal and repressive censorship, especially in the public realm of a democracy, where popular opinion is so vulnerable to demagoguery. Moreover, an acceptable system of liberal censorship is likely to be exceedingly difficult to devise in the United States today, because our educated classes, upon whose judgment a liberal censorship must rest, are so convinced that there is no such thing as a problem of obscenity, or even that there is no such thing as obscenity at all. But, to counterbalance this, there is the further, fortunate truth that the tolerable margin for error is quite large, and single mistakes or single injustices are not all that important.

This possibility of error, of course, occasions much distress among artists and academics. It is a fact, one that cannot and should not be denied, that any system of censorship is bound, upon occasion, to treat unjustly a particular work of art—to find pornography where there is only gentle eroticism, to find obscenity where none really exists, or to find both where its existence ought to be tolerated because it serves a larger moral purpose. Though most works of art are not obscene, and though most obscenity has nothing to do with art, there are some few works of art that are, at least in part, pornographic and/or obscene. There are also some few works of art that are in the special category of the comic-ironic "bawdy" (Boccaccio, Rabelais). It is such works of art that are likely to suffer at the hands of the censor. That is the price one has to be prepared to pay for censorship—even liberal censorship.

But just how high is this price? If you believe, as so many artists seem to believe today, that art is the only sacrosanct activity in our profane and vulgar world—that any man who designates himself an artist thereby acquires a sacred office—then obviously censorship is an intolerable form of sacrilege. But for those of us who do not subscribe to this religion of art, the costs of censorship do not seem so high at all.

If you look at the history of American or English literature, there is precious little damage you can point to as a consequence of the censorship that prevailed throughout most of that history. Very few works of literature—of real literary merit, I mean—ever were suppressed; and those that were, were not suppressed for long. Nor have I noticed, now that censor-

36

37

38

39

---

* It is fairly predictable that someone is going to object that this point of view is "elitist"—that, under a system of liberal censorship, the rich will have privileged access to pornography and obscenity. Yes, of course, they will—just as, at present, the rich have privileged access to heroin if they want it. But one would have to be an egalitarian maniac to object to this state of affairs on the grounds of equality.

ship of the written word has to all intents and purposes ceased in this country, that hitherto suppressed or repressed masterpieces are flooding the market. Yes, we can now read *Fanny Hill*[13] and the Marquis de Sade. Or, to be more exact, we can now openly purchase them, since many people were able to read them even though they were publicly banned, which is as it should be under a liberal censorship. So how much have literature and the arts gained from the fact that we can all now buy them over the counter, that, indeed, we are all now encouraged to buy them over the counter? They have not gained much that I can see.

40   And one might also ask a question that is almost never raised: How much has literature lost from the fact that everything is now permitted? It has lost quite a bit, I should say. In a free market, Gresham's Law[14] can work for books or theater as efficiently as it does for coinage—driving out the good, establishing the debased. The cultural market in the United States today is being preempted by dirty books, dirty movies, dirty theater. A pornographic novel has a far better chance of being published today than a nonpornographic one, and quite a few pretty good novels are not being published at all simply because they are not pornographic, and are therefore less likely to sell. Our cultural condition has not improved as a result of the new freedom. American cultural life was not much to brag about twenty years ago; today one feels ashamed for it.

41   Just one last point, which I dare not leave untouched. If we start censoring pornography or obscenity, shall we not inevitably end up censoring political opinion? A lot of people seem to think this would be the case— which only shows the power of doctrinaire thinking over reality. We had censorship of pornography and obscenity for 150 years, until almost yesterday, and I am not aware that freedom of opinion in this country was in any way diminished as a consequence of this fact. Fortunately for those of us who are liberal, freedom is not indivisible. If it were, the case for liberalism would be indistinguishable from the case for anarchy; and they are two very different things.

42   But I must repeat and emphasize: What kinds of laws we pass governing pornography and obscenity, what kind of censorship—or, since we are still a federal nation, what kinds of censorship—we institute in our various localities may indeed be difficult matters to cope with; nevertheless the real issue is one of principle. I myself subscribe to a liberal view of the

[13] Eighteenth-century novel by John Cleland, originally published as *Memoirs of a Woman of Pleasure* (1749). Its republication in 1963 led to court cases of censorship in three states. In 1966 the Supreme Court ruled against censorship of the book.—Ed.

[14] Law in economics that inferior currency will drive out the superior currency.—Ed.

enforcement problem: I think that pornography should be illegal *and* available to anyone who wants it so badly as to make a pretty strenuous effort to get it. We have lived with under-the-counter pornography for centuries now, in a fairly comfortable way. But the issue of principle, of whether it should be over or under the counter, has to be settled before we can reflect on the advantages and disadvantages of alternative modes of censorship. I think the settlement we are living under now, in which obscenity and democracy are regarded as equals, is wrong; I believe it is inherently unstable; I think it will, in the long run, be incompatible with any authentic concern for the quality of life in our democracy.

Reading and Analyzing

1. Kristol begins his argument (as so many begin) by establishing that a problem exists. His opening has a special twist, though. What is the problem Kristol examines? What is the twist that gives him a clever opening?
2. What is Kristol's position, the claim of his argument?
3. Whom does he hold responsible for the current situation?
4. Those opposing censorship, in Kristol's view, end up "in a mindless insistence on the absurd." What "absurd" or contradictory idea do they hold?
5. How does Kristol define *pornography? Obscenity?* These are complex definitions; be certain that you can explain them in your own words.
6. What does language tell us about the usual human response to "private parts"? What can we learn from primitive cultures about human attitudes toward sex?
7. Why should pornography be viewed as a form of sexism?
8. For what two reasons does Kristol reject the idea that the current popularity of pornography and obscenity will dissipate with time? Explain each reason in your own words.
9. Why, ultimately, should we favor censorship?
10. What does Kristol mean by a "liberal form of censorship"? By what argument does he justify the errors that will occur under this form of censorship?

Responding to the Writer's Ideas

1. Kristol asserts that "none of us is a complete civil libertarian." Unqualified statements are risky; is this one you will accept? Why or why not?

2. Do you accept Kristol's definition of pornography? Is it a clear, working definition? Can we be certain of a work's purpose?

3. Do you agree that pornography and obscenity are "suffusing our entire culture"? Do we have a serious problem that needs to be addressed? Defend your answer.

4. Kristol defends censorship on two philosophical concepts: the quality of life and a definition of democracy as a form of self-government. Do you agree with both concepts, or neither, or do you find one more convincing than the other? Explain.

5. Has Kristol altered your thinking in any way about pornography? If so, how? If not, why not?

6. Kristol's idea of a liberal censorship establishes essentially three positions: no censorship, a liberal censorship, or a more widespread or rigid censorship. Where do you stand on the issue? Why?

❖

Stories the Public Has No
Right to Know

Nat Hentoff

Nat Hentoff (b. 1925) has been a staff writer of the Village Voice *for many years and a* Washington Post *columnist since 1984. Also an author of articles and books on jazz and education, Hentoff is best-known for his syndicated columns on First Amendment issues. One of his "Sweet Land of Liberty" columns, the following defense of media discretion appeared on April 18, 1992.*

After the paper had gone to bed, several New York reporters were sitting in the newsroom telling—without guilt—of stories they had deprived the public of its constitutional right to know, or so our editor at the time had said.   1

One of us had interviewed a former powerful figure in Washington. That person had been out of the news and out of Washington for several years. As the interview proceeded, the person's accounts of civil wars in the administration the interviewee had served sounded disjointed, inconsistent, incoherent. "I realized," the reporter said, "that I was watching someone in the midst of a nervous breakdown or a clinical depression or something very frightening."   2

The reporter told the editor of the paper that there would be no story. The public did not have the right to know, she said, that someone no longer in power was falling apart. The editor was angry and demanded the notes of the interview. The reporter refused. No further action was taken.   3

I told of getting a call early one Saturday morning—a couple of years before gay liberation took hold—from a desk sergeant I knew. "Have I got a story for you!" he said. There had been a routine police raid on a gay bar, and a U.S. senator from another state had been among those packed into a holding cell. The only charge against him and the others arrested was that they were associating with each other. In those days, the First Amendment did not apply to gays.   4

The sergeant gave me the name of the senator. He was well-known, with particular expertise in a field that had nothing to do with homosexuality. He had never denounced that sexual preference, as far as I knew. At that time, if I had run the story, it was very likely that the senator would   5

189

never have been reelected. He might even have had to resign before the end of his term.

6   I did not print the story. I knew that the desk sergeant might well call other reporters with the news, but I felt as William O. Douglas did when he refused to tailor his views to gain a majority on the Supreme Court. "The only soul I have to save is my own," Douglas would say. As it happened, no one else did get the story of the senator's night out, and the republic did not fall.

7   I thought of the senator when Arthur Ashe was forced to give up his privacy because he falls, as he puts it, "under the dubious umbrella of 'public figure.'" Some journalists I have spoken to say that they would not have printed the story, but Sheryl McCarthy of *Newsday* spoke for many reporters and editors when she said the *USA Today* reporter who prepared the story was "just doing his job."

8   The job description, then, entails no possibility, however slight, that not all reporting jobs of this sort are the same because not all illnesses are the same; not all consequences of banner headlines concerning them are the same. And indeed, not all degrees of being a public figure are the same. A reporter, according to conventional journalistic standards, is programmed—like a mechanical greyhound on a track.

9   On the other hand, the New York *Post* is regarded by some as just this side of the newspapers that carry stories about three-headed Martian babies and are sold at supermarket checkout counters. Yet that paper's executive editor, Lou Colasuonno, said: "The *Post* is not in the business of outing people, whether it be their sexuality or their private medical condition."

10   He apparently would be in a minority among the editors of much higher-minded papers. Alex S. Jones of the New York *Times* reported in a spot check that only one of six editors he surveyed in Washington—at the annual convention of the American Society of Newspaper Editors—would not have published the news that Arthur Ashe has AIDS.

11   Jane Healy, associate editor of the Orlando *Sentinel,* explained how editors figure out how to do the right thing. "I can't imagine knowing that information and keeping it quiet," she said. "I think a lot of it comes down to whether there is a real public issue here rather than just titillating the public."

12   What *is* the public issue in printing and broadcasting that Arthur Ashe has AIDS? I would have thought an issue to be debated is privacy, but I am obviously misguided. Is the issue AIDS? Does every public figure with AIDS, as a form of public service conscription, have to be outed so that he can be recruited into the prestigious ranks of those educating the public on how to deal with AIDS?

13   Or, is it at all possible that *USA Today* was about to break the story—as so many papers would have—to give the public a special *frisson* at breakfast. "I read the news today. Oh, boy."

Reading and Analyzing

1. What was the occasion for the writing of this column; that is, what story had just been published?
2. What is Hentoff's attitude toward the press's coverage of private facts about public figures? State the claim of his argument.
3. How does Hentoff develop his argument? What is his primary strategy?
4. According to Hentoff, what, apparently, accounts for reports and editors choosing to publish such facts as Ashe's AIDS condition?
5. Hentoff writes that "a reporter, according to conventional journalistic standards, is programmed—like a mechanical greyhound on a track." What writing technique does he use in this sentence? What attitude toward journalists is revealed by this sentence?
6. The author does not establish specific criteria for determining what stories should not be published. What guidelines can be inferred from the examples he gives and from his comments on the concept of the "public figure"?

Responding to the Writer's Ideas

1. Would you say that all or only some of Hentoff's examples (the former Washington insider, the gay senator, Arthur Ashe) qualify as public figures? If you agree that one or more of these men is not a public figure, then would you, as a reporter or editor, have repressed the story? Should the private lives of private citizens be kept from public knowledge?
2. Clearly the gay senator was a public figure at the time he was arrested (and just as clearly Arthur Ashe is the hardest to categorize); should the sexual orientation of the one and the medical condition of the other become public knowledge? Why or why not?
3. If you agree with Hentoff that some stories should not be published, what guidelines would you establish for journalists?
4. What are some ways to implement guidelines for *not* publishing stories? Are there strategies other than teaching a different code of ethics in journalism classes? What, if any, strategies for implementation are appropriate?
5. Whether or not you agree with Hentoff's position, who do you think is responsible for the situation? Are the reporters to blame? The editors? The consumers—we who read or listen to the news? If consumers want to read about the private lives of well-known figures, is it fair to ask journalists to be "better" than their customers? Why or why not?

❖

Is Pornography a Matter of
Free Expression?

Patty McEntee

Patty McEntee (b. 1961) graduated from college in communications and has been director of public relations for Morality in Media, Inc., a nonprofit organization working to stop pornography. A victim of date rape, McEntee became an activist first by founding a Morality in Media chapter on Long Island, New York, and then taking the position with the national organization. In the following article, published in the August 10, 1991, issue of America, *the author argues for restricting pornographic materials.*

1   On a typical day in New York City, my senses are assaulted by pornographic material almost continuously. On my way to work, I pass newstands with racks of porn magazines, one more explicit than the next. I pick up a newspaper and flip past advertisements for dial-a-porn "services," erotic dancing clubs and video stores with "adult" sections. Small cards advertising dial-a-porn are occasionally scattered all over the sidewalk or placed on car windshields. When I turn on the television, I may come across a talk show host respectfully interviewing porn movie "actresses" or the producers of the homemade porn movies that are now on the shelves of my local video store. Every so often, the mailman delivers an unsolicited envelope of full-color ads for the latest porn videos that are now available through the mail.

2   While not all this material is available in every neighborhood, hi-tech advances have made it almost impossible to shield oneself completely from the pornography industry and its products. What's more, newscasts regularly interview distributors who claim it is their right to display and promote the sale of these items. But whose rights are at stake here? Most Americans get only one side of the story and are repeatedly fed the clichés and distortions of the very people profiting from pornography. So, let's take a look at "censorship," the First Amendment, pornography and obscenity.

3   If I refuse to shop in my neighborhood stationery store because it sells pornographic magazines, am I a "censor"? If Morality In Media (MIM) encourages citizens to urge their district attorney to enforce their state's obscenity law, is it guilty of "censorship"? Although it may surprise

some people, the answer is no. The word censorship has been misused ad nauseam. Censorship is *prior* restraint *by government* of freedom of speech or the press.

Although civil libertarians may not like to say so, the First Amendment is not without limits. Obscenity, slander, libel, perjury, inciting a riot and false advertising are not within the area of constitutionally protected speech or freedom of the press.

"Pornography" is a generic term that includes both hardcore and softcore porn. "Obscenity" is the legal term for "hardcore" pornography, and obscenity is not protected by the First Amendment. Another legal term is "indecency," and it is prohibited in broadcasting (radio and television). The Federal Communications Commission (F.C.C.) has defined indecency as "language or material that depicts or describes, in terms patently offensive as measured by contemporary community standards for the broadcast medium, sexual or excretory activities or organs."

The F.C.C. has also imposed fines on those who broadcast indecency. This 24-hour ban on indecency is, however, currently being challenged in the Federal Court of Appeals in Washington, D.C., by the American Civil Liberties Union, People for the American Way, the television networks and a group ironically calling itself "Action for Children's Television." Morality In Media believes, on the contrary, that the potential flow of indecent broadcasts into the nation's living rooms is a great threat to the country's moral well-being. If the 24-hour indecency ban is struck down, television depictions of oral sex, sodomy, orgies, sadomasochism and bestiality could become commonplace by the turn of the century.

According to the U.S. Supreme Court, materials or performances are "obscene" if: (a) taken as a whole, they appeal to the prurient interest; (b) depict or describe in a patently offensive manner sexual conduct specifically defined, or (c) taken as a whole, lack serious literary, artistic, political and scientific value. Obscenity may apply to magazines, videos, dial-a-porn, cableporn or live performances.

Throughout our history, the Supreme Court, no matter whether characterized as conservative, moderate or liberal, has held that obscenity is not protected by the First Amendment. In 1973, the Court stated: "We hold that there are legitimate state interests at stake in stemming the tide of commercialized obscenity. . . . These include the interest of the public in the quality of life and the total community environment, . . . and, possibly, the public safety itself. . . . There is a 'right of the nation and the states to maintain a decent society.' . . . The sum of experience, including that of the past two decades, affords an ample basis for legislatures to conclude that a sensitive, key relationship of human existence, central to family life, community welfare and the development of the human personality, can be debased and distorted by crass commercial exploitation of sex."

9   In recent years, Federal law enforcement against illegal pornography (obscenity) has increased substantially. Major law enforcement efforts are still needed, however, at the state or local (district attorney) level. Nor are these the only effective measures that can be taken. Meetings with store owners, picketing, public seminars to educate the community and counseling groups for pornography addicts and their wives are also useful. These efforts may be labeled "censorship" by those who don't know what censorship is or who want to confuse the public. But does not our freedom as persons and citizens include the right to try to influence others for good, the right to rebel against total decadence and the right to preserve our cherished Judeo-Christian values? Is it not our *right* to protect our children from sexual abuse and exploitation? Have we not the *right* to try to create safer and more decent communities for these children? It sometimes seems, however, that the right to raise children has taken a back seat to the so-called "right" to distribute hardcore pornography despite a local community's protests.

10   Studies indicate that porn addicts are 40 percent more likely to commit a sex crime than non-addicts, but these are not the only damages that pornography inflicts on our society. Men addicted to porn lose faith in marriage and commitment and are more likely to have extramarital affairs or to visit prostitutes. They think convicted rapists should be given lighter sentences and they persuade themselves that sexual perversions are more common than is the fact ("Everyone's doing it"). Not surprisingly, the marriages of these men often end in divorce.

11   Attorney General Richard Thornburgh said that enforcement of pornography laws would be one of his top five priorities, but the battle continues. Pornography is still a business that makes from $9 billion to $10 billion annually in the United States. It is the third largest profit maker for organized crime after drugs and gambling. As Federal Judge Jose Gonzales remarked in the recent obscenity trial of the 2 Live Crew rap group: "This is a case between two ancient enemies: 'anything goes' and 'enough already!'"

12   That conviction of "enough already" is now widespread. Common sense perceives that pornography is related to sex crimes, promiscuity and the devaluation of committed marriages and family life. Citizens everywhere are tired of the pornographic assault. Since the obscenity law is grounded in contemporary community standards, it is vital that communities loudly and clearly protest against the invasion of their homes and neighborhoods by illegal pornography. If they do not, their silence may be misinterpreted as acceptance.

13   Protests of this sort have grown stronger each year with the Morality In Media-sponsored White Ribbon Against Pornography (WRAP) Campaign.

14   In 1987, a woman named Norma Norris sat in St. Paul's Roman Catholic Church in Butler, Pa., and listened to her pastor, Msgr. Francis

Glenn, lament the pornography epidemic. He said that the local district attorney actually thought people didn't care because he rarely received a complaint. As Norma Norris thought of her 2,000 fellow-parishioners, she concluded, "That can't be—they must care!" She decided then and there to come up with a way to express the community's true standard. Thus was born the WRAP Campaign. It was a huge success that first year in Butler, and it was launched nationally by MIM in 1988.

Last year's WRAP Campaign enrolled over five million partici-   15
pants from all 50 states in activities such as letter-writing campaigns; the display of a white ribbon in porn-free stores; proclamations from governors and mayors; motorcades flying the ribbon from car antennas; presentations of white bows to district attorneys who support obscenity-law enforcement and public seminars in which citizens heard the testimonies of pornography's victims, including reformed porn addicts and former porn actresses. The WRAP campaign continues to expand and is now promoted by groups in Australia, Canada, France and Switzerland. The 1991 WRAP Campaign, Oct. 27–Nov. 3, promises to be the largest yet.

From time immemorial, symbols have conveyed crucial messages.   16
During the Persian Gulf War, support for U.S. troops was symbolized by a yellow ribbon. The white ribbon symbolizes a battle still being fought here at home—the battle against the dehumanizing forces of pornography that strike at the soul of America. Morality In Media urges every citizen to join this moral struggle by taking part in the WRAP Campaign against illegal hardcore pornography.

Reading and Analyzing

1. What does the writer seek to accomplish in the opening two paragraphs? Where does she announce her subject?
2. What is McEntee's attitude toward her subject? Where does she state her claim?
3. McEntee defines several key terms early in her essay. Why is it important to define *censorship* as a part of her argument?
4. What is the relationship between the terms *pornography* and *obscenity*? What, legally, is meant by *indecency*? How does it fit into the issue of First Amendment restrictions?
5. What steps would the author like to see taken at the community level to reduce the amount of illegal pornography? On what argument does she defend these activities?
6. According to McEntee pornography contributes to what social problems? What evidence does she provide? Is the evidence convincing?

7. Analyze McEntee's article as a problem-solution argument. What steps (see Chapter 3) does she include, and what paragraphs are devoted to each step? What solution does she offer?

Responding to the Writer's Ideas

1. In paragraph 12, McEntee asserts that "common sense perceives that pornography is related to sex crimes." Does the appeal to common sense make an effective argument here? What readers are likely to accept common sense as evidence?
2. McEntee also writes that "citizens everywhere are tired of the pornographic assault." Does your experience coincide with this statement? If not, are you prepared to accept it, nonetheless, as probably true? If not, to what extent, if any, does the statement weaken the author's argument as a whole?
3. Were you aware that obscenity and indecency are illegal? Do you anticipate that indecency laws will be struck down? Rather than eliminating the law altogether, what may be more likely to change?
4. Compare this argument to Barbara Dority's argument that follows. Which writer comes closest to expressing your views on this subject? Which writer, in your view, makes the best argument for her position? Defend your answer.
5. Irving Kristol (see pp. 176–87) argues that pornography should be available to those willing to make some effort to obtain it "under the table." However, McEntee asserts that today's technology makes it hard for us to avoid pornography. Does the nature of modern communication technology make Kristol's solution unrealistic? Does it follow that further regulation and/or more aggressive law enforcement is appropriate? If so, what action would you recommend? If not, why not?

❖

Feminist Moralism, "Pornography," and Censorship

Barbara Dority

Barbara Dority (b. 1949), a community organizer and activist, speaks and writes regularly on First Amendment issues. Dority is a founding member and cochairperson of the Northwest Feminist Anti-Censorship Taskforce based in Seattle; she frequently writes op-ed pieces for newspapers; and she writes a regular column, "Civil Liberties Watch," for the Humanist. *Her article, opposing the regulation of pornographic materials, appeared in the* Humanist *in 1989.*

The issue of "pornography" has engendered an intense debate within the feminist movement. Will feminism, having achieved some significant gains, continue to capitulate to moralistic forces, or will it wake up and take a stand for the liberation of women in all domains, including the difficult and often contradictory domain of sexual expression?

Two separate issues are involved in this debate: first, the moralistic feminist condemnation of "pornography"; and, second, the translation of that condemnation by nearly all feminist leaders into calls for various kinds of legislation which would effectively ban "pornographic" imagery and words. Both issues are alarming.

As a feminist secular humanist and a card-carrying member of the American Civil Liberties Union, I believe the writers of the First Amendment meant every word exactly and literally: "Congress shall make no law . . . abridging the freedom of speech or of the press. . . ." No law means *no law.*

The First Amendment does not say there is to be freedom of speech and press provided they are not sexually explicit, offensive, dangerous, or degrading. The authors of the Bill of Rights had learned firsthand why it was absolutely necessary to permit all manner of ideas to be expressed in the new republic. They knew this guarantee could not be confined to the expression of ideas that are conventional or shared by the majority but must include even those ideas considered repugnant or socially undesirable.

In the words of Justice William O. Douglas: "This demands that government keep its hands off all literature. There can be no freedom of expression unless all facets of life can be portrayed, no matter how repulsive these disclosures may be to some people." Justice Douglas later added that, in addition to freedom from government intervention, all manner of literature must remain available in the marketplace of ideas or the purpose of free expression is defeated. In other words, if we protect only the right to publish and then limit availability, we are still limiting freedom of speech.

6   The moralistic pro-censorship mindset has remained the same throughout the history of civilization. The censors aim at protecting us from the perceived harmful effects of what we read, see, and hear. Historically, they did this to protect our souls from blasphemy or society from alien political, social, or economic ideas. Today, it is being done to protect us from explicit sexual imagery and words. The justification, however, remains the same: it is best for us and best for society.

7   The highly subjective term *pornography* is grossly overused and abused. A wide range of materials has been so classified by feminists and summarily condemned, boycotted, picketed, and even banned.

8   The definition of *pornography* from Webster is: "The depiction of erotic behavior (as in pictures or writing) intended to cause sexual excitement." The blanket condemnation of all such materials is cause for grave concern. Obviously, this would include a great deal of advertising, network television, art, film, and a vast array of magazines, books, and videos. Indeed, many feminists have condemned most mainstream advertising and film as degrading and harmful to women. Most members of the feminist movement endorse and promote Minneapolis-style "anti-pornography" ordinances. Many feminists are committed full-time to these pursuits.

9   Despite their claims to a mandate, these women do not speak for all feminists. Scores of women and men dropped out (or were forced out) of the feminist movement when the Equal Rights Amendment was defeated and attention shifted to moralizing and "pornography." We will never know how many feminists were lost to activism, or never activated, as a result of this departure from our basic goals and principles.

10   Many of us believe that feminism and civil liberties are inextricable. We remind our sisters that history has repeatedly shown that censorship and suppression work directly against feminist goals and are always used to limit women's rights in the name of protection. If such censorship laws are passed, we would create the illusion that something is being done to end sexism and sexual violence—a harmful effect in itself.

11   We ask: whose definitions shall we use? Who will decide? Who will make all the necessary individual judgments? Who will distinguish "dehumanizing, objectifying, degrading" materials from "erotica"?

12   Many leaders in the feminist movement assert that the message of all "pornography," even "soft-core," is that women are slaves whose bodies are for sale and available to be used and degraded. Again, this is not the

only feminist view. For example, many feminists do *not* believe that *Playboy* and *Penthouse* are sexist, or that the presentation of the naked female body, whether or not in "inviting positions," is intrinsically sexist. We do not believe that sexually explicit photos and words are intrinsically exploitative, degrading, or objectifying.

Many feminist leaders tell us that "pornography" is sex discrimination and hate literature against women—a violation of women's civil rights. But the history and intent of civil rights law and case law are clear: discrimination is not what people say or write about other people; it is what people *do* to other people. Individuals cannot be persecuted, censored, or condemned for their ideas. In a free society, there are no crimes of thought—only crimes of action.

Certainly some materials are offensive and degrading to many women, and few would claim that sex discrimination and oppression of women no longer exist in our culture. But many materials are offensive and degrading to *men,* blatantly promoting not only their oppression but their brutalization. There are aspects of our culture that oppress Indians, Hispanics, Asians, and homosexuals. Anti-Semitic literature is inarguably harmful to Jews, as is racist literature to blacks. Are we going to offer men and racial, ethnic, and religious minorities a civil right to suppress speech which they find objectionable?

Many feminists tell us that "pornography" *causes* sexism and violence against women. But this claim draws on simplistic behaviorist psychology and has been repeatedly discredited by reputable specialists in sexual behavior. Even the notorious Meese commission reported that no such causal link can be substantiated. Sexist and violent materials are *symptoms* of a sexist and violent society—not the causes.

The claim that certain forms of expression are dangerous and an incitement to violence has been used time after time to try to prohibit speech that some people don't like. Although some of us do not support this exception to the First Amendment, the notion of "a clear and present danger" was evolved to address this threat. For "pornography" to be suppressed under this test, we would have to demonstrate that any viewer is likely to be provoked to sexual violence immediately upon seeing it.

Anecdotal stories of sex offenders who are found to possess "pornography" are often cited. As Sol Gordon has pointed out, a large percentage of these offenders are also found to possess milk in their refrigerators. Sporadic incidents do not prove a correlation, nor does a correlation prove causation.

Even if it is assumed that a small percentage of people are "encouraged" to engage in sexist behavior or commit violent acts after exposure to certain books or films, this still would not justify suppression. Such a "pervert's veto" would threaten a broad range of literature and film. A free society must accept the risks that come with liberty.

19   People receive different messages from sexually explicit material, and it is ridiculous and dangerous to conclude that a picture or an idea will have the same effect on all viewers or readers. Charles Manson testified that he was inspired by the biblical Book of Revelation to commit multiple murders. Youths involved in interracial street fights have said that viewing *Roots* led them to commit their crimes. John Hinckley testified that he knew he had to kill Ronald Reagan after reading *Catcher in the Rye*.

20   If viewing and reading sexually explicit and violent materials caused people to become sex criminals, all the members of the Meese commission would now be dangerous sexual predators. The same would be true of the many sociologists who study this material, countless persons who create, publish, and disseminate it, mental health professionals who work with sex offenders, and all the moralists—on the right and the left—who pore over these materials as they analyze them for the rest of us.

21   In many repressive countries—whether in Central America, Asia, Africa, eastern Europe, or the Middle East—there is practically no "pornography." But there is a great deal of sexism and violence against women. In the Netherlands and Scandinavia, where there are almost no restrictions on sexually explicit materials, the rate of sex-related crime is much lower than in the United States. "Pornography" is virtually irrelevant to the existence of sexism and violence.

22   Nor does a causal relationship exist between an increase in the availability of "pornography" and inequality for women. While "pornography" has increased over the past fifty years, the rights of women have jumped dramatically.

23   "Violent pornography" is viewed by many as the most offensive form of expression. But it can be seen in two ways: as the depiction of consensual sadomasochism or as the depiction of actual coercion and violence against nonconsenting persons. If the latter, *the actual perpetrators of the violence or coercion* have broken the law and should be prosecuted to its full extent. However, not everyone sees the degradation of women in depictions of "violent" sexual activity. What some find degrading, others may find erotic.

24   Human sexual behavior is very complicated. In our society, and all over the world, consenting adults exist who like to engage in sadomasochistic activity and who do so of their own free will. They enjoy publications which depict or describe this behavior. For them, these activities are not designed to degrade or promote violence against women *or men* but, rather, to satisfy a sexual need of the participants. It is not a crime or an issue subject to moral judgment to fantasize about rape, or even for two consenting adults to choose to enact a pretend rape. It is not anyone's right to judge the private sexual fantasies, inclinations, or activities of other consenting adults.

We are told we must especially condemn materials depicting (usually simulated) violence to prove that we are opposed to violence against women. We must, many feminists say, condemn nearly all sexually explicit materials as degrading to women and label "pornography" a principal cause of women's oppression in order to retain our credentials as feminists.

Many feminist humanist women and men refuse to do this. We believe it is possible to be feminists dedicated to equal rights and the elimination of violence against women while defending the freedom of all kinds of sexual expression. It is a tragedy that the feminist movement has been drawn into an anti-sex stance, condemning "deviant" sexual representation and expression. We are horrified by the assertion of many feminists that male sexuality is inherently destructive, violent, and "prorape." We are appalled by the condemnation of men who enjoy "pornography" as sexist and anti-humanist or, in the case of women, by the assertion that they are "brainwashed by patriarchy."

This Victorian imagery—pure women controlling the vile, lustful impulses of men and being unable to think for themselves—is a feminine stereotype we should be working against. In this analysis, women cannot ever freely choose to have sex with men or use "male-identified" imagery in their sexual fantasies or practices. Certainly they cannot freely choose to earn their living by inviting the rapacious male gaze or providing sexual services to men.

Many feminist women and men believe it is moralistic, insulting, and inaccurate to maintain that no "normal" woman rationally chooses or consensually participates in the sex industry. This moralistic position alienates not only women in the sex industry but also women who create their own sexual pleasure without regard for its "political correctness."

We believe that this moralism and the attendant calls for censorship have seriously undermined the integrity of our movement. Being a feminist means being against sexism—not sex. In *Against Sadomasochism*, feminist Ti Grace Atkinson says, "I do not know any feminist worthy of that name who, forced to choose between freedom and sex, would choose sex." This is the choice being presented to feminist women and men. In so doing, the movement betrays its principles and destroys its credibility.

Many of us insist on the right to choose *both* freedom *and* sexuality. We call upon other feminist humanists to do likewise.

Author's note: The access of minors to sexually explicit material is a complex issue which would require another article for proper examination. The Supreme Court has held that minors' access to legally "obscene" materials is not protected by the First Amendment. The Court's nebulous and subjective definition of *obscenity* raises even more definitional problems, and a vast array of materials are currently restricted on the basis of this seriously flawed definition. These restrictions, instituted to protect minors, inevitably affect the freedom of adults. *Legally,* the burden of preventing the exposure of children to offensive or "pornographic" materials *should* rest with parents; as a *practical* matter, parents *must* assume this responsibility.

Reading and Analyzing

1. What subject does Dority examine? How does she choose to divide the issue?
2. What is the author's attitude toward her subject? What words in paragraphs 1 and 2 reveal her attitude?
3. What is Dority's thesis? Where does she state it?
4. The author identifies herself as a "feminist secular humanist" and a member of the ACLU. What does she hope to gain by this? Consider her audience.
5. Why does the author always put the term *pornography* in quotation marks?
6. Summarize Dority's explanation of the meaning and requirements of the First Amendment. What is required to maintain freedom of expression?
7. What has been and continues to be the justification of censorship?
8. According to Dority, what have the antipornography feminists done to the feminist movement?
9. Why are many feminists today opposing pornography? What is Dority's answer to them? What distinction does she make regarding discrimination?
10. What does Dority seek to accomplish when she writes that "some materials are offensive and degrading to many women, and few would claim that sex discrimination and oppression of women no longer exist in our culture"? Why, in spite of this observation, does she refuse to join feminists who oppose pornography? What, for Dority, is the more important fight to fight?
11. Summarize Dority's argument against repression of "pornographic" film and literature. What strategies for ascertaining cause does she use in paragraphs 18–20? (See Chapter 1 for a discussion of causal argument.)
12. The author makes her point quite strongly in her final six paragraphs. What elements of style does she use in these paragraphs to express her position forcefully?

Responding to the Writer's Ideas

1. Dority asserts that pornography that is violent and sexist is not a *cause* of sexism and violence but a *symptom*. Patty McEntee (see pp. 192–95) says that pornography is related to sex crimes. Who is right? Which writer provides the best defense of her assertion? What is the difference between a correlation and a cause? Are you prepared to embrace a position based on one of these articles?

2. The author provides a note regarding "access of minors to sexually explicit material" in which she asserts that parents must take responsibility for protecting their children, practically and legally. Do you agree, or do you think that the society has the legal right and responsibility to protect children from pornography? How would Mill answer this question? If you think that legal restrictions are appropriate, what restrictions would you enact and how would you enforce them? For example, should stores selling porn to minors be fined? Closed down? What about record stores? Or should there be prior censorship of some music and musical videos? What about MTV?

3. Do you agree with Dority that women can be feminists and support the right of others to pornography, or do you share the view of many feminists that they must fight for restrictions on pornographic materials? Defend your position.

The Public and Its Art

John J. Conley, S.J.

*Holding a master's in theology and a Ph.D. in philosophy from
Louvain University in Belgium, Father John Conley (b. 1951) is an
assistant professor of philosophy at Fordham University. He has
published articles on aesthetics, French social philosophy, and ethics
and society in both scholarly and popular journals. In "The Public and
Its Art," published in* Current *in February 1991, Conley makes a case
for some restrictions on public-sponsored art.*

1   The public sponsorship of art raises a series of aesthetic, moral and
political problems. The relationship between public sponsor and commissioned artist has long been stormy. Plato wanted the state to expel the per-
nicious artist in the *Republic,* but to employ the artist for educational purposes in the *Laws.* The medieval church fostered the arts as a privileged
means to glorify God, yet questioned the religious orthodoxy of certain religious works by Michelangelo or El Greco.

2   The contemporary democratic city has made the public sponsorship
of art even more complex. Unlike certain homogeneous societies, the contemporary city defines itself by its ethnic diversity and credal pluralism. In
this merry Babel, the public patron cannot construct a unique temple, or
even a single museum, to fill the naked public square. The recent squabbles
over the "Tilted Arc" at Javits Plaza or the "Many Faces of AIDS" exhibit
in New York City indicate the dilemma of the public urban sponsor. Unlike the private patron, the public sponsor subsidizes works with money
collected from taxpayers rather than with voluntary contributions.

3   Further, the public sponsor chooses works in a framework of values
that are not uniquely aesthetic. Governmental policies concerning the urban
environment, education or ethnic inclusiveness shape the public sponsorship of art. Serving a disparate citizenry that often interprets public art as a
symbolic representation of itself, the public sponsor faces the thorny mission of promoting worthwhile art that benefits all and harms none.

Criteria for Sponsorship

4   To clarify the problem of public urban art, one may examine several
criteria that should guide the public sponsor in the choice of works to
commission or subsidize. Like any patron, a sponsor must (1) evaluate the

formal qualities of the work proposed. The public sponsor, however, must attend to several other criteria of artistic choice; (2) the appropriateness of the work in the framework of public policy; (3) the representativity of artists and style, given the particular ethnic-credal mix of the city; (4) a moral sensitivity to the citizens who fund and experience the work.

The first criterion is *formal*. The public sponsor must evaluate the   5
quality of the work on the basis of its intrinsic values. The evaluation of a painting must attend to the qualities of color, texture and perspective that constitute its formal surface. The judgment of a novel must examine the qualities of prose, characterization and narrative structure that distinguish the literary work. The assessment of a piece of sculpture or architecture must weigh the evidence of integrity, proportion and radiance that characterize its *formal* structure.

This formalist scrutiny of the work constitutes the distinctively aes-   6
thetic moment of public evaluation. The formalist analysis underlines the autonomy of art. In the formalist perspective, the value of a work cannot be reduced to the moral or political veracity of its "message." The work's aesthetic value resides in the quality of its internal organization.

This respect for the formal qualities of a work distinguishes a proper-   7
ly artistic analysis from an instrumental analysis, which simply considers the work a tool of social edification. Mature aesthetic judgment requires the public, as well as the private, judge to distinguish between the formal qualities of a work and the ideology that the work appears to communicate. A capitalist might well appreciate the dramatic structure of Brecht's Mother Courage, while simultaneously denouncing its Marxist theory of history. A Jewish theater-goer might admire the verse of The Merchant of Venice, while criticizing its anti-Semitic stereotypes. A devout Catholic might relish the musical finesse of Massenet's *Thaïs*, while objecting to the opera's puerile anticlerical text. But the exclusion or minimizing of such formalist analysis of a work by the public sponsor risks reducing public art to that of servant for political propaganda in the crankiest tradition of social realism.

Appropriateness

The public sponsor, however, cannot limit evaluation of art to the   8
sole criterion of its formal value. Other criteria legitimately complement, without suppressing, the prime aesthetic measure. The criterion of *appropriateness* assesses the artwork within the framework of the sociopolitical project developed by public authority. In this context, the public sponsor judges the work according to its capacity to fulfill certain goals of the city's cultural, recreational and educational programs.

The criterion of appropriateness emerges most clearly in artworks   9
commissioned by public authority in a program of public works. Every contemporary city has designed, through law and ordinance, a particular

physical and cultural environment for itself. When choosing sculpture for a park or murals for a municipal building or musical compositions for a civic event, the public sponsor may not limit its judgment to purely aesthetic criteria. It must squarely assess whether a proposed work fosters the goals of a particular municipal project.

10   The criterion of appropriateness for the public patronage of art is especially prominent in educational programs. The city routinely funds thousands of school-based orchestras, theatrical groups, art studios and dance troupes. Obviously, the school-based art programs serve in part to cultivate the artistic appreciation and talent of the students. However, these programs are integrated into the broader pedagogical project of the city: the integral formation of the student in intellectual, moral and civic virtue. In choosing artistic works and programs for the school, the public sponsor must weigh heavily the pedagogical appropriateness of the candidate. From the pedagogical perspective, a school-wide finger-painting contest, organized by an amateur artist, might outweigh the value of a professional oil portrait of the school's founder in the main lobby.

11   Ideally, the criterion of appropriateness will prove complementary to the criterion of aesthetic form in the public sponsorship of art. On occasion, however, the criteria conflict. The howling dispute over the Tilted Arc in 1985 illustrates the problem. This enormous curved wall, which intersected Javits Plaza in New York City, provoked an uproar from Government workers in surrounding buildings. At subsequent hearings, they complained that the arc delayed their entry to and exit from their places of work. More tellingly, they argued that "the wall" had destroyed the former social life on the plaza, the sole place in a dreary urban complex where workers could soak up the sun, eat lunch and chat with friends outdoors. The artist, Richard Serra, defended his work as site-specific. The artistic community generally defended the right of an artist to maintain the integrity of his or her work, especially in the face of a hostile public.

12   This dispute reflects the dilemma of the public patron. Art cannot simply be judged as a utilitarian object whose sole purpose is to facilitate public business, like a fire hydrant or a trash can. On the other hand—and this is where the artistic community's prim aestheticism wears thin—publicly commissioned art incorporates a work into a specific political project. In this case, the General Services Administration commissioned the sculpture to enhance the aesthetics and conviviality of a densely used urban space. If the palpable result of the arc's placement is contrary to this aim, the complaints of the aggrieved users at least deserve careful attention. The public sponsor could reasonably decide that the work, while distinguished by undoubted qualities of shape and perspective, simply fails to fulfill its designated function.

Representativity

The third criterion, representativity, reflects the particular demands 13
of the contemporary democratic city. Because of its ethnic diversity and its
ideological pluralism, the contemporary city must carefully apportion its
public sponsorship of art to reflect the racial-credal mosaic of its populace.

In a city like New York, the search for the "balanced ticket" had 14
long influenced public aesthetics as well as electoral politics. Art commis-
sions apportion public monuments among the various religious and ethnic
groups in the city. Public sponsorship of popular artistic events, such as
neighborhood festivals or senior-citizen concerts, seeks rough demographic
balance. Municipal museums usually follow an eclectic approach to exhibitions, with a careful balance of contrasting schools and themes, in order
to reflect the city's present and past composition.

In recent years, however, the criterion of *representativity* has be- 15
come considerably more complex than the simple division of artistic
manna among competing power-blocs. In evaluating art under the
rubric of representativity, the public sponsor has increasingly underscored the voices and visions of population groups that have tended to
be excluded from the mainstream of the city's artistic life. Representativity has increasingly become a criterion of inclusiveness, not without
parallels to the political concepts of redistribution of wealth and affirmative action.

The Bronx Council on the Arts, in New York City's borough of 16
that name, for example, clearly attends to representativity in its choice
of artistic programs for funding through grants. The Council supports
an unusually high number of Hispanic projects in a wide variety of arts.
A glance at the projects indicates that the Council not only respects the
demographic weight of the Hispanic community, numerically the largest
in the borough. The tax-funded Council also promotes a number of projects based in various Hispanic dialects or focused upon different
Caribbean ethnic groups or rooted in distinctive Hispanic artistic motifs
or genres.

Rather than integrating Hispanic artists into the prevailing style of 17
the municipal artistic mainstream, as an earlier policy of civic assimilation
once attempted, the Council appears to privilege the distinctive traditions
of the disparate Hispanic communities that currently occupy much of the
Bronx. Similarly, the Bronx Museum of Art clearly favors exhibitions that
present the work of young and minority artists who would easily be overlooked by a public sponsor who primarily employs formal criteria for any
choice of projects in a competitive art mecca like New York City.

Obviously, the metamorphosis of the criterion of representativity 18
into that of inclusiveness poses certain dangers for the development of
public art. A rigid use of this criterion, comparable to a mathematical

quota, can smother formal considerations by exclusive focus upon political representation. Too heavy an emphasis upon ethnic or ideological representativity can reduce art to a smug folklorism or a series of placards for pet causes. Nonetheless, the criterion of representativity views art not only in a political, but in a distinctively democratic, perspective. Under the rubric of representativity, the public sponsor evaluates art as the symbolic representation of the city, grasped as irreducibly plural.

Moral Sensitivity

19   The final criterion, *moral sensitivity,* has recently proved the most controversial. The successive brawls over the National Endowment for the Arts funding of the Mapplethorpe, Serrano and "Many Faces of AIDS" exhibits reveals the confusion concerning the relevance of this criterion in the public sponsorship of art. For many supporters of these grants, any consideration of the moral qualities of a work, such as its putative obscenity or religious bias, transforms the public sponsor into a censor. After all, spectators are free to attend the exhibits or not. In this aesthetic-libertarian perspective, the public sponsor must evaluate art exclusively on formal criteria.

20   Although the libertarian perspective avoids the reduction of an art work to its moral "message," it inadequately treats the complex moral issues legitimately raised by public sponsored art. The libertarian critique of government censorship is askew here. Technically, state censorship restrains literary/artistic freedom in the private sphere of the city. Publicly sponsored art, however, raises a different set of issues. The question is no longer the state's intervention in privately funded and privately-facilitated interactions between the independent artist and the voluntary spectator. With public sponsorship, the state uses its tax revenue and often its tax-supported institutions to promote certain works of art.

21   It is cold comfort to a taxpayer outraged by the sexism of a film or the obscenity of an exhibition to be told that she need not attend the offensive event when she is being forced by the government to pay for it. When providing public sponsorship for art, the city legitimately ponders whether a given work grievously assaults the moral sensibilities of numerous citizens or whether it promotes certain disvalues (racism, for example) that flagrantly contradict the city's key moral-legal ideals. Even the most tolerant public sponsor cannot ignore that its choice of art serves the state's promotion of the general welfare, and that this welfare involves, in part, certain ethical concerns.

22   The following concrete cases illustrate the moral constraints that might shape the public sponsor's choice of art. A city might tolerate the private screening of "snuff" films, films that graphically depict sexual violence ending in dismemberment, but refuse to publicly fund such a film, even one technically perfect, because of the degradation of women such

films promote. A public school system might recognize the aesthetic merits of D. W. Griffith's "Birth of a Nation," yet decide that the film should not be shown to adolescents, because this film's brutal stereotypes of African-Americans might well foster racism among impressionable viewers. The National Endowment for the Arts' decision not to fund the catalogue for the "Many faces of AIDS" exhibit was rooted in several instances of religious vitriol, among which the comparison of Roman Catholics to "walking swastikas" was the most virulent. The right of artists to express sexual, racial or religious hatred does not imply a correlative duty of the state to promote such expressions.

Obviously, the attempt to exercise moral sensitivity in the public sponsorship of art raises serious problems. The use of this criterion to exclude art deemed "obscene" can easily blind the public sponsor to art whose formal qualities or striking representation of a minority viewpoint outweigh the moral offense that it may provoke among certain spectators. Further, consensus on the content of this moral sensitivity in the evaluation of art is increasingly elusive in a pluralist society where one citizen's blasphemy is another citizen's nirvana. Nonetheless, despite the practical difficulties of consensus on a particular work, public sponsors routinely weigh moral considerations in the choice of art. The most liberal public sponsor recognizes that its moral latitude is more limited than that of the private sponsor, for the simple reason that the public sponsor is employing public funds in the service of a common good broader than pure aesthetic value. The public sponsor cannot evaluate the work in total isolation from the moral horizon of the citizens who fund and will be shaped by public art. 23

In conclusion, public urban art requires an evaluation that is simultaneously autonomous and relational. As art, it manifests a form and beauty that cannot be reduced to social utility, political emblem or moral teacher. It is other. And yet, as public art of a particular city, it does build the urban landscape along with the cloverleafs. It does hold a mirror up to the city's tapestry of colors and creeds. It does touch the moral imagination along with the Decalogue. 24

Undue emphasis upon the relational criteria—those of appropriateness, representativity and moral sensitivity—risks reducing public art to the bland tool of the engineer, the party boss and the puritan. Art's integrity vanishes. But unique emphasis upon the autonomous criterion, that of form, risks another reduction. It obscures the mission of art to foster symbolic community in a city that cannot live on bread alone. 25

Reading and Analyzing

1. What is Conley's subject? What are the particular problems of the public sponsorship of art?

2. What strategy for getting started does Conley use?
3. State in your own words the four criteria that Conley establishes for sponsoring public urban art.
4. In Conley's view, on what bases do we judge a work's aesthetic value? How do these formal elements of judgment allow us to respond to various works?
5. Explain Conley's argument for appropriateness.
6. How has the concept of representativity been redefined by some sponsors in recent years? What is the potential danger to this approach? What is the advantage?
7. What problems are raised by "the attempt to exercise moral sensitivity in the public sponsorship of art"? Why, in Conley's view, must public sponsors consider the moral sensitivities of the citizens?
8. State the claim of Conley's argument.

Responding to the Writer's Ideas

1. Conley believes that all four criteria must be weighed in the public sponsorship of art. Apparently, he means that any one criterion could be a reason for rejecting a particular project. That is, a work that meets the first three criteria could be rejected because it would offend the community's moral sensitivities. Do you agree with Conley's four criteria? Why or why not? Do you agree that all should be considered equally? Why or why not?
2. Those who believe that art should be judged only by aesthetic standards argue that judgment by the criterion of moral sensitivity results in censorship of art. Should public-sponsored art be chosen in consideration of community values or not? One answer is that a community can allow morally "challenging" works but just not sponsor them with public funds. What is the response of the artistic community? Who is right? Why?
3. Conley draws his examples primarily from the visual arts. Extend his argument to books. Could his criteria result in some public libraries' deciding not to spend money on books that may offend a community, books such as *Catcher in the Rye*? Should library books be subject to Conley's criteria, or are the criteria better suited for selecting sculpture or public spaces, or works for museum shows? Explain your position.

❖

Why Tolerate Campus Bigots?

James T. Laney

*An ordained minister who holds a doctorate from Yale University,
James Laney (b. 1927) is president of Emory University in Atlanta. He
has frequently taught and written on ethics and shows his continued
interest in issues of ethical behavior in the article reprinted here from
the April 6, 1990, issue of the* New York Times. *Laney develops his
position in part by defining the university and then examining the rights
and limits of free speech within the university community.*

In recent years, life on the American campus has become ruder, less   1
civil—nastier. It has turned with the general social tide toward a more
anxious self-assertiveness that harbors little respect for the strange or different. Ominously, campuses have proven fertile ground for a renascent
bigotry, with an increasing number of racial incidents and serious crimes.

Because of this development, some universities have proscribed cer-   2
tain kinds of language and behavior. At Emory last year, we banned "discriminatory harassment," defined as "conduct (oral, written, graphic or
physical) directed against any person or group . . . that has the purpose
or reasonably foreseeable effect of creating an offensive, demeaning, intimidating, or hostile environment."

Such policies are criticized by free-speech absolutists and by people   3
who see the university as a forum where all ideas must be aired, where the
false and the odious must be defeated not by sanction but by reason.

I share the ideals of both sorts of critics. If the university stands for   4
anything, it stands for freedom in the search for truth. The university, by
its hard-won freedom from church and state, has demonstrated that truth
is best discovered by the public weighing of claim and counterclaim.

These convictions are really not at issue in the debate over free   5
speech. At issue are two other questions: Can truth have its day in court
when the courtroom is made into a mud-wrestling pit where vicious epithets are flung? And should the university be a place of such severe neutrality about values that mere volubility or numbers can carry the day?

We misconstrue the nature of the university when we operate as if it   6
were value-neutral. Educators are by definition professors of value.
Through education we pass on to the next generation not merely informa-

211

tion but the habits and manners of our civil society. The university differs from society at large in its insistence on not only free expression but also an environment conducive to mutual engagement.

7   The Supreme Court's historic exceptions to the guarantee of free speech are: language posing a "clear and present danger," libel, some forms of obscenity, the use of children in producing pornography and "fighting words." I would suggest that when a fraternity sells T-shirts that portray women in demeaning sexual positions, at least one of those historic exceptions applies.

8   What we intend is not to curb free speech but to make it more probable. To paraphrase John Stuart Mills's dictum about liberty, the restraint of free speech can be justified only if it fosters greater freedom of speech. People do not feel free to speak when they are bullied—when the message they hear is not "I disagree with you" but "I wish you didn't exist."

9   Of course we need to take great care in enforcing our policies. We need to be evenhanded, so that there is no hint of a political agenda. And the policies should serve a pedagogical purpose. There should be no prior restriction of anyone's civil address in classrooms or public meetings.

10   We need to teach adversaries how to speak to each other as members of the same community, each worthy of respect. In the university, learners should be valued as highly as learning. We must be about the business of building up wisdom and knowledge. But we cannot build up wisdom by tearing down people.

11   With care—meaning both "caution" and "nurturing"—we can prove that free speech and freedom from harassment go hand in hand.

Reading and Analyzing

1. What issue is Laney's subject? How does he establish that the issue is a problem? What appear to be causes of the problem?
2. What position has Emory University taken?
3. What groups of people oppose the banning of "discriminatory harassment"? How do they support their position?
4. How does Laney respond to his opponents? What, in his view, are the key questions in the debate?
5. What is the purpose of paragraph 4?
6. What does Laney gain by quoting the Supreme Court's exceptions to free speech? By referring to Mill's views? What is their connection to campus harassment?
7. How does Laney define the university? What should the university be teaching students?

8. Although Laney feels strongly about his university's position, he writes with restraint. What does he do—and not do—to keep to the road of reason and restraint?

Responding to the Writer's Ideas

1. Have you experienced or heard about any incidents of bigotry or harassment directed at any person or group? If so, how did you feel about it?
2. Do you agree with Laney's position? Why or why not? If you disagree, how would you refute his argument?
3. Do you agree with Laney's concepts of the university? Why or why not?
4. What is your attitude toward abusive language in any environment? Should uncivil behavior be tolerated? Why or why not? If you don't want to tolerate it, what solutions do you have to the problem?

❖

Colleges Should Seek Educational Alternatives to Rules That Override the Historic Guarantees of Free Speech

Robert M. O'Neil

A lawyer and law professor who has written extensively on First Amendment issues, Robert M. O'Neil (b. 1934) was president of the University of Virginia from 1985 to 1990. Currently he is director of the Thomas Jefferson Center for the Protection of Free Expression, at the university. His article addressing the issue of restricting free expression on college campuses appeared in the Chronicle of Higher Education *on October 18, 1989.*

1   One of our students wrote me recently to protest the presence in our student daily of an insert that she found deeply offensive. The issue, she argued, was not one of censorship; the material was blatantly sexist. "Discrimination such as this," she insisted, "must not be tolerated." She closed by asking: "What can be done about this incident?"

2   The question is a valid and recurring one at many university campuses across the country. It is a question to which the answers are curiously unsatisfying. Growing numbers of institutions have fashioned new rules to meet the challenge. Such rules may forbid religious or ethnic slurs and stereotyping or ban the use of racist or sexist language.

3   The University of Michigan's rule exemplified such approaches. Before its recent revision, it prohibited "any behavior, verbal or physical, that stigmatizes or victimizes an individual on the basis of race, ethnicity, religion, national origin, sexual orientation, creed, ancestry, age, marital status, handicap, or Vietnam-veteran status." The catalyst for the rule seems to have been an incident last spring in which anti-Semitic remarks and racist jokes were broadcast on a campus radio station; the faculty responded by insisting on more rigorous standards of speech as well as conduct.

4   The Michigan rule did not fare well in the courts. Nor did the courts have much enthusiasm for city ordinances designed several years ago to ban various forms of demeaning material under the rubric of sex discrimination. In such cases, judges found even the most laudable goals insufficient to warrant creating new exceptions to principles of free speech and press.

214

Therein lies the dilemma. The worthiest motives prompt efforts to re-   5
strict speech that may wound, or embarrass, or offend. Proponents of such
measures wish to do more than protect sensitive feelings. They wish also to
maintain or restore civility to an often uncivil environment: they are especially (and rightly) insistent on civility within the academic community.
They are uneasy about the corrosive effect of slurs and epithets on always
fragile intergroup relations in a setting where learning demands tolerance
and understanding.

All these values, and more, underlie rules directed at racist and sexist   6
speech on college campuses. The people who oppose such rules seldom
question the validity of the values or the sincerity of those who invoke
them. Instead, they point to enduring precepts of free expression that compel Americans to tolerate much speech and press that they find offensive or
abhorrent. As recently as last June, in striking down flag-desecration laws,
the Supreme Court reminded us: "If there is a bedrock principle underlying
the First Amendment, it is that Government may not prohibit the expression of an idea simply because society finds the idea itself offensive or disagreeable."

The question then becomes, at its core, whether the special interests   7
that underlie restrictive campus rules can or should override the historic
guarantees of free speech.

The answer is less clear than one might wish. Freedom of expres-   8
sion is not unqualified. Exceptions have been made over the years for
speech that poses a clear and present danger of serious harm, for obscenity, for some forms of libel, and most recently for the use of children in
producing pornography. While any such exception must be defined precisely and proved carefully, speech may be limited in such compelling situations.

None of those exceptions quite covers the issue at hand, but the   9
Supreme Court nearly 50 years ago created one other loophole that may
be more relevant in some cases—for "fighting words" or face-to-face insults likely to bring disputants to blows. That doctrine has seldom been
applied in recent years, but it remains on the books as a possible, if tenu-
ous, ground for banning racially and ethnically demeaning speech.

Finally, conduct that can be separated from expression may be pun-   10
ished even if the related speech must be tolerated. On that basis, the
Supreme Court upheld a federal law that banned destruction of draft
cards, even in protest. The problem here, is whether the conduct and the
expression can be clearly separated; the risk is that ideas or their expression may be suppressed in the guise of regulating behavior.

In this context, the recent campus rules raise constitutional concerns   11
of two types. The definition of the forbidden activity often leaves much to
be desired; the federal judge who recently ruled against the University of
Michigan's rule found its terms unacceptably vague and imprecise.

12   The other flaw is more basic: Most such rules do not rest upon, or limit their terms to, the categories of expression that fall outside constitutionally protected speech or press. Such rules may include, but do not stop with, words that are obscene, defamatory, or almost certain to provoke a fight. To the degree that they go beyond the recognized exceptions, they attempt to restrict activities that the framers of the First Amendment meant us to tolerate.

13   Such rules also embody serious flaws in policy. The premise of such rules is that sexist, racist, and ethnically demeaning speech is so deeply abhorrent that the normal rules do not apply. We can, in other words, set up a double standard if we really object deeply enough to what is being said. Such a claim is tempting indeed, for the case here could hardly be more compelling. Yet the exception we make today to combat anti-Semitism or racism or sexism may well return to haunt us tomorrow in a quite different context that may seem equally compelling to some people—for example, to those offended by taboo words in books and magazines or by references they deem sacrilegious. Only rigorous adherence to a single standard of speech and its regulation avoids that risk.

14   What can a conscientious institution do short of banning racist and sexist speech? There may be several promising avenues. One surely is to explore the full potential of the recognized and established exceptions to the First Amendment. Some racial diatribes and caricatures might indeed be shown to create a clear and present danger. And material demeaning to women might occasionally be proved legally obscene. In some instances, conduct may be sufficiently detached from speech that it can be regulated without stifling ideas and their expression. The occasions for such traditional sanctions would undoubtedly be rare, but not inconceivable. Sanctions might even be imposed against groups and organizations without abridging the speech of individuals. The fraternity that displays a crude effigy or disseminates advertisements that demean women might be denied certain campus privileges, even for transgressions for which an individual could not be punished.

15   More attractive are the essentially educational options befitting an academic community. A faculty and administration that loudly condemn racial caricature and ethnic slur abridge no student's freedom of speech. An educational program, whether optional or required, designed to increase tolerance and eliminate bigotry enhances free expression and inquiry. Inviting formal complaints from people aggrieved by demeaning speech violates no civil liberty as long as punishment reaches only conduct, not thoughts or words.

16   Much creative thought needs to be given to these issues, especially at institutions beset by intergroup tensions. Yet the lesson of recent months is that no campus, however harmonious or tranquil it may seem, is immune. Educational programs, forums, dialogues, and the like should place a high

priority on promoting tolerance, civility, and trust. "If there be time . . . to avert the evil by the process of education," Justice Brandeis insisted 75 years ago, "the remedy to be applied is more speech, not enforced silence."

Reading and Analyzing

1. What is O'Neil's subject? What strategies does he use to introduce his topic?
2. What are the motives of those who want to restrict speech with rules? What do they want to achieve on the college campus?
3. What do those who oppose codes of speech and behavior want to defend?
4. What restrictions to free speech have been legally established? Which restrictions might be legal precedents for "banning racially and ethnically demeaning speech"?
5. What two constitutional problems are found in the campus rules, in O'Neil's view? What third flaw, a policy flaw, does O'Neil find?
6. What is O'Neil's position on restricting speech beyond existing legal restrictions?
7. What solutions does he offer for addressing the problem without resorting to speech codes?
8. Analyze O'Neil's organization. What are the parts of his essay, or the steps in his argument?

Responding to the Writer's Ideas

1. How would you describe the tone of the essay? Is it appropriate for his subject and purpose?
2. Evaluate the quality of this argument. Is it clear and persuasive, regardless of your position on the issue?
3. Compare O'Neil and Laney. Both write with reason and restraint. Which writer best expresses your position? Why?
4. Do you have rules regarding speech on your campus? If so, do you think that they have contributed to a more civil environment? If so, why? If not, why not? If you do not have a speech code, do you think your college should have one? Why or why not?
5. Have you experienced, directly or indirectly, speech or behavior that demeans a particular group? If so, how did the incident make you feel? Has the experience affected your answers to the previous questions?

WRITING SUGGESTIONS

1. Have you read a book that has been restricted by some communities or schools? (Some examples include *Adventures of Huckleberry Finn, The Catcher in the Rye, One Flew Over the Cuckoo's Nest, The Sun Also Rises,* and *The Lottery.*) If so, write an essay in which you defend or object to the restricting of the book. (If not, read one of the books listed here and then address the topic.) You may want to limit your position to one kind of restriction; that is, should the book be generally available but not included in high school libraries? Or should it be supplementary but not required reading in high school, but required reading in college? There are a range of possibilities that you should reflect on before writing.

2. Should there be any restrictions on works assigned or subjects discussed in college classes? Again, if you argue for some restrictions, be specific about the kinds you consider appropriate.

3. Select one of the following words and develop a definition of the word: *censorship, pornography, obscenity, sexism, feminism.* Use several techniques for developing your definition, including contrasting the word with another word that is similar but exactly synonymous. See Chapter 3 for guidelines.

4. Select an article in this chapter with which you disagree and write a refutation of the article. Follow the guidelines in Chapter 3 for preparing and organizing a refutation essay.

5. Nat Hentoff does not think that Arthur Ashe's AIDS condition should have been reported. If you believe journalists were right to publish the story, write an argument supporting that claim. Alternatively, take a position on whether or not former president John F. Kennedy's extramarital sex activities should have been reported while he was president.

6. Journalists report the names of people accused of crimes (that is, when they are arrested, before they are tried), including those accused of rape. However, they do not publish the names of rape victims. In an essay, defend or attack these policies.

7. Much recent debate over restricting free expression has concentrated on music lyrics. Where do you stand on this issue? Should records be labeled, much as films are, to aid parents and restrict minors from adult material? Are there some records that should be banned altogether? Think through your position, use examples, and write with restraint, not with the strong emotion usually associated with this issue.

CHAPTER 6

COPING WITH
CRIME AND
VIOLENCE

❖

Crime and violence in American soci-
ety is news. Television especially, the medium that thrives on vivid pictures, serves up a nightly menu of murders, rapes, high-speed police chas-
es, and grieving families, victims themselves. Is there more violence today,
or are we actually victims of irrational fears kept alive by a news industry
cynically seeking viewers? Certainly one issue needing calm, objective
analysis is the way we learn about what is happening in our world. Ellen
Goodman, in the chapter's first essay, addresses this issue in part, as she
seeks to correct false perceptions about those who are most likely to harm
women.

Richard Cohen, in "Crimes of Dispassion," gives expression to a
changed society, to a society in which people, mostly young people, kill for

a few dollars or a pair of sneakers. What are the facts? Although it is difficult to compare the present to the distant past because of the lack of statistics, we can observe some changes, as Cohen does, in the last twenty years.
Most people concerned about an increase in violence are not concerned
about conflicts within or among various Mob families. They are concerned
about inner-city turf battles among teenaged gangs, battles that are usually
associated with drugs. Of course, youthful gangs have long been a part of
many cities' mean streets, but one significant change has been the arming
of today's gangs and drug pushers with both military-styled weapons and
concealed handguns. Because today's criminals are so young, guns have
entered schools, increasing the fear of students, teachers, and parents.

Whether in school or on the street, an increasing number of victims
are innocents accidentally caught in the crossfire. These accidental deaths
contribute to the average person's fears, particularly of walking city streets
at night. Further, both victims and those committing the violence seem
much younger, and the numbers support this perception. Young people are
more frequently turning to guns to end conflicts that might have been re-
solved with a fist fight in the past. And many children are killing other
children accidentally, as a result of playing with a parent's loaded gun.
There also seem to be more mass killings of innocents in the wrong Mc-
Donald's or office building at the wrong time. There are either more, or
more reported, cases of rape, spouse beatings, and child abuse, events that
suggest to many that "ordinary" people are seeking violent solutions to
their conflicts.

If the reasons for violence and the ages of the violents have changed,
then what has happened to our society to produce these distressing
changes? It seems logical to find the causes of a problem as the first step to
finding solutions. Not surprisingly, much writing on crime and violence
seeks to explain the causes or to imply the causes in the solutions that are
proposed. Although many writers rail against the "breakdown of the family," others focus more specifically on cycles of poverty and the guns themselves. Economic issues, and the effect of economics on families, have to be
part of the problem, so you may want to read articles in Chapter 9 in con-
junction with your study of the issues in this chapter.

Social problems are a complex web of moral, economic, and political
elements. However, the articles gathered here focus on the drugs and
weapons themselves and on how to punish murderers. Edward Abbey and
Josh Sugarmann debate gun control, and Charles Krauthammer examines
the legalization of drugs as one proposed solution to the crime and violence generated by America's appetite for illegal drugs. (Again the facts:
We purchase a disproportionate share of the world's cocaine; we have a
much higher murder rate than that of Western European countries and
Japan; and the numbers of deaths by guns in America is staggering in contrast to Western Europe or Japan.)

Perhaps because of the fears many have about crime and violence, there is a higher approval rating for capital punishment than in the last twenty-five years. Thus the chapter's articles presenting the issues of the capital punishment debate form an appropriate part of this chapter. Know the facts: Thirteen states do not have the death penalty. Fifteen of the states with the death penalty have executed at least one person since the 1976 Supreme Court ruling that capital punishment is constitutional. Texas, Florida, and Louisiana have had the greatest number of executions; the South generally is the region of the country most often using the death penalty. Inmates executed between 1976 and 1990 classified by race add up this way: whites 72, blacks 53, Hispanics 7. Since blacks constitute only about 15 percent of the total population, they account for a disproportionate number of executed persons. You should not be surprised, then, to find that race is a part of the debate. (See Anthony Amsterdam, "Race and the Death Penalty.")

Most of the debate turns on the moral issue of retribution and the pragmatic issue of deterrence. Studies do not demonstrate that capital punishment deters the kinds of crimes that would receive the death penalty. Proponents of the death penalty argue that since so few people are actually executed, capital punishment doesn't get enough attention to act as a deterrent. The opposition counters by pointing to the much lower murder rate in Western European countries, which do not execute criminals. Perhaps, then, capital punishment needs to be debated primarily as a moral issue, not as a solution to the problems of crime and violence. Three writers, a lawyer, a psychoanalyst, and a philosopher, examine the issue in depth and from various angles.

❖

A Murder in Boston

Ellen Goodman

First a feature writer for the Boston Globe, *Ellen Goodman (b. 1941) became a syndicated columnist in 1976. Her columns appear in over 250 newspapers, and many have been reprinted in three collections. A winner of a Pulitzer Prize for distinguished commentary, Goodman examines social problems as well as political issues, as the following column, printed January 6, 1990, demonstrates. The occasion for Goodman's examination of the dangers to women from violent crime was a 1989 Boston murder that received national attention.*

1   BOSTON—It was a classic page-one banner, a reader-grabber. Charles Stuart and his pregnant wife, Carol, middle class, white, suburban, professional—in short, innocent—left a birthing class at a city hospital. Minutes later, the woman was shot dead, the baby inside her was dying and the husband was wounded.

2   The story became an instant sensation, Boston's answer to the Central Park Jogger, another tale of random urban danger. The victims were the right sort in the wrong place. Maybe they made a bad turn like a character out of Tom Wolfe's novel. Maybe the murderer was a druggie. Surely he was black. A stranger.

3   It went out on the wires, got picked up by the networks, *People* magazine, the talk shows. What was happening to our streets? the Rolodex experts were asked. It could have happened to anyone, people told each other, and made a note to avoid certain neighborhoods and lock the car. Can anybody feel safe? File this story under Willie Horton. Color it black and white.

4   But on Thursday morning, three months after the tragedy, the widower drove to the Tobin Bridge, walked out of his car and jumped. The district attorney announced that Chuck Stuart was a suspect in his wife's murder.

5   So in one leap, a classic tale about the fear of crime in our time, a fear of strangers, turned into the classic tale of the reality of crime in our time. Women are in the most danger from those they know.

6   Last year, the national homicide rate went up some 5 percent. One American was murdered every 25 minutes. Three out of four victims were still likely to be men, but over the course of the decade, the violence against women had risen 20 percent.

Nevertheless, only 9 percent of the known murderers of these women   7
were strangers. Women were—are—nearly twice as likely to be murdered
by their husbands as by strangers. Add wives, ex-wives, girlfriends and
common-law wives together and nearly a third of the female victims were
known to be killed by the men in their lives. What is true for women who
are murdered is also true to one degree or another of women who are
"only" battered, abused or assaulted.

Crime by strangers actually went down in the past decade. But fear   8
of crime by strangers, that other urban cancer, went up. What can we
make of the anxiety and the reality?

James Fox, a Northwestern University criminologist, believes that   9
"People get their perceptions based on news, not on crime statistics." So
he pins much of the blame for fear on "the minicam," the video-at-eleven
reporting from the scene of any crime. The "news" has been Willie Horton
and the Central Park Jogger and the Montreal Murderer. These stories,
like the Stuart case, Part I, starred strangers.

It is also true that people don't relate statistics to their own lives.   10
The national figures about spousal murders don't translate into a fear of
being murdered by your own husband. But with homelessness among
the alcoholic, the drug-users and the deranged, the streets simply feel
"scarier."

Women have always felt vulnerable to crime, and have monitored   11
and modified their behavior because of it. But as they've pushed boundaries in the rest of their lives, they are more likely to feel crime as the single
greatest lingering limit on independence, on their daily sense of freedom.

Many feel resentment at crime-induced purdah. And the more they   12
have refused to be shut in by the fear of crime, the more they have also experienced that fear: the fear walking home at night, getting into the car in
a parking garage.

It was no surprise that crime became a powerful women's issue in the   13
last presidential campaign. Nor is it a surprise that in a poll of *New
Woman* readers, some 90 percent agreed that "we are too lenient toward
criminals in this country."

But fear sells more than politics. The Smith and Wesson brochure for   14
its Lady Smith handgun begins with one simple word: "Independence." In
words and images, it suggests that the modern, responsible woman and
mother protects her family with this .38-caliber security. Handgun advocates and manufacturers alike are using fear of strangers to break down
women's longstanding resistance to guns at home.

I don't believe that there is nothing to fear but fear itself. There is   15
much to fear, although it would be wiser to disarm men than to sell
women "the great equalizer." But as this horrifying story of the murder of
Carol Stuart unravels, it is a sordid reminder that the greatest danger is
often very close to home.

Reading and Analyzing

1. What are the facts of the Stuart case?
2. How was Carol Stuart's murder originally explained or "categorized"? What logical fallacy does the explanation illustrate?
3. What does Goodman accomplish by retelling the Stuart story in its original version and reminding readers of the real story only in paragraph 4?
4. What did the original reaction to the event illustrate for Goodman? What do the other cases she mentions have in common with the Stuart case "Part I"? What does Goodman emphasize about American attitudes toward crime by the strategy?
5. How did the case finally demonstrate "the reality of crime in our time"?
6. What is Goodman's thesis? Summarize the evidence that she provides in support of her thesis.
7. What causes the "fear of crime by strangers"? What are some effects of this fear on women?
8. For Goodman, is purchasing a handgun a good solution for women?
9. What is another solution recommended by Goodman? What other "solution" is implied? What else should we be doing to protect ourselves, especially women?

Responding to the Writer's Ideas

1. Did you know that women are more likely to be hurt or killed by men they know? Did you know that crime against women has increased? Did you know that crime by strangers has decreased? What are your reactions to these facts?
2. Prior to reading Goodman, had you shared the prevailing anxiety about "crime in the streets" and a fear of strangers? If so, has reading this article led to any rethinking of those views? Why or why not?
3. One reason for our anxiety about crime is that we do not connect statistics to our particular lives. What do many of us assume about the people we know? What are some other statistics that many people fail to connect to their own lives in a way that would lead to changed behavior?
4. Another influence on our fears about crime may be the news coverage of crime, especially coverage on television. Are the media distorting reality? If so, what, if anything, should be done about it? Explain your views.

❖

Crimes of Dispassion

Richard Cohen

Richard Cohen (b. 1941), a Washington Post *columnist who has been syndicated since 1976, writes about both political issues and contemporary culture. In the following column, which was published December 12, 1990, Cohen paints a dispiriting picture of youthful violence in America.*

Taking the subway home from school last September, Alison Benabe, 15, and her sister Jennifer were attacked by three teenage boys, two of them armed with knives. The *New York Times,* whence these facts are drawn, said the boys menaced the two girls and kicked Alison in the face. "Adults nearby silently looked the other way."

The story of Alison Benabe is both prosaic and momentous. In another era that sentence—"Adults nearby silently looked the other way"— would have produced indignation and a flood of questions: "Why? Don't they care? How could they be so callous?" For explanation, a canard might have sufficed: "That's New York for you." But no more.

Recall Kitty Genovese. In 1964 she was stabbed to death on a Queens, N.Y., street while 38 witnesses did nothing. They heard her screams. Windows were opened. Shades opened. The attack was long, brutal—and yet no one even called the police. Countless imaginary voices admonished, "Don't get involved." Windows closed. Shades were drawn. Kitty Genovese, stabbed three times, died.

But afterward tough and supposedly heartless New York put itself through intensive therapy. How could it happen? Whatever New Yorkers and others made of the episode, there was agreement on this: it was extraordinary, not something that happens or could happen often. Everyone agreed on that.

Not anymore. In the new era, no one would be surprised to read that sentence in The *Times:* "Adults nearby silently looked the other way." Indeed, it would be surprising if anyone intervened—unless it was someone who was armed. The years since 1964 have taught everyone a lesson: Mind your own business—otherwise you could get killed.

Part of the problem is guns. Kids walk around armed like James Bond. The storied zip gun, wildly inaccurate, has gone the way of the zoot suit. Kids now carry weapons of warfare: machine pistols of stunning

225

power. They know their names like they used to know ballplayers: TEC-9, MAC-10. And they can, of course, recite the statistics: weight, muzzle velocity, price—both retail and street. These guns bring status to the owner. They have brought a low-grade panic to the street.

7   The year Kitty Genovese was killed, New York's murder rate was 6.1 per 100,000. In 1989 it was 22.7. Washington's record is even more alarming: from 8.4 in 1964 to 59.5 in 1988 and climbing. Back in 1964 your average murder was a domestic affair—husbands, wives, lovers, and few of them (19 percent in 1960) involved guns. Now strangers kill strangers, and most often (66 percent last year in New York) guns were involved. Crimes of passion have become crimes of total dispassion.

8   But even apart from the guns—the sheer number of them—is the willingness to use them, to kill. Knives or guns, it matters not. The taking of a life is nothing. Cops are numbed by the cold cruelty of children. Each year, Washington careens from one homicide record to another, too much of it attributable to kids. In many other cities, the story is not much different. Sometimes the issue is drugs. Sometimes, though, it's a jacket or that intangible core of machismo, respect. The lack of it can be fatal.

9   In New York last August, a tourist from Utah was stabbed to death when he went to the aid of his parents on a subway station. They were being robbed. After the killing, the gang of youths used the money to buy tickets to a dance hall. That's where the cops found them. They were dancing.

10   New York paused and gagged. This was not a senseless crime, but one that made eminent sense. The kids needed money, and so they looked for someone to rob. They were not feeding a habit, looking for food—nothing like that. They wanted to go dancing. One of their victims balked. He was killed. Did the kids panic? Did they run and hide? No. They went dancing.

11   Ponder that crime a minute, and you will realize how far we have come from the Kitty Genovese era. Oh, how quaint were the days when people were held morally culpable for not coming to the aid of an innocent victim. Now city dwellers are like people in Nazi-occupied Europe. The terror is so great that we tend to suspend moral judgment: Would we have done any differently? Notions of accountability, of what is owed others, no longer apply. In their place is the credo of the city dweller: Mind your own business.

12   Poor Alison Benabe, she's on her own. The greatest military and economic power on Earth can't keep a girl safe on the subway. Mindless policies have taken their toll. The lack of meaningful gun control is one. The inability or refusal to punish and punish swiftly is another. Homicide has become a childhood disease for which there is no inoculation.

13   "Adults silently looked the other way," The *Times* said. Of course. Why should they be different? When it comes to cities, this is what most of the country has been doing for years.

Reading and Analyzing

1. In paragraph 2, Cohen calls the story of Alison Benabe "both prosaic and momentous." In what way is it "prosaic"? In what way "momentous"? (If necessary, check both words' meanings in a good dictionary before answering.)
2. What lesson have we learned since 1964? How have murders changed? What is contributing to the current problem?
3. What kinds of guns are being carried? What seems to be the attitude toward the guns by those carrying them?
4. What does Cohen conclude from the examples and statistics he presents? In other words, what is his thesis, the claim of his argument?
5. How does the example of the Utah tourist's murder help support Cohen's claim? What is particularly shocking about this murder?
6. The terror created by many city streets results, according to Cohen, in what attitudes and responses?
7. Cohen points to two specific causes for the problem he examines. Arguing that these are causes is also to argue for solutions. What does Cohen imply that we should do?
8. Will taking action on the causes solve the problem? What attitudes do the "new" murderers seem to hold that also need addressing before significant changes may be realized?

Responding to the Writer's Ideas

1. Compare Cohen's article to Goodman's. Do they seem to be contradictory? Is Cohen contributing to our fear of strangers, a fear that may be misplaced? Can the two articles be reconciled; that is, can both be accurate analyses of today's society?
2. How would you go about trying to address the crimes of dispassion Cohen writes about? Try making a list of three to five specific steps that we could and should take. Also consider *who* should be responsible for initiating these steps, for example, a local, state, or federal government agency. Do new laws need to be enacted at the state or federal government level to empower these agencies?
3. Do you think more people today are unwilling to become involved in the conflicts of strangers? Is it unrealistic to expect people to become involved? Do you want to live in a community in which no one helps anyone else?

❖

Legalize? No. Deglamorize.

Charles Krauthammer

Charles Krauthammer studied political theory at Oxford University and medicine at Harvard Medical School. Certified as a neurologist and psychiatrist, Krauthammer returned to his first love, political analysis, as an editor for The New Republic *and then as a syndicated columnist and analyst on CBS's* Inside Washington. *He has won a Pulitzer Prize for distinguished commentary. In the following column, published May 20, 1988, Krauthammer presents his views on legalizing drugs.*

1   The idea of the month—to cure the hysteria of the year—is to legalize illegal drugs. The idea has been broached by the mayors of Baltimore and Washington. It has made the front pages of The *Post* and The *New York Times.* It even boasts an academic champion in Ethan Nadelmann, a professor at Princeton University.

2   Now, legalization, unlike militarization, has a logic. (Militarization is Congress' cynical election-year ploy to order the military to play drug policeman and pretend to interdict the problem at the border.) Legalization is the cheap and easy solution. It works instantly. Well, definitionally. By redefining drug use as legal, it eliminates all drug-related crime.

3   Now, legalization does solve the drug enforcement problem. If drugs are legal, there are no profits to be made smuggling, no mafias and drug cartels to be enriched by the trade. No one goes to jail. We save billions in law enforcement and reduce corruption to boot.

4   What legalizers minimize is the catastrophic effect that legalization would have on public health, an effect that would far outweigh the savings in law enforcement. We had an inkling of that during Prohibition. Prohibition was a law enforcement disaster but, during its early years at least, a public health triumph. The rates of such alcohol-related illnesses as cirrhosis of the liver and alcoholic psychosis went down remarkably.

5   Well, you ask, if alcohol is now legal, what is the logic of prohibiting cocaine and heroin? No logic, just history. Alcohol use is so ancient and so universal a practice that it cannot be repealed. The question is not: Which is worse, alcohol or cocaine? The question is: Which is worse, alcohol alone or alcohol *plus* coke and heroin and PCP? Alcohol is here to stay. To legalize other drugs is to declare that the rest of the pharmacy is here to stay too.

Do we really want the additional and permanent burden of the other   6
intoxicants, some of which are infinitely more addictive than alcohol?
Since the January 1987 Amtrak crash in which 16 passengers were killed,
there have been 37 railroad accidents involving drug use. With cocaine and
heroin (and drug cocktails yet to be imagined) readily available, additional
transportation deaths alone—think just of the highway toll—would dwarf
the current number of drug-related deaths.

Even legalization proponents admit that it would increase drug use   7
(though they say it is worth the price). First, legalization gives a social
sanction. A public house dispensing crack invites crack use. Second, it
makes drugs available without risk. Third, it makes them available at a
price that must match or undercut the street price—otherwise, the black
market continues and the whole law-enforcement rationale for legalization
is defeated. All three effects of legalization—making available sanctioned,
safe and cheap drugs—would increase consumption. What we save in law
enforcement we would have to spend many times over in traffic deaths,
lost productivity and hospital costs.

What to do? For any problem that is ultimately cultural, there can be   8
no quick fix. The answer has to be cultural, too, and changing attitudes
takes decades. But it can be done. The great paradigm is the success of the
now 25-year-old antismoking campaigns.

When I was a kid, the most glamorous image one could imagine was   9
Bogie with a cigarette dangling from his lips. No more. Tobacco advertising
is banned on TV, a clear violation of free speech and a good one. A relentless government campaign, finally picked up by Hollywood and the rest of
the culture industry, has thoroughly deglamorized cigarettes. It simply isn't
cool to smoke. It is considered a confession of personal weakness. This is
not the image a person wants to project, and projecting an image is why
people start to smoke in the first place. (Addiction is why they continue.)

The combination of moral suasion, deglamorization and mild repres-   10
sion—segregating smokers, banning TV ads—has led to a dramatic decline
in tobacco usage in one generation. It was 40 percent when the surgeon
general's first report was issued in 1964. It is 30 percent today.

Nancy Reagan's Just Say No to drugs campaign drew ridicule, but it   11
recognized the only nonrepressive way to go after drugs. Do to them what
was done to tobacco: deglamorize. The only way to reduce consumption is
to reverse a cultural impression. In a culture of bright lights and big cities
that cannot be quick and easy, but there is no other way.

Save one. If you want an overnight fix, the only one that will work is   12
a dramatic attack on demand. When the Chinese communists came to
power, they eliminated China's endemic opium problem rather quickly.
They shot, imprisoned or "reeducated" anyone involved with opium.

That is a bit rough for Congress. Nonetheless, in the current hysteria,   13
Congress wants to turn soldiers into drug cops and undermine the cher-

ished American tradition of keeping the military out of police work. Well, if drug abuse is really such a mortal danger that civil liberties need to be trampled, there is a far more effective way to do it: start cracking down hard on users.

14   Not by putting them all in jail. There aren't enough cells to go around. But by imposing stiff sanctions against property—heavy fines and confiscations. When a user has to calculate the price of coke at $100 per gram plus, say, a $10,000 premium thrown in, he might start looking for cheaper forms of recreation.

15   There you have it: four solutions. If you are desperate for a quick fix, either legalize drugs or repress the user. If you want a civilized approach, mount a propaganda campaign against drugs on the scale of the antismoking campaign. And if you are just a politician looking for reelection, send in the Marines and wave to the cameras.

Reading and Analyzing

1. What are the advantages of legalizing drugs? Why do some find this an appealing solution to the drug problem?
2. What, according to Krauthammer, is the chief difficulty with legalizing drugs? What evidence does he offer to support his position?
3. How does the author's opening sentence reveal his attitude toward legalizing drugs? What else does his opening paragraph accomplish?
4. What is Krauthammer's attitude toward politicians who have been calling for some of the more dramatic responses to the drug problem? How do you know?
5. Those who argue that since alcohol is legal, other drugs should also be legalized are using what kind of argument? How does Krauthammer counter the argument?
6. What four solutions does Krauthammer offer?
7. What are his objections to repressing the user and using the military? What is his preferred solution? What reasons does he offer in support of it?
8. Krauthammer uses the word *fix* twice: "an overnight fix" and "a quick fix." What does he gain by this word choice?

Responding to the Writer's Ideas

1. Although the author attacks the argument that drugs should be legal because alcohol is legal, he defends his solution to the drug problem by using a similar argument. Why is Krauthammer's argument the more convincing one?

2. Do you agree that the use of the military is a bad idea? Why or why not? Do you think the solution of fining drug users and confiscating their property has merit? Why or why not?
3. Has the author convinced you that deglamorization is the best solution? Why or why not?
4. Do you have another solution to put forward? If so, what is it? How would you defend your proposal?

❖

The Right to Arms

Edward Abbey

*Edward Abbey (1927–1989) was educated at the University of New
Mexico and served as a National Park Service ranger before devoting
his time to writing. Abbey has written novels* (Good News, 1980),
books on the West (The Hidden Canyon, 1978), *and collections of
essays* (Abbey's Road, 1979). *The following article, from* Abbey's
Road, *expresses, with strong emotion, his views on gun control and the
rights of individuals.*

*If guns are outlawed
Only outlaws will have guns
(True? False? Maybe?)*

1   Meaning weapons. The right to own, keep, and bear arms. A sword
and a lance, or a bow and a quiverful of arrows. A crossbow and darts. Or
in our time, a rifle and a handgun and a cache of ammunition. Firearms.

2   In medieval England a peasant caught with a sword in his possession
would be strung up on a gibbet and left there for the crows. Swords were
for gentlemen only. (*Gentlemen!*) Only members of the ruling class were
entitled to own and bear weapons. For obvious reasons. Even bows and
arrows were outlawed—see Robin Hood. When the peasants attempted to
rebel, as they did in England and Germany and other European countries
from time to time, they had to fight with sickles, bog hoes, clubs—no
match for the sword-wielding armored cavalry of the nobility.

3   In Nazi Germany the possession of firearms by a private citizen of
the Third Reich was considered a crime against the state; the statutory
penalty was death—by hanging. Or beheading. In the Soviet Union, as in
Czarist Russia, the manufacture, distribution, and ownership of firearms
have always been monopolies of the state, strictly controlled and supervised. Any unauthorized citizen found with guns in his home by the OGPU
or the KGB is automatically suspected of subversive intentions and subject
to severe penalties. Except for the landowning aristocracy, who alone
among the population were allowed the privilege of owning firearms, for
only they were privileged to hunt, the ownership of weapons never did become a widespread tradition in Russia. And Russia has always been an au-
tocracy—or at best, as today, an oligarchy.

In Uganda, Brazil, Iran, Paraguay, South Africa—wherever a few rule   4
many—the possession of weapons is restricted to the ruling class and to
their supporting apparatus: the military, the police, the secret police. In
Chile and Argentina at this very hour men and women are being tortured
by the most up-to-date CIA methods in the effort to force them to reveal
the location of their hidden weapons. Their guns, their rifles. Their arms.
And we can be certain that the Communist masters of modern China will
never pass out firearms to *their* 800 million subjects. Only in Cuba, among
dictatorships, where Fidel's revolution apparently still enjoys popular support, does there seem to exist a true citizen's militia.

There must be a moral in all this. When I try to think of a nation that   5
has maintained its independence over centuries, and where the citizens still
retain their rights as free and independent people, not many come to mind.
I think of Switzerland. Of Norway, Sweden, Denmark, Finland. The
British Commonwealth. France, Italy. And of our United States.

When Tell shot the apple from his son's head, he reserved in hand a   6
second arrow, it may be remembered, for the Austrian tyrant Gessler. And
got him too, shortly afterward. Switzerland has been a free country since
1390. In Switzerland basic national decisions are made by initiative and
referendum—direct democracy—and in some cantons by open-air meetings in which all voters participate. Every Swiss male serves a year in the
Swiss Army and at the end of the year takes his government rifle home
with him—where he keeps it for the rest of his life. One of my father's
grandfathers came from Canton Bern.

There must be a meaning in this. I don't think I'm a gun fanatic. I   7
own a couple of small-caliber weapons, but seldom take them off the wall.
I gave up deer hunting fifteen years ago, when the hunters began to outnumber the deer. I am a member of the National Rifle Association, but
certainly no John Bircher. I'm a liberal—and proud of it. Nevertheless, I
am opposed, absolutely, to every move the state makes to restrict my right
to buy, own, possess, and carry a firearm. Whether shotgun, rifle, or handgun.

Of course, we can agree to a few commonsense limitations. Guns   8
should not be sold to children, to the certifiably insane, or to convicted
criminals. Other than that, we must regard with extreme suspicion any effort by the government—local, state, or national—to control our right to
arms. The registration of firearms is the first step toward confiscation. The
confiscation of weapons would be a major and probably fatal step into authoritarian rule—the domination of most of us by a new order of "gentlemen." By a new and harder oligarchy.

The tank, the B-52, the fighter-bomber, the state-controlled police   9
and military are the weapons of dictatorship. The rifle is the weapon of
democracy. Not for nothing was the revolver called an "equalizer." *Egal-
ité* implies *liberté*. And always will. Let us hope our weapons are never

needed—but do not forget what the common people of this nation knew when they demanded the Bill of Rights: An armed citizenry is the first defense, the best defense, and the final defense against tyranny.

10   If guns are outlawed, only the government will have guns. Only the police, the secret police, the military. The hired servants of our rulers. Only the government—and a few outlaws. I intend to be among the outlaws.

Reading and Responding

1. What is the source of the essay's opening lines?
2. What is Abbey's thesis? That is, what assertion does he make about citizen ownership of guns?
3. What is the author's primary argument for gun ownership?
4. What is the purpose of references to gentlemen? To class distinctions in the past? To secret police and military weapons? Do these references provide logical support for Abbey's position? Are they effective emotional appeals?
5. Why does Abbey stress that he is a liberal? How might that assertion serve his purpose? What does he mean when he says he is "no John Bircher"? (If you do not recognize the reference, look it up.)
6. Abbey asserts that "the registration of firearms is the first step toward confiscation." Confiscation will then lead to authoritarian rule. Is there any logic or evidence to support this causal pattern? If not, what logical fallacy is represented?
7. The author asserts that confiscation will result in rule by "a new and harder oligarchy." What is an oligarchy? (If necessary, check your dictionary.)
8. What is the effect of Abbey's use of sentence fragments, especially in paragraph 1? What does he seek to accomplish with this technique?
9. Abbey shifts rapidly among synonyms for guns: "arms," "weapons," "bows and arrows," "firearms." Do these words have the same connotation? If not, is Abbey playing rather loosely with language? What is the effect?
10. Does Abbey's reference to his father's grandfather advance his argument? If so, how? If not, why does he include the reference?
11. When Abbey refers to the Bill of Rights and asserts that "the rifle is the weapon of democracy" to advance his argument, what must he assume for these remarks to be relevant to the debate? Is his assumption a sound one?

Responding to the Writer's Ideas

1. Whatever your position on gun control, do you think that Abbey has written an effective argument? If so, why? If not, why not?
2. If you agree with Abbey's position, are there other arguments you would present?
3. If you disagree with Abbey's position, what reasons would you present to support you argument?

❖

The NRA Is Right, but We Still Need to Ban Handguns

Josh Sugarmann

A graduate in journalism from Boston University, Josh Sugarmann (b. 1960) is executive director of New Right Watch and director of their Firearms Policy Project. He has published many articles, mostly on firearms-related issues, and has appeared on Nightline, ABC's World News Tonight, *and* Cable News Network. *The following article, with its often overlooked facts on firearms deaths, was published in June 1987 in* Washington Monthly *magazine.*

1   One tenet of the National Rifle Association's faith has always been that handgun controls do little to stop criminals from obtaining handguns. For once, the NRA is right and America's leading handgun control organization is wrong. Criminals don't buy handguns in gun stores. That's why they're criminals. But it isn't criminals who are killing most of the 20,000 to 22,000 people who die from handguns each year. We are.

2   This is an ugly truth for a country that thinks of handgun violence as a "crime" issue and believes that it's somehow possible to separate "good" handguns (those in our hands for self-defense) from "bad" handguns (those in the hands of criminals).

3   Contrary to popular perception, the most prevalent form of handgun death in America isn't murder but suicide. Of the handgun deaths that occur each year, approximately 12,000 are suicides. An additional 1,000 fatalities are accidents. And of the 9,000 handgun deaths classified as murders, most are not caused by predatory strangers. Handgun violence is usually the result of people being angry, drunk, careless, or depressed—who just happen to have a handgun around. In all, fewer than 10 percent of handgun deaths are felony-related.

4   Though handgun availability is not a crime issue, it does represent a major public health threat. Handguns are the number one weapon for both murder and suicide and are second only to auto accidents as the leading cause of death due to injury. Of course there are other ways of committing suicide or crimes of passion. But no means is more lethal, effective, or handy. That's why the NRA is ultimately wrong. As several public health organizations have noted, the best way to curb a public health problem is through prevention—in this case, the banning of all handguns from civilian hands.

236

The Enemy Is Us

For most who attempt suicide, the will to die lasts only briefly. Only one   4
out of every ten people attempting suicide is going to kill himself no matter
what. The success or failure of an attempt depends primarily on the lethality of the means. Pills, razor blades, and gas aren't guaranteed killers, and
they take time. Handguns, however, lend themselves well to spontaneity.
Consider that although women try to kill themselves four times as often as
men, men succeed three to four times as often. For one reason: women use
pills or less lethal means; men use handguns. This balance is shifting, however, as more women own or have access to handguns. Between 1970 and
1978 the suicide rate for young women rose 50 percent, primarily due to
increased use of handguns.

Of course, there is no way to lock society's cupboard and prevent   5
every distraught soul from injuring him or herself. Still, there are ways we
can promote public safety without becoming a nation of nannies. England,
for instance, curbed suicide by replacing its most common means of committing suicide—coal stove gas—with less toxic natural gas. Fifteen years
after the switch, studies found that suicide rates had dropped and remained low, even though the number of suicide *attempts* had increased.
"High suicide rates seem to occur where highly lethal suicidal methods are
not only available, but also where they are culturally acceptable," writes
Dr. Robert Markush of the University of Alabama, who has studied the
use of handguns in suicide.

Most murders aren't crime-related, but are the result of arguments   6
between friends and among families. In 1985, 59 percent of all murders
were committed by people known to the victim. Only 15 percent were
committed by strangers, and only 18 percent were the result of felonious
activity. As the FBI admits every year in its *Uniform Crime Reports,* "murder is a societal problem over which law enforcement has little or no control." The FBI doesn't publish separate statistics on who's killing whom
with handguns, but it is assumed that what is true of all murders is true of
handgun murders.

Controlling the Vector

Recognizing that eliminating a disease requires prevention, not treatment,   7
health professionals have been in the forefront of those calling for a national ban on handguns. In 1981, the Surgeon General's Select Panel for
the Promotion of Child Health traced the "epidemic of deaths and injuries
among children and youth" to handguns, and called for "nothing short of
a total ban." It is estimated that on average, one child dies from handgun
wounds each day. Between 1961 and 1981, according to the American Association of Suicidology, the suicide rate for 15- to 24-year-olds increased
150 percent. The report linked the rise in murders and suicides among the

young to the increased use of firearms—primarily handguns. In a 1985 re-port, the Surgeon General's Workshop on Violence and Public Health rec-ommended "a complete and universal ban on the sale, manufacture, im-portation, and possession of handguns (except for authorized police and military personnel)."

8   Not surprisingly, the American Public Health Association, the Ameri-can Association of Suicidology, and the American Psychiatric Association, are three of the 31 national organizations that are members of National Coalition to Ban Handguns (NCBH).

9   Comparing the relationship between handguns and violence to mos-quitos and malaria, Stephen P. Teret, co-director of the Johns Hopkins In-jury Prevention Center, says, "As public health professionals, if we are faced with a disease that is carried by some type of vehicle/vector like a mosquito, our initial response would be to control the vector. There's no reason why if the vehicle/vector is a handgun, we should not be interested in controlling the handgun."

10   The NRA refers to handgun suicides, accidental killings, and murders by acquaintances as "the price of freedom." It believes that handguns right enough wrongs, stop enough crimes, and kill enough criminals to justify these deaths. But even the NRA has admitted that there is no "adequate measure that more lives are saved by arms in good hands than are lost by arms in evil hands." Again, the NRA is right.

11   A 1985 NCBH study found that a handgun is 118 times more likely to be used in a suicide, murder, or fatal accident than to kill a criminal. Be-tween 1981 and 1983, nearly 69,000 Americans lost their lives to hand-guns. During that same period there were only 583 justifiable homicides reported to the FBI, in which someone used a handgun to kill a stranger—a burglar, rapist, or other criminal. In 1982, 19 states reported to the FBI that not once did a private citizen use a handgun to kill a criminal. Five states reported that more than 130 citizens were murdered with handguns for each time a handgun was justifiably used to kill a criminal. In no state did the number of self-defense homicides approach the murder toll. Last year, a study published in the *New England Journal of Medicine* analyzing gun use in the home over a six-year period in the Seattle, Washington, area found that for every time a firearm was used to kill an intruder in self-de-fense, 198 lives ended in murders, suicides, or accidents. Handguns were used in more than 70 percent of those deaths.

12   Although handguns are rarely used to kill criminals, an obvious question remains: How often are they used merely to wound or scare away intruders? No reliable statistics are available, but most police officials agree that in a criminal confrontation on the street, the handgun-toting civilian is far more likely to be killed or lose his handgun to a criminal than successfully use the weapon in self-defense. "Beyond any doubt, thou-sands more lives are lost every year because of the proliferation of hand-

guns than are saved," says Joseph McNamara, chief of police of San Jose, who has also been police chief in Kansas City, a beat cop in Harlem, and is the author of a book on defense against violent crime. Moreover, most burglaries occur when homes are vacant, so the handgun in the drawer is no deterrent. (It would also probably be the first item stolen.)

Faced with facts like these, anti-control advocates often turn to the argument of last resort: the Second Amendment. But the historic 1981 Morton Grove, Illinois, ban on handgun sale and possession exploded that rationale. In 1983, the U.S. Supreme Court let stand a lower court ruling that stated, "Because the possession of handguns is not part of the right to keep and bear arms, [the Morton Grove ordinance] does not violate the Second Amendment."

Criminal Equivocation

Unfortunately, powerful as the NRA is, it has received additional help from the leading handgun control group. Handgun Control Inc. (HCI) has helped the handgun lobby by setting up the perfect strawman for the NRA to shoot down. "Keep handguns out of the wrong hands," HCI says. "By making it more difficult for criminals, drug addicts, etc., to get handguns, and by ensuring that law-abiding citizens know how to maintain their handguns, we can reduce handgun violence," it promises. Like those in the NRA, HCI chairman Nelson T. "Pete" Shields "firmly believe(s) in the right of law-abiding citizens to possess handguns . . . for legitimate purposes."

In its attempt to paint handgun violence solely as a crime issue, HCI goes so far as to sometimes ignore the weapon's non-crime death tally. In its most recent poster comparing the handgun murder toll in the U.S. with that of nations with strict handgun laws, HCI states: "In 1983, handguns killed 35 people in Japan, 8 in Great Britain, 27 in Switzerland, 6 in Canada, 7 in Sweden, 10 in Australia, and 9,014 in the United States." Handguns *killed* a lot more than that in the United States. About 13,000 suicides and accidents more.

HCI endorses a ban only on short-barrelled handguns (the preferred weapon of criminals). It advocates mandatory safety training, a waiting period during which a background check can be run on a purchaser, and a license to carry a handgun, with mandatory sentencing for violators. It also endorses mandatory sentencing for the use of a handgun in a crime. According to HCI communications director Barbara Lautman, together these measures would "attack pretty much the heart of the problem."

HCI appears to have arrived at its crime focus by taking polls. In his 1981 book, *Guns Don't Die—People Do,* Shields points out that the majority of Americans don't favor a ban on handguns. "What they do want, however, is a set of strict laws to control the easy access to handguns by the criminal and the violence prone—*as long as those controls don't jeop-*

ardize the perceived right of law-abiding citizens to buy and own hand-guns for self defense [italics his]." Shields admits "this is not based on any naive hope that criminals will obey such laws. Rather, it is based on the willingness of the rest of us to be responsible and accountable citizens, and the knowledge that to the degree we are, we make it more difficult for the criminal to get a handgun." This wasn't always HCI's stand. Founded in 1974 as the National Council to Control Handguns, HCI originally called a ban on private handgun possession the "most effective" solution to re-ducing violent crime rapidly and was at one time a member of NCBH. Michael Beard, president of NCBH, maintains that HCI's focus on crime "started with a public relations concern. Some people in the movement felt Americans were worried about crime, and that was one way to approach the problem. That's the problem when you use public opinion polls to tell you what your position's going to be. And I think a lot of the handgun control movement has looked at whatever's hot at the time and tried to latch onto that, rather than sticking to the basic message that there is a re-lationship between the availability of handguns and the handgun violence in our society. . . . Ultimately, nothing short of taking the product off the market is really going to have an effect on the problem."

18   HCI's cops and robbers emphasis has been endlessly frustrating to many in the anti-handgun movement. HCI would offer handgun control as a solution to crime, and the NRA would effectively rebut their arguments with the commonsensical observation that criminals are not likely to obey such laws. I can't help but think that HCI's refusal to abandon the crime argument has harmed the longterm progress of the movement.

Saturated Dresser Drawers

19   In a nation with 40 million handguns—where anyone who wants one can get one—it's time to face a chilling fact. We're way past the point where registration, licensing, safety training, waiting periods, or mandatory sen-tencing are going to have much effect. Each of these measures may save some lives or help catch a few criminals, but none—by itself or taken to-gether—will stop the vast majority of handgun suicides or murders. A "controlled" handgun kills just as effectively as an "uncontrolled" one.

20   Most control recommendations merely perpetuate the myth that with proper care a handgun can be as safe a tool as any other. Nothing could be further from the truth. A handgun is not a blender.

21   Those advocating a step-by-step process insist that a ban would be too radical and therefore unacceptable to Congress and the public. A hard-core 40 percent of the American public has always endorsed banning handguns. Many will also undoubtedly argue that any control measure—no matter how ill-conceived or ineffective—would be a good first step. But after more than a decade, the other foot hasn't followed.

In other areas of firearms control there has been increasing recogni-   22
tion that bans are the most effective solution. The only two federal measures passed since the Gun Control Act of 1968 have been bans. In each
case, the reasoning was simple: the harm done by these objects outweighed   &
any possible benefit they brought to society. In 1986, Congress banned
certain types of armor-piercing "cop-killer" bullets. There was also a silver
lining to last year's NRA-McClure-Volkmer handgun "decontrol" bill,
which weakened the already lax Gun Control Act of 1968, making it legal,
for instance, for people to transport unloaded, "not readily accessible"
handguns interstate. A last-minute amendment added by pro-control
forces banned the future production and sale of machine guns for civilian
use.

Unfortunately, no law has addressed the major public health prob-   23
lem. Few suicides, accidental killings, or acquaintance murders are the result of cop-killer bullets or machine guns.

Outlawing handguns would in no way be a panacea. Even if   24
handgun production stopped tomorrow, millions would remain in the
dresser drawers of America's bedrooms—and many of them would
probably stay there. Contrary to NRA fantasies, black-booted fascists
would not be kicking down doors searching for handguns. Moreover,
the absolute last segment of society to be affected by any measure
would be criminals. The black market that has fed off the legal sale
of handguns would continue for a long while. But by ending new
handgun production, the availability of illegal handguns can only decrease.

Of course, someone who truly wants to kill himself can find another   25
way. A handgun ban would not affect millions of rifles and shotguns. But
experience shows that no weapon provides the combination of lethality
and convenience that a handgun does. Handguns represent only 30 percent
of all the guns out there but are responsible for 90 percent of firearms mis-
use. Most people who commit suicide with a firearm use a handgun. At
minimum, a handgun ban would prevent the escalation of killings in segments of society that have not yet been saturated by handgun manufacturers. Further increases in suicides among women, for example, might be
curtailed.

But the final solution lies in changing the way handguns and hand-   26
gun violence are viewed by society. Public health campaigns have changed
the way Americans look at cigarette smoking and drunk driving and can
do the same for handguns.

For the past 12 years, many in the handgun control movement have   27
confined their debate to what the public supposedly wants and expects to
hear—not to reality. The handgun must be seen for what it is, not what
we'd like it to be.

Reading and Analyzing

1. Sugarmann's paradoxical title provides an effective opening. In what way is the NRA right? Why, nevertheless, should handguns be banned?

2. Why is it important for Sugarmann to provide statistics early in his argument? What does he want to accomplish in paragraphs 2 and 3?

3. What, apparently, determines the success of most suicide attempts? Why do you suppose men are more likely than women to use guns in a suicide attempt? What accounts for an increasing number of women using guns in suicide attempts?

4. Examine the statistics in paragraph 6. In 1985, what percentage of murders were committed by "criminals"? Are you surprised by this statistic? How does it help advance the author's argument?

5. Sugarmann develops his argument in part by comparing handgun deaths to a disease. What type of argument is he using here? What is the point of this argument? Is it convincing?

6. Abbey, in "The Right to Bear Arms" (pp. 232–34), builds much of his argument on the rights guaranteed in the Bill of Rights. What evidence does Sugarmann present to challenge the Second Amendment argument?

7. What solutions to the problem of handgun deaths are advocated by Handgun Control Inc. (HCI)? How does their stand help the NRA reinforce its position? How does this irony provide evidence to advance Sugarmann's argument? What does Sugarmann mean when he says that "a handgun is not a blender"?

8. What is a major purpose of Sugarmann's article besides making another statement for banning handguns? How does he want us to see the handgun problem?

Responding to the Writer's Ideas

1. In the "battle" between criminals and citizens with handguns, who is the bigger loser? Having studied the facts that the author has presented, do you agree or disagree with the NRA that citizen deaths are "the price of freedom"?

2. Evaluate Sugarmann's argument. Do the facts warrant redefining the handgun problem as a public health rather than a crime problem? If so, do you agree that the only logical solution is the banning of handguns? If you disagree, what reasons would you give to support your position?

❖

Race and the Death Penalty

Anthony G. Amsterdam

*Holding degrees from Haverford College and the University of
Pennsylvania, Anthony G. Amsterdam is professor of law and director
of the Lawyering Program at New York University Law School. He is
the author of several trial manual texts and many articles. As the
following article (published in* Criminal Justice Ethics *in 1988) reveals,
Amsterdam's scholarship on capital punishment has concentrated on
the role of race in capital punishment sentencing.*

There are times when even truths we hold self-evident require affir- 1
mation. For those who have invested our careers and our hopes in the
criminal justice system, this is one of those times. Insofar as the basic principles that give value to our lives are in the keeping of the law and can be
vindicated or betrayed by the decisions of any court, they have been sold
down the river by a decision of the Supreme Court of the United States less
than a year old.

I do not choose by accident a metaphor of slavery. For the decision I 2
am referring to is the criminal justice system's *Dred Scott*[1] case. It is the case
of Warren McCleskey, a black man sentenced to die for the murder of a
white man in Georgia. The Supreme Court held that McCleskey can be constitutionally put to death despite overwhelming unrebutted and unexplained statistical evidence that the death penalty is being imposed by Georgia juries in a pattern which reflects the race of convicted murderers and
their victims and cannot be accounted for by any factor other than race.

This is not just a case about capital punishment. The Supreme 3
Court's decision, which amounts to an open license to discriminate against
people of color in capital sentencing, was placed upon grounds that impli-
cate the entire criminal justice system. Worse still, the Court's reasoning
makes us all accomplices in its toleration of a racially discriminatory administration of criminal justice.

Let us look at the *McCleskey* case. His crime was an ugly one. He 4
robbed a furniture store at gunpoint, and he or one of his accomplices

---

[1] In 1857 The Supreme Court ruled that Dred Scott, a slave, could not sue his
owner because, as a slave, he did not have the rights and privileges given to citizens, including the right to due process.—Ed.

243

killed a police officer who responded to the scene. McCleskey may have
been the triggerman. Whether or not he was, he was guilty of murder
under Georgia law.

5   But his case in the Supreme Court was not concerned with guilt. It
was concerned with why McCleskey had been sentenced to death instead
of life imprisonment for his crime. It was concerned with why, out of seventeen defendants charged with the killings of police officers in Fulton
County, Georgia, between 1973 and 1980, only Warren McCleskey—a
black defendant charged with killing a white officer—had been chosen for
a death sentence. In the only other one of these seventeen cases in which
the predominantly white prosecutor's office in Atlanta had pushed for the
death penalty, a black defendant convicted of killing a black police officer
had been sentenced to life instead.

6   It was facts of that sort that led the NAACP Legal Defense Fund to
become involved in McCleskey's case. They were not unfamiliar facts to
any of the lawyers who, like myself, had worked for the Legal Defense
Fund for many years, defending blacks charged with serious crimes
throughout the South. We knew that in the United States black defendants
convicted of murder or rape in cases involving white victims have always
been sentenced to death and executed far out of proportion to their numbers, and under factual circumstances that would have produced a sentence of imprisonment—often a relatively light sentence of imprisonment—in identical cases with black victims or white defendants or both.

7   Back in the mid-sixties the Legal Defense Fund had presented to
courts evidence of extensive statistical studies conducted by Dr. Marvin
Wolfgang, one of the deans of American criminology, showing that the
grossly disproportionate number of death sentences which were then being
handed out to black defendants convicted of the rape of white victims
could not be explained by any factor other than race. Prosecutors took the
position then that these studies were insufficiently detailed to rule out the
influence of every possible non-racial factor, and it was largely for that
reason that the courts rejected our claims that our black death-sentenced
clients had been denied the Equal Protection of the Laws. Fortunately, in
1972 we had won a Supreme Court decision that saved the lives of all
those clients and outlawed virtually every death penalty statute in the United States on procedural grounds; and when the States enacted new death-
penalty laws between 1973 and 1976, only three of them reinstated capital
punishment for rape. Now that it no longer mattered much, the prosecutors could afford to take another tack. When we argued against the new
capital murder statutes on the ground that the Wolfgang studies had
shown the susceptibility of capital sentencing laws to racially discriminatory application, the Government of the United States came into the
Supreme Court against us saying, Oh, yes, Wolfgang was "a careful and
comprehensive study, and we do not question its conclusion that during

the twenty years between [1945 and 1965] . . . , in southern states, there was discrimination in rape cases." However, said the Government, this "research does not provide support for a conclusion that racial discrimination continues, . . . or that it applies to murder cases."

So we were well prepared for this sort of selective agnosticism when we went to court in the *McCleskey* case. The evidence that we presented in support of McCleskey's claim of racial discrimination left nothing out. Our centerpiece was a pair of studies conducted by Professor David Baldus, of the University of Iowa, and his colleagues, which examined 2,484 cases of murder and non-negligent manslaughter that occurred in Georgia between 1973, the date when its present capital murder statute was enacted, and 1979, the year after McCleskey's own death sentence was imposed. The Baldus team got its data on these cases principally from official state records, supplied by the Georgia Supreme Court and the Georgia Board of Pardons and Paroles.

Through a highly refined protocol, the team collected information regarding more than five hundred factors in each case—information relating to the demographic and individual characteristics of the defendant and the victim, the circumstances of the crime and the strength of the evidence of guilt, and the aggravating and mitigating features of each case: both the features specified by Georgia law to be considered in capital sentencing and every factor recognized in the legal and criminological literature as theoretically or actually likely to affect the choice of life or death. Using the most reliable and advanced techniques of social-science research, Baldus processed the data through a wide array of sophisticated statistical procedures, including multiple-regression analyses based upon alternative models that considered and controlled for as few as 10 in as many as 230 sentencing factors in each analysis. When our evidentiary case was presented in court, Baldus reanalyzed the data several more times to take account of every additional factor, combination of factors, or model for analysis of factors suggested by the State of Georgia's expert witnesses, its lawyers, and the federal trial judge. The Baldus study has since been uniformly praised by social scientists as the best study of any aspect of criminal sentencing ever conducted.

What did it show? That death sentences were being imposed in Georgia murder cases in a clear, consistent pattern that reflected the race of the victim and the race of the defendant and could not be explained by any non-racial factor. For example:

(1) Although less than 40 percent of Georgia homicide cases involve white victims, in 87 percent of the cases in which a death sentence is imposed, the victim is white. White-victim cases are almost eleven times more likely to produce a death sentence than are black-victim cases.

(2) When the race of the defendant is considered too, the following figures emerge: 22 percent of black defendants who kill white victims are

8

9

10

11

12

sentenced to death; 8 percent of white defendants who kill white victims are sentenced to death; 1 percent of black defendants who kill black victims are sentenced to death; 3 percent of white defendants who kill black victims are sentenced to death. It should be noted that out of the roughly 2,500 Georgia homicide cases found, only 64 involved killings of black victims by white defendants, so the 3 percent death-sentencing rate in this category represents a total of two death sentences over a six-year period. Plainly, the reason why racial discrimination against black defendants does not appear even more glaringly evident is that most black murderers kill black victims; almost no identified white murderers killed black victims; and virtually nobody is sentenced to death for killing a mere black victim.

13   (3) No non-racial factor explains these racial patterns. Under multiple regression analysis, the model with the maximum explanatory power shows that after controlling for legitimate non-racial factors, murderers of white victims are still being sentenced to death 4.3 times more often than murderers of black victims. Multiple regression analysis also shows that the race of the victim is as good a basis for predicting whether or not a murderer will be sentenced to death as are the aggravating circumstances which the Georgia statute explicitly says should be considered in favor of a death sentence, such as whether the defendant has a prior murder conviction, or whether he is the primary actor in the present murder.

14   (4) Across the whole universe of cases, approximately 5 percent of Georgia killings result in a death sentence. Yet when more than 230 non-racial variables are controlled for, the death sentencing rate is 6 percentage points higher in white-victim cases than in black-victim cases. What this means is that in predicting whether any particular person will get the death penalty in Georgia, it is less important to know whether or not he committed a homicide in the first place than to know whether, if he did, he killed a white victim or a black one.

15   (5) However, the effects of race are not uniform across the entire range of homicide cases. As might be expected, in the least aggravated sorts of cases, almost no one gets a death sentence; in the really gruesome cases, a high percentage of both black and white murderers get death sentences; so it is in the mid-range of cases—cases like McCleskey's—that race has its greatest impact. The Baldus study found that in these mid-range cases the death sentencing rate for killers of white victims is 34 percent as compared to 14 percent for killers of black victims. In other words, out of every thirty-four murderers sentenced to death for killing a white victim, twenty of them would not have gotten death sentences if their victims had been black.

16   The bottom line is this: Georgia has executed eleven murderers since it passed its present statute in 1973. Nine of the eleven were black. Ten of the eleven had white victims. Can there be the slightest doubt that this revolting record is the product of some sort of racial bias rather than a pure fluke?

A narrow majority of the Supreme Court pretended to have such doubts and rejected McCleskey's Equal-Protection challenge to his death sentence. It did not question the quality or the validity of the Baldus study, or any of the findings that have been described here. It admitted that the manifest racial discrepancies in death sentencing were unexplained by any non-racial variable, and that Baldus's data pointed to a "likelihood" or a "risk" that race was at work in the capital sentencing process. It essentially conceded that if a similar statistical showing of racial bias had been made in an employment-discrimination case or in a jury-selection case, the courts would have been required to find a violation of the Equal Protection Clause of the Fourteenth Amendment. But, the Court said, racial discrimination in capital sentencing cannot be proved by a pattern of sentencing results: a death-sentenced defendant like McCleskey must present proof that the particular jury or the individual prosecutor, or some other decision-maker in his own case, was personally motivated by racial considerations to bring about his death. Since such proof is never possible to obtain, racial discrimination in capital sentencing is never possible to prove.

17

The Court gave four basic reasons for this result. First, since capital sentencing decisions are made by a host of different juries and prosecutors, and are supposed to be based upon "innumerable factors that vary according to the characteristics of the individual defendant and the facts of the particular capital offense," even sentencing patterns that are explicable by race and inexplicable except by race do not necessarily show that any single decision-maker in the system is acting out of a subjective purpose to discriminate. Second, capital punishment laws are important for the protection of society; the "[i]implementation of these laws necessarily requires discretionary judgments"; and, "[b]ecause discretion is essential to the criminal justice process, we [sh]ould demand exceptionally clear proof before we . . . infer that the discretion has been abused." Third, this same respect for discretionary judgments makes it imprudent to require juries and prosecutors to explain their decisions, so it is better to ignore the inference of racial discrimination that flows logically from their behavior than to call upon them to justify such behavior upon non-racial grounds.

18

Fourth, more is involved than capital punishment. "McCleskey's claim . . . throws into serious question the principles that underlie our entire criminal justice system." This is so because "the Baldus study indicates a discrepancy that appears to correlate with race," and "[a]pparent disparities in sentencing are an inevitable part of our criminal justice system." "Thus," says the Court, "if we accepted McCleskey's claim that racial bias has impermissibly tainted the capital sentencing decision, we could soon be faced with similar claims as to other types of penalty. Moreover, the claim that . . . sentence rests on the irrelevant factor of race easily could be extended to apply to claims based on unexplained discrepancies that correlate to membership in other minority groups, and even to gender"—and

19

even to claims based upon "the defendant's facial characteristics, or the physical attractiveness of the . . . victim." In other words, if we forbid racial discrimination in meting out sentences of life or death, we may have to face claims of discrimination against Blacks, or against women, or perhaps against ugly people, wherever the facts warrant such claims, in the length of prison sentences, in the length of jail sentences, in the giving of suspended sentences, in the making of pretrial release decisions, in the invocation of recidivist sentencing enhancements, in the prosecutor's decisions whether to file charges, and how heavily to load up the charges, against black defendants as compared with white defendants or against ugly defendants as compared with ravishingly beautiful defendants; and of course the whole criminal justice system will then fall down flat and leave us in a state of anarchy. In thirty years of reading purportedly serious judicial opinions, I have never seen one that came as close to Thomas De Quincy's famous justification for punishing the crime of murder: "If once a man indulges himself in murder, very soon he comes to think little of robbing; and from robbing he next comes to drinking and Sabbath-breaking, and from that to incivility and procrastination."

20   Notice that the Court's version of this slippery-slope argument merely makes explicit what is implied throughout its opinion in the *McCleskey* case. Its decision is not limited to capital sentencing but purports to rest on principles which apply to the whole criminal justice system. Every part of that system from arrest to sentencing and parole, in relation to every crime from murder to Sabbath-breaking, involves a multitude of separate decision-makers making individualized decisions based upon "innumerable [case-specific] factors." All of these decisions are important for the protection of society from crime. All are conceived as "necessarily require[ing] discretionary judgments." In making these discretionary judgments, prosecutors and judges as well as jurors have traditionally been immunized from inquiry into their motives. If this kind of discretion implies the power to treat black people differently from white people and to escape the responsibility for explaining why one is making life-and-death decisions in an apparently discriminatory manner, it implies a tolerance for racial discrimination throughout the length and breadth of the administration of criminal justice. What the Supreme Court has held, plainly, is that the very nature of the criminal justice system requires that its workings be excluded from the ordinary rules of law and even logic that guarantee equal protection to racial minorities in our society.

21   And it is here, I suggest, that any self-respecting criminal justice professional is obliged to speak out against this Supreme Court's conception of the criminal justice system. We must reaffirm that there can be no justice in a system which treats people of color differently from white people, or treats crimes against people of color differently from crimes against white people.

We must reaffirm that racism is itself a crime, and that the toleration   22
of racism cannot be justified by the supposed interest of society in fighting
crime. We must pledge that when anyone—even a majority of the Supreme
Court—tells us that a power to discriminate on grounds of race is necessary to protect society from crime, we will recognize that we are probably
being sold another shipment of propaganda to justify repression. Let us
therefore never fail to ask the question whether righteous rhetoric about
protecting society from crime really refers to protecting only white people.
And when the answer, as in the McCleskey case, is that protecting only
white people is being described as "protecting society from crime," let us
say that we are not so stupid as to buy this version of the Big Lie, nor so
uncaring as to let it go unchallenged.

Let us reaffirm that neither the toleration of racism by the Supreme   23
Court nor the pervasiveness of racism in the criminal justice system can
make it right, and that these things only make it worse. Let us reaffirm
that racism exists, and is against the fundamental law of this Nation,
whenever people of different races are treated differently by any public
agency or institution as a consequence of their race and with no legitimate
nonracial reason for the different treatment. Let us dedicate ourselves to
eradicating racism, and declaring it unlawful, not simply in the superficial,
short-lived situation where we can point to one or another specific decision-maker and show that his decisions were the product of conscious bigotry, but also in the far more basic, more intractable, and more destructive
situation where hundreds upon hundreds of different public decision-makers, acting like Georgia's prosecutors and judges and juries—without collu-
sion and in many cases without consciousness of their own racial biases—
combine to produce a pattern that bespeaks the profound prejudice of an
entire population.

Also, let us vow that we will never claim—or stand by unprotestingly   24
while others claim for us—that, because our work is righteous and important, it should be above the law. Of course, controlling crime is vital work;
that is why we give the agencies of criminal justice drastic and unique co-
ercive powers, including the powers of imprisonment and death. And of
course discretion in the execution of such powers is essential. But it is precisely because the powers that the system regulates are so awesome, and
because the discretion of its actors is so broad, that it cannot be relieved of
accountability for the exercise of that discretion. Nor can it be exempted
from the scrutiny that courts of law are bound to give to documented
charges of discrimination on the ground of race by any agency of government. Let us declare flatly that we neither seek nor will accept any such ex-
emption, and that we find it demeaning to be told by the Supreme Court
that the system of justice to which we have devoted our professional lives
cannot do its job without a special dispensation from the safeguards that
assure to people of every race the equal protection of the law.

25   This is a stigma criminal justice practitioners do not deserve. Service
in the criminal justice system should be a cause not for shame but for
pride. Nowhere is it possible to dedicate one's labors to the welfare of
one's fellow human beings with a greater sense that one is needed and that
the quality of what one does can make a difference. But to feel this pride,
and to deserve it, we must consecrate ourselves to the protection of all
people, not a privileged few. We must be servants of humanity, not of
caste. Whether or not the Supreme Court demands this of us, we must demand it of ourselves and of our coworkers in the system. For this is the
faith to which we are sworn by our common calling: that doing justice is
never simply someone else's job; correcting injustice is never simply someone else's responsibility.

Reading and Analyzing

1. In the second sentence, Amsterdam writes of "our careers." Whom
   does he mean besides himself? Who is his primary audience?
2. Explain the *McCleskey* case. What issue was the Supreme Court ruling on? What was it not ruling on?
3. Why does Amsterdam write that McCleskey's "crime was an ugly
   one"? What does he want to establish with readers by that comment?
4. Why were Dr. Wolfgang's studies of racially biased sentencing rejected? How were death-sentenced blacks saved anyway? On what basis
   were his studies dismissed as a challenge to the new death-penalty
   laws?
5. What is Amsterdam's claim about the pattern of death sentencing in
   Georgia, and the South generally?
6. What evidence does he provide? Explain the Baldus studies in your
   own words.
7. How did the Supreme Court rule on the *McCleskey* case? What were
   the four reasons given for their decision?
8. Amsterdam characterizes the Supreme Court's argument as illogical;
   what fallacy does it rest on in his view?
9. What, then, is the connection between the *McCleskey* and *Dred Scott*
   cases? Why does Amsterdam compare them?
10. The author concludes by calling on his readers to react to the ruling.
    What does he want them to do?
11. Observe Amsterdam's language in his concluding paragraphs: "we
    must reaffirm"; "let us dedicate ourselves"; "let us vow." His word
    choice and sentence style are similar to what famous speech? What
    does he accomplish by choosing this style?

Responding to the Writer's Ideas

1. Do the numbers convince you that death sentencing in Georgia is racially motivated? If not, why not?
2. Do you agree with Amsterdam that the Supreme Court's decision is sufficiently serious in denying blacks rights to warrant the comparison to *Dred Scott* ? If not, why not?
3. When Amsterdam challenges readers to reaffirm their commitment to working for justice for all Americans, he is addressing his colleagues in the law. Can a case be made that his challenge can and should be made to all of us, not just lawyers? If you think so, what do you think the rest of us can do, specifically, to improve protection under the law for all? If you think his challenge must be limited to lawyers, explain your reasons.

❖

The Ultimate Punishment: A Defense

Ernest van den Haag

A naturalized citizen born in 1914 in the Netherlands, Ernest van den Haag holds a doctorate from New York University and is a practicing psychoanalyst. Van den Haag has written many articles in both American and European journals and several books on sociological issues, including violence and crime. "The Ultimate Punishment: A Defense" is reprinted (with some footnotes omitted) from the May 7, 1986, issue of the Harvard Law Review. *Van den Haag effectively organizes his defense around the arguments put forward by his opponents.*

1   In an average year about 20,000 homicides occur in the United States. Fewer than 300 convicted murders are sentenced to death. But because no more than thirty murderers have been executed in any recent year, most convicts sentenced to death are likely to die of old age.[1] Nonetheless, the death penalty looms large in discussions: it raises important moral questions independent of the number of executions.

2   The death penalty is our harshest punishment. It is irrevocable: it ends the existence of those punished, instead of temporarily imprisoning them. Further, although not intended to cause physical pain, execution is the only corporal punishment still applied to adults. These singular characteristics contribute to the perennial, impassioned controversy about capital punishment.

I. Distribution

3   Consideration of the justice, morality, or usefulness, of capital punishment is often conflated with objections to its alleged discriminatory or capricious distribution among the guilty. Wrongly so. If capital punishment is immoral *in se,* no distribution among the guilty could make it moral. If capital punishment is moral, no distribution would make it immoral. Improper distribution cannot affect the quality of what is distributed, be it punishments or rewards. Discriminatory or capricious distribution thus could not justify abolition of the death penalty. Further, maldistribution inheres no more in capital punishment than in any other punishment.

252

Maldistribution between the guilty and the innocent is, by defini-   4
tion, unjust. But the injustice does not lie in the nature of the punishment. Because of the finality of the death penalty, the most grievous
maldistribution occurs when it is imposed upon the innocent. However,
the frequent allegations of discrimination and capriciousness refer to
maldistribution among the guilty and not to the punishment of the innocent.

Maldistribution of any punishment among those who deserve it is ir-   5
relevant to its justice or morality. Even if poor or black convicts guilty of
capital offenses suffer capital punishment, and other convicts equally
guilty of the same crimes do not, a more equal distribution, however desirable, would merely be more equal. It would not be more just to the convicts under sentence of death.

Punishments are imposed on persons, not on racial or economic   6
groups. Guilt is personal. The only relevant question is: does the person
to be executed deserve the punishment? Whether or not others who deserved the same punishment, whatever their economic or racial group,
have avoided execution is irrelevant. If they have, the guilt of the executed convicts would not be diminished, nor would their punishment be
less deserved. To put the issue starkly, if the death penalty were imposed on guilty blacks, but not on guilty whites, or, if it were imposed
by a lottery among the guilty, this irrationally discriminatory or capricious distribution would neither make the penalty unjust, nor cause anyone to be unjustly punished, despite the undue impunity bestowed on
others.

Equality, in short, seems morally less important than justice. And   7
justice is independent of distributional inequalities. The ideal of equal
justice demands that justice be equally distributed, not that it be replaced by equality. Justice requires that as many of the guilty as possible be punished, regardless of whether others have avoided punishment.
To let these others escape the deserved punishment does not do justice
to them, or to society. But it is not unjust to those who could not escape.

These moral considerations are not meant to deny that irrational dis-   8
crimination, or capriciousness, would be inconsistent with constitutional
requirements. But I am satisfied that the Supreme Court has in fact provided for adherence to the constitutional requirement of equality as much as
possible. Some inequality is indeed unavoidable as a practical matter in
any system.[2] But, *ultra posse neo obligatur*. (Nobody is bound beyond
ability.)

Recent data reveal little direct racial discrimination in the sentencing   9
of those arrested and convicted of murder. The abrogation of the death
penalty for rape has eliminated a major source of racial discrimination.
Concededly, some discrimination based on the race of murder victims may

exist; yet, this discrimination affects criminal victimizers in an unexpected way. Murderers of whites are thought more likely to be executed than murderers of blacks. Black victims, then, are less fully vindicated than white ones. However, because most black murderers kill blacks, black murderers are spared the death penalty more often than are white murderers. They fare better than most white murderers. The motivation behind unequal distribution of the death penalty may well have been to discriminate against blacks, but the result has favored them. Maldistribution is thus a straw man for empirical as well as analytical reasons.

II. Miscarriages of Justice

10 In a recent survey Professors Hugo Adam Bedau and Michael Radelet found that 7000 persons were executed in the United States between 1900 and 1985 and that 25 were innocent of capital crimes. Among the innocents they list Sacco and Vanzetti as well as Ethel and Julius Rosenberg. Although their data may be questionable, I do not doubt that, over a long enough period, miscarriages of justice will occur even in capital cases.

11 Despite precautions, nearly all human activities, such as trucking, lighting, or construction, cost the lives of some innocent bystanders. We do not give up these activities, because the advantages, moral or material, outweigh the unintended losses. Analogously, for those who think the death penalty just, miscarriages of justice are offset by the moral benefits and the usefulness of doing justice. For those who think the death penalty unjust even when it does not miscarry, miscarriages can hardly be decisive.

III. Deterrence

12 Despite much recent work, there has been no conclusive statistical demonstration that the death penalty is a better deterrent than are alternative punishments. However, deterrence is less than decisive for either side. Most abolitionists acknowledge that they would continue to favor abolition even if the death penalty were shown to deter more murders than alternatives could deter. Abolitionists appear to value the life of a convicted murderer or, at least, his nonexecution, more highly than they value the lives of the innocent victims who might be spared by deterring prospective murderers.

13 Deterrence is not altogether decisive for me either. I would favor retention of the death penalty as retribution even if it were shown that the threat of execution could not deter prospective murderers not already deterred by the threat of imprisonment.[3] Still, I believe the death penalty, because of its finality, is more feared than imprisonment, and deters some prospective murderers not deterred by the threat of imprisonment. Sparing the lives of even a few prospective victims by deterring their murderers is

more important than preserving the lives of convicted murderers because of the possibility, or even the probability that executing them would not deter others. Whereas the lives of the victims who might be saved are valuable, that of the murderer has only negative value, because of his crime. Surely the criminal law is meant to protect the lives of potential victims in preference to those of actual murderers.

Murder rates are determined by many factors; neither the severity nor the probability of the threatened sanction is always decisive. However, for the long run, I share the view of Sir James Fitzjames Stephen: "Some men, probably abstain from murder because they fear that if they committed murder they would be hanged. Hundreds of thousands abstain from it because they regard it with horror. One great reason why they regard it with horror is that murderers are hanged." Penal sanctions are useful in the long run for the formation of the internal restraints so necessary to control crime. The severity and finality of the death penalty is appropriate to the seriousness and the finality of murder.

IV. Incidental Issues: Cost, Relative Suffering, Brutalization

Many nondecisive issues are associated with capital punishment. Some believe that the monetary cost of appealing a capital sentence is excessive. Yet most comparisons of the cost of life imprisonment with the cost of execution, apart from their dubious relevance, are flawed at least by the implied assumption that life prisoners will generate no judicial costs during their imprisonment. At any rate, the actual monetary costs are trumped by the importance of doing justice.

Others insist that a person sentenced to death suffers more than his victim suffered, and that this (excess) suffering is undue according to the *lex talionis* (rule of retaliation). We cannot know whether the murderer on death row suffers more than his victim suffered; however, unlike the murderer, the victim deserved none of the suffering inflicted. Further, the limitations of the *lex talionis* were meant to restrain private vengeance, not the social retribution that has taken its place. Punishment—regardless of the motivation—is not intended to revenge, offset, or compensate for the victim's suffering, or to be measured by it. Punishment is to vindicate the law and the social order undermined by the crime. This is why a kidnapper's penal confinement is not limited to the period for which he imprisoned his victim; nor is a burglar's confinement meant merely to offset the suffering or the harm he caused his victim; nor is it meant only to offset the advantage he gained.[4]

Another argument heard at least since Beccaria is that, by killing a murderer, we encourage, endorse, or legitimize unlawful killing. Yet, although all punishments are meant to be unpleasant, it is seldom argued that they legitimize the unlawful imposition of identical unpleasantness. Imprisonment is not thought to legitimize kidnapping; neither are fines

14

15

16

17

thought to legitimize robbery. The difference between murder and execution, or between kidnapping and imprisonment, is that the first is unlawful and undeserved, the second a lawful and deserved punishment for an unlawful act. The physical similarities of the punishment to the crime are irrelevant. The relevant difference is not physical, but social.[5]

V. Justice, Excess, Degradation

18   We threaten punishments in order to deter crime. We impose them not only to make the threats credible but also as retribution (justice) for the crimes that were not deterred. Threats and punishments are necessary to deter and deterrence is a sufficient practical justification for them. Retribution is an independent moral justification. Although penalties can be unwise, repulsive, or inappropriate, and those punished can be pitiable, in a sense the infliction of legal punishment on a guilty person cannot be unjust. By committing the crime, the criminal volunteered to assume the risk of receiving a legal punishment that he could have avoided by not committing the crime. The punishment he suffers is the punishment he voluntarily risked suffering and, therefore, it is no more unjust to him than any other event for which one knowingly volunteers to assume the risk. Thus, the death penalty cannot be unjust to the guilty criminal.

19   There remain, however, two moral objections. The penalty may be regarded as always excessive as retribution and always morally degrading. To regard the death penalty as always excessive, one must believe that no crime—no matter how heinous—could possibly justify capital punishment. Such a belief can be neither corroborated nor refuted; it is an article of faith.

20   Alternatively, or concurrently, one may believe that everybody, the murderer no less than the victim, has an imprescriptible (natural?) right to life. The law therefore should not deprive anyone of life. I share Jeremy Bentham's view that any such "natural and imprescriptible rights" are "nonsense upon stilts."

21   Justice Brennan has insisted that the death penalty is "uncivilized," "inhuman," inconsistent with "human dignity" and with "the sanctity of life," that it "treats members of the human race as nonhumans, as objects to be toyed with and discarded," that it is "uniquely degrading to human dignity" and "by its very nature, [involves] a denial of the executed person's humanity." Justice Brennan does not say why he thinks execution "uncivilized." Hitherto most civilizations have had the death penalty, although it has been discarded in Western Europe, where it is currently unfashionable probably because of its abuse by totalitarian regimes.

22   By "degrading," Justice Brennan seems to mean that execution degrades the executed convicts. Yet philosophers, such as Immanuel Kant and G. F. W. Hegel, have insisted that, when deserved, execution, far from degrading the executed convict, affirms his humanity by affirming his ra-

tionality and his responsibility for his actions. They thought that execution, when deserved, is required for the sake of the convict's dignity. (Does not life imprisonment violate human dignity more than execution, by keeping alive a prisoner deprived of all autonomy?)

Common sense indicates that it cannot be death—or common fate—   23
that is inhuman. Therefore, Justice Brennan must mean that death degrades when it comes not as a natural or accidental event, but as a deliberate social imposition. The murderer learns through his punishment that his fellow men have found him unworthy of living; that because he has murdered, he is being expelled from the community of the living. This degradation is self-inflicted. By murdering, the murderer has so dehumanized himself that he cannot remain among the living. The social recognition of his self-degradation is the punitive essence of execution. To believe, as Justice Brennan appears to, that the degradation is inflicted by the execution reverses the direction of causality.

Execution of those who have committed heinous murders may deter   24
only one murder per year. If it does, it seems quite warranted. It is also the only fitting retribution for murder I can think of.

Notes

1. Death row as a semipermanent residence is cruel, because convicts are denied the normal amenities of prison life. Thus, unless death row residents are integrated into the prison population, the continuing accumulation of convicts on death row should lead us to accelerate either the rate of executions or the rate of commutations. I find little objection to integration.

2. The ideal of equality, unlike the ideal of retributive justice (which can be approximated separately in each instance), is clearly unattainable unless all guilty persons are apprehended, and thereafter tried, convicted and sentenced by the same court, at the same time. Unequal justice is the best we can do; it is still better than the injustice, equal or unequal, which occurs if, for the sake of equality, we deliberately allow some who could be punished to escape.

3. If executions were shown to increase the murder rate in the long run, I would favor abolition. Sparing the innocent victims who would be spared, *ex hypothesi*, by the nonexecution of murderers would be more important to me than the execution, however just, of murderers. But although there is a lively discussion of the subject, no serious evidence exists to support the hypothesis that executions produce a higher murder rate. *Cf.* Phillips, *The Deterrent Effect of Capital Punishment: New Evidence on an Old Controversy*, 86 AM. J. Soc. 139 (1980) (arguing that murder rates drop immediately after executions of criminals).

4. Thus restitution (a civil liability) cannot satisfy the punitive purpose of penal sanctions, whether the purpose be retributive or deterrent.

5. Some abolitionists challenge: if the death penalty is just and serves as a deterrent, why not televise executions? The answer is simple. The death even of a murderer, however well-deserved, should not serve as public entertainment. It so served in earlier centuries. But in this respect our sensibility has changed for the better, I believe. Further, television unavoidably would trivialize executions,

wedged in, as they would be, between game shows, situation comedies and the like. Finally, because televised executions would focus on the physical aspects of the punishment, rather than the nature of the crime and the suffering of the victim, a televised execution would present the murderer as the victim of the state. Far from communicating the moral significance of the execution, television would shift the focus to the pitiable fear of the murderer. We no longer place in cages those sentenced to imprisonment to expose them to public view. Why should we so expose those sentenced to execution?

Reading and Analyzing

1. What does van den Haag mean by "distribution"? That is, what issue in the death-penalty debate is examined in section I?

2. On what grounds does van den Haag dismiss the issue of possible maldistribution of death sentencing among the guilty? State his argument in your own words.

3. Does van den Haag believe that a significant racial bias can be found in the distribution of capital punishment? Does he offer evidence to support his views? How would Amsterdam respond to his statements? (See "Race and the Death Penalty," pp. 243–50.)

4. What kind of logical fallacy is illustrated by the argument of maldistribution, according to van den Haag?

5. Van den Haag asserts that "punishments are imposed on persons, not on racial or economic groups." Although this is true, does it effectively dismiss the argument that if death sentencing is unevenly distributed, it is wrong? What do you know about stereotyping and prejudice that may lead to a dispute with van den Haag on this issue?

6. On what two grounds does van den Haag dismiss challenges to the death penalty based on miscarriages of justice?

7. Consider the author's word choice in this brief second section. What words does he avoid using that a writer opposed to the death penalty might use instead of "miscarriage of justice" or to refer to the persons executed because of the miscarriage?

8. What do studies show about the death penalty's potential as a deterrent to murder?

9. What is the position on deterrence of those who oppose the death penalty? What does van den Haag conclude about the values of abolitionists?

10. Why does van den Haag dismiss deterrence as an issue in the debate?

11. How might capital punishment serve, indirectly, as a deterrent? What does it tell members of a society about that society's values?

12. Why should costs be considered an irrelevant issue?

13. What is the purpose of punishing a criminal, according to van den Haag? Why is this purpose important to our understanding of death sentencing?

14. How does the author refute the idea that death sentencing legitimizes murder? Those who make this claim are using what type of argument? Van den Haag's refutation employs what strategy designed to reveal a weakness in this type of argument?

15. What, finally, is the author's justification of legal punishment, including the death penalty?

16. To argue that the death penalty is always excessive, what must one believe? Why does van den Haag believe that the death penalty does not degrade? Explain his argument in your own words.

17. Where does van den Haag place his claim, the thesis of his essay? What does he accomplish by this choice?

Responding to the Writer's Ideas

1. Van den Haag and Amsterdam do not agree on the role of racial bias in death sentencing. In your view, who makes the better argument? Why?

2. Van den Haag is prepared to accept some miscarriages of justice (that is, some innocent people will be executed) to achieve the advantages of capital punishment; are you? If you agree with the author, explain why; if you disagree, how would you challenge van den Haag?

3. Van den Haag argues that capital punishment is a just form of retribution for murder, that it is not revenge but justice. Do you agree with his distinction between retribution and revenge? Explain.

4. Evaluate van den Haag's argument. Is it reasoned, thorough, and appropriately serious? Is it logical throughout? Do you think he is right? Why or why not?

❖

Death Is Different

Hugo Adam Bedau

A native of Oregon with a doctorate from Harvard University, Hugo Adam Bedau (b. 1926) teaches in the philosophy department at Tufts University. He is the author of many articles and books on justice and capital punishment, including The Courts, the Constitution and Capital Punishment *(1977) and* Death Is Different *(1987). In the following essay, the concluding chapter of* Death Is Different, *Bedau provides a thorough review of the debating points in the argument over capital punishment.*

1   Insofar as fundamental moral questions are raised by the death penalty, their resolution does not turn on what a majority of the Supreme Court says the Constitution permits or forbids. Nor does it rest on what the tea leaves of public-opinion polls can be construed to mean. Morally speaking, what are at stake are the *reasons* that can be brought forward to support or to criticize this punishment. These reasons—familiar from public debates, letters to the editor, and radio and television talk shows—have not significantly altered over the past generation, and perhaps not even during the past century.

2   In order of increasing importance, the main reasons for support seem to me to be these six: (1) the death penalty is a far less expensive method of punishment than the alternative of life imprisonment; the death penalty is more effective in preventing crime than the alternative because (2) it is a more effective deterrent, and because (3) it more effectively incapacitates; (4) the death penalty is required by justice; (5) in many cases there is no feasible alternative punishment; and (6) the death penalty vindicates the moral order and thus is an indispensable symbol of public authority. I want to evaluate each of these reasons and elaborate especially on those of salient current importance.

The Taxpayer's Argument

3   Is the death penalty really so much less expensive than long-term imprisonment? The answer depends on how one allocates the costs imposed under the two alternatives. The few attempts that have been made to do this in a manner comparable to the way economists try to answer other questions about the cost of alternative social policies are in agreement. In

the words of the most recent study, "A criminal justice system that includes the death penalty costs more than a system that chooses life imprisonment."[1] Why this is true is easily understood. It is mainly a consequence of the commendable desire to afford every protection to a defendant whose life is at stake, and virtually every such defendant avails himself of all these protections. If the defendant is indigent, as are most of those accused of crimes that put them in jeopardy of the death penalty, then society has to foot the bill for the defendant's attorney as well as for the costs involved in the prosecution, jury selection, trial, and appeals. Although in theory these costs would need to be paid even if the defendant were not on trial for his life, in practice the evidence shows that non-death-penalty trials and appeals are generally less protracted and therefore less expensive. So the taxpayer's argument, as I have called it, is simply wrong on the facts.

But, of course, even if it were sound, no decent citizen or responsible legislator would support the death penalty by relying on this argument alone. Those who seriously advance it do so only because they also believe that the criminals in question ought to be executed whatever the cost to society and however galling the expenditure may be. As a consequence, the taxpayer's argument is really no more than a side issue, since defenders and critics of the death penalty agree that economic costs should take a back seat to justice and social defense where human life is concerned. *4*

Uniquely Effective Deterrent

No one has ever offered any scientific evidence that the death penalty is an *5* effective deterrent, or more effective than the alternative of long-term imprisonment, to any such crime as rape, arson, burglary, kidnapping, aircraft hijacking, treason, espionage, or terrorism (which itself typically involves one or more of these other crimes). All arguments for the death penalty that rest on belief in its superior deterrent capacity to prevent or reduce the incidence of these crimes depend entirely on guesswork, common sense, or analogy to its allegedly superior deterrent effects on the crime of murder.

What, then, is the evidence that the death penalty is an effective de *6* terrent to murder? There is little or none. Murder comes in many different forms (gangland killings, murder among family members, murder during armed robbery or burglary, murder in jail or prison, murder for hire, murder to escape custody or avoid arrest), but very little of the research on deterrence has concentrated exclusively on one of these types to the exclusion of all the rest. The threat of executions is conceivably a much better deterrent to some types of murder than to others; but no research currently exists to confirm such a hypothesis.

It doesn't really matter. Deterrence is increasingly a make-weight in *7* the argument for the death penalty. Public opinion surveys indicate that most of those who profess support for the death penalty would support it even if they were convinced—contrary to what they believe—that it is not a better deterrent than life imprisonment.[2] I find this plausible. Although from time to time there is sporadic evidence in favor of the deterrent power of executions (hardly anyone who thinks about it attaches much differential deterrent efficacy to the death penalty *statutes,* all by themselves), none of it survives careful scrutiny very long.[3] If anything, there is a steadily accumulating body of evidence to suggest that on balance the death penalty may cause (or encourage, or set the example for) more homicides than it prevents, because its "brutalizing" effect out-performs its deterrent effect.[4]

8   Furthermore, and quite apart from the status of the evidence on the issue of deterrence vs. brutalization, one would expect that the rationale for deterrence in our society is of slowly declining importance. In previous centuries and up to a generation ago, when our society punished many *non* homicidal crimes with death, deterrence was the most plausible reason for hanging a counterfeiter or a horse thief or a claim jumper. Today, however, with the death penalty applied exclusively to murder, nondeterrent considerations naturally play an increasingly prominent role all the time. Indeed, social science research, public opinion, and Supreme Court rulings all neatly converge at this point. Despite more than a decade of effort to obtain convincing support for rational belief in the superior deterrent power of the death penalty, the evidence points the other way. During the same period, advocates of capital punishment—both those who are and those who are not aware of this lack of evidence—shifted the basis of their support for executions from deterrence to other reasons. Meanwhile, the Supreme Court has said in effect that the death penalty is unconstitutional except where it is not disproportionate to the crime and regardless of its deterrent effects.

9   From a public-policy perspective, one can say this: During the past fifteen years, the legislative re-enactment of death penalty statutes has been no more than a series of stabs in the dark, insofar as these laws have been predicated on their supposed superior deterrence. A legislature ought to have better reasons than this for trying to protect the life of its citizens by imposing the threat of the death penalty. On moral grounds, general deterrence is certainly a legitimate function of the criminal law and therefore a justifiable basis on which to construct a system of punishments under law. Nevertheless, the choice of more rather than less severity in punishment for particular crimes on grounds of better deterrence alone encounters two different objections. One is that we violate moral principles if we are willing to use punitive methods, regardless of their savagery, in order to secure slight improvements in deterrence; the other is that there simply is no adequate evidence in favor of the superior deterrent efficacy of the death penalty.

Incapacitation and Prevention

No one can dispute that capital punishment, when carried out, does effec-   10
tively incapacitate each offender who is executed. (This has nothing to do
with deterrence, however, because deterrence operates by threat and intim-
idation, not by destroying the capacity to break the law.) Does this incapacitation make a significant dent in the crime rate? The Department of
Justice has reported that as of the end of 1984 "approximately 2 of every
3 offenders under sentence of death had a prior felony conviction; nearly 1
out of 10 had previously been convicted of homicide."[5] These data indicate that more than a hundred of those currently under sentence of death
may be some of the worst offenders in the nation—and that several hundred more served a prison term for robbery, assault, or some other crime,
and then, after their release, went on to commit the even graver crime of
murder. (Of course, these data simultaneously show that the vast majority
of condemned prisoners are *not* recidivist murderers.) But do these data
also show that society needs the incapacitating power of death to prevent
more crimes from being committed by convicted capital offenders?

If parole boards and release authorities knew in advance which in-   11
mates would murder after their release, the inmates in question would obviously be prevented from committing these offenses by being kept in some
form of custody. Yet we have no reliable methods for predicting future
dangerousness, and especially not for the propensity of a convicted murderer to murder again.[6] Consequently, the only effective general-policy alternatives to the present one are a system of mandatory death penalties
and a system of mandatory prison terms for life. Even then, if the Bureau's
own statistics are reliable, this would prevent only a tiny fraction of the
twenty thousand or so murders committed in this nation each year. The
truth is, as all release statistics agree, very few of the persons convicted of
homicide and sent to prison are ever convicted of homicide again. Either to
kill all those convicted of murder or to keep them all in prison forever, because of a few exceptions that cannot be identified in advance, would be
an expensive and unjustified policy that very few of us, on reflection,
would want to support.

Opponents of the death penalty encounter their stiffest objections   12
when they try to explain why even the multiple or serial or recidivist murderer should not be executed. Few would disagree that "the thirst for revenge is keenest in the case of mass murder, . . . especially when it includes elements of sadism and brutality against innocent victims."[7]
Revenge apart, incapacitation probably has its most convincing application in such cases. It is hardly surprising that many who generally oppose
the death penalty would be willing to make an exception for such killers.

Let us note first that if the death penalty were confined to such cases,   13
abolitionists would have scored a major victory. The immediate consequence of such a policy would be an unprecedented reduction in the annu-

al number of death sentences—a drop from more than two hundred per year to fewer than twenty, if we can rely on the Bureau of Justice Statistics report quoted above. Any policy change that reduced death sentences by more than 90 percent should be welcomed by opponents of the death penalty as a giant step in the right direction.

14   More controversial is whether abolitionists could accommodate such an exception on moral grounds. The best way to do so, it seems to me, is to argue much as George Bernard Shaw did earlier in this century in his little book *The Crime of Imprisonment* that the execution of such murderers is society's only alternative—we have no nonlethal methods of sedation or restraint that suffice to make certain that such offenders will not and cannot kill yet again. However, this is a factual question, and I (unlike Shaw) think that once the offender is in our custody, we are never in the position where our only recourse is to lethal methods. Others who have studied the problem more carefully agree;[8] there are reasonably humane methods at our disposal for coping with the most difficult and dangerous prisoners.

15   In the end, however, I think one must admit that the refusal to execute a murderer who has repeated his crime—not to mention those who embody murderous evil on a gigantic scale, such as an Adolph Eichmann or a Lavrenti Beria—is evidence of a position on the death penalty that owes something to fanatic devotion as well as to cool reason. Dedicated pacifists and devoutly religious opponents of the death penalty may well be able to embrace such categorical opposition to executions without fear of rebuke from reason. Conscientious liberals, however, cannot so easily refuse to compromise. Do they not already compromise on other life-and-death issues—often tolerating suicide, euthanasia, abortion, the use of lethal force in social and self-defense—thereby showing that they refuse to accept any moral principle that categorically condemns all killing? If so, what is so peculiarly objectionable, from the moral point of view as they see it, in an occasional state-authorized killing of that rare criminal, the murderer who has murdered more than once? I cannot point to any clear and defensible moral principle of general acceptability that is violated by such a compromise, a principle that *absolutely forbids* such executions. If one nonetheless opposes all executions, as I do, then it must be on other grounds.

Retributive and Vindictive Justice

16   Today there is substantial agreement that retribution is an essential aspect of the criminal justice system, and that a general policy of punishment for convicted criminals is the best means to this end. Less agreement exists on whether retribution alone justifies the practice of punishment; and there is no consensus on how to construct a penalty schedule on retributive grounds, matching the severity of punishments to the gravity of crimes. Regrettable confusion of the dangerous (though normal) emotion of anger

and the desire for revenge it spawns—neither of which has any reliable connection to justice—with moral indignation at victimization—which does—often clouds the thinking of those who defend the "morality" of capital punishment.[9] There is also disagreement on whether other considerations of justice—such as equality, fairness of administration, and respect for the rights of the accused—should yield or prevail when they conflict with the demands of retribution.

These issues are inescapably philosophical, and I have my own views on them, which I have explained elsewhere.[10] In a word, the most that principles of retribution can do for the death penalty is to *permit* it for murder; principles of retribution are strained beyond their capacity if they are invoked to justify the death penalty for any other crime. Thus if retribution is the moral principle on which defenders of the death penalty want to rest their case, then morality requires that nonhomicidal crimes must be punished in some less severe manner. However, the principles of retribution do not *require* us to punish murder by death; what they require is the severest punishment for the gravest crime consistent with our other moral convictions. Consequently, the appeal to retribution in the present climate of discussion—and it is a widespread appeal—fails to justify the death penalty.

In fact I think there is considerable self-deception among those who think they rest their defense of the death penalty on the moral principles of just retribution. Those principles cannot explain why society actually executes those few whom it does, and why it sentences to death no more than a small percentage of the murderers it convicts. Retribution is another fig leaf to cover our nakedness, I am afraid, even if it appears to be a respectable line of moral reasoning when taken in the abstract.

In recent years, neo-conservative writers of various sorts—such as columnist George F. Will, New York's Mayor Edward Koch, and academicians Walter Berns and Ernest van den Haag—have made much of the vindictive powers of the death penalty and of the civilizing and moralizing influence it thus wields. Van den Haag writes, "The [death] penalty is meant to vindicate the social order."[11] Berns elaborates the point: "The criminal law must be made awful, by which I mean, awe-inspiring. . . . It must remind us of the moral order by which alone we can live as *human* beings, and in our day the only punishment that can do this is capital punishment."[12] The language is resonant, but the claim is unconvincing.

One purpose of *any* system of punishment is to vindicate the moral order established by the criminal law—and properly so, because that order protects the rights of the law-abiding and because in a liberal society those rights are the basis for self-esteem and mutual respect. To go further, however, and insist that lethal punishment is the "only" appropriate response by society to the gravest crimes is wrong on two counts. The claim itself relies on naked moral intuitions about how to fit punishments to crimes,

17

18

19

20

and such intuitions—with their deceptive clarity and superficial rationale—are treacherous. The least bit of historical sophistication would tell us that our forebears used the same kind of intuitive claims on behalf of maiming and other savageries that we would be ashamed to preach today. Furthermore, the claim makes sense only against the background of a conception of the state as a mystical entity of semi-divine authority, a conception that is hardly consistent with our pluralistic, liberal, nontheocratic traditions.

The Alternative

21 Imprisonment as it is currently practiced in this country is anything but an ideal alternative to the death penalty. Life imprisonment without the possibility of parole has been opposed by all experienced prison administrators as a virtually unmanageable option. The more one knows about most American prisons the more one judges long-term imprisonment to be a terrible curse for all concerned.[13] Defenders of the death penalty rightly point out that persons in prison can and sometimes do murder other inmates, guards, or visitors—although such crimes occur much less frequently than some of those defenders imply. (Nor do they occur with greater frequency in the prisons of states that do not punish these crimes with death than in the prisons of states that do.[14]) So imprisonment for ten or twenty years, not to mention for life, is vulnerable to many objections. Indeed, a cynic might even go so far to say that one of the best reasons for the death penalty is the alternative to it. Nevertheless, I think this alternative is still superior to execution—and will have to suffice until something better is proposed—for at least three important reasons.

22 First, society avoids the unsolvable problem of picking and choosing among the bad to try to find the worst, in order to execute them. Experience ought long ago to have taught us that it is an illusion to expect prosecutors, juries, and courts to perform this task in a fashion that survives criticism. Deciding not to kill any among the murderers we convict enables us to punish them all more equitably, just as it relieves us of the illusion that we can choose the worst among the bad, the irredeemable from the others, those who "deserve to die" from those who really do not.

23 Second, we avoid the risk and costly error of executing the innocent, in favor of the equally risky but far less costly error of imprisoning the innocent. Arresting, trying, convicting, and punishing the innocent is an unavoidable problem, whose full extent in our history is only now beginning to be understood. Recent research on persons erroneously convicted of capital crimes in this century in the United States has identified some 350 such cases.[15] Scores of these convictions occurred in states where there was no death penalty; dozens of these errors were corrected and in some instances the wrongly convicted defendant was indemnified. Not so in all cases in the death penalty states. Where is the necessity—moral or empirical—to run the risk of executing the innocent?[16]

Third, there is a crucial symbolic significance in drawing the line at   24
punishments that deprive the offender of his liberty. Just as we no longer
permit the authorities to use torture to secure confessions or to attack the
body of the convicted offender with whips, branding irons, or other instruments that maim and stigmatize, nor to carry out the death penalty by the
cruelest means our fevered imaginations can devise—even though some
still cry out that social defense and just retribution require it—so we
should repudiate the death penalty. It belongs alongside these other bar-
baric practices, which our society has rejected in principle.

For at least these reasons, the alternative of imprisonment is prefer-   25
able to death as punishment in all cases.[17]

The Symbolism: Death or Life?

During earlier centuries, the death penalty played a plausible, perhaps even   26
justifiable, role in society's efforts to control crime and mete out just
deserts to convicted offenders. After all, the alternative of imprisonment—
the modern form of banishment—had yet to be systematically developed.
Consequently, society in an earlier age could tolerate the death penalty
with a clearer conscience than we can today. For us, however, the true dimension in which to assess this mode of punishment is neither its crime-
fighting effectiveness nor its moral necessity, but its symbolism. Mistaken
faith in deterrent efficacy, confusion over the requirements of justice, indifference to unfair administration, ignorance of nonlethal methods of social
control—all these can explain only so much about the current support for
the death penalty. The rest of the explanation lies elsewhere, in what executions symbolize, consciously or unconsciously, for those who favor
them.

This symbolism deserves a closer look.[18] The death penalty, today as   27
in the past, symbolizes the ultimate power of the state, and of the government of society, over the individual citizen. Understandably, the public
wants visible evidence that the authority of its political leaders is intact,
their powers competent to deal with every social problem, and their
courage resolute in the face of any danger. Anxiety about war, fear of
crime, indignation at being victimized provoke the authorities to use the
power of life and death as a public gesture of strength, self-confidence, and
reassurance. Not surprisingly, many are unwilling to abandon the one
symbol a society under law in peacetime has at its disposal that, above all
others, expresses this power with awe-inspiring finality: the death penalty.

This is precisely why, in the end, we should oppose the death penalty   28
in principle and without exception. As long as capital punishment is available under law for any crime, it is a temptation to excess. Tyrannical governments, from Idi Amin's Uganda to the Ayatollah's Iran, teach this lesson. At best the use of the death penalty here and elsewhere has been and
continues to be capricious and arbitrary. The long history of several of our

own states, notably Michigan and Wisconsin, quite apart from the experience of other nations, proves that the government of a civilized society does not *need* the death penalty. The citizenry should not clamor for it. Their political leaders should know better—as, of course, the best of them do—than to cultivate public approval for capital statutes, death sentences, and executions. Instead a civilized government should explain why such practices are ill-advised, and why they are ineffective in reducing crime, removing its causes, and responding to victimization.

Notes

1. Comment, "The Cost of Taking a Life: Dollars and Sense of the Death Penalty," *U. C. Davis Law Review* 18 (1985):1221–74, at 1270.

2. See *The Gallup Report,* January-February 1986, nos. 244–45, pp. 10–16; and Phoebe C. Ellsworth and Lee Ross, "Public Opinion and Capital Punishment: A Closer Examination of the Views of Abolitionists and Retentionists," *Crime & Delinquency* 29 (1983):116–69, at 147.

3. The findings reported by Isaac Ehrlich, "The Deterrent Effect of Capital Punishment: A Question of Life and Death," *American Economic Review* 65 (1975):397–417 ("[each] additional execution . . . may have resulted . . . in 7 or 8 fewer murders") have been extensively criticized; see, e.g., Lawrence R. Klein, Brian Forst, and Victor Filatov, "The Deterrent Effect of Capital Punishment: An Assessment of the Estimates," in Alfred Blumstein, Jacqueline Cohen, and Daniel Nagin, eds., *Deterrence and Incapacitation: Estimating the Effects of Criminal Sanctions on Crime Rates* (1978), pp. 336–60. The findings reported by James A. Yunker, "Is the Death Penalty a Deterrent to Homicide? Some Time Series Evidence," *Journal of Behavioral Economics* 5 (1976):45–81 ("one execution will deter 156 murders") have been evaluated and found wanting by James Alan Fox, "The Identification and Estimation of Deterrence: An Evaluation of Yunker's Model," *Journal of Behavioral Economics* 6 (1977):225–42. The findings reported by David P. Phillips, "The Deterrent Effect of Capital Punishment: New Evidence on an Old Controversy," *American Journal of Sociology* 86 (1980):139–48 (". . . in the two weeks following a public execution the frequency of homicide drops by 35.7%") has been refuted by William J. Bowers, "Deterrence or Brutalization: What is the Truth About Highly Publicized Executions?" (unpublished). The latest claims in this vein are by Stephen K. Layson, "Homicide and Deterrence: A Reexamination of the United States Time-Series Evidence," *Southern Economic Journal* 52 (1985):68–89 ("the tradeoff of executions for murders is approximately— 18.5," i.e., each execution results in a net decrease of 18.5 murders); for criticism see James Alan Fox, "Persistent Flaws in Econometric Studies of the Death Penalty: A Discussion of Layson's Findings," testimony submitted to the Subcommittee on Criminal Justice, House of Representatives, U.S. Congress, 7 May 1986.

4. See Bowers, "Deterrence or Brutalization."

5. United States, Department of Justice, Bureau of Justice Statistics, *Capital Punishment 1984* (1985), p. 1.

6. Mark H. Moore et al., *Dangerous Offenders: The Elusive Target of Justice* (1984), and Ted Honderich et al., "Symposium: Predicting Dangerousness," *Criminal Justice Ethics* 2 (Winter/Spring 1983):3–17.

7. Jack Levin and James Alan Fox, *Mass Murder: America's Growing Menace* (1985), p. 222. The authors do not support the death penalty for serial, mass, or recidivist murderers.

8. See especially Norval Morris, *The Future of Imprisonment* (1974), pp. 85–121.

9. This is especially true of Walter Berns, *For Capital Punishment: Crime and the Morality of the Death Penalty* (1979), pp. 153ff. The arousal of "anger" is not evidence that anything morally wrong is its cause. There is no reason to believe that the punitive policies adopted by a society "angry" at criminals will be fair or effective in reducing crime. The revenge that "anger" can motivate has no claim as such to the title of just retribution. Moral indignation is another matter. As a feeling, it may be indistinguishable from anger, but its claim for a different status rests on its essential connection to a moral principle; one's indignation is aroused only if an important moral principle has been violated. Even when this happens, the policies inspired by moral indignation are not thereby guaranteed to be just or effective; and the capacity for self-deception about the legitimacy of one's indignation is legendary.

10. See Bedau,"Classification-Based Sentencing: Some Conceptual and Ethical Problems," *New England Journal of Criminal and Civil Confinement* 10 (1984):1–26; Bedau, "Prisoners' Rights," *Criminal Justice Ethics* 1 (Winter/Spring 1982):26–41; Bedau, "Retribution and the Theory of Punishment," *Journal of Philosophy* 75 (1978):601–20; Bedau, "Penal Theory and Prison Reality Today," *Juris Doctor* 2 (December 1972):40–43.

11. Ernest van den Haag, "The death penalty vindicates the law," *American Bar Association Journal* 71 (April 1985):38–42, at 42; cf. van den Haag, "Refuting Reiman and Nathanson," *Philosophy & Public Affairs* 14 (1985):165–76 ("punishment must vindicate the disrupted public order").

12. Berns, *For Capital Punishment*, p. 173.

13. See, e.g., Robert Johnson and Hans Toch, eds., *The Pains of Imprisonment* (1982).

14. See Wendy Phillips Wolfson, "The Deterrent Effect of the Death Penalty upon Prison Murder," in Bedau, ed., *The Death Penalty in America*, 3d ed. (1982), pp. 159–73.

15. Hugo Adam Bedau and Michael L. Radelet, "Miscarriages of Justice in Potentially Capital Cases," presented at the annual meeting of the American Society of Criminology, November 1985.

16. Ernest van den Haag argues, with evident complacency, that the death penalty does "lead to the unintended death of some innocents in the long run"; he goes on to add that this leaves the death penalty precisely where other things of the same sort are: "in the long run nearly all human activities are likely to lead to the unintended deaths of innocents." Van den Haag, "The death penalty vindicates the law," p. 42. This tends to obscure three important points. First, lawful activities that take "statistical lives" (e.g., coal mining) are not designed to kill anyone, whereas every death by capital punishment (whether of a guilty or of an innocent person) is intentional. Second, society permits dangerous commercial and recreational activities on various grounds—it would be wrongly paternalistic to interfere with what people choose to do at their own risk (e.g., scaling dangerous cliffs), and society can better afford the cost of the risky activity than the cost of its complete

prevention or stricter regulation (e.g., public highways crowded with long truck-trailer rigs rather than separate highways for cars and trucks). But these reasons have no bearing on the choice between the death penalty and imprisonment, unless the combined deterrent/incapacitative effects of executions are demonstrably superior to those of the alternative. Since no defender of the death penalty has sustained the burden of the proof on this point—see the papers cited in n. 3 supra—van den Haag's argument is undermined. Van den Haag's position would be less vulnerable to objection if the only executions he favored were of persons convicted of several—serial, multiple, or recidivist—murders. But he does not confine his support for the death penalty to such cases.

17. Michael Davis has recently argued that the death penalty is no more "irrevocable," in any important sense of that term, than many other punishments, including life in prison. See Davis, "Is the Death Penalty Irrevocable?" *Social Theory and Practice* 10 (1984):143–56. Insofar as he addresses the arguments I put forward in Chapter 1, to explain why death is a "more severe" punishment than imprisonment, he does not seem to disagree. On his interpretation, however, the issue of revocability has nothing to do with severity (see p. 147). Basic to his argument that the punishments of death and of life in prison are equally (ir)revocable is the idea that (a) an irrevocable punishment is such that if it is erroneously imposed on someone, then there is no way to compensate the person for the injustice he suffers, and (b) anyone has interests that are not extinguished with the end of natural life (see p. 146). But as compensating a person is not always identical with conferring a benefit on something he is interested in—rather, it is sometimes a matter of benefiting *him*, directly and in his own person—the truth of (a) and (b) do not entail that there is no difference, relative to irrevocability, that distinguishes the punishment of death from a life behind bars.

18. See Barbara Ann Stolz, "Congress and Capital Punishment: An Exercise in Symbolic Politics," *Law & Policy Quarterly* 5 (1983):157–80; and Tom R. Tyler and Renee Weber, "Support for the Death Penalty: Instrumental Response to Crime, or Symbolic Attitude?" *Law & Society Review* 17 (1982):21–45. Tyler and Weber bifurcate all defenses of the death penalty into the "instrumental" and the "symbolic." Thus a retributive defense of the death penalty is, for them, merely "symbolic." Nor do they make it clear whether the "symbolic" role of this punishment is a conscious and intentional one. Stolz is concerned with the conscious symbolism of enacting national (more precisely, federal) criminal penalties; how much of what she reports could be transferred without loss to the reasons for enactment of state death penalty laws or to the reasons the public supports executions (state or federal) is not clear.

Reading and Analyzing

1. On what should the resolution of the death-penalty debate rest? Why?
2. How does Bedau organize his discussion?
3. What are the six arguments in support of capital punishment, according to Bedau? Compare these to the arguments of van den Haag; has Bedau covered the arguments he presents?

4. What two reasons are given for dismissing the "taxpayer's argument"? Compare Bedau and van den Haag on the significance of cost in one's position on the death penalty; do they agree? What might you conclude from your comparison?

5. What is Bedau's position on deterrence? Is there evidence that the death penalty deters murder? Is deterrence a justifiable use of criminal law? Is capital punishment justifiable as a possible deterrent?

6. What are the facts on recidivist murderers? What kind of murderer do many people want executed, even those who generally oppose the death penalty? What would be accomplished if only this kind of murderer were executed? Which group of people will still be unhappy? Why?

7. Does retribution *allow* for the death penalty? Does it *require* it? What distinction does Bedau make between *retribution* and *revenge* ? What does Bedau's distinctions among words illustrate about the nature of good argument?

8. What are Bedau's two arguments for rejecting capital punishment as the necessary response to grave crimes?

9. Bedau begins his discussion of the alternative to the death penalty by agreeing that it is not an ideal alternative. By so doing, what does he accomplish? How does this strengthen his argument?

10. The author offers three reasons for preferring imprisonment to the death penalty; explain each in your own words.

11. What does the death penalty symbolize, according to Bedau? Why is that the very reason to oppose the death penalty?

Responding to the Writer's Ideas

1. Compare Bedau's views on deterrence to van den Haag's. Who makes the better case? Why?

2. Which of the three reasons for supporting imprisonment over death sentencing do you think is the strongest? Why?

3. Could you accept the compromise position of death sentencing only for multiple murderers? Is this a position that we should strive to bring about as the standard in this country? Why or why not?

4. Do you consider the desire for revenge an appropriate justification for the death penalty? If so, how would you refute Bedau on this issue?

5. Has Bedau led you to change your views on capital punishment in any way? Explain.

WRITING SUGGESTIONS

1. In a 500-word essay present a case for restricting television coverage of violent crimes. In addition to making an argument for restrictions, you will need to decide how restrictions should be determined. For example, if news directors should be self-censors, then what criteria should be used for deciding how much and what kind of coverage is appropriate?

2. Prepare a 500-word position paper (a) for or against handgun control or (b) for or against capital punishment. You should, for the most part, use your own words and details to illustrate points. However, if you draw specifically on your reading, be certain to credit sources appropriately.

3. In a 500-word essay, argue that the existing pattern of racial bias is (or is not) a sufficient reason to abolish capital punishment.

4. In a 500-word essay, argue that the possibility of deterrence (as demonstrated by reasoning but not based on clear evidence—the current situation) is (or is not) sufficient cause to maintain the death penalty as a punishment for serious crimes.

5. In a 500-word essay, argue for (or against) the compromise position on the death penalty, namely, that it should be used only for multiple murders or the most heinous murders.

6. Prepare a 500-word position paper on the issue of the public display of executions, that is, on television coverage of executions, whether by lethal injection or the gas chamber or electrocution.

7. In an essay offer your solutions to the problem of street crime. Consider not only what *should* be done but also what, in practical terms, *can* be done to reduce crime, and *how* it can be accomplished. (This topic can also be expanded into a research essay with formal documentation.)

8. In an essay offer your solutions to the problem of drugs. Do not just repeat Charles Krauthammer's solution, but consider other approaches or how, specifically, to implement Krauthammer's solution. (This topic can also be expanded into a research essay with formal documentation.)

9. Do some research into the history of capital punishment laws in your state (if it has had or now has the death penalty) or a state you are interested in that has had or now has the death penalty. Learn about the number of executions and the cases that led to death sentencing, the number of appeals, and the number of murders during the years of capital punishment and without capital punishment. Prepare a report on your study and consider what, if any, conclusions you think can be drawn from the evidence you obtain.

CHAPTER 7

EXPLORING THE
ETHICS AND
POLITICS OF
TODAY'S HEALTH
ISSUES

"**T**he fires are burning" writes Representative Harry Johnston of what Dr. Thomas Bodenheimer calls "the nation's health care chaos." The divisive abortion-rights debate is, Goodman asserts, a "crisis"; and euthanasia is, in the words of Drs. Peter Singer and Mark Siegler, a "perilous public policy." Although the tone of the articles in this chapter is generally serious and restrained, the words used to describe the debated issues are measures of the seriousness of the problems, at least in the eyes of those who have chosen to address them. The nation's health problems, and the health care systems to pay for them, are now firmly on the debate agenda. The debate in some cases, however, is less about what, exactly, we should do and more about the need to do something. Writers still feel compelled to convince readers that the problems are of crisis proportions; hence their choice of language.

The choice of words for the chapter's title also carries a message. For many, health issues such as abortion and euthanasia are ethical issues only, but the reality of these, and other health problems, is that they have become political issues, too. Reproductive decisions such as abortion or controlling the number of pregnancies seem among the most private and personal of decisions, yet, as Ellen Goodman and Jessica Mathews make clear, these have become two of the most virulent issues we face. Goodman addresses the divisiveness of the abortion debate in "Away from Absolutism," calling for both sides somehow to find common ground and reduce the level of conflict. Mathews attacks President Bush directly in "Life and Death: U.S. Population Policy" for his refusal to support organizations that provide family planning education and contraceptives worldwide. Charles Krauthammer in "Who Is Spreading AIDS?" exposes the politicizing of AIDS in the arguments over who are responsible, who are the victims, and what the government should do. Finally, George Will establishes the relationship between smoking and politics when he writes that "the tax treatment of tobacco is relevant to today's entwined arguments about health care and budget deficits." Although smoking is a serious health hazard that increases the cost of health care for all of us and raising taxes on cigarettes could help reduce the deficit, tobacco growers and tobacco companies are not without political leverage and continue to protect their interests.

Part of the ongoing debate over legalizing euthanasia is whether this issue should be discussed only as a private moral decision or as a public-policy decision. Each side has its defender in this chapter. Drs. Peter Singer and Mark Siegler in "Euthanasia: A Critique" provide a detailed review of the debate and also present and support a case against legalizing euthanasia. One of their arguments is that if euthanasia becomes legal, some unwanted people may be euthanized against their will—the poor, the mentally retarded, the elderly, the disabled. This argument could be significant, or it could be a slippery slope fallacy, depending upon the degree of your trust in people or in how well medicine is administered and controlled. Singer and Siegler also raise the issue of the physician's role or relationship to patients. The argument on the other side usually focuses on the individual, the right of the suffering patient to control his or her life, which also means deciding when to end that life. Sidney Hook, writing after heart failure followed by a stroke, makes an emotional plea for the individual's right to choose.

Hook also uses the argument that a very sick elderly person such as himself should not place such a costly burden on health care resources, an argument that underscores the crisis in U.S. health care services. What crisis, many employed, affluent Americans may respond. These Americans have health care benefits through their jobs, and they have the money for extras—good dental care, for example. Representative Johnston addresses his article, "Health Care: Fire Out of Control," to these people who need, in Johnston's view, to recognize that something must be done to provide health care to the many Americans without coverage and to control the spiraling costs of health care, now 14 percent of the country's GNP. Because health care is tied to employment in this country, the unemployed and those working part-time have no insurance, resulting in little health care except for emergencies. What are we to do to provide access to quality care for all Americans without costs becoming prohibitive? Dr. Bodenheimer, a California physician, and Caspar Weinberger, former Secretary of Defense, propose two quite different plans. One proposal is for a national health care program that would continue to provide services through a variety of private physicians and HMOs but would cover everyone regardless of employment. The other proposal is to maintain the existing structure except that the federal government would provide health care insurance for the unemployed. Each writer explains the perceived advantages of his program and attacks the opposition's proposal. If only the solution were as simple as selecting one proposal or the other! Unfortunately for those who continue to live without quality care, several interest groups—physicians, private hospitals, and providers such as Blue Cross/Blue Shield—have used their political leverage to forestall a shift to a national health plan. And so we come full circle, once again recognizing the close connection between the ethics and the politics of today's health issues.

❖

Away from Absolutism

Ellen Goodman

Author of Close to Home *(1979),* At Large *(1981), and* Keeping Touch *(1985), collections of her essays, Ellen Goodman (b. 1940) has been a feature writer for the Boston* Globe *since 1967 and a syndicated columnist since 1976. Her columns appear in over 250 newspapers, and she has won a Pulitzer Prize for her commentary. Goodman examines social problems and changing lifestyles as frequently as political issues, as her columns reprinted here attest. In the following article, published on January 25, 1992, Goodman examines the painfully divisive issue of abortion rights.*

1   BOSTON—The anniversary went as expected. After 19 years of protests and counterprotests that mark the Supreme Court's abortion decision, everyone knows the drill. Placards of fetuses over here, posters of coat hangers over there. Sound bites all around.

2   Of course, the energy level seemed higher this year, and the sense of urgency heightened. That too was to be expected. After all, the Supreme Court has decided to hear the Pennsylvania case this spring. If the justices overturn *Roe v. Wade* or empty it of any last sips of meaning, the date of the protests may change, but the argument will go on.

3   Anyone who doubts that should check the age of the protesters. They are getting younger, not older.

4   What a fix we are in. Pro-life and pro-choice forces are more than polarized; they are mutually demonized. Most Americans feel deeply ambivalent about abortion—with views that are complicated and highly personal. But the issue is as public and oversimplified as a vote. Ambivalence is only heard as two separate voices, arguing in absolutist terms.

5   As a country, we would like the issue to go away, but instead it's shifting into a higher focus. As a people, we rank it low on the list of national priorities, but it's gaining importance in politics. It will rage on in the presidential campaign, in Congress where the Freedom of Choice Act will gain ground, in state legislatures, in the push to import the abortion pill.

6   Even Kate Michelman, the head of the National Abortion Rights Action League, stopped in the middle of the anniversary rituals to acknowledge, "Most Americans are hungry for some kind of solution for the con-

276

troversy. People are tired of battling out the issue in the public domain. They will do battle. But they want to move on and resolve this."

Abortion, she said wearily, "is not a happy event in the lives of women. We don't run around saying this is an experience you need to have a fulfilling life. I work on this issue, but I would like to see nothing more than a country that respects the right and works to reduce the need." 7

That wish may signal a new direction. During all the years of deadlock, those for and against a woman's right to decide have focused far more energy on abortion than on reducing the number of unintended pregnancies. Indeed, as someone who views the loss of abortion rights with alarm and more than that, a sense of betrayal, I share the current sense of crisis. But this is the time to broaden our perspective—not to dilute the energy, but to enlarge the argument and the audience. 8

Americans don't want to talk about rights without also talking about responsibility. We can't talk about how to end pregnancy without also talking about how it begins. 9

As Frances Kissling, the head of Catholics for a Free Choice says, "We who are feminists talk about women's right to control our bodies. For the right-to-lifers, that right ends at pregnancy. But for the pro-choicers, it often sounds as if the right *begins* at pregnancy." 10

The tough reality is that in half of all the abortions performed, neither the women nor their partners had used birth control. Just to raise this issue leaves pro-choice advocates open to charges of "guilt-tripping." We know, after all, about birth control flaws and failures. We know about human frailty as well. We don't subscribe to forced motherhood as a punishment. 11

But it is also true that those of us who defend the right to choose do not comfortably endorse abortion as a first choice. Those who believe that women are more than wombs do not regard the fetus as mere protoplasm. 12

Indeed, the same women and men who believe in women's rights support access to abortion as just one part of a much wider vision—one of women who are raised to be strong, self-confident and responsible. We have to be willing to say in public what we would say to our daughters. And to our sons. 13

It's hard to broaden the debate during a crisis; far easier to raise the same old banners. But maybe we can only lower the decibels of this debate by staking out this common ground. 14

People of strong moral sensibilities disagree violently about abortion. That is not going to change. But as Frances Kissling says, "We're going to have to live together in this country." Sometime, before the 20th anniversary of *Roe*, or the 25th, or the 50th, we have to begin learning how. 15

Reading and Analyzing

1. What anniversary does Goodman refer to at the beginning of her article?
2. The Supreme Court gave its decision on the Pennsylvania case in the summer of 1992. What was their ruling? Did they uphold or overturn *Roe versus Wade,* or keep abortion rights but place further restrictions on *Roe versus Wade?*
3. How do most Americans feel about abortion, according to Goodman?
4. How does Goodman depict the ambivalence in America? What images of the "debate" does she provide?
5. What is Goodman's position on abortion rights?
6. What is Goodman's claim? Be precise; this is not an argument for choice.
7. How does the author think the debate needs to be changed? How can we go about doing that?
8. Goodman has a distinctive writing style. Describe its essential elements. Consider her word choice, sentence patterns, choice of examples, and so on.

Responding to the Writer's Ideas

1. Is Goodman's assessment of American ambivalence accurate, in your view? Are the protesters on both sides not really representative of most people?
2. Where do you stand on the abortion issue?
3. Are you interested, as Goodman is, in trying to find some common ground? Why or why not?
4. Where should the issue be settled? In the Congress? State legislatures? The Supreme Court? Outside abortion clinics? Explain your answer.
5. If we are serious about reducing the need for abortion, we need to reduce the number of unwanted pregnancies. How do you propose that we accomplish that goal? What programs or policies would you initiate?

❖

Tobacco Road

George F. Will

After completing his Ph.D. at Princeton, George Will (b. 1941)
taught for several years before being drawn to Capitol Hill and then
to writing about politics. He has been a syndicated columnist since
1974; is the author of several books, one about his great love—
baseball; and is a regular participant on television programs of
political analysis. The following column, which appeared on February
16, 1992, reveals his broad range of social and political topics and
his biting style.

WASHINGTON—King James I, author of "Counterblast to Tobacco," 1
denounced tobacco as "harmful to the brain and dangerous to the
lungs"—this in the 17th century—and increased taxes on it 4,000 percent.
Now Virginia, the state that began with Jamestown settlement, named
after James I, has flinched from increasing cigarette taxes even half as
much as it should.

A rejected bill would have put the tax at 20 cents a pack. Virginia's 2
tax has been 2½ cents since 1966, when it was cut from 3 cents. The national
average is 24 cents. The nation's highest, Hawaii's, is 47 cents.

Taxing cigarettes when tobacco is the state's largest cash crop may 3
be hazardous to political health, but a 20 cent tax would obviate the need
for many unpopular budget cuts and increases in state fees and charges.
North Carolina, where 56 percent of America's cigarettes are made, recently
was driven by budget problems to raise the per-pack tax from 2 to 5
cents. Tobacco is a waning force there: The number of tobacco farms fell
from 100,000 to 41,800 between the mid-1980s and 1991, and poultry
now is a bigger business.

The tax treatment of tobacco is relevant to today's entwined argu- 4
ments about health care and budget deficits. Americans spend 13 percent
of GNP on health care, $2.2 billion a day. There would be huge savings if
Americans drank moderately, drove sensibly, exercised regularly, ate prudently
and smoked not at all. Two of today's expensive epidemics—crack
and AIDS—also are primarily "chosen calamities"—results of dangerous
behavior.

Smoking is the leading preventable cause of death. It kills more peo- 5
ple than the combined toll of AIDS, cocaine, heroin, alcohol, fire, auto-

279

mobile accidents, homicide and suicide. Today's national campaign against smoking is a paradigm of sound policy against optional problems.

6   Consider California, where in 1988 (the year lung cancer surpassed breast cancer as the leading cause of women's cancer deaths nationwide) voters enacted, by referendum, a 25 cent increase (to 35 cents) in the cigarette tax to fund tobacco education, medical care and research. A small amount of money (a pittance relative to cigarette advertising) has funded anti-smoking broadcast commercials such as:

7   "Only one in four Americans smokes, so chances are every time you light up somebody hates you. What a great way to keep your phone bill down."

8   "I mean, I'm not a businessman but just, I mean, a crazy thought. I mean, why sell cigarettes? Why not just sell phlegm and cut out the middleman?"

9   "I tried it twice, and I, ah, got all red in the face and I couldn't inhale and I felt like a jerk and, ah, never tried it again, which is the same as what happened to me with sex."

10   In three years the percentage of Californians smoking has declined 17 percent.

11   Canadians were heavier smokers per capita than Americans as recently as 1989. No more. Consumption has declined about 25 percent in three years. Virtually all cigarette advertising is banned, and health warnings must cover 20 percent of the front and back of a pack. Most important, since 1984 federal taxes, including sales taxes, have risen from 42 cents to $1.94 a pack. Provincial taxes bring the tax bite to about $3.70, so a pack costs about $5.50. Demand for cigarettes is most price-elastic among teen-agers, those most vulnerable to cigarette addiction.

12   Tobacco companies, denying it all the way, work to hook tomorrow's cancer victims young. Consider Camel's hugely successful advertising campaign featuring Old Joe, the cartoon camel. Strong evidence suggests a causal connection between cigarette advertising and cigarette addiction among young people. Certainly the Old Joe campaign, now four years old, has coincided with a sharp increase in Camel's penetration of the youth market.

13   A coincidence? A study of children aged 3 to 6 showed that Old Joe was not quite as familiar as the McDonald's and Coca-Cola emblems but was more familiar than the Cheerios emblem. An astonishing 91 percent of 6-year-olds recognized Old Joe, about as many as recognized Mickey Mouse. The Camel people say the cartoon is aimed at adults, and they are shocked—shocked!—that anyone suspects otherwise.

14   The issue of health care is hot among politicians just now. They should be asked about tobacco subsidies and other issues relating to a habit that kills 430,000 Americans a year—more than 1,100 a day—at an

annual cost of $52 billion ($221 per American) in health care, insurance and lost productivity.

The growth of the U.S. tobacco industry is primarily overseas. About a quarter of all U.S.-made cigarettes are exported (many to Japan), and about 40 percent of raw tobacco grown here is sold abroad. On the home front, the latest survey of U.S. college freshmen reveals that both liberalism and smoking are again increasing on campus. Foolish choices are still jeopardizing public health.

15

Reading and Analyzing

1. What was the occasion, the political event, that led to Will's column?
2. What is Will's subject? Answer thoughtfully; Will's subject is broader than Virginia's tax on cigarettes.
3. What is Will's thesis, the claim of his argument? What, by statement or implication, does he want to see happen regarding smoking?
4. Will presents many statistics. Summarize the key facts, organizing them by subtopics such as taxing cigarettes, cigarette advertising, and so on.
5. What is the chief advantage of imposing high taxes on cigarettes? What is a second advantage?
6. What seems to be the relationship between advertising and cigarette addiction? Who denies this relationship?
7. Comment on Will's last two sentences. What do they tell you about his politics? What tone do they create?

Responding to the Writer's Ideas

1. Consider some of Will's statistics. Cigarettes are $5.50 a pack in Canada, and there is no advertising. In California strongly worded antismoking ads have been used. In Canada smoking has dropped by 20 percent in three years; in California the drop has been 17 percent. Does it seem logical to infer that price and advertising affect the number of smokers? Why or why not?
2. Consider the other side of the advertising coin. If you agree that no advertising or negative advertising work to decrease smoking, does it follow that positive advertising would increase smoking? If so, should cigarette advertising be eliminated? Why or why not?
3. Will accuses tobacco companies of trying, through advertising, to get young people to start smoking, even though the companies deny it. Who is right? How familiar are you with Joe Camel and other cigarette ads? (Test yourself; can you describe the basic ad strategies of

three or four different cigarettes?) Consider also the evidence that Will provides in paragraphs 12 and 13 when evaluating the purpose of cigarette advertising.

4. As Will explains, cigarette smoking is a major health hazard. So is secondhand smoke. What should be done? Should there be further restrictions on smokers in public places such as restaurants and offices? Should restaurants be fined if they fail to enforce no-smoking codes? Should companies have the right to deny employment to smokers? (Remember that smokers cost companies and other employees money in health care costs.) Should all government tobacco subsidies be eliminated? Should taxes be significantly increased on cigarettes? Should vending machines be eliminated to keep cigarettes from minors? Are there other suggestions that you have? Be prepared to defend your position on each of these suggestions.

❖

Life and Death: U.S. Population Policy

Jessica Tuchman Mathews

A magna cum laude graduate of Radcliffe College, Jessica Tuchman Mathews (b. 1946) received her doctorate in molecular biology from the California Institute of Technology. She is the vice president of World Resources Institute and writes a weekly column for the Washington Post. The column reprinted here, published February 16, 1992, speaks strongly of the need to address the problems of world population growth.

George Bush's hypocritical and cowardly intransigence on world population growth is keeping the United States from offering a choice of life over death to millions of women in developing countries. Recently released population projections shed a new light on the future costs of this harsh policy.

There is no blinking at one devastating fact: Children born less than two years after their next older sibling are almost twice as likely to die as those born more than two years apart. Spacing is the single most important contributor to infant death. Providing the means of spacing births can therefore prevent huge numbers—perhaps one-fifth—of these deaths, and a considerable portion of maternal mortality as well.

This is not a matter of imposing someone else's culturally alien notion of the right number of children on a Kenyan, Indonesian or Saudi couple. It is about providing the means for couples who want to space or limit the number of their children to do so. Demographers call this "unmet demand" for family planning services. They peg it today at 120 million women or couples. They know that to be a gross underestimate, because experience has shown that well-designed family planning programs create demand as word spreads from satisfied users to family, friends and neighbors. The real number lies somewhere between 120 million and the 300 million couples who do not now have access to contraceptives.

The new United Nations projections reveal that it will matter enormously to our grandchildren whether contraceptive use spreads quickly or slowly. They show that the future is far more uncertain, and either much more threatening or a lot more hopeful, than we have been led to think.

5   Until now, official population projections have been built on the assumption that fertility will eventually reach replacement levels (in which each couple reproductively replaces itself by having, on average, 2.1 children) and stay there. After some decades at replacement fertility, populations stabilize. Depending on how fast replacement level fertility is reached, global population has been projected to stabilize at 9 billion to 14 billion people, approximately double to triple today's 5.3 billion.

6   The new U.N. figures expose what has been demographers' dirty little secret: Constant replacement fertility is an assumption adopted for reasons of statistical convenience. There are no grounds for believing that human behavior will actually follow that pattern. Most developed countries are 10 percent to 20 percent below replacement fertility today and may not increase. Other countries may never reach replacement.

7   Here's how much it matters. Sticking with the old assumption and using the most up-to-date data on birth rates, socioeconomic trends and the like, the United Nations now projects global stabilization in 2150 at 11.5 billion (up, incidentally, from its previous estimate of 10.1 billion). If, however, fertility is assumed to be 5 percent higher than replacement, global population in that year would be 20.8 billion and climbing. If fertility is just 5 percent lower, population would be 5.6 billion. (This is not a typo. Those who want to know more about these astonishing numbers can consult a clear, short explanation by the Population Reference Bureau.)

8   Since 1984, the United States has withheld funds from the principal providers of international family planning services, the U.N. Population Fund and private agencies—the former with the concocted excuse that the money might otherwise support forced programs in China, the latter on the grounds that no U.S. money should go to any agency that directly or indirectly provides abortion services, even counseling or referral. The fact that fewer contraceptives means more abortions and more deaths does not seem to trouble those who support these policies.

9   For three years, the president has vetoed or threatened to veto every congressional attempt to overturn these policies and repulsed every effort at compromise. Yet before Bush became Ronald Reagan's vice-president, he was a leading advocate of international family planning, criticizing the "timidity" of agencies that could not understand how "desperately" these services are needed.

10   Politicians have the right to change their minds, but when they do they have to explain why. Bush has never done so. I don't believe that he can. All of the reasons he once cited for making population control a top international priority are far more urgent today than they were 20 years ago.

In a recent speech to the United Nations, former World Bank president Robert S. McNamara outlined an aggressive program to slow global population growth, one pillar of which would be the provision of comprehensive family planning. He estimated the cost in 2000 at $8 billion (in 1990 dollars) most of which would be borne by developing countries. International assistance would need to grow fourfold to $3.5 billion, about 5 percent of all development assistance. That is a pittance.

Whether the motivation is altruistic or selfish, principally to relieve needless human suffering or to ensure the future habitability of the planet, the U.N. numbers make clear that there are urgent reasons—of both fear and hope—for the United States to do its part in providing the means for family planning. Congress is ready to act. This is the president's choice—between reason and conscience or politics as usual.

Reading and Analyzing

1. What is Mathews's subject? What is her attitude toward the topic—her thesis?
2. What is the significance of spacing children? How many women lack the contraceptives that would allow them to space or limit their children?
3. What world population is expected when replacement level fertility is reached?
4. How important is it to reach replacement level fertility soon? What happens to world population figures the longer replacement is not achieved?
5. What money is needed to provide worldwide family planning to stabilize population growth?
6. Why is the United States not providing any of the money? Who, specifically, does Mathews blame for the problem? What does she accuse him of?

Responding to the Writer's Ideas

1. Mathews provides many numbers designed to strengthen her position on family planning. Does she present the numbers clearly? Are her sources reliable? Are you prepared to accept the numbers? (These questions are not meant to imply that the numbers are suspect; rather, they are the kinds of questions that readers must get in the habit of asking about all statistics used to support a claim. See pp. 34–36.)

2. Mathews accuses Bush of being both hypocritical and cowardly. What are the reasons for her judgment? Do you think the labels are justified? Why or why not?
3. Is a steadily increasing world population a problem, or do you think that we will find ways to feed and house everyone? Support your position.
4. Should family planning information and contraceptives be available to all who want them? Why or why not?

❖

Who Is Spreading AIDS?

Charles Krauthammer

One of today's most penetrating and uniquely trained thinkers and writers, Charles Krauthammer (b. 1950) studied political theory at Oxford University after graduating from Canada's McGill University and then went to Harvard Medical School. Board certified as a neurologist and psychiatrist, Krauthammer returned to political analysis as a senior editor at The New Republic *and then as a syndicated columnist. He also is an occasional* Time *essayist and a regular on the political talk show* Inside Washington. *He won a Pulitzer Prize for commentary in 1987. In the following column, which appeared on October 4, 1991, Krauthammer offers some "politically incorrect" insight into the AIDS crisis.*

Kimberly Bergalis, 23 years old and dying of AIDS, came to Washington last week on a crusade. She contracted AIDS from her dentist and wants Congress to impose mandatory AIDS testing for medical workers. She wants to spare others her fate.

Kimberly's story is moving. But mandatory testing is a terrible idea. The numbers just don't add up. In the entire history of AIDS there is but a single case of a doctor giving AIDS to his patients. (Kimberly's dentist.) A million Americans carry the HIV virus. Five got it from medical workers. (All from Kimberly's dentist.)

The American Hospital Association estimates that it would cost about a quarter of a billion dollars every year to test American health care workers for HIV. To save five patients per decade? However heartbreaking Kimberly's story, this is insane public policy. There are a thousand ways to spend that kind of money and save a hundred times more lives (immunizing kids against childhood diseases, for example). To say nothing of the inefficiency arising from the inevitable false negative results (for up to six months the HIV virus may not show up on tests) and the anguish arising from the inevitable false positives.

Kimberly's crusade is so obviously misguided that her story risks being dismissed as a mere tragic aberration. But there is a far deeper meaning to Kimberly Bergalis, and it has nothing to do with health care workers. It has to do with taking responsibility for the spread of AIDS.

Kimberly Bergalis is the first politically incorrect AIDS victim. Instead of hurling *"J'accuse"* at George Bush or Cardinal O'Connor or a

287

bigoted citizenry, she hurled it at another AIDS victim and, by implication, at the entire AIDS community: You killed me.

6   Which is why, as The *Post*'s Malcolm Gladwell pointed out in an acute study of the Bergalis phenomenon, she has been shunned by mainstream gay rights and AIDS activists. None has been in touch with her to express sympathy. Some go further. The executive director of the Lambda Legal Defense Fund in New York, notes Gladwell, calls Bergalis the "HIV version of Willie Horton."

7   In the public mind, the allocation of blame for AIDS has seen three stages. When the cause of AIDS first became known, AIDS patients were seen as victims of their own appetites. Then, with Ryan White, the young hemophiliac, they began to be seen as victims of fate. Now, AIDS activists are trying to portray AIDS patients as the victims of society: of an indifferent majority, of public silence, of government inaction, of drug company avarice, of Catholic homophobia.

8   In the middle of a concerted campaign to persuade the American public that AIDS sufferers are victims of you and me, along comes Kimberly Bergalis and blames an AIDS patient. She reminds the country that for every person who gets HIV, there is an HIV carrier who gave it to her. Generally, of course, the transmission is unwitting. But not always. A study of HIV carriers published in the current issue of the American Journal of Public Health found that 52 percent of those who were sexually active had concealed their condition from a sexual partner.

9   Some epidemics can be laid at the feet of government and some cannot. Cholera is a government-controllable and, in some ways, government-induced epidemic. If you don't treat the sewage, people will die. But that model does not apply to a disease that is not waterborne or airborne but behavior-borne. In a free society, government can do little to influence the spread of a behavioral epidemic, and AIDS is the quintessential behavioral epidemic. In a country where, to judge by the Thomas hearings,[1] the right to choose and the right to privacy are singularly cherished, it is absurd to blame government for a disease that spreads through the most private of acts in the most intimate of settings.

10   The main role of government is to protect the civil rights of AIDS sufferers and to try to find a cure. (The federal government spends a staggering $1.2 billion a year on AIDS research.) The rest depends on the private decisions of individual citizens, and, in particular, of the only ones in a position to spread AIDS: HIV carriers.

11   Kimberly's case brought home a truth as biologically obvious as it is politically unfashionable: HIV is spread by people who already have HIV.

---

[1] Senate hearings on Supreme Court nominee Clarence Thomas; Thomas was appointed to the Court.

Thus, in the absence of effective treatment, the single most effective curb on the spread of AIDS is an ethic of responsibility among HIV sufferers. Reveal or refrain: Either reveal one's status to those one might infect, or, if one prefers the perfectly legitimate option of privacy, refrain from any behavior that might lead someone else unwittingly to contract it. That means lovers telling partners, or, if they don't, abstaining from sex, certainly from unprotected sex. That means doctors telling their patients that they have HIV or, if they prefer not to, retiring from any invasive medical practice.

Universal acceptance of—and social pressure to enforce—such an ethic would do far more to prevent AIDS than mandatory testing of health care workers (or anyone else for that matter). It would do far more, too, than all the blame-everybody AIDS demonstrations that capture the anger but miss the point.

Reading and Analyzing

1. Do you recall Kimberly Bergalis who, while dying, came to Washington to testify on Capitol Hill? She died shortly after her trip, and, as Krauthammer has said, her story is moving. Why does the author express this view in paragraph 2? What does he want to accomplish?
2. What *two* issues does Krauthammer find in Kimberly's story? What does she want? And what is the "deeper meaning" in her story?
3. What is Krauthammer's position on testing medical workers for HIV? What are the arguments in support of his position?
4. Why did gay rights and AIDS activists shun Kimberly?
5. What, in the author's view, have been the three stages of thinking about AIDS? How does Kimberly's crusade connect with these ways of viewing AIDS?
6. What are the responsibilities of the government with regard to AIDS? What is *not* the government's responsibility? Why?
7. What is the best way to control the spread of AIDS?
8. Analyze this essay as a problem-solution argument. What steps does Krauthammer include and in what order? (See Chapter 3.)

Responding to the Writer's Ideas

1. Why is Kimberly's crusade "politically incorrect"? Do you agree that the term fits this situation?
2. Does the government have a special responsibility to find a cure for AIDS, that is, a greater responsibility than for any other disease? Why or why not?

3. On what basis should government funds be allocated for research for cures for diseases? How would you decide on the priority of projects?
4. Do you believe that testing for HIV should be mandatory for medical care workers? Should it be mandatory for anyone? Why or why not?

❖

Euthanasia—A Critique

Peter A. Singer and Mark Siegler

A graduate of the University of Toronto Medical School and holding a master's in public health from Yale University, Dr. Peter A. Singer (b. 1960) is assistant professor of medicine and associate director of the Center for Bioethics at the University of Toronto. He is the author of many articles on bioethics, end-of-life care, and euthanasia. Dr. Mark Siegler (b. 1941) obtained his medical degree from the University of Chicago where he is director for the Center of Clinical Medical Ethics. Dr. Siegler is a recognized authority in the field of clinical medical ethics, having written more than 100 articles, 6 books, and the chapters on clinical ethics in two standard texts on internal medicine. In the following article, published in the New England Journal of Medicine *on June 20, 1990, the authors provide a good review of the issues that are central to the debate on euthanasia and make their case against allowing euthanasia.*

A vigorous medical and political debate has begun again on euthanasia, a practice proscribed 2500 years ago in the Hippocratic oath.[1-4] The issue has been publicized recently in three widely divergent settings: a journal article, a legislative initiative in California, and public policy in the Netherlands.

The case of "Debbie" shows that euthanasia can be discussed openly in a respected medical journal. "It's Over, Debbie" was an anonymous, first-person account of euthanasia, published on January 8, 1988, in the *Journal of the American Medical Association,*[5-8] that stimulated widespread discussion and elicited spirited replies. Later in 1988, perhaps as a result, the Council on Ethical and Judicial Affairs of the American Medical Association reaffirmed its opposition to euthanasia.[9]

In California, a legislative initiative[10,11] has shown that in the near future euthanasia may be legalized in certain U.S. jurisdictions. A bill proposing a California Humane and Dignified Death Act was an attempt to legalize euthanasia through the referendum process, which allows California voters to approve controversial issues directly. Public-opinion polls reported that up to 70 percent of the electorate favored the initiative, and many commentators flatly predicted that the initiative would succeed. Nevertheless, the signature drive failed, collecting only 130,000 of the 450,000 required signatures. Attributing the failure to organizational problems, the proponents vowed to introduce the legislation again in California and in other states in 1990.

4   Experience in the Netherlands has shown that a liberal democratic government can tolerate and defend the practice of euthanasia. Although euthanasia is technically illegal in the Netherlands, in fact it is part of Dutch public policy today.[1,12–16] There is agreement at all levels of the judicial system, including the Supreme Court, that if physicians follow the procedural guidelines issued by a state commission, they will not be prosecuted for performing euthanasia.[16] The Dutch guidelines emphasize five requirements: an explicit, repeated request by the patient that leaves no doubt about the patient's desire to die; very severe mental or physical suffering, with no prospect of relief; an informed, free, and consistent decision by the patient; the lack of other treatment options, those available having been exhausted or refused by the patient; and consultation by the doctor with another medical practitioner (and perhaps also with nurses, pastors, or others).[13] The usual method of performing euthanasia is to induce sleep with a barbiturate, followed by a lethal injection of curare.[1] An estimated 5000 to 10,000 patients receive euthanasia each year in the Netherlands.[16]

5   In view of these developments, we urge physicians to consider some reasons for resisting the move toward euthanasia. This article criticizes the main arguments offered by proponents and presents opposing arguments. The case for euthanasia is described in detail elsewhere.[10,17]

Critique of the Case for Euthanasia

6   In the debate about euthanasia, imprecision of language abounds. For the purposes of this article, euthanasia is defined as the deliberate action by a physician to terminate the life of a patient. The clearest example is the act of lethal injection. We distinguish euthanasia from such other acts as the decision to forgo life-sustaining treatment (including the use of ventilators, cardiopulmonary resuscitation, dialysis, or tube feeding—the issue raised in the Cruzan case[18]); the administration of analgesic agents to relieve pain; "assisted suicide," in which the doctor prescribes but does not administer a lethal dose of medication; and "mercy killing" performed by a patient's family or friends. The Dutch guidelines described above and the terms proposed in the California initiative represent two versions of euthanasia.

7   The case for euthanasia is based on two central claims.[10,17] First, proponents argue that patients whose illnesses cause them unbearable suffering should be permitted to end their distress by having a physician perform euthanasia. Second, proponents assert that the well-recognized right of patients to control their medical treatment includes the right to request and receive euthanasia.

Relief of Suffering   We agree that the relief of pain and suffering is a cru-   8
cial goal of medicine.[19] We question, however, whether the care of dying
patients cannot be improved without resorting to the drastic measure of
euthanasia. Most physical pain can be relieved with the appropriate use of
analgesic agents.[20] Unfortunately, despite widespread agreement that dying
patients must be provided with necessary analgesia,[21] physicians continue
to underuse analgesia in the care of dying patients because of concern
about depressing respiratory drive or creating addiction. Such situations
demand better management of pain, not euthanasia.

Another component of suffering is the frightening prospect of dying   9
shackled to a modern-day Procrustean bed, surrounded by the latest forms
of high technology. Proponents of euthanasia often cite horror stories of
patients treated against their will. In the past, when modern forms of life-
saving technology were new and physicians were just learning how to use
them appropriately, such cases occurred often; we have begun to move beyond that era. The law, public policy, and medical ethics now acknowledge the right of patients to refuse life-sustaining medical treatment, and a
large number of patients avail themselves of this new policy.[22–24] These
days, competent patients may freely exercise their right to choose or refuse
life-sustaining treatment; to carry out their preferences, they do not require
the option of euthanasia.

We acknowledge that some elements of human suffering and mental   10
anguish—not necessarily related to physical pain—cannot be eliminated
completely from the dying process. These include the anticipated loss of
important human relationships and membership in the human community,
the loss of personal independence, the feeling of helplessness, and the raw
fear of death. Euthanasia can shorten the duration of these emotional and
psychological hardships. It can also eliminate fears about how and when
death will occur. Finally, euthanasia returns to the patient a measure of
control over the process of dying. These are the benefits of euthanasia,
against which its potential harms must be balanced.

Individual Rights   The second argument in favor of euthanasia is based   11
on the rights of the individual. Proponents contend that the right of patients to forgo life-sustaining medical treatment should include a right to
euthanasia. This would extend the notion of the right to die to embrace
the concept that patients have a right to be killed by physicians. But rights
are not absolute. They must be balanced against the rights of other people
and the values of society. The claim of a right to be killed by a physician
must be balanced against the legal, political, and religious prohibitions
against killing that have always existed in society generally and in medicine particularly. As the President's Commission for the Study of Ethical
Problems in Medicine and Biomedical and Behavioral Research has observed, "Policies prohibiting direct killing may also conflict with the important value of patient self-determination. . . . The Commission finds

this limitation on individual self-determination to be an acceptable cost of securing the general protection of human life afforded by the prohibition of direct killing."[22] We agree. In our view, the public good served by the prohibition of euthanasia outweighs the private interests of the persons requesting it.

The Case against Euthanasia

12   The arguments against euthanasia are made from two perspectives: public policy and the ethical norms of medicine.

13   *Euthanasia Is Perilous Public Policy*   Proponents of euthanasia use the concept of individual rights to support their claim, but this same concept can be used for the opposite purpose. The argument against euthanasia on grounds of civil rights involves a consideration of the rights not just of those who would want euthanasia themselves but of all citizens. As public policy, euthanasia is unacceptable because of the likelihood, or even the inevitability, of involuntary euthanasia—persons being euthanized without their consent or against their wishes.

14   There are four ways in which a policy of voluntary euthanasia could lead to involuntary euthanasia. The first is "crypthanasia" (literally, "secret euthanasia").[15] In the Netherlands, for instance, it is alleged that vulnerable patients are euthanized without their consent. Dutch proponents of euthanasia disavow these reports and claim that they are unrelated to the toleration of voluntary euthanasia. We suggest, however, that a political milieu in which voluntary euthanasia is tolerated may also foster involuntary euthanasia and lead to the killing of patients without consent. The second way in which involuntary euthanasia may occur is through "encouraged" euthanasia, whereby chronically ill or dying patients may be pressured to choose euthanasia to spare their families financial or emotional strain.[25] The third way is "surrogate" euthanasia. If voluntary euthanasia were permissible in the United States, the constitutional guarantees of due process, which tend to extend the same rights to incompetent as to competent patients, might permit euthanizing incompetent patients on the basis of "substituted judgment" or nebulous tests of "burdens and benefits." Finally, there is the risk of "discriminatory" euthanasia. Patients belonging to vulnerable groups in American society might be subtly coerced into "requesting" euthanasia. In the United States today, many groups are disempowered, disenfranchised, or otherwise vulnerable: the poor, the elderly, the disabled, members of racial minorities, the physically handicapped, the mentally impaired, alcoholics, drug addicts, and patients with the acquired immunodeficiency syndrome. In a society in which discrimination is common and many citizens do not have access even to basic health care, the legalization of euthanasia would create another powerful tool with which to discriminate against groups whose "consent" is already susceptible to coercion and whose rights are already in jeopardy.

The proponents of euthanasia contend that procedural safeguards, such as the five provisions of the Dutch guidelines noted above, will prevent involuntary euthanasia. They claim further that society permits many dangerous activities if adequate procedural safeguards are provided to reduce risk and protect the public. We agree that safeguards would reduce the risk of involuntary euthanasia, but they would not eliminate it entirely. In the case of euthanasia, safeguards have not been adequately tested and shown to be effective. Even in their presence, we are concerned that patients could be euthanized without their consent or even against their wishes. Even one case of involuntary euthanasia would represent a great harm. In the current era of cost containment, social injustice, and ethical relativism, this risk is one our society should not accept.

Euthanasia Violates the Norms of Medicine   In addition to being perilous as public policy, euthanasia violates three fundamental norms and standards of medicine. First, as noted above, it diverts attention from the real issues in the care of dying patients—among them, improved pain control, better communication between doctors and patients, heightened respect for the patient's right to choose whether to accept life-sustaining treatment, and improved management of the dying process, as in hospice care. The hospice movement has demonstrated that managing pain appropriately and allowing patients control over the use of life-sustaining treatments reduce the need for euthanasia.

Second, euthanasia subverts the social role of the physician as healer. Historically, physicians have scrupulously avoided participating in activities that might taint their healing role, such as capital punishment or torture. Physicians should distance themselves from euthanasia to maintain public confidence and trust in medicine as a healing profession.

Third, euthanasia strikes at the heart of what it means to be a physician.[26] Since the time of Hippocrates, the prohibition against it has been fundamental to the medical profession and has served as a moral absolute for both patients and physicians. This prohibition has freed physicians from a potential conflict of interest between healing and killing and in turn has enabled patients to entrust physicians with their lives. It has enabled physicians to devote themselves single-mindedly to helping patients achieve their own medical goals. This prohibition may even have encouraged medical research and scientific progress, because physicians, with the consent of patients, are motivated to perform risky, innovative procedures that are aggressive and sometimes painful, with a total commitment to benefit the patient.

Conclusions

Pressure to legalize euthanasia will surely increase in an era of spiraling health care costs, but it must be resisted. Euthanasia represents a development that is dangerous for many vulnerable patients and that threatens the moral integrity of the medical profession. Physicians must become more responsive to the concerns of patients that underlie the movement for euthanasia and must provide better pain management, more compassionate terminal care, and more appropriate use of life-sustaining treatments. But physicians need to draw the line at euthanasia. They and their professional associations should defend the integrity of medicine by speaking out against the practice. Finally, even if euthanasia is legalized in some jurisdictions, physicians should refuse to participate in it, and professional organizations should censure any of their members who perform euthanasia.

References

1. Angell M. Euthanasia. N Engl J Med 1988; 319:1348–50.
2. Singer PA. Should doctors kill patients? Can Med Assoc J 1988; 138:1000–1.
3. Kinsella TD, Singer PA, Siegler M. Legalized active euthanasia: an Aesculapian tragedy. Bull Am Coll Surg 1989; 74(12):6–9.
4. Wanzer SH, Federman DD, Adelstein SJ, et al. The physician's responsibility toward hopelessly ill patients: a second look. N Engl J Med 1989; 320:844–9.
5. It's over, Debbie. JAMA 1988; 259:272.
6. Vaux KL, Debbie's dying: mercy killing and the good death. JAMA 1988; 259:2140–1.
7. Gaylin W, Kass LR, Pellegrino ED, Siegler M. 'Doctors must not kill.' JAMA 1988; 259:2139–40.
8. Lundberg GD. 'It's over, Debbie' and the euthanasia debate. JAMA 1988; 259:2142–3.
9. The Council on Ethical and Judicial Affairs of the American Medical Association. Euthanasia. Report: C (A-88). AMA council report. Chicago: American Medical Association, 1988:1.
10. Risley RL. A humane and dignified death: a new law permitting physician aid-in-dying. Glendale, Calif.: Americans Against Human Suffering, 1987.
11. Parachini A. Mercy, murder, & morality: perspectives on euthanasia: the California Humane and Dignified Death Initiative. Hastings Cent Rep 1989; 19(1):Suppl:10–2.
12. Pence GE. Do not go slowly into that dark night: mercy killing in Holland. Am J Med 1988; 84:139–41.
13. Rigter H, Borst-Eilers E, Leenen HJJ. Euthanasia across the North Sea. BMJ 1988; 297:1593–5.
14. Rigter H. Mercy, murder, & morality: euthanasia in the Netherlands: distinguishing facts from fiction. Hastings Cent Rep 1989; 19(1):Suppl:31–2.
15. Fenigsen R. Mercy, murder, & morality: perspectives on euthanasia: a case against Dutch euthanasia. Hastings Cent Rep 1989; 19(1):Suppl:22–30.
16. de Wachter MAM. Active euthanasia in the Netherlands. JAMA 1989; 262:3316–9.
17. Humphry D, Wickett A. The right to die: understanding euthanasia. New York: Harper & Row, 1986.
18. Angell M. Prisoners of technology: the case of Nancy Cruzan. N Engl J Med 1990; 322:1226–8.

19. Cassell EJ. The nature of suffering and the goals of medicine. N Engl J Med 1982; 306:639–45.
20. Foley KM. The treatment of cancer pain. N Engl J Med 1985; 313:84–95.
21. Angell M. The quality of mercy. N Engl J Med 1982; 306:98–9.
22. President's Commission for the Study of Ethical Problems in Medicine and Biomedical and Behavioral Research. Deciding to forego life-sustaining treatment: a report on the ethical, medical, and legal issues in treatment decisions. Washington, D.C.: Government Printing Office, 1983.
23. The Hastings Center. Guidelines on the termination of life-sustaining treatment and the care of the dying: a report. Briarcliff Manor, N.Y.: Hastings Center, 1987.
24. Emanuel EJ. A review of the ethical and legal aspects of terminating medical care. Am J Med 1988; 84:291–301.
25. Kamisar Y. Some non-religious views against proposed "mercy-killing" legislation. Minn Law Rev 1958; 42:969–1042.
26. Kass LR. Neither for love nor money: why doctors must not kill. Public Interest 1989; 94(winter):25–46.

Reading and Analyzing

1. What debate do the authors join in with their essay?
2. Examine the format of this essay; what kind of paper is it?
3. How many people in the Netherlands apparently employ euthanasia each year? Summarize the required guidelines physicians must follow to use euthanasia without prosecution.
4. What do the authors want to accomplish in their opening references to the article, the California initiative, and the practice of euthanasia in the Netherlands?
5. What position do Singer and Siegler take on euthanasia?
6. Analyze the essay's organization, indicating the paragraphs which belong in each part.
7. How do Singer and Siegler define *euthanasia*? What is not included in their definition?
8. What are the two claims of those who argue for euthanasia? Summarize the authors' critique of each claim.
9. What do the authors accomplish in paragraph 10?
10. What two approaches do Signer and Siegler take in arguing against euthanasia?
11. Why is euthanasia bad public policy? What could voluntary euthanasia lead to? What characteristics of modern society make legalizing euthanasia too risky?
12. Why is euthanasia inconsistent with the norms of medicine?
13. To resist the current pressure to legalize and employ euthanasia, what should physicians do?

Responding to the Writers' Ideas

1. Do you agree that interest in euthanasia is increasing; that is, if you oppose it, do you see a problem developing? What evidence would you cite to support your answer?
2. Which of the two arguments in favor of euthanasia is the most convincing, in your view? Which of the arguments against euthanasia do you find most convincing? Why?
3. Do you agree with the authors when they write that we live in an "era of cost containment, social injustice, and ethical relativism"? Why or why not? The authors do not provide evidence for this assertion; what evidence can you provide either to support or deny the assertion?
4. Where do you stand on the issue of legalizing euthanasia? Be prepared to defend your position.

❖

In Defense of Voluntary Euthanasia

Sidney Hook

A philosopher, educator, and author, Sidney Hook (1902–1989) taught philosophy at New York University and was a senior research fellow at the Hoover Institution. He published numerous articles and books on philosophy throughout his busy career, and his autobiography, Out of Step: An Unquiet Life in the Twentieth Century, *appeared in 1987. The following emotional argument for euthanasia, incorporating his personal experience with grave illness, was published in the* New York Times *in 1987.*

A few short years ago, I lay at the point of death. A congestive heart failure was treated for diagnostic purposes by an angiogram that triggered a stroke. Violent and painful hiccups, uninterrupted for several days and nights, prevented the ingestion of food. My left side and one of my vocal cords became paralyzed. Some form of pleurisy set in, and I felt I was drowning in a sea of slime. At one point, my heart stopped beating; just as I lost consciousness, it was thumped back into action again. In one of my lucid intervals during those days of agony, I asked my physician to discontinue all life-supporting services or show me how to do it. He refused and predicted that someday I would appreciate the unwisdom of my request.

A month later, I was discharged from the hospital. In six months, I regained the use of my limbs, and although my voice still lacks its old resonance and carrying power I no longer croak like a frog. There remain some minor disabilities and I am restricted to a rigorous, low sodium diet. I have resumed my writing and research.

My experience can be and has been cited as an argument against honoring requests of stricken patients to be gently eased out of their pain and life. I cannot agree. There are two main reasons. As an octogenarian, there is a reasonable likelihood that I may suffer another "cardiovascular accident" or worse. I may not even be in a position to ask for the surcease of pain. It seems to me that I have already paid my dues to death—indeed, although time has softened my memories they are vivid enough to justify my saying that I suffered enough to warrant dying several times over. Why run the risk of more?

4   Secondly, I dread imposing on my family and friends another grim round of misery similar to the one my first attack occasioned.

5   My wife and children endured enough for one lifetime. I know that for them the long days and nights of waiting, the disruption of their professional duties and their own familial responsibilities counted for nothing in their anxiety for me. In their joy at my recovery they have been forgotten. Nonetheless, to visit another prolonged spell of helpless suffering on them as my life ebbs away, or even worse, if I linger on into a comatose senility, seems altogether gratuitous.

6   But what, it may be asked, of the joy and satisfaction of living, of basking in the sunshine, listening to music, watching one's grandchildren growing into adolescence, following the news about the fate of freedom in a troubled world, playing with ideas, writing one's testament of wisdom and folly for posterity? Is not all that one endured, together with the risk of its recurrence, an acceptable price for the multiple satisfactions that are still open even to a person of advanced years?

7   Apparently those who cling to life no matter what, think so. I do not.

8   The zest and intensity of these experiences are no longer what they used to be. I am not vain enough to delude myself that I can in the few remaining years make an important discovery useful for mankind or can lead a social movement or do anything that will be historically eventful, no less event-making. My autobiography, which describes a record of intellectual and political experiences of some historical value, already much too long, could be posthumously published. I have had my fill of joys and sorrows and am not greedy for more life. I have always thought that a test of whether one had found happiness in one's life is whether one would be willing to relive it—whether, if it were possible, one would accept the opportunity to be born again.

9   Having lived a full and relatively happy life, I would cheerfully accept the chance to be reborn, but certainly not to be reborn again as an infirm octogenarian. To some extent, my views reflect what I have seen happen to the aged and stricken who have been so unfortunate as to survive crippling paralysis. They suffer, and impose suffering on others, unable even to make a request that their torment be ended.

10   I am mindful too of the burdens placed upon the community, with its rapidly diminishing resources, to provide the adequate and costly services necessary to sustain the lives of those whose days and nights are spent on mattress graves of pain. A better use could be made of these resources to increase the opportunities and qualities of life for the young. I am not denying the moral obligation the community has to look after its disabled and aged. There are times, however, when an individual may find it pointless to insist on the fulfillment of a legal and moral right.

What is required is no great revolution in morals but an enlargement   11
of imagination and an intelligent evaluation of alternative uses of community resources.

Long ago, Seneca observed that "the wise man will live as long as he   12
ought, not as long as he can." One can envisage hypothetical circumstances in which one has a duty to prolong one's life despite its costs for
the sake of others, but such circumstances are far removed from the ordinary prospects we are considering. If wisdom is rooted in knowledge of the
alternatives of choice, it must be reliably informed of the state one is in
and its likely outcome. Scientific medicine is not infallible, but it is the best
we have. Should a rational person be willing to endure acute suffering
merely on the chance that a miraculous cure might presently be at hand?
Each one should be permitted to make his own choice—especially when no
one else is harmed by it.

The responsibility for the decision, whether deemed wise or foolish,   13
must be with the chooser.

Reading and Analyzing

1. What subject is introduced in Hook's opening two paragraphs? What
   strategy does he use as an introduction?
2. What have some people seen in his experience? For what two reasons
   does Hook disagree with them?
3. What is Hook's position on euthanasia? Where does he state his
   claim?
4. Analyze the nature of Hook's argument. What kind of evidence does
   he provide?
5. When others observe the pleasures of life that the author can still experience, what are his responses? Summarize his reasons for not
   wanting to continue to live on in his eighties.

Responding to the Writer's Ideas

1. Hook concludes by asserting that he should be free to make choices
   about his life—or death—as long as he does not harm others. John
   Stuart Mill (see pp. 167–74) asserts much the same philosophy with
   regard to freedom of expression. Is the philosophy appropriate for
   both kinds of situations? Is there a significant difference between arguing for euthanasia and acting on your belief by seeking euthanasia? Is there any purpose in our being free to hold and express the
   idea if we are forbidden to put the idea into action? Debate this
   issue.

2. Can Hook actually assert that "no one else is harmed by" the decision of a very sick person to seek euthanasia? He mentions a (presumably) loving family; should he have to get assurances from them that his death would not harm them? What might be Hook's response to this idea?

3. Hook speaks of "intelligent evaluation," of "wisdom," "knowledge," and "a rational person." How would you characterize his philosophical stance? What does he value as essential to decision making, as essential to being human?

4. What is your position on euthanasia? What are your reasons?

5. The previous article by Drs. Singer and Siegler and this essay by Hook make for interesting contrasts beyond their differing views on euthanasia. Do a comparative analysis of the style of the two pieces. Which type of approach to this particular issue do you find most effective? Does the answer to this question depend in part on the audience for each piece?

❖

Health Care: Fire out of Control

Harry Johnston

*Harry Johnston (b. 1931) is the U.S. representative from the Palm
Beach area of Florida. Holding a JD from the University of Florida Law
School, the former Florida state senator serves on the Foreign Affairs
and the Science, Space, and Technology Committees in the House. In
the following article, published in the* Washington Post *on November
13, 1991, Johnston stresses the seriousness of the health care situation
in the United States.*

Imagine if fire departments were modeled on our current health care   1
system. Your access to fire department services would depend on the quality of your fire insurance. If private market forces operated as they do in
health care, 37 million people would not have fire insurance, and 60 million more Americans would have only limited fire insurance. Moreover, if
you were previously a victim of fire, your fire insurance agent would raise
your premium due to your preexisting condition of bad luck.

While it is possible you could feel secure if you had quality fire insur-   2
ance, you might begin to wonder when your neighbor's house sets ablaze.
Is his employer still providing his fire insurance, or is he one of the 29 million working uninsured? Absurd, isn't it?

Fortunately, our society has decided that protection from fire is a   3
community responsibility; it is time that we made the same distinction for
health care. It is a historic accident that health care coverage has fallen to
the responsibility of business. After World War II, America continued a
policy of wage controls as our troops returned home and flooded the labor
market. Facing labor shortages and unable to increase wages, businesses
competed for workers by offering benefits such as health insurance.

Relying on employers to manage health insurance has resulted in a   4
piecemeal system of coverage that is inefficient and ineffective. With business affiliation providing the basis of forming insurance pools, private insurance companies have isolated pockets of our population that can be
manipulated to generate a profit. There is no rationale why two individuals with the same health status may face drastically different insurance
costs because of their business affiliation or lack of it.

Our health insurance system's moral deficiencies translate into eco-   5
nomic inefficiencies. The complexity of our current system is a nightmare

303

for health care providers. Picture a firefighter searching through files to determine whether a desperate caller is insured and if so what services are covered. This is what our physicians face every day, and this inefficiency has contributed to the highest administrative cost of any health care system in the industrialized world.

6   The American economy suffers from a stranglehold of these soaring health care costs. Businesses that provide health insurance for their employees are crippled in the international market. Currently, Chrysler's health insurance costs force the price of its automobiles up by $700 compared with the $300 expense incurred by a comparable German car company.

7   Responsibility for insuring health care is misplaced; it is as if we were telling businesses that they must manage the provision of fire insurance in our community. America's health care crisis derives from a core misconception, and incremental solutions will not deliver a cure. Increasing coverage in this inefficient system will exacerbate our runaway health costs and, therefore, lead to poorer access to services.

8   As a pretext to any serious reform, we must resolve that health care is a community responsibility. First, we must declare that providing health insurance entails an obligation to cover a comprehensive population dispersing our shared risk of illness in a large insurance pool. We can no longer provide private insurance for the healthy and the affluent and leave the ill and the poor for a public program.

9   Second, we must establish a structure of health care budgets at the state, district and institutional level. Hospitals should receive a budget target with which to provide an expected level of services. District and state health boards would review each institution's performance with respect to its budget target rewarding efficient providers and weeding out inefficient practices. Physicians, not insurance companies, would have greater responsibility for managing our health care.

10   America deserves a better health insurance system. I find it sadly amusing that amid our talk of the community of nations, we have forgotten to safeguard the foundations of our own communities. The fires are burning.

Reading and Analyzing

1. What argumentative strategy does Johnston use in his opening paragraphs? Analyze his argument.
2. What is Johnston's claim? Where does he state it?
3. Why is health care coverage tied to employment?
4. What are the problems that result from employers' managing health care?

5. What idea, in Johnston's view, must be embraced before meaningful reform can take place? Once the idea is embraced, what two steps are necessary?
6. Explain Johnston's concluding sentence.
7. What is the author's purpose in writing? What part of the problem of current health care does Johnston focus on?

Responding to the Writer's Ideas

1. Evaluate Johnston's analogy. Is it effective as an argument? Is it effective as a clever comparison providing emotional appeal?
2. Were you aware of the "historic accident" that shaped our current health care system? Does this knowledge affect your attitude toward the prospects of changing the system? Why or why not?
3. What is accomplished by increasing the insurance pool? Can you explain this concept in your own words? How does the concept serve as an argument for national health insurance?
4. Are you convinced that our health care system is in trouble and needs to be changed? Why or why not?
5. Do you agree with Johnston that health care is, like fire protection, a community responsibility? Why or why not?

❖

The Way to Real Health Security

Thomas Bodenheimer

Dr. Thomas Bodenheimer (b. 1939) obtained his medical degree from the Harvard Medical School and is in private practice in internal medicine in the San Francisco area. He is a member of Physicians for a National Health Program, an organization of 4,000 physicians who support universal health insurance, and he has written many articles on national health care. In "The Way to Real Health Security," published in the Nation *on December 16, 1991, Bodenheimer presents an argument for a national health insurance system that would be delivered in much the same way that health care is provided today.*

1   More than 37 million Americans are without any health insurance, and an additional 56 million have insurance so inadequate that a serious illness could throw them into bankruptcy. At the same time, U.S. health care costs are the highest in the world and are rising at nearly twice the general rate of inflation.

2   How do we solve the two-part health crisis, the crisis of access and the crisis of cost? At first glance, proposed solutions appear abundant. On May 15, *The Journal of the American Medical Association,* with full media fanfare, published no fewer than thirteen proposals for insuring the uninsured. But on closer inspection, twelve of them are virtually identical. Our nation must choose between two proposals for solving the health care crisis. The contestants are the "private insurance reform package" and the "health security approach."

3   The private insurance reform package is a concoction of the health care industry: physicians, hospitals, commercial insurers, Blue Cross/Blue Shield, pharmaceutical companies, the medical supply industry—in short, the people who make money from the sickness of others. The health security approach, modeled on the Canadian system, is favored by the people; in a 1990 Harris poll, 66 percent favored such a plan. Let's take a look at these alternative solutions to the nation's health care chaos.

4   The private insurance reform package has two main components: a program for unemployed people with no insurance (Medicaid expansion) and a separate plan for the employed who are uninsured (employer-mandated health insurance).

Medicaid Expansion

One-third of uninsured adults are either unemployed or have in-   5
comes below the poverty line. The easiest way to insure this group is to expand Medicaid, the federal-state program that covers 40 percent of the
poor. This approach is supported by the American Medical Association
and the private insurance industry. For insurers, removing the poor (who
cannot afford insurance) from the private market relieves the industry of
responsibility for a portion of those who lack insurance without encroach-
ing on an area of possible insurance expansion.

The main weakness of this program is its high cost. Medicaid expan-   6
sion would cost an estimated $14 billion in its first year, and Health Care
Financing Administration chief Gail Wilensky has stated that no funds are
available. Another problem with Medicaid expansion is that many states
pay physicians' fees that are half or less those paid by Medicare or private
insurers. My own group medical practice receives $14.60 for a Medicaid
patient visit; we lose money each time such a patient walks in the door.
More and more doctors are refusing to see Medicaid patients or are limiting the number of such patients.

Employer-Mandated Health Insurance (E.M.H.I.)

Two-thirds of the uninsured are employed or dependents of   7
working people; most work in small companies that cannot afford to
buy health insurance for their employees. E.M.H.I. is the American
Medical Association's favored plan for covering uninsured working
people. The hospital industry is also supportive. The Congressional
Democratic leadership is calling for E.M.H.I., as is the National Leadership Coalition for Health Care Reform (which includes major
unions and corporations such as the United Steelworkers, Chrysler, International Paper and Lockheed) and the Pepper Commission, chaired
by Senator Jay Rockefeller. Hawaii, Massachusetts and Oregon have
passed E.M.H.I. laws; several others have versions of E.M.H.I. on
their legislative agendas.

For budget-squeezed politicians, E.M.H.I. looks like manna from   8
heaven. Pass a law forcing all businesses either to purchase health insurance for their employees or to pay a tax to fund coverage for the uninsured—"pay or play," as it is known. Lo and behold, the majority of the
uninsured are suddenly insured, at no cost to the government. Great idea?
Well, let's take a closer look.

Most large employers already provide health insurance. So E.M.H.I.   9
forces small companies to come up with much of the financing for the employed who lack coverage. Thus, companies with the smallest profit mar-
gins will be saddled with most of the burden. In Massachusetts E.M.H.I. is
estimated to increase labor costs for small employers by 12 percent of the

first $14,000 of every employee's wages. How will employers respond? According to the Partnership on Health Care and Employment, a national E.M.H.I. plan could force companies to lay off between 5.4 million and 8.6 million people. Blue Cross/Blue Shield vice president Donald Cohodes says, "Mandating health insurance coverage for employees of small employers may be tantamount to mandating employer bankruptcy."

10   E.M.H.I. would also be an administrative nightmare. According to Professor Alvin Schorr's 1990 *New England Journal of Medicine* study, companies with uninsured workers have a high-turnover work force. The average time on the job is between five and eleven months, with an average of seven and a half weeks unemployed between jobs. An employer would take a month or two to process health insurance papers for a newly hired employee, and the employee would spend another month or two making arrangements with a health maintenance organization or other health provider. By this time, many newly insured employees would be leaving the job, Schorr points out. After a few months of unemployment, the employee would find another job and begin the bureaucratic treadmill all over again.

11   A basic flaw of E.M.H.I. is the linkage of health insurance to employment. Millions of workers change jobs each year; employees offered coverage by one health maintenance organization (H.M.O.) may, upon changing jobs, be forced to sign up with a different H.M.O. and thus lose their family physician. Those with pre-existing illnesses may face major restrictions in new health insurance policies. Workers who are laid off or who leave jobs for health reasons may lose their employer-sponsored insurance at critical times in their lives. Spouses and children of insured workers may also lose their insurance. Divorces may leave children and spouses uninsured if coverage is based on one family member's job.

12   Of all the problems with the private insurance reform package, none are more damaging than its failure to control costs. The Bush Administration and health insurers claim to have a new solution to health cost inflation: managed care. In an attempt to contain costs, most managed care plans restrict patients' freedom to choose their physicians. Yet managed care has an undistinguished track record on cost control. While H.M.O.s, the main weapon in managed care's arsenal, can boast success in cutting hospital use, that success does not translate into long-term savings. Between 1961 and 1981, H.M.O. costs inflated as fast as overall health care costs. In the late 1980s, even with managed care accounting for at least three-quarters of all group insurance plans, premiums for group health insurance rose by 18 percent a year.

13   It is impossible to improve health care access without simultaneously containing costs. Look at Medicare: Its costs have skyrocketed, and the elderly now have to spend a greater proportion of their income on health care than they did before Medicare was created in 1965. Check out Medic-

aid: As costs climbed, state and federal governments cut the program. The proportion of the poor covered by Medicaid has dropped from 70 percent to 40 percent. Take private health insurance: As costs have climbed, so have premiums, forcing businesses to shift more health costs onto employees or stop insuring their employees altogether. The message should be clear: As costs go up, access to care goes down. The access crisis and the cost crisis must be solved together. The health security approach does just that.

Social Security collects payments from virtually everyone in society and provides benefits to everyone upon retirement. A health security system would copy this model: Just as we all have a Social Security card, so we would have a health security card, entitling us to care at any doctor's office, hospital or group practice we choose. The system would cover hospital and physician care; labwork, X-rays and other ancillary services; prescription drugs; mental health services; and long-term care.

14

Socialized medicine? No. Most hospitals would continue to be privately owned, and outpatient care would be delivered by the same pluralistic mix of private physicians, H.M.O.s, community clinics and local public health facilities we have now. The health security approach meshes public insurance and private medicine.

15

Patients would never see a hospital or a medical bill. Rather, the single health care trust fund set up in every state, under federal guidelines, would pay each hospital a lump-sum budget negotiated yearly with the hospital. Physicians would be prohibited from sending bills to patients and would be paid fees by the health care trust fund.

16

Where would the money come from? The funds would derive from the same places they come from now: employer and employee premiums for group health insurance and taxes that currently finance such programs as Medicare and Medicaid. The only change would be that money currently going to private insurance companies would be rerouted to the health care trust fund in each state. The money currently paid in out-of-pocket medical bills or cash at the time of receiving service would be converted to prepayment. That is, all funds would be paid to the health care trust fund either through premiums or earmarked health care taxes that are graduated by income so that wealthy people would pay higher rates than lower- and middle-income people. Remember, any new taxes or premiums would replace, rather than add to, current family health expenses. Most families would pay less rather than more for health care than they do under the current system.

17

How about the uncontrollable rise in health costs? Under the health security approach, cost control is simple. Evidence from other nations—Canada and Germany are two examples—demonstrates that when hospitals and doctors are reimbursed by a single payment mechanism, total health costs can be budgeted and runaway health care inflation can be

18

stopped. If health care inflation is reduced from its present 8.3 percent a year to 6 percent, in the year 2000 we will spend hundreds of billions less on health care than under the proposed health insurance reform package, which lacks a serious cost-control program.

19   While the private insurance reform package would cost as much as $50 billion to $80 billion per year in new dollars, the health security approach would not cost the nation one extra cent. In 1991 the nation will spend about $700 billion on personal health care services. At least 25 percent of this sum, $175 billion, goes for administration—paper pushing by hundreds of insurance companies, more paper pushing by hospitals that have to bill hundreds of insurance companies, and yet more paper pushing by doctors billing those same hundreds of companies. The replacement, within each state, of these multiple insurers by one public insurance fund would save the nation an estimated $67 billion each year. That is enough money to insure all of the 37 million uninsured and to improve the coverage of the 56 million underinsured, with plenty to spare for transition costs to the new health security system. These administrative savings would be achieved by abolishing most private health insurance and by converting hospital and physician administrative expenses into the provision of more medical care.

20   Because so much money would be saved from cutting administrative waste, there would be no need to ration needed services or to force people into long waits for medical services. Some people argue that Canada, utilizing a similar system, requires people to wait for months for certain surgical procedures. But let's keep in mind that Canada spends about 9 percent of its gross national product on health care, while the United States spends more than 12 percent. With our well-financed health system, there would be no need for such waiting lists in the United States.

21   The nation's health care industry is at a historic crossroad. Do we join the rest of the civilized world and provide health services to everyone at a cost we all can afford, utilizing the well-recognized principle of universal public insurance? Or do we bumble along with a bureaucratically top-heavy mixture of inflationary programs marred by gaps and uncertainties in insurance coverage, punishing those with lower incomes and higher ages?

22   Extending current policies through the insurance reform package would perpetuate the effective division of society into two groups. To use insurance industry terminology, the first is the "preferred risk grouping," which consists of younger, healthier and more affluent people who pay for their own health insurance either directly or indirectly as a fringe benefit (which comes out of their paychecks). The second is the "unacceptable risk grouping," which comprises chronically ill or elderly people, whom private insurers do not want to cover, and low-income people, who cannot afford private insurance; health care for this group is either subsidized by taxpay-

ers through Medicare and Medicaid or is paid for by increases in the premiums of privately insured people.

By separating society into those two groups, our health system gives those who are in the preferred risk category the impression that they are paying twice: once for their own health insurance and again through taxes or higher premiums for the "unacceptable" risk group. Moreover, the media have conveyed the impression that the unacceptable risks are mainly unemployed, homeless, minority people who may be alcoholics, drug abusers, mentally ill and/or infected with HIV. This group is seen as the enemy, soaking up much of the health care dollar. Such a perception undermines popular support for public funding of health care and obstructs the passage of health care reforms that cost tax dollars that appear to benefit someone else.

23

This perceived division of society is largely false. In fact, the great majority of unacceptable risks are the elderly, who have the highest rate of illness and on whose behalf most health care dollars are spent. The enemy, in other words, is ourselves—a few years down the road. Almost everyone will at some time pass from the preferred to the unacceptable risk group by getting older or by getting sick. The best way to guarantee fairness in health insurance is to place the entire population in a single risk pool and to spread the risk from the disabled and elderly to the healthy and young—the health security approach. Our health care system should reflect the reality that we are all in this together.

24

Reading and Analyzing

1. What does Bodenheimer seek to accomplish in his opening paragraph?
2. What, in the author's view, are the two parts of the health care problem?
3. What are the two basic solutions to the health care problem?
4. Examine Bodenheimer's word choice in paragraph 3. From his word choice, what can you conclude about the author's preferred health care system?
5. Explain the elements of the "private insurance reform package." What, in the author's view, are the problems with this proposed solution?
6. What is the relationship between cost and access?
7. Explain the "health security approach." What will it be modeled on? Why is it not socialized medicine? Where will the money come from? How will it keep costs down? Why will it avoid waiting periods for receiving health care?
8. How does Bodenheimer's organization help to reinforce his position?

9. What people make up the unacceptable risk group? Why should that encourage us to support the health security approach?

Responding to the Writer's Ideas

1. Health insurance issues are quite complicated. What, if anything, did you learn from this essay that you did not know before reading?
2. Bodenheimer argues that the "pay or play" approach will hurt small companies and force them to lay off many employees. Does this scenario make sense to you? If it is an accurate prediction, does it influence your attitude toward this proposed plan? Why or why not?
3. Bodenheimer argues that the health security approach will not increase costs or produce long waiting periods for care because "so much money would be saved from cutting administrative waste." Are you prepared to accept this argument? Why or why not?
4. Of the two proposals outlined in this article, which one makes the most sense to you? Why or why not?

❖

Health Care for All—Without Government Control

Caspar W. Weinberger

A graduate of Harvard College and Harvard Law School, Caspar Weinberger (b. 1917) was Secretary of Health, Education, and Welfare from 1973 to 1975 and Secretary of Defense from 1981 to 1987. He is the author of Fighting for Peace: Seven Critical Years in the Pentagon *(1990), a memoir that defends his stewardship of the Defense Department; a member of an international law firm; and the publisher of* Forbes, *a magazine devoted to business and investment. In the following article (published February 3, 1992), one of his regular columns in* Forbes, *Weinberger makes the case for keeping health care in the private sector.*

The combination of a presidential election and legitimate calls for less expensive health care for all—including the 31 million to 36 million Americans currently uninsured—will produce some extremely undesirable proposals. Here is a set of suggestions that could accomplish the main objectives without involving the federal government in the follies of full national health insurance. 1

All employers would provide health insurance to all employees. The self-employed would be required to secure their own insurance, much as they now pay their own Social Security. The federal government would be required to provide health insurance for the unemployed, much as it now helps fund unemployment insurance. 2

The critical factor in this plan is that *all* this insurance would have to be secured from *private* insurance companies. The fact that there would be more companies competing, coupled with the enormous increase of those insured (literally the whole population), would guarantee that the cost of comprehensive insurance would be far lower than it is now. And that would be good news for the American economy, because one of the principal factors that make our automobiles so expensive to produce is the ever rising cost of medical care for each employee paid for by employers. 3

The federal government's role would be limited to certifying that the insurance is sufficiently comprehensive and that the companies providing it are found to be financially sound by state authorities. There would be no 4

313

mandate for specialized coverages. Those could be arranged by private negotiation, if desired.

5   This program would be vastly less expensive for both federal and state governments than the present enormously costly hodgepodge of systems. It would also serve our senior citizens and others far better than the expensive Medicare and Medicaid systems. And, since private insurance companies would have a strong interest in not making unnecessary payments, there would be real market incentives to reduce costs in all ways. Of course, *necessary* medical and hospital care claims would have to be paid if insurance companies wished to stay competitive, and some co-payments would be desirable to discourage overuse.

6   Readers may hear some familiar echoes in this proposal because it is basically the plan I advanced when Secretary of Health, Education & Welfare in the 1970s. That plan was derailed when the attention of the chairman of the relevant House committee focused on other objectives. Up to that point, it had begun to attract support from industry, much of which was providing insurance for its employees; from unions, whose members would, of course, benefit; and from the insurance industry itself.

7   Most were attracted by the federal government's minimal role contrasted with either a Canadian- or British-style approach or the full national health insurance proposals of Senator Kennedy and others. Under their plans, the federal government would be in complete charge of health care, and all doctors, hospitals and other providers would work virtually full time for the government.

8   Another useful reform—which the Administration is reported to be sponsoring—would be to reduce the huge additional costs resulting from the ever growing number of malpractice suits. We should eliminate or sharply curtail contingent fee contracts that induce lawyers to generate a great many of these suits. Doctors feel compelled to order many unnecessary, expensive procedures to protect themselves from this type of litigation.

9   Obviously, this is but the barest outline for a bold and far-reaching proposal requiring much study, analysis and refinement. But it seems to me that with the features of universal coverage, minimal government involvement, and heavy reliance on the private sector and market system, it is a far better approach than simply having the government provide, manage and pay for health care for all.

10   We need to keep the best of our existing standards of medical care and extend it to all citizens without turning to the government to pay for and control the whole system. But we also need to reduce the veritable hemorrhage of medical costs. In 1992 the U.S. will pay $817 billion, or a record 14% of our GNP, on medical care.

11   This proposal could, I believe, help us achieve all of our objectives at much lower cost.

Reading and Analyzing

1. What possible outcome of the health care debate concerns Weinberger?
2. What is Weinberger's proposal for health care? State all three parts of his proposal in your own words.
3. What, in the author's view, is the critical factor in his plan? What does he think will result from this factor?
4. What would be the role of the federal government in Weinberger's plan?
5. Why, according to Weinberger, would this program be cheaper for federal and state governments?
6. What additional reform does Weinberger want? What would it accomplish?
7. On what basis does the author attack "full national health insurance proposals"?

Responding to the Writer's Ideas

1. Weinberger asserts that his proposal would rely on "the private sector and market system" rather than a government-managed and government-financed system. Is that an entirely accurate assertion? What would be the roles of government under his plan? How extensive do these roles seem to you?
2. Weinberger argues that costs will be kept down because insurance companies will want to avoid "unnecessary payments." Does the author establish *how* distinctions will be made between necessary and unnecessary costs or *who* will make them? Do you want more details on this point, or are you satisfied with the author's explanations? Explain.
3. Weinberger asserts that with a national health program, "doctors, hospitals and other providers would work virtually full time for the government." First, how does Weinberger expect his readers to react to this statement? Second, is it necessarily an accurate statement? Review Bodenheimer's proposal for a national health care system before answering.
4. Who, in your view, has the better proposal, Bodenheimer or Weinberger? Or, is there yet another plan that you would put forward? Explain your views.

WRITING SUGGESTIONS

1. Have you experienced someone close to you dying after considerable suffering? If so, use this personal experience as part of your argument for or against legalizing euthanasia.
2. Develop an argument that either supports or opposes legalizing euthanasia. Include in your argument counterarguments of the opposing position.
3. Experts estimate that one-third of Americans are overweight and out of shape. Many children and teenagers are also in poor physical health. What should be done? Write an essay that develops a plan for addressing either the problem of obesity in America or the problem of the poor physical conditioning of young people.
4. In an essay develop a proposal for moving "away from absolutism" in the abortion debate. What can be done to ease tensions and find some middle ground?
5. What, if anything, should be done to further protect nonsmokers from secondhand smoke? Develop your position on this issue in a reasoned discussion.
6. What needs to be done to continue to discourage Americans from smoking? In an essay explain and support your proposals.
7. What is your proposal for health care coverage for this country? Develop your position on a plan that will both control cost and provide access to quality care.
8. George Will ("Tobacco Road") asserts that tobacco ads are targeted to young people to encourage them to start smoking, but the tobacco companies disagree, asserting that they are only seeking to influence brand choice. A study of cigarette ads seems in order. Collect at least 25 different ads and analyze the techniques used to sell the product. See what types of strategies are used and in what frequency. Organize your information, provide percentages for the frequency of appeals and use representative ads to illustrate the various strategies. After introducing your topic, explain, early in your essay, how you gathered your evidence; then present and analyze the evidence for readers.

CHAPTER 8

LOOKING AT AMERICAN SOCIETY: CONFLICTS OF GENDER, CLASS, AND RACE

F. Scott Fitzgerald, seeking to characterize three cultures, suggested that if France was a land and England a people, then America was an idea. Many have tried to define the idea that is America, but few have disputed the importance of America's conception of itself. Recently, some have questioned whether the idea of America is an unrealistic ideal, or whether Americans still have the will to make this the land of the free for everyone, not just for some.

What is the idea of America? Is it to be found in those principles expressed in the Declaration of Independence, or illustrated in the life of the most famous self-made American, Ben Franklin? Two Frenchmen have written important explanations of America, explanations that have con-

tributed to the country's image of itself. Crèvecoeur in the eighteenth century gave us the concept of the melting pot, and de Tocqueville in the nineteenth century sought to explain the effects of a belief in equality and the
individual. But de Tocqueville also examined the tyranny of the majority,
one of the dangers of democracy in his view; Elizabeth Cady Stanton, in
her nineteenth-century Declaration of Sentiments underscored the truth
that the freedoms of the original Declaration applied only to white males
with property; and Martin Luther King, Jr., in 1963 had to call on America to truly extend the rights and privileges of the Constitution to all Americans. Surely the idea of America incorporates both the ideals of freedom,
of the rule of law, of the opportunity to exceed the potential suggested by
one's roots, and the constant vigilance of a people striving to realize the
ideal, to expand the reality of the idea of America to an increasingly larger
share of Americans and to newcomers from all parts of the world.

Some who have recently questioned America's ability to make the
idea reality have looked at the country's place in the world. Books describing the end of history, the decline of the United States' superpower position, or the country's loss of economic supremacy have been best sellers.
Others, many others, have turned their analyses to the problems within, to
the conflicts among groups within the society, to the seeming disintegra-
tion of community. Concerns about the country's place in a world economy will be addressed in Chapter 9; this chapter looks at the problems
within, at the issues that divide rather than bring together, that hold people back rather than provide opportunities for growth.

Although the battle of the sexes is by no means unique to American
culture, it seems ironic that a country founded on liberty has had to struggle so hard to allow—and encourage—the liberation of women. Stanton,
in her Declaration of Sentiments, reminds us of just how exclusive were
the rights provided by the new United States, and how long and hard the
struggle has been to provide equality under the law. But a society does not
operate purely on legal relationships; rather, it operates on the more subtle
and, according to John Stuart Mill, more powerful, expectations of behavior taught to each new generation. And so, even though more than half of
American women are in the workforce, they are still hard to find in CEO
offices or in the U.S. Senate. The chapter's second article, a report of research on playing dumb by sociologists Michael Hughes and Walter Gove,
examines some assumptions about how men and women behave.

The struggle of women for equality in the armed forces continues because while they are now accepted into the services, they are not allowed
in combat, which means that promotions will not come as easily as to
those who have been able to distinguish themselves as leaders under pressure. The more notable conflict in the services today, however, has been
generated by a law prohibiting homosexuals from serving at all. Three
people speak to this issue in the following pages: Representative Patricia

Schroeder, who has introduced a bill prohibiting the exclusion of homosexuals from the military; Colin Powell, Chairman of the Joint Chiefs of Staff; and David Hackworth, a much-decorated retired colonel. The issue of gays in the military is significant in itself, but it also serves to represent attitudes that extend into other work environments.

Unfortunately, women were not the only group left out when the men who gathered in Philadelphia created a new nation. The treatment of Native Americans and African Americans is hardly an attractive part of our past, a past that reaches into the present in the form of a disproportionate number of racial minorities living in poverty, excluded from opportunities to seek the American dream. Ethnic minorities, also struggling to achieve the dream, find themselves in conflict with both the white majority and with other ethnic groups crowded into inner-city neighborhoods and competing with one another for scholarships, jobs, or business loans. The anger and frustration continuing to smolder in poor inner-city neighborhoods flamed into violence in Los Angeles in the spring of 1992 following the acquittal of white Los Angeles police officers accused of viciously beating an unarmed black motorist. Two authors, Elaine Kim and Lance Morrow, examine the causes and consequences of racial and ethnic tensions in the context of the Los Angeles riots. Both define the problem as the consequence of what is missing: economic opportunity, stable families, and sense of identity and self-worth.

A less than perfect melting pot has caused leaders within various groups to encourage their members to find self-esteem in a strong group identity, even in a rejection of the dominant Western culture, while at the same time seeking opportunities for economic advancement with the dominant culture. Some of the tensions within our multicultural society are addressed in other chapters, specifically, in the chapters on education and economics. This chapter concludes with two studies of our ethnic-racial-class conflicts. Andrew Hacker provides interesting data to challenge several ideas some people hold about differences between blacks and whites. And Arthur Schlesinger, Jr., defends the idea of America as a melting pot, multicultural but unified.

❖

Declaration of Sentiments

Elizabeth Cady Stanton

Elizabeth Cady Stanton (1815–1902) was one of the most important leaders of the women's rights movement. Educated at a local academy and then the Emma Willard Seminary in Troy, New York, Stanton studied law with her father before her marriage. She was an active reformer in the abolition and temperance movements, later focusing her attention on women's issues. At the Seneca Falls Convention in 1848, Stanton gave the opening speech and read her Declaration of Sentiments. She founded and became president of the National Women's Suffrage Association in 1869. The Declaration of Sentiments, patterned after the Declaration of Independence, lists the grievances of women suffering under the tyranny of men.

1   When, in the course of human events, it becomes necessary for one portion of the family of man to assume among the people of the earth a position different from that which they have hitherto occupied, but one to which the laws of nature and of nature's God entitle them, a decent respect to the opinions of mankind requires that they should declare the causes that impel them to such a course.

2   We hold these truths to be self-evident: that all men and women are created equal; that they are endowed by their Creator with certain inalienable rights; that among these are life, liberty, and the pursuit of happiness; that to secure these rights governments are instituted, deriving their just powers from the consent of the governed. Whenever any form of government becomes destructive of these ends, it is the right of those who suffer from it to refuse allegiance to it, and to insist upon the institution of a new government, laying its foundation on such principles, and organizing its powers in such form, as to them shall seem most likely to effect their safety and happiness. Prudence, indeed, will dictate that governments long established should not be changed for light and transient causes; and accordingly all experience hath shown that mankind are more disposed to suffer, while evils are sufferable, than to right themselves by abolishing the forms to which they were accustomed. But when a long train of abuses and usurpations, pursuing invariably the same object evinces a design to reduce them under absolute despotism, it is their duty to throw off such government, and to provide new guards for their future security. Such has been

the patient sufferance of the women under this government, and such is now the necessity which constrains them to demand the equal station to which they are entitled.

The history of mankind is a history of repeated injuries and usurpa- [3] tions on the part of man toward woman, having in direct object the establishment of an absolute tyranny over her. To prove this, let facts be submitted to a candid world.

He has never permitted her to exercise her inalienable right to the [4] elective franchise.

He has compelled her to submit to laws, in the formation of which [5] she had no voice.

He has withheld from her rights which are given to the most ignorant [6] and degraded men—both natives and foreigners.

Having deprived her of this first right of a citizen, the elective fran- [7] chise, thereby leaving her without representation in the halls of legislation, he has oppressed her on all sides.

He has made her, if married, in the eye of the law, civilly dead. [8]

He has taken from her all right in property, even to the wages she [9] earns.

He has made her, morally, an irresponsible being, as she can commit [10] many crimes with impunity, provided they be done in the presence of her husband. In the covenant of marriage, she is compelled to promise obedience to her husband, he becoming, to all intents and purposes, her master—the law giving him power to deprive her of her liberty, and to administer chastisement.

He has so framed the laws of divorce, as to what shall be the proper [11] causes, and in case of separation, to whom the guardianship of the children shall be given, as to be wholly regardless of the happiness of women—the law, in all cases, going upon a false supposition of the supremacy of man, and giving all power into his hands.

After depriving her of all rights as a married woman, if single, and [12] the owner of property, he has taxed her to support a government which recognizes her only when her property can be made profitable to it.

He has monopolized nearly all the profitable employments, and from [13] those she is permitted to follow, she receives but a scanty remuneration. He closes against her all the avenues to wealth and distinction which he considers most honorable to himself. As a teacher of theology, medicine, or law, she is not known.

He has denied her the facilities for obtaining a thorough education, [14] all colleges being closed against her.

He allows her in Church, as well as State, but a subordinate position, [15] claiming Apostolic authority for her exclusion from the ministry, and, with some exceptions, from any public participation in the affairs of the Church.

16   He has created a false public sentiment by giving to the world a different code of morals for men and women, by which moral delinquencies which exclude women from society, are not only tolerated, but deemed of little account in man.

17   He has usurped the prerogative of Jehovah himself, claiming it as his right to assign for her a sphere of action, when that belongs to her conscience and to her God.

18   He has endeavored, in every way that he could, to destroy her confidence in her own powers, to lessen her self-respect, and to make her willing to lead a dependent and abject life.

19   Now, in view of this entire disfranchisement of one-half the people of this country, their social and religious degradation—in view of the unjust laws above mentioned, and because women do feel themselves aggrieved, oppressed, and fraudulently deprived of their most sacred rights, we insist that they have immediate admission to all the rights and privileges which belong to them as citizens of the United States.

20   In entering upon the great work before us, we anticipate no small amount of misconception, misrepresentation, and ridicule; but we shall use every instrumentality within our power to effect our object. We shall employ agents, circulate tracts, petition the State and National legislatures, and endeavor to enlist the pulpit and the press in our behalf. We hope this Convention will be followed by a series of Conventions embracing every part of the country.

Reading and Analyzing

1. Summarize the ideas of paragraphs 1 and 2 in your own words.
2. What is Stanton's claim? What does she charge men with?
3. What are the first three facts given by Stanton? Why are they presented first?
4. How have women been restricted by law if married or owning property?
5. How have women been restricted in education and work?
6. How have they been restricted psychologically?
7. What do women demand?
8. How will they seek their goals?

Responding to the Writer's Ideas

1. Analyze the similarities and differences in Stanton's version and the original Declaration. (See pp. 15–18.) What are the significant differences in wording and content?

2. Do some research to determine when specific grievances were eliminated. See how many you can put a date to.

3. Most of the charges have been redressed, however slowly. What charges continue to be legitimate complaints, at least in part?

4. Do we need a new declaration of sentiments for women? If so, what specific charges would you list? If not, why not?

5. Do we need a declaration of sentiments for other groups—children, minorities, gays, veterans? If so, what specific charges should be listed? Select one group that you think needs a list of complaints and prepare a declaration of sentiments for that group.

6. What can be done to eliminate the need for future declarations? What recommendations would you make to eliminate the battle of the sexes?

❖❖

Playing Dumb

Michael Hughes and Walter R. Gove

Michael Hughes (b. 1944) completed his doctorate in sociology at Vanderbilt University and is associate professor of sociology at Virginia Polytechnic Institute and State University. Hughes has published articles in academic journals reporting on his research in the sociology of mental health. Walter R. Gove (b. 1938) is a professor of sociology at Vanderbilt and director of graduate studies. A list of his published books, articles, and reviews runs to many pages. The following article, published in October 1981 in Psychology Today, *is a nonscholarly version of a report of research that originally appeared in* Social Psychology Quarterly. *Hughes and Gove present interesting data that challenge current assumptions about those who play dumb and the effects of doing so.*

1   Several years ago, when we and our colleagues at Vanderbilt University put together a national survey of sex roles, marital roles, and mental health, we included a group of questions about playing dumb—that is, consciously deciding not to display one's knowledge or intelligence. The survey was designed to measure a number of factors that might make women more likely than men to develop mental problems. At least one previous study had suggested that having to feign inferiority in some social situations—particularly on dates—might be one of the major stresses on women. We wanted to find out if playing dumb could account for the differences researchers have found in the mental health of men and women.

2   The sample was sizable. The survey included 2,247 men and women, 18 years old and older, weighted to be representative of Americans living in the 48 contiguous states. We recently analyzed the data on playing dumb and found that they contradicted most common assumptions. On the basis of our sample, we conclude that, in fact, more men than women play dumb in nearly every situation—with friends and strangers, with bosses and coworkers, with dates and children—and that such behavior is most common among people with more education and high-status jobs.

3   The widespread impression that women play dumb more often than men was created in part by two articles published by sociologists more than 30 years ago that have frequently been mentioned since in newspapers and popular magazines as well as in the psychological literature. In a

1946 piece in the *American Journal of Sociology,* Mirra Komarovsky reported that 40 percent of the female students she had interviewed at a prestigious eastern university admitted they had occasionally hidden their academic achievements from the men they dated, pretended ignorance, or allowed their dates to beat them in athletic or intellectual competition. Komarovsky concluded that for women in our society, the desire for academic and career achievement comes into conflict with the attributes that make women attractive to men; this conflict causes women to behave in ways that are inconsistent with their self-image, producing a significant amount of psychological distress.

After studying 163 female college students, Paul Wallin published an article in the *American Sociological Review* in 1950 that showed essentially the same thing—women occasionally play dumb on dates. Wallin suggested that the women did not think of playing dumb as particularly distressing but accepted it as part of conventionalized dating behavior, a ploy that they dropped when relationships became serious.

Those studies have been cited by behavioral scientists for more than 30 years to demonstrate that, because of their lower social status, women often act less intelligent than they are, not only on dates but in many other situations as well. Dwight Dean and his colleagues at Iowa State University reported in a 1975 article in *Sociological Quarterly* that a casual search of the sociological literature had turned up 20 uncritical citations of the two journal articles and none that questioned the validity of the studies, despite the fact that neither study considered cases of men who play dumb or women who don't.

Dean and his colleagues also told about a study of their own, in which about equal numbers of college men and women said they played dumb on dates. Indeed, the same researchers found that more than 90 percent of the students in their study—and in Wallin's—said either that they had never played dumb or that they had done so only a few times in their lives.

The Dean study had not been published when we designed and conducted our original study at Vanderbilt University, although we did consider it in the analysis reported here. What we knew at the time was that some evidence showed that college women played dumb on dates and that Komarovsky claimed it produced psychological distress; that Wallin claimed that it did not, but that neither had any real indicators of the mental state that accompanied the behavior.

The question we decided to ask our respondents was: "Have you ever pretended to be less intelligent or knowledgeable than you really are?" Note that the wording of the question was such that people who answered yes were presumably not *feeling* dumb; that is, they were confident of their knowledge and intelligence and were only pretending to be ignorant in a given circumstance. If they answered yes, they were then asked how often they had pretended to be less intelligent or knowledgeable—

very often, pretty often, not too often, or not at all often. We also asked them in what situations they had ever played dumb. The categories were: (1) with a date, (2) with your spouse, (3) with your boss, (4) with your coworkers, (5) with friends, (6) with strangers, (7) with children.

9   We were surprised by the answers, which showed that more men than women admitted to having played dumb—31 percent to 23 percent. Since the earlier research had led us to expect the opposite, we looked for an explanation. Perhaps more men play dumb at some time, but women do so more frequently. That idea proved false. Among those who had played dumb, only about 18 percent of both sexes said they had done so very often or fairly often.

10   Taking another tack, we wondered whether there were differences in *when* men and women played dumb. To find out, we analyzed the answers in each of the seven categories separately. For dates, we confirmed what Dean had found: no significant differences in the propensity of men and women to play dumb on dates. That is true of the never-married (16 percent of the men, 15 percent of the women); the divorced (13 percent, men; 12 percent, women); the widowed (1 percent, men; 4 percent, women); and the married—we presume their responses were completely retrospective (7 percent, men; 9 percent, women).

11   Men were roughly twice as likely to say that they have played dumb on the job as were women. That was true both with the boss (15 percent, men; 7 percent, women) and with their coworkers (17 percent, men; 9 percent, women).

12   The responses were similar with friends (13 percent, men; 9 percent, women); with strangers (16 percent, men; 8 percent, women); and with children (9 percent, men; 7 percent, women). The only situation in which women were significantly more likely to report playing dumb was with their spouses. They were nearly twice as likely to say they play dumb with their husbands (13 percent) as men were to say they play dumb with their wives (7 percent).

13   We then decided to see what personal characteristics other than sex were involved. We looked at age, education, income, occupation, marital status, ethnicity, and mental health to see if any of those characteristics were related to the tendency to feign ignorance. We did two separate analyses: one to see how the characteristics related to ever having played dumb, and another to see how they related to playing dumb in each situation (with a date, with a friend, and so on).

14   We found that age was the strongest overall predictor, relating significantly to playing dumb with dates, spouses, friends, strangers, and children. Young people consistently play dumb more often than older people. People with more education are more likely to play dumb, particularly with coworkers, strangers, and children. In contrast, those with lower incomes play dumb more often, especially in dealing with bosses, friends,

and coworkers. People in high-status occupations also play dumb more often, especially with the boss, with friends, and with strangers. Whether people are married or not doesn't seem to matter, but ethnicity does, in one case. Jews reported playing dumb more often than blacks, Hispanics, Orientals, and non-Jewish white Americans.

We were particularly interested in whether mental health and playing dumb were related, since Komarovsky, Wallin, and Dean had disagreed on the point. We looked at several indicators of mental health—self-esteem, happiness, psychiatric symptoms, and alienation—as shown by answers to questions in the survey. Without exception, we found that those who played dumb very often were worst off, while people who said they played dumb "not at all often" were in the best mental health. In between, going from poorer to better mental health, were those who said they feigned ignorance "pretty often," "not too often," or never. Apparently the willingness to seem dumb occasionally—to ingratiate yourself with others, perhaps, or to tease information out of them subtly—is consistent with good psychological adjustment.

Most of our findings contradicted our original suppositions. To account for both the findings and the contradictions, we must start with one of the basic tenets on which American society and democracy are based: that we are similar in intelligence to most of those around us. If you are— or feel you are—clearly more intelligent or knowledgeable than those around you, you will feel considerable pressure to hide that fact. People play dumb when they have a strong commitment to a relationship with others and are concerned with how others will evaluate them. But they may also play dumb in another kind of situation, when they do not particularly care about the others involved. Then they may pretend to be dumb simply to promote smooth social interaction and to avoid situations embarrassing to themselves or others.

In our study, we were primarily concerned with playing dumb in relationships that involve a strong commitment—to dates, spouses, friends, bosses, and coworkers. That means we were trying to explain behavior that occurs relatively infrequently but is usually important when it does occur. As we've mentioned, we have found that it occurs most often among males, the young, and the highly educated; among Jews, people with relatively low income, and people in high-status occupations. There are four factors or conditions consistent with our findings that we feel provide a framework for understanding why and in what situations people play dumb.

1. They must be intelligent and knowledgeable, or at least believe they are.
2. Knowledge and intelligence must be valued by everyone involved.
3. Their intelligence and knowledge must be taken seriously by others involved in the situation.

4. What they gain from playing dumb must be greater than what it costs them.

18   Unless the first two points apply to a situation, playing dumb has no point. Unless the second two points apply, it is difficult to imagine any motivation for playing dumb. According to social stereotypes, distorted as they may be, the first and second points are attributes of those with a good education and high-status jobs, of males, and (among ethnic groups) of Jews—the same groups who, according to our study, play dumb the most.

19   Within our framework, it makes sense that young people play dumb more often than old people, since they are more likely to meet situations in which competition and ambition are important; to hold low-status positions at work, and, at the same time, to be more educated than their elders. As a result, they face more situations in which playing dumb may be useful, compared with older people, who generally meet few persons to whom they find it necessary to defer.

20   The relationship between playing dumb and low income is also consistent with our framework; it provides a motive for acting in an ingratiating manner. That is especially true where the relationship between low income and playing dumb was particularly strong—on the job.

21   Since in America today women are less likely than men to encounter situations in which all four criteria apply, it is not surprising that men play dumb more often. The situation is changing as more women reach responsible positions in the working world, but a higher percentage of men are still channeled into situations that value knowledge and competition.

22   Our interpretation is strengthened by what happens in marriage, the one situation in which women are more likely than men to play dumb. It is also the one situation in which women consistently meet our four criteria for playing dumb. In some areas of marriage, such as homemaking and childrearing, women are considered particularly intelligent and knowledgeable and are valued for their special ability (factors 1 through 3). In other areas—financial matters or world affairs, for example—women are frequently constrained to play dumb to avoid undercutting their husband's supposed special competence (factor 4).

23   We have provided some evidence that disputes the belief that women play dumb more than men because of social stereotypes and pressures. But what does that tell us? Given our analysis, the fact that fewer women pretend to do so simply means that women have less opportunity or reason to play dumb. Even among the majority of women who work, many are channeled into low-status, low-paying jobs. At home or at work, they are less likely than men to see themselves as intelligent, to meet others who value knowledge highly, or to be taken seriously by those in authority. Cold comfort for anyone who believes in sexual equality.

Reading and Analyzing

1. What is the definition of "playing dumb"?
2. What assumptions did the authors want to test? What previous studies are cited, and what did they seem to suggest?
3. What do the authors conclude based on their study? That is, what is the claim of their argument?
4. What type of argument is this?
5. Summarize the results of the study as presented in paragraphs 9 through 14. What is the study's most significant result with regard to gender? In what situation do women play dumb more than men?
6. What relationship did the authors find between playing dumb and mental health?
7. Why do those who play dumb the most do so? What do they seek to accomplish from this behavior?
8. How do the authors account for the fact that women rarely have the opportunity to play dumb?

Responding to the Writers' Ideas

1. Do you ever play dumb? If so, how often and in what circumstances?
2. Does your experience coincide with the study result showing that young people are more likely to play dumb than older people? Why or why not?
3. Do you think that people should play dumb? If so, in what situations? Would you encourage your children to play dumb? Would you encourage female friends to play dumb in school or on dates to please men? Why or why not?
4. Is the need some people feel to play dumb a sign of courtesy (of smoothing social relations) or a sign of distorted values and expectations? Explain.
5. The authors seek to explain the results of their study by noting the American tenet that "we are similar in intelligence to most of those around us." Do you agree that most Americans adhere to this belief? Do you agree with the belief? Why or why not?

❖

A Case for the Military
Freedom Act

Patricia Schroeder

*Holding a law degree from Harvard University, Patricia Schroeder (b.
1940) has been the U.S. representative from the Denver area for twenty
years. She chairs the Select Committee on Children, Youth, and Families
and serves on the Judiciary, Post Office, and Armed Services
committees. In 1992 Representative Schroeder introduced legislation
prohibiting discrimination against gay and lesbian Americans in the
armed forces. The following pieces represent some of her work on this
issue. The first, the introduction to the proposed legislation, is followed
by correspondence between Representative Schroeder and General
Colin Powell, chairman of the Joint Chiefs of Staff, on the issue of gays
in the military. Questions to guide reading and responding follow the
three pieces.*

On The Introduction of the Military Freedom Act of 1992

1   One Vietnam veteran's tombstone inscription reads, "When I was in
the military they gave me a medal for killing two men and a discharge for
loving one."

2   For the first 150 years of our country's history, gay and lesbian
Americans served in our country's military. And for the past fifty years,
these same Americans, regardless of their conduct, devotion, and their accomplishments have been told they need not apply to any branch of the
Armed Forces. Fortunately, this has not stopped brave, patriotic gay and
lesbian Americans from serving their country. But these brave Americans
put themselves at risk twice every time they answer a call to service. First,
they put their lives on the line for their country. Second, they risk being
disgracefully cashiered if their sexual orientation is discovered. We should
be thankful that they have ignored this stupid policy. Our nation's defense
has gained the service of thousands of good soldiers and sailors. You will
hear from these veterans today.

3   Department of Defense Directive 1332.14, which says homosexuality
is incompatible with military service, is un-American because it judges people by their being rather than their conduct and because it arbitrarily excludes and denies Americans equal opportunities, particularly women,

who are three times more likely than men to be investigated and discharged under this policy.

We have waited patiently for the courts to overturn this ban on the   4
grounds that it is unconstitutional. We have appealed to the President and
the Secretary of Defense with the argument that one's sexual orientation is
irrelevant, and that the military is being denied skilled, valued personnel.
Even Lawrence Korb, former Assistant Secretary of Defense for Manpower
in the Reagan Administration, and officials within Army Headquarters
have argued for repeal. Those pleas have all gone unanswered. Now, Congress must take it upon itself to change the policy.

We can be silent about this invidious discrimination no more: Silence   5
is tantamount to complicity in the perpetuation of prejudice, discrimination, and fear.

Today I am joined by twenty-four of my colleagues, gay and lesbian   6
veterans from three wars, and representatives of the Military Freedom Project, a group of organizations fighting to repeal the ban, in introducing the
Military Freedom Act of 1992, which will end the arbitrary elimination of
individuals because of their sexual orientation.

Congress of the United States
House of Representatives
Washington, DC 20515-0601

April 28, 1992

General Colin L. Powell
Chairman
Joint Chiefs of Staff
The Pentagon
Washington, DC 20301

Dear Colin:

For some time, I have been troubled by your comments before Congress in February about the suitability of gay and lesbian Americans for service in our nation's Armed Forces.

On the one hand, I was pleased to see you admit that the exclusionary policy is no longer defended for national security purposes. As you know, two PERSEREC reports from the Department of Defense—which, I fear, are merely collecting dust on some desk at the Pentagon—concluded, "Both patriots and traitors are drawn from the class American citizen and not specifically from the class heterosexual or homosexual."

You also admitted that the exclusion doesn't exist because gay and lesbian Americans "are not good enough." Rather, you explained, "homosexual behavior is inconsistent with maintaining good order and discipline."

Indulge me further, as I underscore your words: "I mean it is difficult in a military setting where there is no privacy, where you don't get a choice of association, where you don't get a choice of where you live, to introduce a group of individuals . . . who favor a homosexual lifestyle, and put them in with heterosexuals who would prefer not to have somebody of the same sex find them sexually attractive, put them in close proximity, ask them to share the most private facilities together, the bedroom, the barracks, latrines, the showers."

You'll have to forgive me—once a history major, always a history major—because your shower apprehensions or privacy fears could have been written in 1942 from the Chairman of the General Board to the Secretary of the Navy:

Men on board ship live in particularly close association; in their messes, one man sits beside another; their hammocks or bunks are close together; in their common tasks they work side by side, and in their particular tasks such as those of a gun's crew, they form a closely knit highly coordinated team. How many white men would choose, of their own accord, that their closest associates in sleeping quarters, at mess, and in a gun's crew should be of another race? How many would accept such conditions, if required to do so, without resentment and just as a matter of course? The General Board believes that the answer is "Few, if any," and further believes that if the issue were forced, there would be a lowering of contentment, teamwork and discipline in the service.

I am sure you are aware that your reasoning would have kept you from the mess hall a few decades ago, all in the name of good order and discipline and regardless of your dedication and conduct.

On a related matter, enclosed is a letter that twenty-five of my Congressional Caucus for Women's Issues colleagues and I sent to the Defense Advisory Committee on Women in the Service, which explains how lesbian-baiting is used to harm female service members, regardless of sexual orientation.

As I can't make much sense of your privacy defense, particularly because of its past abuse against blacks and women, would you explain it to me?

All my best,

Patricia Schroeder
Congresswoman

CHAIRMAN OF THE JOINT CHIEFS OF STAFF
WASHINGTON, D.C. 20318-0001

8 May 1992

The Honorable Patricia Schroeder
House of Representatives
Washington, DC 20515-0601

Dear Pat,

Thank you for your recent letter concerning the position I took before Congress in February concerning homosexuals serving in the Armed Forces. I have given a great deal of thought to my position and continue to hold the view that the presence of homosexuals in the military is prejudicial to good order and discipline.

This is the policy of the Department of Defense and is supported by all of the Joint Chiefs of Staff. It is also a view held by experts who have studied the sociology of the military for many years. I am including a recent article by Charles Moskos on the subject.

I am well aware of the attempts to draw parallels between this position and positions used years ago to deny opportunities to African-Americans. I know you are a history major, but I can assure you I need no reminders concerning the history of African-Americans in the defense of their Nation and the tribulations they faced. I am a part of that history.

Skin color is a benign, non-behavioral characteristic. Sexual orientation is perhaps the most profound of human behavioral characteristics. Comparison of the two is a convenient but invalid argument. I believe the privacy rights of all Americans in uniform have to be considered, especially since those rights are often infringed upon by the conditions of military service.

As Chairman of the Joint Chiefs of Staff, as well as an African-American fully conversant with history, I believe the policy we have adopted is consistent with the necessary standards of good order and discipline required in the Armed Forces.

Sincerely,

Colin L. Powell
Chairman of the
Joint Chiefs of Staff

Reading and Analyzing

INTRODUCTION

1. What is Schroeder's position on excluding homosexuals from the armed forces?
2. What reasons are given in support of her position?
3. What does the author accomplish by including references to veterans and army officials?
4. What does the author accomplish with her opening two paragraphs? What is the basis of her persuasive appeal in these paragraphs?

LETTER TO COLIN POWELL

1. On what basis were homosexuals excluded from the military in the past? Now, according to General Powell, why are homosexuals excluded?
2. Schroeder provides two long quotations in her letter: General Powell's words and those from 1942. What do these quotations have in common? How do they differ significantly? How can Schroeder use the similarities to her advantage in her letter to Powell?
3. What is "lesbian-baiting"? How does this issue connect to the subject of Schroeder's letter?
4. How would you describe the tone of this letter? What details help create the tone?

LETTER TO REPRESENTATIVE SCHROEDER

1. What position on the issue does Powell reaffirm in his letter?
2. How does Powell defend his position and counter the argument in Schroeder's letter?
3. What is the purpose of paragraph 2?
4. How would you describe the tone of this letter? What details help create the tone?

Responding to the Writers' Ideas

1. Is the current law excluding homosexuals from the military discriminatory? Why or why not?
2. If it is discriminatory, is it nonetheless necessary to maintain military order and discipline? Why or why not? Is it possible to defend dis-

crimination in one situation without allowing for discrimination in other situations?

3. If the law is necessary for discipline, then does it follow that women should be excluded from combat for similar reasons—lack of privacy and so on? Why or why not?

4. Who "won" the letter exchange? Support your answer.

❖

The Case for a Military Gay Ban

David H. Hackworth

The most decorated living American veteran, David H. Hackworth (b. 1931) rose from private to colonel before retiring from the U.S. Army in 1971. Hackworth is an expert on guerrilla warfare, has written many articles in military periodicals, is a contributing editor for defense at Newsweek, *and has written critically of today's army in his autobiography* About Face: The Odyssey of an American Warrior *(1989). In "The Case for a Military Gay Ban," which appeared in the* Washington Post *on June 28, 1992, Hackworth defends the ban on homosexuals serving in the military.*

Rep. Pat Schroeder of Colorado wanted to give women "equality and opportunity" by making them rucksack-toting grunts. Now she aims at putting homosexuals in the foxholes to "end the final bastion of discrimination."

I cannot think of a better way to destroy fighting spirit and gut U.S. combat effectiveness. My credentials for saying this are over four decades' experience as a soldier or military reporter.

Despite the ban on service by homosexuals, gays have long served in the armed forces, some with distinction. Many perhaps felt no sexual inclination toward their heterosexual fellow soldiers. If they did, they had their buddies' attitudes and the Uniform Code of Military Justice hanging over their heads. Still, I have seen countless examples of inappropriate and morale-busting behavior.

In Italy, for example, in the postwar occupation, a gay soldier could not keep his hands off other soldiers in my squad. He disrupted discipline, mangled trust among squad members and zeroed out morale. In the same unit, the personnel major was gay. He had affairs with ambitious teenage soldiers in exchange for kicking up their test scores. This corrupted the command's promotion system and led to the commissioning of William Calley-like[1] lieutenants not fit to lead combat soldiers.

During my second tour in the Korean War, a gay commanding officer gave combat awards to his lovers who had never been on the line. In

---

[1] Officer court-martialed during the Vietnam War for leading a raid on a village, giving orders to kill everyone in the village.—Ed.

Vietnam, a young captain in my unit was asked by the commander to go to bed with him. This almost destroyed the esprit of a fine parachute unit.

6   These are not isolated incidents: During my Army career I saw countless officers and NCOs who couldn't stop themselves from hitting on soldiers. The absoluteness of their authority, the lack of privacy, enforced intimacy and a 24-hour duty day made sexual urges difficult to control. The objects of their affection were impressionable lads who, searching for a caring role model, sometimes ended up in a gay relationship they might not have sought.

7   A majority of American citizens, according to polls, support Schroeder's bill. Many people look at the armed forces as they do the post office, the Bank of America or General Motors—an 8-to-5 institution where discrimination on the basis of sexual orientation is against basic freedom, human rights and the American way of life. If these polls are true, a lot of people don't understand what war is about.

8   Sure, banning gays from defending their country is discriminatory. But discriminations are necessary when a larger public purpose is being served. Civilian standards of fairness and equality don't apply down where the body bags are filled.

9   On the battlefield, what allows men to survive is combat units made up of disciplined team players, who are realistically trained and led by caring skippers who set the example and know their trade. When all of these factors are in synch, a unit has the right stuff. It becomes tight, a family, and clicks like a professional football team. Spirited men who place their lives in their buddies' hands are the most essential element in warfare. The members of such combat teams trust one another totally.

10   One doesn't need to be a field marshal to understand that sex between service members undermines those critical factors that produce discipline, military orders, spirit and combat effectiveness. Mix boys and girls, gays and straights in close quarters such as the barracks or the battlefield, and both sexual contact and the consequent breakdown of morale are inevitable.

11   Many bright people are pushing for the ban to be lifted. I suspect that few if any have been down in the trenches, but I have no doubt their psychological/sociological/political clout will have considerable influence even if they don't have a clue what combat is about.

12   Unfortunately, most of the top brass won't sound off. They duck and weave and offer hollow and spurious Pentagonese double-talk reasons for continuing the ban—reasons that only fuel the pro-gay argument. But they have told me in the "G" ring of the Pentagon that they're "against it, but sounding off would be the kiss of death, like opposing women in combat—a career killer, you know."

13   I hope that our lawmakers will visit Quantico and Fort Benning before they vote, and ask Marine gunnery sergeants and Army platoon

sergeants what a few gays would do to the fighting spirit of units. These pros told me: Gays are not wanted by straight men or women in their showers, toilets, foxholes or fighting units. They say that in combat young men face death constantly, and what allows them to make it through the hell of it all is a feeling of toughness, invincibility and total trust in their buddies.

My experience with warriors in over eight years of roaming the killing fields in seven wars confirms what these old salts are saying. 14

A serving lieutenant general recently wrote to me, "Ask Pat Schroeder if she'd like her kids under a gay first sergeant who might use his rank and authority to demand sexual favors from his subordinate 18-year-old kids. We just had that occur in my command." 15

No doubt advocates of gays in combat units will argue that they don't approve of demanding sexual favors and that the first sergeant deserved what he got—a court-martial. The problem is, all the court-martials and regulations in the world can't prevent the kind of morale problems that a change in the law is bound to create. Sure, the first sergeant is serving hard time at Fort Leavenworth, but Pat Schroeder and the two dozen lawmakers who support her bill must also ask themselves what happened to the morale and fighting spirit of his unit. 16

Reading and Analyzing

1. What is Hackworth's subject? What is his position on this subject?
2. Why does the author begin with a reference to Representative Patricia Schroeder?
3. What are Hackworth's arguments in defense of his position? List his points.
4. What is the source of Hackworth's evidence? What credentials for his evidence does he provide?
5. Hackworth gives, as evidence, the view of "pros" that "gays are not wanted by straight men or women" because to survive the horrors of war they need a "feeling of toughness, invincibility and a total trust in their buddies." Although this may well be how some people feel, is it a logical argument? Should people be excluded from a job because others don't want them? Is there any reason, other than stereotyping, for straight men not to trust gays?
6. What people does Hackworth blame for contributing to the possibility of gays' being allowed in the military?
7. How would you describe the tone of this article? What elements help to shape tone?

Responding to the Writer's Ideas

1. How convincing are Hackworth's examples as evidence supporting his claim? What is the assumption underlying the relationship of evidence to claim? How emotionally persuasive are the examples?
2. Hackworth asserts that banning gays is discriminatory, but "discriminations are necessary when a larger public purpose is being served." Do you accept this argument? How has this kind of argument been used in the past to justify other patterns of discrimination? Is this situation really different, or is it another area of discrimination that needs changing? Support your position.
3. Should gays be allowed in the military? Why or why not?

❖

They Armed in Self-Defense

Elaine H. Kim

Holding a doctorate from Berkeley, Elaine Kim (b. 1942) is a professor
of Asian-American Studies at the University of California, Berkeley.
Kim has worked on several radio and television shows about Asian
Americans and participated in organizations for Asians in the Bay area.
She has written Asian American Literature: An Introduction to the
Writings and Their Social Context *(1982) and* With Silk Wings: Asian
American Women at Work *(with Janice Otani, 1983). In her May 18,*
1992,"My Turn" article in Newsweek, *Kim seeks to create a different*
image of Korean Americans than that which emerged from the Los
Angeles riots.

When images of armed Korean shopkeepers and headlines about
conflicts between African-Americans and Korean-Americans were suddenly beamed from Los Angeles two weeks ago, seemingly out of nowhere
and without history or context, I knew it was another case of visual media
racism. The disembodied images implied that both groups come from cultures more violent and racist than the dominant culture. They also diverted
attention away from a long tradition of racial violence that was not created by African-Americans or Korean-Americans.

The tensions among people of color are rooted in racial violence
woven into U.S. history for the past 500 years and evidenced today in a judicial system that can allow the men who beat Rodney King to escape conviction. The so-called black-Korean problem is a decontextualized manifestation of a much larger problem. The roots lie not in the
Korean-immigrant-owned corner store situated in a community ravaged by
poverty and police violence, but stretch far back to the corridors of corporate and government offices in Los Angeles, Sacramento and Washington,
D.C. Without an understanding of our histories, Korean-Americans and
African-Americans, it seems, are ready to engage in a zero-sum game over
the crumbs of a broken society, a war in which the advancement of one
group means deterioration for the other.

I have lived all my life in the United States. Even though people still
compliment me occasionally on my ability to speak English and ask me
when I am returning to "my country," I don't consider myself Korean. I
am Korean-American. My consciousness was shaped by the civil-rights

341

movement led by African-Americans, who taught me to reject the false choice between being treated as a perpetual foreigner and relinquishing my own identity for someone else's Anglo-American one. For me, African-Americans permanently redefined the meaning of "American." I came to understand how others had also been swept aside by the dominant culture: my schooling offered nothing about Chicanos or Latinos, and most of what I was taught about African-Americans was distorted to justify their oppression and vindicate the forces of that oppression.

4   Likewise, Korean-Americans have been and continue to be used for someone else's agenda and benefit, whether we are hated as foreigners who refuse to become "good Americans," stereotyped as diligent work machines or simply treated as if we do not exist. Throughout my childhood, the people who continually asked, "What are you?" knew nothing of Korea or Koreans. "Are you Chinese or Japanese?" they would ask confidently, as if there were no other possibilities. The "world history" courses I took started with Greece and Rome; China and Japan were barely mentioned— and Korea never was.

5   Like many Korean exiles whose political consciousness ripened under Japanese colonialism, my father was a fierce nationalist fond of talking about Koreans as a people of great courage and talent. When we were small, he regaled us with tales of heroes like Sohn Kee-chung, the Korean marathon runner who proved the bankruptcy of Hitler's notion of the Aryan "master race" when he won a gold medal in the 1936 Olympics in Nazi Germany. My father also claimed that Koreans were responsible for astounding and important inventions, such as gunpowder and movable type, as well as one of the world's oldest astronomical observatories.

6   Although I searched and searched, I could find no trace, in the America outside our house, of the things my father told us about. Because of Korea's suzerain relationship with China, Korean inventions such as gunpowder are commonly thought to be Chinese. Likewise, Sohn Kee-chung ran the marathon in a Japanese uniform because Korea was a colony of Japan at the time. The gold medal went to Japan. Later, I began to wonder if my father had made up these things. It was almost as if Korea had never existed, or its existence made no difference.

7   Why did my parents talk so much about Korea? After all, they both lived most of their lives in the United States. Why didn't they take on an "American" identity? My mother grew up on the plantations and tenant farms of Hawaii and California. Although she did not visit Korea until she was in her 60s, she considered herself a Korean. My father came to Chicago as a foreign student in 1926. He lived in the United States for 63 years. My parents didn't embrace an American identity because racism did not give them that choice. My mother arrived in Hawaii as an infant in 1903,

but she could not vote until she was in her 50s, when laws prohibiting persons born in Korea from becoming naturalized U.S. citizens were overturned. My father never became a U.S. citizen, at first because he was not allowed to and later because he did not want to. He kept himself going by believing that he would return to Korea in triumph someday. Instead, he died in Oakland at 88, and we buried him in Korea in accordance with his wishes.

When the Los Angeles Police Department and the state government   8
failed to respond to the initial outbreak of violence in South-Central, I suspected that Korean-Americans were being used as human shields to protect the real source of rage. Surveying the charred ruins of Koreatown, Korean-American newcomers must feel utterly betrayed by what they had believed was a democratic system that would protect life, liberty and property. The shopkeepers who trusted the government to protect them lost everything. In a sense, they may have finally come to know what my parents knew more than half a century ago: that the American Dream is only an empty promise.

I only hope that we can turn our outrage into energy, because I still   9
want to believe the promise is real.

Reading and Analyzing

1. What event is the occasion for Kim's article?
2. What is the claim of her argument?
3. Explain in your own words the ideas in paragraph 2. What does Kim mean by "a decontextualized manifestation of a much larger problem"? What is the "larger problem" she refers to?
4. What is the point of Kim's reference to personal experience in sentence 2 of paragraph 3? What did Kim learn from African Americans in the civil-rights movement? What was she taught in school?
5. What are the details of Kim's and her parents' experience designed to illustrate about America? What, in Kim's view, is the context in which the rioters must be understood?
6. Does Kim believe in the possibility of the American dream?

Responding to the Writer's Ideas

1. Has your schooling included study of Latin America, Africa, and Asia? If so, do you think that study has helped you understand and relate to Hispanic Americans, African Americans, and Asian Americans? If not, why not?

2. Kim accuses the television coverage of the riots of media racism. Do you agree with her charge? Is it the responsibility of TV news camera crews to somehow provide "context" when they are on the site of a riot in progress?

3. Would providing a context of racism in America justify the rioting and looting and attacks on passersby captured on video tape? In other words, did the rioters act in self-defense? And if so, does that justify their behavior? Why or why not?

❖

Video Warriors in Los Angeles

Lance Morrow

Lance Morrow (b. 1939) is a senior writer at Time *magazine who contributes to cover stories and the* Time *essay section. Morrow has also written several books, including* The Chief: A Memoir of Fathers and Sons *(1985), a study of the author's relationship with his famous journalist father Hugh Morrow. In 1981, Morrow received the National Magazine Award for his* Time *essays. In his* Time *essay "Video Warriors in Los Angeles" (May 11, 1992), Morrow offers an interesting perspective on the causes of the Los Angeles riots.*

The final episode of *The Cosby Show* ran on the second night of the riots.

1

Theo Huxtable graduated from New York University with a bachelor's degree in psychology. The large and loving family gathered: the plot's only crisis had something to do with whether Theo could find enough tickets to the ceremony for all the friends and neighbors and family who had assembled to hug one another and make fond jokes. Dr. Huxtable (Bill Cosby) was goofy with pride. He had a flashback to the time some years before when Theo announced he wanted to forget about school and get a job: Dr. Huxtable, stern and loving, laid down the law. And then at the end of the show, Cosby and his television wife, Phylicia Rashad, walked off the stage set, out of fantasy into real time, as the studio audience applauded.

2

Now Dr. Huxtable is gone. What are Americans to do for fathers? Ronald Reagan was a hologram of American Dad. George Bush is, so to speak, a less vivid absence than Reagan. He seems to be away a lot, either physically or morally. When he does come home to try to focus, Americans almost wish he would not: He has been going too often into his '50s flustery, dufus mode. Mario Cuomo is the only Democrat who looks and talks like a father, but he refused to accept the role, and that amounted to abandonment. He left the Democratic race to the sibling rivals (Clinton, Kerrey, Brown, Tsongas and so on), who have spent the season gouging one another the way kids in a big unhappy family do.

3

Love is a zero-sum game in America, and the children riot over it. Or rather, they riot in the absence of it: it is usually the want of love that makes children vicious and sends them out of control. It seemed perfect that Cosby, America's ideal fantasy father (black) should vanish just at that moment: video metaphysics. Cosby-Huxtable was a heartbreaking

4

345

American illusion. There is no deeper need among the nation's most deeply needy blacks than perfect fathers, Dr. Huxtables, role models for male children, grown men who will do the first, indispensable thing for children: make them safe and happy. Then teach them how to grow up, how to be intelligent and responsible and how to raise children of their own. Without all that, nothing can be done. It must be hard for some young blacks not to think of *The Cosby Show* as a species of fraud, a looking glass into a never-never America for them. The set goes blank.

5   America makes itself insane with the envies and needs that its self-images create. To have and have not is relative. Last year's movie *Boyz N the Hood* was set in the same South Central Los Angeles that was burning in last week's riots. The characters, the boyz, were supposed to represent the dead-end hopelessness of black ghetto males. And they did. They also lived in relatively pleasant homes and drove customized cars and watched enormous color TV sets in a life-style that most of the residents of Kinshasa or Cairo would consider upper-middle class—nearly luxurious. An objective, literal-minded Marxist might wonder what the boyz' whining was all about. But the terrible American lovelessness and exclusion and self-pity— the fatherlessness, the leaderlessness—gave the boyz a ring of truth. Grievance is comparative. If you feel inferior and hopeless and lost, especially compared with the Big White Other, why then you are. And you may go around blowing each other's heads off: the most literal enactment of brainlessness.

6   Without grownups to sort out right and wrong, what is acceptable and what is not, judgments that should belong to the moral-responsible realm fall to that of sensational empathy, of momentary response. Discussion is reduced to jolts of electric horror and freezes instantly as attitude— as racial stereotype. Society becomes a war of videos, in which orderly brainwork, any reasoning over rights and wrongs, is impossible. Cosby gave way on American television screens to endlessly reduplicated, hall-of-mirrors replays of the Rodney King video and the truck-driver video: the truck-driver video being the one shot from a helicopter when a group of blacks dragged a white driver from his vehicle and beat him almost to death (he survived).

7   In the moral flatness of button-pushing sensation, the truck-driver video accomplished the amazing task of nullifying the Rodney King video. The dumb, blunt message of the Rodney King video was: white cops are monsters beating defenseless blacks. The bottom-feeders' message of the truck-driver video was that blacks are savage, racist animals who would beat a man virtually to death because he is white. On that level of discourse, if Americans choose to stay there, there can only be a gridlock of rage: blacks make demons of whites, whites make demons of blacks.

8   America is in certain ways a country out of control: drugs, crime, what has become a morally borderless wandering. The two videos are a

matched pair, complementary. They are choreographed like MTV, performed by Road Warriors. The Rodney King video shows cops in the stylized tribal rioting that men in groups on dangerous excursions sometimes use as a form of bonding—solidarities of atrocity on the late shift. The truck-driver video looked like ritual sacrifice, the helicopter circling overhead, the rioters circling the trucker's flung body. Both videos recorded naked power dances, conscienceless, brainless, evil, pain inflicting: *I have your life under my boot.* To look at them last week was to see Americans of both races going backward at the speed of light.

Reading and Analyzing

1. What, according to Morrow, does Dr. Huxtable represent?
2. What does his "disappearance" at the time of the riots symbolically suggest to Morrow?
3. How does the author connect some political leaders to the father-family subject? What does Morrow mean when he describes Reagan as a "hologram of American Dad"? What does he mean when he says that Bush is a "less vivid *absence* [emphasis mine] than Reagan"?
4. What does Morrow assert to be a cause of the riots?
5. What do good fathers give to children? How do children feel without the direction of fathers?
6. When young people are not taught how to make moral judgments, what is likely to guide their decision making? How has modern technology influenced the way we think, the expectations we have, the way we react to events?
7. What was the result of the two endlessly replayed videos? What did they show us of the police officers and the black rioters?
8. Explain Morrow's final sentence.
9. What is Morrow's thesis, the claim of his argument?
10. The author draws connections among a number of different subjects. Analyze the essay's structure. Is there a pattern or logic to the organization? If not, how would you describe the "pattern"? Is this a flaw in the essay? What might Morrow want to suggest by the way he writes this piece?

Responding to the Writer's Ideas

1. Morrow writes: "If you feel inferior and hopeless and lost, especially compared with the Big White Other, why then you are." Does this idea make sense to you? Can it apply to anyone, regardless of race or degree of affluence, who does not feel loved and valued? Explain.

2. In spite of many specific references, Morrow's essay is essentially philosophical; that is, he presents no data, survey results, and so on, to support his assertions. Do you agree that we are in "a morally borderless wandering," a "country out of control"? Why or why not?

3. Morrow suggests that television depicts an ideal world that many people do not experience. Explore this idea. What shows (and what commercials) may be creating, for many of us, a world we cannot, realistically, hope to duplicate in our own lives? Try collecting some evidence to support this idea.

4. Do you agree with Morrow's analysis of the "war of videos" producing racial stereotypes that make reasoning about racial conflicts almost impossible? What environment is needed for race conflicts to be eased?

5. Morrow offers some harsh comments on various political leaders. Do you disagree with any of his observations? If so, prepare a counterargument in support of *one* politician in Morrow's list.

❖

The Myths of Racial Division

Andrew Hacker

*A graduate of Amherst, Oxford, and Princeton, Andrew Hacker
(b. 1929) has been a political science professor at Queens College of the
City University of New York since 1971. Hacker has written many
articles and books, including* The Study of Politics *(1963; 1973),* The
End of the American Era *(1970), and* U.S.: A Statistical Portrait of the
American People *(1983). The following article, published in the* New
Republic *on March 23, 1992, offers a counter to the many works
emphasizing racial divisions in America.*

The urge to emphasize racial division in America is hard to resist.   1
Few nations have etched so deep a black-and-white separation as our own.
Even South Africa allows for Coloureds, while Latin countries have mulat-
tos and mestizos, as well as Creoles and quadroons. But here even children
of mixed marriages end up regarded as black. And while citizens may cherish their European origins, being white retains primacy in most of their
minds. At times, race seems to surpass even gender as our major schism.

It shouldn't. We now have information about how much impact race   2
has in areas such as school achievement, hiring, family life, and crime—
and it should spur us to rethink the actual impact of race and ethnic separatism. If anything, there is evidence that race is becoming a *less* salient
factor for growing groups of Americans. Here follows a brief debunking of
a variety of black-and-white myths, which, upon inspection, turn out to be
grayer realities.

The black family is disintegrating, while the white family remains in-   3
tact. Since Daniel Patrick Moynihan's 1965 report found black families
trapped in a "tangle of pathology," conditions seem to have gotten worse.
Two-thirds of black babies are now born outside of wedlock, and more
than half of black homes are headed by women. A majority of black
youngsters live only with their mother; and in most of these households
she has never been married.

Almost everyone agrees that the increases in nonmarital births and   4
female-headed households are causes for dismay. But why should race be
the crucial variable? Readily available reports show that low income and
education outweigh race in causing family instability. Absent fathers
abound in depressed counties where the residents are almost wholly white.

349

In rural Maine, for example, out-of-wedlock rates exceed those for blacks in several states.

5   As it happens, extramarital births and households headed by women are subject to social trends, which touch all races and classes in similar ways. The Census figures for female-headed families for the last four decades show that both black and white families have disintegrated at virtually identical rates. In 1950, 17.2 percent of black families were headed by single women, against 5.3 percent of white families (a black-white multiple of 3.2). In 1990, the figures are 56.2 percent and 17.3 percent respectively (a black-white multiple of 3.2). Plainly, what we have been seeing are not so much race-based differences as concurrent adaptations to common cultural conditions. True, the black figure has always been three times larger, and here is where "racial" reasons have an influence of their own. But those forces were at work well before 1950, prior to talk about "pathology." Of course, the current 56.2 percent rate for black households is depressingly high. But then the 1990 figure for whites is almost identical to the one for blacks lamented in Moynihan's report.

6   The point here is not whether family structure is important, but whether its dynamic over the last thirty years has been different along racial lines. It hasn't been. Given the ubiquity of absent fathers—black and white—little will be gained by lecturing one race on its duties. To call on black Americans to show greater discipline would seem to suggest that only they have deviated from national norms. Black families will become more stable when all households evolve a stronger structure.

7   Where out-of-wedlock births are concerned, there is actual racial convergence. What we hear most is that 66 percent of black births are to girls and women who are not married. However, close study of the figures reveals that the black-white multiple is less than half of what it was forty years ago. So while black out-of-wedlock births are at an all-time high, the white ratio has been ascending at a far faster rate. Even in typical mid-American cities such as Davenport, Iowa, and Dayton, Ohio, the current white figures are 27.8 percent and 31.4 percent. In 1950, 16.8 percent of black births were out of wedlock, while 1.7 percent of white births were (a black-white multiple of 9.9). In 1970, the proportions were 37.6 percent and 5.7 percent respectively (a multiple of 6.6). Today, the figures are 66 percent and 16 percent (a multiple of 4.1). The chief reason for the decrease in the multiple is the availability of abortion. Although black women constitute only 13 percent of women of childbearing age, they account for more than 30 percent of the pregnancies terminated each year.

8   *Blacks are far more likely to commit crimes than whites.* When we hear allusions to "crime," our first image tends to be of violent assaults—rape, robbery, murder—not insider trading or embezzling. And "black crime" conjures up Willie Hortons, whose acts of terror forever scar their victims' lives. By every measure we have, black felons commit far more

than their share of the most dreaded crimes. While constituting only about 12 percent of the population, they account for 43.2 percent of arrests for rape, 54.7 percent of murders where the perpetrator is known, and 69.3 percent of reported robberies.

Does this mean that blacks on the whole are less law-abiding? Bruce Wright, a black New York judge, came close to saying just that when he argued that felons of his own race are simply breaking "a social contract that was not of their making in the first place." In fact, we know much less about offenses by whites, since their crimes tend to be office-based, or involve insurance claims or tax evasion, fewer of which are uncovered or apprehended. Although white-collar crooks can and do end up behind bars, many more do not. There is reason to believe that larcenous proclivities exist in members of every race but since more alternatives are open to whites, they have less need for thievery that threatens physical harm. (Class constraints are also more likely to make whites repress hatred or rage that could propel them to rape or murder.)

Because we fear more for our bodies than our bank accounts, violent crimes are more apt to bring prison terms, which explains the disproportionate number of blacks behind bars. But how far is their race the reason? What we can say with some assurance is that people who end up as inmates tend to be lower class, and represent a rougher and tougher element within that economic stratum. The prison rolls in West Virginia and Idaho are overwhelmingly white, and most inmates were convicted of crimes that in other states tend to be associated with blacks. (While West Virginia's and Idaho's overall crime rates are relatively low, their ratios of violent to non-violent crimes do not differ significantly from those of states having larger black populations.)

Blacks now outnumber whites in our penal institutions, but this was not always so. In 1930, 76.7 percent of inmates were white; as recently as 1970 the number was 60.5 percent. In contrast, blacks made up 22.4 percent of the prison population in 1930 and now make up a staggering 45.3 percent. This would suggest that black men were much more law-abiding half a century ago, since most then lived in the South, where they could have been sent to the chain gang with relative ease. In fact, controls exerted by churches, the authority of elders, and community pride combined to deter conduct that could land black men in trouble. Given the depth of poverty and endless humiliations, this discipline is all the more striking.

At the same time, the past had a much larger class of whites who used or threatened violence. The Jimmy Cagneys of New York's Hell's Kitchen and the George Rafts who filled the cells at Sing Sing portrayed an actual segment of the population. Indeed, what is often seen today as "black crime" used to be predominantly white. Since those days many if not most whites have moved up to the middle class, so those who are drawn to larceny have less need to commit face-to-face felonies. The flip side is that blacks now constitute a much larger share of the poor, and more of them live in urban centers where earlier controls no longer apply. As a result, they preponderate among those being charged and imprisoned for the kinds of crimes poorer people are more likely to commit.

12   *Blacks score less well on objective IQ tests.* Ours is an age of machine-graded tests, so much so that a single score can determine a person's future. The Scholastic Aptitude Test, which more than a million high school seniors take every year, is the first thing colleges consider when assessing applicants. Do the tests discriminate? Quite obviously they do. Children from better-off families usually do better, since they go to schools that familiarize them with the format. Students with a mathematical bent usually score well throughout the SAT, as do those with a flair for solving puzzles at a one-a-minute rate.

13   The problem is that black Americans as a group do not do well on standardized tests. This holds true for job applicants and civil service promotions, even when special courses have been arranged. An analysis of the SAT results shows that blacks still lag behind other groups even when they come from homes with comparable incomes and parental educations. The average SAT scores for students whose parents earn between $50,000 and $60,000 are 955 for Asians, 947 for whites, 879 for Hispanics, and 790 for blacks. For those whose parents have a graduate degree, the average SAT scores are 1053 for Asians, 1018 for whites, 897 for Hispanics, and 830 for blacks. Can there be a bias in the SAT that hampers even privileged blacks?

14   The first answer is that if there is a bias, it is not "white" in character. As the scores show, Asians rank ahead of whites when backgrounds are held constant, just as Hispanics outperform blacks. Asians and Hispanics do better on this American test because they study longer and harder, pay attention to the rules, and are less likely to cavil about the oddities of the test. If there is a bias to the multiple-choice matrix, it favors what might be called a technocratic mentality, which is emerging in Seoul and Bogotá as much as in Seattle or Baltimore.

15   But why so visible a black gap at every social level? Here the causes are explicitly racial, in that they stem from the segregation that affects even black youngsters from professional homes. Simply stated, the intellectual processes most black children learn, which tend to be at odds with technocratic modes, are reinforced by spending much of their time among people of their own race. The persistence of segregation—residential and social—draws a sharp dividing line between blacks and whites of all classes. In consequence, black intellectual styles remain more discursive than linear, which can be a drawback when facing a multiple-choice format. Indeed, one of the early arguments for integration was that in mixed classes, black students would learn "white" modes of interpretation and analysis, thus eroding the SAT gap. Yet white scores have been on the decline for at least twenty years, so whites may not be the best model.

Whites have been hurt by affirmative action. Whether affirmative   16
action involves "quotas" or "goals," in practice it means exempting
some people from customary requirements and qualifications. In fact,
such policies have been around for a long time. For example, colleges
occasionally decide to admit some students from Montana, to ensure a
diverse entering class. Even if their grades aren't very good, coming
from a distant state is seen as a compensatory credential. And to make
room for them, abler applicants from other states end up being turned
down. Today affirmative action aims at raising black ratios in education
and employment. As with coming from Montana, being black becomes
a credential.

No one can say with certainty how many white Americans have been   17
bypassed or displaced because of preferential policies. Alan Bakke sued a
University of California medical school because he believed that a place he
deserved had gone to a minority applicant. He obviously felt injured. But if
his record was creditable, he would probably have been admitted to some
other schools, which should have cushioned the blow. With this caveat in
mind, we can try to gauge how far affirmative action has been edging out
whites.

At last count, ten top-rated schools—Amherst, Brown, Cornell,   18
Dartmouth, Harvard, MIT, Northwestern, Princeton, Stanford, and
Yale—had a total of 9,555 black, Hispanic, and Native American students out of an overall 107,409 enrollment. Unfortunately, colleges do
not report academic records for subgroups. So for present purposes,
using nationwide SAT figures, I will assume that three-fifths of the minority students accepted had records that were inferior to those of other
applicants who were turned away. Three-fifths of 9,555 works out to
5,733 unadmitted whites and Asians, who had to settle for lesser
schools. (Had these colleges imposed their customary criteria, their aggregate minority ratio would have stood at 3.6 percent, rather than the
8.9 percent they attained through affirmative action.) Still, 101,676
whites and Asians *were* admitted, a fairly hefty number. And in many if
not most cases, those rejected simply traded down within the Top Ten.
It's also worth considering that not all admitted whites are potential Phi
Beta Kappas. In addition to Montana residents, even the Iviest schools
bend rules for alumni offspring, and even Harvard has been known to
favor football players.

White displacement in employment is less easy to compute, since hir-   19
ings and promotions are more apt to involve intangible judgments. Still,
figures for occupations yield some answers. In most professional, white-
collar, and craft fields, recent years have seen an increased bloc of blacks;
and affirmative action has undoubtedly played some role. There is much
talk about whites who feel they are being bypassed, with not a few filing
lawsuits. In the academic world, white men seeking instructorships have

good reason to believe that their résumés will be relegated to the bottom of the pile. After all, it is hard to find a department that has not given high priority to recruiting a black colleague.

20   The blue-collar world has young men who aspire to careers as police officers or fire fighters, often to carry on a long family tradition. Although not usually studious, they cram hard for the tests; but those who pass at the margin see appointments going to blacks with lower scores.

21   But how typical are stories like these? The Census and Bureau of Labor Statistics collate figures on racial distributions within various occupations. As the accompanying table shows, despite all the efforts of medical schools and college faculties, the black proportions of physicians and professors have barely budged over twenty years.

Black Representation in Occupations

	1970	*1990*	*Share of New Jobs*
Physicians	2.2%	3.0%	3.8%
Lawyers	1.3	3.2	4.3
College professors	3.5	4.5	6.3
Electricians	3.0	6.2	12.7
Bank tellers	4.3	9.9	16.3
Bus drivers	14.3	24.4	33.8
Police officers	6.3	13.5	41.1
Total work force	9.6%	10.1%	11.0%

Indeed, blacks filled only 6.3 percent of the new faculty positions created between 1970 and 1990. So if white men haven't gotten posts, it wasn't due to extensive black hiring, but rather to a preference for women, who received more than half of the new academic openings. Among doctors and lawyers, black gains were even smaller, in part because expansions in both professions brought in even more whites. Nor are all advances by blacks due to preferential policies. There are more black bus drivers and bank tellers; while one reason is that blacks have been upgrading their skills, another may be that fewer whites find they are attracted to those jobs.

22   Although the percentage of black electricians doubled, it yielded them little more than their overall share of new jobs, so hardly any whites lost out. The real shift was in police selection, where blacks received more than 40 percent of the 100,000 new posts in law enforcement. Here, clearly, affirmative action has worked against white applicants. Unlike the stu-

dents rejected by Amherst, who go on to Lehigh, whites who don't make it into the police haven't as consoling a second option. But in the end black Americans remain a relatively small minority, so there are limits to how many whites they can displace even with aggressive affirmative action re-cruiting. At the college level, the real competition for whites comes from Asians, who are winning places not through preferential policies but on academic merit.

Overall, persons with racial identities—black and white Americans—   23
constitute a declining portion of the population. Since 1970 individuals of European ancestry, or Caucasoid stock, have declined from 83.3 percent to 75.3 percent of the national total. And during these decades, Americans of African ancestry, or the Negroid race, rose by only one percentage point—from 10.9 to 11.9 percent—and that was largely due to new ar-rivals from the Caribbean. By the next census, it is likely that blacks will have lost out to Hispanics—whose share of the population has more than doubled in the last twenty years—as America's largest minority group. In-deed, this has already happened in twenty states, including Massachusetts, California, and Colorado.

The nation's fastest-growing groups are rejecting racial designa-   24
tions. For example, we hardly ever hear allusions to the "yellow" or "Mongoloid" race, just as "Oriental" has all but disappeared. Chinese and Japanese and Koreans have chosen to emphasize their separate na-tional identities rather than evoke a common heritage. Unfortunately the media have adopted the umbrella term "Asian," which tells us little about those under it, since they could equally well be Afghans or Lao-tians or Filipinos.

Hispanics are also finding no need for a racial category. This, too, is   25
a recent development. In responding to the 1970 census, fully 98 percent said they wanted to be classified as black or white. In 1990, however, over half shunned those racial options and chose to check "Other." By doing this, they were signaling that their Hispanic identity was all they wanted or needed. Even less than Asians, Hispanics are hardly a race. If anything, Latin America has been the world's leading melting pot, yielding every possible mixture of European and African and indigenous strains. Even Latino lobbyists limit themselves to calling for preserving regional histo-ries, languages, and cultures rather than racial roots.

In the past, also, many persons of indigenous stock would report that   26
they were white, perhaps hoping to gain such benefits as that designation might bring. Recently we have seen displays of pride among these groups, reflected in what they tell the census. Since 1970 persons listing themselves as Native Americans, Hawaiians, Aleuts, or Eskimos have increased by al-most 90 percent, which comes to seven times the increase for the nation as a whole. Moreover, these affinities tend to be tribal or regional, rather than racial.

27   Of course, it could be argued that it doesn't much matter if the "dis-uniting of America"—Arthur Schlesinger's phrase—is along racial or other lines. Blacks and Puerto Ricans and Aleuts all claim preference under affirmative action; and supposed disadvantages can have varied sources. Still, my own observations have been that Asians and Hispanics and others who want to make it on their own have seen the harm that being "racial" can do. To define one-self as black or white—or to have those origins assigned to you—assigns overwhelming weight to a primordial ancestry. With race can come a genetic determinism, often suggesting higher or lower locations on an evolutionary ladder. Hence the choice of Asians to put their nationalities first, while Hispanics prefer to stress the culture they created and sustain as a matter of choice. They are also aware of the hostilities and tensions dividing blacks and whites, and have chosen not so much a middle ground as seats off to the side.

28   If the United States becomes less racial, does this mean it will emerge as a more "multiethnic" society? Don't bet on it. The great majority of recent immigrants, like their counterparts in the past, intend to become mainstream Americans. They did not make the trek here to change the rules and regimens of a society in which they want to succeed. Too much heed has been paid to Latino and kindred publicists, who make careers calling for the preservation of what are essentially folktales and folkways. (They get as much attention as they do by playing on white guilt, which regards tribal rites in the same vein as the spotted owl.)

29   Statistically, the advent of Hispanics and Asians—joined by new immigrants from the Middle East—will spell further white decline. Yet if most of those arriving have no wish to become white, not many see themselves as "people of color." They want their children to get traditional American educations and graduate to assimilated suburbs. As recent books by Linda Chavez and Rosalie Pedalino Porter have shown, Hispanic students tend to be shunted into special classes by self-serving bureaucrats rather than at the behest of their parents. And the families of my immigrant students in Queens regard the borough as a way-station prior to a suburban move. Moreover, once they become middle-class, they will have little or no difficulty entering what were once all-white neighborhoods. (For that reason, they are at pains to dissociate themselves from black Americans; just listen to some of their remarks.) In return, middle-class America is prepared to absorb newcomers who show a willingness to adapt. Even George Bush boasts of his Hispanic daughter-in-law, and she is one of almost 30 percent of Hispanics who marry outside their culture. But that hardly matters, since most people come here to become Americans, and they have a good eye and ear for how and where to adapt.

Reading and Analyzing

1. What is Hacker's claim? Where does he state it?
2. What is the warrant, the underlying assumption, of his argument?
3. State each of the myths about blacks and whites in your own words, and then summarize the evidence presented that challenges each myth.
4. What seems to be the "bias" of the SAT? What, according to Hacker, accounts for blacks', as a group, doing less well than any other group on the SAT?
5. In what kinds of jobs has affirmative action worked well for blacks? For women?
6. How is the American population changing? How do Asians and Hispanics, in general, want to be identified? What seems to be their motivation?
7. Hacker supports his debunking of myths by providing what kind of evidence? In other words, what kind of argument is this?
8. Hacker concludes by asserting that the U.S. population, although becoming less racial, is not likely to become more multiethnic because most ethnic groups want to become Americans, to be assimilated into the middle class. What evidence does he provide to support this observation?
9. What is the tone of the essay? Does the tone help to make the argument convincing? Why or why not?

Responding to the Writer's Ideas

1. Hacker provides some startling figures about U.S. families. Which figures do you find most discouraging? Why?
2. Do the numbers demonstrate the inaccuracy of the myth about families as Hacker has stated it? Does Hacker's comparison of black and white families remove concern for black families in particular? Explain.
3. Hacker's analysis of crime statistics demonstrates, in his view, that violent crime correlates more with class and family-community structures than with race. Does his analysis make sense to you? If it is valid, what strategies for addressing violent crime seem most appropriate?
4. If the SAT is biased in favor of a "technocratic mentality," does that mean that we should reject the test as part of one's application to college? Why do colleges value the SAT so much?
5. Has Hacker's analysis of the effects of affirmative action in college admissions convinced you that white students, in general, ought not

to be angry that blacks are "taking places meant for them"? If not, how would you refute or counter his argument?

6. Do your experiences with Asian, Hispanic, and mid-Eastern students confirm the author's concluding assertion that ethnic groups want to be assimilated into the American melting pot? When you talk with students of different ethnic backgrounds, what future goals (regarding careers, marriage, lifestyles) do they express? What evidence do you have either to support or challenge Hacker's views?

❖

The Disuniting of America

Arthur Schlesinger, Jr.

Respected historian, successful author, and adviser to presidents, Arthur Schlesinger, Jr. (b. 1917), is the Albert Schweitzer Professor in the Humanities at the City University of New York. A native of Columbus, Ohio, and son of the historian Arthur Schlesinger, he was educated at Harvard, taught at Harvard, was special assistant to Presidents Kennedy and Johnson, and has been at CUNY since 1966. Schlesinger is the author of numerous books and articles, many of which have won major awards, and all of which are valued both for the scholarship they reflect and for the quality of writing they sustain. His three-volume The Age of Roosevelt *is recognized as a standard study of the period. His* John F. Kennedy biography A Thousand Days *(1965) won a Pulitzer Prize, and* Robert Kennedy and His Times *(1978) won a National Book Award. "The Disuniting of America" is excerpted from his most recent book,* The Disuniting of America *(1992). Here Schlesinger argues for a unified nation, not a divisive collection of ethnically diverse groups.*

Is the Western tradition a bar to progress and a curse on humanity? 1
Would it really do America and the world good to get rid of the European legacy?

No doubt Europe has done terrible things, not least to itself. But 2
what culture has not? History, said Edward Gibbon, is little more than the register of the crimes, follies, and misfortunes of mankind. The sins of the West are no worse than the sins of Asia or of the Middle East or of Africa.

There remains, however, a crucial difference between the Western 3
tradition and the others. The crimes of the West have produced their own antidotes. They have provoked great movements to end slavery, to raise the status of women, to abolish torture, to combat racism, to defend freedom of inquiry and expression, to advance personal liberty and human rights.

Whatever the particular crimes of Europe, that continent is also the 4
source—the *unique* source—of those liberating ideas of individual liberty, political democracy, the rule of law, human rights, and cultural freedom that constitute our most precious legacy and to which most of the world today aspires. These are *European* ideas, not Asian, nor African, nor Middle Eastern ideas, except by adoption.

5   The freedoms of inquiry and of artistic creation, for example, are Western values. Consider the differing reactions to the case of Salman Rushdie[1]: what the West saw as an intolerable attack on individual freedom the Middle East saw as a proper punishment for an evildoer who had violated the mores of his group. Individualism itself is looked on with abhorrence and dread by collectivist cultures in which loyalty to the group overrides personal goals—cultures that, social scientists say, comprise about 70 percent of the world's population.

6   There is surely no reason for Western civilization to have guilt trips laid on it by champions of cultures based on despotism, superstition, tribalism, and fanaticism. In this regard the Afrocentrists are especially absurd. The West needs no lectures on the superior virtue of those "sun people" who sustained slavery until Western imperialism abolished it (and, it is reported, sustain it to this day in Mauritania and the Sudan), who still keep women in subjection and cut off their clitorises, who carry out racial persecutions not only against Indians and other Asians but against fellow Africans from the wrong tribes, who show themselves either incapable of operating a democracy or ideologically hostile to the democratic idea, and who in their tyrannies and massacres, their Idi Amins and Boukassas,[2] have stamped with utmost brutality on human rights.

7   Certainly the European overlords did little enough to prepare Africa for self-government. But democracy would find it hard in any case to put down roots in a tribalist and patrimonial culture that, long before the West invaded Africa, had sacralized the personal authority of chieftains and ordained the submission of the rest. What the West would call corruption is regarded through much of Africa as no more than the prerogative of power. Competitive political parties, an independent judiciary, a free press, the rule of law are alien to African traditions.

8   It was the French, not the Algerians, who freed Algerian women from the veil (much to the irritation of Frantz Fanon, who regarded deveiling as symbolic rape); as in India it was the British, not the Indians, who ended (or did their best to end) the horrible custom of *suttee*—widows burning themselves alive on their husbands' funeral pyres. And it was the West, not the non-Western cultures, that launched the crusade to abolish slavery—and in doing so encountered mighty resistance, especially in the Islamic world (where Moslems, with fine impartiality, enslaved whites as well as blacks). Those many brave and humane Africans who are struggling these days for decent societies are animated by Western, not by African, ideals. White guilt can be pushed too far.

---

[1] Author of *Satanic Verses*, a work that led the late Ayatollah Khomeini of Iran to place a sentence of death on him, which required Rushdie to live in hiding.—Ed.

[2] Former brutal dictators in Uganda and the Central African Republic.—Ed.

The Western commitment to human rights has unquestionably been   9
intermittent and imperfect. Yet the ideal remains—and movement toward
it has been real, if sporadic. Today it is the *Western* democratic tradition
that attracts and empowers people of all continents, creeds, and colors.
When the Chinese students cried and died for democracy in Tiananmen
Square, they brought with them not representations of Confucius or Bud-
dha but a model of the Statue of Liberty.

The great American asylum, as Crèvecoeur called it, open, as Wash-   10
ington said, to the oppressed and persecuted of all nations, has been from
the start an experiment in a multiethnic society. This is a bolder experiment than we sometimes remember. History is littered with the wreck of
states that tried to combine diverse ethnic or linguistic or religious groups
within a single sovereignty. Today's headlines tell of imminent crisis or impending dissolution in one or another multiethnic polity—the Soviet
Union, India, Yugoslavia, Czechoslovakia, Ireland, Belgium, Canada,
Lebanon, Cyprus, Israel, Ceylon, Spain, Nigeria, Kenya, Angola, Trinidad,
Guyana. . . . The list is almost endless. The luck so far of the American
experiment has been due in large part to the vision of the melting pot. "No
other nation," Margaret Thatcher[3] has said, "has so successfully combined
people of different races and nations within a single culture."

But even in the United States, ethnic ideologues have not been with-   11
out effect. They have set themselves against the old American ideal of assimilation. They call on the republic to think in terms not of individual but
of group identity and to move the polity from individual rights to group
rights. They have made a certain progress in transforming the United
States into a more segregated society. They have done their best to turn a
college generation against Europe and the Western tradition. They have
imposed ethnocentric, Afrocentric, and bilingual curricula on public
schools, well designed to hold minority children out of American society.
They have told young people from minority groups that the Western democratic tradition is not for them. They have encouraged minorities to see
themselves as victims and to live by alibis rather than to claim the opportunities opened for them by the potent combination of black protest and
white guilt. They have filled the air with recrimination and rancor and
have remarkably advanced the fragmentation of American life.

Yet I believe the campaign against the idea of common ideals and a   12
single society will fail. Gunnar Myrdal was surely right: for all the damage
it has done, the upsurge of ethnicity is a superficial enthusiasm stirred by
romantic ideologues and unscrupulous hucksters whose claim to speak for
their minorities is thoughtlessly accepted by the media. I doubt that the
ethnic vogue expresses a reversal of direction from assimilation to

---

[3] Former prime minister of Great Britain.—Ed.

apartheid among the minorities themselves. Indeed, the more the ideologues press the case for ethnic separatism, the less they appeal to the mass of their own groups. They have thus far done better in intimidating the white majority than in converting their own constituencies.

13   "No nation in history," writes Lawrence Fuchs, the political scientist and immigration expert in his fine book *The American Kaleidoscope,* "had proved as successful as the United States in managing ethnic diversity. No nation before had ever made diversity itself a source of national identity and unity." The second sentence explains the success described in the first, and the mechanism for translating diversity into unity has been the American Creed, the civic culture—the very assimilating, unifying culture that is today challenged, and not seldom rejected, by the ideologues of ethnicity.

14   A historian's guess is that the resources of the Creed have not been exhausted. Americanization has not lost its charms. Many sons and daughters of ethnic neighborhoods still want to shed their ethnicity and move to the suburbs as fast as they can—where they will be received with far more tolerance than they would have been 70 years ago. The desire for achievement and success in American society remains a potent force for assimilation. Ethnic subcultures, Stephen Steinberg, author of *The Ethnic Myth,* points out, fade away "because circumstances forced them to make choices that undermined the basis for cultural survival."

15   Others may enjoy their ethnic neighborhoods but see no conflict between foreign descent and American loyalty. Unlike the multiculturalists, they celebrate not only what is distinctive in their own backgrounds but what they hold in common with the rest of the population.

16   The ethnic identification often tends toward superficiality. The sociologist Richard Alba's study of children and grandchildren of immigrants in the Albany, New York, area shows the most popular "ethnic experience" to be sampling the ancestral cuisine. Still, less than half the respondents picked that, and only one percent ate ethnic food every day. Only one-fifth acknowledged a sense of special relationship to people of their own ethnic background; less than one-sixth taught their children about their ethnic origins; almost none was fluent in the language of the old country. "It is hard to avoid the conclusion," Alba writes, "that ethnic experience is shallow for the great majority of whites."

17   If ethnic experience is a good deal less shallow for blacks, it is because of their bitter experience in America, not because of their memories of Africa. Nonetheless most blacks prefer "black" to "African-Americans," fight bravely and patriotically for their country, and would move to the suburbs too if income and racism would permit.

18   As for Hispanic-Americans, first-generation Hispanics born in the United States speak English fluently, according to a Rand Corporation study; more than half of second-generation Hispanics give up Spanish altogether. When *Vista,* an English-language monthly for Hispanics, asked its

readers what historical figures they most admired, Washington, Lincoln, and Theodore Roosevelt led the list, with Benito Juárez trailing behind as fourth, and Eleanor Roosevelt and Martin Luther King Jr. tied for fifth. So much for ethnic role models.

Nor, despite the effort of ethnic ideologues, are minority groups all   19
that hermetically sealed off from each other, except in special situations, like colleges, where ideologues are authority figures. The wedding notices in any newspaper testify to the increased equanimity with which people these days marry across ethnic lines, across religious lines, even, though to a smaller degree, across racial lines. Around half of Asian-American marriages are with non-Orientals, and the Census Bureau estimates one million interracial—mostly black-white—marriages in 1990 as against 310,000 in 1970.

The ethnic revolt against the melting pot has reached the point, in   20
rhetoric at least, though not I think in reality, of a denial of the idea of a common culture and a single society. If large numbers of people really accept this, the republic would be in serious trouble. The question poses itself: how to restore the balance between *unum* and *pluribus?*

The old American homogeneity disappeared well over a century ago,   21
never to return. Ever since, we have been preoccupied in one way or another with the problem, as Herbert Croly phrased it 80 years back in *The Promise of American Life,* "of preventing such divisions from dissolving the society into which they enter—of keeping such a highly differentiated society fundamentally sound and whole." This required, Croly believed, an "ultimate bond of union." There was only one way by which solidarity could be restored, "and that is by means of a democratic social ideal. . . ."

The genius of America lies in its capacity to forge a single nation   22
from peoples of remarkably diverse racial, religious, and ethnic origins. It has done so because democratic principles provide both the philosophical bond of union and practical experience in civic participation. The American Creed envisages a nation composed of individuals making their own choices and accountable to themselves, not a nation based on inviolable ethnic communities. The Constitution turns on individual rights, not on group rights. Law, in order to rectify past wrongs, has from time to time (and in my view often properly so) acknowledged the claims of groups; but this is the exception, not the rule.

Our democratic principles contemplate an open society founded on   23
tolerance of differences and on mutual respect. In practice, America has been more open to some than to others. But it is more open to all today than it was yesterday and is likely to be even more open tomorrow than today. The steady movement of American life has been from exclusion to inclusion.

Historically and culturally this republic has an Anglo-Saxon base;   24
but from the start the base has been modified, enriched, and reconstituted

by transfusions from other continents and civilizations. The movement from exclusion to inclusion causes a constant revision in the texture of our culture. The ethnic transfusions affect all aspects of American life—our politics, our literature, our music, our painting, our movies, our cuisine, our customs, our dreams.

25   Black Americans in particular have influenced the ever-changing national culture in many ways. They have lived here for centuries, and, unless one believes in racist mysticism, they belong far more to American culture than to the culture of Africa. Their history is part of the Western democratic tradition, not an alternative to it. Henry Louis Gates Jr. reminds us of James Baldwin's[4] remark about coming to Europe to find out that he was "as American as any Texas G.I." No one does black Americans more disservice than those Afrocentric ideologues who would define them out of the West.

26   The interplay of diverse traditions produces the America we know. "Paradoxical though it may seem," Diane Ravitch has well said, "the United States has a common culture that is multicultural." That is why unifying political ideals coexist so easily and cheerfully with diversity in social and cultural values. Within the overarching political commitment, people are free to live as they choose, ethnically and otherwise. Differences will remain; some are reinvented; some are used to drive us apart. But as we renew our allegiance to the unifying ideals, we provide the solvent that will prevent differences from escalating into antagonism and hatred.

27   One powerful reason for the movement from exclusion to inclusion is that the American Creed facilitates the appeal from the actual to the ideal. When we talk of the American democratic faith, we must understand it in its true dimensions. It is not an impervious, final, and complacent orthodoxy, intolerant of deviation and dissent, fulfilled in flag salutes, oaths of allegiance, and hands over the heart. It is an ever-evolving philosophy, fulfilling its ideals through debate, self-criticism, protest, disrespect, and irreverence; a tradition in which all have rights of heterodoxy and opportunities for self-assertion. The Creed has been the means by which Americans have haltingly but persistently narrowed the gap between performance and principle. It is what all Americans should learn, because it is what binds all Americans together.

28   Let us by all means in this increasingly mixed-up world learn about those other continents and civilizations. But let us master our own history first. Lamentable as some may think it, we inherit an American experience, as America inherits a European experience. To deny the essentially European origins of American culture is to falsify history.

---

[4] African-American novelist and essayist, 1924–1987.—Ed.

Americans of whatever origin should take pride in the distinctive in-   29
heritance to which they have all contributed, as other nations take pride in
their distinctive inheritances. Belief in one's own culture does not require
disdain for other cultures. But one step at a time: no culture can hope to
ingest other cultures all at once, certainly not before it ingests its own. As
we begin to master our own culture, then we can explore the world.

Our schools and colleges have a responsibility to teach history for its   30
own sake—as part of the intellectual equipment of civilized persons—and
not to degrade history by allowing its contents to be dictated by pressure
groups, whether political, economic, religious, or ethnic. The past may
sometimes give offense to one or another minority; that is no reason for
rewriting history. Giving pressure groups vetoes over textbooks and courses betrays both history and education. Properly taught, history will convey
a sense of the variety, continuity, and adaptability of cultures, of the need
for understanding other cultures, of the ability of individuals and peoples
to overcome obstacles, of the importance of critical analysis and dispassionate judgment in every area of life.

Above all, history can give a sense of national identity. We don't   31
have to believe that our values are absolutely better than the next fellow's
or the next country's, but we have no doubt that they are better *for us,*
reared as we are—and are worth living by and worth dying for. For our
values are not matters of whim and happenstance. History has given them
to us. They are anchored in our national experience, in our great national
documents, in our national heroes, in our folkways, traditions, and standards. People with a different history will have differing values. But we believe that our own are better for us. They work for us; and, for that reason, we live and die by them.

It has taken time to make the values real for all our citizens, and we   32
still have a good distance to go, but we have made progress. If we now repudiate the quite marvelous inheritance that history bestows on us, we in-
vite the fragmentation of the national community into a quarrelsome spat-
ter of enclaves, ghettos, tribes. The bonds of cohesion in our society are
sufficiently fragile, or so it seems to me, that it makes no sense to strain
them by encouraging and exalting cultural and linguistic apartheid.

The American identity will never be fixed and final; it will always be   33
in the making. Changes in the population have always brought changes in
the national ethos and will continue to do so; but not, one must hope, at
the expense of national integration. The question America confronts as a
pluralistic society is how to vindicate cherished cultures and traditions
without breaking the bonds of cohesion—common ideals, common political institutions, common language, common culture, common fate—that
hold the republic together.

Our task is to combine due appreciation of the splendid diversity of   34
the nation with due emphasis on the great unifying Western ideas of indi-

vidual freedom, political democracy, and human rights. These are the ideas that define the American nationality—and that today empower people of all continents, races, and creeds.

35   "What then is the American, this new man? . . . Here individuals of all nations are melted into a new race of men."[5] Still a good answer—still the best hope.

Notes on Sources

For more information about the collectivist cultures on p. 360, see the research described by Daniel Goleman, "The Group and the Self: New Focus on a Cultural Rift," *The New York Times,* December 25, 1990.

The passage on p. 360 concerning Algerian women is from Frantz Fanon's book *A Dying Colonialism* (London, 1965), pp. 37, 46.

Margaret Thatcher's quotation on p. 361 is from David S. Broder's article "Her View of the U.S. Had a Euro-Cynical Bent," *International Herald Tribune,* March 13, 1991.

Lawrence Fuchs's quotation on p. 362 is from *The American Kaleidoscope,* p. 492.

Stephen Steinberg's quotation on p. 362 is from his book *The Ethnic Myth,* p. 257.

Richard Alba's quotation on p. 362 is from his book *Ethnic Identity: The Transformation of White America.* See the discussion in Andrew Hacker's article "Trans-National America," *The New York Review of Books,* November 22, 1990.

The passages on pp. 362–63 concerning Hispanic-Americans and historical leaders are from Lawrence Fuchs's *The American Kaleidoscope.*

The statistics concerning Asian-American marriages on p. 363 are from Stephan Thernstrom's article "Is America's Ethnic Revival a Fad Like Jogging?" *U.S. News & World Report,* November 17, 1980.

The statistics from the Census Bureau on p. 363 are from Gregory Stephens' letter "Interracial Marriage," *San Francisco Chronicle,* December 24, 1990.

Herbert Croly's quotations on p. 363 are from his book *The Promise of American Life* (New York, 1909), pp. 139, 194. Croly was talking about class, not ethnic, divisions—indeed, he rather believed in the inferiority of blacks—but his general point remains sound.

The James Baldwin quotation on p. 364 is from his essay "The Discovery of What It Means to Be an American," quoted by Henry Louis Gates, Jr., *Nation,* July 15/22, 1991.

Diane Ravitch's quotation on p. 364 is from her article "Multiculturalism," p. 339.

Reading and Analyzing

1. What is Schlesinger's thesis, the claim of his argument? (There is a complex set of interrelated ideas here, so you may need more than one sentence in which to state the author's central point.)

[5] Quotation from Crèvecoeur's *Letters from an American Farmer* (1782).

2. Examine Schlesinger's opening two paragraphs. What is the author reacting to? What is his purpose in writing?
3. What is unique about the evils of the European culture? What ideas have emerged from the European culture?
4. Summarize the examples given to illustrate the Western tradition of human rights and the examples given to illustrate the limitations of human rights in other cultures.
5. Whom does Schlesinger blame for encouraging ethnic group identity and separatism in the United States? How successful does he think they will be?
6. What forces are working against those fighting for ethnic separation?
7. Explain Ravitch's comment that "the United States has a common culture that is multicultural."
8. Why should history be taught, and how should it be taught? What do we gain from the study of history—a history that is not rewritten to satisfy some group?
9. How would you describe Schlesinger's tone?

Responding to the Writer's Ideas

1. Schlesinger is not gentle when he defends the European tradition, but he does make some conciliatory statements. Do you agree that he is fair and balanced in his comments? If so, why? If not, why not?
2. The author objects to the teaching of multiculturalism *instead of* Western civilization. Does your campus offer various cultural studies courses? If so, are they electives or requirements? Are American history and Western civilization required? Which courses, in your view, should be required, which elective? Why?
3. Schlesinger remains hopeful that American culture will endure as a unified culture that embraces ethnic diversity. Are you hopeful, too? If so, why? If not, why not?
4. Do you agree with Schlesinger that we should work toward unity, or should we embrace ethnic separatism? Explain your position.

WRITING SUGGESTIONS

1. Prepare an argument modeled on Stanton's Declaration of Sentiments for a group that, in your view, has grievances against those in control of our society. Possibilities include women, gays, children, ethnic or racial minorities, the disabled.

2. The many books on gender issues seem to be a comment on a battle of the sexes that continues in spite of changes in laws and lifestyles. Is there one area of conflict in particular that bothers you? If so, what can be done to reduce this particular conflict? Develop an essay in which you present and argue for your solutions to that gender problem.

3. In an essay make a case for encouraging young people *not* to play dumb in the classroom or on dates.

4. Develop an argument for—or against—restricting homosexuals from the armed forces. Use a reasoned, not emotional, approach.

5. Some have opposed having known homosexuals teaching in elementary or secondary schools. Develop an argument either in support of this position or challenging this position. Use a reasoned, not emotional, approach.

6. Lance Morrow asserts that we are a "country out of control." Defend or challenge this assertion. Think carefully about the kind of evidence you need to support whichever position you take, and then organize your reasons and examples. Do not just complain about life in general or, conversely, write about how universally wonderful life is.

7. Have you experienced any racial or ethnic or gender conflict or issue on your campus? If so, were you satisfied with how the incident was handled, or were you distressed by the entire incident? Take a stand on the incident and support your position. Write to an audience who may not be familiar with the incident, so be sure to provide a clear, detailed, and fair explanation of the event.

8. If you have evidence from personal experience of the desire of ethnic minorities (or one particular group) either to remain separate or to become a part of mainstream America, then organize your evidence in support of the position that your evidence leads to.

9. Develop a theoretical argument that supports (1) the virtues of America as a melting pot and thus the need to encourage minorities to become part of American culture or (2) the virtues of strong ethnic identification and separatism to maintain that identity.

CHAPTER 9

DIVIDING THE
PIE: ECONOMICS
AND COMMUNITY

"**R**ich and poor have lived together, always uncomfortably and sometimes perilously, since the beginning of time" writes John Kenneth Galbraith, one of the most influential economists of our time. When then-president Reagan convinced Congress to accept supply-side economic theory and approve a tax cut that primarily benefited the rich, many Democrats objected. "The politics of envy" the Republicans shot back. Was it "mere" envy, or a disagreement over economic theory, or a difference of values? Certainly the conflict extended beyond an intellectual debate over various proposals for economic growth.

Economics cannot be studied independently of the values that shape public policy. The sophisticated training needed for statistical analyses and computer modeling does not alter the fact that the numbers economists collect and study are given meaning only when they are used in the service of economic theory and specific policies. The study of economics is directly descended from the study of political philosophy, however much the discipline today may appear to be an objective intellectual debate about market forces. We must not leave the issues of how wealth is to be shared, who has access to the best jobs, and what government is expected to do to manage a prosperous economy only to the specialists, for these are issues that directly touch the lives of each one of us.

The universality in the problems of rich and poor struggling to live together in social harmony is underscored by Galbraith in "How to Get the Poor Off Our Conscience" when he quotes the first-century Greek writer Plutarch: "An imbalance between the rich and poor is the oldest and most fatal ailment of republics" and when he takes a historical approach to his topic. Galbraith begins with the Bible and reminds readers of the philosophies of various important economists such as Malthus and Adam Smith to provide a context for the contemporary debate over what to do with the poor, and how to justify whatever is, or is not, done. This chapter provides additional historical perspective with its opening piece by the eighteenth-century writer Jonathan Swift. Swift's vicious attack on unfeeling landlords and a do-nothing government establishes the fact that poverty is not only a private, but a public-policy, problem. A second theoretical piece to accompany Galbraith's, Robert Samuelson's "Economics: The Cheery Science" explores America's faith in a never-ending expansion of economic prosperity, and the pessimism currently spawned by economists and politicians who have not been able to deliver endless prosperity. The study of attitudes and expectations gets support from Donald Barlett and James Steele's presentation, in "America: What Went Wrong?," of many of the facts that may account for the current pessimism Americans feel.

How do we recharge an ailing economy, expand exports, and see new jobs created by the increased economic activity? But, even if new jobs are created by reenergized American business and industry, is there any guarantee that these jobs will be here in the United States? Not necessarily, for we live now in a global economy characterized by companies' importing materials from one country, assembling those materials in another country, and financing the endeavor in a third. Further, the modern world of business and industry is a high-tech world, requiring skills many would-be American workers do not have. Many without education and skills, without hope, contribute not only to the country's economic woes but also to its social problems. These and other related issues of the workplace are explored in several of the following articles, notably by Lester Thurow in "The New Economics of High Technology," by Robert Reich in "The Three Jobs of the Future," and by Arthur Ashe in "Can a New 'Army' Save Our Cities?"

No study of contemporary economic and job issues can ignore both the history of economic deprivation for women and minorities and the anger some have expressed over current affirmative-action policies designed to redress the discrimination of the past. Two articles, completing the chapter, address these issues. First, Stephen Steinberg in "Occupational Apartheid" reviews the history of job segregation in America to demonstrate the need for continuing affirmative action. George Weimer expresses an opposing view, by use of analogy, in "Fires, Factories, Football." Whatever position one takes on the various specific proposals for helping those who have been left out, or left behind, there is no escaping the reality that economic "life" is not fair and that there is nothing sacred or free about "free-market forces." We choose our economic policies based on our values, not on economic "laws."

❖

A Modest Proposal
For Preventing the Children of Poor People in Ireland from Being a Burden to Their Parents or Country, and for Making Them Beneficial to the Public

---

Jonathan Swift

One of the most important eighteenth-century authors, Jonathan Swift (1667–1745) led several lives. Born in Dublin, he graduated from Trinity College, was ordained in the Anglican Church, and spent many years as dean of Saint Patrick's in Dublin. But Swift was also involved in the political and social life of London for some years, and throughout all parts of his career he kept busy writing, sometimes imaginative literature, sometimes political treatises. His most famous imaginative work is Gulliver's Travels, *published anonymously in 1726. Almost as well-known is the essay that follows, published in 1729. In "A Modest Proposal," as in all his satiric works, Swift's biting irony is present, but so also is his concern to improve humanity.*

1   It is a melancholy object to those who walk through this great town[1] or travel in the country, when they see the streets, the roads, and cabin doors crowded with beggars of the female sex, followed by three, four, or six children, all in rags, and importuning every passenger for an alms. These mothers, instead of being able to work for their honest livelihood, are forced to employ all their time in strolling to beg sustenance for their helpless infants, who, as they grow up, either turn thieves for want of work, or leave their dear native country to fight for the pretender[2] in Spain, or sell themselves to the Barbados.

2   I think it is agreed by all parties that this prodigious number of children in the arms, or on the backs, or at the heels of their mothers, and frequently of their fathers, is in the present deplorable state of the kingdom a very great additional grievance; and therefore, whoever could find out a fair, cheap, and easy method of making these children sound and useful members of the commonwealth would deserve so

---

[1] Dublin.—Ed.

[2] James Stuart, claimant to the British throne lost by his father, James II, in 1688.—Ed.

well of the public as to have his statue set up for a preserver of the nation.

But my intention is very far from being confined to provide only for the children of professed beggars; it is of a much greater extent, and shall take in the whole number of infants at a certain age who are born of parents in effect as little able to support them as those who demand our charity in the streets.

As to my own part, having turned my thoughts for many years upon this important subject, and maturely weighed the several schemes of other projectors,[3] I have always found them grossly mistaken in the computation. It is true a child just dropped from its dam may be supported by her milk for a solar year with little other nourishment; at most not above the value of two shillings, which the mother may certainly get, or the value in scraps, by her lawful occupation of begging; and, it is exactly at one year that I propose to provide for them in such a manner as instead of being a charge upon their parents or the parish, or wanting food and raiment for the rest of their lives, they shall on the contrary contribute to the feeding, and partly to the clothing, of many thousands.

There is likewise another great advantage in my scheme, that it will prevent those voluntary abortions, and that horrid practice of women murdering their bastard children, alas, too frequent among us, sacrificing the poor innocent babes, I doubt, more to avoid the expense than the shame, which would move tears and pity in the most savage and inhuman breast.

The number of souls in this kingdom being usually reckoned one million and a half, of these I calculate there may be about two hundred thousand couples whose wives are breeders; from which number I subtract thirty thousand couples who are able to maintain their own children, although I apprehend there cannot be so many, under the present distress of the kingdom; but this being granted, there will remain a hundred and seventy thousand breeders. I again subtract fifty thousand for those women who miscarry, or whose children die by accident or disease within the year. There only remain a hundred and twenty thousand children of poor parents annually born. The question therefore is, how this number shall be reared and provided for, which, as I have already said, under the present situation of affairs, is utterly impossible by all the methods hitherto proposed. For we can neither employ them in handicraft or agriculture; we neither build houses (I mean in the country) nor cultivate land. They can very seldom pick up a livelihood by stealing until they arrive at six years old, except where they are of towardly parts,[4] although I confess they learn the rudiments much earlier, during which time they can, however, be

---

[3] Planners.—Ed.

[4] Innate abilities.—Ed.

properly looked upon only as probationers, as I have been informed by a principal gentleman in the country of Cavan, who protested to me that he never knew above one or two instances under the age of six, even in the part of the kingdom renowned for the quickest proficiency in that art.

7   I am assured by our merchants that a boy or a girl before twelve years old is no saleable commodity; and even when they come to this age they will not yield above three pounds, or three pounds and half a crown at most, on the exchange; which cannot turn to account either to the parents or the kingdom, the charge of nutriment and rags having been at least four times that value.

8   I shall now therefore humbly propose my own thoughts, which I hope will not be liable to the least objection.

9   I have been assured by a very knowing American of my acquaintance in London that a young healthy child well nursed is at a year old a most delicious, nourishing, and wholesome food, whether stewed, roasted, baked, or boiled; and I make no doubt that it will equally serve in a fricassee or ragout.

10   I do therefore humbly offer it to public consideration that of the hundred and twenty thousand children, already computed, twenty thousand may be reserved for breed, whereof only one fourth part to be males, which is more than we allow to sheep, black cattle, or swine; and my reason is that these children are seldom the fruits of marriage, a circumstance not much regarded by our savages, therefore one male will be sufficient to serve four females. That the remaining hundred thousand may at a year old be offered in sale to the persons of quality and fortune, through the kingdom, always advising the mother to let them suck plentifully in the last month, so as to render them plump and fat for a good table. A child will make two dishes at an entertainment for friends; and when the family dines alone, the fore or hind quarter will make a reasonable dish, and seasoned with a little pepper or salt will be very good boiled on the fourth day, especially in winter.

11   I have reckoned upon a medium that a child just born will weigh twelve pounds, and in a solar year if tolerably nursed encreaseth to twenty-eight pounds.

12   I grant this food will be somewhat dear, and therefore very proper for landlords, who, as they have already devoured most of the parents, seem to have the best title to the children.

13   Infant's flesh will be in season throughout the year, but more plentiful in March, and a little before and after. For we are told by a grave author, an eminent French physician,[5] that fish being a prolific diet, there are more children born in Roman Catholic countries about nine months

---

[5] François Rabelais.—Ed.

after Lent than at any other season; therefore reckoning a year after Lent, the markets will be more glutted than usual, because the number of popish infants is at least three to one in this kingdom; and therefore it will have one other collateral advantage, by lessening the number of Papists among us.

I have already computed the charge of nursing a beggar's child (in   14
which list I reckon all cottagers, laborers, and four-fifths of the farmers) to be about two shillings per annum, rags included; and I believe no gentleman would repine to give ten shillings for the carcass of a good fat child, which, as I have said, will make four dishes of excellent nutritive meat, when he hath only some particular friend or his own family to dine with him. Thus the squire will learn to be a good landlord, and grow popular among his tenants; the mother will have eight shillings net profit, and be fit for work until she produces another child.

Those who are more thrifty (as I must confess the times require) may   15
flay the carcass; the skin of which artificially dressed will make admirable gloves for ladies and summer boots for fine gentlemen.

As to our city of Dublin, shambles[6] may be appointed for this pur-   16
pose, in the most convenient parts of it, and butchers we may be assured will not be wanting; although I rather recommend buying the children alive, and dressing them hot from the knife as we do roasting pigs.

A very worthy person, a true lover of his country, and whose virtues   17
I highly esteem, was lately pleased in discoursing on this matter to offer a refinement upon my scheme. He said that many gentlemen of this kingdom, having of late destroyed their deer, he conceived that the want of venison might be well supplied by the bodies of young lads and maidens, not exceeding fourteen years of age nor under twelve, so great a number of both sexes in every county being now ready to starve for want of work and service; and these to be disposed of by their parents, if alive, or otherwise by their nearest relations. But with due deference to so excellent a friend and so deserving a patriot, I cannot be altogether in his sentiments. For as to the males, my American acquaintance assured me from frequent experience that their flesh was generally tough and lean, like that of our school-boys, by continual exercise, and their taste disagreeable; and to fatten them would not answer the charge. Then as to the females, it would, I think with humble submission, be a loss to the public, because they soon would become breeders themselves; and besides, it is not improbable that some scrupulous people might be apt to censure such as a practice (although indeed very unjustly) as a little bordering upon cruelty; which, I confess, hath always been with me the strongest objection against any project, how wellsoever intended.

---

[6] Butcher shops.—Ed.

18   But in order to justify my friend, he confessed that this expedient was put into his head by the famous Psalmanazar,[7] a native of the island Formosa who came from thence to London above twenty years ago, and in conversation told my friend that in his country when any young person happened to be put to death, the executioner sold the carcass to persons of quality as a prime dainty; and that in his time the body of a plump girl of fifteen, who was crucified for an attempt to poison the emperor, was sold to his Imperial Majesty's prime minister of state, and other great mandarins of the court, in joints from the gibbet, at four hundred crowns. Neither indeed can I deny that if the same use were made of several plump young girls in this town, who without one single groat to their fortunes cannot stir abroad without a chair, and appear at the playhouse and assemblies in foreign fineries which they never will pay for, the kingdom would not be the worse.

19   Some persons of a desponding spirit are in great concern about that vast number of poor people who are aged, diseased, or maimed, and I have been desired to employ my thoughts what course may be taken to ease the nation of so grievous an incumbrance. But I am not in the least pain upon that matter, because it is very well known that they are every day dying and rotting by cold and famine, and filth and vermin, as fast as can be reasonably expected. And as to the younger laborers, they are now in almost as hopeful a condition. They cannot get work, and consequently pine away for want of nourishment to a degree that if at any time they are accidentally hired to common labor, they have not strength to perform it; and thus the country and themselves are in a fair way of being soon delivered from the evils to come.

20   I have too long digressed, and therefore shall return to my subject. I think the advantages by the proposal which I have made are obvious and many, as well as of the highest importance.

21   For, first, as I have already observed, it would greatly lessen the number of Papists, with whom we are yearly overrun, being the principal breeders of the nation as well as our most dangerous enemies; and who stay at home on purpose with a design to deliver the kingdom to the pretender, hoping to take their advantage by the absence of so many good Protestants, who have chosen rather to leave their country than stay at home and pay tithes against their conscience to an idolatrous Episcopal curate.

22   Secondly, the poorer tenants will have something valuable of their own, which by law may be made liable to distress,[8] and help to pay their landlord's rent; their corn and cattle being already seized, and money a thing unknown.

---

[7]A known imposter who was French, not Formosan as he claimed.—Ed.
[8]Can be seized by lenders.—Ed.

Thirdly, whereas the maintenance of a hundred thousand children,   23
from two years old and upwards, cannot be computed at less than ten
shillings a piece per annum, the nation's stock will be thereby increased
fifty thousand pounds per annum, besides the profit of a new dish introduced to the tables of all gentlemen of fortune in the kingdom who have
any refinement in taste. And the money will circulate among ourselves, the
goods being entirely of our own growth and manufacture.

Fourthly, the constant breeders, besides the gain of eight shillings   24
sterling per annum by the sale of their children, will be rid of the charge of
maintaining them after the first year.

Fifthly, this food would likewise bring great custom to taverns,   25
where the vintners will certainly be so prudent as to procure the best receipts for dressing it to perfection, and consequently have their houses fre-
quented by all the fine gentlemen, who justly value themselves upon their
knowledge in good eating; and a skillful cook, who understands how to
oblige his guests, will contrive to make it as expensive as they please.

Sixthly, this would be a great inducement to marriage, which all wise   26
nations have either encouraged by rewards or enforced by laws and penalties. It would increase the care and tenderness of mothers towards their
children, when they were sure of a settlement for life to the poor babes,
provided in some sort by the public, to their annual profit instead of expense. We should soon see an honest emulation among the married
women, which of them could bring the fattest child to the market. Men
would become as fond of their wives during the time of their pregnancy as
they are now of their mares in foal, their cows in calf, or sows when they
are ready to farrow; nor offer to beat or kick them (as it is too frequent a
practice) for fear of a miscarriage.

Many other advantages might be enumerated. For instance, the addi-   27
tion of some thousand carcasses in our exportation of barrelled beef, the
propagation of swine's flesh, and improvement in the art of making good
bacon, so much wanted among us by the great destruction of pigs, too frequent at our tables, which are no way comparable in taste or magnificence
to a well-grown fat, yearling child, which roasted whole will make a considerable figure at a lord mayor's feast or any other public entertainment.
But this and many others I omit, being studious of brevity.

Supposing that one thousand families in this city would be constant   28
customers for infants' flesh, besides others who might have it at merry
meetings, particularly weddings and christenings, I compute that Dublin
would take off annually about twenty thousand carcasses, and the rest of
the kingdom (where probably they will be sold somewhat cheaper) the remaining eighty thousand.

I can think of no one objection that will possibly be raised against   29
this proposal, unless it should be urged that the number of people will be
thereby much lessened in the kingdom. This I freely own, and it was in-

deed one principal design in offering it to the world. I desire the reader will observe that I calculate my remedy for this one individual kingdom of Ireland and for no other that ever was, is, or I think ever can be upon earth. Therefore let no man talk to me of other expedients: of taxing our absentees at five shillings a pound: of using neither clothes nor household furniture except what is of our own growth and manufacture: of utterly rejecting the materials and instruments that promote foreign luxury: of curing the expensiveness or pride, vanity, idleness, and gaming in our women: of introducing a vein of parsimony, prudence and temperance: of learning to love our country, wherein we differ even from Laplanders and the inhabitants of Topinamboo[9]: of quitting our animosities and factions, not act any longer like the Jews, who were murdering one another at the very moment their city was taken[10]: of being a little cautious not to sell our country and consciences for nothing: of teaching landlords to have at least one degree of mercy towards their tenants. Lastly, of putting a spirit of honesty, industry, and skill into our shopkeepers; who, if a resolution could now be taken to buy only our native goods, would immediately unite to cheat and exact upon us in the price, the measure, and the goodness, nor could ever yet be brought to make one fair proposal of just dealing, though often and earnestly invited to it.

30   Therefore I repeat, let no man talk to me of these and the like expedients, till he hath at least a glimpse of hope that there will ever be some hearty and sincere attempt to put them in practice.

31   But as to myself, having been wearied out for many years with offering vain, idle, visionary thoughts, and at length utterly despairing of success, I fortunately fell upon this proposal, which, as it is wholly new, so it hath something solid and real, of no expense and little trouble, full in our own power, and whereby we can incur no danger in disobliging England. For this kind of commodity will not bear exportation, the flesh being of too tender a consistence to admit a long continuance in salt, although perhaps I could name a country which would be glad to eat up our whole nation without it.

32   After all, I am not so violently bent upon my own opinion as to reject any offer proposed by wise men, which shall be found equally innocent, cheap, easy, and effectual. But before something of that kind shall be advanced in contradiction to my scheme, and offering a better, I desire the author, or authors, will be pleased maturely to consider two points. First, as things now stand, how they will be able to find food and raiment for a hundred thousand useless mouths and backs. And secondly, there being a

[9] An area in Brazil.—Ed.

[10] Some Jews were accused of helping the Romans and were executed during the Roman siege of Jerusalem in 70 A.D.—Ed.

round million of creatures in human figure throughout this kingdom whose whole subsistence put into a common stock would leave them in debt two millions of pounds sterling, adding those who are beggars by profession to the bulk of farmers, cottagers, and laborers, with their wives and children who are beggars in effect; I desire those politicians who dislike my overture, and may perhaps be so bold to attempt an answer, that they will first ask the parents of these mortals whether they would not at this day think it a great happiness to have been sold for food at a year old in the manner I prescribe, and thereby have avoided such a perpetual scene of misfortunes as they have since gone through by the oppression of landlords, the impossibility of paying rent without money or trade, the want of common sustenance, with neither house nor clothes to cover them from the inclemencies of weather, and the most inevitable prospect of entailing the like or greater miseries upon their breed forever.

I profess, in the sincerity of my heart, that I have not the least personal interest in endeavoring to promote this necessary work, having no other motive than the public good of my country, by advancing our trade, providing for infants, relieving the poor, and giving some pleasure to the rich. I have no children by which I can propose to get a single penny, the youngest being nine years old, and my wife past childbearing. 33

Reading and Analyzing

1. Swift was a minister, but he writes this essay as if he were in a different vocation. What *persona* does he assume here? In what early paragraph does he reveal his persona? What are the traits of this persona?
2. How is the writer's argument organized? What is accomplished in paragraphs 1 through 7? In paragraphs 8 through 16? In paragraphs 17 through 19? In paragraphs 20 through 28? In paragraphs 29 through 33?
3. What specific advantages does the writer offer in defense of his proposal?
4. What specific passages and connotative words make you aware that this is a satirical piece? What is Swift's chief device for creating satire?
5. What do you conclude to be Swift's purpose in writing?
6. From reading this essay, what can you conclude about some of the problems in eighteenth-century Ireland and some of the English attitudes toward the Irish?
7. Can you find passages in which Swift offers some direct condemnation of existing conditions and attitudes?
8. What actual reforms would Swift like to see to improve life in Ireland?

Responding to the Writer's Ideas

1. What does Swift gain by approaching his subject and purpose in this way? What is the risk of using this strategy?

2. Swift paints a gloomy picture of many families trapped in a web of poverty, hunger, disease, and unemployment. Is his description still applicable today? Has life for the very poor changed much? Explain.

3. Swift's gruesome proposal is based on the expectation that the poor will continue to have children for which they can not adequately care, a reality today as well. Some have recommended that welfare benefits be taken away from those who continue to have children. Do you support or disapprove of this proposal? Explain your position.

4. The author's proposer defends his proposal in part by complaining that he has "been wearied out for many years with offering vain, idle, visionary thoughts." Are we still being wearied with "visionary thoughts" instead of concrete proposals? Are there specific proposals that you think need implementation, or a more widespread implementation? What proposals for helping the poor should be implemented?

❖

How to Get the Poor Off Our Conscience

John Kenneth Galbraith

One of the most influential of contemporary economists, John Kenneth Galbraith (b. 1908) was educated at the Universities of Toronto and California and was, for many years, the Paul M. Warburg Professor of Economics at Harvard. Galbraith has also served as ambassador to India (1961 to 1963), national chairman of Americans for Democratic Action, and presidential adviser to both Kennedy and Johnson. Galbraith has a long list of books and articles to his credit, but perhaps the best known are The Affluent Society *(1959),* The New Industrial State *(1967), and* Economics and the Public Purpose *(1973). The* Affluent Society, *standard reading in college courses, has been translated into a dozen languages. Galbraith is a broadscope or philosophical economist, raising moral issues and questioning social priorities, such as how wealth should be divided. In the following article, adapted from several speeches and published in the November 1985 issue of* Harper's, *he examines some contemporary philosophies for coping with society's poor and then offers his views.*

I would like to reflect on one of the oldest of human exercises, the process by which over the years, and indeed over the centuries, we have undertaken to get the poor off our conscience.

Rich and poor have lived together, always uncomfortably and sometimes perilously, since the beginning of time. Plutarch was led to say: "An imbalance between the rich and poor is the oldest and most fatal ailment of republics." And the problems that arise from the continuing coexistence of affluence and poverty—and particularly the process by which good fortune is justified in the presence of the ill fortune of others—have been an intellectual preoccupation for centuries. They continue to be so in our own time.

One begins with the solution proposed in the Bible: the poor suffer in this world but are wonderfully rewarded in the next. Their poverty is a temporary misfortune; if they are poor and also meek, they eventually will inherit the earth. This is, in some ways, an admirable solution. It allows the rich to enjoy their wealth while envying the poor their future fortune.

Much, much later, in the twenty or thirty years following the publication in 1776 of *The Wealth of Nations*—the late dawn of the Industrial

Revolution in Britain—the problem and its solution began to take on their modern form. Jeremy Bentham, a near contemporary of Adam Smith,[1] came up with the formula that for perhaps fifty years was extraordinarily influential in British and, to some degree, American thought. This was utilitarianism. "By the principle of utility," Bentham said in 1789, "is meant the principle which approves or disapproves of every action whatsoever according to the tendency which it appears to have to augment or diminish the happiness of the party whose interest is in question." Virtue is, indeed must be, self-centered. While there were people with great good fortune and many more with great ill fortune, the social problem was solved as long as, again in Bentham's words, there was "the greatest good for the greatest number." Society did its best for the largest possible number of people; one accepted that the result might be sadly unpleasant for the many whose happiness was not served.

5   In the 1830s a new formula, influential in no slight degree to this day, became available for getting the poor off the public conscience. This is associated with the names of David Ricardo, a stockbroker, and Thomas Robert Malthus, a divine. The essentials are familiar: the poverty of the poor was the fault of the poor. And it was so because it was a product of their excessive fecundity: their grievously uncontrolled lust caused them to breed up to the full limits of the available subsistence.

6   This was Malthusianism. Poverty being caused in the bed meant that the rich were not responsible for either its creation or its amelioration. However, Malthus was himself not without a certain feeling of responsibility: he urged that the marriage ceremony contain a warning against undue and irresponsible sexual intercourse—a warning, it is fair to say, that has not been accepted as a fully effective method of birth control. In more recent times, Ronald Reagan has said that the best form of population control emerges from the market. (Couples in love should repair to R. H. Macy's, not their bedrooms.) Malthus, it must be said, was at least as relevant.

7   By the middle of the nineteenth century, a new form of denial achieved great influence, especially in the United States. The new doctrine, associated with the name of Herbert Spencer, was Social Darwinism. In economic life, as in biological development, the overriding rule was survival of the fittest. That phrase—"survival of the fittest"—came, in fact, not from Charles Darwin but from Spencer, and expressed his view of economic life. The elimination of the poor is nature's way of improving the race. The weak and unfortunate being extruded, the quality of the human family is thus strengthened.

8   One of the most notable American spokespersons of Social Darwinism was John D. Rockefeller—the first Rockefeller—who said in a famous speech: "The American Beauty rose can be produced in the splendor and

---

[1] Author of *The Wealth of Nations.*—Ed.

fragrance which bring cheer to its beholder only by sacrificing the early buds which grow up around it. And so it is in economic life. It is merely the working out of a law of nature and a law of God."

In the course of the present century, however, Social Darwinism came to be considered a bit too cruel. It declined in popularity, and references to it acquired a condemnatory tone. We passed on to the more amorphous denial of poverty associated with Calvin Coolidge and Herbert Hoover. They held that public assistance to the poor interfered with the effective operation of the economic system—that such assistance was inconsistent with the economic design that had come to serve most people very well. The notion that there is something economically damaging about helping the poor remains with us to this day as one of the ways by which we get them off our conscience.   9

With the Roosevelt revolution (as previously with that of Lloyd George in Britain), a specific responsibility was assumed by the government for the least fortunate people in the republic. Roosevelt and the presidents who followed him accepted a substantial measure of responsibility for the old through Social Security, for the unemployed through unemployment insurance, for the unemployable and the handicapped through direct relief, and for the sick through Medicare and Medicaid. This was a truly great change, and for a time, the age-old tendency to avoid thinking about the poor gave way to the feeling that we didn't need to try—that we were, indeed, doing something about them.   10

In recent years, however, it has become clear that the search for a way of getting the poor off our conscience was not at an end; it was only suspended. And so we are now again engaged in this search in a highly energetic way. It has again become a major philosophical, literary, and rhetorical preoccupation, and an economically not unrewarding enterprise.   11

Of the four, maybe five, current designs we have to get the poor off our conscience, the first proceeds from the inescapable fact that most of the things that must be done on behalf of the poor must be done in one way or another by the government. It is then argued that the government is inherently incompetent, except as regards weapons design and procurement and the overall management of the Pentagon. Being incompetent and ineffective, it must not be asked to succor the poor; it will only louse things up or make things worse.   12

The allegation of government incompetence is associated in our time with the general condemnation of the bureaucrat—again excluding those concerned with national defense. The only form of discrimination that is still permissible—that is, still officially encouraged in the United States today—is discrimination against people who work for the federal government, especially on social welfare activities. We have great corporate bureaucracies replete with corporate bureaucrats, but they are good; only public bureaucracy and government servants are bad. In fact, we have in   13 the United States an extraordinarily good public service—one made up of talented and dedicated people who are overwhelmingly honest and only rarely given to overpaying for monkey wrenches, flashlights, coffee makers, and toilet seats. (When these aberrations have occurred, they have, oddly enough, all been in the Pentagon.) We have nearly abolished poverty among the old, greatly democratized health care, assured minorities of their civil rights, and vastly enhanced educational opportunity. All this would seem a considerable achievement for incompetent and otherwise ineffective people. We must recognize that the present condemnation of government and government administration is really part of the continuing design for avoiding responsibility for the poor.

14   The second design in this great centuries-old tradition is to argue that any form of public help to the poor only hurts the poor. It destroys morale. It seduces people away from gainful employment. It breaks up marriages, since women can seek welfare for themselves and their children once they are without their husbands.

15   There is no proof of this—none, certainly, that compares that damage with the damage that would be inflicted by the loss of public assistance. Still, the case is made—and believed—that there is something gravely damaging about aid to the unfortunate. This is perhaps our most highly influential piece of fiction.

16   The third, and closely related, design for relieving ourselves of responsibility for the poor is the argument that public-assistance measures have an adverse effect on incentive. They transfer income from the diligent to the ideal and feckless, thus reducing the effort of the diligent and encouraging the idleness of the idle. The modern manifestation of this is supply-side economics. Supply-side economics holds that the rich in the United States have not been working because they have too little income. So, by taking money from the poor and giving it to the rich, we increase effort and stimulate the economy. Can we really believe that any considerable number of the poor prefer welfare to a good job? Or that business people—corporate executives, the key figures in our time—are idling away their hours because of the insufficiency of their pay? This is a scandalous charge against the American businessperson, notably a hard worker. Belief can be the servant of truth—but even more of convenience.

17   The fourth design for getting the poor off our conscience is to point to the presumed adverse effect on freedom of taking responsibility for them. Freedom consists of the right to spend a maximum of one's money by one's own choice, and to see a minimum taken and spent by the government. (Again, expenditure on national defense is excepted.) In the enduring words of Professor Milton Friedman,[2] people must be "free to choose."

---

[2] President Reagan's first chairman of the Council of Economic Advisers.—Ed.

This is possibly the most transparent of all of the designs; no mention [18] is ordinarily made of the relation of income to the freedom of the poor. (Professor Friedman is here an exception; through the negative income tax, he would assure everyone a basic income.) There is, we can surely agree, no form of oppression that is quite so great, no constriction on thought and effort quite so comprehensive, as that which comes from having no money at all. Though we hear much about the limitation on the freedom of the affluent when their income is reduced through taxes, we hear nothing of the extraordinary enhancement of the freedom of the poor from having some money of their own to spend. Yet the loss of freedom from taxation to the rich is a small thing as compared with the gain in freedom from providing some income to the impoverished. Freedom we rightly cherish. Cherishing it, we should not use it as a cover for denying freedom to those in need.

Finally, when all else fails, we resort to simple psychological denial. [19] This is a psychic tendency that in various manifestations is common to us all. It causes us to avoid thinking about death. It causes a great many people to avoid thought of the arms race and the consequent rush toward a highly probably extinction. By the same process of psychological denial, we decline to think of the poor. Whether they be in Ethiopia, the South Bronx, or even in such an Elysium as Los Angeles, we resolve to keep them off our minds. Think, we are often advised, of something pleasant.

These are the modern designs by which we escape concern for the [20] poor. All, save perhaps the last, are in great inventive descent from Bentham, Malthus, and Spencer. Ronald Reagan and his colleagues are clearly in a notable tradition—at the end of a long history of effort to escape responsibility for one's fellow beings. So are the philosophers now celebrated in Washington: George Gilder,[3] a greatly favored figure of the recent past, who tells to much applause that the poor must have the cruel spur of their own suffering to ensure effort; Charles Murray,[4] who, to greater cheers, contemplates "scrapping the entire federal welfare and income-support structure for working and aged persons, including A.F.D.C., Medicaid, food stamps, unemployment insurance, Workers' Compensation, subsidized housing, disability insurance, and," he adds, "the rest. Cut the knot, for there is no way to untie it." By a triage, the worthy would be selected to survive; the loss of the rest is the penalty we should pay. Murray is the voice of Spencer in our time; he is enjoying, as indicated, unparalleled popularity in high Washington circles.

---

[3] Author of *Wealth and Poverty* (1981), a book that influenced the economic thinking of the Reagan administration.—Ed.

[4] A senior research fellow at the Manhattan Institute for Policy Research and author of *Losing Ground: American Social Policy, 1950–1980* (1984).—Ed.

21   Compassion, along with the associated public effort, is the least comfortable, the least convenient, course of behavior and action in our time. But it remains the only one that is consistent with a totally civilized life. Also, it is, in the end, the most truly conservative course. There is no paradox here. Civil discontent and its consequences do not come from contented people—an obvious point. To the extent that we can make contentment as nearly universal as possible, we will preserve and enlarge the social and political tranquility for which conservatives, above all, should yearn.

Reading and Analyzing

1. Galbraith says that he wants to reflect on the ways we explain (and thus justify) the discrepancy between rich and poor. How do you know that his purpose is not only to analyze economic theories but to express an attitude about the appropriate way to respond to the poor? From the first two paragraphs, what clues do you get about his attitude?
2. Make a list of the specific explanations and justifications for poverty in Galbraith's historical review, beginning with the Bible.
3. What made the Roosevelt era's view of the poor different from previous periods?
4. State, in your own words, the five contemporary designs for getting the poor off our conscience.
5. How does Galbraith challenge each modern attitude?
6. What does Galbraith want us to feel—and to do—about the poor? What, then, is the claim of his argument?
7. By what argument does the author support his position? Explain why he considers his position the "truly conservative course."
8. Galbraith's essay is neatly organized. Analyze his organization, and prepare, from your analysis, a detailed outline.

Responding to the Writer's Ideas

1. Do you share the antibureaucratic attitude that Galbraith refers to? Do you agree that it is widespread? What reasons does Galbraith offer for rejecting the view? Are his reasons convincing?
2. The novelist F. Scott Fitzgerald once said that the rich are different from the poor, to which Ernest Hemingway responded that, yes, they have more money. What is the difference that Fitzgerald understood and that Galbraith also emphasizes?
3. Do you agree with Galbraith's assertion that there is "no form of oppression that is quite so great, no constriction on thought and effort

quite so comprehensive, as that which comes from having no money at all"? If so, why? If not, why not?

4. Galbraith asserts that one strategy for "dealing" with the poor is denial. Do you ever use this strategy, or do you agree that many people do? If the assertion is sound, then what needs to be done to make people more responsive to the problems of the poor?

❖

Economics: The Cheery Science

Robert J. Samuelson

Journalist Robert Samuelson (b. 1945) began his career as a
Washington Post *reporter after earning a B.A. degree in government
from Harvard University. He is now a syndicated columnist whose
columns are printed weekly in many papers and biweekly in* Newsweek
*magazine. Samuelson's usual topics are from economics, or, as the
following column (*Washington Post, *January 8, 1992) illustrates, about
cultural attitudes that affect or are affected by economic elements.*

1   Just about the most backward idea around is that economics is the
"dismal science." Quite the opposite: Economics—since at least the time of
Adam Smith in the 1700s—has devoted itself to improving the human condition by promoting policies to reduce material want. Never before was
the promise so great as during the decades after World War II. The crumbling of our faith in economics now underlies much of today's pessimism
and anxiety.

2   The promise was for a constant rise in living standards and an end to
business cycles. Economics sold itself as a science that, if followed, would
enable society to achieve the ageless ambitions of social stability and ever-
ascending abundance. From these triumphs would flow more caring government and greater individual liberty. Today's disillusion is so profound
because this vision completely captured mass psychology and politics.

3   It served as our national religion, writes economist Robert Nelson in
a new book, "Reaching for Heaven on Earth" (Rowman & Littlefield). We
believed in the future as economists sketched it. Correct economic policies
would "solve not only practical but also spiritual problems," because "material scarcity and the resulting competition for limited resources [are] the
fundamental causes of human misbehavior"—everything from crime to
war. Eliminate scarcity, and good would flourish. Economists could do
that by engineering perpetual prosperity.

4   Popular disillusion is surely warranted—though why it should be so
acute now is less clear. We have had nine recessions since World War II.
You would think people would no longer be shocked. They are. Every economic expansion, it seems, recreates false hopes that recessions are a thing
of the past. The delusion is fostered by politicians and economists who
refuse to talk about the inevitability of the next recession. The 7½-year expansion of the 1980s saw this phenomenon in full swing.

388

Living standards are another source of obvious disappointment. Between 1950 and 1970, median family income rose 85 percent. Since 1970, the increase has been only 13 percent. Similar slowdowns have occurred in most industrial nations. Economists now refer to the period between the late 1940s and the early 1970s as the "golden age" and wonder why growth was so fast.

Perhaps it merely reflected a catch-up from the Great Depression and World War II. There were huge backlogs of demand for houses, cars and appliances. New technologies (television, plastic and antibiotics, among others) were ready to be exploited. Europe and Japan had to be rebuilt. But this is only one theory among many, and no one really knows why growth has now become so much more grudging.

The search continues for salvation: sustained, higher growth. As Nelson shows, economists have differences. Some favor more government, while others trust markets. But the basic gospel—the belief in social progress through rational policies—is widely embraced. It was this faith that permeated popular consciousness and created confidence in the future. In effect, economics became the cheery science. But it did not seem so. Economists projected themselves as sober pragmatists. The contrast between their demeanor (hard-nosed, even dour) and their message (desirable and glorious) actually made the message more believable.

Government is now expected to deliver on the promises even when—as more and more economists concede—the promises are extravagant. Failure to do so is taken as evidence of incompetence and sows huge doubts about the future. This is one cause of today's pessimism. (It isn't, however, the only cause. Another is higher unemployment among white-collar workers who thought themselves invulnerable to a slump. Insecurity has spread among a whole new class of people.)

Curiously, pessimism about our economic prospects may now be overdone—just as optimism was before. The truth is that, although recessions haven't disappeared, they've become much less violent or frequent than before World War II. Between 1875 and 1918, the average recession involved a decline of 5 percent in national output. In the Great Depression, the drop exceeded 30 percent. Since World War II, the average decline has been about 2.5 percent. In the latest slump, it was 1.6 percent.

One reason for this is that the service sector represents a bigger share of employment—and spending on services isn't so erratic. "People postpone replacement of old cars," says economist Victor Zarnowitz of the University of Chicago. "For services, you can't do that." Another reason is that the gold standard (effectively abandoned in 1933) often worsened slumps by weakening the banking system. Finally, economists today better understand how to combat recession by changing interest rates. Economists are like doctors. Their knowledge and therapeutic powers, though imperfect, have improved.

11   Gloom over living standards is also exaggerated. Between 1950 and 1970, productivity—the basic source of higher living standards—grew about 3 percent annually. In the past decade, growth has been about 1 percent. Although that's lousy, it's not stagnation.

12   Up to a point, our new skepticism about the future isn't bad. Foolish optimism is more than foolish. It's also self-defeating. It promotes carelessness and irresponsibility. Why worry if the future is fated to turn out all right? This casual approach to things may help explain why Americans save so little or why our companies often become uncompetitive. Insecurity can prevent complacency. Paradoxically, a little less optimism might be good for America.

13   But describing things as worse than they are can also be self-defeating. It spawns cynicism and obscures the fact that some policies are better (or worse) than others. It fosters unrealistic public impatience and creates suspicion of our institutions. Obsessive pessimism can be immobilizing, both for people and societies. It promotes precautionary behavior—an aversion to risks—that can be crippling. A frightened society can talk itself into economic stagnation or political crisis. We need to control our anxieties. Otherwise, they will control us.

Reading and Analyzing

1. What is Samuelson's thesis, the claim of his argument? Where does he state it?
2. What was the promise of economics? What problems would economic policies solve?
3. What are the causes of the current disappointment?
4. Why can't the economists tell us how to maintain high, sustained economic growth?
5. Why are recessions less violent than in the past?
6. Why is the pessimism of the early 1990s unwarranted?
7. Why is a little less optimism good for America? Why is excessive pessimism also a problem? Which, in Samuelson's view, might be the worse attitude?

Responding to the Writer's Ideas

1. Samuelson quotes Robert Nelson's idea that conflict over limited resources is the major cause of "human misbehavior." Does this idea make sense to you? If so, then does it follow that a country's economic and tax policies and programs for the disadvantaged are of fundamental importance? Explore these ideas.

2. Do you agree with Nelson—and Samuelson—that an ever-increasing prosperity is America's "national religion"? In what ways is Nelson using the word *religion* in this context?

3. Do you agree with Samuelson that a religion of perpetual prosperity is an unhealthy faith? If not, how would you counter Samuelson's view?

4. Do you agree that "obsessive pessimism can be immobilizing" for a society? If not, why not? Samuelson suggests that such thinking can also be unhealthy for individuals; what kinds of negative behavior might it lead to in individuals?

America: What Went Wrong?

Donald L. Barlett and James B. Steele

Donald Barlett and James Steele have been investigative reporters at the Philadelphia Inquirer *since 1970. A number of their stories, which usually focus on urban affairs, have led to books, including* Oil: The Created Crisis *(1973),* Forevermore: Nuclear Waste in America *(1985), and* America: What Went Wrong? *(1992), from which the following excerpt is taken. In 1975, Barlett and Steele won the Pulitzer Prize for national reporting. Their reliance on facts a trademark of their style, Barlett and Steele have been described as the "most systematic and thorough investigative reporting team in the U.S. today." Their emphasis on the facts is demonstrated in the following pages, the prologue to* America: What Went Wrong?

1   Listen to the people in charge of the American economy tell how well the recovery was going in 1991.

2   Listen to them explain, month after month, how economic conditions were improving for you.

3   On Dec. 16, 1990, Nicholas Brady, secretary of the United States Treasury, told a television audience: "I have great conviction the American economy is strong. We're in a cyclical downturn. It'll return to a good strong level sometime in 1991. . . . We'll be back on the growth path, jobs, investment, during that year."

4   On Feb. 4, 1991, the Council of Economic Advisers, headed by Michael J. Boskin, reported: "The downturn in the U.S. economy in the latter part of 1990 does not signal any decline in its long-run underlying health or basic vitality. . . . Several factors suggest that the economic downturn is not likely to last long and that a recovery will begin by the middle of 1991."

5   On June 11, 1991, President Bush told the National Advertising Federation: "If I can borrow a term from Wall Street, I am bullish on the economy. . . . While some sectors are still sluggish, on the whole, a turnaround in the economy appears to be in the making. . . . Things are beginning to move forward. And as far as your industry is concerned, I'm optimistic that it, too, will pick up as the rest of the economy gathers steam."

On July 10, 1991, Alan Greenspan, chairman of the Federal Reserve   6
Board, told a news conference: "I think the evidence is increasing week
by week that the bottom is passed and the economy is beginning to move
up. . . . I think it's a pretty safe bet at this stage to conclude that the decline is behind us and the outlook is continuing to improve."

On Oct. 4, 1991, President Bush told a news conference: "I think the   7
economy is recovering. I think it will be more robust as we go along here.
Job creation is fast."

Job creation fast?   8

You might have a different view. Especially if you were one of the   9
74,000 workers destined to lose their jobs at General Motors Corporation,
the world's largest car manufacturer.

Or one of the 2,500 workers whose jobs were eliminated at TRW   10
Inc., the space and defense contractor with interests in information services
and automotive equipment.

Or one of the 8,000 workers whose jobs were eliminated at GTE   11
Corporation, the telephone operations and telecommunications company.

Or one of the 4,000 workers whose jobs were eliminated at Westing-   12
house Electric Corporation, the diversified broadcasting, energy and elec-
tronic systems company.

Or one of the 5,000 workers whose jobs were eliminated at Allied-   13
Signal Inc., the aerospace, automotive and engineered-materials (synthetic
fibers and plastics) company.

Or one of the 1,000 workers whose jobs were eliminated at First   14
Chicago Corporation, the global corporate bank.

Or one of the 4,000 workers whose jobs were eliminated at J.I. Case,   15
the construction and farm-equipment maker.

Or one of the 20,000 workers destined to lose their jobs at Interna-   16
tional Business Machines Corporation, the computer company with a
decades-old reputation of guaranteeing job security.

You also might have a different view if you are one of the millions of   17
workers competing for a shrinking number of manufacturing jobs. Preliminary figures show that in 1991 about 18.4 million men and women were
employed in manufacturing, earning middle-class wages. Ten years earlier,
in 1981, there were 20.2 million men and women at work in manufacturing. Between 1981 and 1991, a total of 1.8 million manufacturing jobs
vanished in the United States—a decline of 9 percent.

This at the same time the population 16 and older rose from 171.8   18
million to 191.2 million—an increase of 11 percent. In other words, while
the potential work force grew by 19.4 million persons, the number of
manufacturing jobs shrank by 1.8 million.

You also might have a different view if you are a member of Ameri-   19
ca's disappearing middle class—whether blue-collar, white-collar, middle-
level manager or professional.

20   And you especially might have a different view if you are one of the millions of Americans seeking to attain a middle-class status that you now find beyond your reach. But that's because you have a skewed vision. You are on the bottom looking up.

21   Those in charge, on the other hand, are on the top looking down. They see things differently. Call it the view from Washington and Wall Street.

22   It is a view that can be documented by a mountain of statistics. Such as the amount of money you receive in your weekly paycheck, contrasted with the paychecks of more affluent citizens.

23   Take 1989, the latest year for which complete data, as compiled from federal income tax returns, are available. That year, the top 4 percent of all wage earners in the country collected as much in wages and salaries as the bottom 51 percent of the population. Mull over the numbers carefully: The top 4 percent of American's work force earned as much as the bottom 51 percent. That is in wages and salaries alone. In more precise numbers, 3.8 million individuals and families at the top earned as much from their jobs as did 49.2 million individuals and families at the bottom.

24   The view from Washington and Wall Street was not always so distorted. In 1970, the top 4 percent earned as much on the job as the bottom 38 percent. And in 1959, they earned as much as the bottom 35 percent.

25   Now put the numbers in order, as viewed from the bottom: In 1959—a time of growing middle-class prosperity—the bottom 35 percent of the work force earned as much as the top 4 percent. By 1970, it took the wages of the bottom 38 percent of the work force to match the top 4 percent.

26   By 1989—a time of middle-class decline—it took the wages and salaries of the lowest 51 percent of the workers to equal the wages and salaries of the 4 percent at the top.

27   If the trend continues, sometime early in the next century the top 4 percent of individuals and families drawing paychecks will earn as much on the job as 60 percent of the rest of American workers.

28   Keep in mind these numbers deal only with wages and salaries. They do not include interest and dividends; gains from the sale of stocks, bonds and other capital assets; or income from other investments, indeed, from any other sources. This income, too, flows overwhelmingly to the top 4 percent.

29   For a growing number of individuals and families, the exploding difference in wages and salaries among the people at the top and everyone else means the end of the American dream. Call it the relentless shrinking of the middle class.

30   Not to worry. The people in Washington want to help. Democrats, for example, have proposed both tax cuts and tax credits for the middle class. But lest you believe Democrats at work in the nation's capital have

an edge over Republicans—who through most of 1991 insisted all was well—in dealing with the economy, ponder the words of one party leader. In a speech to his colleagues in October 1991, Richard A. Gephardt, the Missouri Democrat who is the majority leader of the House of Representatives, criticized President Bush and other Republicans for their tax policies of the last decade.

Gephardt zeroed in on the generous tax cuts that were handed out to the wealthy in the 1980s at the expense of those in the middle: "For the last ten years, Democrats have warned of a day of reckoning. We warned that excessive tax cuts for the rich, wasteful military spending, and neglect of the middle class would someday combine to dampen our abundance and diminish our prospects." 31

Five years earlier, Gephardt delivered quite a different message to lawmakers while urging them to approve the Tax Reform Act of 1986, the legislation that provided hefty tax cuts for the wealthy. Said Gephardt in September 1986: "[This bill] does give a tax cut . . . To ordinary, average taxpayers. It does not give the lion's share to people at the top. It helps people at the bottom . . . [and] people in the middle, the people we are supposed to be worrying so much about." 32

It didn't. But that's another matter. 33

Everyone, to be sure, has a definition of middle class. It is a term that conjures up varying images for sociologists and economists, politicians and ordinary folks. In Washington, for example, it is often said that the top of the middle class is whatever salary is earned by members of Congress. That is $125,100 a year in 1992. But that is more money than 97 percent of the households in America earn. Similarly, many families that earn $80,000 in wages and salaries a year consider themselves middle class. But that income actually puts them in the top 6 percent of American households that file income tax returns. 34

For these reasons we have defined the heart of the middle class as those wage-earners who reported incomes between $20,000 and $50,000 on their tax returns in 1989. Median family income that year was $34,213, meaning half of all Americans earned more and half earned less. All told, just under thirty-four million individuals and families filed tax returns reporting incomes between $20,000 and $50,000. They accounted for 35 percent of all tax returns. 35

A definition of an extended middle class might include all households with reported income between $15,000 and $75,000. While individuals or families in New York would be living in poverty if they earned $15,000, the same individuals or families could well achieve a middle-class lifestyle in, say, Sedalia, Missouri. 36

Slightly under ten million tax returns were filed by the $15,000-to-$20,000 income group. That represented 10 percent of all returns. At the other end of the extended middle class are people earning $50,000 to 37

$75,000. A total of 9.2 million returns were filed by that income group, accounting for 10 percent of all returns.

38   Overall, 53.2 million individuals and families in the extended middle class—with income between $15,000 and $75,000—filed tax returns. They accounted for 55 percent of all returns. That put 37.3 million individuals and families at the bottom, with incomes below $15,000. They represented 39 percent of total returns. While this figure includes returns filed by teenagers working part-time, the overwhelming majority are married couples, single persons and single parents who represent the working poor.

39   In fact, the fastest-growing group of persons filing tax returns is made up of heads of households. They include a single parent caring for a child and a person who provides support for a relative, often an aging parent. Their numbers have shot up 1,100 percent over the last three decades, rising from one million in 1960 to an estimated twelve million in 1989.

40   They represent part of the changing face of America. In 1960, a majority of all tax returns filed—62 percent—were submitted by married couples. By 1989, that figure had fallen to an estimated 44 percent or less. During the same period, returns filed by single persons rose from 33 percent to an estimated 44 percent of the total.

41   Now consider the incomes of these different groups: 94 percent of all returns filed by heads of households and married persons living separately reported incomes of less than $40,000 in 1988, the latest year for which there is a detailed accounting.

42   As for married couples, keep in mind that the government statistics on median family income exaggerate the financial condition of families, especially when looked at in historical terms. In the 1950s, median family income was derived largely from the wages and salaries of one working spouse. In the 1990s, median family income represents, in a majority of cases, the wages and salaries of a husband and wife who both work. Thus, goods and services that once could be purchased with a single income now require two incomes.

43   Whatever your status—a married couple with children, a single person, a married couple without children, a single parent with children—if you work for a living and if you are in the middle-class income range defined here, the chances are that your standard of living is falling or will do so in the coming years. If you are striving to join the middle class, you are working against long odds.

44   None of this, it must be emphasized, is related to the recession, which, depending upon your economist of choice, began in July 1991 and ended, or will end, on a date uncertain.

45   In the early days of the recession, Treasury Secretary Brady dismissed the seriousness of what he then labeled an "economic slowdown" by saying: "I don't think it's the end of the world even if we have a recession. We'll pull back out of it again. No big deal."

That is true—recessions do end. But when that day comes, your standard of living—over the long term—will continue to decline. That is because the plight of America's middle class is rooted in serious structural problems within both the economy and society that go beyond the recession.

To correct those problems will require comprehensive changes in government laws and regulations on a scale of the sweeping legislative revisions of the 1930s. In the absence of such action, the future will remain bleak for the middle class.

This is especially true for the generation now entering the work force. For those at the lower end of the middle class clinging to a lifestyle once promised to everyone. For those at the bottom struggling to move up. And for those who will be retiring early in the next century.

This is one reason why the stories you read in newspapers and magazines, the reports you watch on television, and those you listen to on radio seem disconnected from your personal situation. For the fact is you are adrift in uncharted economic waters.

The experts—the economists, Wall Street analysts, the politicians— talk in traditional terms, use traditional navigational measures to pinpoint the economy's location. Like interest rates.

On Feb. 21, 1991, the *Washington Post*, relating the testimony of Alan Greenspan, the Federal Reserve Board chairman, before a congressional committee, reported; "Greenspan did note that interest rate cuts engineered by the Fed over the past three months are finally bearing fruit, but he carefully sidestepped questions about whether future rate cuts are needed."

On Mar. 9, 1991, the *Chicago Tribune* reported: "The Federal Reserve moved to lower a key interest rate Friday just hours after the government reported that the nation's jobless rate jumped unexpectedly last month to 6.5 percent, the highest rate in four years. . . . Since October the Fed has pushed the rate 2.25 percentage points lower in an effort to encourage borrowing and stimulate growth."

On May 1, 1991, the *Boston Globe* reported: "The Federal Reserve yesterday gave up all hope that post–Persian Gulf War euphoria will lift the nation from recession and cut the discount rate it charges banks by half a point to 5.5 percent in an effort to reverse the economic slide. . . . The rate cut signals the Fed has returned to its pre-war strategy of cautiously cutting the cost of borrowing to jump start the economy back to growth."

On June 6, 1991, the *Washington Post* reported: "Federal Reserve Board Chairman Alan Greenspan said today that recent evidence suggests the U.S. economy has begun to recover from recession, a prospect that makes unlikely further cuts in interest rates by the central bank to spur growth."

55   On Nov. 7, 1991, the *Los Angeles Times* reported: "Acting for the second time in as many weeks to pump more money and confidence into a faltering economy, the Federal Reserve moved decisively Wednesday to reduce interest rates by lowering its benchmark discount rate to an 18-year low of 4.5 percent. The half-point reduction . . . was clearly designed to force down interest rates paid by business and consumers in an effort to stimulate more borrowing and to breathe new life into the apparently faltering recovery."

56   And on Dec. 21, 1991, the *New York Times* reported: "In a bold move to revive the slumping economy, the Federal Reserve chopped its bedrock discount rate by a full point, to 3½ percent, the lowest level since 1964. The surprisingly big cut was seen as part of a broad effort to stimulate borrowing and perk up an economy whose signs of recovery from recession have all but vanished."

57   Label it the interest-rate obsession.

58   But for a different view, listen to an exchange between Richard Ford, a reporter with KSDK-TV in St. Louis, Missouri, and President Bush, that took place on Nov. 13, 1991:

59   President Bush—"Interest rates are down, and today yet there's—another very important credit card company came down on their rates. At some point when those rates are, people see the rates are where they are, I believe you're going to see confidence start back in housing or in consumer buying. And that's what the economy needs."

60   Ford—"But people don't have jobs, sir. They don't have any income. They don't care what the interest rate is. They can't spend any money. They can't borrow any money."

61   Indeed so. Nonetheless, the experts continue to talk of interest rates and gross national product and gross domestic product and savings rates. Once upon a time, the measures served a purpose. Their usefulness today, in assessing the current and future state of Americans at work in a global economy, operating without restraints, is doubtful.

62   For the middle class, there are more relevant measures. For example: What is the rate at which new jobs that pay middle-class wages—upwards of $20,000 a year—are being created? What is the rate at which such jobs are being eliminated?

63   How much of your weekly paycheck is being transferred to wealthy investors in the form of interest payments on the national debt? What percentage of your paycheck do you have left over after deductions for Social Security and federal, state, and local taxes? How does that percentage compare with, say, the percentage retained by persons earning more than $100,000 a year? What is the rate of job loss attributable to unrestrained imports?

64   How much of your paycheck is going for health-care costs? What is the percentage of the work force that will receive a guaranteed annual pension?

You might think of what is happening in the economy—and thereby   65
to you and your family—in terms of a professional hockey game, a sport
renowned for its physical violence. Imagine how the game would be played
if the old rules were repealed, if the referees were removed.

That, in essence, is what is happening to the American economy.   66
Someone changed the rules. And there is no referee. Which means there is
no one looking after the interests of the middle class.

They are the forgotten Americans.   67

Reading and Analyzing

1. What was the message in 1991 from those "in charge of the American economy"?
2. By contrast, what was happening in the economy? What *kinds* of jobs were lost? What, at the same time, happened to the workforce?
3. What has happened to America's middle class? What figures do Barlett and Steele examine to demonstrate the change taking place?
4. What is the authors' definition of the middle class? Of the extended middle class? Why is someone earning $80,000 a year not really middle class?
5. What percentage of Americans is classified as the working poor?
6. What do the authors predict will happen to the middle class's standard of living in the coming years?
7. The authors provide seven different quotations (including one from President Bush) on declining interest rates. Why? What point do they want to establish?
8. What measures of the economy are more relevant than interest rates?
9. The authors offer a metaphor to explain what is happening to the economy. Explain the metaphor.
10. What is the claim of this argument? What kind of evidence is provided to support the claim? What type of argument is this?

Responding to the Writers' Ideas

1. Barlett and Steele present many statistics; are some of them surprising, even shocking, to you? If so, which ones? And why are you surprised? What did you think were the facts?
2. Do you know people who make $80,000 to $90,000 a year? If so, do they consider themselves middle class? Would you call them middle class? Are these labels significant? Why or why not?
3. Some have suggested that part of our problem grasping the reality of a shrinking middle class is that most people, if asked, would identify

themselves as middle class. Does this correspond to your experience? If so, how do you account for people—rich or poor—choosing to label themselves middle class?

4. The authors' presentation of quotations about interest rates suggests that politicians, and the economists who work for them, are out of touch with the realities of the average person's life. Is this, in your view, a fair assessment? Why or why not?

5. What are your expectations for annual earnings upon graduation? Or by the time you are forty-five? Do you expect to have a higher or lower standard of living than your parents? If you expect it to be higher, on what basis do you hold that view? If you expect it to be lower, is this because of the economic analysis of Barlett and Steele, or for other reasons?

❖

The New Economics of High Technology

Lester C. Thurow

A graduate of Williams College and a Rhodes Scholar, Lester C. Thurow (b. 1938) earned his Ph.D. at Harvard and is now the Gordon Y. Billard Professor of Management and Economics at MIT. He is also a consultant to various government agencies and private companies and a productive writer, having contributed to a long list of collections on economics and public policy, written more than sixty articles for both professional journals and popular magazines, and authored more than a half-dozen books, among them The Zero-Sum Society *(1980),* The Zero-Sum Solution *(1985), and* Dangerous Currents *(1984). The following article, published in* Harper's *in March 1992, explores the economics of high tech and has advice for U.S. firms and American workers.*

In the past, the nations that succeeded economically were those whose businesses invented new products. The British in the nineteenth century and the Americans in the twentieth century got rich by doing this. In the twenty-first century, sustainable competitive advantage will come not from new-product technologies but from new-process technologies—those that enable industries to produce goods and services faster, cheaper, and better. 1

American firms currently spend two-thirds of their R&D money on new products and one-third on new processes. The Japanese do exactly the opposite—one-third on new products, two-thirds on new processes. Not surprisingly, both sets of firms do well where they concentrate their talent: The Americans earn higher rates of return on new-product technologies; the Japanese earn higher rates of return on new processes. 2

Someone, however, is making a mistake. Both strategies cannot be correct. In this case, the someone is the United States. Its spending patterns are misguided, reflecting economic thinking that is thirty years out of date. In the early 1960s the rate of return on investment in new-product R&D was almost always higher than that on new-process R&D. A new product gave the inventor the monopoly power to set higher prices and earn higher profits. With a new product, there were no competitors. 3

In contrast, a new manufacturing or production process left the inventor to fend for himself in an existing, competitive business. Competi- 4

401

tors also knew how to make the product, and they would always lower their prices to match the inventor's. It was simply rational to spend most of a firm's R&D money on new-product development.

5   But while Americans focused on product technologies, Japan and Germany focused on process technologies. They did so not because they were smarter than Americans but because the United States had such a technological advantage in the 1950s and 1960s that it was virtually impossible for either Japan or Germany to become leaders in the development of new products. They could only hope to compete in existing markets. As a result, Japan and Germany invested more heavily in process R&D. They had no choice.

6   But what was a good American strategy thirty years ago—a focus on product technologies—is today a poor strategy. Levels of technical sophistication in Germany, Japan, and the United States are not very different, and reverse engineering—the art of developing a new manufacturing process for an existing product—has become a highly developed art form. The nature of the change can be seen in the economic history of three of the most successful products introduced into the mass consumer market in the past two decades—the video recorder, the fax, and the CD player. Americans invented the video recorder and the fax; Europeans (the Dutch) invented the CD player. But measured in terms of sales, employment, and profits, all three have become Japanese products.

7   The moral of the story is clear. Those who can make a product cheaper can take it away from the inventor. In today's world it does very little good to invent a new product if the inventor is not also the cheapest producer of that product. What necessity forced upon Germany and Japan thirty years ago happens to be the right long-run R&D strategy today.

8   This reality will eventually force the United States to alter its R&D spending patterns, but it also requires a much more difficult shift in human-resource allocation. Over time, the pay and promotion curve for American managers and engineers in production has fallen behind that in other parts of a firm. Since production isn't seen as the key to a firm's success, it has ceased to be the route to the top. Only 4 percent of American CEOs come from production; America's best and brightest, aware of this trend, have not gone into processes. Reversing this allocation of talent is now very difficult, since traditional salary scales and promotion practices will have to be disrupted.

9   In order to profit from technological advancement, firms need CEOs who understand process technologies. Large investments in revolutionary technologies will only be made quickly if the man or woman at the top appreciates those technologies. Yet American CEOs are much less likely to be technologically aware than those in either Japan or Europe. In those countries 70 percent of CEOs have technical backgrounds; in the United States 30 percent do. This difference in educational background is not unrelated

to the fact that in industry after industry, American firms have been slow to adopt revolutionary new-process technologies. One striking example: Twenty-five years ago the leaders of the American steel industry failed to comprehend the technology revolution that was under way and chose not to make the massive investments in oxygen furnaces and continuous casters being made elsewhere in the world. American steel companies have been playing an unsuccessful game of catch-up ever since.

The management of technology is usually seen as something of relevance to manufacturing but not to the rest of the economy. Here again, what was historically true is no longer true. In the twenty-first century there will be high-tech and low-tech products, but almost every product will be produced with high-tech processes. The automobile is a low-tech product; the robots that make it are high-tech. Gaining an edge in high-tech processes will be important in almost every industry—from fast food to textiles—and mastering process technologies will become central to the success of almost every firm.

The new information and telecommunication technologies that are being developed are also going to make most service industries into high-tech process industries. In retailing, those who survive will have the inventory-control systems that best reduce costs. Stores will be directly linked to suppliers to minimize the time lags between the customer's purchase of some particular item and the restocking of that item. Even now, American firms such as The Limited, a clothing retailer, are converting retailing into a high-tech competition. The Limited's inventory-control, telecommunication, and CAD-CAM (computer-aided design/computer-aided manufacturing) systems allow it to know what women are buying and to put precisely those clothes in their stores within twenty-eight days; their competitors take as long as six months. The result: They win, and their slower competitors lose.

While technology creates competitive advantage, seizing that advantage requires a work force skilled from top to bottom. When the route to success is inventing new products, the education of the smartest 25 percent of the labor force is critical: Someone in that top group can be counted on to invent the new products of tomorrow. But when success depends on being the cheapest and best producer of products, the education of the bottom 50 percent of the population becomes a priority. This is the part of the population that must operate those new processes. If the bottom 50 percent cannot learn what must be learned, new high-tech processes cannot be employed.

Information technologies need to be integrated into the entire production process, from initial designs through marketing to final sales and supporting services such as maintenance. To do this requires workers in the office, the factory, the retail store, and the repair service to have levels of education and skill that they have never had to have in the past.

14   If sustainable competitive advantage depends on work-force skills, American firms have a problem. Human-resource management is not traditionally seen as central to the competitive survival of the firm in the United States. Skill acquisition is considered an individual responsibility. Labor is simply another factor of production to be hired—rented at the lowest possible cost—much as one buys raw materials or equipment.

15   The lack of importance attached to human-resource management can be seen in the corporate pecking order. In an American firm the chief financial officer is almost always second in command. The post of head of human-resource management is usually a specialized job, off at the edge of the corporate hierarchy. The executive who holds it is never consulted on major strategic decisions and has no chance to move up to CEO. By way of contrast, in Japan the head of human-resource management is central—usually the second most important executive, after the CEO, in the firm's hierarchy.

16   While American firms often talk about the vast amounts spent on training their work forces, in fact they invest less in the skills of their employees than do either Japanese or German firms. The money they do invest is also more highly concentrated on professional and managerial employees. And the limited investments that are made in training workers are also much more narrowly focused on the specific skills necessary to do the next job rather than on the basic background skills that make it possible to absorb new technologies.

17   As a result, problems emerge when new breakthrough technologies arrive. If American workers, for example, take much longer to learn how to operate new flexible manufacturing stations than workers in Germany (as they do), the effective cost of those stations is lower in Germany than it is in the United States. More time is required before equipment is up and running at capacity, and the need for extensive retraining generates costs and creates bottlenecks that limit the speed with which new equipment can be employed. The result is a slower pace of technological change. And in the end the skills of the bottom half of the population affect the wages of the top half. If the bottom half can't effectively staff the processes that have to be operated, the management and professional jobs that go with these processes will disappear.

Reading and Analyzing

1. What is Thurow's claim? Where does he state it?
2. Who is Thurow's audience? What is his purpose in writing?
3. What is meant by *process technologies?* By *R&D money?*
4. What portion of R&D money do American firms devote to new products? To new processes? How does this contrast with Japanese and German companies?

5. Why did Japanese and German firms start spending more on new processes?
6. What is meant by *reverse engineering?*
7. What does the history of the development of the video recorder, the fax, and the CD player teach us? Who now makes the most money on these products?
8. To redirect U.S. research-and-development money to processes, what else will need to be changed in U.S. firms?
9. Why will high-tech processes be central to the successful economy of the next century?
10. For U.S. firms to use high-tech processes in a competitive fashion, what is required of American workers? Are American firms currently preparing workers for new technologies, in Thurow's view?

Responding to the Writer's Ideas

1. To test yourself on the distinction between products and processes, make a list of four high-tech products and four high-tech processes.
2. Had you thought about the distinction between products and processes before reading Thurow's article? Does the distinction, and the importance of the processes, make sense to you? Has Thurow convinced you of the need for U.S. firms to put more emphasis on high-tech processes? Why or why not?
3. Is it possible that Americans have stressed the making of products because the culture is, in general, product oriented? That is, are Americans more likely than those from other cultures to value things more than ideas, or products more than plans for making better or cheaper products? Explore these ideas.
4. Are you ready for a high-tech workplace? What are some of the things that those who are not ready need to do to become ready?
5. Whose responsibility is it to prepare a workforce for the high-tech jobs of the next century: the schools or the companies? Should high school (or college) graduates be ready for the workplace, or should the firms they join be required to provide the needed training, or is there some middle ground? What should be the responsibility of the schools and the companies?

The Three Jobs of the Future

Robert B. Reich

Economist Robert B. Reich, currently the Secretary of Labor, is also on the faculty of the Harvard University John F. Kennedy School of Government, a contributing editor of The New Republic, *and the author of many articles and books, including* The Next American Frontier *(1983),* Tales of a New America *(1987), and* The Work of Nations *(1991), from which the following excerpt is taken. In this section from* The Work of Nations, *Reich gives his analysis of the changing job market, in the light of a changing economy, and describes three categories of jobs based on what people do.*

1   The usual discussion about the future of the American economy focuses on topics like the competitiveness of General Motors, or of the American automobile industry, or, more broadly, of American manufacturing, or, more broadly still, of the American economy. But these categories are becoming irrelevant. They assume the continued existence of an American economy in which jobs associated with a particular firm, industry, or sector are somehow connected within the borders of the nation, so that American workers face a common fate; and a common enemy as well: The battlefields of world trade pit our corporations and our workers unambiguously against theirs.

2   No longer. In the emerging international economy, few American companies and American industries compete against foreign companies and industries—if by *American* we mean where the work is done and the value is added. Becoming more typical is the global web, perhaps headquartered in and receiving much of its financial capital from the United States, but with research, design, and production facilities spread over Japan, Europe, and North America; additional production facilities in Southeast Asia and Latin America; marketing and distribution centers on every continent; and lenders and investors in Taiwan, Japan, and West Germany as well as the United States. This ecumenical company competes with similarly ecumenical companies headquartered in other nations. Battle lines no longer correspond with national borders.

3   So, when an "American" company like General Motors shows healthy profits, this is good news for its strategic brokers in Detroit and its American investors. It is also good news for other GM executives world-

wide and for GM's global employees, subcontractors, and investors. But it is not necessarily good news for a lot of routine assembly-line workers in Detroit, because there are not likely to be many of them left in Detroit, or anywhere else in America. Nor is it necessarily good news for the few Americans who are still working on assembly lines in the United States, who increasingly receive their paychecks from corporations based in Tokyo or Bonn.

The point is that Americans are becoming part of an international labor   4
market, encompassing Asia, Africa, Latin America, Western Europe, and, increasingly, Eastern Europe and the Soviet Union. The competitiveness of Americans in this global market is coming to depend, not on the fortunes of any American corporation or on American industry, but on the functions that Americans perform—the value they add—within the global economy. Other nations are undergoing precisely the same transformation, some more slowly than the United States, but all participating in essentially the same transnational trend. Barriers to cross-border flows of knowledge, money, and tangible products are crumbling; groups of people in every nation are joining global webs. In a very few years, there will be virtually no way to distinguish one national economy from another except by the exchange rates of their currencies—and even this distinction may be on the wane.

Americans thus confront global competition ever more directly, un-   5
mediated by national institutions. As we discard vestigial notions of the competitiveness of American corporations, American industry, and the American economy, and recast them in terms of the competitiveness of the American work force, it becomes apparent that successes or failures will not be shared equally by all our citizens.

Some Americans, whose contributions to the global economy are   6
more highly valued in world markets, will succeed, while others, whose contributions are deemed far less valuable, fail. GM's American executives may become more competitive even as GM's American production workers become less so, because the functions performed by the former group are more highly valued in the world market than those of the latter. So when we speak of the "competitiveness" of Americans in general, we are talking only about how much the world is prepared to spend, *on average,* for services performed by Americans. Some Americans may command much higher rewards; others, far lower. No longer are Americans rising or falling together, as if in one large national boat. We are, increasingly, in different, smaller boats.

2

In order to see in greater detail what is happening to American jobs and to   7
understand why the economic fates of Americans are beginning to diverge, it is first necessary to view the work that Americans do in terms of categories that reflect their real competitive positions in the global economy.

8   Official data about American jobs are organized by categories that are not very helpful in this regard. The U.S. Bureau of the Census began inquiring about American jobs in 1820, and developed a systematic way of categorizing them in 1870. Beginning in 1943, the Census came up with a way of dividing these categories into different levels of "social-economic status," depending upon, among other things, the prestige and income associated with each job. In order to determine the appropriate groupings, the Census first divided all American jobs into either business class or working class—the same two overarching categories the Lynns had devised for their study of Middletown—and then divided each of these, in turn, into subcategories.[1] In 1950, the Census added the category of "service workers" and called the resulting scheme America's "Major Occupational Groups," which it has remained ever since. All subsequent surveys have been based on this same set of categories. Thus, even by 1990, in the eyes of the Census, you were either in a "managerial and professional specialty," in a "technical, sales, and administrative support" role, in a "service occupation," an "operator, fabricator, and laborer," or in a "transportation and material moving" occupation.

9   This set of classifications made sense when the economy was focused on high-volume, standardized production, in which almost every job fit into, or around, the core American corporation, and when status and income depended on one's ranking in the standard corporate bureaucracy. But these categories have little bearing upon the competitive positions of Americans worldwide, now that America's core corporations are transforming into finely spun global webs. Someone whose job falls officially into a "technical" or "sales" subcategory may, in fact, be among the best-paid and most influential people in such a web. To understand the real competitive positions of Americans in the global economy, it is necessary to devise new categories.[2]

10   Essentially, three broad categories of work are emerging, corresponding to the three different competitive positions in which Americans find themselves. The same three categories are taking shape in other nations. Call them *routine production services, in-person services,* and *symbolic-analytic services.*

---

[1] See Alba M. Edwards, *U.S. Census of Population, 1940: Comparative Occupation Statistics, 1870–1940* (Washington, D.C.: U.S. Government Printing Office, 1943).

[2] Because much of the information about the American work force must be gleaned from the old categories, however, the only way to discover who fits into which new category is to decompose the government's data into the smallest subcategories in which they are collected, then reorder the subcategories according to which new functional group they appear to belong in. For a similar methodology, see Steven A. Sass, "The U.S. Professional Sector: 1950 to 1988," *New England Economic Review,* January–February 1990, pp. 37–55.

Routine production services entail the kinds of repetitive tasks performed by the old foot soldiers of American capitalism in the high-volume enterprise. They are done over and over—one step in a sequence of steps for producing finished products tradeable in world commerce. Although often thought of as traditional blue-collar jobs, they also include routine supervisory jobs performed by low- and mid-level managers—foremen, line managers, clerical supervisors, and section chiefs—involving repetitive checks on subordinates' work and the enforcement of standard operating procedures.

Routine production services are found in many places within a modern economy apart from older, heavy industries (which, like elderly citizens, have been given the more delicate, and less terminal, appellation: "mature"). They are found even amid the glitter and glitz of high technology. Few tasks are more tedious and repetitive, for example, than stuffing computer circuit boards or devising routine coding for computer software programs.

Indeed, contrary to prophets of the "information age" who buoyantly predicted an abundance of high-paying jobs even for people with the most basic of skills, the sobering truth is that many information-processing jobs fit easily into this category. The foot soldiers of the information economy are hordes of data processors stationed in "back offices" at computer terminals linked to worldwide information banks. They routinely enter data into computers or take it out again—records of credit card purchases and payments, credit reports, checks that have cleared, customer accounts, customer correspondence, payroll, hospital billings, patient records, medical claims, court decisions, subscriber lists, personnel, library catalogues, and so forth. The "information revolution" may have rendered some of us more productive, but it has also produced huge piles of raw data which must be processed in much the same monotonous way that assembly-line workers and, before them, textile workers processed piles of other raw materials.

Routine producers typically work in the company of many other people who do the same thing, usually within large enclosed spaces. They are guided on the job by standard procedures and codified rules, and even their overseers are overseen, in turn, by people who routinely monitor—often with the aid of computers—how much they do and how accurately they do it. Their wages are based either on the amount of time they put in or on the amount of work they do.

Routine producers usually must be able to read and to perform simple computations. But their cardinal virtues are reliability, loyalty, and the capacity to take direction. Thus does a standard American education, based on the traditional premises of American education, normally suffice.

By 1990, routine production work comprised about one-quarter of the jobs performed by Americans, and the number was declining. Those who dealt with metal were mostly white and male; those who dealt with fabrics, circuit boards, or information were mostly black or Hispanic, and female; their supervisors, white males.[3]

17   *In-person services,* the second kind of work that Americans do, also entail simple and repetitive tasks. And like routine production services, the pay of in-person servers is a function of hours worked or amount of work performed; they are closely supervised (as are their supervisors), and they need not have acquired much education (at most, a high school diploma, or its equivalent, and some vocational training).

18   The big difference between in-person servers and routine producers is that *these* services must be provided person-to-person, and thus are not sold worldwide. (In-person servers might, of course, work for global corporations. Two examples: In 1988, Britain's Blue Arrow PLC acquired Manpower Inc., which provides custodial services throughout the United States. Meanwhile, Denmark's ISS-AS already employed over 16,000 Americans to clean office buildings in most major American cities.) In-person servers are in direct contact with the ultimate beneficiaries of their work; their immediate objects are specific customers rather than streams of metal, fabric, or data. In-person servers work alone or in small teams. Included in this category are retail sales workers, waiters and waitresses, hotel workers, janitors, cashiers, hospital attendants and orderlies, nursing-home aides, child-care workers, house cleaners, home health-care aides, taxi drivers, secretaries, hairdressers, auto mechanics, sellers of residential real estate, flight attendants, physical therapists, and—among the fastest-growing of all—security guards.

19   In-person servers are supposed to be as punctual, reliable, and tractable as routine production workers. But many in-person servers share one additional requirement: They must also have a pleasant demeanor. They must smile and exude confidence and good cheer, even when they feel morose. They must be courteous and helpful, even to the most obnoxious of patrons. Above all, they must make others feel happy and at ease. It should come as no surprise that, traditionally, most in-person servers have been women. The cultural stereotype of women as nurturers—as mommies—has opened countless in-person service jobs to them.[4]

20   By 1990, in-person services accounted for about 30 percent of the jobs performed by Americans, and their numbers were growing rapidly. For example, Beverly Enterprises, a single nursing-home chain operating

---

[3] For an illuminating discussion of routine jobs in a high-technology industry, see D. O'Connor, "Women Workers in the Changing International Division of Labor in Microelectronics," in L. Benerici and C. Stimpson (eds.), *Women, Households, and the Economy* (New Brunswick, N.J.: Rutgers University Press, 1987).

[4] On this point, see Arlie Russell Hochschild, *The Managed Heart: The Commercialization of Human Feeling* (Berkeley: University of California Press, 1983).

throughout the United States, employed about the same number of Americans as the entire Chrysler Corporation (115,174 and 116,250, respectively)—although most Americans were far more knowledgeable about the latter, including the opinions of its chairman. In the United States during the 1980s, well over 3 million *new* in-person service jobs were created in fast-food outlets, bars, and restaurants. This was more than the *total* number of routine production jobs still existing in America by the end of the decade in the automobile, steelmaking, and textile industries combined.[5]

Symbolic-analytic services, the third job category, include all the problem-solving, problem-identifying, and strategic-brokering activities. Like routine production services (but *unlike* in-person services), symbolic-analytic services can be traded worldwide and thus must compete with foreign providers even in the American market. But they do not enter world commerce as standardized things. Traded instead are the manipulations of symbols—data, words, oral and visual representations.

Included in this category are the problem-solving, -identifying, and brokering of many people who call themselves research scientists, design engineers, software engineers, civil engineers, biotechnology engineers, sound engineers, public relations executives, investment bankers, lawyers, real estate developers, and even a few creative accountants. Also included is much of the work done by management consultants, financial consultants, tax consultants, energy consultants, agricultural consultants, armaments consultants, architectural consultants, management information specialists, organization development specialists, strategic planners, corporate headhunters, and systems analysts. Also: advertising executives and marketing strategists, art directors, architects, cinematographers, film editors, production designers, publishers, writers and editors, journalists, musicians, television and film producers, and even university professors.

Symbolic analysts solve, identify, and broker problems by manipulating symbols. They simplify reality into abstract images that can be rearranged, juggled, experimented with, communicated to other specialists, and then, eventually, transformed back into reality. The manipulations are done with analytic tools, sharpened by experience. The tools may be mathematical algorithms, legal arguments, financial gimmicks, scientific principles, psychological insights about how to persuade or to amuse, systems of induction or deduction, or any other set of techniques for doing conceptual puzzles.

Some of these manipulations reveal how to more efficiently deploy resources or shift financial assets, or otherwise save time and energy. Other manipulations yield new inventions—technological marvels, innovative legal arguments, new advertising ploys for convincing people that certain

21

22

23

24

---

[5] U.S. Department of Commerce, Bureau of Labor Statistics, various issues.

amusements have become life necessities. Still other manipulations—of sounds, words, pictures—serve to entertain their recipients, or cause them to reflect more deeply on their lives or on the human condition. Others grab money from people too slow or naïve to protect themselves by manipulating in response.

25   Like routine producers, symbolic analysts rarely come into direct contact with the ultimate beneficiaries of their work. But other aspects of their work life are quite different from that experienced by routine producers. Symbolic analysts often have partners or associates rather than bosses or supervisors. Their incomes may vary from time to time, but are not directly related to how much time they put in or the quantity of work they put out. Income depends, rather, on the quality, originality, cleverness, and, occasionally, speed with which they solve, identify, or broker new problems. Their careers are not linear or hierarchical; they rarely proceed along well-defined paths to progressively higher levels of responsibility and income. In fact, symbolic analysts may take on vast responsibilities and command inordinate wealth at rather young ages. Correspondingly, they may lose authority and income if they are no longer able to innovate by building on their cumulative experience, even if they are quite senior.

26   Symbolic analysts often work alone or in small teams, which may be connected to larger organizations, including worldwide webs. Teamwork is often critical. Since neither problems nor solutions can be defined in advance, frequent and informal conversations help ensure that insights and discoveries are put to their best uses and subjected to quick, critical evaluation.[6]

27   When not conversing with their teammates, symbolic analysts sit before computer terminals—examining words and numbers, moving them, altering them, trying out new words and numbers, formulating and testing hypotheses, designing or strategizing. They also spend long hours in meetings or on the telephone, and even longer hours in jet planes and hotels—advising, making presentations, giving briefings, doing deals. Periodically, they issue reports, plans, designs, drafts, memoranda, layouts, renderings, scripts, or projections—which, in turn, precipitate more meetings to clarify what has been proposed and to get agreement on how it will be implemented, by whom, and for how much money. Final production is

[6]The physical environments in which symbolic analysts work are substantially different from those in which routine producers or in-person servers work. Symbolic analysts usually labor within spaces that are quiet and tastefully decorated. Soft lights, wall-to-wall carpeting, beige and puce colors are preferred. Such calm surroundings typically are encased within tall steel-and-glass buildings or within long, low, postmodernist structures carved into hillsides and encircled by expanses of well-manicured lawn.

often the easiest part. The bulk of the time and cost (and, thus, real value) comes in conceptualizing the problem, devising a solution, and planning its execution.

Most symbolic analysts have graduated from four-year colleges or   28
universities; many have graduate degrees as well. The vast majority are white males, but the proportion of white females is growing, and there is a small, but slowly increasing, number of blacks and Hispanics among them. All told, symbolic analysis currently accounts for no more than 20 percent of American jobs. The proportion of American workers who fit this category has increased substantially since the 1950s (by my calculation, no more than 8 percent of American workers could be classified as symbolic analysts at midcentury), but the pace slowed considerably in the 1980s— even though certain symbolic-analytic jobs, like law and investment banking, mushroomed.[7]

3

These three functional categories cover more than three out of four Ameri-   29
can jobs. Among the remainder are farmers, miners, and other extractors of natural resources, who together comprise less than 5 percent of American workers. The rest are mainly government employees (including public school teachers), employees in regulated industries (like utility workers), and government-financed workers (American engineers working on defense weapons systems and physicians working off Medicaid and Medicare), almost all of whom are also sheltered from global competition.

Some traditional job categories—managerial, secretarial, sales, and   30
so on—overlap with more than one of these functional categories. The traditional categories, it should be emphasized, date from an era in which most jobs were as standardized as the products they helped create. Such categories are no longer very helpful for determining what a person actually does on the job and how much that person is likely to earn for doing it. Only some of the people who are classified as "secretaries," for example, perform strictly routine production work, such as entering and retrieving data from computers. Other "secretaries" provide in-person services, like making appointments and fetching coffee. A third group of "secretaries" perform symbolic-analytic work closely allied to what their bosses do. To classify them all as "secretaries" glosses over their very different functions in the economy. Similarly, "sales" jobs can fall within any one of the three functional groups: some salespeople simply fill quotas and orders; others

---

[7] Sass's definition of "professional worker" overlaps significantly with my definition of symbolic analyst (although not all symbolic analysts are professionals, and not all professionals are symbolic analysts). Sass finds that by 1988 professional workers comprised 20 percent of the American labor force. See Sass, op. cit.

spend much of their time performing in-person services, like maintaining machinery; and some are sophisticated problem-identifiers no different from high-priced management consultants. "Computer programmers" (one of the more recent additions to the standard list of occupations) are as varied: They might be doing routine coding, in-person troubleshooting for particular clients, or translating complex functional specifications into software.

31   That a job category is officially classified "professional" or "managerial" likewise has little bearing upon the function its occupant actually performs in the world economy. Not all professionals, that is, are symbolic analysts. Some lawyers spend their entire working lives doing things that normal people would find unbearably monotonous—cranking out the same old wills, contracts, and divorces, over and over, with only the names changed. Some accountants do routine audits without the active involvement of their cerebral cortices. Some managers take no more responsibility than noting who shows up for work in the morning, making sure they stay put, and locking the place up at night. (I have even heard tell of university professors who deliver the same lectures for thirty years, long after their brains have atrophied, but I do not believe such stories.) None of these professionals is a symbolic analyst.

32   Nor are all symbolic analysts professionals. In the older, high-volume economy, a "professional" was one who had mastered a particular domain of knowledge. The knowledge existed in advance, ready to be mastered. It had been recorded in dusty tomes or codified in precise rules and formulae. Once the novitiate had dutifully absorbed the knowledge and had passed an examination attesting to its absorption, professional status was automatically conferred—usually through a ceremony of appropriately medieval pageantry and costume. The professional was then authorized to place a few extra letters after his or her name, mount a diploma on the office wall, join the professional association and attend its yearly tax-deductible meeting in Palm Springs, and pursue clients with a minimum of overt avarice.

33   But in the new economy—replete with unidentified problems, unknown solutions, and untried means of putting them together—mastery of old domains of knowledge isn't nearly enough to guarantee a good income. Nor, importantly, is it even necessary. Symbolic analysts often can draw upon established bodies of knowledge with the flick of a computer key. Facts, codes, formulae, and rules are easily accessible. What is much more valuable is the capacity to effectively and creatively *use* the knowledge. Possessing a professional credential is no guarantee of such capacity. Indeed, a professional education which has emphasized the rote acquisition of such knowledge over original thought may retard such capacity in later life.

4

How, then, do symbolic analysts describe what they do? With difficulty.   34
Because a symbolic analyst's status, influence, and income have little to do
with formal rank or title, the job may seem mysterious to people working
outside the enterprise web, who are unfamiliar with the symbolic analyst's
actual function within it. And because symbolic analysis involves processes
of thought and communication, rather than tangible production, the content of the job may be difficult to convey simply. In answering the question
"What did you do today, Mommy (or Daddy)?" it is not always instructive, or particularly edifying, to say that one spent three hours on the telephone, four hours in meetings, and the remainder of the time gazing at a
computer screen trying to work out a puzzle. . . .

Years ago, fortunate and ambitious young people ascended career   35
ladders with comfortable predictability. If they entered a core corporation,
they began as, say, a second assistant vice president for marketing. After
five years or so they rose to the rank of first assistant vice president, and
thence onward and upward. Had they joined a law firm, consulting group,
or investment bank, they would have started as an associate, after five to
eight years ascended to junior partner, and thence to senior partner, managing partner, and finally heaven.

None of these predictable steps necessitated original thought. Indeed,   36
a particularly creative or critical imagination might even be hazardous to
career development, especially if it elicited questions of a subversive sort,
like "Aren't we working on the wrong problem?" or "Why are we doing
this?" or, most dangerous of all, "Why does this organization exist?" The
safest career path was the surest career path, and the surest path was sufficiently well worn by previous travelers so that it could not be missed.

Of course, there still exist organizational backwaters in which career   37
advancement is sequential and predictable. But fewer fortunate and ambitious young people dive into them or even enter upon careers marked by
well-worn paths. They dare not. In the emerging global economy, even the
most impressive of positions in the most prestigious of organizations is
vulnerable to worldwide competition if it entails easily replicated routines.
The only true competitive advantage lies in skill in solving, identifying, and
brokering new problems.

Reading and Analyzing

1. What changes in the way companies and industries work are altering
   the way we discuss the future of the American economy?
2. How must American competitiveness now be understood?
3. Why are the Census Bureau's job categories no longer meaningful, in
   Reich's view?

4. What three categories of work does Reich put forward? Explain each category: where the people work, how they are paid, what kinds of things they do.
5. What did the term *professional* used to mean? How does the professional fit into Reich's categories?
6. What are the key marks of the work of a symbolic analyst?
7. How have the emergence of a global web and the work of symbolic analysts altered the process of moving ahead in one's career?
8. What is the primary purpose of this section of Reich's book? What is the implied conclusion we are to draw from Reich's analysis?

Responding to the Writer's Ideas

1. Is Reich's analysis of job types new to you? Does it make sense? Is his approach to job descriptions more helpful than the old categories? Explain.
2. Think of one traditional job category you are familiar with. Are there some people in this job who fit into each one of Reich's categories? If so, describe the three kinds of work that can be found in this job category, much as Reich describes secretaries whose actual duties will place them in one of the three categories.
3. Reich is making much the same point that Lester Thurow makes: Americans must understand that they are part of a global economy, and they must adjust their thinking about "what is good for America" to correspond to the new economic realities. To illustrate the point, explain why it may be "good for America" for Americans to buy a great many Hondas.
4. Based on the author's descriptions of the kinds of tasks and kinds of traits needed for each of his three job categories, which type of work do you think you are most suited for? How does your answer fit in with your career plans? That is, if you were thinking of majoring in business, can you continue with that plan and imagine a type of work in business that fits the Reich category that would suit you? Be prepared to explain how you could pursue the traditional major of your choice and find job duties that would suit you.
5. Reich places government employees and schoolteachers in a separate category outside his three main groupings. Take one of these groups and analyze the work they do. Do some people in the group belong in each of Reich's categories? Explain.
6. Both Lester Thurow and Robert Reich warn American workers of hard times ahead in a global economy unless workers are properly educated and trained. What knowledge, skills, and personality traits seem to be most important for success in the high-tech global web the two authors describe?

❖

Can a New "Army" Save
Our Cities?

Arthur Ashe

A graduate of UCLA, a former tennis champion, and a Davis Cup captain, Arthur Ashe (1943–1993) was a contributor to the Washington Post *sports section, a sports commentator on ABC and HBO, a lecturer, and an author.* A Hard Road to Glory *(1988) is Ashe's history of African-American athletes, and* Off the Court *(1981) is his autobiography. In the following article, printed in the* Post *shortly after the Los Angeles riots in the spring of 1992, Ashe offers a plan for redirecting the lives of inner-city youth.*

Once again, seething, residual anger has burst forth in an American   1
city. And the riots that overtook Los Angeles 10 days ago were a reminder
of what knowledgeable observers have been saying for a quarter-century:
America will continue paying a high price in civil and ethnic unrest unless
the nation commits itself to programs that help the urban poor lead productive and respectable lives.

Once again, a proven program is worth pondering: national service.   2

Somewhat akin to the military training that generations of American   3
males received in the armed forces, a 1990s version would prepare thousands of unemployable and undereducated young adults for quality lives in
our increasingly global and technology-driven economy. National service
opportunities would be available to any who needed it and, make no mistake, the problems are now so structural, so intractable, that any solution
will require massive federal intervention.

In his much-quoted book, "The Truly Disadvantaged," sociologist   4
William Julius Wilson wrote that "only a major program of economic reform" will prevent the riot-prone urban underclass from being permanently locked out of American economic life. Today, we simply have no choice.
The enemy within and among our separate ethnic selves is as daunting as
any foreign foe.

Families rent apart by welfare dependency, job discrimination and in-   5
tense feelings of alienation have produced minority teenagers with very little self-discipline and little faith that good grades and the American work
ethic will pay off. A military-like environment for them with practical domestic objectives could produce startling results.

417

6   Military service has been the most successful career training program we've ever known, and American children born in the years since the all-volunteer Army was instituted make up a large proportion of this targeted group. But this opportunity may disappear forever if too many of our military bases are summarily closed and converted or sold to the private sector. The facilities, manpower, traditions, and capacity are already in place.

7   Don't dismantle it; rechannel it.

8   Discipline is a cornerstone of any responsible citizen's life. I was taught it by my father, who was a policeman. Many of the rioters have never had any at all. As an athlete and former Army officer, I know that discipline can be learned. More importantly, it *must* be learned or it doesn't take hold.

9   A precedent for this approach was the Civilian Conservation Corps that worked so well during the Great Depression. My father enlisted in the CCC as a young man with an elementary school education and he learned invaluable skills that served him well throughout his life. The key was that a job was waiting for him when he finished. The certainty of that first entry-level position is essential if severely alienated young minority men and women are to keep the faith.

10   We all know these are difficult times for the public sector, but here's a chance to add energetic and able manpower to America's workforce. They could be prepared for the world of work or college—an offer similar to that made to returning GIs after World War II. It would be a chance for 16- to 21-year-olds to live among other cultures, religions, races and in different geographical areas. And these young people could be taught to rally around common goals and friendships that evolve out of pride in one's squad, platoon, company, battalion—or commander.

11   We saw such images during the Persian Gulf War and during the NCAA Final Four basketball games. In military life and competitive sports, this camaraderie doesn't just happen; it is taught and learned in an atmosphere of discipline and earned mutual respect for each other's capabilities.

12   Ethnic hatred, like that portrayed in Los Angeles, is also taught and learned.

13   A national service program would also help overcome two damaging perceptions held by America's disaffected youth: that society just doesn't care about minority youngsters and that one's personal best efforts will not be rewarded in our discriminatory job market. Harvard professor Robert Reich has opined that urban social ills are so pervasive that the upper 20 percent of Americans—that "fortunate fifth" as he calls them—have decided quietly to "secede" from the bottom four-fifths, and the lowest fifth in particular. We cannot countenance such estrangement on a permanent basis. And what better way to answer skeptics from any group than by certifying the technical skills of graduates from a national service training program?

Now, we must act decisively to forestall future urban unrest. Republicans must put aside their aversion to funding programs aimed at certain cultural groups. Democrats must forget labels and nomenclature and recognize that a geographically isolated subgroup of Americans—their children in particular—need systematic and substantive assistance for at least another 20 years.   14

The ethnic taproots of minority Americans are deeply buried in a soil of faith and fealty to traditional values. With its accent on discipline, teamwork, conflict resolution, personal responsibility and marketable skills development, national service can provide both the training and that vital first job that will reconnect these Americans to the rest of us. Let's do it now before the fire next time.   15

Reading and Analyzing

1. What is the context in which Ashe writes, the problem that he will address?
2. What is Ashe's proposal?
3. Who is the targeted group for the proposal? What are their problems? What will national service do for this group, in Ashe's view?
4. What two programs will national service be similar to? What similarity does Ashe find in military service and competitive sports?
5. How will national service be financed? How does Ashe justify the cost?
6. Ashe refers to Robert Reich's idea that the wealthiest, that is, the top fifth, of Americans "have decided quietly to'secede'" from the rest. Explain Reich's point. How does the idea contribute to Ashe's argument?
7. Who is Ashe's audience? Whom does he need to sell his proposal to?

Responding to the Writer's Ideas

1. Do you know people who are or have been in the armed services? If so, have they expressed views similar to Ashe's, namely, that they learned discipline, self-esteem, and skills for a job? If not, what were their views?
2. If young people in the underclass need what the military has been able to provide most, if not all, of those who have participated, does it seem logical to you to try a similar program for the disadvantaged? If not, why not?
3. Ashe argues for economic aid to the disadvantaged very much as Galbraith does (see pp. 381–86), namely, that it is in everyone's best

interest to provide for the poor. In what specific ways does the entire society benefit when the urban underclass is trained and able to get jobs? Do these benefits justify, in your view, the costs of a national service program? If not, why not?

4. Do you have suggestions for improving the economic potential of America's bottom fifth, keeping in mind that two-thirds of the poor are white and many do not live in inner-city ghettos? What policies and programs would you push for along with or instead of Ashe's national service plan?

❖

Occupational Apartheid

Stephen Steinberg

A professor in the department of urban studies at Queens College, Stephen Steinberg (b. 1940) is a research sociologist and author of books and articles on prejudice and ethnic issues, including The Ethnic Myth: Race, Ethnicity and Class in America *(1981). In "Occupational Apartheid" (* Nation, *December 9, 1991), Steinberg reviews the history of labor patterns in the United States to explain how African Americans have been denied job opportunities and to make the case for continuing affirmative-action policies.*

In the United States the essence of racial oppression is a racial division of labor, a system of occupational segregation that relegates most blacks to the least desirable jobs or that excludes them altogether from legitimate job markets. 1

The racial division of labor has its origins in slavery, when over half a million Africans were imported to provide cheap labor for the South's evolving plantation economy. During the century after slavery ended, the United States had the perfect opportunity to integrate blacks into the North's burgeoning industries. *Northern* racism prevented this outcome. Instead, the North relied exclusively on European immigrants, most of whom, like blacks, came from peasant origins and had no previous industrial experience. In effect, a system of labor deployment evolved whereby blacks provided the necessary labor for Southern agriculture and white immigrants provided the necessary labor for Northern industry. 2

This regional and racial division of labor cast the mold for generations more of racial inequality and conflict. Not until the mechanization of agriculture in the decades after World War II were blacks finally liberated from their historic role as agricultural laborers in the South's feudal economy. Thus it was that in one century white planters went all the way to Africa to import black laborers, and in another century the descendants of those planters gave the descendants of those African slaves one-way bus tickets to Chicago and New York. 3

When blacks finally arrived in the North, they encountered a far less favorable structure of opportunity. Not only were these labor markets staked out by immigrant groups, who engaged in a combination of nepotism and unabashed racism, but the occupational structures themselves 4

421

were changing. William Julius Wilson has argued that deindustrialization is the principal factor in the genesis of the black underclass. However, Wilson does not explain why blacks, who were never heavily represented in the industrial sector in the first place, were not absorbed into the expanding service sector. He neglects two other factors: (1) racism, which still pervades the occupational world, especially in the service sector, where the personal traits of workers play a key role in employment decisions, and (2) immigration policy, which has encouraged the influx of more than 12 million people since 1965. Thus, at the same time that we are exporting jobs, we are importing workers—at an even higher rate! In New York City, for example, there were 493,000 post-1965 immigrants employed in 1980, accounting for 17 percent of the total work force.

5   Nor is it the case that immigrants take only jobs that native workers spurn. Large numbers are found in such coveted job sectors as construction, hotels and restaurants, health care, and building management. It is difficult to escape the conclusion that recent immigration has had a detrimental impact on the job prospects of African-Americans and other native workers, not to speak of already settled immigrant workers. Here was another missed opportunity to upgrade the skills of marginal workers and lower racist barriers throughout the workplace.

6   Thus, despite the much-touted progress of the black middle class, the racial division of labor is very much intact. By some estimates, as many as half of black men of working age lack steady employment. Countless others, men and women alike, work at poverty wages, or have no job security or health benefits and are only a paycheck away from poverty. This job crisis is the single most important factor behind the familiar tangle of problems that beset black communities.

7   Tragically, this nation does not have the political will to confront its racist legacy, even if that means nothing more than providing jobs at decent wages for the descendants of slaves who continue to be relegated to the fringes of the job market. Instead, a mythology has been constructed that, in ways reminiscent of slavery itself, alleges that blacks are inefficient and unproductive workers, deficient in the work habits and moral qualities that have delivered other groups from poverty. We are used to hearing this from Nathan Glazer, Thomas Sowell, Shelby Steele and others on the right, but recently even voices on the left have succumbed to gratuitous clucking about "Nihilism in Black America," to use the title of Cornel West's recent disquisition in *Dissent* (Spring 1991). What is the failure to deliver jobs to yet another generation of black youth if not nihilism on a grand scale? Jim Sleeper preaches hard work and moral discipline in New York, a city where 101,000 people recently took the civil service exam for 2,000 expected openings in the Sanitation Department. Still others on the left have declared that the problems confronting black America have less to do with race than with class, a strange message for the millions of

twelfth-generation Americans still condemned to live out their lives in impoverished ghettos. By reifying "class" and shifting the focus away from "race," these would-be progressives unwittingly undermine the antiracist movement. They absolve the nation of the moral and political responsibility for making restitution for its 300-year crime, and play into the hands of those on the right who have already succeeded in removing race from the national agenda.

The pivotal issue today is affirmative action. The significance of affirmative action is that it amounts to a frontal assault on the racial division of labor. Even those who support the liberation struggle often fail to appreciate the profound impact that affirmative action has had in breaking the caste system in the occupational world. Before affirmative action, the black middle class—the one that E. Franklin Frazier lampooned in *Black Bourgeoisie*—consisted of a few businessmen and professionals anchored in the ghetto economy. It was affirmative action that opened up access to *mainstream* occupations—not just the professions and corporations but also the blue-collar and government jobs that are the staple of black employment. Despite its limitations, affirmative action has produced the first significant departure from the occupational caste system that has prevailed since slavery.

The current attack on affirmative action is reminiscent of the retrenchment at the end of the nineteenth century. America did not return to slavery, but it turned the clock back on progress made during Reconstruction. Today, it is inconceivable that there could be a return to official segregation. However, the impending evisceration of affirmative action will reinforce current patterns of occupational segregation and deepen the racial crisis. Are the American people condemned to wait until the smoldering resentments within the black community again reach an explosive climax before our political leaders take decisive action against the enduring system of occupational apartheid? What will it take to convince whites that it is in their interest, and the interest of the nation, to eliminate the vestiges of slavery?

Reading and Analyzing

1. Explain the "regional and racial division of labor" described by Steinberg.
2. When did blacks start their northward migration looking for employment? What did they find?
3. How does Wilson explain employment problems in the North for blacks? Why does Steinberg consider this explanation to be incorrect?
4. What two factors better explain employment problems for African Americans?

5. Explain the details of the black "job crisis" as Steinberg summarizes it.

6. Instead of responding positively to racism in the workplace, what have we done? How do we explain away the problems of black unemployment?

7. What has been the impact of affirmative action on "occupational segregation"? Why, in Steinberg's view, should Americans remain strongly committed to affirmative action?

8. What is Steinberg's thesis, the claim of his argument? Where does he state his thesis? What does the author gain from his organizational strategy?

Responding to the Writer's Ideas

1. Look again at the publication date of Steinberg's article. What words in his final paragraph have become prophetic? Does the turn of events give more weight to his argument?

2. Steinberg refers to the "current attack on affirmative action" without providing much information. Who is attacking affirmative action? From whom do you hear complaints?

3. Does the author's historical review and current economic analysis provide convincing evidence of occupational segregation? If not, why not?

4. Steinberg concludes with an argument that parallels Galbraith's (see pp. 381–86) and Ashe's (see pp. 417–19) argument that it is in everyone's interest to eliminate occupational racism. Does the fact that these three writers make the same point have an impact on your thinking? Are you prepared to join these three different writers on this issue? Why or why not?

5. If you agree that the country must do something to help the unemployed, underemployed, and minorities in particular, what would you advise as a series of programs? Suppose you were an adviser to the president. Would you recommend strong federal support for affirmative action? Would you recommend Ashe's idea of a national service? What else, or what instead of these programs, would you advise the president to support?

❖

Fires, Factories, Football

George Weimer

A graduate of Case Western Reserve University, George Weimer (b.
1941) has worked in journalism and public relations. He is currently
executive editor of Industry Week *and writes a regular column in that*
journal. In the following article, one of his columns, published on
November 18, 1991, Weimer challenges the concept of affirmative
action.

Want to start a real revolution in America, one that could put 1776   1
to shame? Want to see the country united as never before? All you have
to do to get this mass revolt going is to change one small aspect of television.

To start this second American Revolution, we need only apply the   2
hiring rules we already live with in industry (and that our safety forces
must conform to as well) to Sunday football. Do it to baseball, basketball,
and golf, too.

Make it a requirement that the Browns and the Bengals, the 49ers   3
and the Celtics, must reflect the racial, sexual, religious, ethnic, and age
groups of their audiences. What's it called? Why, politically correct football, of course!

Think about it. So many of this group. So many of that. Otherwise,   4
no play! Clearly we'd have to add quite a few positions to basketball, and
golf matches would become especially long.

Do all of the above, and I guarantee the biggest mass revolt in the   5
history of the U.S. of A. Such a move would empty the bars and living
rooms of the country. Not a politician in the land would be safe.

People in this country respect excellence and admire competition pas-   6
sionately in at least one area: sports and particularly professional sports.

At any rate, none of these favorite American pastimes reflects any
issue in hiring at all except excellence and appropriateness.

Can't you see it? Congress says all of the above are now to move to-   7
ward an affirmative-action mode in all hiring, with all of the many kinds
of Americans represented. Failure to do so will mean big trouble for owners and managers and directors and conductors.

No more best man or woman. No more best running back or best   8
pitcher. First check the colors, the ethnicity, the group they represent. Priority One is to make sure the team reflects its audience's history—not
whether it's the best human assembly possible.

425

9   Ridiculous? Yes. Nonsense? Yes. Silly even? Absolutely. Yet we are doing exactly this to organizations far, far more important to America than our football teams. We do it to our safety forces and to business in general and that most important player in business—manufacturing.

10   We have placed the enormous burden of redressing the perceived wrongs of the past upon the producers and protectors of the present. We are diverting industry in particular from its job, which is, like any athletic team, to compete in the world.

11   In attempting to eliminate bias in hiring, are we not moving the country to mediocrity or worse? If we do not consider capability and appropriateness first (isn't that the proper bias?) then what happens to excellence in performance? The answer would be as clear on the football field as it is in the factory world.

12   Yes, we need to consider justice in all aspects of life. Yes, we need to feel compassion for those who for millions of different reasons may have a more difficult time making it in life. But, is that the issue here? Who will benefit from this approach to hiring?

13   Is the country served well by its free-enterprise sports industry? Hard to say no. Isn't it the wish of the people to live in safety from crime and fire? Obviously. Is the country served well by its free-enterprise manufacturing industry? So far.

14   But if industry is going to have to keep its eye on everything but talent and appropriateness in its searches for people, then the manufacturing Super Bowl is going to get pretty depressing for America.

15   What we need in industry and on our streets is what we already have in football when it comes to hiring. Namely, a search for the best person available for the job. Wasn't it Knute Rockne who lo these many years ago said, "Whatever your background was I don't care. If you can play football, I want you on the team." Should any less be asked by business?

16   Meanwhile, consider this next time you lock your doors and sit down in front of the tube. When the bureaucrats and social engineers are done with manufacturing and the men and women in blue, where do they go next? So get ready for some pretty lousy football—or for one helluva revolution!

Reading and Analyzing

1. What requirement does Weimer think will start another revolution in America? Why will it generate a revolution?
2. What is the point of Weimer's opening? Does he expect to see professional sports subject to affirmative action?
3. What type of argument is Weimer using? What is the function of his references to sports?

4. Who, in Weimer's view, is a "most important player in business"? Is his view here surprising?

5. What groups, in addition to industry, does Weimer include in his coverage?

6. The author writes of the "perceived wrongs of the past." What is suggested by his word choice in this passage?

7. What is the author's purpose in paragraph 12? What does he seek to accomplish?

8. What is the claim of the author's argument?

9. What are Weimer's reasons in support of his claim?

10. What is the warrant, the underlying assumption, in this argument?

Responding to the Writer's Ideas

1. Weimer writes that we should have compassion "for those who for millions of different reasons may have a more difficult time making it in life." Is this a fair statement with regard to the women and minorities targeted for affirmative-action benefits? Are we talking about *millions* of reasons that *may* have caused difficulties, or are we talking about *one* reason that *has* caused difficulties? What does Weimer gain by suggesting that there are many reasons for people's economic troubles? How would Galbraith (see pp. 381–86) describe this kind of manoeuver?

2. Weimer's audience is people involved in industry. Why does he also include police officers and firefighters as groups that ought not be subjected to affirmative action? Does this strike you as an odd collection of workers to group together?

3. Evaluate Weimer's analogy. Are the points of comparison valid for industry? How can this argument be challenged?

4. Where do you stand on continuing affirmative-action policies? If you oppose affirmative action, what reasons do you have to support your position?

WRITING SUGGESTIONS

1. You are a member of the President's Council of Economic Advisors. What one proposal would you support to aid the poor, the bottom fifth of the population? In an essay present and argue for your proposal.

2. Several writers in this chapter have argued that part of the problem in dealing with the poor is the lack of will among the better-off to address the problems of poverty. If you agree with this view, prepare an argument, addressed to college students, that seeks to convince them that they must be concerned about the problems of poverty. If you draw on other writers, such as those in this chapter, be sure to acknowledge their ideas or facts in your essay (for example, "as John Kenneth Galbraith observes, . . .).

3. In an essay argue for or against the claim that conflict over dividing the economic pie is the major cause of "human misbehavior." Think carefully about the kinds of evidence you need, and then organize your evidence effectively.

4. In an essay argue for or against the claim that faith in an ever-increasing prosperity is our national religion. Think carefully about the kinds of evidence you need, and then organize your evidence effectively.

5. What education and skills do young people need so that they will be ready for jobs in a global economy in the twenty-first century? Reflect on what you have read in this chapter and what you know about the world of work, and then develop an argument in support of your views on this issue.

6. Make an argument for or against a national service program. If you draw on Arthur Ashe's article, be sure to acknowledge the material taken from him. If you oppose the program, make your argument a refutation of Ashe's article.

7. Make an argument for or against continuing affirmative action in the workplace. To prepare to write on this topic, you may want to read Andrew Hacker's article "The Myths of Racial Division" in Chapter 8 in addition to the relevant articles in this chapter. Again, if you draw on your reading, be sure to acknowledge the authors from whom you have borrowed material.

CHAPTER 10

CARING FOR THE PLANET AND ITS VARIED INHABITANTS

"There was once a town in the heart of America where all life seemed to live in harmony with its surroundings." These are the words with which Rachel Carson began "A Fable for Tomorrow," the opening to her influential 1962 book *Silent Spring*. Her fable continues: "Then a strange blight crept over the area" and created "a spring without voices." Carson's silent landscape, destroyed by the poison of pesticides, gave the first resounding cry of the environmental movement. Since then countless scientists and poets, citizen activists and political candidates have raised their voices in a chorus of concern that government, industry, and the ordinary citizen all become more committed to preserving, protecting, and living in harmony with the Earth and all its inhabitants.

We may appropriately ask, thirty years later, if our springs are silent or if an increased awareness has led to a cleaner, greener, healthier world. Some would say that we are better off today, that we live longer in a less polluted land that we share with many species we have brought back from near extinction. Gregg Easterbrook, in "Green Cassandras," complains about the doom-and-gloom voices of environmentalists who, in Easterbrook's view, address problems in panicked overstatement, most notably at the 1992 Earth Summit in Rio. Easterbrook's is a minority voice, but one whose argument and evidence must be evaluated along with the many voices calling attention to a host of environmental problems.

It may be true that some environmentalists express their views with strong emotion, but there are at least a couple of reasons for presenting a powerful message. Activists believe, and rightly so, that they must sell readers on the seriousness of environmental problems if their solutions, however brilliant, will ever be initiated. How many people care enough about the slaughter of the rhino to demand that governments ban the sale of items made from their horns? Environmentalists know that the issues that get addressed, the problems that get funded, are often those that get media attention. Cleaning up the Chesapeake Bay is a hard sell in western Maryland unless television specials portray the loss to state revenues from failed boating and fishing businesses on a polluted bay. You will find that while the writers in this chapter do not succumb to excessive emotional appeals, they do present evidence to underscore the seriousness of the problems they examine. Suzanne Winckler, for example, in "Stopgap Measures," provides detailed evidence of the limitations of our attempts to save species to convince readers that gap analysis should be tried. And Mark Pagel and Ruth Mace bring their specialized knowledge to bear on the issue of maintaining a ban on ivory as the best strategy for protecting the African elephant from extinction.

Environmentalists also write movingly about problems because they have a particularly strong attachment to the Earth and all living things, and they may well believe that spreading their feelings is important for protecting the Earth. Most discussions today emphasize the interrelatedness of living organisms and the causal connections among population, poverty, and destruction. British botanist Chillean Prance begins the chapter with a quietly moving description of the richness of rainforests in "Rainforested Regions of Latin America." Frances Moore Lappé and Rachel Schurman, also concerned about conserving the rainforests, take a different approach in "Taking Population Seriously: Power and Fertility": Poor people lacking power over their lives have many children for security and cannot worry about conservation. We cannot, these authors believe, expect to protect the rainforested regions important to all of us when these areas are home to many poor people.

If the causes of environmental problems are complex, the solutions must be global, according to most writers. Polluted air doesn't stop at state borders, polluted rivers carry garbage to the oceans, and greenhouse gases spread global warming. John Gribben, in "Hothouse Earth: What to Do?" argues that countries must work together to slow down the process of global warming, with the industrialized North helping Third World countries to progress without pouring excessive amounts of carbon dioxide into the skies. Vice President Albert Gore, Jr., focusing primarily on ozone depletion, also stresses that global problems require global solutions. Is one such solution energy that is "green" (friendly to the environment), that is, nuclear energy? Gribben says no, but Dixy Lee Ray argues that the nuclear alternative to burning fossil fuels is the solution to balancing energy needs with protecting the world from global warming.

Although some species have been lost in the last thirty years, our springs are not yet silent. But neither are those concerned with conserving our Earth and bringing us into balance with nature.

❖

Rainforested Regions of Latin America

Chillean T. Prance

Born in Suffolk, England, Chillean Prance (b. 1937) obtained his B.A. in botany in 1960 from Keble College, Oxford, and his Ph.D. in 1963, also from Oxford University. He has worked with the New York Botanical Garden and has spent over eight years in field work in Amazonian Brazil. Currently Prance is director of the Royal Botanic Gardens in Kew, outside London. He is also the author of more than 200 articles and nine books, some scholarly on plant systematics, others, directed to a general audience, on conservation. In the following essay, drawn from Lessons of the Rainforest, *a collection of articles by different authors published in 1990, Prance provides both a wealth of information on tropical rainforests in the Americas and a clear stand on protecting these areas.*

1   The tropical rainforests of the Americas are located in five main regions: Mexico and Central America (Mesoamerica), Pacific Coastal Colombia and Ecuador, the Caribbean Islands, the Guianas and Amazonia, and the Atlantic Coastal region of Brazil. The forests in these five areas are similar to each other in the many aspects that define rainforests, but numerous regional differences also exist due to history, topography, geology, and climate. For example, some common rainforest plant species occur throughout the region. Other species are restricted to one, or even a small part of one, of the five regions.

2   Central American rainforests are located from Mexico south to Panama in the wetter lowland areas, which tend to occur more on the Atlantic side of the various countries. Rainforest is the natural cover for part of each of the Central American republics; however, it has been greatly reduced, and completely eliminated from El Salvador and much of Honduras. The rainforest of the Osa peninsula in Costa Rica, now protected in a forest reserve, is particularly important since it contains the northernmost distributions of many South American rainforest species. The southernmost country of this region, Panama, is still well endowed with rainforest, especially in the province of Darién.

3   Caribbean rainforest occurs, or formerly occurred, scattered throughout this archipelago in areas where rainfall is high enough to sustain it.

This is mainly in areas where the presence of mountains increases rainfall, such as the northern part of eastern Cuba, eastern Hispaniola in the area of Sierra de Bahoruco, northeastern Puerto Rico around the Luquillo mountains, and small patches in some of the Lesser Antilles.

Pacific Coastal South America, commonly known as the Chocó, extends from the Panama border south to northern Ecuador, and it all lies to the west of the Andes. It is the wettest region in the world and an important center of rainforest endemism—that is, it contains many species that are found nowhere else. In terms of overall rainforest diversity, this narrow strip of forest, which runs between the western slopes of the Andes and the Pacific Ocean, is one of the most important in the world. But the Ecuadorean part is almost entirely destroyed, apart from the tiny Río Palenque reserve; and the Colombian part is severely threatened by logging.

Amazonia and the Guianas contain the largest contiguous rainforest in the world. It includes part of the territory of eight countries: Bolivia, Brazil, Colombia, French Guiana, Guyana, Peru, Suriname, and Venezuela; and covers an area of approximately seven million square kilometers. The region with the highest known rainforest diversity occurs in Amazonian Peru at Yanomono, with 300 species of trees recorded from a single hectare.[1]

Although rainforest is the predominant forest cover in the region, it is by no means the only type of vegetation. The region is covered by a mosaic of rainforest, floodplain forest, savanna, and white sand formations; and there are great variations within the Amazonian rainforests themselves due to local variations in climate, soil, and topography.

Atlantic Coastal Brazil is a narrow rainforest belt, 120 to 160 kilometers wide, that formerly stretched along the coast of Brazil from Rio Grande do Norte south to Rio Grande do Sul; only about 4 percent remains. This area has a high degree of plant endemism, which makes the forest destruction all the more tragic. For example, 53.5 percent of the woody forest species are endemic to that region.[2] These forests also harbor many interesting and important species of animals such as the woolly spider monkey, the lion tamarins, and an endemic sloth—each of which is almost extinct.

Biogeographical History

Many popular and scientific publications have referred to the stability of Latin American rainforests over time. But recent evidence indicates that this region has been anything but stable over the last hundred thousand years. There have been many fluctuations in vegetation cover; areas where the natural vegetation seems always to have been rainforest have not necessarily always been forested. Changes in vegetation in tropical regions have corresponded to the natural cycles of glaciation in the temperate regions. With each ice age a cooler and drier climate in the tropics has favored savanna and other, more arid vegetation types. The rainforests were pushed into smaller regions where the climate was still humid enough to support them. Each region that remained forested through these climatic transitions is called a refugium.

9   These refugia are thought to have been the evolutionary nurseries of the rainforests. In them, species became isolated and concentrated; and faster-breeding organisms quickly evolved into new species—one cause of the incredible diversity of life in contemporary rainforests. Refugia theory, the idea that patches of forest become isolated and grow back together over time, also helps to explain why certain species are found only in specific areas and nowhere else.[3] Because of their diversity, these refugia are now an important focus for conservation efforts.

10   By studying changes in forest cover we can learn much about the make-up and evolution of the rainforest. In the past, the forest was reduced in area by natural causes and recuperated naturally to again cover large areas as climate changed. Although the rainforest does express recuperative power when given the right conditions, the current spread of human-induced deforestation is much more rapid than was gradual climate-induced change. Because of this heightened pace of deforestation, many more species are becoming extinct. Information about rainforest recuperation and coalescence is vital for contemporary management and conservation. This information helps to unravel the complexities of species diversity and gives us tools for preventing extinction, revealing the ecological patterns of deforestation, increasing the benefits of forests that must be used, and regenerating forests on once-forested lands. All this knowledge can help us to minimize forest destruction.

The Forest

11   The Latin American rainforest is an awesome place. Its tall trees produce a dense overhead canopy that keeps all but a tiny fraction of sunlight from reaching the forest floor. This semidarkness is filled with thousands of different species of trees, many with strangely shaped trunks, no two alike. Any visitor to the Latin American rainforest has been spellbound by the haunting sound of the howler monkey echoing for kilometers over the forest. How many times have I been attacked by the spider monkey as it either tries to throw tree branches or urinate on the human invader of its territory—presenting a fascinating experience for a naturalist but an easy target for the hunter.

12   These are the forests that house the capybara, the world's largest rodent; the tapir; and the jaguar. My favorite of all animals is the giant otter. How privileged I feel to have been in a canoe on the Uraricoera River in Roraima territory, Brazil, and on the Rio Negro of Mato Grosso, surrounded by a group of these curious beasts popping out of the water and barking right beside the canoe. Again, alas, an easy target for the marks-

man. This animal has provided me with more pleasure than any other I have met, yet it is now confined to only a few of the least disturbed areas of forest where hunters have not eliminated it.

The plants are equally intriguing, varying from enormous buttressed trees—such as the giant angelim in the legume family, whose trunk frequently attains three meters in diameter—to small flowers growing inconspicuously among the litter layer of the forest floor. Bizarrely contorted vines are abundant, and varied in shape and form—and fascinating also for their diverse chemical potency, which has been put to many uses by the Indians. It is from vines that curare, the arrow poison and the muscle-relaxing drug, is extracted; *timbo,* used for poisoning fishes, contains the insecticide rotenone and comes from the *Lonchocarpus* vine; and the stems of the caapi vine are the basis for the hallucinogenic beverage ayahuasca. | 13

The animals and plants of the Latin American rainforests are legion. This diversity is linked together in a large web of food chains, defense mechanisms against predators, pollination and dispersal interactions, and links between fungi and tree roots that are essential for the rapid recycling of nutrients. The study of one organism in the forest soon leads to the others with which it interacts. | 14

For example, I have studied many aspects of the *castanha-degalinha,* a common tree in the forests of Brazil around Manaus. The flowers open at night and are born on long peduncles that hang below the branches. This makes them easily accessible to the nocturnal bats that visit the flowers to feed on the abundance of nectar that they produce. The bats brush against the mass of pollen-filled stamens and are dusted with pollen. As they fly from tree to tree each night, they cause pollination by transporting the pollen from one tree to another. After pollination the fruit gradually matures. The egg-shaped fruit falls to the forest floor, where it is collected up by agoutis. These rodents scatter-hoard fruit and nuts the way a squirrel does in the temperate region. Some of their caches are forgotten, and so dispersal of the seed from the mother tree takes place. On the underside of the leaves and the outside of the sepals are small nectaries that secrete sugar. Ants drink this nectar and when other insects land on the leaves or flower-buds they are driven off by the aggressive ants that are fed by the plants. In return for nectar the tree has an army of small protectors. The wood of the *castanha-de-galinha* is very hard. This is because it is full of small silica or sand grains. This serves as good protection against the hordes of wood-boring insects that are to be found in the tropical rainforest. This single species of tree links together a species of bat, the agouti, and ant into the web of interactions that make up the Amazon rainforest. | 15

Indigenous Populations

No account of the Latin American rainforests would be complete without reference to the indigenous peoples who were originally to be | 16 found in all the major regions of rainforest, varying from Maya people in Mexico and Guatemala, through the Kuna of the isthmus of Panama, to the numerous groups of forest Indians in Brazil. The surprising and most significant fact in the history of these people is that, although in pre-Columbian times there was an extremely large human population, *the rainforests were largely intact.* Early accounts of exploration in Amazonia describe large quantities of what are now rare animals, such as turtles, manatees, piraracu fish, and jaguar; yet they also describe large groups of Indians such as the Omagua and the Tapajós, which would indicate a population density that far exceeded later populations.[4]

17   Since the sighting of the first Carib Indians by Columbus, the native populations of the Americas have had their rights severely abused, whether in the North or the South. What we have left today are the scattered remnants of some 500 distinct rainforest groups. Many of the original ethnic groups have disappeared along with an enormous body of cultural information about living in the rainforest. Recently anthropologists, ethnologists, biologists, and ethnobotanists have been conducting many studies on the remaining Indians. These have concentrated more on their ecology, agriculture, and management practices. The further we study these peoples, the more we begin to respect their wisdom and their knowledge of the forest.

18   A study of quantitative ethnobotany of four groups of Indians showed the extent to which the Indians use rainforest trees. The Chácobo of Bolivia have uses for 78.7 percent of the tree species in a sample hectare, or 92 percent of the individual trees. The Panare Indians of Venezuela use 48.6 percent of the species on a sample hectare. The Ka'apor Indians of Brazil use 78.6 percent, and the Tembé 61.3 percent.[5] The difference between the Indians and contemporary settlers in the Amazon is that the Indians live with and use the forest diversity, whereas the settler wants to cut the forest down and replace it with monoculture. Indigenous systems of cultivation make use of diversity rather than monoculture and rely more on woody perennials than on short-lived herbaceous crops. Both these management practices are far more suitable for the fragile soils of Amazonia than are monocultures of grass for cattle pasture or of *Gmelina* for timber plantations.

Historical Settlement

19   The destruction of the Latin American rainforests began with the arrival of Europeans in the New World. Early destruction focused more on the indigenous inhabitants than on the forest, and so the great Aztec and Inca civilizations soon fell to the conquistadors. The Caribs, who knew so much about the Caribbean forest, were some of the first people to be eliminated because of the utility of their island territory for such crops as sugar cane.

Each rainforest region has its own history of genocide and slavery as   20
the thirst for land, gold, and territory became the dominant motive of
countries and individuals. For example, in Amazonia, after the initial battle for territory between the Indians and the Spanish and Portuguese colo-
nizers, the worst atrocities were committed in the wake of the discovery of
the rubber vulcanization process.

Some of the most lucrative Amazonian rainforest species were   21
brought near to extinction in those early days, long before any "red
books" of threatened and endangered species were known. In the rainforests of eastern Brazil, a tree called pau-brasil yielded a purple dye that
became a much-sought-after item of commerce for European fashion. This
tree also gave its name to what is now the largest country in Latin America. Pau-brasil is scarcely known in the wild today because it was mined
out of the forests for its dye and for wood used in constructing musical instruments. The story is the same for several other species.

When the rubber boom ended with the establishment of lower-cost   22
rubber tree plantations in tropical Asia, the destruction caused by the
hunger for rubber continued on Henry Ford's million-acre plantation,
Fordlandia in the Rio Tapajós region of Brazil. This was the first of many
attempts to introduce large-scale monoculture plantations into Amazonia.
Needless to say, like many plantations, it was a failure. Fordlandia failed
because of two ecological factors: the use of a floodplain forest species on
the upland terra firma, and a leaf rust fungus disease that attacked the
leaves. Like most species, the rubber tree is adapted to a certain niche
within the complexity of habitats in Amazonia, and becomes vulnerable
when moved to the habitat of the plantation.

In Central America, especially in Guatemala, Honduras, and   23
Nicaragua, the early part of the century saw large areas of species-rich
rainforest turned into banana plantations. In the banana republics created
by the United Fruit Company the land tenure policies are responsible for
much of the tension in regional politics today, which in turn leads to further destruction as landless peasants are pushed into the rainforest.

Recent Settlement

Although the early settlement of the tropical American rainforests   24
had a devastating effect on indigenous cultures and on the vast body of
their ecological wisdom, it did not have an extensive effect on the forest
cover of the region. The last two decades have changed the whole picture
and led us to the current and well-justified concern for the Latin American
rainforests.

The causes of the current wave of destruction are many but they have   25
been associated largely with two factors: increased population growth and
therefore increased pressure on the land, and readily available international capital from the developed countries in the form of loans and invest-

ments. These two factors have been closely linked in some of the vast settlement programs, such as Polonoroeste, in Rondônia, funded by international capital. A few of the most important examples of forest destruction, especially in Amazonia, will illustrate the seriousness of the crisis.

26   Amazonian forest destruction really began in earnest in 1971, with the commencement of the Transamazon Highway in Brazil. President Médici visited the drought-stricken northwest of Brazil in March 1971 and was appalled by what he saw. His solution to the plight of the northwesterners was a highway linking that region to the rest of Amazonia. This was accompanied by an ambitious colonization plan to resettle the drought-stricken people in the lush, always humid Amazon rainforest. By July 1971, legislation for the road was passed by Congress, and by October the bulldozers were rolling. The first settlers soon began to migrate into the region, and farms, towns, and villages sprung up along the eastern part of the highway near Altamira. The settlers were given land, a house, and agricultural advice—most of it to do with planting upland rice. The first rice harvests fared poorly and showed what ecologists had long said: that this was an inappropriate use of the soil. The news got back to the northwest that Amazonia was not the paradise it was expected to be, and the migration slowed down.

27   By the time the next president, Ernesto Geisel, assumed power, it was obvious that the trans-Amazon settlement program was not a success. He blamed this on the quality of the settlers and their lack of capital, and thus the small size of the farms. So his policy was to encourage large investors to open up huge tracts of land for cattle ranches by introducing favorable tax incentives and the availability of loans through a rural credit program. Companies could invest profits from the south of Brazil in ranches rather than pay income tax. The late 1970's was a time of vast destruction of forests as industries from the south of Brazil and abroad all invested in cattle. Today there is much abandoned cattle pasture and much poor-quality pasture supporting less than one cow per hectare. The investors have lost little because profits have been made on tax incentives and speculation in land prices. However, as of 1983 the tax incentives and loans are no longer available for new cattle projects because of the failure of this scheme.[6]

28   In 1968 billionaire Daniel Ludwig thought that he had the answer to a predicted shortage of the world supply of paper. His solution was a reputedly fast-growing tree in the teak family called *Gmelina arborea*. From the Brazilian government he bought a tract of land on the Jarí River that was almost the size of Connecticut, and began to plant *gmelina*. The trees did not grow as fast as expected, because by clearing the forest with bulldozers he removed all the nutrients, which were in the forest, not in the soil. He replaced bulldozers with workgangs to fell trees with axes and plant *gmelina* among the debris. This worked in some areas but not in oth-

ers. It was then found that the Jari property was on two major soil types, clay and sand. The *gmelina* grew well in clay soils but not in sand, so he had to import the slower growing Caribbean pine for sandy soils. In 1984 he finally sold the project to a consortium of Brazilian companies at a financial loss of $600 million. This is another example of vast deforestation for a poorly researched and economically unsound project.[7] Finally, in October 1988, President Sarney, in his first environmental speech, promised to end all tax incentives in Amazonia and take many other measures to protect the forest.

However, hydroelectric dams are another major threat to the Amazon rainforest still occupying the planning boards. The giant Tucurí Dam on the Tocantins River is now functioning and providing electric power for the city of Belém, the Carajás iron mine, aluminum refineries, and the new railroad to São Luís. That dam was probably a regional necessity. On the other hand, the Balbina Dam north of Manaus is a complete ecological disaster that should never have been built. It floods a larger area of rainforest than Tucurí and has the potential to produce only one-tenth of the energy. Balbina is flooding the territory of the Waimari-Atroari Indians, a center of rainforest species endemism. The lake depth in many places is only three meters. Balbina was partially funded by the World Bank, and Brazil has a whole series of yet other dams planned for Amazonia that it hopes to fund with international loans. This is a case for concerted, logical activism by all people concerned about rainforest destruction.

The state of Rondônia, in the west of Brazilian Amazonia where it borders Bolivia, is the site of another World Bank–financed fiasco called Polonoroeste. The bank funded the paving of a road across Rondônia and the construction of many lateral feeder roads. As a result, the forests of Rondônia have disappeared at an alarming rate. In August 1987 a satellite passed over a small band in the south of Rondônia, north of Mato Grosso and south of Pará states. The images clearly show a huge smoke cloud over the region and 6,803 individual sources of fire. These were 6,803 fires large enough to be seen burning an estimated 12,000 square kilometers of forest.[8] Recently it was noted that there was a marked reduction in the ozone layer of the atmosphere shortly after those fires. It is the first time that rainforest destruction has been connected to ozone depletion, a loss that affects every citizen on this planet.

There now remains only about 3.5 percent of the rainforest of Atlantic Coastal Brazil, due to devastation by farming, colonization, and especially by sugar cane and cocoa plantations to satisfy the world demand for chocolate. Because the area was home to an extremely high percentage of endemic species, many extinctions have already occurred in eastern Brazil.

The Panama Canal is threatened by rainforest destruction in two ways. Deforestation on the isthmus has reduced rainfall so that there is not enough water to replace what is lost as ships pass through the canal. Also, deforestation has caused soil erosion that is silting the canal so that the deeper-draft ships will have difficulty passing through.

33   This catalog of Latin American rainforest destruction could be vastly extended, but the above is surely enough to demonstrate the gravity of the problem of rainforest destruction from Mexico to Brazil. Population growth, poor distribution of land, debt, and greed have led to unprecedented levels of destruction. It is a crisis that demands our response.

The Lessons

34   Rather than dwell on the unfortunate past, let us ask what lessons can be learned from the world's most species-diverse forest and its terrifying history of the wholesale destruction of life. The most important lesson is the interdependence of all living creatures. The global ecosystem is now threatened because of the extent of deforestation in Latin America. The impact of the fires is now so great as to affect the ozone layer of the upper atmosphere and world climate patterns. Regional systems of interaction are being broken down. Trees are no longer being pollinated properly because their animal pollinators are being eliminated or replaced by introduced organisms. One example is the Africanized honeybee, which has outcompeted many of the natural pollinators from South America. To maintain a future for the human race, the other creatures upon which we depend must be preserved and defended.

35   Our future depends on diversity. Latin American rainforests, with up to 300 species of trees per hectare, epitomize diversity. Many of these species may yield useful drugs and other products of economic potential, but we must not look on the forests merely as sources of future economic gain. They are sustainers of life on Earth, the organisms that regulate the balance of gases in our atmosphere to maintain human and all other forms of life.

36   The history of the Latin American rainforest demonstrates the failures of our current economic systems. Human greed, excessively luxurious lifestyles, and fixation on short-term profit have been the moving forces in our society, and this has been accompanied by a loss of spiritual values. Nature is rebelling and telling us that we cannot continue this process indefinitely. We would do well to go back and look at the concepts of those who have lived closer to Nature. American Indian culture, for instance, is based on consideration for the needs of the seventh unborn generation. How differently we would manage the rainforests of Latin America if we were thinking of our great-great-great-great-great-grandchildren rather than short-term personal profit or the reaction of current shareholders. Our society would do well to regain the art of sharing, and of caring for the sacredness of all forms of life.

37   The lesson from the Latin American rainforest is loud and clear: one

organism has dominated, to the exclusion and at the expense of all others upon which it depends. This could bring about the destruction of all organisms—of life on Earth—through the breakdown of interdependent chains of interactions, through the excessive use of natural resources, and through the inability to control population growth. The study of the wonders of rainforest biology helps us to gain a renewed respect for all life, which must in turn lead to reforms that will ensure the sustainability of life on our planet. If we have learned anything from the rainforest, it is that we are responsible for using this knowledge to rescue our world from impending disaster.

Notes

1. A. Gentry, "Tree Species Richness of Upper Amazonian Forests," *Proc. Natl. Acad. U.S.A.* 85 (1988), pp. 156–59.

2. Scott A. Mori, B. M. Boom, and G. T. Prance, "Distribution Patterns and Conservation of Eastern Brazilian Coastal Forest Tree Species," *Britainia* 33 (1981), pp. 233–45.

3. G. T. Prance, ed., *Biological Diversification in the Tropics* (New York: Columbia University Press, 1982), p. 714; T. C. Whitmore and G. T. Prance, eds., *Biogeography and Quarternary History in Tropical America. Oxford Monographs on Biogeography* 3 (Oxford: Clarendon Press, 1987); J. Haffer, "Speciation in Amazonian Forest Birds," *Science* 165 (1969), pp. 131–37; K. S. Brown, Jr., "Geographical Patterns of Evolution in Neotropical Lepidoptera. Systematics and Derivation of Known and New Heliconiini (Nymphalidae: Nymphalinae)," *Jour. Ent. B* 44 (1976), pp. 201–42; C. Schubart, "Climatic Changes During the Last Glacial Maximum in Northern South America and the Caribbean: A Review," *Interciencia* 13 (1988), pp. 128–37.

4. William Denevan, ed., *The Native Population of the Americas in 1492* (Madison: University of Wisconsin Press, 1976).

5. W. Balée, "Análise Preliminar de Inventário Florestal e a Etnobotânico Ka'apor (Maranhão)," *Bol. Mus. Paraense Emílio Goeldi* 2:2 (1986), pp. 141–67, and "A Etnobotânica Quantitativa dos Indios Tembe (Rio Gurupi, Pará)," *Bol. Mus. Par. Emílio Goeldi, Sér. Bot.* 3:1(1987), pp. 29–50; B. M. Boom, "Useful Plants of the Panare Indians of the Venezuelan Guayana," *Adv. Econ. Bot.* 8 (in press), and "Ethnobotany of the Chácobo Indians, Beni, Bolivia," *Advances in Economic Botany 5* (New York Botanical Garden, 1987); and G. T. Prance et al., "Quantitative Ethnobotany and the Case for Conservation in Amazonia," *Conservation Biology* 1 (1987), pp. 296–310.

6. J. O. Browder, "The Social Costs of Rain Forest Destruction: A Critique and Economic Analysis of the 'Hamburger Debate,'" *Interciencia* 13 (1988), pp. 115–20; S. B. Hecht, "Environment, Development and Politics: Capital Accumulation and the Livestock Sector in Eastern Amazônia," *World Development* 13 (1985), pp. 663–84; D. R. Shane, *Hoofprints on the Forest: Cattle Ranching and the Destruction of Latin America's Tropical Forests* (Philadelphia: Institute for the Study of Human Values, 1986).

7. P. M. Fearnside, "Jari at Age 19: Lessons for Brazil's Silviculture Plans at Carajás," *Interciencia* 13 (1988), pp. 12–24.

8. J. P. Malingreau and C. J. Tucker, "Large-Scale Deforestation in the Southeastern Amazon Basin of Brasil," *Ambio* 17 (1988), pp. 49–55.

Reading and Analyzing

1. Locate the rainforested areas of the Americas on a map to get a visual sense of the areas Prance describes. Your library will have a topographical atlas that shows the areas of rainforest. Which is the wettest of the rainforest regions? What other topography will be found in the region containing Amazonia?
2. What is meant by the term *edemism*?
3. What is a *refugium*? Explain refugia theory. Why are the refugia so important?
4. Why is deforestation a problem for the rainforests?
5. What is Prance's purpose in paragraphs 11 through 15? How does this section contribute to his argument?
6. How do the Indians native to the Amazon rainforest use the forest? What are their management strategies? Why are these strategies superior to those of contemporary settlers?
7. Summarize the history of the rainforests of the Americas. How was the area first damaged by colonialism? How has it more recently been damaged? What have been the causes of destruction?
8. What is the most important lesson of the rainforest? What do we need to learn from native Americans, or relearn?
9. What is Prance's thesis? How does he want to change our understanding, our values, our actions, with regard to the rainforest?

Responding to the Writer's Ideas

1. Has Prance given you new information about the rainforests, their locations in the Americas, their history, their current problems? If so, what are the most important facts that you have learned?
2. Has Prance's discussion changed your thinking about the rainforest? If so, in what ways?
3. Analyze the author's argumentative approach. How has he sought to build an argument?
4. Is the author's approach an effective argument for conservation? Is so, why? If not, why not?

❖

Hothouse Earth: What to Do

John Gribben

Born in 1946 in Maidstone, Kent, in England, John Gribben holds two degrees from Sussex University and a Ph.D. in astrophysics from Cambridge University. A respected scientist, Gribben has written several science fiction novels and numerous articles and books on topics that include meteorology, geology, and astronomy. Among his books are Our Changing Universe *(1976),* Spacewarps *(1983),* Genesis: The Origins of Man and the Universe *(1981), and* Hothouse Earth: The Greenhouse Effect and Gaia *(1990), from which the following excerpt is taken. In the following pages, Gribben offers specific suggestions for coping with the greenhouse effect.*

Nobody can predict exactly what will happen to the climate in the twenty-first century, nor how society will respond to the growing awareness of the threat. But change, in both climate and society, is inevitable. It is too late for even the most draconian measures to prevent a further rise in global mean temperatures of at least 1° C, and part of any long-term planning for the future should take account of this. One response to the growing strength of the greenhouse effect is adaptation—which might mean anything from an individual decision to stop taking summer holidays in places like Spain or Greece to a farming community's decision to shift from wheat to maize, or a government's plan to build new reservoirs. But if the increase in the greenhouse effect cannot be stopped, it can certainly be slowed. The second response to the perception of the reality of the greenhouse threat should be action at all levels, from individuals to international agreements, to keep the pace of change down to something that we might have a chance of adapting to.

Neither you nor I can wave a magic wand and ensure that appropriate action to minimize the build-up of greenhouse gases is taken—in the real world, decisions on the construction of power stations and transport networks, for example, are made on political grounds, taking into consideration a variety of factors, including the politicians' wish to be re-elected. But I can tell you what sort of decisions ought to be taken if the greenhouse threat is, as I believe it to be, of overriding importance. If enough people feel the same way, and make their views known, then the politi-

1

2

443

cians' wish for re-election may itself ensure that they take the greenhouse threat seriously.

3   One of the most interesting features of any discussion of policies to minimize the global rise in temperatures is that in almost every case these are policies that are desirable on other grounds as well. The problem of CFCs provides a good example. These gases entered the arena of political debate because of the damage they are doing to the ozone layer of the stratosphere. But they are also powerfully effective greenhouse gases, making a major contribution to the shift of the Earth into a hothouse state. Agreements aimed at limiting damage to the ozone layer so far talk only of reducing the rate of release of CFCs to about half of the 1988 level, but most scientists who have studied the problem are now calling for a complete ban on the use of these gases, except in a very limited number of 'essential' applications, notably medical. Such a total (*and immediate*) ban on CFC emissions would not solve the greenhouse problem, but could, on its own, give us a breathing space of perhaps ten years before the date when the effective carbon dioxide concentration of the atmosphere reaches twice the pre-industrial level. Ten years is not long, but in the situation we now face every little helps. There are those, indeed, who think that this is more important than limiting the damage to the ozone layer. Jim Lovelock, who invented the CFC sniffer and was the first person to use it to trace the spread of CFCs around the globe, once said, in a paper in *Nature* in 1973, that the presence of these gases in the atmosphere 'constitutes no conceivable hazard'. At an international meeting on ozone depletion held in London at the end of November, 1988, he ruefully reminded the audience of this remark, and said that he had since revised his opinion. He now sides, he said, with those who feel that an immediate and total ban on all emissions of CFCs is necessary—because of the implications for the greenhouse effect. Of course, whatever your motive for pressing for such controls on CFC emissions, there will be an additional benefit in the form of a reduction in the damage being caused to the ozone shield. There is, though, another side to the coin. Those who are pressing for CFC controls on the grounds of the damage being done to the ozone layer must take care to ensure that any substitutes developed for these CFCs are not only 'ozone friendly' but are also 'climate friendly' and do not contribute to the greenhouse effect.

4   Controlling CFC emissions is easy, in the sense that we can imagine a world without the convenience that these gases provide. But we cannot imagine our society adapting to a world without power stations, steel mills, high speed transport and intensive agriculture. That is why the temperatures in the global hothouse will continue to rise, and why even slowing the rate of that rise will be difficult and painful—but not as painful, ultimately, as the consequences of letting the temperature rise proceed unchecked.

Burn Less

The most direct way to reduce emissions of greenhouse gases (after a ban on   5
CFCs) is to burn less fossil fuel—more realistically, we should aim to minimize the increase in the rate at which such fuels are being consumed. There
is no way in which we can stop adding carbon dioxide to the atmosphere,
but many studies have shown that it is possible to reduce the rate at which
the carbon dioxide concentration is building up, even while maintaining
economic growth and coping with an increasing human population (but remember that carbon dioxide contributes only half of the greenhouse problem). Ninety per cent of the commercial production of energy in the world
today is from fossil fuel, but a great deal of the energy that is produced is
wasted—a hangover from the days of cheap energy. Just how wasteful we
used to be is reflected in the way the growth in world energy consumption
declined from a rate of nearly five per cent a year in the early 1970s to two
per cent a year now, following oil price rises and economic recession. Part
of the reason for this decline is that some consumers use energy more efficiently simply because it costs more; on that basis, energy is still far too
cheap, and a suitable tax might focus the minds of individuals and industries even more firmly on how to save energy (with the added bonus that
revenues from the tax could be used for research into ways to alleviate the

*Past changes in the concentration of carbon dioxide in the atmosphere (based on a
slightly low estimate of the pre-industrial concentration of 260 ppm), and two
projections into the future. (Source: Will Kellogg, NCAR)*

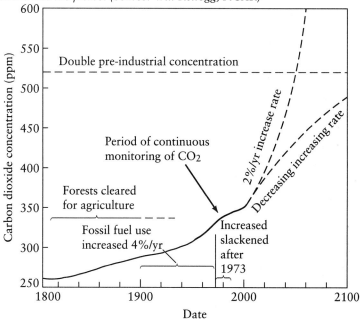

impact of the greenhouse effect). Many of the appropriate measures to save energy are familiar from the long debate about the way we ought to live. Better insulation in houses and other buildings (it doesn't cost any more to build a properly insulated house than to build one which leaks heat); cars that use fuel more efficiently (prototypes already exist that will run for ninety-eight miles on a gallon of fuel, although most cars in the US manage less than a quarter of this figure); improving the efficiency with which energy gets from the power station to the consumer (in the UK, more than sixty per cent of the energy available in coal, oil or gas literally goes up in smoke and never reaches the user).[1]

6   Some of these changes require action at government level, but even individuals can make their own contribution. All those things we were encouraged to do the last time an 'energy crisis' hit—sharing cars, riding bicycles, turning the central heating down a couple of degrees and wearing a sweater—are still relevant. And there is new technology available to make you feel less guilty about using electricity. Compact fluorescent light bulbs that provide the same light as conventional incandescent bulbs but use only a quarter of the electricity are in the shops (some shops) today. At present, these bulbs cost more than conventional bulbs, but last more than five times as long. Replacing a single seventy-five-watt incandescent bulb by a fluorescent bulb that uses only eighteen watts of electricity but is just as bright eliminates the burning of 180 kilogrammes of coal over the lifetime of the bulb, and saves the consumer money in the form of a smaller electricity bill. If electricity prices were higher, the incentive to use these bulbs would be greater, their cost would come down as more were sold, and the value of the new bulbs to the household would be greater still—a beneficial example of positive feedback.

7   Even before this invention became available, a study carried out by researchers at Harvard University at the end of the 1970s concluded that the energy consumption of the US could be reduced by thirty to forty per cent with 'virtually no penalty for the way Americans live'.[2] Advocates of the 'green' movement would like to see humankind living more in tune with the environment and with other species of life on Earth for many rea-

---

[1] This isn't due to incompetence, but a result of the basic physics of the way heat is generated and converted into electricity. One way to get more useful energy out of the same amount of coal or oil is to build small power stations close to the communities they serve, so that the heat that would otherwise be wasted as so much hot air can be piped to the buildings people live and work in to heat radiators or water. Such systems are known as combined heat and power, or CHP, installations, and we need a lot more of them, instead of huge, remote electricity generating stations, to help slow the growth of the greenhouse effect.

[2] R. Stobaugh and D. Yergin, editors, *Energy Future* (Random House, New York, 1979).

sons, but the problem of the greenhouse effect is certainly one of them. Studies such as Amory Lovins's classic *Soft Energy Paths* show how virtually all of the energy requirements of the developed world could be met in the mid-twenty-first century by a combination of environment friendly systems, such as solar energy, wind and wave power, geothermal heat and controlled use of biomass, including wood. Such an extreme view of what some see as an ideal world would involve dramatic changes in society, and has little or no prospect of becoming reality. Nevertheless, many of the possibilities discussed by the idealists could be incorporated into society to some extent without major disruption; and, once again, every little helps.

Overall, in the industrialized world the present consumption of energy per head could be cut in half by the year 2050 with the aid of better insulation in buildings, refrigerators (already designed) that use thirty per cent less electricity, cars that use a third as much fuel as the present generation, and so on and so on. Look at it this way. Demand for energy is scarcely growing at all in the rich world, so we need only make our use of energy more efficient by one per cent each year to cut demand in half, in the developed world, by the middle of the next century. Just which technologies or economies are used to achieve this scarcely matters as long as the job gets done.   8

But what of the Third World? It is all very well arguing for more efficient use of energy in countries such as the US and the members of the European Community, where a little belt-tightening wouldn't cause much pain. But if the poor regions of the world are to achieve a satisfactory standard of living they will need to increase their use of energy. The best any optimist might hope for is that this increase might be countered by improved efficiency in the rich world, leaving annual emissions of carbon dioxide constant at present levels, steadily strengthening the greenhouse effect; but this is not very likely. In one sense, though, the problem faced by developing countries is more straightforward than that faced by the developed world. Rich countries have to undo some of the mistakes made in the past. But countries that lack an infrastructure of existing inefficient energy production and use are well placed to build efficient systems from the start—provided they have the money to pay for them. Once again, the correct response to the greenhouse problem strikes at the heart of another major global issue. Third World countries are poor, in large measure, because they are servicing crippling interest charges on their debts to the rich north. This is immoral and inexcusable on many grounds; wiping out those interest charges, or writing off the debts themselves, could go a long way towards providing the funds for investment in appropriate energy technologies. Indeed, provision of such energy policies could be a condition of the agreement under which the debts were eased. Rich countries might feel, at first sight, that easing the financial burden on the Third World might damage their own economies; but apart from the moral issue   9 this might well be cheaper, in the long run, than waiting for increasing temperatures and rising sea levels to do their own damage to the economies of countries such as the US and Britain.

10   Not that there need be much philanthropy in any of this. Investing in more efficient sources of energy is an attractive prospect for even the most ardent free-market capitalist. One study of energy usage in Brazil, for example, showed that investment in more efficient refrigerators, street lighting and lighting in buildings, at a cost of about ten billion dollars, would save forty-four billion dollars between 1985 and 2000. The investment has not been made, but the example is still valid. At an even more fundamental level, one of the major problems in the poorest parts of the world is obtaining wood for cooking fires. As populations have increased, forests have been stripped, contributing to the greenhouse effect and causing erosion of valuable land. Closed cooking stoves require only half the fuel of traditional open fires, and it has been estimated that it would cost about one billion dollars a year to provide efficient stoves to all rural households in the Third World. This is a tiny proportion of the Gross Global Product, but would provide benefits to millions of people and to the environment.[3]

Change the Mix

11   Still on the subject of fossil fuel, in the short term we could gain some breathing space by changing the mixture of fuels being burnt. Coal produces more carbon dioxide than oil, and oil much more than natural gas, if each type of fuel is used to provide the same amount of energy. Synthetic fuel oils derived from coal—substitutes for oil and gasolene—produce even more carbon dioxide than coal itself, which is the main reason for the opposition among environmentalists to the US 'synfuels' programme of the 1970s. Switching the source of energy for power stations from coal to natural gas would be a help in slowing the growth of the greenhouse effect. Unfortunately, sixty-five per cent of total energy production already comes from oil and gas, and these two sources only account for sixteen per cent and ten per cent, respectively, of known fossil fuel reserves. Even in the medium term, let alone the long term, their contribution to the fuel mix is likely to diminish, not increase. But even though the scope for changing the mix of fuels in use today is limited and short term, providing an option for the next two or three decades only, that is no reason to ignore it. In fact, natural gas associated with oil fields is still very often thrown away—either allowed to escape into the atmosphere, or 'flared off', burning at the drilling site itself and contributing to the greenhouse effect without ever being used to generate useful energy. It simply is not cost effective for all

---

[3] Both these examples are taken from the Friends of the Earth report *The Heat Trap,* written by J. W. Karas and P. M. Kelly (FoE, London, 1988).

of the gas to be husbanded and transported to places that need energy. Once again, the way to make this cost-effective might be through a system of differential taxation, which hits hardest at fuels that produce more carbon dioxide (as against the present policy, in many parts of the world, of *subsidizing* coal-based energy generation in order to make it competitive with oil). This, however, would exacerbate another potential problem: it is possible to argue that reserves of oil should be saved for other uses, not burnt as fuel. Oil provides the raw material for a huge chemical industry producing, among other things, the plastics that have transformed our lives over the past half century. To take just one example: without plastics to use as insulators our entire global communications network would break down (TV sets built in the 1930s used *paper* to insulate their wiring; under modern safety regulations, such lethal objects would never be allowed in the home). Our descendants may well curse the wastrels of the twentieth century who squandered such a valuable resource as oil by burning it.

So once again, alternative sources of energy come into the picture.   12
They can be made to work, but it won't necessarily be easy. One criticism of systems such as solar energy or wave power schemes is that they produce energy all right, but out at sea or in the desert, not in the places where it is needed. There is an answer to this criticism, but it still needs careful study. Electricity produced from wave power, for example, could be used to crack water into its component parts, hydrogen and oxygen. The hydrogen could be stored under pressure, transported around the world and used as a fuel, while the oxygen is released into the air. When the hydrogen burns, it combines with oxygen to make water again. It sounds very attractive, clean and simple. Indeed, the Soviet Union is developing an aircraft which uses liquid hydrogen as its fuel; in West Germany several car manufacturers, including BMW, have plans to develop internal combustion engines that run on hydrogen. The note of caution comes in because we cannot yet be sure that emitting large quantities of water vapour into the atmosphere will be a thoroughly good thing. With any luck, the water from car exhausts would condense and run away back into the sea pretty quickly. But what if the world's fleet of aircraft switched to hydrogen fuel? Remember that water vapour is itself a greenhouse gas, so it might make the world warmer. On the other hand, emitting large amounts of water high in the atmosphere might encourage clouds to form, reflecting away incoming solar heat and cooling the globe. As with all technological fixes, there is a danger that the cure will be at least as bad as the disease. And that certainly applies to the biggest and most widely touted technofix for the greenhouse effect.

What Not To Do

The naive 'solution' to the problem of a build-up of carbon dioxide   13
in the atmosphere is to suggest a switch to nuclear power. Nuclear power

stations emit no carbon dioxide, and do not cause acid rain. They are, in a sense, environmentally clean. Even Britain's Prime Minister, Margaret Thatcher, made a comment, in an interview in *The Times* in 1988, to the effect that nuclear power is 'greener' than coal. But a close look at the implications of going for an all-nuclear programme of power generations shows that things are not as simple as they seem at first sight.

14   The first important point is that any attempt to make nuclear power replace a significant portion of the existing world energy generation capacity would itself consume a great deal of energy. It isn't just the nuclear power plants themselves that have to be built, but the industrial infrastructure required to build the power stations and to ensure that they are kept supplied with fuel. While the world was in the process of switching to nuclear energy generation, it would be using up fossil fuel far more rapidly than it does today because of all this industrial activity. The so-called 'energy payback' time for a nuclear power station is very long; it doesn't produce as much energy as was used in building it for many years. The building programme itself would take decades, and the benefits in terms of carbon dioxide concentration of the atmosphere would not be felt for further decades, by which time the Arctic ice would probably have melted. So a rush programme of building new nuclear power stations and scrapping existing coal-fired power stations would do more harm than good, simply in terms of the amount of carbon dioxide released over the next few crucial decades.

15   Nor would such investment be cost effective in other terms. Bill Keepin and Gregory Kats, of the Rocky Mountain Institute in Snowmass, Colorado, carried out a major investigation of the problem, which they published in 1988 and which provided the basis for testimony by Keepin to the House of Representatives on 29 June that year. Leaving aside the question of how much energy is used (and carbon dioxide released) in the building of a nuclear plant, they pointed out that the cost of energy generation from new US nuclear plants is 13.5 cents per kilowatt hour, in 1987 dollars. But the cost of saving electricity through improved efficiency (measures such as insulation of buildings) is only two cents per kilowatt hour. *Even if the nuclear power plants already existed* and were waiting to come on stream, if you have a limited amount of money to spend and the choice is between buying nuclear electricity to replace coal-generated electricity, or making investments in energy conservation so that you use less electricity, conservation will be nearly seven times as effective in reducing the amount of coal being burnt.[4] Looking at it from a slightly different angle,

---

[4] The cost of the coal-fired electricity doesn't change the calculation significantly. The 'marginal' cost of the nuclear electricity is the amount by which the nuclear cost exceeds the coal-fired cost, and this makes the ratio smaller. But with conservation, you save the money that would have been spent on electricity, which makes the ratio bigger again. The Snowmass study takes account of all this.

for every hundred dollars invested in new nuclear power, about one tonne of additional carbon is added to the air as carbon dioxide, compared with the amount that would have been released if the same money had been spent on improving efficiency of energy use.

Nevertheless, Keepin and Kats developed a scenario to give some idea of the amount of work involved in 'solving' the greenhouse problem with the aid of nuclear power. Again, they ignored the input of carbon dioxide into the atmosphere caused by the construction itself, and they made deliberately optimistic assumptions about the cost of each power station and the time it would take to build, set at six years instead of the ten to twelve years that has been experienced recently in the US. Allowing for the need both to replace existing coal-fired power stations and to cope with increasing energy demand worldwide, they found that a new thousand-megawatt nuclear plant would have to be completed roughly every two days for the next forty years. A great deal of this nuclear activity would be going on in the Third World; it would cost some six hundred billion dollars a year; and even while it was going on carbon dioxide from plants fuelled by oil and natural gas would still be adding to the burden of greenhouse gases in the atmosphere.

Quoting a report in the April 1988 issue of *Scientific American,* Keepin told the House that, by contrast, if all new buildings were designed to be energy efficient, the US alone would save the equivalent of eighty-five such power plants and two Alaskan oil pipelines in fifty years' time. More efficient energy use would save consumers $110 billion a year, but would cost no more than fifty billion dollars a year. 'It's as if,' he said, 'we were offered sixty billion dollars a year to live in a cleaner environment.' And that is by no means the limit of potential savings. Raising the average fuel efficiency of US cars from about eighteen miles per gallon (the present figure) to just twenty-eight mpg (still below the average in the European Community today) would save the equivalent of *all* OPEC imports into the US.

As long as new power stations continue to be built, there will always be a case, on specific occasions, that nuclear power may be the best option, and in that way nuclear power can indeed (and does already) do something to reduce the amount of carbon dioxide getting into the air. But it is by no means 'the' solution. Nor is the other bright idea of the techno fans, that of taking carbon dioxide out of the factory and power station chimneys and getting rid of it underground or in the sea.

Once again, the idea is attractive at first sight, even if you 'buy' the nuclear option. After all, nuclear power stations cannot displace a very large proportion of greenhouse gas emissions. Only half of the present greenhouse emissions are carbon dioxide, and fossil fuel-fired power stations contribute only fifteen per cent of all carbon dioxide emissions. Extracting carbon dioxide from stack gases could be applied not only to power stations but to factory smokestacks as well—if only it were not prohibitively expensive in terms of both money and, you guessed, energy.

20   At least fifty per cent of the carbon dioxide in stack gases can be recovered, in principle. But if we consider the specific example of a coal-fired power station, the energy needed to extract something over half the carbon dioxide would be forty per cent of the energy produced by burning the coal in the first place (and a comparable amount of energy would be needed to remove carbon dioxide from the gases emitted by, say, a steel mill). The gases have to be captured (probably by electrically powered fan systems), compressed, cooled, perhaps treated chemically and stored at low temperatures, all of which takes energy. If it takes nearly half the energy of the power station to remove just over half of the carbon dioxide, you have to build another power station the same size to make up for the shortfall in energy, and you end up with very nearly as much carbon dioxide going into the air while the cost of electricity has almost doubled—the economics of the madhouse.[5]

21   There is also the problem of what to do with all the carbon dioxide once it has been captured. The most widely touted bright idea is to inject it into the oceans, either as a cold, dense liquid or as a solid, so that it would sink into the deep currents and be removed from contact with the atmosphere for hundreds or thousands of years. Apart from the fact that shipping the carbon dioxide off to a suitable site would use up yet more energy, there are two strikes against this idea. The first is that we do not know how such a major change in the amount of carbon dioxide dissolved in sea water will affect natural carbon cycles. The second is that this is no solution to the problem at all, but at best postpones the day of reckoning for a few centuries, leaving our descendants to cope with our mess when the deep currents return to the surface and the stored carbon dioxide comes into contact with the atmosphere.

22   Probably the maddest of all such proposals, though, is the idea that carbon dioxide from the emissions of fossil fuel-fired power plants could be turned back into useful fuel using energy from solar or nuclear power stations. This breathtakingly bizarre scheme would involve the construction of about six thousand plants, each using a thousand megawatts of energy. As well as all the problems of the carbon dioxide released during

---

[5] Activists in the 'green' movement also face a conflict of interests in trying to clean up other emissions from fossil fuel-fired power plants, such as the sulphur dioxide that causes acid rain. Flue gas desulphurization at a major power station takes energy, and in effect reduces the efficiency of the power plant by about five per cent. This means that about five per cent *more* carbon dioxide gets into the air than from a comparable power station without desulphurization, while the cost of electricity generated by the station increases by about ten per cent because only about half of the energy produced gets to the consumer in a useful form.

their construction, this additional number of large energy sources on the surface of the Earth would produce so much waste heat that they could change the climate directly, without any help from the greenhouse effect. I have, perhaps, travelled too far into the realms of science fiction. But there are less crazy ways in which carbon dioxide might be taken out of the air, using far less technology and working with the natural cycles of Gaia herself.

The Return of Johnny Appleseed?

If the technology of removing carbon dioxide from the air is imprac- [23] tical, can biology help? Trees and other plants are largely made of carbon, obtained from the carbon dioxide in the air, and some trees have very long lifetimes. The greenhouse effect has certainly been made stronger in the past by destruction of forests, and it would be very pleasing if we could alleviate the greenhouse problem, if only in the relatively short term, by planting new forests and letting them grow. It sounds like a hippy fantasy; but for once the appealing 'natural' option does have something more going for it than wishful thinking. Reforestation is being taken seriously as a policy option, not only because every little helps in our efforts to slow the growth of the greenhouse effect, but also because forests slow erosion, increase the availability of water, provide some timber even if the bulk of the trees are being left to grow, and provide a home for the diversity of life that is in danger in many parts of the world today. Even if efforts at reforesting large parts of the world do not turn out to have much impact on the build-up of carbon dioxide, no harm will have been done by planting the trees, and a great deal of benefit will have accrued in other ways—so why not give it a go?

Gregg Marland, of Oak Ridge National Laboratory, in Tennessee, [24] has carried out a major study of what might be involved in any serious attempt to control the greenhouse effect by planting trees, and he testified on the subject to the Senate energy committee in Washington in 1988. The amount of carbon getting into the atmosphere as carbon dioxide from the burning of fossil fuels is about five billion tonnes each year. To provide a rough guide to what might be achieved by biological fixation of atmospheric carbon, Marland calculated how many trees would be needed to convert this much carbon into wood each year. He based his calculations on the American sycamore, a species that has been well studied and which has a good carbon uptake rate. Other species growing in the tropics would probably be even more effective at absorbing carbon dioxide, but on a tree plantation in Georgia one hectare of sycamores can absorb 7.5 tonnes of carbon every year as the trees grow. To fix five billion tonnes of carbon a year would need seven million square kilometres of young trees, an area about the size of Australia. As it happens, this is also about the area of all the tropical forest cleared as a result of human activities since the end of the latest ice age, most of it during the past few hundred years.

25   A forest the size of Australia does seem rather large. But the trees need not all be in one place, and nobody would seriously try to absorb *all* of the carbon dioxide being emitted by power stations, transport and industry each year. Half the carbon dioxide being produced is already being absorbed by natural sinks,[6] so a forest just half as big might be enough to halt the build-up of this particular greenhouse gas, while one even a quarter the size would make a valuable contribution to reducing the growth of the greenhouse effect. An area roughly equal to the land mass of Zaire would be ample to do the job.[7]

26   Of course, even if it could be achieved, storing carbon in trees is only a temporary solution to the problem. Eventually the trees mature, and sooner or later the carbon they store will be released back into the atmosphere as they die. Some of the trees might be used as fuel for power stations, instead of coal, while new trees are planted to replace them; some of the mature trees might be cut down and stored underground (in abandoned coal mines?) But maybe these are worries that we could reasonably leave to the next generation; if we can slow the build-up of greenhouse gases enough to give society time to adapt to the changing climate and to reduce its dependence on fossil fuels, deciding what to do with the new forests when they mature in the twenty-first or twenty-second centuries shouldn't be an insuperable problem.

27   Although it might seem foolish to begin replanting at a time when many tropical forests, in particular, are still being destroyed, reforestation also has the advantage that it provides a way for anybody to do something useful to help. In October 1988, the American power company Applied Energy Services, of Arlington, Virginia, agreed to help offset the production of carbon dioxide from a new power station in the US by planting fifty-two million trees in Guatemala. The scheme—the first of its kind in the world—will operate through CARE, the international relief and development agency, which is being given two million dollars by AES to help forty thousand farmers to plant the trees during the 1990s, as part of a land development programme. A further sixteen million dollars for the

---

[6] But every time I see that statistic I worry that those natural sinks may be getting overloaded and that some day soon they may stop taking up so much carbon dioxide, leaving us with an even bigger problem on our hands.

[7] A related idea, which might be easier in practice, is to fertilize the oceans by spreading nitrogen and phosphorus compounds (and perhaps iron compounds) on the surface to encourage the growth of phytoplankton. But this is more likely to have unpredictable and perhaps unwelcome repercussions on the natural carbon cycles, whereas planting trees would, in a sense, simply be restoring the status quo that existed before human intervention.

project comes from American government aid agencies. The power station will emit 387,000 tonnes of carbon dioxide each year during its forty-year life, and the growing trees will absorb at least that much carbon dioxide, as well as providing other benefits to the Guatemalan farmers.

Saving existing tropical forests from destruction would be just as beneficial, in terms of the greenhouse effect. This would also be beneficial for many other reasons, often aired in debate about the damage we are doing to our planet. In one season in 1988 an area of rainforest the size of Scotland was burned in Brazil to provide pasture land for cattle. The cattle, in many cases, provide meat for North America hamburgers; the pasture lasts only a few years before the soil is worked out and destroyed, then another huge area of forest is burned (in fact, this much forest is cleared *every year* in a continuous cycle). The problem is inextricably linked with the crisis of development facing the poor regions of the world. Brazil is one of those countries with a huge foreign debt, which must be serviced by earning foreign currency. If the way to get that currency is to burn the forest and rear hamburger meat, can the Brazilians really take sole blame for the damage that is done to the planet—Gaia— as a whole? Global problems need global solutions, and if the rich countries of the world are worried about rising sea levels and other consequences of the greenhouse effect, why shouldn't they offer simply to buy the forest for the cost of the Brazilian debt or even for more, on the single condition that it is left alone? At worst, that might mean a temporary and minor tax hike for citizens of the rich world; I'll gladly pay my share, and do without hamburgers. Or do the people of North America actually value their cheap burgers more than they value the stability of the climate? The 'solution' may be naive and simplistic; but at least it indicates the magnitude of the changes required even to bring the build-up of carbon dioxide under some sort of control. And that still leaves other greenhouse gases to worry about.

Reading and Analyzing

1. State the claim of Gribben's argument.
2. What is his purpose in writing? That is, what does he seek to accomplish in this section of his book?
3. What specific actions does the author recommend?
4. What are the advantages of a ban on CFCs?
5. What is one governmental strategy for reducing energy consumption?
6. What can individuals do to reduce the energy they use without significantly changing lifestyles?
7. What does Gribben think the industrialized North should do to help Third World countries develop a higher standard of living without adding too much to the greenhouse effect?

8. What are some alternative fuels that might be used?
9. What, in Gribben's view, is the alternative that we ought definitely to avoid? Summarize the reasons he presents to support his position.
10. How significant is reforestation? Or ceasing to destroy the rainforest regions?

Responding to the Writer's Ideas

1. Gribben argues that controlling carbon dioxide is a global issue and an "us" (the industrialized North) versus "them" (the Third World countries, most of which are in the southern hemisphere) issue requiring global solutions and financial aid from the industrialized nations. These points were also underscored at the Earth Summit in Rio in the spring of 1992. Are you convinced that many environmental issues, just like many economic issues (see Chapter 9), are international in scope? If not, why not? If so, then how do we go about addressing these problems? Are there procedures and/or institutions in place that can be used? What proposals would you make?

2. Gribben is strongly opposed to any increased use of nuclear power. Has he made a convincing case? If so, why? If not, why not?

3. Both Prance and Gribben have argued for preserving what is left of the rainforests, although their reasons are different. Which writer, in your view, has the best argument? Have they convinced you that the preservation is important? Why or why not?

4. Gribben mentions a number of specific actions that individuals can take to help reduce carbon dioxide emissions. Are you prepared to start acting on one or more of these suggestions? If so, which one(s)? If not, why not?

5. If you were a presidential advisor advocating one or more actions individuals can take to help slow down the greenhouse effect, what strategies would you propose for getting people to start appropriate actions? How would you educate and motivate individual Americans?

❖

The Greenhouse Blues: Keep Cool about Global Warming

Dixy Lee Ray

A marine biologist educated at Mills College and Stanford University, Dixy Lee Ray (b. 1914) chaired the U.S. Atomic Energy Commission from 1973 to 1975 and was the governor of Washington from 1977 to 1981. The recipient of many honors and awards, Ray has long been known as an advocate of the nuclear energy alternative, and she continues to be involved in environmental studies. In 1990 her book (with Lou Guzzo) Trashing the Planet: How Science Can Help Deal with Acid Rain, Depletion of the Ozone, and Nuclear Waste *was published. In the following article, which appeared in the summer 1989 issue of* Policy Review, *Ray expresses skepticism about the dangers of global warming but also calls for greater use of nuclear power for energy.*

The year 1988 ended on a high note of hysteria, one that was to con- 1
tinue well into 1989. The issue fueled by an unusually hot, dry summer, was global warming. NASA's James Hansen testified at a Senate hearing that the high temperatures presaged the onset of the long-debated "greenhouse effect" and global warming due to buildup of carbon dioxide in the atmosphere. Forgotten were the harsh winters of 1978 (when barges carrying coal and heating oil froze in river ice and more than 200 people lost their lives in the cold weather) and 1982.

Memory is a capricious thing. Perhaps the early winter months of 2
1989 will remind prophets of global warming that nature can be fickle. Only days after *Time* magazine featured as its "Man" of the Year for 1988 a doomed Planet Earth, perishing from human mismanagement and greenhouse overheat, Alaska experienced the worst cold in its history. Twenty locations in our most northerly state recorded their lowest-ever temperatures, mainly in the range of −50 to −65 degrees Fahrenheit. The cold did not begin to move south until the first week in February, when it seeped down from Alaska on both sides of the Rocky Mountains, bringing near-record lows to the Pacific Northwest and throughout the Midwest, south to Texas, and eventually to the mid-Atlantic and New England states. Proponents of the "greenhouse-effect-is-here-global-warming-has-begun" theory were very quiet during these weeks.

457

Seeing Infrared

3   To be fair, even if there is a potential for increased temperatures due to enhancement of the greenhouse effect, no one would expect it to occur all at once or without intervening cold spells. So let us examine the situation more closely.

4   Earth, with its blanket of atmosphere, constitutes a "greenhouse." This fact has never been at issue. Indeed, were it not for the greenhouse function of air, the Earth's surface would be like the moon's, bitterly cold (–270 degrees Fahrenheit) at night and unbearably hot (+212 degrees) during the day. Although the amount of solar energy reaching the moon is similar to that reaching the Earth, the Earth's atmosphere permits incoming solar radiation to penetrate. When that warms the surface, infrared heat is radiated back. The "greenhouse gases"—carbon dioxide, water vapor, methane, hydrocarbons—all absorb longwave (infrared) radiation. This process moderates the surface temperature. Let us therefore rejoice and be glad that the Earth does indeed function as a greenhouse!

5   In addition, the greenhouse gases are all produced by nature as well as by human activity. For example, carbon dioxide comes from the respiration of all living things, and from forest fires, decaying vegetation, and volcanoes, as well as from humans burning fossil fuel. The total amount divides about 50/50 between what nature produces and what people can be blamed for. Hydrocarbons come from growing plants, especially evergreens such as the pines and firs that cause the "blue haze" of the Great Smoky Mountains and other areas where coniferous forests abound. Hydrocarbons also come from various industrial activities and incomplete combustion in automobiles. Both hydrocarbons and methane enter the atmosphere from the "burping" of cows and other ruminants. The contribution of hydrocarbons to our air is also about evenly divided between nature and human activities. Methane comes from swamps, termites, coal mines, and rice paddies. Approximately 90 percent of methane comes from nature and only about 10 percent from human activity.

Contrary Computer Models

6   These gases have always been present in the atmosphere, but in total they have been increasing during the last century. Carbon dioxide, the most carefully measured, has increased 25 percent since the Industrial Revolution. The current rate of increase in carbon dioxide plus the other greenhouse gases is about 1 percent a year. Assuming this rate continues, the amount of greenhouses gases will double in this century.

7   According to the leading computer models of climate scientists, the rise in carbon dioxide concentration since the middle of the 19th century should have caused measurable warming of 1 to 5 degrees centigrade (2 to 9 degrees Fahrenheit). But it hasn't! The temperature has oscillated and the overall rise is in the range of 0.3 to 0.7 degrees centigrade. (Nobody

knows what has happened in the Southern Hemisphere, which is 90 percent ocean, because oceanic temperature measurements are so scarce.)

Recall that the public furor started June 1988, when NASA scientist James Hansen testified in the U.S. Senate that the greenhouse effect was here and changing the climate. He said he was 99 percent sure of it and that "1988 would be the warmest year on record . . . unless there is some remarkable, improbable cooling in the remainder of the year." Well, there was. (Ask them in Alaska!) While Hansen was testifying, the eastern tropical Pacific Ocean cooled drastically. The temperature dropped 7 degrees quite suddenly and is now at near-record lows. No one knows why. The phenomenon is called La Niña, to contrast it with the warmer El Niño current. Such cooling has occurred 19 times in the last 102 years. But Hansen didn't consider La Niña because his computer model didn't take sea temperatures into account even though sea water covers 73 percent of Earth's surface. When a NASA scientist talks "global" it's hard to imagine that he would ignore 73 percent of the globe's surface—but he did.

Another possible explanation for the absence of the warming predicted by the computer models: both carbon dioxide and water vapor have several absorption bands besides the infrared. While longwave (infrared) radiation may be kept *in,* some shorter waves of the incoming solar radiation may be kept *out* (by the combined effect of carbon dioxide and water) so that less heat becomes available to be trapped in the first place. Nature has many feedback and self-regulating mechanisms of which this is only one.

Eddy's Sun Spots

There also may be cosmic forces at work that influence Earth temperatures more than does the greenhouse effect. John Eddy of the National Center for Atmospheric Research has found an interesting correlation between decades of low sunspot activity and cold periods such as the "Little Ice Age" of the 17th century, when there was a virtual absence of sunspot activity between 1645 and 1715. (During the winter of 1683–84, recorded in the novel *Lorna Doone,* the trees of Somerset could be heard bursting in the cold.) Conversely, Eddy found that decades of high sunspot activity coincided with warm temperatures on Earth. If Eddy's theory holds up, the high solar activity of the mid-20th century accounts for the period's unusual warmth, and Earth may soon enter a slow return to colder temperatures. (Ice ages recur about every 10,000 to 12,000 years, and it is now 11,000 years since the last one.)

While most environmentalists blame deforestation and the burning of fossil fuel for the carbon dioxide increase, they generally fail to take into account the role of volcanoes in affecting the composition of the atmosphere. We are currently near the peak of a 500- to 600-year cycle of volcanic activity, which may have something to do with the carbon dioxide increase. The quantity of air-polluting materials produced by man during his entire existence on Earth does not begin to equal the quantities of toxic gases and particulates spewed forth into the atmosphere from just three volcanic eruptions: Krakatau in Indonesia in 1883, Mount Katmai in Alaska in 1912, and Hekla in Iceland in 1947. Mount St. Helens pumped out 910,000 metric tons of carbon dioxide during six months in 1982, not including the eruption.

Switch to Nuclear

12   Despite the uncertainty about whether we are now experiencing global warming, it is prudent to reduce the production of greenhouse gases through human activity. Because no one really knows what the ultimate consequences of the increases in carbon dioxide and other greenhouse gases might be, we should reduce man's contribution wherever possible. While there is no need to take draconian measures that would damage our standard of living, there are several things we can do.

13   For starters, we can phase out the use of fossil fuel for generating electricity and turn to technology with no known adverse impact on the atmosphere—nuclear power. We can shift to an essentially all-electric economy. We can turn, once again, to electric buses and trains and eventually to electric automobiles. For air travel we could replace fossil fuels with hydrogen. New ceramics materials and ceramics-metal compounds can overcome the former problem of embrittlement resulting from the absorption of hydrogen into metal. Recent advances in storage technology promise to ease the necessity for large, heavy, high-pressure, low-temperature hydrogen storage tanks.

Sapling Hopes

14   We can also take advantage of photosynthesis to absorb carbon dioxide and produce oxygen. Those who urge preservation of old growth, or "climax," forests on the basis of their contribution to the oxygen-carbon dioxide balance in the atmosphere overlook the fact that old trees metabolize far less rapidly than young ones (like humans and most living things). Indeed, old trees contribute little to removing carbon dioxide or producing oxygen, whereas a forest of young trees will remove carbon dioxide from the air at a rate of five or six tons per acre. Reforestation, therefore, is far more effective in carbon dioxide reduction than is preservation of existing forests. We should also vastly increase the use of plants in urban areas, where air pollution is usually worse than in rural regions.

15   In considering possible carbon dioxide mitigating actions, it is important to keep in mind that these steps are feasible for an advanced, highly technical industrialized society with plenty of electricity. Around the world, however, fossil fuel burning will inevitably continue for many

years. In China, for example, 936 million metric tons of coal were burned in 1987–88. Who is going to tell them to stop or to change? What alternatives do they have? No matter what we do in the United States, or even throughout the Western world, the carbon dioxide from man-made sources is bound to rise. Should global warming occur, it is estimated that no nation, acting alone, could affect it by more than 10 percent. We should nevertheless do what we can to reduce our own carbon dioxide contribution—proper stewardship of the Earth demands nothing less.

To do so, we need not be panicked into precipitous and costly "corrective" actions that only reduce our standard of living. We can phase out fossil fuels—replacing them with nuclear power and other fuels such as hydrogen—in a deliberate, responsible way. We can also plant lots of trees.   16

Apocalypse No

A final note on the supposedly dire consequences of a global temperature rise of 1.5 to 4.5 degrees centigrade over the next 50 years: Such a climate change, should it occur, is not nearly so drastic a change for humans as a move by an Alaskan to Palm Springs. Elevated temperatures would have greater impact on agriculture and vegetation in general. But with plants, temperature is hardly the only determinant of growth. Perhaps as important are the duration and quality of light (latitude is significant here), soil moisture, and the amounts, timing, and duration of rainfall, and the possibilities for irrigation. A warmer Earth—and the changes in rainfall that might accompany it—would make some areas of farmland more fertile or less fertile than today. But that hardly constitutes global environment doom.   17

Nor do the predictions of melting ice caps and possible inundation of low-lying areas. Most weather specialists predict that a global temperature rise of 1.5 to 4.5 degrees centigrade—enough to dislodge Antarctica ice submerged under the surface—would cause the sea level to rise by one and a half to four and a half feet. Should this happen, a number of cities would be vulnerable to flooding of the sort that Venice and Holland have coped with for centuries. Some beachfronts would be gradually moved back a few miles, and some people would have to move. The inconvenience of all this should not be minimized, but it is hardly apocalypse.   18

Is a global warming on the way? Maybe sometime, but it is not here now. Why do so many people believe in the dire forecasts? Perhaps the historian Hans Morgenthau was right when he wrote in 1946, "The intellectual and moral history of mankind is the story of insecurity, of the anticipation of impending doom, of metaphysical anxieties." John Maddox, editor of the British journal *Nature,* says, "But these days there also seems to be an underlying cataclysmic sense among people. Scientists don't seem to be immune to this."   19

20   Well, they ought to be. What the greenhouse debate needs most is a dose of healthy skepticism.

Reading and Analyzing

1. Ray announces her subject but not her thesis in her opening two paragraphs. What is her subject? What is her attitude toward that subject? How do you know from her opening?
2. The author provides important facts in paragraphs 3 through 5. What else does she seek to accomplish in this section?
3. What several events may affect Earth's temperatures in addition to the solar rays that are caught in the Earth's atmosphere? What is one significant natural source of carbon dioxide?
4. Ray concedes that it is wise to reduce greenhouse gases. What actions does she recommend?
5. If global warming should occur, what will be the consequences, in Ray's view?
6. How should we approach the greenhouse debate?

Responding to the Writer's Ideas

1. Ray recommends a shift to nuclear power. Should you be surprised by her recommendation? Explain.
2. Ray and Gribben differ in two ways: the seriousness of the problem and the best solutions. First, compare them on the problem of global warming. Which one do you find more convincing? Why?
3. Ray argues for a shift to nuclear power as one solution, an approach Gribben argues against. Who has the more convincing argument on this issue? Why?
4. Ray explains that reforesting will do more to counter global warming than preserving older forests. Does this explanation serve as a counterargument to Prance's plea for preserving the rainforests, or can both positions be right? Explain.
5. Many of the writers in this chapter can be described or labeled as "environmentalists," or "conservationists." They hold a set of values about the Earth and all that lives on it. How would you characterize Ray? What is she committed to? Where is she "coming from"? What evidence can you point to in her article to support your inference?

❖

The Ozone Catastrophe: Warning from the Skies

Al Gore

Albert Gore, Jr. (b. 1948), is the Vice President of the United States. He was educated at Harvard and Vanderbilt University Law School and worked as an investigative reporter before entering politics. As a senator from Tennessee, Gore chaired the Senate Subcommittee on Science, Technology, and Space. The following article, printed in the Washington Post *on February 9, 1992, is adapted from his book* Earth in the Balance: Ecology and the Human Spirit *(1992).*

The rapid deterioration of the stratospheric ozone layer is but one signal of an environmental crisis that is revealing itself all over. Suddenly, the disturbing news carries with it a threat to all of us.

The infamous ozone "hole" that opens each winter over Antarctica is now threatening to open over Kennebunkport and a sizeable portion of North America, exposing densely populated areas for the first time to significantly increased doses of dangerous ultraviolet radiation. Scientists have recorded higher levels of ozone-depleting chlorine over northern New England and Canada than they have ever recorded over Antarctica or anywhere else. And the emergency described by NASA scientists is only going to get worse throughout the coming decade.

Indeed, a global ecological crisis is now banging down the door, announcing itself in various ways:

- Increasing emissions of carbon dioxide and other greenhouse gases are fueling increases in Earth's temperature that foreshadow catastrophic consequences.
- Forests are being destroyed at one and a half acres per second, and with them thousands of species that can never be replaced.
- Each day, almost 40,000 children under the age of 5 are dying from hunger and malnutrition caused in significant part by ecological devastation.
- We continue to generate waste in the United States at a rate that exceeds twice the average body weight of every American every day.
- Dead dolphins wash up along the Mediterranean Coast, their immune systems weakened by too much pollution; within the last few

years, several million starfish washed up over miles of the White Sea; thousands of seals washed up on the shores of the North Sea; our own children dodged hypodermic needles washing in with the waves.

4   It's beginning to resemble what the comedian A. Whitney Brown called, "A nature hike through the Book of Revelations."

5   All these ecological crises are symptoms of the same underlying crisis: a relatively recent and dramatic change in our relationship to Earth, which has led to a collision between industrial civilization and the ecological system of the planet. Like an alcoholic who has a string of drunk-driving accidents, but sees each one as an isolated incident with a separate explanation, we're failing to recognize the pattern connecting these environment catastrophes. Our civilization is, in effect, addicted to the voracious consumption of Earth itself.

6   We can discern this pattern better if we begin to think in terms usually used by the military. There are "local" skirmishes, "regional" battles and "strategic" conflicts. This third category is reserved for threats to a nation's survival and must be understood in a global context, like our long and successful struggle against Soviet communism.

7   In the same way, most instances of water pollution, air pollution and illegal waste dumping are essentially local in nature. And we now recognize that problems like acid rain and the contamination of large underground aquifers are fundamentally regional. But we now face a new class of environmental problems that affect the entire global ecological system and are fundamentally strategic in nature—the ozone "hole" now threatening to open above our heads is but one example.

8   Ozone depletion is, in fact, just one of three strategic threats to the entire global atmosphere; the others are diminished oxidation and global warming. All three have the power to change the makeup of the atmosphere and, in the process, disrupt its crucial balancing role in the global ecological system.

9   Ozone depletion changes the atmosphere's ability to protect Earth's surface from harmful quantities of short-wave (ultraviolet) radiation. Decreased oxidation potentially damages the atmosphere's ability to cleanse itself of pollutants like methane. Global warming increases the amount of long-wave (infrared) radiation retained in the lower atmosphere and thereby inhibits the atmosphere's ability to maintain temperatures within the relatively constant range that provides stability for the global climate system.

10   In all three cases, the changes are ubiquitous and persistent.

11   A thinner ozone layer allows more ultraviolet radiation to strike Earth's surface. Many life forms are vulnerable to large increases in this radiation, including plants that normally remove huge quantities of CO_2 from the atmosphere through photosynthesis. The scientific evidence indicates that these plants, when exposed to increased ultraviolet radiation,

can no longer photosynthesize at the same rate, thus further raising the levels of CO_2 in the atmosphere.

We too are affected. The best known consequences of extra ultraviolet radiation include skin cancer and cataracts, both of which are increasingly common, especially in areas of the Southern Hemisphere such as Australia, New Zealand, South Africa and Patagonia.

Residents of the area already inside the Southern Hemisphere's ozone hole, in Patagonia, have been advised by the Argentine Health Ministry to stay indoors as much as possible during September and October. In Queensland, in northeastern Australia, more than 75 percent of citizens who have reached the age of 65 have some form of skin cancer, and children are required by law to wear large hats and neck scarves to and from school to protect against ultraviolet radiation. In Patagonia, hunters now report finding blind rabbits; fisherman catch blind salmon.

When the international Ozone Trends Assessment Panel reported its findings last fall—ozone depletion occurring 200 percent faster, during the summer months as well as winter, and over mid-latitudes and not just the poles—they warned it could mean hundreds of thousands of deaths and more than 1 million new cases of skin cancer.

Less well known are the effects of extra ultraviolet radiation on the human immune system. Still, it is clear that increased levels suppress the immune system and so may actually increase our vulnerability to diseases of the immune system, all of which, incidentally, have increased dramatically in the last two decades. The scientists said that skin pigmentation and most sun screens would offer little protection from this threat.

Although other chemicals have contributed to the ozone depletion crisis, the principal damage has been done by chlorofluorocarbons (CFCs). The fact that CFCs have been produced for fewer than 60 years and yet have had such a sweeping impact should make us consider how many of the other 20,000 chemical compounds introduced each year may, when mass-produced, cause other significant changes in the environment. Very few are extensively tested for environmental impact before they are used—although, ironically, CFCs were. It was their benign chemical stability in the lower atmosphere that enabled them to float slowly, unimpeded, to where ultraviolet rays finally sliced them into corrosive pieces.

Today, even as we try to understand the enormity of this, we continue putting the same chemicals into the environment. What does it mean to redefine one's relationship to the sky? What will it do to our children's outlook on life if we have to teach them to be afraid to look up?

Considering the Bush administration's slow response to ozone depletion, it is frightening to think what kind of environmental disaster it will take to get the White House moving on the even more serious threat of global climate change.

19   In the past, it was safe to assume that nothing we could do would have any lasting effect on the global environment. But it is precisely that assumption which must now be discarded so that we can think strategically about our new relationship to Earth.

20   We must do no less than make the rescue of the global environment the central organizing principle for our post-Cold War civilization. Adopting a central organizing principle—one agreed to voluntarily by nations around the world—means embarking on an all-out effort to use every policy and program, every law and institution, every treaty and alliance, every tactic and strategy.

21   Marginal adjustments in ongoing programs, moderate improvements in laws and regulations, rhetoric offered in lieu of genuine change—these are all forms of appeasement, designed to satisfy the public's desire to believe that a wrenching transformation of society will not be necessary. The Neville Chamberlains of this crisis carry not umbrellas but "floppy hats and sunglasses"—the palliative allegedly suggested by a former secretary of the interior as an appropriate response to the increased ultraviolet radiation caused by the thinning of the ozone layer.

22   What is needed is a plan—call it a Global Marshall Plan for the environment—that combines large-scale, long-term, carefully targeted financial aid to developing nations; massive efforts to design and then transfer to poor nations the new technologies needed for sustained economic progress, a world-wide program to stabilize world population and binding commitments by the industrial nations to accelerate their transition to an environmentally responsible pattern of life.

23   To work, however, any such effort will also require wealthy nations to make a transition that in some ways will be more wrenching than that of the Third World, simply because powerful established patterns will be disrupted. It must emphasize cooperation—in the different regions of the world and globally—while carefully respecting the integrity of individual nation states.

24   The world's most important supranational organization—the United Nations—has a role to play, though I am skeptical about its ability to do very much. The U.N. might, though, consider establishing a Stewardship Council to deal with matters relating to the global environment—just as the Security Council now deals with war and peace. Such a forum could be increasingly useful as the full extent of the environmental crisis unfolds.

25   Similarly, it would be wise to establish environmental summit meetings, much like the annual economic summits of today that only rarely find time to consider the environment. The preliminary discussions of a Global Marshall Plan would, in any event, have to take place at the highest level. And, unlike economic summits, these discussions must involve heads of state from both the developed and developing world.

Some strategic goals are obvious. For example, world population   26
should be stabilized, with policies designed to create the conditions necessary for the so-called demographic transition—the historical and well-doc-
umented change from a dynamic equilibrium of high birth rates and death
rates to a stable equilibrium of low birth rates and death rates. This
change has taken place in most of the industrial nations and in virtually
none of the developing nations. It is no secret that President Bush has opposed an active U.S. role in population stabilization.

But we also need to rapidly create and develop environmentally ap-   27
propriate technologies—especially in energy, transportation, agriculture,
building construction and manufacturing.

In this regard, I have proposed a Strategic Environment Initiative   28
(SEI), a worldwide program that would discourage and phase out older,
inappropriate technologies and develop and disseminate a new generation
of sophisticated and environmentally benign substitutes. As soon as possible, the SEI should be the subject of intensive international discussions,
first among the industrial nations and then between them and the developing world.

And we need to re-think the economic "rules of the road," by which   29
we measure the impact of our decisions on the environment. We must establish—by global agreement—a system of economic accounting that assigns appropriate values to the ecological consequences of both routine
choices in the marketplace by individuals and companies and larger,
macroeconomic choices by nations.

The nations of Earth need a new generation of agreements that will   30
embody the regulatory frameworks, specific prohibitions, enforcement
mechanisms, cooperative planning, sharing arrangements, incentives, penalties and mutual obligations necessary to make the overall plan a success.
These agreements must be especially sensitive to the vast differences of capability and need between developed and undeveloped nations. The process
will begin at the Earth Summit in Brazil this June. President Bush is the only
major world leader who has refused to announce his participation there.

What is needed, finally, is this: an ecological perspective that does   31
not treat Earth as something separate from human civilization. We, too,
are part of the whole, and looking at the whole ultimately means also
looking at ourselves. If we do not see that we are a powerful natural force
like the winds and tides, we cannot see how we threaten to push Earth out
of balance.

Reading and Analyzing

1. What is Gore's subject? What is the relationship between atmospheric ozone depletion and Gore's subject?

2. List the ecological crises described by Gore, using just a phrase for each one (for example, ozone depletion or greenhouse effect). Which is the more effective strategy: your list or Gore's first four paragraphs? Support your answer.

3. Gore sees a connection among these specific crises; what is it?

4. What type of argument does the author use in paragraphs 6 and 7? Explain the point of the argument.

5. Explain each of the "strategic threats" in your own words.

6. What are the two most common consequences of ozone depletion for humans? What evidence is there that the ozone layer is diminishing?

7. What additional medical problems might be caused by ozone depletion?

8. Explain Gore's reference to Neville Chamberlain.

9. State the author's claim.

10. What does Gore want us to do to address environmental crises? What role might the United Nations play?

11. Explain Gore's Strategic Environment Initiative.

12. Analyze Gore's argument. What kind of argumentative purpose and pattern do you find here? Find the pattern in Chapter 3, and determine the steps that Gore includes and the paragraphs devoted to each one.

Responding to the Writer's Ideas

1. Gore makes several references to former president Bush. What attitude toward Bush is revealed? Compare Gore's statements with Jessica Mathews's about Bush's position on world population (see pp. 283–85). What is your view on the relationship between population and other environmental problems? What should the U.S. policy be? Why?

2. Both Gore and John Gribben (see pp. 443–55) speak movingly about our relationship to the Earth, our need to be in balance or in harmony with the Earth. Does this attitude make sense to you? Do you feel an emotional attachment with the Earth, or do you not think about it very much?

3. Is attitude an important part of the problem, requiring change before people will establish the needed environmental policies? If you agree with Gore that attitude is important, what strategies would you recommend for encouraging people to develop the right attitude?

4. Examine Gore's specific proposals. Do you agree with all, or some, or none of them? Explain your position.

5. Gore concentrates primarily on one crisis, ozone depletion. Of the several problems mentioned by Gore, which one do you think is the most serious? Why?

❖

Green Cassandras

Gregg Easterbrook

Gregg Easterbrook is a contributing editor to Newsweek *and the* Atlantic. *In the following article, published in the* New Republic *on July 6, 1992, Easterbrook questions both the accuracy of and the motivation for the environmentalists' emotionally charged analyses of environmental issues.*

The distinction between a bicycle accident and the end of civilization   1
has seldom been so blurred as at the Earth Summit, recently concluded in Rio de Janeiro. There, discussion of palpable threats to nature mixed in equal proportion with improbable claims of instant doom. Environmentalists, who would seem to have an interest in separating the types of alarms, instead encouraged the confusion on doctrinal grounds, namely, that all environmental news should be negative. This worldview may be appropriate for fund-raising and faculty sherry hours, but it can backfire in the realm of public policy.

Consider the interplay between global warming hype and the Earth   2
Summit. Most U.S. pollution controls exceed those of other nations, including Japan and Western Europe. Carbon emissions are the one important environmental category where America is the worst offender. So in the conferences that preceded Rio, environmentalists and Southern diplomats relentlessly hammered Washington about the greenhouse effect, because this is where the United States can be made to seem the wolf, all other gentle ewes.

This swirl of overstatement managed to convince everyone, including   3
the White House, that global warming was the principal issue to be addressed at Rio—though artificial warming is strictly a speculative threat, secondary or even tertiary compared with confirmed problems such as species extinction or, in the Third World, unsafe drinking water and poor sanitation. When it came time for Northern governments to offer the South new funds for addressing the low-profile issues that really matter, the rich countries (even the Scandinavians) said, "Sorry, we've made this huge commitment to greenhouse controls, no money left over." It may be years until the moment is ripe for the Third World to ask again.

There is something bordering on indecent about the world's heads of   4
state gathering to bestow many tens of billions of dollars upon a hypothet-

469

ical ecological concern like greenhouse warming while not lifting a finger to assist the 3.2 million impoverished Southern children who die each year of diarrheal diseases communicated through impure water. Yet this ordering of priorities is in sync with current environmental rhetoric.

5   Consider also last winter's ozone scare. NASA made an announcement that sounded as if the agency were saying that a stratospheric ozone hole had been detected over the populous regions of North America. (The ozone breaches so far have occurred above the Antarctica, where there is little life to harm.) Breathless network reports and magazine covers followed, adorned with the photos of blondes in bikinis that are necessary for coverage of this issue. Senator Al Gore of Tennessee declared the findings "an immediate, acute emergency threat . . . the single most important issue facing this country and this Earth."

6   It's just that, ummm, there never was any Northern ozone hole. What NASA monitors found were precursor chemicals that are sometimes, but not always, associated with ozone depletion. No actual breach had been detected, and none developed. The precursor compounds can derive from CFCs; they can also stem from volcanism, and last year there was an eruption of unusual power at Mount Pinatubo in the Philippines. These annoying details were dismissed in the name of a good panic.

7   This is especially frustrating because the straightforward case for CFC abolition (that there's nothing to fear now, but why gamble with radiation?) is sufficient. Increasingly, environmental advocates seem to think reforms can be sold only with benevolent Big Lies. If it is someday shown that stratospheric ozone trends are primarily natural—a possibility—the doomsday proclamations about depletion will be used to ridicule the premises of environmentalism.

8   It's worrisome that Gore in particular, the bright light of political environmentalism, seems increasingly to believe that the only correct stance is to press the panic button on every issue. For instance, in his book *Earth in the Balance,* Gore describes in affectionate detail his association with the late ecologist Roger Revelle. Revelle is the modern father of greenhouse science, having in the 1950s pioneered the study of atmospheric carbon dioxide. As a Harvard undergraduate Gore met the great researcher; later he often called on Revelle to testify before congressional hearings. Gore cites Revelle as leading him toward his view that an emergency program of gas reductions is required because the greenhouse effect is "extremely grave . . . the most serious crisis that we have ever faced."

9   *Earth in the Balance* does not mention that before his death last year, Revelle published a paper that concludes, "The scientific base for greenhouse warming is too uncertain to justify drastic action at this time. There is little risk in delaying policy responses." A lifetime of study persuaded Revelle that carbon emissions should be restricted but are far less hazardous than initially feared. That position isn't bleak enough for current

enviro cant, so Revelle is being eased out as a hero of the movement. As is the English scientist James Lovelock, co-author of the Gaia hypothesis and once an environmental demigod. Lovelock has become persona non grata by saying that the ecosphere is so resilient no amount of human malfeasance, including nuclear war, could end life.

Gore occupies a precarious position in the web of ecological events. His commitment to environment reform is genuine; he became involved long before the issue was trendy. And his reputation for intellect and dedication is deserved. But increasingly his environmental oratory is out of control. In Gore's standard after-dinner talk, declaiming coming ecological catastrophes, he works in continental drift, chaos theory, and even black holes.   11

Gore, and environmentalists generally, find it especially painful to acknowledge that there has been significant ecological progress on most fronts in the United States in recent decades. Air, water, toxic, landfill, and sewage pollution are steadily declining, even as population increases (Los Angeles today has significantly less smog than it did twenty years ago); the number of trees is greater than at the turn of the century; CFCs are being abolished; driftnet fishing, Alaskan and offshore oil exploration are down or out; energy use per dollar of GNP is falling; the list goes on. There's a weird sense that this good news should be hushed up. Shouldn't it instead be offered to the public as happy proof that environmental efforts pay off in surprisingly little time?   12

Lately Gore and the distinguished biologist Paul Ehrlich have ventured into dangerous territory by suggesting that journalists quietly self-censor environmental evidence that is not alarming, because such reports, in Gore's words, "undermine the effort to build a solid base of public support for the difficult actions we must soon take." Skeptical debate is supposed to be one of the strengths of liberalism; it's eerie to hear liberal environmentalists asserting that views they disagree with ought not to be heard. More important, the desire to be exempt from confronting the arguments against one's position traditionally is seen when a movement fears it is about to be discredited. Why not defuse environmental rhetoric before an implosion?   13

In exemplary doublespeak, some enviros put forth that dissenting views should be suppressed in the name of balance. Gore, for example, asserts that reporters should attach little weight to scientists who question greenhouse emergency claims, because perhaps 2 percent of credentialed researchers feel that way. This simply isn't true. Greenpeace recently surveyed climatologists, doubtless hoping for evidence of global warming panic; instead it found that the largest group of respondents, 47 percent, believe a runaway greenhouse effect is nearly impossible. The two source authorities of the greenhouse business, reports by the National Academy of Sciences and the U.N.-affiliated Intergovernmental Panel on Climate   14

Change, contain hundreds of pages of credentialed misgivings. Recently I attended the climate change sessions of the annual meeting of the American Association for the Advancement of Science. There was clear agreement that recent temperatures are up, that they might or might not continue to go up, and that the sky is blue.

14   One factor in environmental overstatement is the belief that only end-of-the-world locution can hold public attention. This assumption is wrong. Voters care about many issues that pose no threat to life, and they would continue to support environmentalism even if the rhetoric were more veracious, because the plain-spoken case for the environment is strong enough. At any rate, end-of-the-world environmental issues have been in short supply recently. Toxic wastes once seemed like a threat to general well-being, but experience has shown their impact locally confined and nowhere near as severe as assumed. Ozone depletion someday may imperil life, but with CFCs being banned there's little left to advocate, unless you know of a means to plug volcanos. Global warming holds out the appeal of a sweeping calamity, a bad science fiction movie come true. Enviros now seem almost to be rooting for temperature increases.

15   Well, enviro fund-raisers are, at least. As the movement has advanced from a low-budget operation to a branch office of the status quo, the need to acquire ever larger sums has driven many green groups to rely on direct mail. The direct-mail business is based on scare tactics, conspiracy theories, bogeymen, and preposterous levels of exaggeration. Some enviros now eagerly promote (to credulous acceptance in the big-deal press corps) the notion that EPA administrator William Reilly is a mere pawn before shadowy forces on Dan Quayle's Competitiveness Council. In fact, the council is a pipsqueak organization, and Reilly just persuaded Bush to go to Rio over the combined objections of numerous leading administration figures. But turning on a conspiracy theory, the notion makes for snazzy direct mail.

16   Supposedly Reilly recently was bested by Quayle's council in the writing of a Clean Air Act regulation regarding toxic emissions. Front-page stories devoted many paragraphs to interpretation of the event as a sign of impending environmental doom, while skipping glissando over what exactly happened, except to say, as the *New York Times* did, that Quayle's action granted companies the freedom to "increase air pollution without prior notice." Strictly speaking that is true, but only in the sense that the *Times* is free to publish libel without prior notice; legal penalties make it unlikely this will happen. The regulatory question was whether companies with valid air permits must go through a formal public hearing sequence to obtain a new permit each time they want to install new factory process equipment. Reilly thought they should, Quayle thought they shouldn't. Unaltered by the dispute, and unmentioned in the stories, was that if factory process changes do increase pollution, companies must disclose that fact and pay fines.

Once you know that, the incident is a mere technical skirmish about   17
how best to minimize regulatory transaction costs. But what if enviro attacks on Reilly succeed in convincing Washington that he has lost power,
and a self-fulfilling prophecy results? Thinking in terms of what may sell to
the bulk-rate donor list engages the risk that, like politicians believing their
own press releases, environmentalists will believe their own direct mail.
This in turn raises the worst aspect in which ecological hype may backfire—the New Right parallel.

At one time the New Right consisted of underfunded voices crying in   18
the wilderness. Then Ronald Reagan came to power and made some of the
changes his backers favored. Rather than celebrating, many on the New
Right became yet more strident, if only to differentiate themselves from a
mainstream that had shifted somewhat in their direction. A dynamic took
hold in which numerous conservative factions were more concerned about
crazy claims for fund-raising purposes than about the actual condition of
the real world. The public ceased believing conservative alarms: unstop-
pable as the New Right seemed in the early 1980s, it now borders on in-
significance.

Enviros today risk the same progression of events. Once they were   18
disfranchised outsiders, invariably right where industry was invariably
wrong. Now the movement is a monied faction of the establishment, with
many satisfying right/wrong distinctions blurred by the very reforms environmentalists set in motion. Like the New Right, enviros are evolving an
internal dynamic of self-satisfaction based on mutual displays of stridency,
with the state of the real world a subsidiary concern. That certainly
seemed to be the name of the game at Rio. If environmentalists keep pro-
claiming that nature is ending when daily the sun continues to rise, they
may find the public's "oh, shut up" point can be reached on environmentalism, too.

Reading and Analyzing

1. What is Easterbrook's subject? What is his thesis, the claim of his argument?
2. What does he accuse environmentalists of doing?
3. Since Easterbrook is objecting to the view of environmental problems
presented by environmentalists, his article can appropriately be characterized as what kind of argumentative essay?
4. For what environmental problem is the United States the worst offender?
5. What Third World problems should we be devoting money to?
6. What environmental problem does Easterbrook describe as "hypothetical"? What evidence does he provide?

7. What environmental "problem" was greatly exaggerated, in Easterbrook's view?

8. Explain the term *doublespeak*. What bothers the author about the way environmentalists present their case?

9. What is the message for environmentalists in Easterbrook's comparison with the New Right?

10. How would you describe the article's tone? What specific elements of style create Easterbrook's tone?

Responding to the Writer's Ideas

1. At one level Easterbrook's essay is a counter to the preceding article by Gore. Whom do you believe? Is ozone depletion a serious problem or not? What else have you read or heard on this issue that might influence your response to this question?

2. Easterbrook asserts that the problems most needing our attention are water and sanitation problems in Third World countries. Can you comment on the seriousness of these problems through experience visiting or living in a Third World country? If so, how would you seek to convince Americans of their need to help?

3. Evaluate Easterbrook's argument. Has he convinced you that he has a valid point? Why or why not? Is it possible for both Easterbrook, on the one hand, and Gribben and Gore, on the other, to be right? Explain.

❖

Taking Population Seriously:
Power and Fertility

Frances Moore Lappé and Rachel Schurman

A graduate of Earlham College, Frances Moore Lappé (b. 1944) is a cofounder and staff member of the Institute for Food and Development Policy in San Francisco. She is the author of Diet for a Small Planet *(1971) and* Food First: Beyond the Myth of Scarcity *(1977). Rachel Schurman has completed her master's at Tufts University and is a doctoral student in sociology at the University of Wisconsin. A research assistant at Lappé's Institute, Schurman coauthored, with Lappé,* Betraying the National Interest *(1988). In the following essay, from the collection* Lessons of the Rainforest *(1990), the authors ask readers to take a different look at the causes of population problems in Third World countries.*

Since 1950 the world's population has doubled, and 85 percent of that growth has occurred in the Third World, where today's population growth rates are unprecedented. Because the fastest rates of growth are in many rainforested countries—Brazil, the Philippines, Indonesia, Guatemala—we cannot hope to protect rainforests without asking, What set off this population explosion? And how can we defuse it to help bring human population into balance with the Earth's ecology?

To answer these questions, we present a "power-structures perspective,"[1] focusing on the multilayered arenas of decision-making power that shape people's reproductive choices, or lack of them. This perspective shows how the powerlessness of the poor often leaves them little option but large families. Indeed, high birth rates among the poor can best be understood as a defensive response against structures of power that fail to provide—or actively block access to—sources of security beyond the family.

When we ask what can be learned from the handful of Third World countries that have been extraordinarily successful in reducing fertility, we find this thesis reinforced. In each, far-reaching social changes have empowered people, especially women, thereby facilitating alternatives to child bearing as a source of income, security, and status.

Population: What's the Problem?

4   In the most widely held definition of the population problem, growing numbers of people are pitted against limited amounts of resources. In
this food-versus-resources perspective, humanity is fast overrunning the
Earth's capacity to support us; indeed, current environmental degradation
and hunger prove that in some places we've already pushed beyond the
Earth's limits.

5   Our prior work has demonstrated that it is incorrect to explain hunger
by blaming high population density when the two are not demonstrably related.[2] China, for instance, has only half as much cropped land per person
as India, yet Indians suffer widespread and severe hunger and the Chinese
do not. Costa Rica, with less than half the cropped acres per person of Honduras, boasts a life expectancy—one indicator of nutrition—14 years longer
than that of Honduras, and close to that of the industrial countries.[3]

6   Obviously, many factors other than sheer numbers determine
whether people eat adequately, such as whether people have access to fertile land to grow food, or have jobs providing them with money to buy it.

7   The same simplistic formulation must be rejected when it comes to
environmental destruction. Within this century, forests in the tropical
Third World have declined by nearly half. Much of the damage is attributed to peasants practicing slash-and-burn agriculture. But if land in
Brazil, for example, were not the monopoly of the few—with 2 percent of
the landowners controlling 60 percent of the arable land—poor Brazilians
would not be forced to settle in the Amazon, destroying the irreplaceable
rainforest.[4] In Indonesia, commercial logging is a major source of the destruction. There, lumber multinationals Weyerhauser and Georgia-Pacific
have leveled an estimated 800,000 hectares a year—at least four times
more than the area affected by peasant slash-and-burn farming.[5]

8   Surely in some locales populations already exceed the size at which
they can coexist healthily with the environment, but "to blame colonizing
peasants for uprooting tribal people and burning the rainforest," write two
rainforest ecologists, "is tantamount to blaming soldiers for causing wars."[6]

The Emerging "Power Structures Perspective"

9   Over the past two decades, a more sophisticated social analysis of the
population problem has begun to emerge. It points to economic, social,
and cultural forces that keep Third World fertility high: among them the
low status of women, the high death rates of children, and the lack of old-
age security. From this social perspective, high fertility becomes an effect
more than a cause of poverty and hunger.

10   This essay seeks to synthesize crucial insights emerging from this perspective, while adding a critical dimension: social power. By social power
we mean, very concretely, the relative ability of people to have a say in decisions that shape their lives. To understand why populations are explod-

ing in the Third World, one must understand how choices about reproduction—those most personal, intimate choices—are influenced by structures of decision-making power. These structures include the distant arena of international finance and trade, and extend downward to the level of national governments, on through the village, and, ultimately, to relationships within families.

"Power structure" is not a mysterious concept. It simply refers to the   11
rules, institutions, and assumptions that determine both who is allowed to participate in decisions and in whose interests decisions are made. The decisions most relevant to the population question are those governing access to and use of life-sustaining resources—land, jobs, health care, and the education needed to make the most of them—and contraceptive resources.

Decision-making structures can most usefully be characterized as   12
falling along a continuum from what we call democratic to antidemocratic. By democratic we mean decision-making structures in which those most affected by the decisions have a say, or that minimally include consideration of the interests of those affected. In no polity or other social institution is power shared in completely equal measure, but in our definition, democratic organization exists to the extent that power is dispersed and no one is utterly powerless. In contrast, antidemocratic structures are nonparticipatory when those most affected have no say, or unequal when power is so concentrated that a few decide exclusively in their own interests. Our thesis is that antidemocratic power structures create and perpetuate conditions keeping fertility high.

In Western societies one tends to think of democracy as strictly a polit-   13
ical concept, and of power as exercised only in the political arena. We in the West also assume that because the communist state is the antithesis of political democracy, any use of the term *democratic* is inappropriate when describing communist societies. However, power is a critical variable in both political and economic affairs, as well as in social and cultural life. And the labels *democratic* and *antidemocratic*—describing structures of decision-making power in a multiplicity of social institutions—are most usefully applied not to societies *in toto*, but to the many arenas of life within societies.

Within any given society, power is not necessarily structured along   14
the same lines throughout the political, economic, and social sectors. These varied sectors influence each other, but asymmetry is more the norm: a society might be highly antidemocratic in the way political power is wielded but might allow considerable sharing of economic control over essential resources. Take China. Under the former collectivized system, everyone had the right to participate in economic life and share in the fruits from the land. At the same time, political leadership was not freely chosen and people's right to political expression was not protected.

The converse is probably more common. In a number of societies—   15
the United States is an example—political participation and expression are

protected, but citizens' rights to economic resources are not. So a significant share of the population goes without enough income to provide adequate food, housing, and health care.

16   Structures of economic and political power differ by level as well: although they may be relatively participatory at, say, the national political level, they may remain grossly unequal at another level—for example, when it comes to relations between men and women within the family.

17   When this power-structures perspective is applied to the population problem, it reveals the ways in which structures of power—interpersonal to international—influence reproductive choices.

Power and Reproductive Choice

18   In largely agrarian societies, the most accurate indicator of the economic power structure is the control of farmland, for access to land determines a family's security.

19   What are the consequences for fertility when at least one billion rural people in the Third World have been deprived of farmland? In many countries, including Brazil, Mexico, the Philippines, India, and most of the Central American countries, landholdings have become increasingly concentrated in the hands of a minority during the period of rapid population growth. When the more powerful have an incentive to expand—such as the chance to grow lucrative export crops—and have military backing, they can quite easily seize the land of the less powerful. They might do it legally, by calling in the loan of a heavily indebted peasant family, or not so legally, by simply bulldozing the peasant's land and laying claim to it. The peasant family has no legal title or lawyer to back up its claim in court.

20   In this context, without adequate land or secure tenure—and with no old-age support from the government or any other source of support outside the family—many poor people understandably view children as their sole source of power. Indeed children can be critical to their very survival.

21   For those living at the economic margin, children's labor can augment meager family income by freeing adults and elder siblings to earn outside income, or by bringing in money directly. Furthermore, in most Third World societies, parents rely on their children to care for them in old age. Children's earnings also provide insurance against risk of property loss for many rural families for whom a bad crop year or unexpected expense can spell catastrophe.

22   Adding pressure for high birth rates are high infant death rates in the Third World, for to enjoy the possible benefits of children eventually, the poor realize they need to have many children initially.

23   Of course, the value of children to their parents cannot be measured just in hours of labor or extra income. The intangibles may be just as important. In community affairs, bigger families carry more weight and sta-

tus. And for poor parents—whose lives are marred so much by grief and sacrifice—the role children play in fulfilling the very real human need for joy and satisfaction cannot be underestimated.

High birth rates reflect, moreover, the disproportionate powerlessness of women. With no say in many decisions that determine their role in the family, as well as in the society at large, many women have little opportunity for pursuits outside the home. Perpetual motherhood becomes their only "choice."   24

Women's subordination to men within the family cuts to the core of the population issue because it often translates into a direct loss of control over their own fertility. After several births, many Third World women want to avoid or delay pregnancy. But they simply do not have the power to act on their desire. As one doctor in a Mexican clinic explained, "When a wife wants to . . . [try] to limit the number of mouths to feed in the family, the husband will become angry and even beat her. He thinks it is unacceptable that she is making a decision of her own. She is challenging his authority, his power over her—and thus the very nature of his virility."[7] Patriarchal family and community attitudes may also pressure a woman to keep having children until she gives birth to a son, regardless of her own wishes or even possible jeopardy to her health.   25

The power-structures perspective helps explain the high birth rates where women are subordinated within the family and the society, but also it recognizes that the men who hold power are often themselves part of a subordinate group—those with little or no claim to income-producing resources. Denied sources of self-esteem through productive work and access to the resources needed to shoulder responsibility for their families, such men are likely to cling even more tenaciously to their superior power vis-à-vis women. In many cultures, men unable to earn enough money to support dependents feel inadequate and unable to maintain a permanent household. The resulting self-blame can contribute to a behavior pattern of men moving in and out of relationships, fathering even more children.   26

Taking the Broader View

Thus, the power-structures analysis stresses the impact on fertility of women's subordination to men, a condition that contributes to the social pressure for many births. But it places this problem within the context of unjust social and economic structures that deny women realistic alternatives to unlimited reproduction, structures that encompass far more than the family or even the community. From the level of international trade and finance, down to jobs and income available to men as well as women, antidemocratic structures of decision-making set limits on people's choices, which in turn influence their reproductive options.   27

Consider the global "debt crisis." In the 1970's, Third World governments received large loans from banks in the industrial nations and in-   28 vested the money in big-ticket projects—airports, arms, nuclear power plants, and so on—responding to the interests of their wealthiest citizens. In the 1980's, many of these loans came due, just as the interest rates climbed and prices of raw material exports from the Third World hit a 30-year low. As a result, between 1982 and 1987, the net transfer from poor countries to banks and governments in the rich countries totaled $140 billion, or the equivalent of two Marshall Plans.[8]

29   How did Third World countries come up with such sums? Health and welfare budgets and food subsidies got slashed first. And, to earn foreign exchange, land and credit increasingly went toward export crops. But reduced health care budgets mean that more babies die and fewer resources are available for comprehensive family planning care. More resources devoted to crops for export means that, locally, food becomes more scarce and more expensive. Understandably, nutrition and health worsen.

30   Thus, the "international debt crisis," seemingly remote from intimate reproductive behavior, ends up affecting the conditions of basic family security, health, and nutrition known to influence fertility.

31   This discussion of the layers of decision-making power shaping rates of human reproduction might make the reader draw back with skepticism, for could not virtually every economic, political, and cultural fact of life be viewed within such a broad perspective? Our response is that to achieve a holistic understanding, one's view must necessarily be far-reaching. But such an approach need not lack coherence. The pivot on which our perspective turns is the concept of power. Without it we believe it is impossible to understand the complex, interrelated problems of poverty, hunger, population growth, and ecological stress, much less act effectively to address them.

Solutions from the Power-Structures Perspective: The Evidence

32   A power-structures perspective holds that far-reaching economic and political change is necessary to reduce birth rates to replacement levels. Such change must enhance the power of the poorest members of society so that they no longer feel the need to cope with economic insecurity by giving birth to many children. Social arrangements beyond the family—jobs, health care, old-age security, and education (especially for women)—must offer both security and opportunity. At the same time, acceptable birth control devices must be made universally available.

33   Consider the population trends over the last 20 years in the 70-odd countries designated "low" and "lower-middle" income by the World Bank, countries that are home to three-fourths of the world's people.[9] Although average annual population growth rates in the industrial countries have been below 2 percent a year for decades, among the more than 70 poor countries only six had both reduced their population growth to less than 2 percent by the period 1980–85 and cut total fertility rates by one-

third or more since 1960. The six are China, Sri Lanka, Colombia, Chile, Burma, and Cuba. Although not a country, the Indian state of Kerala also meets these criteria.[10]

Population growth in these seven societies has slowed at a much faster rate than occurred in the now industrialized countries during their transition from high to low growth. What do these population success stories tell us?

Is it that these seven have carried out the most aggressive family planning programs? In general, no. A 1985 study rated most Third World countries according to what demographers call "family planning effort"— the prevalence and strength of organized family planning programs. The study included the six countries we are focusing on here (Kerala was not included because it is not a country). It found that two had weak or very weak family planning effort (Chile, Burma); one showed moderate effort (Cuba); and three showed strong effort (China, Sri Lanka, Colombia).[11]

What made the strong family planning efforts in those three countries so successful were the social changes introduced that allowed people to take advantage of birth control programs. What significant developments took place in these disparate societies that may hold the key? For one thing, in striking contrast to most Third World societies, four of the seven have assured their citizens considerable security through access to a basic diet: China, Kerala, Cuba, and Sri Lanka.

Of these seven societies, to us the most intriguing demographic case study is that of Kerala state in India. Its population density is three times the average for all India,[12] yet commonly used indicators of hunger and poverty—infant mortality, life expectancy, and death rate—are all considerably better in Kerala than in most low-income countries as well as in India as a whole. Its infant mortality is less than one-third the national average.[13]

Other measures of welfare also reveal the relatively better position of the poor in Kerala. In addition to a grain distribution system that keeps the cost of rice and other essentials within their reach, social security payments, pension, and unemployment benefits transfer resources to the poorest groups. Expenditures on public health in Kerala have historically been high, and the female literacy rate is two-and-a-half times the all-India average. Although land reform left significant inequality in land ownership, it did abolish tenancy, providing greater security to many who before were only renters.

But perhaps the most fundamental difference is that from the 1950's onward, political organization among Kerala's poor led to greater self-confidence. The poor came to see health care as their right, not a gift bestowed upon them. And among agricultural workers, grassroots political organization has also been the key to making land reform meaningful, to keeping wages relatively high, and to securing old-age pensions.

39   Although more complex, China's recent demographic history is equally telling. From 1969 to 1979, China achieved a dramatic transition from high to low rates of fertility, often attributed simplistically to an aggressive family planning program. Through a network of "barefoot doctors," family planning programs reached into every village, making birth control freely available and relying on group persuasion to change attitudes toward childbearing and family size.

40   Unarguably, such a concerted effort helps explain the dramatic fall in China's fertility rate in the 1970's. But China's family planning program did not arise out of thin air; it reflected prior, massive political change. We can unequivocally condemn China's totalitarian features while recognizing that a shift in power from a leadership long ignoring the needs of the Chinese peasantry to one attempting to address those needs was a prerequisite to China's population success record.

41   It was in 1979 that China's family planning policies took a new tack, when the Deng Xiaoping government instituted the world's most restrictive family planning program. Material incentives and penalties began to be offered to encourage all parents to bear only one offspring, and enormous pressure was brought to bear on those who become "unofficially" pregnant. At the same time, China's post-1979 approach to economic development began to undercut guaranteed employment, and old-age and medical security. In agriculture, the "individual responsibility" system replaced collective production; private entrepreneurship is now encouraged.

42   Thrown back on their own family's resources, many Chinese again see having many children—especially boys—as beneficial, both as a substitute for lost public protections and as a means of taking maximum advantage of the new economic system.[14] Since 1980, in fact, China's birth rates have *risen*.[15] This fertility rise is not due solely to these economic and social changes, but surely these underlying changes add to pressure for higher fertility.[16]

Reflections and Implications for Action

43   In our view, the population puzzle is impossible to solve without employing the concept of social power. The very great diversity of these societies underscores our earlier point that power is not a monolithic concept, moving uniformly through the many sectors and levels of a society. It is diverse, characterized by uneven development. But within each of these successful societies, shifts in power relations in key aspects of family, community, and national life have made lowered fertility possible: the enhanced power of women, through basic literacy, education, and employment; the heightened power of peasants to provide food and income for themselves because of land reforms; the bolstered power of consumers to secure adequate nutrition where deliberate policies have been implemented to keep basic food staples within reach of all; the enhanced capacity of people to

protect their health as medical care becomes accessible; and the heightened power of women to limit their births through birth control. These are some vital measures of changes needed for people to be able to choose fewer children.

In recent years, however, especially with the advent of the debt crisis, some have suggested that Third World countries are just too poor to address rapid population growth through economic and social development. Surely our examples demonstrate the fallacy of this easy out. Of the seven societies we cite for their exceptionally rapid drop in fertility, four are among the world's poorest: China, Sri Lanka, Burma, and the Indian state of Kerala. Poverty is no excuse for the continuing violation of basic human rights to essential resources.

Effective Responses to the Population Problem

Since the 1960's, those operating from the people-versus-resources perspective have linked the specter of famine to overpopulation and, in challenging this view, structural analysts have understandably focused on food, too. They have shown that hunger is not caused by inadequate resources.[17] Those using the power-structures perspective must now make clear that although hunger is not caused by too many people, for many other reasons one might well judge a nation to have too many people.

To thrive, human beings need a pollution-free environment to protect health, and enough physical space to allow for intellectual and spiritual growth. Ecosystem services such as adequate clean water, cool breezes, clean air, and diverse natural resources all support humans in their day-to-day activities. Human well-being is also enhanced by the opportunity to enjoy an environment undefaced and untransformed by human manipulation. The power-structures perspective emphasizes the quality of human relations but this can hardly be described without attention to the larger natural world we inhabit.

This analysis can therefore serve all those concerned about the quality of life for yet unborn generations. At the same time, it can incorporate the insights of ecological thinkers who challenge the assumption that if humans are thriving, then everything is all right. The accelerating destruction of irreplaceable rainforests is only one example of environmental assault, which threatens far more than humanity's well-being. This perspective can affirm that the infinitely rich biosphere itself must be considered of innate worth.

In other words, the power-structures analysis can show how the same antidemocratic structures that keep fertility high also play a central role in environmental destruction. Further, it can incorporate the insights of those questioning *any* model of development that perceives the environment merely as a pool of resources for human use.

In recent years it has become commonplace to acknowledge the complex social roots of the population problem. But when attention turns to solutions, this social analysis is foregone. It is assumed that regardless of the real roots of the problem, better birth control programs are all that the industrial West can offer.

50   We do not accept this view, especially as U.S. citizens. As a major world power, the U.S. government directly and indirectly shapes the behavior of many foreign governments. It is inconceivable that the United States would ever stop using its foreign policy to aid those governments it deems supportive of its own interests. But until our government transcends its deep fear of redistributive change abroad, our tax dollars will go on supporting governments that block the very changes we outline in this chapter as necessary to allow people the option of smaller families.

51   U.S. policy toward the Philippines illustrates our point. The population growth rate in the Philippines is among the highest in Asia, and its people are among the poorest and hungriest. Seventy percent of the rural people either lack land altogether or lack secure tenure to the land they farm. The United States supplied billions of dollars to maintain the former martial law government of Ferdinand Marcos, which not only refused to reform this gross imbalance in access to resources, but furthered economic concentration. Since 1986, the Philippines' new government remains unwilling to confront the underlying insecurity at the root of hunger and high birth rates; yet, it too receives enormous U.S. military, economic, and diplomatic support.

52   Unfortunately, the Philippines is the rule, not the exception. Rarely has the United States made its economic and political support conditional on domestic policies addressing the undemocratic economic structures that stand in the way of a significant drop in birth rates.

53   We argue that such a change in policy cannot come about until U.S. citizens reorient their government's understanding of what is in our own interests.[18] Simply funding a family planning initiative in the Philippines or in Honduras, for example, is woefully inadequate. If U.S. citizens are serious about confronting the worldwide population problem and related ecological problems, we must be willing to do that which is much more controversial: explicitly to identify the link between U.S. policies and the antidemocratic structures of decision-making power that keep birth rates high to begin with, and to use our rights as citizens to alter those policies.

54   Taking population seriously thus means incorporating the concept of social power as an indispensable tool of analysis and facing the logical consequences. It means learning from the historical evidence: without more democratic structures of decision-making power, from the family to the global arena, there is no solution—short of dehumanizing coercion or plagues—to the population explosion. The fate of the Earth hinges on the fate of today's poor majorities. Only as they are empowered to achieve greater security and opportunity—can population growth halt.

Notes

1. This chapter is excerpted from "The Missing Piece in the Population Puzzle: Power and Fertility," *Food First Development Report #4* (Summer 1988). Available from The Institute for Food and Development Policy, 145 Ninth St., San Francisco, CA 94103.

2. Frances Moore Lappé and Joseph Collins with Cary Fowler, *Food First: Beyond the Myth of Scarcity* (New York: Ballantine, 1977); Frances Moore Lappé and Joseph Collins, *World Hunger: Twelve Myths* (New York and San Francisco: Grove Press/Food First Books, 1986).

3. Per capita cropland data from Francis Urban and Thomas Vollrath, "Patterns and Trends in World Agricultural Land Use," *Foreign Agricultural Economic Report, no. 198* (Washington, DC: U.S. Dept. of Agriculture, Economic Research Service, 1984), table 2; Life expectancy from World Bank, *World Development Report 1985,* (New York: Oxford University Press, 1985), table 1, p. 174.

4. At least half of that lies completely idle. See "The IMF and the Impoverishment of Brazil," *Instituto Brasileiro de Analises Socias e Economicas (IBASE)* (Rio de Janeiro, September 8, 1985), p. 18. See also, Mac Margolis, "Land Disputes Trigger Wave of Violence in Brazil," *Washington Post* (August 29, 1985).

5. For more on the forces behind rainforest destruction in Indonesia, see K. Kartawinata and A. P. Vayda, "Forest Conversion in East Kalimantan, Indonesia: The Activities and Impact of Timber Companies, Shifting Cultivators, Migrant Pepper-Farmers and Others," in F. DiCastri et al., eds., *Ecology in Practice* (Paris: UNESCO).

6. Val Plumwood and Richard Routley, "World Rainforest Destruction—The Social Factors," *The Ecologist* 12:1 (1982), p. 14.

7. Perdita Huston, *Message from the Village* (New York: The Epoch B Foundation, 1978), p. 119, cited in Hartmann, *Reproductive Rights and Wrongs*, p. 48.

8. Susan George, *Fate Worse than Debt* (New York: Grove Press/Food First Books, 1988).

9. World Bank, *World Development Report 1987,* table 27. We've included Cuba in this list of 74 low and lower-middle income countries because it was so classified for the first period of our time series. Only in recent years has the World Bank reclassified Cuba as a "nonreporting nonmember economy." Countries of a million or fewer in population are excluded from the bank's statistics.

10. According to the Indian Census, the population growth rate of Kerala averaged 1.8 percent annually between 1971 and 1981 (*Census of India,* Kerala State, Part 2A, Statements 3 and 8, pp. 28 and 32). Interview with Dr. K. C. Zachariah at the World Bank, Population and Human Resources Division, April 1986.

11. Robert J. Lapham and W. Parker Mauldin, "Contraceptive Prevalence: The Influence of Organized Family Planning Programs," *Studies in Family Planning* 16 (May–June 1985), pp. 177–237.

12. A. V. Jose, "Poverty and Inequality: The Case of Kerala," in Azizur Rahman Khan and Eddy Lee, eds., *Poverty in Rural Asia* (Bangkok: International Labour Organization, Asian Employment Programme, 1983), p. 108.

13. *World Development Forum 6* (Feb. 29, 1988), p. 1, quoting the New Delhi Family Planning Foundation. The infant mortality rate in India is 100; in Kerala it is 30.

14. This may well explain the rise in female infanticide in China since the 1979 change in policy. See "The Threat of Population Growth," *World Press Review* (Aug. 1987), p. 59.

15. Ratcliffe, "China's Population Policies." See also news release from the Population Reference Bureau (Apr. 28, 1988).

16. The fertility rise may also be a consequence of the Chinese government's 1980 decision to relax its stringent policy governing age at marriage, and its recent relaxation in enforcement of the one-child policy.

17. See, for instance, Lappé and Collins, *Food First and World Hunger: Twelve Myths.*

18. Frances Moore Lappé, Rachel Schurman, and Kevin Danaher, *Betraying the National Interest* (New York and San Francisco: Grove Press/Food First Books, 1988).

Reading and Analyzing

1. What problem will the authors examine? What is the connection between rainforest protection and population growth?
2. Explain the concept of a "power-structures perspective."
3. What is the authors' claim?
4. The authors challenge a causal relationship between hunger and population size. What are other possible explanations?
5. Similarly, how should rainforest destruction be understood? Who is causing the destruction?
6. Explain, in your own words, the idea of the democratic to antidemocratic continuum and its application at various levels.
7. What does a power-structure perspective tell us about the "choice" of Third World peasant families to have many children?
8. How does the subordination of women contribute to high birth rates?
9. How has the international debt crisis impacted on population growth?
10. What solutions do the authors recommend?
11. Can poor countries make the needed changes? What evidence do the authors provide to answer this question?
12. What should the United States do to help?
13. In this problem-solution paper, which steps get the greatest emphasis? In other words, what is the authors' primary purpose in writing?

Responding to the Writers' Ideas

1. Once again we see writers connecting population size to preserving rainforests and conserving the Earth's resources in general. Is this a

new way for you to look at environmental problems? If so, does it make sense to you? Why or why not?

2. Is Lappé and Schurman's power-structures approach a new idea for you? If so, have the authors presented a convincing argument for the approach? Does it make sense to you that poor farmers would value large families for security?

3. Lappé and Schurman also see the subjection of women in terms of power. Does it make sense that poor men, those who have little feeling of power and control, would seek dominance over their families? (You might do some research on the economic distribution of family size. Is there an inverse correlation between income and family size?)

4. The authors have argued that a redefining of the problem leads to an understanding that different solutions are needed. Have the authors made a convincing argument that hunger is not caused simply by high population density? Or that poor countries cannot be expected to control population growth? Why or why not?

5. Evaluate Lappé and Schurman's proposed general solution. Does the idea that the United States should tie its aid to a country's willingness to provide more democratic structures follow logically from the authors' analysis? Is the solution one you accept? Why or why not?

❖

Keeping the Ivory Trade Banned

Mark Pagel and Ruth Mace

Mark Pagel (b. 1954) has a Ph.D. in statistics and has taught at the University of Washington and Oxford University. He is currently a research fellow exploring biological evolutionary theory in the School of Mathematical Sciences at the University of London. British born Ruth Mace (b. 1961) took her doctorate in zoology at Oxford University and went on to postdoctoral work at the University of London. She is currently a lecturer in biological anthropology at the University of London's University College. Both authors have published articles in their fields, and Pagel has coauthored The Comparative Method in Evolutionary Biology *(1991). In the following article, published May 23, 1991, in the British journal* Nature, *Pagel and Mace refute arguments for lifting the ban on selling ivory and present an argument for maintaining the ban.*

1   The international moratorium on the trade of ivory agreed at the Convention on International Trade in Endangered Species (CITES) meeting in 1989 is under siege. The ban was already somewhat tattered at birth because several key ivory-exporting countries refused to cooperate with it. But it has achieved a greatness of sorts: after eight frenzied years in which poachers reduced the African elephant populations by 50 per cent or more, by all accounts poaching has plummeted along with the price of ivory.[1-3] Elephant tusks that would have fetched perhaps $100 per kilogram for a poacher in 1989, currently find few buyers at $2–3 per kilogram, according to Richard Leakey, director of the Kenya Wildlife Service.[2] Leakey adds that elephants are beginning to return to parts of northern Kenya from which they had been eradicated or fled.[3] But rumblings from ivory-exporting and importing nations to lift the ban have placed it squarely on the agenda of the next CITES meeting in Japan during January 1992.

2   It is easy to be cynical about this issue. Pressures to lift the ban derive from its success: ivory-exporting countries are feeling the pinch of having lost their markets, ivory importers are chafing to resume business, and the decline in poaching has created a sense that elephants are, perhaps, not as threatened as once feared. Moreover, arguments against bans seem to be fashionable in the environmental economics and development literature, in academic enclaves, among science journalists, and even among some con-

488

servation organizations.[2,4,5-7] Politicians have been quick to seize this momentum. The British Trade Secretary David Heathcoat-Amory, following a short debate in the House of Commons last August, said "there are indications that the ban on the trade of ivory is proving effective. . . . I hope that should the situation continue to improve it may be possible to in the not too distant future allow the ban to be lifted in some respects" (ref. 1). But despite the fall in ivory prices, poaching is still occurring.

More thoughtful attempts to argue against the ban have been mooted by the economists.[4,6,7] An indefinite ban on the trade in ivory, the argument goes, causes an initial drop in demand and price as legal demand for ivory declines. But due to latent consumer demand for ivory, some of the formerly legal demand will be shifted into illegal demand (that is, demand that can only be satisfied by illegal supply). This argument assumes, probably correctly, that any ban will be cheated upon because some countries will ignore it either by allowing the killing of elephants for ivory, or by allowing the sale of ivory products. The result of increasing the demand on a subset of the total supply (that is, on the supply that is obtained by poaching) is to raise the price of ivory, and thereby promote poaching. Over time the amount of illegal demand may even increase if more and more of the formerly legal demand shifts to illegal demand, or if new consumers enter the market. The result is even more poaching. Lifting the ban, it is argued, would prevent this upward spiral of poaching.

The spectre of a brutish hobbesian underworld of ivory poachers slaked by illegal consumer demand for ivory is distressing. Nevertheless, the economic arguments hide the gruesome fact that nearly all of the so-called legal supply of ivory has in the past been obtained illegally by poaching. Only two countries—Zimbabwe and South Africa—have legal culling programmes and they provide only a small fraction of the total ivory that is traded.[5] The remainder of the ivory has been confiscated from poachers by governments and sold. This point is overlooked by every economic argument advanced against the ban, and yet it is crucial to understanding why lifting the ban must be avoided. Governments that confiscated poached ivory were, under CITES pre-ban Appendix II regulations, able to sell this ivory legally. Appendix II regulations allow some legal trade in ivory whereas the more restrictive Appendix I regulations—in force under the current ban—prohibit trade in elephant products of any kind. Therefore, countries whose elephant populations were being drastically reduced by poaching were still selling 'legal' ivory. Furthermore, given such rules, there was great temptation for government 'confiscators' to team up with 'poachers', leading in some cases to the ivory being 'confiscated' directly from the elephant.

When weighing arguments against the ban, it must also be borne in mind that total demand for ivory is lower if there is at least one honest ivory trader who does not respond to the ban by seeking illegal supplies, or at least one obedient consumer who decides not to buy ivory products. So, if the goal is fewer elephants killed, a ban will probably work. The success of the current ban attests to this. But those opposed to a ban argue that a potential difficulty arises because poaching is not easily stopped. Regardless of how one feels about killing elephants, there is some amount of ivory that could be obtained each year that would be sustainable over the long term. If enough countries were to ignore the ban, especially the importing nations which create the demand for ivory, poaching might exceed this. Again, however, such arguments ignore the fact that the proportion of the total world demand for ivory that was being met before the ban by truly legal culling was very small. Concern about the amount of poaching under a ban misses this important point.

6   Other arguments against the ivory ban rely on the idea that a legal trade in ivory gives governments an incentive to keep poaching at a minimum as a way of protecting a valuable export commodity.[4-7] Economists turned conservationists, the environmental economists, argue that elephants, like other environmental resources, can be "sustainably managed" or "sustainably developed" once they are properly valued.[6-9] The idea of sustainable development is that a resource has some estimable value to society and to future generations. Using or consuming the resource in a sustainable way can mean a variety of things, but the key point seems to be that the resource is preserved for future generations. For example, if the resource is clean water, then one might want to tax polluters as a way of either giving them an incentive to pollute less, or as a way of accumulating money which is spent on cleaning the water. If the resource is consumed but is renewable, like trees, the idea is to charge a high enough price for them to ensure that there is roughly a balance between consumption of trees and planting of new trees so that the resource will not be used up. In theory, the price attached to the resource should be sufficient to guarantee that the resource is properly managed.

Sustainable Development

7   These ideas are now being applied to elephants.[6,7] The argument is that if the revenues from sustainable development of elephants, that is from culling or hunting programmes, are higher than those which can be obtained from short-term eradication, there will be an incentive to conserve the elephants. But such schemes can never work for elephants so long as they are a 'commons' or nonexcludable resource. If an ivory trade is resumed in the form of some countries attempting to run sustainable development programmes, the consumer-driven demand for ivory will return. This will be true even if only a small number of countries are given the right to trade in ivory. The demand created by the legal sale of ivory will provide incentives to poachers. If poachers can kill elephants and sell their ivory, the short-term payoffs of doing so will be much more valuable to

them than the idea of preserving the elephant for possible long-term advantages to society—the 'intergenerational equity' of the green economists.[9] Only if all elephants—not just those in one or a few countries—could be rounded up and put in a pen would such a sustainable development programme have a chance of working. Then the death of each elephant, perhaps from government culling for later sale or from a tourist hunter's rifle could be 'appropriately' valued. But, like air, large migratory animals tend to be found all over.

Countries that want to preserve their elephants but still engage in a legal ivory trade will always suffer the costs of stopping the illegal killing of elephants for their ivory. No matter that only some ivory would be 'legal': smugglers are notoriously good at getting around legal strictures, and certificates of legality can and have been forged.[4,10] Further, attempts by governments to stop poaching will always have to bridge a fundamental asymmetry between poachers and governments. Poaching is a livelihood for many poachers. Stopping poaching is a policy that can return benefits, but not ones on which the livelihood of the government rests. There are analogies here to the state of nature: a rabbit's life depends upon not getting caught by the fox chasing it. Not catching a rabbit means the fox may go without its dinner. Running fast brings higher rewards to rabbits than to foxes.[11] Aesop knew this.

Managing elephants for long-term yields is also difficult to sustain because of the presence of other nations that want to make a profit from their ivory. If one or two countries were to be granted trading status, and they were to make money from ivory, it would only encourage other nations to do the same. Managing for long-term sustained yields would require cartel-like cooperation among these nations to prevent increased ivory production by one or more of them. Where the attraction of short-term economic gains—often to ameliorate domestic ructions—can easily outweigh the more abstract promise of sustainable but lower long-term yields, this is unlikely: cartels are unstable, just look to OPEC.

The most effective way to stop the killing of elephants is to reduce demand for ivory. This is best achieved by banning the trade in ivory and making social outcasts of those in possession of it; strategies that seem to be working for furs. Allowing even a small legal trade in ivory will make this impossible: the existence of any socially acceptable ivory would confuse public opinion, and keep consumer demand alive. The reduction in demand that has been brought about by the publicity of the current ban has probably been the most important reason behind its success in reducing poaching.[4] Bans or partial bans enacted by Britain, the nations of the European Community, the United States, Dubai and Japan may all have been a response to public pressure. A ban is the only option that avoids public confusion and which greatly reduces the demand for ivory, even if some countries ignore it. It is the much more trying option: a ban will create social disruption as ivory carvers lose their market, and it will witness the temporary degradation of habitats as some elephant populations grow large. But elephants have proven to be a great attraction to tourists—thus generating jobs, and revenues—and nature has long known how to regulate natural populations. Moreover, elephants as a tourist attraction do not require the elephant-containing nations to cooperate like a cartel: there are no incentives to cheat on the elephants. Just the opposite behaviour—competition for tourists—will be favoured.

Tourism

11   Tourism also provides a dependable incentive for stopping poaching. In addition to the money that tourism funnels into local economies, tourists may even be willing to pay an elephant surcharge.[5] If elephants are worth more alive than dead then they will not be killed. This is different from the sustainable development idea, which attempts only to value appropriately each kill, and which by placing ivory in the marketplace keeps demand alive. Kenya is already profiting handsomely from showing off its elephants to tourists. The key to the success of tourist programmes such as Kenya's is to direct the profits just as much as possible into improving the standard of living of the local people involved in the tourist trade, and into improving the management and facilities of national parks.

12   Just such a programme has been highly successful at providing protection for the mountain gorillas in Zaire.[12] Poaching had reduced the population to around 260 but now the ranks are increasing. Receipts from allowing groups of just six tourists at a time to visit gorilla families rose from zero to about £23,000 per month between 1984 and 1987 (ref. 12). Guards are provided with uniforms, boots, warm clothing, sleeping bags and wet-proofs.[12]

13   Any other option for the ivory trade, such as relying upon centralized trading exchanges[2,6,7] as a way of monitoring where and how the ivory was obtained (for example, by using isotope analysis of tusks[13,14]), and to whom it will be sold, will only encourage the demand for ivory products and suffer from the weaknesses discussed here. Such schemes reflect economic and market ideals, fanned by current scholarly fashion, more than reality in an industry that has proven adept at getting its product (legal and illegal) to market so long as there is demand for it.

References

1. *New Scient.* **127**, 26 (1990).
2. *The Economist* **318** (7696), 16 (1991).
3. *The Economist* **318** (7696), 42 (1991).
4. *The Economist* **312** (7609), 15 (1989).
5. *The Economist* **313** (7624), 19 (1989).
6. Barbier, E. & Swanson, T. *New Scient.* **127**, 52 (1990).

7. Barbier, E., Burgess, J., Swanson, T. & Pearce, D. *Elephants, Economics, and Ivory* (Earthscan, London, 1991).

8. *The Economist* **312** (7620), 77 (1989).

9. Pearce, D., Markyanda, A. & Barbier, E. *Blueprint for a Green Economy* (Earthscan, London, 1991).

10. Milner-Gulland, E. J. & Mace, R. *Biol. Conserv.* **55**, 215–229 (1991).

11. Dawkins, R. & Krebs, J. R. *Proc. R. Soc.* B **205**, 489–511 (1979).

12. Aveling, C. & Aveline, R. *Oryx* **23**, 64–70 (1989).

13. Vogel, J. C., Eglington, B. & Auret, J. M. *Nature* **346**, 747–749 (1990).

14. van de Merwe, N. J. *et al. Nature* **346**, 744–746 (1990).

Reading and Analyzing

1. What is the authors' subject?
2. What is the specific occasion that provides a context for the article?
3. What evidence do the authors cite to demonstrate the ban's success?
4. What, ironically, is one of the best pieces of evidence that the ban has been working?
5. Explain, in your own words, the argument for lifting the ban because it encourages poaching.
6. Explain the term *hobbesian* in paragraph 4.
7. How do the authors counter the arguments against the ban?
8. Explain the concept of sustainable development. Why is this concept inappropriate when applied to preserving elephants?
9. What is the authors' claim? Where do they state it?
10. What do the authors offer as an alternative source of revenue for countries making money (legally or illegally) from the ivory trade?

Responding to the Writers' Ideas

1. The authors' argument is a tightly constructed web of ideas. How would you describe the essay's tone? Is the tone appropriate for the essay's audience? (What do you know—or can you learn—about the journal *Nature*?)
2. Do you find the approach of the authors to be persuasive, effective? If not, why not? What approach would work better for you? Why?
3. Analyze the argument as a refutation. Have the authors presented the opposing arguments clearly and then offered clear and relevant points refuting the opposition? Can you use this as a good model of a clear and effective refutation? If so, what can you learn from this model about writing effective refutations?
4. Which of the authors' arguments for maintaining a ban on ivory do you find most convincing? Why?

Stopgap Measures

Suzanne Winckler

Suzanne Winckler wrote two volumes of the twelve-volume
Smithsonian guide to historic America: The Great Lakes *(1988) and*
The Plains States *(1989). She is a contributing editor to the* Texas
Monthly. *In "Stopgap Measures," published in the January 1992 issue*
of Atlantic, *Winckler analyzes existing problems in meeting the goals of*
the Endangered Species Act and argues for an alternative approach.

1   To say that the Endangered Species Act is not working is to sound ungrateful for what it has accomplished. Inasmuch as tens, if not hundreds, of organisms that would undoubtedly be extinct by now—including the Attwater's prairie chicken, the Florida panther, the black-footed ferret, the Kirtland's warbler, and the Puerto Rican parrot—are instead hanging on by a thread, the act has been a success.

2   The continued existence, however precarious, of these species is deeply satisfying to many people. The creatures are beautiful (the whooping crane); they stand for ideals that are important to us culturally (the bald eagle); they exhibit incredible behavior (the Attwater's prairie chicken); they are stunning emblems of the closest we can come to pristine wilderness (the grizzly bear). Our knowledge of their presence in the wild helps assuage our guilt about what we've done to them in particular and to the natural world in general, which might imply that the Endangered Species Act is ultimately designed to treat our own brand of sickness and not theirs. Regardless of what these animals do to make us feel better, they are the walking wounded of the world, and it costs millions of dollars to keep them out there.

3   That it saves organisms from extinction is faint praise for a law with the far loftier aspiration of "better safeguarding, for the benefit of all citizens, the Nation's heritage in fish, wildlife, and plants." It is the stated purpose of the law not just to keep species from going extinct but to return them to viability. In this regard it is failing.

4   The Endangered Species Act takes under its wing an array of taxa—from full species (whooping crane) to subspecies (Attwater's prairie chicken) to discrete populations of species (the Mojave population of the desert tortoise). "Taxon" (plural "taxa") refers to any of the groupings into which taxonomists classify organisms. As of last November the federal

government listed 1,196 taxa around the world—more than half of them occurring in the United States and its territories—as either endangered or threatened, one of which dubious distinctions is necessary for care under the act. Another 3,500 or so are waiting for review. Among this second group—known as candidate species or Category 1 and Category 2 species—are many plants and animals acknowledged by scientists to be in far worse danger than species that have already qualified. They languish in bureaucratic limbo because of a perennial problem of the act: it never has enough funding. A number of candidate species have gone extinct before they could be considered for listing.

The process for listing threatened and endangered species is complicated, but if there is an overriding criterion for listing, it is that the species is demonstrably imperiled. John Fay, a botanist with the Division of Endangered Species of the U.S. Fish and Wildlife Service, explains the implicit ranking process: "We try to set our priorities so that those species that face the greatest threat are the ones we address first. The alternative—intervening with things that are in better shape—would mean losing a substantial number of species in immediate danger. And within the terms of the Endangered Species Act that's unacceptable."

This is what critics point to as a major failing of the act. It intervenes in a way that no intelligent nurse, paramedic, or doctor would under analogous circumstances. It has thrown out the window any concept of triage. It does not sort and care for species in such a way as to maximize the number of surviving species. On the contrary, it attempts to save the hardest cases, the equivalent of the terminally ill and the brain-dead. It pays less attention to species that would be easier and cheaper to save—species that require treatment akin to minor surgery, a splint, or a Band-Aid. The act has no concept of preventive medicine, of keeping healthy species from peril. Consequently, many animals and plants that were common twenty years ago—were even considered in some realms to be pests—are now entitled to care under the Endangered Species Act.

One reason the act eschews triage is that its enforcers, not to mention many endangered-species watchdogs, do not want—and do not want to allow anyone else—to "play God." There is no doubt that such a role confers awesome responsibilities. The triage of species and the triage of individuals of one species (as it is practiced in emergency rooms and on battlefields) differ by several orders of magnitude. Few people would want the ethical burden of deciding the fate of a whole species—of saying, for instance, that the blunt-nosed leopard lizard can go but the humpback whale stays. John Fay says, "All we can do is try to preserve our options. My absolutely favorite quote is from Aldo Leopold: 'To save every cog in the wheel is the first precaution of intelligent tinkering.' That's what we're trying to do. We don't know which ones are important. We don't know which ones are going to disappear."

8   Moral neutrality is noble, but it creates problems in the categories of money (there has never been enough allocated to save every cog; there is no promise of more in the future) and biology (the cogs we are saving are so crippled, so compromised, that they can barely perform their assigned functions in their respective niches). To refuse to play God is to play the devil by default.

9   It's also true that saving species that don't need much fixing is boring. We thrive on crisis management, and we love things that are rare much more than things that are common. The people in the public and private sectors who work on policy that actually attempts to protect species before they become endangered—for instance, the Fish and Wildlife Service's Office of Migratory Bird Management, the Nature Conservancy, and the International Council for Bird Preservation—receive precious little attention from the media for their work, because what they do is tedious and unglamorous: it does not play well in measured media doses the way a hand puppet feeding a nestling condor does.

Uncertain Return on Investment

10   In 1988 Congress began to require that the Fish and Wildlife Service submit annual reports on federal expenditures for the U.S. roster of endangered and threatened species. (The federal government spends little money on foreign species.) This is not an easy task—at least thirteen federal agencies make regular outlays of money for endangered species. Nor are the reports ever likely to be more than a best guess of expenditures, since endangered-species activities often merge with other operations. For example, prescribed burning—setting fires to remove the brushy vegetation once held at bay by natural fires—is a management tool at Francis Marion National Forest, in coastal South Carolina, which aids not only endangered red-cockaded woodpeckers but also game species like turkey and quail.

11   While there is much to be said for making the protectors of endangered species accountable for how they spend our money, the expense reports (two have been prepared so far, for 1989 and 1990) are sadly divisive documents that reinforce the individual-species thrust of the Endangered Species Act. They provide ammunition not only for those who are alarmed by how much we're spending on, say, the Higgins' eye pearly mussel ($437,700 in 1989; $367,000 in 1990) but also for those who are upset at what we're *not* spending on, say, the desert tortoise, a species that because of a strange upper-respiratory disease is dropping dead at an alarming pace in the Mojave Desert. The tortoise got almost $500,000 in 1989. Its advocates saw that boosted to more than $4 million in 1990.

12   By focusing on individual species, the expenditure reports perpetuate a chronic lack of attention to the big picture. Environmentalists are defending expenditures for the plants and animals to which they have, for whatever reason, chosen allegiance when instead they should be addressing

a whole different set of questions and concerns. Why does the list of endangered and threatened species keep getting longer? Why have only a few species ever been taken off the list? Where on earth will the money come from to care for every new addition to the lengthening list?

The biggest question the expenditure reports should provoke is this: 13
Why is half of all the money earmarked for endangered and threatened species being spent on only twelve of them? In 1990, of $102 million apportioned among 591 taxa, a total of $55 million went to twelve. They are, in descending order of expenditures, the northern spotted owl, the least Bell's vireo, the grizzly bear, the red-cockaded woodpecker, the Florida panther, the desert tortoise, the bald eagle, the ocelot, the jaguarundi, the peregrine falcon, the California least tern, and the Chinook salmon. The apportionment does not become much more equal after this first dozen. The next dozen species—which include the gray wolf, the southern sea otter, and the Puerto Rican parrot—received the next $19 million. In other words, the remaining quarter of funding—$28 million—was shared among about 570 other organisms.

The fortunate two dozen or so creatures that command three quar-   14
ters of the money are among the most beautiful on earth. They have captured the hearts of a wide assortment of people. These people would better serve the objects of their affections if they cared for whole ecosystems—the degradation of which is largely responsible for our degraded wildlife—with the same fervor.

Intensive care for animals and plants is costly. It is not cheap to hire   15
airplanes and helicopters for the surveillance of populations (as was done before the last California condors were taken from the wild), set up captive-breeding facilities (for the bald eagle, the peregrine falcon, the whooping crane, and the black-footed ferret), translocate animals, either in order to get them away from the threat of people or in order to invigorate isolated gene pools (the grizzly bear, the red-cockaded woodpecker), release individuals back into the wild (successfully accomplished with the peregrine falcon), attempt to establish breeding populations (tried and failed with the whooping crane), or keep parasitic cowbirds out of the nests of endangered birds (being done year in and year out for the Kirtland's warbler, the golden-cheeked warbler, and the black-capped vireo). When we focus treatment on the most afflicted, we can expect to pay.

It is true that the Endangered Species Act inherited some desperate   16
cases when it went into effect. The whooping crane, the California condor, and the Kirtland's warbler are examples of species that were rare to begin with and suffered from the presence of people within their ranges. Thirty years before the Endangered Species Act, biologists had begun the arduous and expensive endeavor of bringing the whooping crane back, from a single flock of fourteen individuals in the wild. After fifty years of intensive management, the wild flock of whooping cranes numbers about 140 birds.

This population—like all small populations—is intensely vulnerable: last winter nine birds, representing six percent of the flock, were lost.

17   It is also true that many endangered and threatened species need only moderate sums of money to survive. For instance, certain narrowly endemic plants—plants that have evolved in rare microhabitats, such as the bunched cory cactus and the McKittrick pennyroyal—require little more than the purchase of the land on which they grow, and small outlays for monitoring and law enforcement (cacti, for example, are particularly susceptible to rapacious collectors).

18   But for every one of these bargain species there is a very expensive one waiting for a constituency to care enough, waiting to get a little more endangered, or waiting for its recovery plan to be approved. To name just a few, they include the black-capped vireo, the golden-cheeked warbler, several of the Columbia River salmon stocks, the humpback whale, the San Marcos gambusia, Texas wild rice, and the thirty-odd species of freshwater mussels now menaced by the accidental introduction of the alien zebra mussel.

Last-Ditch Spending

19   The conventional wisdom is that money will save these mortally damaged species. And more money is on the way. Since the Reagan years, when funding for and morale within the Division of Endangered Species fell to all-time lows, its fortunes have enjoyed a reversal. President George Bush's appointment of John Turner as the director of the U.S. Fish and Wildlife Service has restored a sense of mission and esprit de corps to the division, and Bush's 1992 budget included a record request of almost $60 million for the endangered-species program. Although these developments are salutary, they are the sort of modest encouragement that rewards the status quo and inhibits critical assessment of a noble piece of legislation that is fraught with problems.

20   All bird watchers have had the gut-wrenching experience of returning to a woods, marsh, or stream that has transmogrified into a condominium project or a cornfield or a parking lot. Their local, subjective sense of loss can be objectified and magnified across the continent. In 1987 the Office of Technology Assessment published a document called "Technologies to Maintain Biological Diversity." It is full of depressing information, including this rueful sentence: "Natural ecosystem diversity has declined in the United States historically, and no evidence suggests that this long-term trend has been arrested." The authors continue, "Twenty-three ecosystem types that once covered about half the conterminous United States now cover only about 7 percent."

21   The recent book *Where Have All the Birds Gone?*, by the biologist John Terborgh, is a long lament over the loss of habitat in North America: only a fraction of a percent remains of the virgin forests that once covered

the continent east of the Rockies; more than 90 percent of the woodlands along rivers and streams in the arid West have been eliminated, for the sake of flood control or irrigation; 99 percent of Iowa's wetlands, 90 percent of Nebraska's and Missouri's, 89 percent of Illinois's, and 80 percent of Minnesota's have been drained and converted to cropland.

In order to save the most-endangered species, the act diverts attention and money from the much more crucial goal of preserving overall biological diversity—that is, preserving the maximum number of healthy species in ecosystems that require a minimum of maintenance. The way to save species is to save the places where they live. By extension, the way to save the greatest number of species is to save the places that house the richest biological inventory. One example is the 17,800-acre Sacramento National Wildlife Refuge, where, according to J. Michael Scott, a research biologist with the U.S. Fish and Wildlife Service, and his colleagues, there are 257 vertebrate species, 170 of which have resident populations. "The populations of many of these species number in the tens of thousands," Scott et al. write. "The annual cost of managing this system, estimated at one million dollars, is less than the annual expenditures on the recovery effort for the critically endangered California condor." The comparatively low cost of maintenance leads Scott and his colleagues to conclude, "Prevention is cheaper than treatment."

The Endangered Species Act has institutionalized the bizarre notion that the primary legal justification for the preservation of an ecosystem is a species teetering on the brink of extinction. That it is one of the most magnificent landscapes in North America is somehow no longer reason enough to preserve the last remnants of the Pacific old-growth forest. Instead, the only legal mechanism available is to require the preservation of some minimum configuration of that forest in hopes of keeping the northern spotted owl—one species among thousands that dwell there—from going extinct. At the same time, the boreal forests of Minnesota, Wisconsin, and upper Michigan, the marshes and wetlands rimming our coasts, the prairie potholes of the Midwest, the riparian woodlands along streams in the West, and other ecosystems will continue to shrink until they yield evidence of the endangered species that will warrant their preservation.

These ecosystems are well on their way to providing the requisite crippled species. Of particular concern to biologists is the roster of declining birds, any one of which may soon vie with the northern spotted owl for attention in the media. They are the common loon, the wood thrush, the Swainson's warbler, and the marbled murrelet, which rely on various forest ecosystems; the reddish egret, a coastal species; the surfbird, the bristle-thighed curlew, and the buff-breasted sandpiper, highly migratory shorebirds; and the vermilion flycatcher, the loggerhead shrike, and the grasshopper sparrow, denizens of various grassland, prairie, and plains ecosystems.

25   These problems point to an obvious conclusion: the Endangered
Species Act is treating the symptom and not the disease. The increasing
numbers of plants and animals that are becoming biological wards of the
government are a manifestation of what can only be described as an
ecosystems crisis. Yet the servants of the Endangered Species Act, charged
explicitly with habitat conservation, have never excelled at the real-estate
business. They have come to rely on heroic measures for saving one species
at a time in large part because they have failed at the alternative of saving
habitat. The act has continually gone against the grain of the American desire to exploit the natural resources of this continent, its arterial system of
fresh water, and its surrounding seas without considering the consequences.

26   Defenders of the act, many of whom know exactly what's wrong
with it and willingly discuss its flaws in private, worry that public criticism
will play into the hands of the pro-development groups who perennially
try to weaken it. Many environmentalists are girding for just such an assault this spring, when the act comes up in Congress for reauthorization.
They should not fear criticism from within their own ranks, however.
When adversaries of the act assail its shortcomings—when, for example,
they complain that we are spending too much money on endangered
species—environmentalists have an obvious counteroffensive: The reason
the act has engendered a costly and unwieldy bureaucracy for the perpetual care of compromised organisms is that pro-development groups have
been so successful at evading the central principle of the act—the preservation of ecosystems. The very people who complain about the act are the
ones who have made it malfunction.

Gap Analysis

27   Over the past decade steadily increasing numbers of zoologists,
botanists, geneticists, environmental-policy makers, land managers, geographers, and developers have been making the case that it is time to focus
on the rational, systematic, continent-wide preservation of those ecosystems that support maximum biological diversity. A leader in this cause has
been J. Michael Scott, who was the project leader for the California-con-
dor recovery program from 1984 to 1986, and before that spent ten years
in Hawaii, which harbors the greatest concentration of endangered birds
in the world. Hawaii also holds an appalling number of endangered plants,
of which the Cooke's kokio, a tree, is considered the most endangered
species in the world. Only half of one Cooke's kokio exists; it is grafted
onto a related species in a botanical garden in Hawaii.

28   On behalf of the Fish and Wildlife Service, Scott and a team of twenty-six ornithologists, botanists, and statisticians were assigned the task of
conducting an inventory of the forest birds of the Hawaiian Islands; they
produced one of the classic documents in field ornithology, *Forest Bird*

Communities of the Hawaiian Islands. During years of camping in the rain and slogging in the mud (Hawaii harbors the wettest places on earth) and worrying about the people on his team ("I count as our biggest achievement outside the scientific realm that we got through six years of that kind of survey in remote country and we didn't lose a single person"), Scott began to get his first inklings of what was wrong with the management of endangered species. He began to see the gaps.

For their study Scott and his team made Mylar maps of the vegetation of each island, of the range of each species of bird, and of the existing federal, state, and private land holdings that preserved the presumed habitats of these species. When the maps were laid on top of one another, the lack of overlap was glaringly apparent: the areas of greatest avian diversity were outside the protection of preserves. 29

In this simple fashion Scott performed one of the first exercises in what has come to be called "gap analysis" (F. William Burley, an Oregon biologist and rancher, is usually credited with coining the term). Gap analysis looks for unprotected landscapes that are rich in species. Far faster than a man stacking maps, and with the ability to manipulate much more information, computers store, manage, retrieve, and analyze vast amounts of information from satellite imagery and data bases that show for a particular landscape the different species on it, their distribution, and various habitat factors (vegetation, soil type, geologic elements) and cultural features (zoning, roadways, land ownership, dominant land use). Much of the species information being used comes from information gathered by the Nature Conservancy, a private land-preservation organization that has been a leader in the assessment of ecosystems in North America. 30

The development of gap analysis as a technique for locating areas of rich biological diversity has coincided with increased concern about rapidly dwindling tropical ecosystems. Biologists and policy-makers working in the tropics have been quick to use gap-analysis approaches to try to find and save the richest examples of those ecosystems. Scott came up against endangered-species bias when he began looking for funding to start doing some gap analysis of North American ecosystems. "I got no buyers for two years," he says. He kept hearing, "'Come back in twenty-five years and we'll talk to you. Right now we're up to our eyeballs in endangered species.' But look, I said, this is the way to get around it." Scott and his colleagues, funded by the Idaho Department of Fish and Game, the U.S. Fish and Wildlife Service, and the National Fish and Wildlife Foundation, have completed a gap analysis for Idaho. "The same sorts of patterns we were finding in Hawaii hold true for Idaho," Scott says. "Even with a state that has more than fifty percent federal land ownership, we're still finding large numbers of natural vegetation types that are completely outside natural preserve areas." Gap analysis is also in progress or about to begin for seventeen other states. 31

32   Analyzing the gaps in protected biological diversity across North America will be merely a stimulating computer game for a handful of biologists and geographers unless the new method is applied to rethinking and rearranging land use on the continent. "What I envision," Scott says, "is making this information available to people who are in a position to make management decisions—federal landowners, for instance, who can see how their property plays a role in the protection of biological diversity, where a shift in land management could afford more protection to an area of high species richness or to a vegetation type that is unprotected in other areas. That requires no expenditures of dollars. That's simply a shift in management."

33   Scott believes that gap analysis can steer bureaucracies toward buying unprotected areas that are rich in species—and away from ecosystems that, however beautiful to behold, are already adequately protected. Gap analysis promotes the greatest biodiversity at the least cost to the taxpayer. By also identifying areas of potential conflict (areas where oil exploration is occurring, for example), gap analysis allows buyers to find the species-rich land least encumbered by controversy. Gap analysis locates lands owned by willing sellers, not by parties who are intractable and litigious—and this is its strongest virtue.

34   Perhaps Michael Scott has impossibly lofty goals for gap analysis; perhaps he is simply tired of the good fight; perhaps the evolved policies of the Endangered Species Act are the best we can hope for in an imperfect world. But when I think of biologists frantically building nest holes for red-cockaded woodpeckers, or keeping vigil under the last few Puerto Rican parrot nests in the wild, or watching black-footed ferrets die of canine distemper, or abandoning their efforts to establish another flock of whooping cranes at Grays Lake, Idaho, or pitching cowbirds out of the nests of Kirtland's warblers year in and year out, I no longer call to mind the words of Aldo Leopold or Henry David Thoreau or John Muir or any of the Native American chiefs who spoke so eloquently long ago about the sacredness of the earth and mankind's debt to the beasts. Instead, I think of Hampton Carson, a geneticist and an authority on endangered Hawaiian flora and fauna, who once wrote, "Nature is a better stockkeeper than we are."

Reading and Analyzing

1. What situation is Winckler reacting to? Why is the situation a problem, in her view?
2. What does the author seek to accomplish by her opening paragraphs?
3. Explain the concept of *triage*. How does Winckler apply the concept to saving species?

4. Why do the enforcers of the Endangered Species Act refuse to apply triage? Why is there little support for this approach? What, in Winckler's view, is the result?
5. What is Winckler's thesis, the claim of her argument? What, in other words, is her solution to the problem?
6. Preserving ecosystems is contrary to what trend in the United States? Who are helping to make the Endangered Species Act malfunction?
7. Explain gap analysis in your own words. How can it be used to preserve endangered species? Why is it, in Winckler's view, the better approach?

Responding to the Writer's Ideas

1. Winckler recommends triage because of the continually inadequate funding of the Endangered Species Act. Did you know how much funding is being provided before reading this article? If not, are you surprised by the amount? If so, because it seems so little, or so much? Do you need to reassess your understanding of what it costs to save the condor, for example?
2. Do you think the federal government should spend more money for the act? Why or why not?
3. Assuming that the act is not likely ever to be funded adequately to save all endangered species, does Winckler's proposal make sense as a different approach? Why or why not?
4. The author suggests that the media have something to do with which species get the attention, and then the funding to be saved. (The spotted owl in the Pacific Northwest is one good recent example.) Assess your own degree of concern for endangered species. Do you worry about protecting nature? Do you get moved only for one species or another from time to time as they are given attention by the media? Do you generally not think much about the problem—but you are happy to know that some effort is being made to protect endangered species? Or, do you think the government is spending too much money on a fruitless endeavor that doesn't really matter? Where do you stand along the continuum suggested by these questions? Defend your position.
5. Evaluate Winckler's argument. Does she provide convincing evidence that there is a problem? Does her proposal follow logically from her analysis of the problem? Winckler refers to many different animals in the course of her essay; how do those references enhance her argument?

WRITING SUGGESTIONS

1. Make a case for or against the need to preserve what is left of the rainforest throughout the world. If you argue in favor of conservation, consider also offering some plan for accomplishing the conservation. (For example, should the United States—or the United Nations—try to get an international treaty signed? Should Third World debts be forgiven in exchange for no further cutting? Something else?)

2. Make a case for or against developing nuclear power as an alternative to carbon dioxide–creating fossil fuels. If you argue for its use, you will need to address the potential dangers. If you argue against its use, you will also have to address the potential danger of increasing greenhouse gases.

3. Propose two or three actions that individuals should take to help slow down the greenhouse effect. Your purpose will be to persuade the average citizen to start incorporating these activities into their lives.

4. Are you an "environmentalist," agreeing with many of the writers in this chapter that we need to live in harmony with the Earth and to cherish all living things? If so, make a case for the attitudes and values that combine to make the environmentalist's position. Conversely, if you oppose the environmentalist's perspective, make a case for a different position, a different set of values.

5. Each writer in this chapter has his or her particular concern: greenhouse gases, ozone depletion, population increases, rainforest depletion, water and sanitation problems in Third World countries, species loss. Do you feel that there is one problem that stands out as more significant than the others? If so, develop an argument that supports your choice as the most serious environmental problem we face today.

6. Should the Endangered Species Act be better funded? Should it refocus to include the use of gap analysis? Develop an argument for or against increased funding, or for or against the use of gap analysis. (Be certain to explain the concept of gap analysis.)

Permissions Acknowledgments

James A. Banks, "Multicultural Education: For Freedom's Sake," *Educational Leadership*, Dec. 1991/Jan. 1992, 49, 4:32–36. Reprinted with permission of The Association for Supervision and Curriculum Development and James A. Banks. Copyright © 1991 by the Association for Supervision and Curriculum Development. All rights reserved.

Albert Shanker, "The Pitfalls of Multicultural Education," *The Education Digest*, Dec. 1991. Copyright © 1991 by Prakken Publications, Inc., Ann Arbor, MI. Reprinted with perrmission of the publisher.

"Pornography, Obscenity, and the Case for Censorship" from *Reflections of a Neoconservative* by Irving Kristol, Copyright © 1983 by Basic Books, Inc. Reprinted by permission of Basic Books, a division of HarperCollins Publishers Inc.

Nat Hentoff, "Stories the Public Has No Right to Know," *The Washington Post*, April 18, 1992, Copyright © 1992 Nat Hentoff, reprinted by permission of NEA, Inc.

Patty McEntee, "Is Pornography a Matter of Free Expression?" *America*. Copyright © 1991 by American Press, Inc. Reprinted with permission from the publisher.

"Feminist Moralism, 'Pornography', and Censorship" by Barbara Dority first appeared in the Nov/Dec 1989 issue of *The Humanist* and is reprinted with permission.

John J. Conley, S. J., "The Public Art in the Plural City," *America*, June 23, 1990. Reprinted with permission of America Press, Inc. 106 West 56th Street, New York, NY 10019. © 1990 All Rights Reserved.

James T. Laney, "Why Tolerate Campus Bigots," *New York Times* April 6, 1990 Op-Ed. Copyright © 1990 The New York Times Company. Reprinted by permission.

Robert M. O'Neil, "Colleges Should Seek Educational Alternatives to Rules That Override the Historic Guarantees of Free Speech," *Chronicle of Higher Education*, Oct 18, 1989. Copyright © 1989 by Robert M. O'Neil. Reprinted with permission of the author.

Ellen Goodman, "A Murder in Boston," *Washington Post*, Jan. 6, 1990. Copyright © 1990, The Boston Globe Newspaper Co./Washington Post Writers Group. Reprinted with permisson.

Richard Cohen, "Crimes of Dispassion," *Washington Post*, Dec. 12, 1990. Copyright © 1990, Washington Post Writers Group. Reprinted with permission.

Charles Krauthammer, "Legalize? No. Deglamorize." *Washington Post*, May 20, 1988. Copyright © 1988, Washington Post Writers Group. Reprinted with permission.

"The Right To Arms", from *Abbey's Road* by Edward Abbey. Copyright © 1972, 1975, 1976, 1977, 1978, 1979 by Edward Abbey. Used by permission of the publisher, Dutton, an imprint of New American Library, a division of Penguin Books USA Inc.

Josh Sugarmann, "The NRA Is Right, but We Still Need to Ban Handguns," *Washington Monthly*, June 1987. Reprinted with permission from *The Washington Monthly*. Copyright by the Washington Monthly Company 1611 Connecticut Avenue, NW, Washington D.C. 20009. (202) 462-0128.

Index